Irish Music Handbook

2nd Edition

Music Network
The Coach House
Dublin Castle
Dublin 2

Tel: +353 1 6719429
Fax: +353 1 6719430
Email: info@musicnetwork.ie
Website: www.musicnetwork.ie

ARTS
COUNCIL
of Northern Ireland

Irish Music Handbook 2nd Edition

First published in 2000 by:
Music Network
The Coach House
Dublin Castle
Dublin 2
Republic of Ireland
Tel: +353 1 6719429
Fax: +353 1 6719430
Email: info@musicnetwork.ie
Website: www.musicnetwork.ie

ISBN: 0-9528783-4-8

DESIGN AND TYPESETTING:
Brosna Press Ltd, Church Street, Ferbane, Co. Offaly

PRINTED AND BOUND IN THE REPUBLIC OF IRELAND BY:
Colourbooks Ltd, Baldoyle Industrial Estate, Dublin 13

DISCLAIMER:
While Music Network has taken every care in collecting the information for this book, and in preparing the printed publication, it does not assume, and hereby disclaims any liability to any party for loss or damage caused by errors or omissions in the Irish Music Handbook 2nd Edition.

Contents

Editor
Gillian Keogan

Assistant Editor
Des FitzGerald

Project Contributor
Michelle Hoctor

Acknowledgements

Many thanks to the staff of Music Network, both past and present, Deirdre McCrea, Orla Moloney and Alison Browne in relation to adminstrative aspects of the project, Sinéad Collins and Peter Mangan for their work on advertising and marketing and John O'Kane, Assumpta Lawless, Catherine Carey, Joan Dempsey and Gráinne O'Driscoll for their advice and support. Also to Agnes O'Kane of the Irish Association of Youth Orchestras; Margaret O'Sullivan of Cumann Náisúnta na gCór and Barbara Heas formerly of Cumann Náisúnta na gCór; David Byers BBC Northern Ireland; Lesley Ann Wilson and Martin Dowling of the Arts Council of Northern Ireland; Nick Costello of Opera Theatre Company; Michael Dervan of the Irish Times; Angela Dorgan of the Federation of Music Collectives; Nicholas Carolan of the Irish Traditional Music Archive; Martin Whelan of Siamsa Tíre; EPTA Ireland; ESTA Ireland; Sandra Ellis, Caroline Wynne, Peter Senior, Richard Brennan, Jim Cosgrove, Phil Mullen, Eileen Quilter Williams, Dr. Leonard Condron and the arts officers through-out Ireland.

Finally a special thanks to Maura Eaton and Maeve Giles of the Arts Council and Pamela Smith of the Arts Council of Northern Ireland, for their help with this project.

Music Network, the ESB sponsored national music development organisation, was established by the Arts Council in 1986 to develop music in Ireland on a nationwide basis.

Music Network aims to make music accessible to all, regardless of circumstance or location, by supporting partnerships with locally-based organisations.

Music Network
The Coach House
Dublin Castle
Dublin 2

Tel: 01 6719429
Fax: 01 6719430
Email: info@musicnetwork.ie

Programme

Live Music Concerts
north and south in classical, traditional and jazz.

Participative Programmes
in music education and healthcare.

Local Development Initiatives
including the development of regional "ensembles-in-residence" and ongoing support for "Music County 2000" in Kerry and Waterford.

Information Service
publishing the **Irish Music Handbook** (2nd Edition) and the **Directory of Musicians in Ireland**.

What is Music Network?

Music Network is the national music development organisation, established in 1986 by the Arts Council to develop music nationwide. The organisation aims to give everyone in Ireland access to musical activity of the highest quality. Music Network provides access to music through the delivery of a range of high quality music services. The delivery of all Music Network services is realised at a local level through a commitment to work in partnerships with communities throughout Ireland.

Among Music Network's key services are a range of performance based activities, including a touring programme and a complementary Musicwide scheme, both of which offer concerts of classical, jazz and traditional Irish music to an ever expanding network of partner promoters in locations across the country, North and South. Other performance based services now extend to participative programmes exploring the provision of access to music in community contexts including education and healthcare settings.

In addition, Music Network has pioneered new models of regional music development through a series of partnerships with key local and national agencies. These have included the Vogler Quartet in Sligo residency which has been designed to combine the twin concepts of access to music with artistic excellence. It was established through a partnership with Sligo County Council, Sligo Corporation and the Arts Council. A contrasting model was previously pioneered in two county based pilot projects, Kerry Music County and Waterford Music City and County.

Music Network's Information Service provides access to information on all aspects of non-commercial music in Ireland. Key publications now include the 2nd edition of the Irish Music Handbook and the Directory of Musicians in Ireland (1998).

Music Network is core funded by the Arts Council and receives significant sponsorship from ESB.

Foreword

Arts Council of Ireland by
Patrick J. Murphy, Chairman

I am pleased to welcome the publication of this second edition of the Irish Music Handbook. An Chomhairle Ealaíon/The Arts Council has identified as a strategic priority the need for arts organisations to develop audiences for and participation in the arts. Publications such as this provide a valuable service by alerting people to the great richness and diversity of arts activities in their areas. We thus applaud Music Network, which was established by An Chomahirle Ealaíon in 1986 to develop music in Ireland, for putting together such a comprehensive guide to the wide spectrum of musical activity taking place throughout this island.

The Handbook gives an insight into the tremendous range of musical activity going on in Ireland. There are entries for everything from festivals and summer schools to workshops, competitions and scholarships. The island of Ireland dimension of the Handbook is particularly commendable - I believe that there is considerable scope for publications such as this to document the island-wide nature of so much artistic activity. My colleagues in the Arts Council of Northern Ireland are to be congratulated for their ongoing support of this particular initiative.

The Irish Music Handbook will prove to be a valuable resource to anyone with an interest in music in Ireland. I wish Music Network every success with this publication.

Patrick J. Murphy
Chairman An Chomhairle Ealaíon/The Arts Council

Foreword
Chairman of ACNI

The Arts Council of Northern Ireland welcomes the second edition of the Irish Music Handbook. Building on the success of the first edition, and revealing the fruits of ongoing research by Music Network over recent years, the Handbook is one of the most comprehensive sources of information about music in the island of Ireland.

The increased size of the new Handbook reflects the enormous amount of musical activity in the country and the interconnections that exist between different groups, which continually refresh and enrich our common cultural life. New information on community musicians, music educators, music therapists and musicians' health, to focus on just a few areas, will be very valuable in widening access to musical life for all sections of the community.

The Handbook has benefited from close collaboration between Music Network and the Arts Council of Northern Ireland. Cross-border partnerships of this kind have always been endorsed by the Council, and are likely to assume even greater importance in the Council's new strategy as we move into the new Millennium.

I hope that readers and entrants alike will discover Ireland's musical wealth in the pages of the Handbook, and I congratulate all who have contributed to this fine publication.

Brian Walker
Chairman Arts Council of Northern Ireland

Sponsors Message

As Chief Executive of ESB I am delighted that we are associated with Music Network in promoting good music all over Ireland.

Over the last seventy years, ESB has contributed to the development of communities nationwide, both rural and urban. We have contributed not only to the supply of electricity but also to the development of a quality service to our customers. We have also contributed to these communities by supporting a variety of initiatives, be they of an enterprise, education, environment or cultural nature. Our partnership with Music Network builds on this and, over the last few years, we have witnessed a remarkable programme of top class Irish and international musicians who have toured Ireland on ESB sponsored Music Network tours.

Building an awareness of music and its associated industry is an important part of Music Network's activities and this Handbook will help considerably in this task.

I hope that it will become an invaluable aid to all those working in, promoting or supporting that music industry.

Ken O'Hara
Chief Executive ESB

Introduction

Participation in music making, no matter what the level of accomplishment, is an enjoyable, life enriching activity, integral to the lives of a great many people all over Ireland. In compiling this publication, which builds upon the success of the Irish Music Handbook 1st Edition, we have sought to reflect the richness and diversity of musical life by recording information on many of the individuals and organisations whose collective endeavours contribute greatly to the music sector. As a result, we hope that whether you are looking for a 'left hand instrument' maker, tuition on the Tibetian singing bowl or advice on how to cope with a repetitive strain injury induced by too much piano practising, that this one-stop guide to classical, jazz and traditional music will assist you.

In compiling this publication we have been struck many times by the obvious growth in the music sector since the publication of the 1st edition, both in terms of the establishment of new organisations and also the many new channels for the performance and use of music. The content of the Irish Music Handbook 2nd Edition represents this growth by introducing a series of new categories which include music educationalists, community musicians, health and musicians, arts consultants, music therapists, piano tuners, event management companies, winter schools and short courses. It seems clear that these new categories reflect not only the burgeoning of new activity in specific areas such as music education but, more generally, a growing reponse to the self-evident need to provide increased levels of access to music for everyone.

One key factor which drives this increased activity is the collective efforts of committed individuals and organisations from across the country, many of whom feature in this publication. Without their co-operation it would not have been possible to compile this handbook and we thank them again for their continuing support.

The gathering, updating and storing of information on a computer database is an integral part of the work of Music Networks' Information Service. Not only does this enable us meet the continuous demand for information provision, for example through our telephone enquiry service, but also enables us to undertake the production of publications such as the 2nd edition of the Irish Music Handbook. In this regard, we wish to acknowledge the contribution of both Ann Swift and Michelle Hoctor, who were the original pioneers of the Irish Music Handbook 1st Edition 1996, and who set in motion Music Networks ongoing committment to comprehensive information provision.

The Irish Music Handbook 2nd Edition is the result of intensive planning and research which has taken place over a two year period. As with its predecessor, this publication does not attempt to cover every musical genre or every type of musical activity in Ireland. For the most part, information relates to activity relating to the practice of classical, jazz and traditional Irish music. In particular, the handbook has tried to avoid significant duplication or replication of information provided in an in-depth manner by other service providers. Compiling the information involved targeting two groups of potential data entries, i.e. for existing categories and for a number of new categories. Every potential entry identified was circulated with a category-specific questionnaire upon which to provide their details. Questionnaires that were not returned initially were followed up with phone calls. While every care has been taken in the compilation of this publication to ensure that we have represented the music sector to its fullest, we apologise in advance for any inevitable omissions and hope that future editions will rectify these.

In response to the changing expectations of information provision at the present time, the information gathered in the preparation of this publication has been stored in a format suitable for electronic transmission via the internet. As a result, the contents of the Irish Music Handbook 2nd edition will shortly be made available on the Music Network website which is currently under construction and is due to be launched by the end of this year.

Music Network would like to thank our key funders An Chomhairle Ealaíon/Arts Council, the Arts Council of Northern Ireland and IMRO for their assistance, advice and financial support with regards to the preparation of this handbook. A special word of thanks must also go to our corporate sponsors, ESB, whose continuing support has also helped make this publication possible.

We hope that the 2nd edition of the Irish Music Handbook will prove to be a useful tool for all who use it. For some, this is likely to mean that the handbook will act as an occasional point of reference. For others, we have reason to believe that, like its predecesssor, it may well become a constant, well-thumbed companion. Whatever the category that you are likely to find yourself in, we trust that you will find this handbook accurate, easy to use and informative.

Gillian Keogan
Editor

Notes for using this Handbook

- In detailing telephone and fax numbers for Northern Ireland we have used the standard dialling access code from the Republic of Ireland to Northern Ireland, which is 048. In the case of callers from Great Britain to Northern Ireland the access code is 028. The international access code for Northern Ireland is +44 28 and the local 8 digit number. Telephone numbers for the Republic of Ireland have been listed with the standard international dialling code, for example +353 1 6719429. For callers within the Republic of Ireland the local code is used e.g 01 6719429.

- We have used symbols in some sections which we found would be lengthy otherwise. For example, and in particular with the venues section, we have detailed the list of symbols on the title page of that section for your reference. These symbols serve to illustrate amenities, services, facilities and also to highlight important detail such as the availablility of an instrument bank since the first edition of the Irish Music Handbook.

- You will note that some of the sections, for example venues and promoters, have been listed county by county, the media section is further divided by region and instrument makers and repairers are categorised by their instrument family. We hope that this categorisation will help you find what you are looking for easily.

- The words RTÉ (Radio Telifis Éireann) and CCÉ (Comhaltas Ceoltóirí Éireann) are abbreviated in the text. Many music colleges, orchestras, organisations and venues are also abbreviated. For example, when a college is mentioned for the first time in each entry, it will be given its full name. However for any subsequent mentions within that entry, it will be abbreviated.

- In addition to the A-Z index at the back of the book we have also supplied an index of advertisers for your reference.

Organisations

A number of organisations in the following sections do consider applications for grant aid, although this is not always explicitly stated in their entry. We have used the following symbol to indicate funding:

€

In the case of organisations that provide an instrument bank service we have used the following symbol:

⊟

STATUTORY ORGANISATIONS

An Chomhairle Ealaíon - The Arts Council
Maura Eaton
Music Officer
70 Merrion Square
Dublin 2

Tel/Fax: +353 1 6180200 or +353 1850 392492/+353 1 6761302 or +353 1 6610349
Email: info@artscouncil.ie
Website: www.artscouncil.ie

The development agency for the arts in Ireland. It is an independent state body, established by the Arts Act of 1951 to promote and assist the arts. In fulfiling its remit, the Council provides advice, assistance and support to individuals, arts organisations and a wide range of governmental and non-governmental bodies and it provides financial assistance to individuals and organisations for artistic purposes. Its state grant in 2000 was £34.5 m. The Council consists of 16 members and a chairperson appointed by the Minister for Arts, Heritage, Gaeltacht and the Islands for a period of not more than five years. The present Council was appointed in 1998. The Council also partly funds county and city arts officers throughout the country (see advert page 7).

An Post National Lottery Company
Ray Bates
National Lottery Director
Abbey Street Lower
Dublin 1

Tel/Fax:+353 1 8364444/+353 1 8366034
Email: webmaster@lottery.ie
Website: www.lotto.ie
Other key staff: Malachy Moynihan (Sales & Marketing Manager), Noel Browne (Chief Accountant), Cathal McNally (Operations Manager)

The purpose of the An Post National Lottery is to generate funds for the designated beneficiaries while operating the National Lottery in accordance with the highest standards of integrity, credibility and security. The beneficiary sections which receive funding are as follows: youth, sport, recreation and amenities; arts, culture and national heritage; health and welfare; Irish language. The undertaking to establish a National Lottery in Ireland was first set out in the Government White Paper of October 1984, 'Building on Reality'. 'The National Lottery Act', 1986, was passed in Dáil Éireann on the 15th July 1986, enabling the setting up of a National Lottery. The Government awarded the franchise to establish and operate a National Lottery to An Post, which set up a subsidiary, An Post National Lottery Company, to which the lottery license was issued. An Post owns 80% of the shares in the lottery, with the balance held by the Minister For Finance. The newsletter 'Beneficiary Newsletter' is issued on a quarterly basis.

Aosdána
Patricia Quinn
Registrar
70 Merrion Square
Dublin 2

Tel/Fax: +353 1 6180200/+353 1 6761302 or +353 1 6610349
Email: aosdana@artscouncil.ie
Website: www.artscouncil.ie
Other key staff: Dermot McLaughlin (Deputy Registrar), Bernadette O'Leary (Executive Assistant)

Aosdána is an affiliation of not more than 200 artists engaged in literature, music and the visual arts, established by the Arts Council in 1981 to honour those artists whose work has made an outstanding contribution to the arts in Ireland, to encourage and assist members in devoting their energies full-time to their art, and to give artists a voice in the wider community. There are currently 173 members in Aosdána. Membership is attained following a process of nomination and election. Aosdána is not an academic institution, nor does it offer any award or qualification other than the honorary title of 'Saoi'. The composer members are Gerald Barry, Seóirse Bodley, Brian Boydell, John Buckley, Frank Corcoran, Raymond Deane, Jerome de Bromhead, Roger Doyle, Eibhlís Farrell, Fergus Johnston, John Kinsella, Philip Martin, Kevin O'Connell, Jane O'Leary, Eric Sweeney, Ian Wilson and James Wilson.

Arts Council of Northern Ireland
Pamela Smith
Music and Opera Officer
MacNeice House
77 Malone Road
Belfast BT9 6AQ
Northern Ireland

Tel/Fax: 048 9038 5200/048 9066 1715
Email: performance@artscouncil-ni.org
Other key staff: Martin Dowling (Traditional Arts Officer), Philip Hammond (Performing Arts Director)

The ACNI develop the arts in Northern Ireland so that as many people as possible can enjoy as many forms of art as possible, to as high a standard as possible. Aim to encourage access to, appreciation of and participation in a broad spectrum of arts, to promote creative and performing arts of quality, and to increase resources for the arts, and ensure their effective and efficient use.

Arts Council of Northern Ireland National Lottery Fund
Tanya Greenfield
Lottery Director
MacNeice House
77 Malone Road
Belfast BT9 6AQ
Northern Ireland

Tel/Fax: 048 9066 7000/048 9066 4766
Email: lottery@artscouncil-ni.org
Other key staff: Lorraine McDowell (Monitoring Officer), Damien Coyle (Development Officer), Punam McGookin (Case Officer)

The National Lottery was established by an Act of Parliament and aims to raise money for worthwhile causes. The Arts Council of Northern Ireland receives approximately £7.5m per year and has the responsibility of distributing funds to arts projects which benefit the people of Northern Ireland. The Arts Council of Northern Irelands National Lottery Fund offers four grant programmes: 'Capital Programme' towards buildings and equipment, 'New Work Programme' towards the creation of new work in all art forms, 'Access to the Arts' towards project costs in all art forms, 'Film Programme' towards development and production. Applications should be made on official application forms.

Bord na Gaeilge
Méabh Ní Chatháin
Public Relations Officer
7 Cearnóg Mhuirfean
Baile Átha Cliath 2

Tel/Fax: +353 1 6398400/+353 1 6398401
Email: eolas@bnag.ie
Website: www.bnag.ie
Other key staff: Micheál Ó Gragáin (Chief Executive)

Bunaíodh Bord na Gaeilge mar Bhord stáit i 1978 chun polasaí agus pleanáil stáit don Ghaeilge a chomhordú agus chun seasamh na Gaeilge a chinntiú mar theanga labhartha ar fud na tíre. Tugann an Bord comhairle agus cabhair ar gach gné den Ghaeilge agus oibríonn sé leis an earnáil phoiblí agus an earnáil phríobháideach chun

polasaithe dátheangacha a fhorbairt agus a chur i bhfeidhm. Fuair an Bord fáltas £3.55 m i 1999 ón Roinn Ealaíon, Oidhreachta, Gaeltachta agus Oileán agus faoi láthair tá 30 ag obair sa Bhord.

Bord na Gaeilge was established in 1978 as a statutory semi-state body to co-ordinate state policy and planning for Irish and to seek to ensure the survival of Irish as a spoken language throughout the country. The Bord provides advice and assistance on all aspects of the Irish language and works closely with the private and public sectors in developing and implementing policies for bilingualism. The Bord received a grant of £3.55m from the Department of Arts, Heritage, Gaeltacht and the Islands in 1999 and currently has a staff of 30. The newsletter 'Saol' is issued on a monthly basis.

Combat Poverty Agency
Hugh Frazer
Director
Bridgewater Centre
Conyngham Road
Islandbridge
Dublin 8

Tel/Fax: +353 1 6706746/+353 1 6706760
Email: info@cpa.ie
Website: www.cpa.ie

The aim of the Combat Poverty Agency is to promote a more just and inclusive society by working for the prevention and elimination of poverty and social exclusion. The agency pursues its aim through four main functions set out in the Combat Poverty Agency Act 1986: policy advice, project support and innovation, research and public education. It prepares policy proposals to government on aspects of economic and social planning in relation to poverty. It has a monitoring and evaluation role for the Government's National Anti-Poverty Strategy. It commissions and publishes research on poverty and related issues. Acting as the national community development resource centre, it supports local community development as an anti-poverty strategy. It currently supports an innovative programme to demonstrate integrated responses to educational disadvantage. It also administers a grants scheme, 'Working for Change', which supports the community and voluntary sector to influence policy relating to poverty. The agency provides a drop-in library and information service, promotes media interest in poverty, supports curriculum development at post-primary level, and publishes a range of materials on poverty and community development. A grants brochure, a publications catalogue and a leaflet on the library service are all available free of charge. Newsletter 'Poverty Today' is issued on a quarterly basis.

Crafts Council of Ireland
Joanna Quinn
Information Officer
Castle Yard
Kilkenny

Tel/Fax: +353 56 61804/+353 56 63754
Email: ccoi@craftscouncil-of-ireland.ie
Other key staff: Breda Kennedy (Administrative Assistant), Jolly Ronan (Information Assistant)

The Crafts Council of Ireland is the national design and economic development agency for the crafts in Ireland, funded by the Government and the European Union. The Council acts in an advisory and promotional capacity to other state agencies and the crafts sector. Key activities include 'Training Showcase Ireland' (The Trade fair), outreach programmes and information services. There is a register of craftworkers (1300), some of whom are musical instrument makers (available to buyers). The newsletter 'Stopress' is issued on a monthly basis.

Department of Arts, Heritage, Gaeltacht and the Islands
Etain Murphy
Higher Executive Officer
Dun Aimhirgin
43-49 Mespil Road
Dublin 4

Tel/Fax: +353 1 6670788/+353 1 6670824
Other key staff: Dermot Burke (Principal Officer), Seamas Lynam (Assistant Principal), Rosaleen Fleming (Clerical Officer)

The Department was established in 1993 and is responsible for the formulation of national policy relating to Arts and Culture - An Chomhairle Ealaíon comes under its aegis; the promotion of cultural, social and economic welfare of the Gaeltacht and the preservation and extension of the use of Irish as a vernacular language; the National Museum, National Library, National Gallery of Ireland, National Archives, National Concert Hall, National Heritage Council and the Irish Museum of Modern Art, the formulation of national policy relating to the broadcasting and the audio-visual industry, Heritage Services including Inland Waterways, National Parks and Wildlife as well as National Monuments and Historic Properties, certification of qualifying projects in the music industry for the purposes of the BES taxation incentive scheme and the implementation of the recommendations of FORTE, the task force on the popular music industry.

€

Department of Education and Science
John Denehy
Secretary General
Marlborough Street
Dublin 1

Tel/Fax:+353 1 8734700/+353 1 8786712 or +353 1 8789553
Email: hynes@educ.irlgov.ie
Website: www.irlgov.ie/educ
Other key staff: Oliver Hynes (Post Primary Inspector of Music, Dublin), Jerome Leonard (Post Primary Inspector of Music, Cork), Micheál Ó hEidhin (District Post Primary Inspector, Spiddal)

The mission of the Department of Education and Science is to ensure the provision of a comprehensive, cost-effective and accessible education system of the highest quality, as measured by international standards, which will enable individuals to develop to their full potential as persons and to participate fully as citizens in society and to contribute to social and economic development. The Department of Education and Science is responsible for the administration of public education, primary, post primary and special education. State subsidies for universities and third level colleges are channelled through this department. Regular publications and press releases can be made available.

€

Department of Education and Science - Youth Affairs Section
Brian P. Power
Higher Executive Officer
Tullamore
Co. Offaly

Tel/Fax: +353 506 21363/+353 1 506 41052
Email: powerb@educ.irlgov.ie
Other key staff: P.J Breen (Principal Officer), Máire Ní Fhlaithbheartaigh (Assistant Principal Officer)

The work of the Youth Affairs Section of the Department of Education & Science is in the sphere of informal education and the department is continuing its efforts to make informal education services available to young people. This is principally done through the provision of financial assistance to special projects for disadvantaged young people and to national youth organisations. Youth projects and organisations present valuable opportunities for the social and personal development of young people. Qualities and skills such as leadership, co-operation, decision making, motivation and self responsibility can be acquired in a learning-by-doing manner. The aim of the youth service is to assist all young people to become active participants in a democratic society. This participation, essential to the full development of young people extends to involvement in institutions of social, political, cultural and economic life. In essence, therefore, the primary tasks of the youth service are regarded as being to help realise the potential of each young person and to facilitate full participation in community life. The Youth Affairs Section supports the provision of youth services by way of policy development, consultation with statutory, voluntary and community interests, and the administration and monitoring of a number of grant initiatives: Grant Scheme for Special Projects to assist disadvantaged youth; approximately 200 community based and special projects in disadvantaged areas throughout the country. Youth Service Grant Scheme for the support of national voluntary youth organisations. Youth Information Fund: supporting a national network of 22 Youth Information Centres. Gaisce, The President's Award: a programme of merit awards for young people between the ages of 15 and 25. Léargas, The Exchanges Bureau: for the provision of international youth exchange programmes, including the 'Youth For Europe' initiative. Advisory and monitoring committees have been established in the areas of youth information, youth health and youth arts. The Youth Arts Initiative provides for the employment of youth arts development officers in association with the National Association of Youth Drama and the National Youth Council of Ireland.

Department of Education for Northern Ireland

Roger Jarvis
Music Inspector
Rathgael House
Balloo Road
Bangor
Co. Down BT19 7PR
Northern Ireland

Tel: 048 9127 9726
Email: roger.jarvis@dem.gov.uk
Website: www.nics.gov.uk/demhome.htm
Other key staff: John McFall (Permanent Secretary), Tom Shaw (Chief Inspector), Pat Higgins (Head of Arts, Libraries & Museums Branch)

The Department of Education aims to strengthen society and the economy, enrich the quality of life and promote learning. With particular regard to the arts, the Department seeks "...to enrich the life and personal development of as many people as possible through the creativity of the arts...". The Department has a strategic

role in developing and implementing education policies, and is responsible for legislation and financial control of the education and library services. It is concerned with the whole policy responsibility for sport and recreation, youth services, arts and culture and the development of community relations between schools. The main source of professional advice within The Department is the education and training inspectorate.

€

Department of Foreign Affairs Cultural Relations Committee

Secretary of the Cultural Relations Committee
Department of Foreign Affairs
69-71 St. Stephens Green
Dublin 2

Tel/Fax: +353 1 4780822/+353 1 4082611

The Cultural Relations Committee is appointed by the Minister for Foreign Affairs to advise on artistic and cultural activity likely to promote a knowledge and appreciation of Ireland's cultural life in other countries. Grants may be made to organisations, groups or individuals who apply for assistance for participation in projects abroad, normally involving exhibition or performance. These grants are not available for study or training purposes.

European Commission Representation in Ireland

Paul Gormley
Head of Information Policy
European Union House
18 Dawson Street
Dublin 2

Tel/Fax: +353 1 6625113/+353 1 6625118
Email: paul.gormley@cec.eu.int
Website: www.europa.eu.int
Other key staff: Peter Doyle (Director), Philip Ryan (Deputy Director)

The European Commission Representation in Ireland is based in Dublin, and represents the Commission in Ireland informing the Irish public of developments at EU level and keeps the Commission abreast of developments in Ireland of interest to the rest of the EU. The Representation offers general information about the EU through a public information centre (EPIC) as well as a mobile information vehicle (EPIC roadshow), containing innovative and modern means of information presentation. For specific information needs, there is a library and research centre which has a comprehensive range of EU publications, including a complete set of the official journals covering current legislation and new proposals. The Representation provides a broad range of services to both the media and the general public, co-operating actively with a network of relays around the country. To assist in the dissemination of information on the EU, the Representation has established 'Team Europe' a speakers panel whose members are available to speak at conferences or on local radio.

European Commission Representation in Northern Ireland

Jim Dougal
Head of Representation
Windsor House
9-15 Bedford Street
Belfast BT2 7EG
Northern Ireland

Tel/Fax: 048 9024 0708/+44 9024 8241
Email: jim.dougal@uk.dg10-bur.cec.be
Website: www.cec.org.uk

Represents the voice of the commission to all sectors in Northern Ireland. Ensures that information on the EU is reported accurately and it keeps the commission up to date with developments in the region, mainly political, economical and social. The EC Information point is opened from 9.30-5.00pm daily and holds a comprehensive range of EU and European related publications. The reference library is open from 2.30-5.00pm and has access to all EU legislation and information on policies and programmes. Information officers are on hand to offer assistance. The newsletter 'Network Europe' is issued on a monthly basis.

Údarás na Gaeltachta

Mícheál Ó Fearraigh
Feidhmeannach Forbartha Ealaíon
Doirí Beaga
Léitir Ceanainn
Tír Chonaill

Tel/Fax: +353 75 60100/+353 75 60101
Email: eolas@udaras.ie
Website: www.udaras.ie
Other key staff: Eibhlín de Paor (Áistheoir Ealaíon), Gearóid Ó Smolain (Áisitheoir Ealaíon), Nóirín Ní Ghrádaigh (Áisitheoir Ealaíon)

An tÚdarás' activity is concerned with developing and enhancing the community life of the Gaeltacht, thereby ensuring its preservation as a wellspring of the Irish language. Údarás na Gaeltachta combines an economic development role with community, cultural and language development activities, working in partnership with local communities and organisations. Most of the cultural activities, from single events to full-scale festivals, are community based and organised.

Visiting Arts

Nelson Fernandez
Assistant Director
11 Portland Place
London W1N 4EJ
England

Tel/Fax: +44 20 7389 3019/+44 20 7389 3016
Email: office/visitingarts.demon.co.uk
Website: www.britcoun.org/visitingarts/
Other key staff: Terry Sandell (Director), Camilla Edwards (Deputy Director), Melissa Edwards (Assistant Director)

Visiting Arts is a joint venture of The British Council, The Foreign Office, The Arts Councils of England, Scotland, Wales and Northern Ireland and The Crafts Council. Visiting Arts aims to promote cultural relations between the United Kingdom and the rest of the world by encouraging and assisting the presentation in the UK of the the arts of other countries. Visiting arts promotes the presentation of performances and exhibitions of the arts of other countries. The organisation supports this activity through advise and consultancy and funding support. The newsletter 'Visiting Arts' is issued on a quarterly basis.

OTHER ORGANISATIONS AND PROJECTS

Access Music Project

Kevin McNicholas
Co-ordinator
c/o Galway City Partnership
Kiltartan House
Forster Street, Galway

Tel/Fax: +353 91 566617/+353 91 566618

Aims to provide people who are long-term unemployed with the skills, knowledge and training they require to gain sustainable employment in the general music industry, and to access further education. Access Music Project provides a two year training programme with modules covering instrumental tuition, music teaching skills, song-writing and composition, music technology, community music skills and self-employment skills. The programme also includes placements in schools, community groups and the music industry.

The Arts Council
An Chomhairle Ealaíon

The Arts Council supports organisations and individuals working in music to produce excellent and innovative work and to develop participation in, and audiences for, music. A brochure providing details of grants available from the Arts Council is published each January, and information can be obtained from:

Maura Eaton, Music Officer, The Arts Council, 70 Merrion Square, Dublin 2.
Telephone: 1850 392 492; **Fax:** 01 6761302
E-Mail: info@artscouncil.ie

CUMANN NÁISIÚNTA na gCÓR
Association of Irish Choirs

CNC is a national organisation, funded by the Arts Council/An Chomhairle Ealaíon, which provides for the needs of amateur Irish choirs and their conductors.

• Membership Scheme for Choirs Schools & Individuals •
• Regional Courses & Choral Days •
• Choral Music Publications •
• Administration of the Irish Youth Choir •
• Annual Summer School for Choral Conductors, Teachers & Students •
• Choral Music Library Service •
• Public Liability Insurance Scheme •
• Newsletter *In-Choir* •

CUMANN NÁISIÚNTA na gCÓR
Drinan Street, Cork, Ireland
Tel. 021 - 4312296
Fax 021 - 4962457
email cnc@iol.ie

The Arts Council
An Chomhairle Ealaíon

Irish Association of Youth Orchestras

- Annual Festival of Youth Orchestras
- Penneys/IAYO Youth Orchestra
- Achievement Awards
- Conductors Workshops
- National Chamber Music Workshops
- Music Library
- Instrument Bank

An Association for all Youth Orchestras in Ireland

iayo

For further information please contact:
IAYO
6, Alexandra Place,
Wellington Road, Cork
Tel/Fax: (021) 4507412

The Arts Council
An Chomhairle Ealaíon

Advisory Committee on Church Music

Rev Patrick Jones
National Secretary for Liturgy
National Centre for Liturgy
St. Patricks College
Maynooth
Co. Kildare

Tel/Fax: +353 1 7083478/+353 1 7083477
Other key staff: Professor Gerard T. Gillen
(Chairperson), Sr Moira Bergin (Secretary)

Set up by the Irish Episcopal Commission for Liturgy in light of the liturgical renewal of the Second Vatican Council, as a consultative body on liturgical music.

African Cultural Project

Adekunle Gomez
Director
Ulster Bank Chambers
4 Lower O'Connell Street
Dublin 1

Tel/Fax: +353 1 8780613/+353 1 8780615

Established as a cultural and educational organisation in Ireland. Co-ordinates a multi-disciplinary year-round programme of arts and educational events. Works in partnership with a network of bodies throughout Ireland. Organises a multi-disciplinary programme of arts events for the Africa Festival. Co-ordinates workshops in African arts in schools and with community and youth groups. Resource organisation for African artists. The newsletter 'African Expressions' is issued on a quarterly basis.

AHEAD - Association for Higher Education Access and Disability

Caroline McGrath
Director
Newman House
86 St. Stephen's Green
Dublin 2

Tel/Fax: +353 1 4752386/+353 1 4752387
Email: ahead@iol.ie
Website: www.ahead.ie
Other key staff: Pauline Ryder (Office Manager), Pat Hoey (Research Co-ordinator)

AHEAD is an all-Ireland association established to promote access to and full participation of students with disabilities in higher education and employment. Broadly speaking AHEAD is a research based organisation, as opposed to direct service providers. Aims to promote and develop good policies and practices in the higher education sector to enable full participation of disabled students, and to promote good practices and policies in the recruitment of graduates with disabilities. The newsletter 'AHEAD' is issued on a yearly basis.

AIMS - Association of Irish Musical Societies

Frank Foley
National Secretary
25 Harcourt Lodge
Inchicore
Dublin 8

Tel/Fax: +353 1 4536406
Other key staff: Connie Tantrum (Choral Festival Administrator), Alice Hughes (PRO and Information Officer), Anne-Marie Heskin (Journal Liaison Officer)

AIMS represents over 120 musical societies which spend over £2 million annually, providing quality theatre for audiences which exceed 1.5 million. The primary function of the organisation is to act as a catalyst that will help individuals and societies to attain even higher standards to the benefit of those members, their audiences and musical theatre in general. To fulfil this function, AIMS provides a range of services and activities to its members: an adjudication and awards scheme; workshops; library and information; choral festival. AIMS also organises an annual week-long youth workshop in all aspects of musical theatre, which is held in Thurles each year. Journal 'Showtimes' is published by AIMS.

The following societies are members of AIMS:

Region West
Athenry Musical Society
Castlebar Choral Society
Castlerea Musical Society
Ennistymon Choral Society
Galway Musical Society
Headford Choral Society
Kiltimagh Musical Society
Lackagh Musical Society
Loughrea Musical Society
Marian (Tuam) Choral Society
Patrician Musical Society, Galway
St. Mary's (Ballinrobe) Choral Society
Taibhdhearc Na Gaillimhe

Region South West
Carrick-on-Suir Amateur Musical Society
Cecilian Musical Society

Clonakilty Singing Club
Dungarvan Musical and Choral Society
Ennis Musical Society
Fermoy Choral Society
Killarney Musical Society
Nenagh Choral Society
Roscrea Operatic Society
St. Mary's (Clonmel) Choral Society
Shannon Musical Society
Slievenamon Musical Society
Thurles Amateur Musical Society
Tipperary Musical Society
Tralee Musical Society

Region South East
Athy Musical Society
Avonmore Musical Society, Arklow
Carnew Musical Society
De La Salle Musical Society
Dolmen Music Theatre, Carlow
Edmund Rice Choral and Musical Society
Enniscorthy Musical Society
Gorey Musical Society
Kilkenny Musical Society
New Ross Musical Society
Premier Productions, Waterford
Tramore Musical Society
Tramore Schools Musical Society
Wexford Light Opera Society

Region North
Ballyshannon Musical Society
Banbridge Choral Society
Bangor Amateur Operatic Society
Belfast Operatic Company
First Act Musical Company
Fortwilliam Musical Society
Lisnagarvey Operatic and Drama Society
Londonderry Amateur Operatic Society
Lurgan Operatic and Dramatic Society
New Lyric Opera Company
Newcastle Glee Singers
Newry Musical and Orchestral Society
Portrush Musical Society
St. Agnes Choral Society
St. Patrick's Choral Society
The Ulster Operatic Company

Region Midlands
Athlone Musical Society
Ballinasloe Choral Society
Clara Musical Society
Lakeland Productions, Mullingar
Laois Musical Society
Newbridge Musical Society
St. Brendan's Community School Musical Society, Birr
St. Mel's (Longford) Musical Society
Tullamore Musical Society

Region East
Arthur's Team Musical Society
Baldoyle Musical and Dramatic Society
Bank of Ireland Group Musical Society
Blessington Musical Society
Bray Musical Society
Cameron Musical and Dramatic Society
Cavan Musical Society
Celbridge Musical Society
Clane Musical Society
Coolmine Musical Society
Coolock Musical Society
Corpus Christi Musical and Dramatic Society
Dublin Area Youth Musical Society
Dublin Musical and Dramatic Society
Dublin Musical Theatre Players
Dundalk Musical Society
Dundrum Musical and Dramatic Society
Dunshaughlin Musical Society
Fast Forward Productions
Glencullen Musical and Dramatic Society
Harold's Cross/Tallaght Musical Society
Kells Musical Society
Kilcock Musical and Dramatic Society
Kill Musical and Dramatic Society
Kilmacud Musical and Dramatic Society
Leixlip Musical and Variety Group
Malahide Musical and Dramatic Society
Marian (Skerries) Musical and Dramatic Society
Midas Music Company
Naas Musical Society
Navan Road Musical and Dramatic Society
O'Connell Musical Society
Playback Productions
Portmarnock Musical Society
Portmarnock Singers
Rathmines and Rathgar Musical Society
Rush Musical Society
St. Mary's Musical Society, Navan
St. Michael's Musical Society, Inchicore
Stillorgan Musical Company
Stillorgan Youth Musical Company
The Glasnevin Musical Society
Trim Musical Society
West County Musical Society

AIMS - Association of Irish Musical Societies (Northern Region)
Winston Johnston
Chairperson
6 Springhill Avenue
Bangor
Co. Down BT29 3NT
Northern Ireland

Tel: 048 9146 3153
Other key staff: Brendan Keohane (Vice

Chairman), Olive Melville (Secretary), Thompson Steel (Treasurer)

AIMS Northern Region was formed 25 years ago. Committee meetings are held monthly which consist of representatives from 17 member societies. Main activities include co-ordination with statutory bodies vis a vis grants and training facilities. Active as a representative body of the amateur performing arts groups engaged in musicals, operettas and concerts at national and community levels. Workshops in performance, dance, singing and make-up. Music and information library service available. Newsletter 'Showtimes' is issued on a monthly basis.

AOIFE - Association of Irish Festivals and Events
Karen Bonner
Secretary
Administration Office
1 Upper Main Street
Arklow
Co. Wicklow

Tel/Fax: +353 402 32732/+353 402 91030
Email: aoifeirl@iol.ie
Other key staff: Dan O'Donoghue (Chairperson), Grainne McLoughlin (Vice-Chairperson), Colm Croffy (PRO)

Formed in March 1993, AOIFE aims to bring together the organisers of festivals and events in Ireland, to act as a forum for the sharing of ideas and to endeavour to resolve a number of common areas of concern. Since its inception, over 350 festivals have affiliated, ranging from prestigious international events to a host of smaller town/village festivals throughout the 32 counties. AOIFE also has 150 associate members. Operates an annual weekend conference and trade show, a festival insurance scheme and advisory council. Produces an annual directory, and bi-monthly newsletters. Maintains close contact with all relevant tourist bodies, festival and event organisations and related fields. AOIFE's newsletter 'AOIFE Update' is available bi-monthly.

The Ark - A Cultural Centre for Children
Martin Drury
Director
Eustace Street
Temple Bar
Dublin 2

Tel/Fax: +353 1 6707788/+353 1 6707758
Email: info@ark.ie

Website: www.ark.ie
Other key staff: Clodagh O'Brien (General Manager), Miriam O'Sullivan (Music Programmer), Ken Hartnett (Technical Manager)

The Ark is a custom-designed arts centre for children, with a theatre, gallery and workshop. The ark is committed to creating high quality encounters for children with arts and artists of all disiplines. Presents 8-10 programmes annually ranging across the arts. Since it opened in 1995 The Ark has held an annual music festival in spring and presents several original pieces of music theatre, as well as a new childrens opera. Proposals for innovative music works for children are always welcome.

Armagh Pipers Club
Brian Vallely
Secretary /Public Relations Officer
14 Victoria Street
Co. Armagh BT61 9DT
Northern Ireland

Tel/Fax: 048 3751 1248
Email: jbv@ukgateway.net
Other key staff: Eithne Vallely (Director of Music), Patricia Daly (Harp Tutor), Eamon Curran, Brian Vallely (Uilleann-Pipes Tutor)

Armagh Pipers Club was founded in 1966 with the initial aim of promoting uilleann-piping & harp playing through classes, publications and recordings, public sessions, concerts, festivals, workshops, summer schools and participation in events such as Slogah, National Festival of Music for Youth and Fleadh Cheoil. The club now aims to consolidate the community aspect of traditional music through an inclusion policy drawing on related music of Scotland, Wales and Cape Breton. Provide classes for 135 pupils which are divided into 18 childrens and 4 adult classes, teacher training courses and preparation for the London College of Music traditional music exams. Publication of tutors cassettes for uilleann-pipes, fiddle, tin whistle, singing, flute and collections of tunes. Promotion of piping festival and dance festival. Instrument loan scheme from stock of 43 instruments including pipes, fiddles, harps, flutes, concertinas, accordions. Classes in all instruments and traditional singing in Irish and English. The newsletter 'Monthly Bulletin' is issued on a monthly basis.

Arts and Business (formerly ABSA - Association for Business Sponsorship of the Arts)
Hilary McGrady
Director
53 Malone Road

Belfast BT9 6RY
Northern Ireland

Tel/Fax: +48 9066 4736/+48 9066 4500
Email: northern.ireland@aandb.org.uk
Website: www.aandb.org.uk
Other key staff: Colleen Murray (Manager),
Alice O'Rawe (Manager of Pairing Scheme),
Paul Smith (Manager of Professional
Development Programme)

Arts & Business, formerly ABSA, advises on and develops all aspects of arts and business partnerships. It advises business members on arts sponsorship programmes and can advise arts organisations about improving relationships with the private sector. Seeks to develop partnerships in addition to sponsorship, including management development and bringing the arts into work. Key activities include: the Pairing Scheme which can match sponsorships with an award of Government money, the Professional Development Programmes which develop arts and business managers; the Development Forum, a national body for arts fundraising professionals; and Arts @ Work, which encourages the integration of the arts into work and the workplace.

Arts in Transition
Karen Brady
c/o West Cork Arts Centre
North Street
Skibbereen
Co. Cork

Tel/Fax: +353 28 40111 or +353 28 22090/
+353 28 23237
Other key staff: Teresa O'Sullivan (PR Co-ordinator)

The Arts in Transition project has been devised in response to transition year students needs. The project began in June 1997 and was implemented in three local schools in September 1997. At present the project works with approximately 100 students. The project consists of seven 8-10 week courses in a number of artistic disciplines, delivered by professional artists working within the region. Its objective is to promote the arts as an accessible form of enjoyment and to make pupils aware of the opportunities provided by the arts in further education and as a career. It aims to provide a genuine insight into the life of the artist, to encourage young people to develop their own critical powers, have confidence to make informal judgements and learn about the culture of their region and others.

ArtsCare
Ronnie Dunn
Chairman
25 Adelaide Street
Belfast BT2 8FH
Northern Ireland

Tel/Fax: 048 9053 5639/+48 9023 2304
Other key staff: Gloria Bryans (Personal
Assistant/Administrator)

ArtsCare has been created to assist with the provision of recreational, educational and entertaining arts programmes in various healthcare locations. From a focal point, ArtsCare hopes to stimulate, assist and co-ordinate each individual undertaking, providing ideas, advice and support for the artists and the centre in which they work. It is anticipated that ArtsCare groups will be formed in many of the locations benefiting from its work. Hospitals, hospices, community and health centres will hopefully each soon see their own ArtsCare committees concerned with the special aims and interests of their particular needs. ArtsCare involves the complete artistic spectrum - painting, drama, music and dance. Any visual or performance art is a positive expression, and is therefore significant to the healing process. By directly involving art, patients and staff are given an interest in their surroundings and an interest in themselves. ArtsCare intend patients to be participants as well as spectators. Over the years ArtsCare has developed throughout Northern Ireland. There are currently 23 ArtsCare groups. Also 13 artists are resident working 2/3 days a week at each health location. Newsletter 'ArtsCare Matters' is issued on a quarterly basis.

Artscope
Caroline Wynne
Director
Abbeytown
Boyle
Co. Roscommon

Tel/Fax: +353 79 62963
Email: artscope@eircom.net
Other key staff: Sally Maidment (Administration)

Artscope uses the arts as a means of education and personal development. It aims to increase an awareness of the arts through energetic and interactive programmes. Artscope's policy is to be as inclusive as possible to provide a wide variety of programmes which can be adapted to suit individual needs and resources.

ASCI - Association of Songwriters and Composers of Ireland

Lorraine O'Reilly
General Secretary
1 Oakleigh Court
Dublin Road
Malahide
Co. Dublin

Tel/Fax: +353 1 8450389/+353 1 8450365
Email: lor@iol.ie
Other key staff: Gay Woods (Chairperson), Mike Hanrahan (Vice-Chairperson), Ron Brooks (Treasurer), Pete St. John (PR)

In February 1999 an open meeting for songwriters and composers took place in Dublin. As a result, a new association was formed in early March 1999 with a steering committee of 15 songwriters and composers. The committee has met once a month to discuss various ways that a songwriters' association can make a difference in the music business. The ASCI is at embryonic stage at this time, with limited funds and a small budget. There is no initial fee for joining ASCI at this time. The association is seeking sponsorship from sources who may wish to support its aims, which are as follows: initiation of registration/database of all Irish songwriters home and abroad, the perpetuity of copyright law, to seek a 40% content, (Irish product ruling on all licensed radio stations in Ireland), to promote the standing of Irish songwriters in professional life, to inform its members of their rights, to increase the all round earning power of its members, to advise members of the organisations operating inside the music business with direct, immediate association with the songwriters compositions for commercial presentations, to be a basic association enabling new songwriters to have a place to get the correct "start-up" information to pursue a professional career in the music business. ASCI is not a royalty collection organisation. Sponsored by IMRO.

Association of Irish Composers

John McLachlan
Executive Director
Copyright House
Pembroke Row
Dublin 2

Tel/Fax: +353 1 4961484
Email: aic@eircom.net

The Association of Irish Composers (AIC), is the representative body of composers of contemporary music in Ireland. The association aims to improve standards of composition, and to obtain support and recognition for composers and their work at home and abroad. It repre-sents members' interests at IMRO (Irish Music Rights Organisation), MCPS (Mechanical Copyright Protection Society), SIPTU (Services Industrial Professional Technical Union) and ISCM (International Society of Contemporary Music). With the assistance of IMRO, members can avail of informed advice on local and administrative matters, e.g. contracts royalties. Through the association's regular newsletter, members can keep in touch with developments in Irish contemporary music. The association promotes concerts of contemporary music around Ireland, and under its International Exchange Programme, it arranges concerts abroad with return visits by foreign ensembles and/or composers. Members receive discounts on certain music supplies/services. The newsletter 'AIC News' is issued to members only on a quarterly basis.

Association of Medical Advisors to The British Orchestras - Northern Ireland

Dr Christine Hunter
Honorary Medical Advisor to
the Ulster Orchestra
47 Maryville Park
Belfast BT9 6LP
Northern Ireland

Tel: 048 9032 0919
Email: christinehunter@netscapeonline.co.uk
Other key staff: Dr Meuros Fitch (Honourary Medical Advisor to the Ulster Orchestras), Dr Tony Stevens (Honourary Medical Advisor to the Ulster Orchestra).

The Association of Medical Advisors to the British Orchestras (AMABO), is affiliated to the British Association of Performing Arts Medicine (BAPAM). AMABO has biannual meetings for training in performing arts medicine. Dr Hunter, Dr Fitch and Dr Stevens are setting up a network of consultants who have an interest in performing arts medicine in Northern Ireland.

Association of Music Typesetters in Ireland

Debbie Metrustry
78 St. Lawrence Road
Chapelizod
Dublin 20

Tel/Fax: +353 1 6761409
Mobile: +353 86 2446256
Email: toptype@gofree.indigo.ie
Other key staff: Andrew Mackriell

This association is for all computer music typesetters, to

provide a forum for discussion and negotiation of sales and contracts. It is linked to typesetters' associations outside of Ireland and provides members with contact to others. All professional and semi-professional computer music typesetters are welcome to apply to join.

Belfast and District Set Dancing and Traditional Music Society

Mary Fox
Chairperson
38 Milltown Lane
Portadown
Co. Armagh BT62 1TB
Northern Ireland

Tel/Fax: 048 3885 2469
Other key staff: Peter Woods (Secretary), Pauline Torrens (Treasurer), Ursula Morrow (Publicity Officer)

The society is a registered charity which has been in operation for seven years. Its aims are to promote traditional dance and music and bring it to a wider community, hence encouraging membership from all cultural traditions in Northern Ireland. Monthly dance céilís and regular workshops are held in Ashleigh Hall, Windsor Avenue, Belfast 9. Ongoing music classes cater for all age groups covering tin whistle, flute, button accordion, fiddle, bodhrán, guitar and uilleann pipes. Classes are held in The Crescent Arts Centre, University Road, Belfast 7.

British Kodály Academy

Enid Conaghan
BKA Representative in Ireland
20 St. Johns Park West
Clondalkin
Dublin 22

Tel: +353 1 4570393
Other key staff: John Wood (Chairman), Brenda Harris (Secretary), Celia Cviic (Treasurer)

Founded in 1981 as the British Kodály Society. The organisation's title changed to BKA in 1989. Affiliated to the International Kodály Society and has a membership of 286. Aims to further disseminate the philosophy and practice of music education found in the work of Zoltan Kodály, and to relate it to British and Irish musical heritage and to improve British and Irish music education by means of courses, demonstrations, publications, and co-operation with other like minded bodies and authorities. The British Kodály Academy operates an annual summer school whose tutors include Hungarians

of international repute, part-time training courses at elementary, intermediate and advanced levels for all wishing to improve their own musicianship, teach or communicate music to others, early childhood music education courses, INSET in teacher's own locality, conferences workshops, demonstrations and introductory courses. Most courses are accredited by Trinity College of Music . The 'BKA Newsletter' is issued on a quarterly basis.

British Trombone Society

Stephen Cairns
Northern Ireland Representative
8 Malory Gardens
Lisburn
Co. Antrim BT28 3JX
Northern Ireland

Tel/Fax: 048 9260 2646
Email: spcairns@globalnet.co.uk
Website: www.nthwood.demon.co.uk/bts/index.htm
Other key staff: Anthony Parsons (Editor), John Edney (Membership Secretary), Steve Greenall & Simon Hogg (Advertising).

The British Trombone Society (BTS), promotes the trombone and its repertoire in all musical styles. Formed in 1985, BTS is for everyone interested in the trombone and makes no distinction based on age, ability or any other considerations. BTS commissions new compositions, arranges concerts, workshops, lectures and holds a major festival each year. The newsletter 'The Trombonist' is issued on a quarterly basis and is free to members.

CAFE - Creative Activity for Everyone

Simeon Smith
Membership Development Worker
143 Townsend Street
Dublin 2

Tel/Fax: +353 1 6770330/+353 1 6713268
Email: cafe@connect.ie
Other key staff: Wes Wilkie (Director), Nuala Hunt (Education/Training Worker)

CAFE is the umbrella body for community based activities in Ireland. Set up in 1983 by community arts workers to support the development of their work. CAFE's policy is a commitment to achieving social and cultural equality through creative action. It recognises the importance of collective creative action as a means of achieving social change and aims to promote the use of the arts as a means of education, personal and community development, particularly in areas and communities of disad-

'The Cockpit'

32-Track Digital Recording Facility using
ProTools D.24

Extremely Competitive Rates for
Demos & CD Mastering

Supported by FAS and the EU under the
North Dublin URBAN Initiative

Glenhill House, Glenhill Est.,
Finglas, Dublin 11.
Tel: 8643354
Fax: 8642141
e-mail: fusebox@tinet.ie

Services of
FUSEBOX

Music Workshops
(Personal development through music)

Free Information Service with internet access

Electric & Acoustic Gigs

Instrument Tuition
(Guitar,Keyboards,Bass Guitar)

Graphics Service

---

fmc

Did you know that there is an organisation within 5 miles of you that can help you get a record deal, who can help you fine tune your guitar skills, put you in a recording studio for next to nothing or help your band organise a tour around the country???
EVER HEAR OF A MUSIC COLLECTIVE? Well, there are over 30 of them around the country and if there isn't one in your backyard yet, there's probably one being started in your area right now as you read this . . .

Music Collectives have much to offer for all of you musicians, potential musicians and adventurous bands. Some of the stuff you can expect to find at your local collective:
- information & contacts within the music industry
- business advice for your band or music career
- music related, music biz workshops in your area
- rehearsal & recording studios you can access
- advice and contacts on how to record your demos
- how to design the ideal press pack to promote your music
- music training courses
- bringing music into your community & schools
- how to get involved in starting up a collective in your area

The Federation of Music Collectives (fmc) will help you get started. Contact them to find out about the COLLECTIVES in your area or ways you can help start one of your own.

The Arts Council
An Chomhairle Ealaíon

Angela Dorgan @ FMC Space 28 North Lotts Dublin 1. PH: 01 8782244 / 8721882 FAX: 01 8726827 EMAIL: fmc@1mn.ie vantage. CAFE operates in the areas of information, networking and training. Over the past eight years CAFE has developed a community arts database, CAFEdata, and disseminated through a telephone and mail enquiry service, a bimonthly newsletter, consultancies, research, publication and outreach projects. Access to the service is provided free.

Cairdeas na bhFidileiri

Caoimhin MacAoidh
Registrar
Tullyhorkey
Ballyshannon
Co. Donegal

Tel: +353 72 52144
Email: dldclk1@iol.ie
Other key staff: Rab Cherry (Chairman)

Cairdeas na bhFidileiri aims to promote the playing and appreciation of Donegal fiddle music and to collect and record the music and its history. Runs the Donegal Fiddlers Summer School in Glencolmkill, Co. Donegal during the first week in August and the Donegal Fiddlers Weekend, which is usually held in Glenties, Co. Donegal. Offers help to communities in Co. Donegal who are trying to promote fiddle playing by organising weekend schools.

Cairde na Cruite

Aibhlin McCrann
Secretary
50 Wyvern
Killiney
Co. Dublin

Tel/Fax: +353 1 2856345/+353 1 6768007
Email: mccranna@indigo.ie
Website: www.harp.net/cnac/cnac.htm
Contact: Gráinne Yeats (Chairperson), Joe Joyce (Treasurer), Ann Jones Walsh (Membership/Newsletter)

Founded in the early sixties with the aim of reviving and fostering an interest in the Irish harp and its music. Runs an annual summer course for students of the Irish harp of all standards and ages. Based in Ireland and overseas with a particular emphasis on the interpretation and performance of traditional music. Has published four books of graded pieces for the Irish harp, and organises sessions and workshops for young players. The newsletter 'Cairde na Cruite Newsletter and Season' is issued on a quarterly basis.

Cape Breton - Ireland Musical Bridge

Liz Doherty
Director
Music Department
University College Cork
Cork

Tel/Fax: +353 21 4903139/+353 21 4271595
Email: lizdoherty@ucc.ie

Aims to to promote and encourage musical links between the two islands of Cape Breton, Nova Scotia, Canada and Ireland. The Bridge emerged as a direct result of the 1993 Éigse na Laoi Festival organised by the Music Department of University College Cork, which focused on the music and dance of Cape Breton Island. Royalties from the album recorded by Nimbus Records provided the funds for the establishment of the Bridge. The Cape Breton/Ireland Musical Bridge is primarily concerned with facilitating contact between musicians, dancers, and music enthusiasts from both Cape Breton and Ireland. Its main function will be as a resource centre, providing information on festivals and events in both areas, contacts for those wishing to tour, a bibliography and discography of Cape Breton and Irish Music. Information on ordering albums/books through mail order etc. The Nimbus album Traditional Music from Cape Breton Island will also be available through the Cape Breton/Ireland Musical Bridge.

Ceoil Productions Ireland Ltd

Derek Gleeson
Director
PO Box 4716
Dublin 1

Tel/Fax: +353 1 6235744
Email: ceoilpro@indigo.ie
Website: www.ceoilproductions.com
Other key staff: Ken Kiernan (Producer), Debbie Smith (Engineer), Brendan Hayes (Administrator)

Ceoil Productions aims to develop and produce music projects for CD, CD-ROM, film & theatre, interactive home entertainment and other creative music and/or technologically driven endeavours having similar characteristics. In addition Ceoil and Screen Training Ireland have developed a film scoring program to prepare resident composers for work in Ireland in developing film and television industry. Key activities include the running of music production company, music consultancy, a recording studio and film and television scoring.

Ceol Uíbh Ráthaigh

Pat Kavanagh
Chairperson
Kells Post Office
Kells
Co. Kerry

Tel/Fax: +353 66 9477632/+353 66 9462059
Other key staff: Sarah O'Brien (Cultural Development Officer), Ena Sweeney (Secretary), Shane O'Driscoll (PRO)

Ceol Uíbh Ráthaigh is a local voluntary initiative dedicated to the promotion of high quality music performance and education for the communities of the Iveragh Peninsula in South Kerry. The organisation was established in 1995 as part of Kerry Music County 2000 under Music Networks Regional Development Programme and with the continued assistance of the South Kerry Development Partnership Ltd. Ceol Uíbh Ráthaigh promotes and organises an annual series of winter concerts of varying musical types in the area from Kells to Castlecove. The organisation also has a strong educational remit and organises workshops, masterclasses, schools visits and music appreciation talks in conjunction with performances.

Childrens World Music Centre

Ken McCue
Director
c/o Ewan Mac Coll Centre For the Arts
4 Great Strand Street
Dublin 1

Tel/Fax: +353 1 8735077/+353 1 8735078
Email: dublinarts@ireland.com
Other key staff: Fergus Egan (Co-ordinator)

Research is currently underway to establish a centre of world music for children in association with Marketown Music Collective and the Improvised Music Company. The centre will be located in Dublin's Inner City and will provide a base for the Yehudi Menuhin Foundation Mus'E' project. This will incorporate a strong multi-culture and anti-racist focus.

Choral Ireland

Mr Frank McMullan
Moderator

Email: choralireland-owner@egroups.com
Websites: http://listen.to/choralireland or www.egroups.com/group/choralireland/info.html

Choral Ireland is a web-based information, discussion and upcoming event publicity resource for all enthusiasts, leaders, performers and audience members throughout Ireland. It covers choral singing of all genres from opera to musicals and barbershop to oratorio. Choral Ireland functions via two websites, the first giving an introduction to the group. The second is an e-mail discussion list with many added features for members including calendar, links and database sections. These provide notification of upcoming events and e-mail media publicity contacts. Lists all known Irish choirs with links to those with websites and web-based 'press cuttings', and a discography of Irish choral recordings.

City Arts Centre

Sandy Fitzgerald
Executive Director
23-25 Moss Street
Dublin 2

Tel/Fax: +353 1 6770643/+353 1 6770131
Email: cityartscentre@eircom.net
Website: www.homepage.eircom.net/~cityarts/
Other key staff: Alison Rogers (Music Map Course Director), John Lalor (Studios Manager), Collette Farrell (Programming Manager)

City Arts Centre was founded in 1973. Aims to put arts to work for the community in a way that is relevant, practical, accessible and exciting. Encourages learning through the arts. Based on a policy of equality for people to have a cultural voice to celebrate difference. Key music activities include music rehearsal studios, 'Music Map' (music, media & communications course for people with disabilities), annual DIY Music Festival. Facilities include studios, venue, workshops, gallery, cafe, education and training space available for workshops, rehearsals and meetings. A newsletter is available on a quarterly basis. Full disabled access.

Classical Guitar Society of Northern Ireland

Gerry O'Gorman
Chairman
7 Chapel Lane
Drumaroad
Co. Down BT31 9PQ
Northern Ireland

Tel: 048 4481 1522
Email: secretary@cgsni.freeserve.co.uk
Website: www.cgsni.freeserve.co.uk

The Classical Guitar Society of Northern Ireland aims to encourage the appreciation of the classical guitar. Founded by David McKittrick and Jim McCullough the society has been running for over ten years. Key activities include: workshops, recitals, members recitals, discussions and lectures.

Co-Operation Ireland

Sharon Woods
Senior Media and Information Officer
37 Upper Fitzwilliam Street
Dublin 2

Tel/Fax: +353 1 6610588/+353 1 6618456
Email: swoods@co-operation-ireland.ie
Website: www.co-operation-ireland.ie
Other key staff: Theresa Cullen (Manager -
Youth, Education and Community Programme),
Matthew Kennedy (Project Officer - Community),
David Holloway (Project Officer - Community)

Co-Operation Ireland is a voluntary organisation committed to the belief that a lasting peace can only be achieved when people respect, trust and understand one another. Its aim is to promote improved relations between the people of Northern Ireland and the Republic of Ireland. Co-Operation Ireland's role is as a facilitator and catalyst, making change happen by enabling people to come together. Its activities target young people, community groups, those involved in small to medium sized enterprises, tourism, agriculture, as well as politicians and the media. Through a managed process of reciprocal exchanges which have been adapted and refined over twenty years, the organisation gives thousands of people annually the opportunity to come together to explore issues and from that go on to develop mutual understanding and respect for those of another identity. The newsletter 'Co-Operation Ireland News' is issued on a quarterly basis.

The Columba Initiative

Ms Michelle Ní Chróinín
Project Officer
f/ch Udarás Na Gaeltachta
Na Forbacha
Co. Na Gaillimhe

Tel/Fax: +353 91 503278/+353 91 503101
Email: ccille@udaras.ie
Other key staff: Maolcholam Scott (Project
Officer Northern Ireland), Dohmnall Angaidh
MacLennan (Project Officer, Scotland)

The Columba Initiative aims to develop strategies and projects in which the Gaelic language in Ireland and Scotland can draw together people from diverse backgrounds, within and between each country and region. The Columba Initiative builds upon present cultural exchanges and creates new links. Scotland, Ireland and Northern Ireland participate in the initiative and there is a project officer in each area. This initiative was set up by Mr Brian Wilson, MP and announced by Mary Robinson during the Summer of 1997. Also aims to facilitate practical and sustainable co-operation between communities, networks and speakers of Irish and Scottish Gaelic in the arts, and in social and cultural matters. The Columba Initiative identifies, initiates and develops projects and partnerships between the three partner areas Ireland, Northern Ireland and Scotland.

Comhaltas Ceoltóirí Éireann

Labhrás Ó Murchú
Director General
32 Belgrave Square
Monkstown
Co. Dublin

Tel/Fax: +353 1 2800295/+353 1 2803759
Email: enquiries@comhaltas.com
Website: www.comhaltas.com
Other key staff: Séamus MacMathúna (Timire
Cheoil), Bernard O'Sullivan (Project Officer),
C.M. Hodge (Rúnaí Oifige)

Founded in 1951 to promote Irish traditional music, song, dance and the Irish language. 400 branches and 600 classes worldwide. 44 Fleadhanna Cheoil each year attracting 20,000 competitors. Over 1 million people attend CCÉ functions each year. Responsible for Cultúrlann na hÉireann (Irish Cultural Institute) and 9 other Regional Cultural Centres and holds an extensive National Archive of traditional music and song. Also services worldwide requests for information on Irish music, song, dance and the Irish language and provides lecturers for these subjects. Runs a Diploma Course for Irish traditional music teachers (over 400 already qualified) along with Scoil Éigse, an annual Summer College attended by up to 600 eligible students each year, most on scholarships. In addition organises annual concert tours (national and international), publishes TREOIR magazine and several tutors, produces tapes and CDs and, together with RTÉ, regularly produces TV and local radio programmes.

Community Arts Forum

Martin Lynch
Co-ordinator
15 Church Street
Belfast BT1 1ER
Northern Ireland

Tel/Fax: 048 9024 2910/048 9031 2264
Email: caf@cinni.org
Website: www.cinni.org/caf
Other key staff: Joan Reid (Information Officer),
Pauline Hadaway (Development Officer),
Kate Muldoon (Administrator)

The Community Arts Forum (CAF) was founded at a meeting of community arts groups and activists in 1993 in Belfast. From an initial membership of 10 groups, it has grown to 154 groups and 77 individual affiliated artistes. Membership is from all over Northern Ireland. It aims to service the Community Arts sector and all it constituent parts in Northern Ireland by: supporting and extending community based opportunities for people of participate in and control arts activities; creating a membership organisation to secure long term sustainable development of community arts organisations and groups; developing understanding and standards of practice of community arts through training, education and information; encouraging co-operation and partnership between individuals and groups committed to arts and community development; raising awareness of and support for community arts at neighbourhood, city and national levels.

Contemporary Music Centre
Jonathan Grimes
Information and Outreach Manager
19 Fishamble Street
Temple Bar
Dublin 8

Tel/Fax: +353 1 6731922/+353 1 6489100
Email: info@cmc.ie
Website: www.cmc.ie
Other key staff: Eve O'Kelly (Director), Nicola Murphy (Promotions Officer)

The Contemporary Music Centre is an all Ireland archive and resource centre which promotes and documents the music of modern Irish classical music composers. Services include: a major library of scores and information materials; a sound archive and an information service. It also publishes the free periodical, 'New Music News', which is issued three times per year, in February, May and September.

Copyright Association of Ireland
Helen Sheehy
Secretary
PO Box 29
8 Adelaide Street
Dun Laoghaire
Co. Dublin

Tel/Fax: +353 1 2800340/+353 1 2803101
Email: hsheehy@pals.ie
Website: www.cai.ie

The Association was formed by a group of people who have an interest in copyright law whether as legal prac-

titioners, creators of copyright works or as academics. It is a company limited by guarantee having the following objectives: the promotion of informed debate on copyright; the promotion of awareness of copyright among users and creators of copyright works and the public generally, the examination of legislative measures having an effect on copyright. Also promotes informed debate and awareness of copyright by holding conferences and seminars. Membership open to individuals and businesses. Affiliated to the International Federation on Copyright (ALAI) and has the right to appoint one member to the Board of ALAI. A newsletter, 'Copyright' is issued.

COTHÚ -
Business Council For the Arts
Brigid Roden
Chief Executive
44 East Essex Street
Temple Bar
Dublin 2

Tel/Fax: +353 1 6766966/+353 1 6766997
Email: info@cothu.ie
Website: under construction
Other key staff: Audrey Phelan (Director of Communications), Sharon Stanford (Director of Programmes)

Cothú's mission is to promote and encourage business sponsorship of the arts, to represent the interests of its members to provide them with relevant services, and to foster mutually beneficial business/arts alliances. The organisation administers the Arts Sponsor of the Year Awards, provides a range of membership services for its corporate members, provides advice, information and guidance to arts organisations concerning arts sponsorship and funding, and runs the INFORM programme which provides management and business training for arts managers and administrators.

Council of the Heads of
Music in Higher Education
Pamela Flanagan
Secretary
Royal Irish Academy of Music
Westland Row
Dublin 2

Tel/Fax: +353 1 6764412 / +353 1 6622798
Other key staff: Prof. David Harold Cox (Chairman)

The Council includes every third level institution in Ireland offering music as part of a degree programme. Aims to represent the interests of its member institutions on all the issues involving music education in Ireland today. Information day on postgraduate courses in music held in Dublin, annually every February or March. Booklet published on third-level undergraduate and post-graduate courses in Ireland.

Cultural Diversity Programme of the Northern Ireland Community Relations Council

Dr Tony Langlois
Project Officer
6 Murray Street
Belfast BT1 6DN
Northern Ireland

Tel/Fax: 048 9043 9953/048 9023 5208
Email: info@community-relations.org.uk
Website: www.community-relations.org.uk
Other key staff: Joanne Murphy (Project Officer)

Assists people and organisations in Northern Ireland to address issues of communal division. Through its Cultural Diversity Programme it aims to promote an awareness and respect for cultural diversity in Northern Ireland. Financial and practical support of groups engaged in challenging cultural projects which may include musical, artistic, historical, linguistic and educational elements. Key activities include three small grant schemes, aimed at cultural projects which contribute to debate and dialogue. This grant scheme covers publications, radio, film and multi-media. The resources scheme commissions research and develops materials for use in community relations work. The newsletter 'CRC News' is issued on a quarterly basis.

Cumann Cheoil Tíre Éireann - Folk Music Society of Ireland

Ellen MacIsaac
Honorary Secretary
15 Henrietta Street
Dublin 1

Tel: +353 1 8730093

Established in 1971 in Dublin with the objective of promoting the study and practice of traditional music. The aims of the society, as set forth in its constitution, are to encourage an informed interest in traditional music, to preserve this music and sustain its traditions, and to promote the study of traditional music. Meetings are held in Dublin during the winter season, and these meetings take the form of illustrated lectures, recitals, seminars etc. Topics of these meetings cover all aspects of the Irish tradition - singing in Irish and English, dance music and other instrumental music, dancing, instru-

ments, collections and collectors, means of transmission - and also the folk music of other countries, especially the Celtic countries.

Cumann Náisiúnta na gCór - Association of Irish Choirs

Margaret O'Sullivan
Acting Chief Executive Officer
Drinan Street
Cork City
Co. Cork

Tel/Fax: +353 21 4312296/+353 21 4962457
Email: cnc@iol.ie

Established in 1980 in response to growing interest in choral music and choral singing in Ireland this association is grant-aided by the Arts Council. It is an national organisation committed to the provision of access to a wide variety of services for choral representatives and teachers, and the stimulation of interest in choral music throughout the country. Organises courses for conductors, choristers and teachers on a regional level. Presents an annual Summer School for Choral Conductors and Teachers. Administers the 120 mixed voice Irish Youth Choir. Publishes choral music with an emphasis on works by contemporary Irish composers. Operates a choral music library service for study copies of part-songs, a membership scheme, an insurance scheme and provides a broad based information and advisory service. The newsletter 'In-Choir' is issued on a quarterly basis for choristers.

(See advert page 7.)
The following choirs are members of CNC:

Dublin/Midlands/East region
Alexandra College Choir, Milltown, Dublin
Ashbourne Senior Church Choir, Meath
Assumption Secondary School Choir, Walkinstown, Dublin
Athlone Choral Society, Westmeath
Ballinteer Male Singers, Dublin
Blackrock College Choirs, Dublin
Blakestown Choristers, Mulhuddart, Dublin
Bray Choral Society, Wicklow
Camarata, Drogheda, Co. Louth
Cameron Singers, Ratheny, Dublin
Cantairí Avondale, Dublin
Cantairí Naomh Bríd, Blackrock, Dublin
Cantairí Óga Átha Cliath, Rathmines, Dublin
Cappella, Dublin
Carlton Singers, Navan, Co. Meath
Cavan Singers, Cavan
Choir of Whitefriar St. Church, Dublin
Christ Church Cathedral Choirs, Dublin
Church of Ireland Choral Union, Dublin
Clongowes Wood College Choir, Naas, Co. Kildare
Coláiste Bhríde Choir, Carnew, Co. Wicklow

Collon Senior Choir, Co. Louth
Culwick Choral Society, Dublin
DIT Choral Society, Dublin
Draíocht, Dublin
Dublin Boy Singers
Dublin County Choir
Dublin Welsh Male Voice Choir
East Glendalough School, Wicklow
Eblana, Dublin
Enchiriadis Treis, Malahide, Co. Dublin
Gaudete Singers, Dublin
Géis, Dublin
Goethe Institute Choir, Dublin
Guinness Choir, Dublin
Holy Child Community School, Dublin
Holy Family Sec School Choir, Newbridge, Co. Kildare
Inver Ladies Choir, Arklow, Co. Wicklow
Italian Cultural Institute Choir, Dublin
John Scotus Choir, Donnybrook, Dublin
Kings Hospital Chamber Choir, Dublin
Lassus Scholars/Piccolo Lasso, Dublin
Lindsay Singers, Dublin
Loreto Balbriggan Senior Choir, Dublin
Loreto Junior Schools Choirs, Dublin
Manor House School Choirs, Raheny, Dublin
Maynooth University Choral Society, Kildare
Meánscoil Iognáid Rís, Naas, Co. Kildare
Mercy Secondary School Choir, Ballymahon, Longford
Midland Arts Education Scheme, Westmeath
Mullingar Choral Society, Westmeath
Nás na Rí Singers, Kildare
National Chamber Choir, Dublin
National Children's Choir, Dublin
Navan Male Singers, Meath
Newbridge College Choir, Kildare
Notre Dame des Missions Choir, Churchtown, Dublin
Our Lady of Mercy College Choir, Beaumont, Dublin
Our Lady's Bower Secondary School Choir, Athlone, Co. Westmeath
Our Lady's Choral Society, Dublin
Parc Singers, Dublin
Peoples College Choir, Dublin
Pontana, Drogeda, Co. Louth
Portmarnock Singers, Dublin
Rockford Manor Sec School Choir, Blackrock, Dublin
RTÉ Philharmonic Choir, Dublin
Sacred Heart School Choir, Tullamore, Co. Offaly
Schola Cantorum, Mullingar, Co. Westmeath
Setanta, Dundalk, Co. Louth
Skerries Community Choir, Dublin
St. Cecilia Singers, Dublin
St. Dominic's College School Choir, Cabra, Dublin
St. Joseph's Church Choir, Dublin
St. Laurence's School, Greystones, Co. Wicklow
St. Louis Secondary School Choir, Dundalk, Co. Louth
St. Mary's College Choir, Arklow, Co. Wicklow
St. Patrick's Church Choir, Maynooth, Co. Kildare
St. Peter's College Choir, Dunboyne, Co. Meath

Studio 3 Singers, Mullingar, Co. Westmeath
Tourdion, Dublin
Trim Choral Society, Meath
Ulysses Choir, Dublin
Virginia Singers, Cavan

South/South West region

Ardscoil Rís Boys Choir, Limerick
Blackpool Church Choir, Cork
Broadford Church Choir, Limerick
Cantairí an Phiarsaigh, Farranree, Cork
Cantairí Ghort Alainn, Mayfield, Cork
Cantairí Mhuscraí, Ballincollig, Co. Cork
Cantare, Ennis, Co. Clare
Carbery Choral Society, Skibbereen, Co. Cork
Carrigaline Singers, Cork
Cashel Community School Choir, Tipperary
Choirs of the Cork School of Music
Choirs of University College Cork
City of Cork Male Voice Choir
Coláiste Josaef Choir, Kilmallock, Co. Limerick
Coláiste Mhuire Choir, Ennis, Co. Clare
Commodore Male Voice Choir, Cobh, Cork
Cór Cilliath, Killeagh, Co. Cork
Cór Cluain Lara, Clonlara, Co. Cork
Cór Cois Abhann, Cork
Cór Cois Farraige, Ballycotton, Co. Cork
Cór Coláiste Choilm, Ballingcollig, Co. Cork
Cork Airport Singers
Cork Garda Choir
Crescent College Comprehensive Choir, Limerick
Crosshaven Singers, Cork
Desmond Singers, Rathkeale, Co. Limerick
Douglas Harmonia Singers, Cork
Duneaskey Singers, Tipperary
East Cork Choral Society, Midleton, Co. Cork
Ennis Pro-Cathedral Choir, Clare
Geiptine Singers, Askeaton, Co. Limerick
Glounthaune Church Choir, Cork
Holy Family Boys School Choir, Tralee, Kerry
IMP Folk Choir, Midleton, Co. Cork
Kerry Choral Union, Tralee, Co. Kerry
Laurel Hill Coláiste FCJ Choir, Limerick
Limerick Choral Union
Limerick Singers
Loreto School Choirs, Fermoy, Co. Cork
Loreto Secondary School Choirs, Youghal, Co. Cork
Madrigal '75, Cork
Non Nobis Donime Choir, Ennis, Co. Clare
Presentation Sec School Choir, Ballyphehane, Cork
Presentation Sec School Choir, Clonmel, Co. Tipperary
Redemptorist Church Senior Choir, Limerick
Roscrea Community Choir, Tipperary
Sacred Heart School Choir, Thurles, Co. Tipperary
Scariff Community College Choir, Clare
Schull Community College Choir, Cork
Scoil an Athar Maitiú Choirs, Cork
Scoil Carmel Choirs, Caherdvin, Limerick

Scoil Ide Choir, Corbally, Limerick
Scoil Mhuire Choir, Cork
Scoil Mhuire School Choir, Carrick-on-Suir, Co. Tipperary
Sliabh Féilim Singers Choir, Cappamore, Co. Limerick
South Kerry Choir, Kenmare, Co. Kerry
St Aloysius College Choir, Cork
St Joseph's Church Choir, Limerick
St Mary's High School Choirs, Midleton, Co. Cork
St Mary's Sec School Choir, Mallow, Co. Cork
St Mary's Sec School Choir, Nenagh, Co. Tipperary
St Mary's Senior Church Choir, Clonmel, Co. Tipperary
St Vincent's Secondary School Choir, Cork
Tipperary Singers
Tralee CBS Boys Choir, Co. Kerry
Turners Cross/South Parish Choir, Cork
UCC Choral Society, Cork
University of Limerick Choir
Ursuline Convent School Choir, Cork
Voices of Limerick
West Clare Singers, Kilkee, Co. Clare
West Cork Choral Singers, Skibbereen, Cork
Wilcollane Singers, Cork
Youghal Choral Society, Cork

South East region

Blackwater Singers, Lismore, Co. Waterford
Brigidine Secondary School, Mountrath, Co. Laois
Carlow Choral Society
Carlow Young Artists Choir, Carlow
Castlecomer Community School Choir, Kilkenny
Castlecomer Male Voice Choir, Kilkenny
CBS Secondary School Choir, Kilkenny
De La Salle College Choir, Waterford
Enniscorthy Choral Society, Wexford
Good Counsel Choir, Waterford
Gorey Choral Group, Wexford
Kilkenny CBS Boys Choir, Kilkenny
Lismore Choir, Waterford
Loreto Secondary School Choirs, Wexford
Madrigallery, Waterford
Mount Sion CBS Primary Choir, Waterford
New Ross Singers, Wexford
Newtown Senior Choir, Waterford
Presentation Primary School Choirs, Waterford
Presentation Sec School Choirs, Kilkenny
Edmond Rice Choral Society, Waterford
Smithwicks/Kilkenny Youth Choir, Kilkenny
St Canice's Choral Group, Kilkenny
St Leo's College Choir, Carlow
St Mary's Choir, New Ross, Co. Wexford
Unity Singers, Kilkenny
Waterford Boy Singers
Waterford City Choir
Wexford Festival Singers
Wexford Ladies Choir
WIT Choral & Orchestral Society, Waterford

West/North West/North

Ballyhaunis Community School Choir, Mayo

Ballymote School Choir, Sligo
Black Majic Choir, Belleek, Fermanagh
Breffini Singers, Manorhamilton, Co. Leitrim
Cantairí Béal Atha h-Amhnais, Ballyhaunis, Co. Mayo
Carraig Choral Group, Carrickmacross, Co. Monaghan
Castlebar Choral Society, Co. Mayo
Ceol na Mara, Co. Galway
Cois Cladaigh Chamber Choir, Co. Galway
Colmcille Ladies Choir, Co. Derry
Convent of Mercy Sec School, Co. Roscommon
Cór na Mara, Co. Galway
Doire Calgach Singers, Co. Derry
Dominican College Choir, Co. Galway
Donegal Abbey Singers
Galway Baroque Singers
Galway Boy Singers
Glendoon Singers, Letterkenny, Co. Donegal
Grace Notes, Ballyhaunis, Co. Mayo
Mayo Choral Union
Mercy College Choir, Sligo
Mount St. Michael Choir, Claremorris, Co. Mayo
Moy Singers, Ballina, Co. Mayo
Omagh County Primary School, Co. Tyrone
Scoil Mhuire, Shrude, Co. Mayo
Scoil Mhuire Girls Choirs, Ballinasloe, Co. Galway
Sligo Orpheus Choir, Co. Sligo
St. Eugene's Cathedral Choirs, Co. Derry
St. Ignatius Parish Choir, Co. Galway
St. Louis Community School Choir, Kiltimagh, Co. Mayo
St. Mary's College Choir, Ballygar, Co. Galway
St. Murdach's Cathedral Choir, Co. Mayo
Voice Matters, Ballinasloe, Co. Galway
Westport Choral Society, Co. Mayo
Yeats County Singers, Co. Sligo

Drake Music Project Ireland

Dr Michelle McCormack
Project Leader
Head Office
Unit 5 RDC
Win Business Park, Canal Quay
Newry
Co. Down BT35 6PH
Northern Ireland

Tel/Fax: 048 3026 4294/048 3026 2100
Email: drakemusicireland@compuserve.com
Other key staff: Therese Burns (Project Co-ordinator), Dr. Frank Lyons (Training Officer)

Drake Music Project Ireland (DMPI), is a registered charity which exists in order to enable children and adults with physical disabilities to compose and perform music using specialist computer technology. This new technology, which is specially designed within the project, enables everyone to participate on an equal and independent basis in music making. Weekly workshops currently take place in Newry, Dublin, Belfast, Armagh, Dungannon, Monaghan, Dunleer, Dundalk, Lisburn, Derry and Bray. DMPI exist in order to enhance ability, not to make an issue of disability, to provide a sense of empowerment to people with disabilities. Through regular weekly workshops in music technology, training programs, composition courses, residential courses and public performances; DMPI provides equal opportunities and a sense of social inclusion for people involved in music making, for all ages, interests, abilities and from all sections of the community. The Newsletter 'ExposAbility' is issued on a quarterly basis.

Dublin Arts Office
c/o REC Studios Ltd
Emer McLoughlin
Manager
1st Floor
4 Great Strand Street
Dublin 1

Tel/Fax: +353 1 8735077/+353 1 8735078
Email: dublinarts@ireland.com
Other key staff: Catherine Talbot (Manager)

Established in 1997 Dublin Arts Office is a community employment project which undertakes arts initiatives within the inner city. It is sponsored by BEC Studios Ltd in association with FÁS and has opened an arts development/advisory agency. Dublin Arts Office exists to work in partnership with all facets of the arts and the cultural sector, providing a professional consultancy service. BEC's other activities include: consultancy services in areas of feasibility studies; funding proposals; festival/event management and marketing services.

Dublin Film Office-Script to Screen
Lez Barston
Managing Director
Ewan Mac Coll Centre For the Arts
4 Great Strand Street
Dublin 1

Tel/Fax: +353 1 8735023/+353 1 8735078
Email: lez@script2screen.net
Website: www.script2screen.net
Other key staff: Ken McCue (Chairman), Mary Keane (Special Projects Director)

Established in 1998, this organisation is a screenwriters agency and film production development organisation. Aims to develop the film industry in Dublin's Inner City and the representation of screenwriters at home and abroad. The Music on Film section will be developed in 2000 in conjunction with Liverpool film office and the Institute of Popular Music at Liverpool University. Key activities include an internet site providing information to producers and writers; seminars, workshops and screen writing courses for writers; information for other film offices regarding film production in Dublin and the creation of jobs for inner city residents in the industry.

Dublin Jazz Society
Ralph O'Callaghan
Secretary
4 Knocknacree Park
Dalkey
Co. Dublin

Tel/Fax: +353 1 2851114/+353 1 2800094
Email: jazzirl@indigo.ie
Website: www.indigo.ie/~jazzirl
Other key staff: John P. Holmes (Chairman), Dave Dempsey (Treasurer), Carole Devaney (Publicity)

Established in 1994, Dublin Jazz Society (DJS), is a voluntary, non-profitmaking organisation, dedicated to the promotion of live jazz in Dublin. It organises concerts on a regular monthly basis, featuring world-renowned international jazz artists backed by top Irish jazz musicians. Admission to concerts is open to members and non-members. Profits made are re-invested in promoting further concerts. Membership is approximately 400. Previous concerts over the years featured Scott Hamilton, Art Farmer, Charles MacPherson and Louis Stewart. Managed by a voluntary committee of enthusiasts. Produces the quarterly 'DJS Newsletter' in printed and on the on-line form (at the DJS web site), which gives jazz news on the Irish and international scene, reviews of gigs, books and CDs. Back issues of the 'DJS Newsletter' are featured on the on-line archive. Contains a biographical archive of previous concerts, with reviews, artists details and photographs. The DJS web site was first published in 1998 and is updated regularly to include news of current and forthcoming concerts.

Dublin Philharmonic Society
N. Vincent O'Neill
Director
25 Westland Square
Pearse Street
Dublin 2

Tel/Fax: +353 1 6770542/+353 6770160
Email: fci@eircom.net
Other key staff: Catherine O'Loughlin (Administrator), R.J. O'Kelly (Membership Secretary)

IBEC Music Industry Group

The Music Industry Group was formed under the auspices of IBEC in 1994. It formulates policies for the development of the music industry, and keeps Government and other appropriate bodies briefed on all matters relating to the industry. Policy documents include "Striking the Right Note" and "Raising the Volume" as well as submissions to government on Copyright. MIG also organise seminars and publishes on its website a series of factsheets on the industry.

The members of the Music Industry Group are as follows:

Concert Promoters
Entertainers / Songwriters
Jobs in Music
Irish Music Rights Organisation - IMRO
Irish Recorded Music Association - IRMA
Mechanical Copyright Protection Society (Ireland) Limited - MCPS
Music Publishers Association of Ireland - MPAI
Phonographic Performance (Ireland) Limited - PPI

For further information contact:

Music Industry Group,

Confederation House, 84-86 Lower Baggot Street, Dublin 2.

Tel: 01-605 1562. Fax: 01-638 1562. Website: www.mig.ie E-mail: info@mig.ie

Tommy McCabe, Director. Niamh Collins, Secretariat.

Formed in 1979 The Dublin Philharmonic Society provides peripatetic third level tuition in musical performance. Key activities include masterclasses, concerts, lectures - including contemporary music by Irish composers. The newsletter 'Philharmonic News' is issued occasionally.

Dungannon Disability Arts Studio

Ms Sharon Turtie
Disability Arts Officer
Unit 40 Dungannon Enterprise Centre
2 Coalisland Road
Dungannon
Co. Tyrone BT71 6JT
Northern Ireland

Tel/Fax: 048 8775 3626/048 8775 3789
Minicom: 048 8772 6685
Email: ddas@talk21.com
Other key staff: Iain Davidson (Disability Arts Officer)

Aims to provide access to the highest quality participatory artistic experience and support the development of creative involvement for disabled people on their own terms, towards a true understanding of disability. The Studio is a developmental disability arts project. Key activities includes facilitation of projects of a collaborative nature, requested or inspired and developed in collaboration with users and user organisations. The Studio offers opportunity to empower disabled people through the development of disability arts and culture. As both premises and project, it is a resource for day centres, special schools, voluntary groups and individuals of all ages and disability.

Early Music Organisation of Ireland

Siobhan Armstrong
Chairperson
Kilballyquilty
Carrick-on-Suir
Co. Waterford

Tel/Fax: +353 51 646286
Email: sarm@eircom.net
Other key staff: Maura Uí Chróinín (Secretary), Lindsay Armstrong (Treasurer)

Founded in 1986, the Early Music Organisation of Ireland (EMOI), is a non-profit making all-Ireland organisation. It supports performance and educational opportunities in all areas of early music and provides an Irish forum and information point for people interested in early music. The definition of early music is broad, with an emphasis on historically informed performance. EMOI has initiated a tuition scheme for students of early instruments, currently violin, continuo, lute, cello, voice and harps. EMOI produces a register of early music in Ireland. EMOI ran the Dublin Early Music Festival 1988-1992 and is instrumental in the foundation and development of Christ Church Baroque. The newsletter 'Early Music Ireland' is issued on a quarterly basis giving news, an event guide, reviews of concerts, publications and recordings, editorial opinion, letters and articles.

The Elgar Society

Elizabeth Craven
29 Foxfield St. John
Raheny
Dublin 15

Tel: +353 1 8323952
Website: www.elgar.org
Other key staff: Wendy Hillary (Honorary Secretary), Andrew Neill (Honorary Chairman), John Grieg (Honorary Treasurer)

This society was formed in 1951 to promote the study, performance and appreciation of the works of Sir Edward Elgar, including research into his life and music. The society has a membership of 1,500 worldwide, with 10 branches in the UK. The society sponsors CDs on a regular basis, and treats sympathetically requests for loan of scores etc. It meets each June to celebrate Elgar's birthday and hold its AGM. It awards the Elgar medal, as appropriate. Newsletters, 'Elgar Journal' and 'Elgar News', are issued three times per year, in March, July and November. These include articles on Elgar's life and music, list concerts featuring Elgar's music and book and CD reviews.

EPTA Ireland - European Piano Teachers Association Ireland

Eithne Gallagher
Administrator
16 Rowanbyrn
Blackrock
Co. Dublin

Tel: +353 1 2899367
Other key staff: Elizabeth Fuller (Chairperson), Kathleen Hegarty (Treasurer), Eileen Brogan (Public Relations Officer)

A member of EPTA Europe, the organisation is a non-profit making association with approximately 240 members, founded in 1982 with the aims of raising the standards of piano teaching, establishing links between piano teachers and performers and organising piano teachers workshops and conferences. Membership is open to all practising piano teachers in Ireland and to those interested in advancing the aims of EPTA. Key activities and services include monthly meetings/workshops with speakers from Ireland and overseas, regular circulars giving information on EPTA events and other matters of musical interest, private register of members issued annually, information leaflets, a 'vacancies' scheme whereby prospective students are put in contact with EPTA members, a register of teachers who would be available as deputy teachers either for private teachers or for music schools.

ESTA Ireland - European String Teachers Association Ireland

Prof Ronald Masin
Chairman
21 The Close
Cypress Downs
Dublin 6W

Tel/Fax: +353 1 4905263/+353 1 4920355
Other key staff: Alan Smale (Vice Chairman), Elizabeth Csibi (Administrator), David Lillis (Editor - ESTA Magazine)

Founded by Marianne Kroemer in Graz (Austria) in 1972, following the prinicple that the problems of young string players can only be solved by the organised exchange of experience, and to date there are nineteen member countries. Aims to raise the standard of string playing by improving the quality of teaching, to provide a forum for the exchange of ideas on all matters relating to string teaching and performance, to promote conferences, workshops, lectures, discussions and to sponsor professional publications. ESTA's main concern is the promotion and further education of all eager string teachers, irrespective of the school from which the have graduated and whether or not they are private teachers.

European Cultural Foundation - Irish Committee

Dr Miriam Hederman O'Brien
32 Nassau Street
Dublin 2

Tel/Fax: +353 1 6714300/+353 1 6798203

The European Cultural Foundation (ECF), aims to promote European co-operation in cultural, social, educational, and scientific activities. It is an international, non profit making, non governmental organisation. The Irish National Committee was established in 1984 to ensure Irish participation in the work of the foundation and to represent it in Ireland. The Irish Committee promotes

the aims of the ECF and ensures Irish participation in the work of the foundation in Europe. The Foundation headquarters in Amsterdam operates a grants scheme to support European cultural projects. The grants fund is small in relation to the variety and range of projects that seek support. The Foundation gives priority to proposals that involve at least three European countries. Grants are awarded twice yearly and these details can be obtained from the Amsterdam office at 5 Jan Van Goyenkade, 1075 HN Amsterdam, The Netherlands Tel/Fax: +31 20 6760222/+31 20 6752231.
All enquiries regarding funds should be directed to the Dutch headquarters and not the Dublin office.

€

Federation of Music Collectives - Republic of Ireland Branch

Angela Dorgan
Director
Space 28
North Lotts
Dublin 1

Tel: +353 1 8782244 or +353 1 8721882
Fax: +353 1 8726827
Email: fmc@imn.ie
Website: under construction
Other key staff: Tony Doherty (Project Development Officer, Northern Ireland)

The Federation of Music Collectives (FMC), are a cross border umbrella organisation who support, encourage and develop the work of music collectives in Ireland. This is achieved through education and masterclasses initiatives so that members can facilitate the grass roots needs of musicians to the best standards. To act as a contact point for music collectives /resource centres. To provide training opportunities for member collectives. To assist in the set up of new collectives. To facilitate the work of existing collectives. To raise the profile of the FMC and its members. Offers information and advice resource for members. To act as a conduit form the industry/arts to grass roots musicians. The newsletter 'The Fed' is issued on a quarterly basis (see advert page 14).

Federation of Music Collectives - Northern Ireland Branch

Tony Doherty
Project Development
531 Falls Road
Belfast BT19 9AA
Northern Ireland

Tel: 048 9030 1033

Aims to support new start-up music collectives in Northern Ireland.

Federation of Music Societies Northern Ireland

Leonard Pugh
Chairperson
147a Kings Road
Belfast BT5 7EG
Northern Ireland

Tel: 048 9048 3459
Email: leonard@nfms-nich.freeserve.co.uk
Other key staff: Mary Allen (Secretary)

This federation has three main functions, advocacy, representation and lobbying, members services & training and development. The federation was founded in 1935 and has 2000 member in the UK. The Northern Ireland branch represents the development of choirs, instrumental groups and music societies. The newsletter 'Noteworthy' is issued.

Feis Ceoil Association

Carmel Byrne
Administrator
37 Molesworth Street
Dublin 2

Tel/Fax: +353 1 6767365/+353 1 6767425

Feis Ceoil Association is a voluntary organisation founded in 1896. Feis Ceoil runs a competitive music festival each year. Competitions cover all instruments including voice, plus five composition competitions. There are approximately 165 competitions in total.

Flutewise

Colin Fleming
2 Colin View
Ballyclare
Co. Antrim BT39 9AR
Northern Ireland

Tel/Fax: 048 9335 4529/048 9335 4962
Email: pyramid@iol.ie

Flutewise was established in 1988. Originally aimed at young people learning to play the flute, it now has members of all ages and abilities from all over the world. The aim of Flutewise is to promote flute playing on every level, but especially amongst the young. Events are held with the help and support of professional flute players worldwide. Issues a quarterly magazine which aims to be educational, informative and entertaining.

Forum for Music in Ireland- Fóram Don Cheol in Éirinn

Nicola Murphy
Administrator
19 Fishamble Street
Temple Bar
Dublin 8

Tel/Fax: +353 1 6731922/+353 1 6789100
Email: info@cmc.ie
Website: www.cmc.ie
Other key staff: Dr. Joseph Ryan (Chairperson), Eve O'Kelly (Treasurer)

The Forum for Music in Ireland was founded in June 1999 as an umbrella body for organisations and individuals interested in music in Ireland. The Forum's aims are to create an active network of those interested in music in Ireland, to give voice to music in Ireland and to influence action in the support of it. Membership is open to all organisations and individuals whether professional or amateur, working in or concerned with music in Ireland.

Foundation for the Preservation of the Irish Concertina Heritage

Noel Hill
Director
Mill Lodge
Mill Lane
Shankill
Co. Dublin

Tel/Fax: +353 1 2823249/ +353 1 2823249
Mobile: +353 87 2339062

The foundation was set up to promote and encourage Irish concertina heritage and tradition, for the collection of materials relating to the tradition and for the recording of many older players of the instrument, many of whom have never been recorded before.

The Percy French Society

Jack Johnston
Honorary Secretary
10 Old Windmill Road
Crawfordsburn
Bangor
Co. Down BT19 1XH
Northern Ireland

Tel: 048 9183 2754
Email: doublejay@clara.net
Website: www.dmc-ni.co.uk/percyfrench

Aims to encourage a wider understanding and greater

appreciation of the works of Percy French, and to promote concerts, exhibitions, lectures, meetings and social events to achieve this. Endeavours to arrange an annual festival, and to work towards the establishment of a permanent collection of paintings and memorabilia from the life and works of Percy French. Organises regular members musical and social evenings (October-May). Exhibitions of paintings by Percy French and other memorabilia, an annual festival of concerts, coach tours and watercolour competition/exhibition in North Down, concerts throughout Ireland by the society's 'Concert Party', and publication of books relating to the life of Percy French, together with the society's own newsletter.

FUAIM - The Association for the Promotion of Primary Level Music Education
Regina Murphy
Chairperson
37 Beech Park
Lucan
Co. Dublin

Tel/Fax: +353 1 6280502/+353 1 6219739
Email: fuaim@esatclear.ie
Website: www.esatclear.ie/~fuaim
Other key staff: Christine Ferguson (Secretary), John Gearty (Treasurer), Siobhan Keane (Newsletter Editor)

FUAIM was founded early in 1997 by a group of primary teachers in Ireland. The organisation exists for all those with a professional interest in the music education of primary school children. Membership is open to all Department of Education and Science registered primary teachers. Associate Membership is open to all others with an interest and/or involvement in primary level music education. FUAIM's aims are to promote the musical development of all children at primary level, and to support the needs of those involved in primary level music education. Other activities include: in-career development courses and workshops; networking with other primary teachers; representation in music curriculum matters; liaison with other organisations; information on activities for children and teachers; and access to resources and materials. The newsletter 'FUAIM Newsletter' is issued on a quarterly basis.

Galway Early Music
Justina McElligott
Treasurer
5 Cashel Court
Galway

Tel/Fax: +353 91 528166/+353 91 565314

Email: justina@iol.ie
Website: www.wombat.ie/pages/
Other key staff: Ann McDonagh (Chairperson), Janet Vinnell (Secretary)

Founded in 1996, Galway Early Music (GEM), encourages interest and participation in the music and dance of the 12th-18th century in the context of Galway's medieval heritage. As well as bringing professional performers to Galway, GEM also promotes local involvement in and performance of music and dance. GEM also encourages interest in costume and street performance. GEM presents annually the Galway Early Music Festival, holds regular public events to which performers are invited for informal music making and dancing, organises workshops and talks on aspects of performance for schools and the general public, holds performance evenings for interested amateur players, organises the Galway Children's Medieval Band and Children's Dance Troupe, is associated with the Early Music Organisation of Ireland and the Association of Irish Festivals and Events (AOIFE).

Handbell Ringers of Great Britain
Andrew S. Hudson
Life Vice President
131 Galgorm Road
Balymena
Co. Antrim BT42 1DE
Northern Ireland

Tel/Fax: 048 2565 8896/048 2540 489

Aims to promote the art of handbell music playing. Key activities include masterclasses, concerts, music publication and handbell insurance.

IBEC Music Industry Group
Tommy McCabe
Director
Confederation House
84-86 Lower Baggot Street
Dublin 2

Tel/Fax: +353 1 6051562/+353 1 6381562
Email: info@mig.ie
Website: www.mig.ie
Other key staff: Niamh Collins (Secretariat), John Sheehan (Chairman)

The Music Industry Group was formed under the auspices of the Irish Business and Employers Confederation (IBEC), in 1994. It formulates policies for the development of the music industry and keeps government and other appropriate bodies briefed on all matters relating

to the industry. The key activities of the Music Industry Group are: to promote the development of Ireland's music industry; to represent the views of members to the public, local and national government, as well as European Union institutions; to seek increased co-operation with the EU for the development of the music industry in Ireland and to develop contact with counterpart groups at European and international level.
(See advert)

Improvised Music Company

Gerry Godley
Chief Executive Officer
50 South William Street
Dublin 2

Tel/Fax: +353 1 6703885/+353 6703890
Email: imcadmin@eircom.net

The Improvised Music Company (IMC), is an Arts Council funded organisation set up in 1991 to aid the development of jazz and improvised music in Ireland. There are over 150 concert promotions annually, from venues like the Pendulum Club to the National Concert Hall. The IMC recording label has released 15 CDs to date. Other key activities include regional tours, workshops and masterclasses. 'Open Jazz', the annual open day, recently attracted 3,000 people. The IMC also promotes ESB Dublin Jazz Week, a capacity developing festival which takes place in late September.

IMRO

Copyright House
Pembroke Row
Lower Baggot Street
Dublin 2

Tel/Fax: +353 1 6614844/+353 1 6763125
Email: info@imro.ie
Website: www.imro.ie
Other key staff: Donal McGuirk (Membership Services Manager), Sean Stokes (Operations Manager)

Established in 1988 the Irish Music Rights Organisation (IMRO) is a non-profit organisation owned by its members which are made up of songwriters, composers and music publishers. Administers copyright in music on behalf of its members and on behalf of the members of the overseas societies affiliated to it. Royalties become due when music is broadcast, publicly performed or used in cable transmission (see advert page 30).

International Songwriters Association Ltd

James D. Liddane
Chairman
PO Box 46
Limerick

Tel/Fax: +353 61 228837/+353 61 229464
Email: jliddane@songwriter.iol.ie
Website: www.songwriter.co.uk
Other key staff: Anna Sinden (General Secretary)

Founded in Limerick in 1967, the International Songwriters Association (ISA), now has members in more than fifty countries worldwide, predominantly the UK, USA, Australia and South Africa. The ISA services semi-professional and professional songwriters, music publishers and song contest organisations. The ISA publishes Songwriter Magazine, founded in 1967, which is distributed monthly to its members. Other publications include the Songseller Professional Directory, published twice each year, the UK Music Business Directory and the UK Stars Directory, both published annually. Other publications include Jim Liddane's 'Basic Course in Songwriting', and Bill Miller's 'The Best of the Songwriter'. The ISA also provides copyright, assessment and advice services to members.

Irish Association of Brass and Concert Bands

Gillian Mohan
General Secretary
28 Millmount Terrace
Drogheda
Co. Louth

Tel/Fax: +353 41 9835799

The national umbrella body representing amateur brass and concert bands in the Republic of Ireland. Key activities include: annual national championships, Irish youth brass, which is a 55 player youth brass band, regional competitions and workshops, annual national conference, advocacy on behalf of member bands and the raising of standards of players and teachers. A newsletter is issued for members.

Irish Association of Creative Arts Therapists

Jim Cosgrove
Training Officer
PO Box 4176
Dublin 1

Tel: +353 1 8386171

Other key staff: Gerri Geoghegan (Chairperson), Pauline Sweeney (Secretary), Denise Burke (Treasurer)

The Irish Association of Creative Arts Therapists (IACAT), was formally launched in 1994. Aims to promote and protect the practice of the creative arts therapies in Ireland. Acts as the professional registration body for therapists practising music therapy, drama therapy, art therapy and dance movement therapy. IACAT offers associate membership which is open to all interested in creative arts therapy. Workshops and presentations are held throughout the year (minimum twice a year). IACAT is working on gaining statutory recognition for creative arts therapists and to monitor training and work practices in Ireland. The newsletter 'IACAT News' is issued on a quarterly basis.

The Irish Association for Cultural, Economic and Social Relations

Austin Finnerty
Director
52 Woodbine Road
Raheny
Dublin 5

Tel/Fax: +353 1 8488215/+353 1 8471818
Email: afinn@iol.ie
Website: www.irish-association.ie
Other key staff: Dr Dennis Kennedy (President), Terry Stewart (Vice President), Paul McErlean (Vice President)

Founded in 1938, the association's programme of activities operates under three main headings: political dialogue - the promotion of more political dialogue through a series of seminars and conferences; social and economic affairs, detailed examination of the more immediate communication problems and opportunities; cultural and religious heritage, the pursuit of mutual understanding of the different strands of cultural and religious traditions on the island. Key activities include: conferences, lectures, open debates, exhibitions, theatre sponsorship and production of publications.

Irish Association of Youth Orchestras

Agnes O'Kane
Honorary Administrator
6 Alexandra Place
Wellington Road
Cork

Tel/Fax: +353 21 4507412
Email: agnesokane@eircom.net

Other key staff: Hugh Maguire (President), John O'Brien (Chairman), Kay O'Sullivan (Honorary Treasurer)

The Irish Association of Youth Orchestras (IAYO) represents more than 60 member youth orchestras throughout Ireland, in schools, schools of music, colleges, universities and community based organisations. Promotes the development of youth orchestras by creating a national network for advice and information and provides access to an instrument bank and music library. The IAYO Festival of Youth Orchestras provides a national platform for performance by member orchestras. The annual programme of orchestral clinics and workshops, chamber music weekends and conductors workshops provide support services. The newsletter 'Newsnotes' is issued on a quarterly basis which features the growing network of those involved in music (see advert page 7).

Irish Federation of Musicians and Associated Professionals

Peter Pringle
Secretary
63 Lower Gardiner Street
Dublin 1

Tel/Fax: +353 1 8744645
Other key staff: Richard Glynn (General President)

Trade Union established by dance band musicians in 1936 for the safeguarding and advancement of the interest of working musicians in their dealings with employers, music promoters and the other areas of music. Services to members include music and employment promotion, music tuition, licensed club, credit union, legal service, insurance contacts offering reasonable terms for motor insurance, establishment of terms and conditions of employment per negotiation etc.

Irish Marching Bands Association

John Whelan
Secretary
57 Alderwood Avenue
Springfield
Tallaght
Dublin 24

Tel/Fax: +353 1 4521239/+353 1 8735066
Email: designf@indigo.ie
Other key staff: Paddy Hayden (Chairman), Chris Furlong (Treasurer), Gerry Kelly (Honorary President)

The Irish Marching Bands Association, currently in its 11th year of operation, is a national organisation,

Striking   *Making*   *Hitting the*

a Chord   *Arrangements*   *Right Note*

for   *for*   *for*

Composers   *Arrangers*   *Songwriters*

IRISH MUSIC RIGHTS ORGANISATION
COPYRIGHT HOUSE, PEMBROKE ROW, LOWER BAGGOT STREET, DUBLIN 2.
TELEPHONE 01 - 661 4844 FAX 01 - 676 3125
INTERNET www.imro.ie E-MAIL info@imro.ie

whose purpose it is to assist all marching bands. The intention is to extend the range of assistance to bands. Information services to all bands, linking Irish bands with overseas groups and activities. Organises figure marching contests during the summer and also provides out of season seminars and training weekends developing and supporting new bands. The newsletter 'On Parade' is issued on a quarterly basis.

Irish Music Net

Feargal McKay
Editor
26 South Frederick Street
Dublin 2

Tel/Fax: +353 1 6713664/+353 1 6710763
Email: info@imn.ie
Website: www.imn.ie

Irish Music Net is an online music information resource which includes editorial content.

Irish Pipe Band Association

Brian MacMahon
Honorary Secretary
39 Pondfields
New Ross
Co. Wexford

Tel/Fax: +353 51 422531
Mobile: +353 86 8326316
Email: ipba@iol.ie
Website: www.iol.ie/~ipba/bands
Other key staff: Con O'Conaill (President), Ciaran Mordaut (Chairman), Margaret Saunders (Treasurer)

Established in 1946, The Irish Pipe Band Association (IPBA) endeavours to promote piping and drumming in Ireland and improve standards of musicianship and knowledge of music theory within the organisation. The IPBA caters for 45-50 pipe bands in 26 countries and has close ties to sister organisations in Northern Ireland and Scotland. The IPBA organises solo and band contests including the jointly organised All-Ireland band championships and solo championships. The IPBA has its own College of Piping and Drumming which holds courses in music therapy and musicianship and also holds examinations and awards certificates. The IPBA publishes its own magazine and web page. The newsletter 'Tartan and Green' is issued on a quarterly basis.

Irish Society for Archives

Kieran Hoare
Honorary Secretary
James Hardiman Library
National University of Ireland
Galway

Tel/Fax: +353 91 524411 Ext. 3636/
+353 91 522394
Email: kieran@sulaco.library.nuigalway.ie
Website: www.library.nuigalway.ie
Other key staff: Dr. Kenneth Milne (Chairperson), Tom Quinlan (Honorary Treasurer), Rena Lohan/ Tom Quinlan (Honorary Co-editors)

Founded in 1970 as an all-Ireland voluntary body to promote the preservation of, and access to archives which as primary source material, are essential for accurate and informed research. Membership is open to all interested in these objectives and includes professional archivists, academics, local historians, genealogists and students of all levels, as well as archival institutions and libraries. The activities of the society range from lobbying for the preservation of archives, arranging lectures and visits to places of archival interest and the publication of its journal 'Irish Archives'. The journal attempts to provide accurate and authoritative description and analysis of archives, to advertise the existence of new archival sources and also to discuss research and archival preservation methodologies.

Irish Traditional Music Archive - Taisce Cheol Dúchais Éireann

Nicholas Carolan
Director
63 Merrion Square
Dublin 2

Tel/Fax: +353 1 6619699/+353 1 6624585
Website: www.itma.ie
Other key staff: Róisín Ní Bhriain (Secretary), Sadhbh Nic Ionnraic (Administrative Officer), Glenn Cumiskey (Sound Engineer), Maeve Gebruers (Printed Materials Officer), Joan McDermott (Sound Recording Officer)

Founded in 1987 to collect, preserve, organise and give public access to the materials of Irish traditional music: sound recordings, books, song sheets, videos etc. Now contains the largest such collection in existence with detailed information control. Offers public access to collections and to an information database, a query service, consultancy service and field collection.

Irish World Music Centre

Paula Dundon
Administrator
Foundation Building
University of Limerick
Limerick

Tel/Fax: +353 61 202590/ +353 61 202589
Email: paula.dundon@ul.ie
Web: www.ul.ie/~iwmc

Established in 1994, the Irish World Music Centre at the University of Limerick is a postgraduate centre for the performing arts of music and dance. It offers ten post-graduate programmes in a spectrum of music and dance specialisations. Emphasis on student's own artistic journey. The centre is also home to the Irish Chamber Orchestra and Daghdha Dance Company. Provision of postgraduate music and dance studies at Masters and PhD levels in both academic and performance areas (see advert page 75).

IRMA Trust

Jessica Fuller
Manager
PPI House
1 Corrig Avenue
Dun Laoghaire
Co. Dublin

Tel/Fax: +353 1 2845505/+353 1 2845285
Freephone: +353 1800 923 017
Email: info@irmatrust.ie
Website: www.irmatrust.ie
Other key staff: Padraig O'hUiginn (Chairman), Clive Leacy (Company Secretary)

The Irish Recorded Music Association was founded in 1997 by the record industry in Ireland to assist young Irish musicians. Funding was granted initially through Phonographic Performance of Ireland Ltd. It is expected that further funding will be attracted from the corporate sector. The role of the Trust is to enable and assist the development of young musicians in Ireland. The Trust is overseen by a board of nine trustees, representing all areas of the music community in Ireland. Applications for funding are accepted on an ongoing basis and should be directed to the Manager. The broad objective is to enable and assist in the development of young musicians in Ireland. The Trust will work in partnership with relevant organisations and agencies to advance music activity and will support sustainable initiatives for the creators, performers and ancillary services in music in Ireland. Currently funds projects and supports activities through programme areas which include masterclasses, bursaries, scholarships, event sponsorship

(limited) and an instrument bank. Music instruments and equipment will be available through a loan scheme to organisations and groups from January 2000.

Jeunesses Musicales Ireland

Patricia Durnin
Honorary Secretary
19 Ludford Park
Ballinteer
Dublin 16

Tel/Fax: +353 1 2987596/+353 1 2960109
Email: joanna@iol.ie
Other key staff: John Hayden (Higher Education Authority/Honourary Chairman), Andrew Macknell (Dublin Boy Singers/Honorary Treasurer), Peter Crooks (National Youth Orchestra & Dublin Youth Orchestra/Newsletter and String Ensemble)

Jeunesses Musicales Ireland (JMI), is a member section of Jeunesses Musicales International, the international federation which unites young people through music and which is the largest cultural organisation in UNESCO. The aim and objective of JMI is "...to help young people develop musically across all boundaries within Ireland and within the network of member countries of JM International, valuing, equally all forms of music...". Key activities include the administration of auditions for the JM International World Youth Orchestra and World Youth Choir and JMI acts as a link for musical organisations looking for international contacts. Annual concerts are held for children 'Make Friends with Music'. JMI cross border string ensemble initiative began in October 1999. Concerts in national schools initiative began in September 1999 'Live Music in Schools'. The newsletter 'JM Ireland News' is issued on a quarterly basis.

Jobs in Music

Val James
5-6 Lombard Street
Dublin 2

Tel/Fax: +353 1 6793364/+353 1 6710421
Email: valjames@excite.com
Other key staff: Ann-Marie Walsh

Jobs in Music is a lobby group promoting Irish music of all genres.

Kerry Music County Ltd.
c/o Martin Whelan
General Manager
Siamsa Tíre
Town Park
Tralee
Co. Kerry

Tel/Fax: +353 66 7123055/+353 66 7127276

Kerry Music County was initiated in partnership with Music Network to support and develop music in Kerry. Kerry Music County is now an independent body with members from the arts, statutory, education and community development sectors working together to achieve more music access for all people in the county. Key activities include: supporting existing music resources in Kerry; exploring new models of music access for all people in Kerry; improving the range and choice of music opportunities for people of the county; developing and facilitating a music development plan for Kerry; hosting an annual Kerry music forum; providing a database of music resources in Kerry and assisting others to implement innovative music projects.

Live Music Now! Ireland
Robert A. Wilson
Director
22 Brooklands Park
Whitehead
Carrickfergus
Co. Antrim BT38 9SN
Northern Ireland

Tel/Fax: +48 9337 3942/+48 9337 8836
Email: livemusicireland@btconnect.com
Other key staff: David Openshaw (Music Advisor), Dr. Michael Swallow OBE (Music Advisor)

Founded in 1977 by Yehudi Menuhin, this charity was established to help both young musicians and members of the community, who for various reasons are unable to gain access to professional concerts. Organises concerts in hospitals, schools, hospices, disabilities centres and prisons. Provides advice for musicians in general and represents solo musicians in classical, traditional and rock music. Musicians are chosen by audition. The newsletter 'Live Wire' is issued on a quarterly basis.

MCPS - Mechanical Copyright Protection Society Ireland Ltd
Victor Finn
Chief Executive
Copyright House
Pembroke Row
Baggot Street
Dublin 2

Tel/Fax: +353 1 6766940/+353 1 6611316
Email: vfinn@indigo.ie
Other key staff: Greg McAteer (Licensing Manager), Stephen Goetens (Financial Accountant), Hilary Reid (Distribution Supervisor)

Society of music publishers, composers and songwriters who licence, collect and distribute mechanical royalties arising in the Republic of Ireland on products such as CDs, cassettes, videos, CD-ROMs, multi media products and on-line products. Also issues synchronisation licences in respect of television programmes, films, radio and television adverts.

The Molly Malone Ballad Company
Mary Ryan
Artistic Director
40 Dundela Haven
Sandycove
Co. Dublin

Tel/Fax: +353 1 2300171
Mobile: +353 87 2272918
Email: molly.malone@oceanfree.net
Other key staff: Aidín Gohery (Choreographer)

The Molly Malone Ballad Company explores Irish ballads using theatre, dance, music and literary history to harmonise the songs, tell their stories and perform from the work of writers they inspired. The company celebrates songs in Irish and English and explores the importance of social documents and entertainment throughout the ages. Key activities include musical theatre based on traditional song. The company is made up of professional singers, actors, musicians and dancers who promote performances based around the songs. Performances are aimed at corporate groups, incentive tours, language schools, art and music festivals. Each performance is tailored to the demands of the venue (musical and literary associations of the area) and client requirements. The company is researching songs in Irish and English, their history and literary connections.

Thomas Moore Society
Anne McEvoy
Chairperson
Shalom
Newpark Drive
Kilkenny
Co. Kilkenny

Tel: +353 56 65063
Other key staff: Kay Sheehy (Secretary)

The Thomas Moore Society was established in 1987 to promote an interest in the life and works of Thomas Moore who worked as an actor with the Kilkenny Theatricals and met his wife Betsy Dyke while in Kilkenny. The main activities of the organisation is the Thomas Moore Young Singers Competition open to secondary and primary school children, residing in and attending school in Kilkenny. Occasionally the society holds a fundraising concert/recital.

Music Association of Ireland Ltd
Rodney Senior
Chairman
69 South Great Georges Street
Dublin 2

Tel/Fax: +353 1 4785368/+353 1 4754426
Email: how@indigo.ie
Other key staff: Howard Freeman (FÁS Supervisor)

The Music Association of Ireland Ltd (MAI) was founded in 1948 by Brian Boydell, Frederick May, Edgar Deale and Michael Mullin. It was intended to be a pressure group dedicated to the promotion of excellence of music in Ireland. Key activities include the organisation of music in the classroom both at primary and secondary levels, under the title of 'Music in Time' and co-ordinating a FÁS performing arts project which brings interactive entertainment to institutes for the disabled and also to senior citizen centres. The 'Music Events Diary' is issued on a monthly basis.

Music Instrument Fund of Ireland
Prof Ronald Masin
Artistic Director
21 The Close
Cypress Downs
Dublin 6W

Tel/Fax: +353 1 4905263/+353 1 4920355

Its objective is to obtain a pool of quality string instruments and bows and lend them to young gifted musicians for a period of time.

Music Map@City Arts Centre
Colm Downes
Administrator
23-25 Moss Street
Dublin 2

Tel/Fax: +353 1 6770643/+353 1 6770131
Email: musicmap@eircom.net
Other key staff: Justin Rami (Training Manager), Alison Rogers (Course Director), John Lalor (Studio Manager)

This project is open to those over 18 years who have a disability. City Arts Centres commitment of "...putting the arts to work for the community in a way that is relevant, practical and exciting..." is the basis for Music Map training project. It is now entering its third year and changes with the music industry. Focuses on 'hands on' learning in areas of the music business such as communications, video production, graphic design, developing skills in MIDI recording and 'staging your own event'.

Music Network
Gillian Keogan
Information Service
The Coach House
Dublin Castle
Dublin 2

Tel/Fax: +353 1 6719429/+353 1 6719430
Email: gillian@musicnetwork.ie
Website: www.musicnetwork.ie
Other key staff: John O'Kane (Chief Executive), Assumpta Lawless (PR Manager), Catherine Carey (Performance Programme)

Music Network is the national music development organisation established by the Arts Council to develop music nationwide. An integrated series of programme activities focuses on providing people with access to music in the context of their own communities. This includes assisting communities all over Ireland, both North and South, to promote live music concerts in the classical, jazz and traditional Irish genres; performance programmes in diverse community settings, including music education and healthcare environments; developing large scale partnership style regional development projects such as a programme of 'ensembles-in-residence' which now includes the Vogler Quartet in Sligo project. Working in conjunction with local partnerships helps ensure that all initiatives are designed according to the principles of sustainable development. Other initiatives offer Irish musicians professional development opportunities including the expanding 'Musicwide' performance scheme, an international exchange programme and a Continuing Professional Development programme. An Information Service publishes two key publications; the Irish Music Handbook and the Directory of Musicians in Ireland. The organisation is funded by the Arts Council and receives sponsorship from ESB. The newsletter 'Musiclinks' is issued on a quarterly basis (see advert page vi, 373).

Na Píobairí Uilleann Teoranta

Liam McNulty
Administrator
15 Henrietta Street
Dublin 1

Tel/Fax: +353 1 8730093/+353 1 8723161
Email: npupipes@iol.ie
Website: www.iol.ie/~npupipes/npuhome.htm
Other key staff: Paula Roche (Administrative
Assistant), Liam McNulty (Administrator)

Na Píobairí Uilleann Teoranta is a specialist society existing to promote uilleann piping. Founded in 1968, it has
a worldwide membership and is service orientated to
help members, and all interested in uilleann piping and
Irish traditional music generally. Provides tuition weekly
and monthly at regional events and at summer schools.
Publication of videos, books, recordings of uilleann piping. The newsletter 'An Píobaire' is issued quarterly to
members.

National Archives of Ireland

Aideen Ireland
Archivist
Bishop Street
Dublin 8

Tel/Fax: +353 1 4072300/+353 1 4072333
Email: mail@nationalarchives.ie
Website: www.nationalarchives.ie

The National Archives is an amalgamation of the older
State Paper Office and the Public Record Office of
Ireland. It retains collections created by central government which are over 20 years old. It also collects private
accessions and business accessions. It operates a public
reading room. Key activities include the provision of
research services, publication of finding aids, travelling
exhibitions, Director's reports and the reports of the
National Archives Advisory Council which keep the public informed of developments.

The National Association for Youth Drama

Sarah Fitzgibbon
Development Officer
34 Upper Gardiner Street
Dublin 1

Tel/Fax: +353 1 8781301/+353 1 8781302
Email: nayd@indigo.ie
Other key staff: Eilis Mullan (National Director),
Kate McSweeney (Administrator), Julie Cronin
(Publications and Information Officer)

The National Association of Youth Drama (NAYD) is the
umbrella organisation for youth drama and youth theatre
in Ireland. Founded in 1980, there are now over sixty
affiliated youth theatre groups in Ireland. NAYD aims to
promote a greater understanding of the potential of
drama as a medium for learning and as a means of
expression for young people. To promote drama and
youth arts generally as an integral component of youth
work, to promote the personal, social and aesthetic
development of young people through drama and performance related skills such as music and movement.
NAYD provides a central resource, information and advice
facility which serves youth theatre groups and individuals
throughout the country. NAYD organises workshops,
courses and seminars on drama, theatre, movement,
music and related areas for youth leaders and teachers,
the National Festival of Youth Theatres, 'Reach Out'
(youth theatre for the deaf). Also organises workshops ,
courses and seminars on drama/theatre and related areas
for youth leaders/ teachers. Participates in the European
Youth Theatre encounter and National Youth Theatre.
The newsletter 'Youth Drama Ireland' is issued annually.

National Youth Federation

Tony Murphy
Chief Executive
20 Lower Dominick Street
Dublin 1

Tel/Fax: +353 1 8729933/+353 1 8724183
Email: info@nyf.ie
Website: www.iol.ie/~nyf

A co-ordinating agency for 19 local independent youth
services throughout the country.

NODA - National Operatic and Dramatic Association

Laura Carr McKee
Regional Representative in Northern Ireland
10 Ashford Avenue
Bangor
Co. Down BT19 6DD
Northern Ireland

Tel: 048 9147 3630

NODA is the umbrella body for the amateur theatre.
The organisation's services include discounted sales of
scripts, make-up and insurance, summer schools and
conferences. The newsletter 'NODA News Northwest'
issued on a quarterly basis.

North of Ireland Bands' Association

William J. Clements
Secretary
28 Knockfergus Park
Green Island
Carrickfergus
Co. Antrim BT38 8SN
Northern Ireland

Tel: 048 9086 6179
Other key staff: Douglas Gormley
(Chairperson), George McFadden (Registration
Secretary), John Patton (Treasurer)

The North of Ireland Bands Association is a non-sectarian organisation, founded in 1907 to promote the knowledge of band music. The Association is the co-ordinating body for a number of separate leagues for different band types (i.e accordion, brass, concert and flute) each with its own independent activity. The Association organises the Irish Band Championships and the individual leagues organise solo, quartet and other band contests. The newsletter 'Noteworthy' is issued on a quarterly basis.

Northern Ireland Musicians' Association

Harry Hamilton
NIMA Organiser
Unit 4 Fort William Business Park
Dargan Road
Belfast BT3 9J4
Northern Ireland

Tel/Fax: 048 9037 0037
Email: information@nimaonline.freeserve.co.uk
Website: www.nimaonline.freeserve.co.uk

The Northern Ireland Musicians' Association is a trade union, set up to ensure fair treatment and satisfactory rates of pay for musicians in Northern Ireland. Key activities include negotiations with the media, with music venues and promoters and with music licensing organisations.

Northern Ireland Festivals Forum (formerly The British Federation of Festivals for Music, Dance and Speech - The Irish Area Council)

Carolyn McCabe
Chairperson
The Hollow
Bachelors Walk

Portadown
Co. Armagh BT63 5BQ
Northern Ireland

Tel/Fax: 048 3833 1046
Other key staff: Mary Riddell, (Secretary),
Joan Houston, (Treasurer)

Northern Ireland Festivals Forum is the umbrella organisation for 17 festivals in the province affiliated to the British Federation of Festivals for Music, Dance and Speech. These festivals provide the stimulus for preparing for a public occasion, the opportunity to hear the work of others, and the chance to receive advice from a professional adjudicator. Also aim to develop the audiences of the future. Key activities include the cross community festivals activity (in 1999 over 40,000 performers took part in this), which includes classes for music, dance, speech and folk dancing. All age groups are involved with many school children participating in all the disciplines.

Northern Ireland Music Therapy Trust

Karen Diamond
Team Leader
Graham House
Knockbracken Healthcare Park
Saintfield Road
Belfast BT8 8BH
Northern Ireland

Tel/Fax: 048 9070 5854
Other key staff: Dr Michael Swallow (Secretary to the Board)

The Northern Ireland Music Therapy Trust was established in 1990 to promote music therapy in Northern Ireland, to employ registered music therapists, and to fundraise to support these aspirations. The trust provides a clinical music therapy service to special schools, hospitals, day centres and community programmes throughout Northern Ireland. It also offers training programmes and workshops, a student information service, and carers support programmes.

Northern Ireland Voluntary Trust

Kate Campbell
Community Project Officer
22-24 Mount Charles
Belfast BT7 1NZ
Northern Ireland

Tel/Fax: 048 9024 5927/048 9032 9839
Email: info@nivt.org

An independent charitable grant making organisation whose aim is to create a more just and caring society by enabling people to engage in positive action. The Trust will fund and support community development, and will assist groups to tackle the causes and effects of inequality, poverty and disadvantage at local and regional level. As part of its grant making programme to support community development, the Northern Ireland Voluntary Trust is keen to encourage peoples creativity and self expression through participation in a range of art activities. Grants for a range of community arts activities are available to community organisations which offer people opportunities to become actively involved in arts and cultural projects.

€

Open Arts

Kate Ingram
Director
Crescent Arts Centre
2-4 University Road
Belfast BT7 INH
Northern Ireland

Tel/Fax: 048 9031 2515/048 9024 6748
Email: openarts@aol.com
Other key staff: Beverly Whyte (Musical Workshop facilitator)

Open Arts was formed in 1992. The organisation works with all disabled people in all art forms. In music it facilitates professional musicians to work with disabled people, whilst being properly paid. Key activities include information dissemination, project development and workshops.

Orff Society

Olive Mulcahy
Director
2 Seaview Terrace
Donnybrook
Dublin 4

Tel/Fax: +353 1 2838574/+353 1 6676266
Email: ab@iol.ie
Other key staff: Anne Brady (Treasurer), Peggy McGennis (PRO)

Set up in 1974 to promote Carl Orff's Schulwerk - 'Music for Children'. This is a system devised by the German composer and teacher in 1930's Bavaria. His educational work has spread to more than twenty countries worldwide. This system helps young children to develop as people through the medium of music. The Orff Society organises music for children classes which involves music, dance, speech & drama, summer camps

and class performances. There are also workshops for primary teachers interested in 'Music for Children'.

Pact@Temple Bar and Aberystwyth Arts Centre

Bernice Turner
Project Manager
18 Eustace Street
Temple Bar
Dublin 2

Tel/Fax: +353 1 6772255/+353 1 6772525
Email: pact@temple-bar.ie
Other key staff: Zita Griffin (Administration Assistant)

Pact@Temple Bar and Aberystwyth Arts Centre is an Interreg Programme to promote performing arts co-operation and touring between South East Ireland (Carlow, Dublin, Kildare, Kilkenny, Meath, South Tipperary, Waterford, Wexford and Wicklow) and West Wales (Anglesey, Gwynedd, Ceredigion, Pembrokeshire, and Carmarthen). It endeavours to maximise networks and to improve contacts between venues and performing arts companies offering direct practical and financial support to performing arts companies. Funding is available for performance fees, travel, subsistence, marketing and publicity costs. Deadlines for receipt of applications in the year 2000 by 27th October.

Pavee Point Travellers Centre - Travellers Cultural Heritage Centre

Ruth Swanton
Co-ordinator of TCHC
46 North Great Georges Street
Dublin 1

Tel/Fax: +353 1 8780255/+353 1 8742626
Email: pavee@iol.ie
Website: //homepages.iol.ie/~pavee/
Other key staff: Kay Lawrence

The Travellers Cultural Heritage Centre (TCHC) was set up in 1990 with the following aims: to research and document Travellers history which had previously not been recorded which leads to the development of appreciation of the Travellers cultural heritage; to promote travellers positive identity as an ethnic group and to enhance their cultural identity and self determination; to resource the traditional skills of Travellers as well as stimulating creative development and re-interpretation of these arts and to improve knowledge and opportunities of interculturisation in Ireland. Key activities of the heritage team at present include compiling a collection of music, singing and storytelling from the 1960s. The TCHC are working with Na Píobairí Uilleann on a joint project for the 50th anniversary of the death of Traveller Piper Johnny Doran, which began in January 2000. Na Píobairí Uilleann have offered to train several young Travellers in the pipes, traditional singing and dancing.

Performing Arts Medicine Trust
Dr Íde Delargy
37 Seapoint Avenue
Blackrock
Co. Dublin

Tel: +353 1 2302659
Email: idedelargy@eircom.net

Aims to provide a medical service to musicians which is sensitive to the problems experienced by them. It has an educational remit in terms of preventing injuries, and is available to discuss prevention with students. Provides general practitioner assessment and quick and easy access to physiotherapy. Offers a network of specialists who understand the particular problems of musicians.

Post-Primary Music Teachers Association
Carmel Dooley
Secretary
98 Knockaphunta Park
Castlebar
Co. Mayo

Tel/Fax: +353 94 27063/+353 94 81661
Other key staff: Chris Kinder (Chairperson)

The association aims to keep its members fully informed about music education developments in Ireland. Key activities include: liaising with other music education organisations, providing a network for music teachers throughout the country and acting as a review body for the examinations council. The association issues the 'PPMTA Journal', which is produced three times per year.

PPI - Phonographic Performance Ireland Ltd
Dick Doyle
Chief Executive
PPI House
1 Corrig Avenue
Dun Laoghaire
Co. Dublin

Tel/Fax: +353 1 2805977/+353 1 2806579
Email: ppiltd@iol.ie
Other key staff: Clive Leacy (Head of Finance), Sean Murtagh (Head of Operations), Ciarán Keaney (Head of Legal Affairs)

Phonographic Performances Ireland Ltd (PPI) was established by the record companies of Ireland to administer their rights to collect equitable remuneration for the public performance of their repertoire (CD, tape, LP etc). PPI on behalf of its members controls the public performance of recordings by discos, public houses, hotels and restaurants as well as the broadcasting of sound recordings by national and independent broadcasters. All of PPI's income (less running costs) is distributed every year to its members and to performers.

Pre-Historic Music
Maria Cullen O'Dwyer
Manager
Crimlin
Corr Na Móna
Co. Galway

Tel/Fax: +353 92 48396/+353 92 48396
Email: bronzeagehorns@eircom.net
Website: //homepage.eircom.net/~bronzeagehorns/
Other key staff: Simon O'Dwyer (Manufacturer/Researcher)

Pre-Historic Music was founded by Maria and Simon O'Dwyer to research the area of music and instruments from pre-historic times. This area covers a timescale from early stone age (10,000 B.C) through to the Bronze and Iron Ages to 800 A.D. Instruments from this time include: stone and bone whistles, bronze horns and bells, war trumpets, drums and many sea shell and animal horn instruments. Key activities include combining practical research into the ancient music traditions of the world with the reproduction of the surviving instruments of these traditions.

PRS - Performing Right Society
Alison Cooper
Team Manager
3 Rothesay Place
Edinburgh EH3 7SL
Scotland

Tel/Fax: +44 845 3093090/+44 870 0101384
Email: info@prs.co.uk
Website: www.prs.co.uk

Founded in 1914, PRS is the UK association of composers, songwriters and music publishers. It administers the 'performing right' in their music both in the UK and, by agreement, with similar societies abroad on a world wide basis. At any one time PRS licenses millions of organisations - from advertising jingles to entire symphonies, and every kind of music in between. PRS works for music creators by issuing licenses to cover the public performance and broadcast of their music and collecting the fees due on their behalf. By taking out a single PRS license and paying the appropriate fee any music user can legally use any copyright music which the Society controls.

RDS - Royal Dublin Society

Adrienne Dunne
Development Executive - Arts
Ballsbridge
Dublin 4

Tel/Fax: +353 1 6680866 Ext. 211/
+353 1 6604014
Email: adrienne.dunne@rds.ie
Website: www.rds.ie
Other key staff: Niamh Kelly (Marketing Manager), Eddie McCarron (Booking Enquiries)

The RDS was established in 1731 to promote arts, agriculture, science and industry. Over the years the RDS has contributed to cultural development in Ireland. The encouragement and promotion of excellence in music has been one of the foundation's core areas of activity. A number of music events and concerts are organised annually, including spring and autumn recital series, which allow audiences to hear top musicians perform, and the 'A Spotlight on Youth Series', which gives young musicians an opportunity to gain recital experience. The RDS also contributes to the development of music by running a number of education al seminars and workshops for musicians and music practitioners. The newsletter 'RDS Members Newsletter' is issued on a quarterly basis.

Ronanstown Music and Drama Programme

Marie Carey
Co-ordinator
c/o Ronanstown Youth Service
Clondalkin
Dublin 22

Tel/Fax: +353 1 4570363 or +353 1 4575943/
+353 1 4578505
Other key staff: John Burke (Music Tutor/ Assistant), William LaCambre (Music Tutor/ Assistant)

The Ronanstown Music and Drama Programme is a community youth training programme run by FÁS and

sponsored by CYC. It is a twenty-six week programme run for sixteen to twenty-five year olds, to introduce them to the areas of music and drama. Modules on the course include drama, social skills, theory of music, sound production, history of music, song-writing, and a number of musical instrument workshops. Guest speakers are invited in to give the programme. Certificates from FÁS and a music theory examination associated with Victoria College, London, are given to successful students.

Royal Musical Association

Hilary Bracefield
Convenor - Irish Chapter
Music Department
University of Ulster at Jordanstown
Newtownabbey
Co. Antrim BT37 0QB
Northern Ireland

Tel/Fax: 048 9036 6955/048 9036 6870
Email: hm.bracefield@ulst.ac.uk
Website: www.soton.ac.uk/~stilwell/rma.html

The Royal Musical Association aims to promote musicology in the United Kingdom and Ireland. The Association organises an annual meeting (usually in May), the venue of which alternates between the North and South of Ireland. Scholarly papers are read at the meeting. The Association links with the parent body in London which holds regular meetings and an annual conference. A journal is also published.

Royal School of Church Music Ireland (formerly The Joint Committee For Church Music In Ireland)

Donald Maxwell
Honorary Secretary
68 Granville Road
Dun Laoghaire
Co. Dublin

Tel/Fax: +353 1 2852974/+353 1 2847230
Email: maxwellj@eircom.net
Other key staff: John Crothers (Joint Chairman), Rev. Tom Gordon (Co-Ordinator), Gordon Appleton (Regional Director)

The name under which the Royal School of Church Music and the Church of Ireland Choral Union operate in Ireland aims to serve the Christian Church (all denominations) by providing training and encouragement for church musicians whatever their ability. Organises training courses, summer schools, one day and evening courses for organists (all levels), conductors, instrumentalists, workshop leaders and clergy (in conjunction with

Braemor Institute at the Church of Ireland Theological College, Dublin 14). The 'JCCMI Newsletter' is available on a quarterly basis.

Scoraíocht Lann Léire

Seán Ó Flanagáin
Uachtarán
Scioból Mór
Lann Léire
Co. Lú

Tel: +353 41 6861033

Scoraíocht Lann Léire was formed in 1974 to promote Irish culture in mid-Louth. It has now developed into an organisation with its own premises in Dunleer, where it undertakes music and drama classes on a weekly basis. The main activities of Scoraíocht Lann Léire include kitchen ceilidhes, music, dance and art classes.

Share Centre

Dawn Latimer
Director
Share Holiday Village
Smiths Strand
Lisnaskea
Co. Fermanagh BT92 0EQ
Northern Ireland

Tel/Fax: 048 6772 2122/048 6772 1893
Email: share@dnet.co.uk
Website: www.sharevillage.org

Established in 1981, the Share Holiday Village is a registered charity providing residential facilities for educational, recreational and artistic activities. Dedicated to promoting integration between able-bodied and people with special needs, Share is run by a small core staff including two arts development workers and a team of over 300 volunteers. Situated on the shores of Upper Lough Erne, the on-site residential accommodation for 200 is purpose built for use by disabled visitors. Share is an outdoor activity centre. Facilities include the leisure suite with swimming pool, sauna, steam room and gymnasium. Share's purpose built Arts Arena hosts an extensive arts programme with full artistic support. A theatre, full conference facilities, exhibition and reception areas and dining and bar facilities are available. The arena offers a professional pottery suite, craft, dance, drama and music studios are available for residential use or external hire. An experienced arts team is available to co-ordinate and design programmes or advise and assist with requirements.

Share Music

Dr Michael Swallow
Director
15 Deramore Drive
Belfast BT9 5JQ
Northern Ireland

Tel/Fax: 048 9066 9042

Share Music promotes one week courses/workshops in music and theatre with special facilities for young adults with physical disabilities to take part in a variety of musical activities, often with elements of theatre and visual arts. This is carried out in the company of other musicians and voluntary helpers, and with guidance from professional tutors who have experience in working with special needs groups. The courses are all residential and are held at venues which provide total access for wheelchairs. Each course has a slightly different emphasis but all work towards a final performance given to an invited audience at the end of the week.
Founded in 1985 and works throughout the United Kingdom and the Republic of Ireland. Share Music will be held at the Cuisla Centre Co. Roscommon in the year 2000.

Songlines

Michele Bibby
Co-ordinator
Ewan MacColl Centre for the Arts
4 Great Strand Street
Dublin 1

Tel/Fax: +353 1 8735077/+353 1 8735078
Email: dublinarts@ireland.com
Other key staff: Marie Collins (Researcher)

Dublin Inner City community based audio visual project established during 'International Year For the Older Persons' is dedicated to recording, through music and the spoken word, the experience of senior citizens in the wake of the socio-economic cultural and environmental change in modern Irish society. Key activities include: intergenerational workshops involving school children and senior citizens groups using photographs, moving image and music to stimulate discussion of peoples experiences living and working in Inner City Dublin and research work in the pilot area in conjunction with Heritage Area Rejuvenation Project (and production of a CD and video for sale).

The Songworks

(formerly The Songwriters Workshop)
Tom Byrne
Director
Unit 6

3 Hanover Street East
Dublin 2

Tel/Fax: +353 1 6793880/+353 1 6793876
Email: info@thesongworks.com
Website: www.thesongworks.com
Other key staff: Colin Turner (Music Producer)

The Songworks is a recording and production studio for singers and songwriters, backing track composition and song arrangement and CD masters. Has a 16 track digital studio with a selection of musical equipment. Key activities include producing demos for songwriters, music production, backing tracks, recording for song contests and providing session singers. The newsletter 'Songworks Info' is issued on a quarterly basis.

The Sound Access Programme
Finola McTernan
Project Co-ordinator
Clarence House
Clarence Street
Dun Laoghaire
Co. Dublin

Tel/Fax: +353 1 2301303
Email: aap@iol.ie
Website: www.soundaccess.org
Other key staff: Jody Ackland (Project Administrator)

Sound Access is a music, sound technology and music industry training initiative for people with disabilities who wish to develop as musicians or sound technicians in further education and/or work. Aims to promote equal access and opportunity through a series of linked progression routes namely 'Sound Reach', 'Sound Step' and 'Sound Link'. The courses are free and the pilot programme was funded under the E.U Employment Horizon initiative and the Arts Council. 'Sound Reach' to date comprises of 14 six month regional musician-in-residence projects in National Training and Development Centres nationwide. 'Sound Step' is a six week foundation course exploring various musical styles and genres, with an introduction to sound, midi and radio. 'Sound Link' is a full time NCVA accredited course in 'Music - Performing Arts'.

Suzuki Education Institute of Ireland
Sheila Benny
13 Cois Sleibhe
Southern Cross
Bray
Co. Wicklow

Tel: +353 1 2829798
Other key staff: Magsi Goor
Tel/Fax: +353 1 2868297/+353 1 2864355

Founded in 1986 under the presidency of Dr. Shin'ichi Suzuki, the Institute is the authorised representative of Suzuki education at home and abroad. It works in conjunction with the European and International Suzuki Associations, forming part of a well established global network. Main aims are to further the Suzuki teaching method and philosophy of education of very young children throughout Ireland, to provide teacher training and to maintain professional standards and best practice. Key activities and services include teacher training and local administration of internationally recognised qualifications. Professional services are offered to qualified Suzuki method teachers. Provision of holiday courses, national days and local workshops for children. Lists of qualified teachers and media information are provided to the general public. The journal 'SENSEI' is published, containing reports of activities and articles on teaching/learning topics.

Temple Bar Music Centre
Paddy Dunning
Managing Director
Curved Street
Temple Bar
Dublin 2

Tel/Fax: +353 1 6709202/+353 1 6709105
Email: tbmusic@indigo.ie
Website: www.tbmc.ie
Other key staff: Colm Sexton (Chief Executive), Aoife Woodlock (Venue Bookings Manager)

The Temple Bar Music Centre aims to provide assistance to young emerging talent and industry professionals in the areas of information, recording and rehearsal studios, and training courses. The Centre also houses a 341 seater venue. A newsletter is issued on a quarterly basis (see advert page 42)

Temple Bar Properties
Grainne Millar
Events Programming Manager
18 Eustace Street
Temple Bar
Dublin 2

Tel/Fax: +353 1 6772255/+353 1 6772525
Email: info@temple-bar.ie
Website: www.temple-bar.ie

Temple Bar Properties cultural programme involves

enhancing the relationship between cultural activity in the area and the public in a number of ways including: programming free, quality, outdoor events on Meeting House Square and Temple Bar Square; presenting a diverse programme of live contemporary music by Irish and international composers and musicians and improving opportunities for artists to work in the area through use of the international artists apartment and writers studio. Meeting House Square is a purpose built outdoor performance space with a 35 mm projection screen, slide projector, use of stage and facilities to seat up to 600 people. A programme of free, outdoor events is produced in all artistic disciplines during the summer months with a year-round visual arts programme. Temple Bar Square and Curved Street are also available for programming.

Tóstal

c/o Caroline Senior
Artistic Director
The Garter Lane Arts Centre
22a O'Connell Street
Waterford

Tel/Fax: +353 51 877153/+353 51 871570
Email: admin@garterlane.ie
Website: www.garterlane.ie
Other key staff: Lilly O'Reilly (General Manager)

Tóstal is a network of Arts Council funded Irish arts centres set up to support and develop its members. Tóstal members work with a wide range of art forms. The organisation responsibility for co-ordination of Tóstal members changes each year. The network can be contacted collectively or individually by getting in touch with the arts centre director.

Toyota Ireland

Ian Corbett
Marketing Department
Killeen Road
Dublin 12

Tel/Fax: +353 1 4190200/+353 1 4190273
Email: info@toyota.ie
Website: www.toyota.ie
Other key staff: Dave Shannon (Managing Director, Toyota Ireland), Denis Smyth (Managing Director Killeen Auto Group), Steve Torney (Marketing Manager)

It is a key goal of Toyota Ireland's sponsorship programme to invest maximum available finance in support of Irish language and Irish music related projects, with a view to contributing as meaningfully as possible to cultural and social activities of short and long term significance to our country. Current key activities of the Toyota Arts Initiative include annual sponsorship of the National Youth Orchestra of Ireland, five-year £100,000 p.a sponsorship of the Irish World Music Centre in the University of Limerick, £10,000 p.a. five-year sponsorship of the provision of an Irish Language Chair at the University of Cork, annual sponsorship of the North Monastery Language laboratory, sponsorship of the National Irish Council for the Blind through Golf As Gaeilge nationwide competitions and annual sponsorship of An Feis Cheoil.

Ulster Arts Club

Paddy McCoy
Club Secretary
56 Elmwood Avenue
Belfast BT9 6AZ
Northern Ireland

Tel: 048 9066 0844
Other key staff: Pedro Donald (Club Stewart)

Aims to further the cause of art by promoting the social environment of persons practising or having a sympathetic interest in any of the arts, whether pure or applied, and by encouraging artistic activities within the club.

Ulster Society of Organists & Choirmasters

Rodney Bambrick
Honorary Secretary
1b Beverley Hills
Bangor BT20 4NA
Northern Ireland

Tel: 048 9146 5222
Other key staff: Alasdair Mac Laughlin (Honorary Treasurer), Timothy Allen (President)

Founded in 1918 as a forum for church musicians of all denominations, amateur and professional in Ulster. Principal aims are: to promote high standards in the selection and performance of church music, organ & choral; to uphold the status of the profession and safeguard its interests and to promote a wider public interest in organ and choral music. Its monthly meetings include visits to churches with organs and/or choirs of particular interest, choral workshops, lectures and discussions on all aspects of church music. An annual weekend tour to places outside Ireland is also arranged. Affiliated to the UK Incorporated Association of Organists. A newsletter is issued on a monthly basis.

Very Special Arts Ireland
c/o City Arts Centre
23-25 Moss Street
Dublin 2

Tel/Fax: +353 1 6770643/+353 1 6770131

Aims to promote the creative power in people with disabilities.

Voluntary Arts Network (UK)
Ginny Brink
Information Officer
PO Box 200
Cardiff CF5 1YH
Wales

Tel/Fax: +44 29 2039 5395/+44 29 2039 7397
Email: info@voluntaryarts.org or
info@vanmail.demon.co.uk
Website: www.voluntaryarts.org
Other key staff: Rodger Fox (Chief Executive)

Voluntary Arts Network (VAN), is the UK development agency for the voluntary arts, recognising that the arts are a key part of culture and that they are vital to our health, social and economic development. VAN provides advocacy, information and training for those who participate in the voluntary arts sector. This includes approximately 300 national and regional umbrella bodies, and through them, their member groups of local voluntary arts practitioners. VAN aims to support those participating in the voluntary arts and encourage others to take part, to celebrate cultural diversity, increase equality of opportunity and to promote the role of the arts in the well-being of individuals and communities. Holds information about voluntary arts groups of all ages across a wide range of artforms such as choirs, orchestras, drama, dance, literature, needlework, folk art, media, music, visual arts, crafts and applied arts, and festivals. The newsletter 'Update' is issued on a quarterly basis.

Waterford Music City & County
Linda O'Donnell
Administrative Assistant
7 Lombard Street
Waterford City
Co. Waterford

Tel/Fax: +353 51 857055 or +353 58 45977/
+353 51 879124
Email: waterfordmusic@eircom.net

Waterford Music City & County has, from the start, worked on a number of levels to develop music in Waterford, by setting up structures which facilitate co-operation between locally based groups and organisations involved in the music/arts, community development and education sectors. It provides an information service, and has compiled a Waterford music database. The organisation has also been involved in community based capacity building projects in Waterford County, and aims to improve music accessibility throughout the county to communities, schools, musicians, etc.

PERFORMANCE ORGANISATIONS

Castleward Opera
Hilda Logan
General Manager
737 Lisburn Road
Belfast BT9 7GU
Co. Antrim
Northern Ireland

Tel/Fax: 048 9066 1090/048 9068 7081
Other key staff: Ian Urwin (Joint Artistic Director), Jack Smith (Joint Artistic Director), Michael McGuggin (Musical Director)

Castleward Opera aims to provide a platform for young professional singers, orchestral players and production managers. Key activities include an annual festival every June, various concerts and an opera season in February.

Irish Chamber Orchestra
John Kelly
Chief Executive
Irish Chamber Orchestra
Foundation Building
University of Limerick
Limerick

Tel/Fax: +353 61 202620/+353 61 202617
Email: ico@ul.ie
Other key staff: Fionnuala Hunt (Artistic Director), Imelda Dervin (Administrator/PRO), Margaret McConnell (Friends/Advertising Co-ordinator)

The Irish Chamber Orchestra is an ensemble of professional musicians committed to excellence in the performance of classical and contemporary music. Under the artistic direction of Fionnuala Hunt, the orchestra continues to give a new perspective and approach to performance. The orchestras activities include: a full concert schedule at both national and international levels; recording contemporary work; commissioning and performing new work form Irish and overseas composers; organising the annual Killaloe Music Festival and managing an outreach programme in schools and communities around Ireland.

Opera Ireland

David Collopy
General Manager
John Player House
276-288 South Circular Road
Dublin 8

Tel/Fax: +353 1 4535519/+353 1 4535521
Email: info@opera-ireland.ie
Website: www.opera-ireland.ie
Other key staff: Kay Keilthy (Administrator),
Taragh Loughrey-Grant (Marketing Executive)

Opera Ireland aims to provide full scale opera, produced
to a high standard and presented to the widest possible
audience in Ireland. Opera Ireland presents four opera
productions each year with international casts, usually in
Dublin's Gaiety Theatre. Its associated company, Co-
Opera tours specially adapted versions of the popular
repertoire to the regions. In addition the company promotes concerts, lecture series and fundraising events.
Opera Ireland News newsletter is available to members
on a quarterly basis.

Opera Theatre Company

Gemma Murray
Administrator
Temple Bar Music Centre
Curved Street
Dublin 2

Tel/Fax: +353 1 6794962/+353 1 6794963
Email: info@operatheatreco.com
Website: www.imn.ie/otc
Other key staff: James Conway (Director), Nick
Costello (Marketing/Education Officer), Jan Duffy
(Public Relations Officer), Sadhbh O'Connor
(Administrative Assistant)

Opera Theatre Company produces and tours opera in
Ireland. It is grant aided by both Irish Arts Councils.
Productions generally tour with a chamber orchestra or
ensemble, although there are occasional collaborations
with RTÉ. The company has a special interest in contemporary work, and in opera for young people. A newsletter
is issued on a quarterly basis.

RTÉ Performing Groups

Niall Doyle
Director of Music
Music Division
RTÉ
Donnybrook
Dublin 4

Tel/Fax: +353 1 2083143/+353 1 2082511
Email: doylen@rte.ie
Website: www.rte.ie/music/index.html
Other key staff: Miriam McDonald (General
Manager of Marketing and Communications),
Martyn Westerman (General Manager of the
National Symphony Orchestra), Gareth Hudson
(Executive Producer of RTÉ Concert Orchestra).

Radio Telefís Éireann (RTÉ) is the National Broadcasting
Authority of Ireland. Niall Doyle, Director of Music is
responsible for the Music division in RTÉ, which com-
prises a number of performing groups: The National
Symphony Orchestra - 88 players, Conductor Alexander
Anissimov, The RTÉ Concert Orchestra - 44 players,
Principal Conductor Prionnsias O Duinn, The RTÉ
Vanbrugh String Quartet, The RTÉ Philharmonic Choir
and Cór Na nÓg (The Childrens' Choir). The National
Symphony Orchestra operates an annual subscription
series at the National Concert Hall, Dublin and performs
in a number of other major events in Ireland annually.
Both orchestras run a series of tours around the country
each year and tour internationally. They have a number
of commercial recordings and regularly contribute to
television and radio broadcast. The RTÉ Vanbrugh String
Quartet, based in Cork performs throughout Ireland and
has made a number of commercial recordings.

Ulster Orchestra Society Ltd

David J.L Fisk
Chief Executive
Elmwood Hall at Queen's
89 University Road
Belfast BT7 INF
Northern Ireland

Tel/Fax: 048 9066 4535/048 9066 2761
Email: david@ulstero.freeserve.co.uk
Other key staff: James Stewart OBE
(Chairman), Paul McKinley (Librarian)

Ulster Orchestra Society Ltd aim to provide the highest
standard of classical music for all the people of Northern
Ireland. Based in Belfast, the orchestra was founded in
1966 and established itself as one of the major symphony orchestras in the United Kingdom. It is Northern
Irelands only full-time professional orchestra. The
orchestra has gained an international reputation through
its overseas tours, which in 1999 included Germany,
Holland and Hong Kong. The orchestra has made over
50 commercial recordings and each year records 12
weeks of output for the BBC. Key activities include
orchestral concerts (in 1999-2000 performances of 25
concerts in 11 venues across Northern Ireland) and education and outreach programme in the region. Belfast
venues include The Waterfront Hall and The Ulster Hall.

Wexford Festival Opera

Jerome Hynes
Chief Executive
Theatre Royal
High Street
Wexford

Tel/Fax: +353 53 22400/+353 53 24289
Email: info@wexfordopera.com
Website: www.wexfordopera.com
Other key staff: Luigi Ferrari (Artistic Director),
Phil Keeling (Administrator), Sue Hackett (Press
Officer)

Wexford has been described as "the opera lover's perfect treat, the town has an exquisite small theatre which stages little known operas in elegantly economical productions". The Festival itself takes over the town with a festival air permeating every side street. The traders compete with each other for the prize of best festival window. The artists and audiences mingle in cafes and bars along the main street. Audiences gather from all over the world for this international festival with opera at its core. Eighteen performances are given, six of each of the three operas by a Wexford Festival company of international artists. Over forty other daytime events take place.

LOCAL AUTHORITY ARTS OFFICERS REP. OF IRELAND €

Carlow County Council

Caoimhín Corrigan (Arts Officer)
Carlow County Council
Athy Road
Co. Carlow

Tel/Fax: +353 503 70300/+353 503 41503
Email: art@carlowcoco.ie

Cavan County Council

Catriona O'Reilly (Arts Officer)
Cavan County Council
17 Farnham Street
Co. Cavan

Tel/Fax: +353 49 4331799 Ext. 7350/
+353 49 4362127

Clare County Council

Siobhán Mulcahy (Arts Officer)
Library Headquarters

Harmony Row
Ennis
Co. Clare

Tel/Fax: +353 65 6821616/+353 65 6842462

Cork Corporation

Mark Mulqueen (Arts Officer)
Cork Corporation
City Hall
Cork

Tel/Fax: +353 21 4924298/+353 21 4314238
Email: arts@corkcorp.ie
Website: www.corkcorp.ie

Cork County Council

Ian McDonagh (County Arts Officer)
Cork County Library
County Hall
Cork

Tel/Fax: +353 21 4346210/+353 21 4343254
Email: cosec@corkcoco.ie
Website: www.corkcoco.com

Donegal County Council

Traolach Ó Fionnáin (Arts Officer)
c/o Donegal County Library
Rosemount
Letterkenny
Co. Donegal

Tel/Fax: +353 74 21968/+353 74 26402

Dublin Corporation

Jack Gilligan (Arts Officer)
20 Parnell Square North
Dublin 1

Tel/Fax: +353 1 8722816/+353 1 8722933
Email: arts@dubc.iol.ie

Dundalk Urban District Council

Brian Harten (Arts Officer)
Arts Office
Market Square
Dundalk
Co. Louth

Tel/Fax: +353 42 9332276/+353 42 9336761
Email: dundarts@eircom.net

Dun Laoghaire/ Rathdown County Council
Clíodhna Shaffrey (Arts Officer)
County Hall
Marine Road
Dun Laoghaire
Co. Dublin

Tel/Fax: +353 1 2054749 or
+353 1 2054719/+353 1 2806969
Email: arts@dlrcoco.ie
Website: www.dlrcoco.ie

Fingal County Council
Rory O'Byrne (County Arts Officer)
2-3 Parnell Square
Dublin 1

Tel/Fax: +353 1 8727777 Ext. 2244/
+353 1 8727914
Email: fincoart@club.ie

Galway Corporation/ Galway County Council
James Harrold (Arts Officer)
Wood Quay Court
Wood Quay
Galway

Tel/Fax: +353 91 563841/+353 91 561328
Email: jcharrold@hotmail.com
Website: under construction

Kerry County Council
Kate Kennelly (Arts Officer)
c/o Kerry County Council
Rathass
Tralee
Co. Kerry

Tel/Fax: +353 66 7121111/+353 66 7122466
Email: kcc@kerrycoco.ie
Website: www.kerrycoco.ie

Kildare County Council
Mary Lenihan (Arts Officer)
County Library

Athgarvan Road
Newbridge
Co. Kildare

Tel/Fax: +353 45 431215/+353 45 432490
Email: kap@eircom.net
Website: www.kildare.ie/arts

Kilkenny County Council
Margaret Cosgrave (Arts Organiser)
County Hall
Kilkenny County Council
John Street
Co. Kilkenny

Tel/Fax: +353 56 52699/+353 56 63384
Email: mcosgrav@kilkenny.ie
Website: www.kilkenny.ie

Laois County Council
Muireann Ní Chonaill (Arts Officer)
Laois Arts Office
Áras An Chontae
Portlaoise
Co. Laois

Tel/Fax: +353 502 22044/+353 502 22313

Leitrim County Council
Terre Duffy (Arts Officer)
Park Lane House
Carrick on Shannon
Co. Leitrim

Tel/Fax: +353 78 20005/+353 78 20925
Email: artsoff@leitrimcoco.ie

Limerick Corporation
Sheila Deegan (Arts Officer)
City Hall
Merchants' Quay
Limerick

Tel/Fax: +353 61 415799 Ext. 225/+353 61 415266
Email: artsoff@limerickcorp.ie

Limerick County Council
Joan MacKernan (County Arts Officer)
Limerick County Council
County Buildings
79-84 O'Connell Street
Limerick

Tel/Fax: +353 61 318477/+353 61 317280
Email: artoffice@limerickcoco.ie

Longford County Council
Fergus Kennedy (Arts Officer)
Longford County Council
Áras An Chontae
Great Water Street
Longford

Tel/Fax: +353 43 48376/+353 43 41125
Email: longfordcoco@eircom.net

Mayo County Council
The Arts Officer
The Arts Office
Mayo County Council
Mountainview
Castlebar
Co. Mayo

Tel/Fax: +353 94 24444 Ext 577/+353 94 24774
Email: mayococoarts@hotmail.com

Meath County Council
Gerardette Bailey (Arts Officer)
The Arts Office
Dunshaughlin Library
Main Street
Dunshaughlin
Co. Meath

Tel/Fax: +353 1 8240000/+353 46 21463
Email: gbailey@meathcoco.ie

Monaghan County Council
Somhairle MacConghail (Arts Officer)
1-2 Hill Street
Monaghan

Tel/Fax: +353 47 82928/+353 47 71189
Email: harvestblues@eircom.net

Offaly County Council
Noreen O'Hare (Arts Officer)
The Arts Office
The Courthouse
Tullamore
Co. Offaly

Tel/Fax: +353 506 46830/+353 506 46868
Email: artsoff@offalycoco.ie

Roscommon County Council
The Arts Officer
Roscommon County Council
Abbey Street
Roscommon

Tel/Fax: +353 903 26100/+353 903 25477

Sligo County Council
Mary McAuliffe (Arts Officer)
County Council Offices
Riverside
Sligo

Tel/Fax: +353 71 56629/+353 71 41119
Email: arts@sligococo.ie

South Dublin County Council
Emily Jane Kirwan (Arts Officer)
Council Town Centre
Tallaght
Dublin 24

Tel/Fax: +353 1 4149000 Ext. 3314/3345/
+353 1 4149106
Email: artsofficer@sdublincoco.ie
Website: www.sdcc.ie

Tipperary North County Council
Melanie Scott (Arts Officer)
The Courthouse
Nenagh
Co. Tipperary

Tel/Fax: +353 67 31771/+353 67 33134
Email: artsoffice@northtippcoco.ie

Waterford Corporation
Derek Verso (Arts Officer)
City Hall
The Mall
Waterford City

Tel/Fax: +353 51 309983/+353 51 879124
Email: art@waterfordcorp.ie

Waterford County Council
Margaret Fleming (Arts Officer)
Civic Offices
Davitts Quay
Dungarvan
Co. Waterford

Tel/Fax: +353 58 41416/+353 58 42911

Wexford County Council
Lorraine Comer (County Arts Officer)
Arts Office
Wexford County Council
Wexford

Tel/Fax: +353 53 42211 Ext. 369/+353 53 43532
Email: lcomer@wexfordcoco.ie
Website: www.wexford.ie

Wicklow County Arts Office
Leah Coyne (Arts Officer)
St. Manntan's House
Kilmantin Hill
Wicklow

Tel/Fax: +353 404 20155/+353 404 66057 or
+353 404 20079
Email: wao@eircom.net
Website: www.wicklow.ie/arts

LOCAL AUTHORITY ARTS OFFICERS NORTHERN IRELAND €

Antrim Borough Council
Gary Shaw
(Art & Heritage Development Officer)
Clotworthy Arts Centre
Antrim Castle Gardens
Randalstown Road
Antrim BT41 4LH
Northern Ireland

Tel/Fax: 048 9442 8000/048 9446 0360

Ards Borough Council
Eilis O'Baoill (Arts Officer)
Ards Arts Centre
Town Hall
Conway Square
Newtownards
Co. Down
Northern Ireland

Tel/Fax: 048 9181 0803/048 9182 3131
Email: angelahaley@ards-council.gov.uk

Ballymena Borough Council
Rosalind Lowry (Arts Officer)
Aldeevin
80 Galgorm Road
Ballymena
Co. Antrim BT42 1AB
Northern Ireland

Tel/Fax: 048 2566 0387/048 2566 0400
Email: william.young/ballymenabc@ballymena.gov.uk

Ballymoney Borough Council
Margaret Higgins (Cultural Services Officer)
Riada House
14 Charles Street
Ballymoney
Co. Antrim BT53 6DZ
Northern Ireland

Tel/Fax: 048 2766 2280/048 2766 7659
Email: ballymoneybc@psilink.co.uk
Website: www.ballymoney.gov.uk

Banbridge District Council
Vanessa Miller (Arts & Events Officer)
Banbridge District Council
Civic Building
Downshire Road
Banbridge
Co. Down
Northern Ireland

Tel/Fax: 048 4066 0605/048 4066 0601
Email: info@banbridgedc.gov.uk
Website: www.banbridgedc.com

Belfast City Council
Chris Bailey (Arts & Heritage Manger)
Belfast City Council
Cecil Ward Building
4-10 Linenhall Street
Belfast BT2 8BP
Northern Ireland

Tel/Fax: 048 9032 0202/048 9027 0325
Email: baileyc@belfastcity.gov.uk

Carrickfergus Borough Council
Colin Ellis (Community Relations Officer)
Community Relations Unit
Heritage Plaza

Antrim Street
Carrickfergus
Co. Antrim BT38 7DG
Northern Ireland

Tel/Fax: 048 9336 6455/048 9335 0350
Email: cellis@carrickfergus.org

Castlereagh Borough Council

James D. Rose (Director of Leisure and
Community Services)
111 Old Dundonald Road
Dundonald
Co. Down BT16 1XT
Northern Ireland

Tel/Fax: 048 9048 2611/048 9048 9604
Email: leisure@castlereagh.gov.uk

Coleraine Borough Council

Malcolm Murchison (Arts Centre Manager)
Flowerfield Arts Centre
185 Coleraine Road
Portstewart BT55 7HU
Northern Ireland

Tel/Fax: 048 7083 3959/048 7083 5042
Email: flowerfield@dnet.co.uk
Website: under construction

Cookstown District Council

Linda McGarvey
(Arts & Cultural Development Officer)
Cookstown District Council
Burn Road
Cookstown
Co. Tyrone BT80 8DT
Northern Ireland

Tel/Fax: 048 8676 2205 Ext. 219/
048 8676 4360
Email: econdev@cookstown.gov.uk
Website: www.cookstown.gov.uk

Craigavon Borough Council

Rosaleen McMullan
(Arts Development Officer)
Pinebank Arts & Resource Centre
Tullygally Road
Craigavon

Co. Antrim BT65 5BY
Northern Ireland

Tel/Fax: 048 3834 1618/048 3834 2402

Derry City Council

David McLaughlin (Arts officer)
Rialto Entertainment Centre
5 Market Street
Derry BT48 6EF
Northern Ireland

Tel/Fax: 048 7126 4177/048 7126 0688
Email: derrytheatre@yahoo.com
Website: www.derrytheatre.com

Down District Council

Jill Holmes (Arts Officer)
Down County Museum
The Mall
Downpatrick
Co. Down BT30 6AM
Northern Ireland

Tel/Fax: 048 4461 5218/048 4461 5590
Email: jholmes@downdc.gov.uk

Dungannon District Council

Theresa McNicholl (Arts Officer)
Circular Road
Dungannon
Co. Tyrone BT71 6DT
Northern Ireland

Tel/Fax: 048 8772 0300/048 8772 0368
Email: theresa.mcnicholl@dungannon.gov.uk

Fermanagh District Council

Geraldine O'Reilly (Arts Officer)
Town Hall
Enniskillen
Co. Fermanagh BT74 7BA
Northern Ireland

Tel/Fax: 048 6632 5050/048 6632 2024

Larne Borough Council

H.G Francis (Tourism & Community
Development Manager)
Smiley Buildings

Victoria Road
Larne
Co. Antrim BT40 1RU
Northern Ireland

Tel/Fax: 048 2827 2313/048 2826 0660
Email: mail@larne-bt.com

Limavady Borough Council
S. Bell (Community Relations Officer)
7 Connell Street
Limavady
Co. Londonderry
Northern Ireland

Tel/Fax: 048 7776 0304 or 048 7772 2226/
048 7772 2010

Lisburn Borough Council
Siobháin Stewart (Arts Development Officer)
Harmony Hill Arts Centre
54 Harmony Hill
Lisburn
Co. Down BT27 4ES
Northern Ireland

Tel/Fax: 048 9227 8219/048 9266 2679
Email: manager.hhac@lisburn.gov.uk

Magherafelt District Council
Sean Henry (Community Relations Officer)
50 Ballyronan Road
Magherafelt
Co. Derry BT45 6EN
Northern Ireland

Tel/Fax: 048 7939 7979/048 7939 7980
Email: mdc@magherafelt.demon.co.uk
Website: www.magherafelt.demon.co.uk

Moyle District Council
Pauline Russell (Arts Co-ordinator)
Sheskburn House
7 Mary Street
Ballycastle
Co. Antrim BT54 6QH
Northern Ireland

Tel/Fax: 048 2076 2225/048 2076 2515
Email: dev@moyle-council.org
Website: www.moyle-council.org

Newry & Mourne District Council
Mark Hughes (Arts Administrator/Facilitator)
Newry & Mourne Arts Centre
1a Bank Parade
Newry
Co. Down BT35 6HP
Northern Ireland

Tel/Fax: 048 3026 6232/048 3026 6893

Newtownabbey Borough Council
Cathy Cole (Development Arts Officer)
Department of Leisure & Technical Services
49 Church Road
Newtownabbey
Co. Antrim BT36 7LG
Northern Ireland

Tel/Fax: 048 9086 8751/048 9036 5407

North Down Borough Council
Lorna Hastings (Arts Officer)
Tower House
34 Quay Street
Bangor
Co. Down BT20 5ED

Tel/Fax: 048 9127 8032/048 9146 7744

Omagh District Council
Jean Brennan (Arts Development Officer)
The Grange
Mountjoy Road
Omagh
Co. Tyrone BT78 7BL
Northern Ireland

Tel/Fax: 048 8224 5321/048 8224 3888
Email: jean.brennan@omagh.gov.uk
Website: www.omagh.gov.uk

Strabane District Council
Karen McFarland (Community Services Officer)
47 Derry Road
Strabane
Co. Tyrone BT82 8DY
Northern Ireland

Tel/Fax: 048 7138 2204/048 7138 2264

ADDITIONAL CULTURAL & EDUCATION OFFICERS

City of Dublin VEC - Education Service to Prisons
Vincent Sammon
Prison Education Organiser
Teachers Centre
Mountjoy
North Circular Road
Dublin 7

Tel/Fax: +353 1 8062833/+353 1 8301175
Email: prisoned@indigo.ie

The Education Service within prisons places a strong emphasis on the creative arts in prison education nationwide, and offers programmes in arts, crafts, drama, music (which includes sound recording and production), creative writing, video, photography and publications.

County Kilkenny VEC - Arts Education Organiser for the South East
Proinsias Ó Drisceoil
Arts Education Organiser for the South East
Ormond Road
Kilkenny

Tel/Fax: +353 56 65103 or +353 56 51847/ +353 56 51094
Email: aaed@indigo.ie
Other key staff: Mary Fennelly, Anne Marie Donnelly

The VEC Arts Education Office was established by Co. Kilkenny VEC and the Department of Education in order to reverse the historic neglect of the arts in Irish education. The office takes a particular interest in the development of the arts in the formal education system at second level and in adult education. The office has immediate and long term objectives and functions in relation to the provision of an appropriate curriculum in arts subjects and the provision of arts in schools, in service training, and courses aimed at increasing proficiency in the arts. The office urges the establishment of teaching posts in the arts on school authorities.

County Sligo VEC - Arts Education Organiser
Leo Regan
Arts Education Organiser
VEC

Riverside
Sligo

Tel/Fax: +353 71 45844/+353 71 43093
Email: sligovec@iol.ie
Other key staff: Michael Burke (Adult Education Organiser), Loman Conway (Chief Executive Officer)

The arts education programme was established in 1980 to promote the arts in education in Sligo and Leitrim. The primary resource is provision of teaching hours in vocational schools for art and music. Teaching assistance is provided for workshops from traditional music to classical music as master classes. The VEC hold a collection of brass instruments for student use. Classes of tuition in traditional music and classical music are provided on a self-financing basis in Sligo county and Sligo Town. Performances and recitals in schools, particularly post-primary schools in Sligo and Leitrim, are organised by the Arts Education Organiser.

County Westmeath VEC - Arts Education Organiser
Bernadette Cleary
Arts Education Organiser
Westmeath VEC
Midland Arts Office of The Committee
Bellevue Road
Mullingar
Co. Westmeath

Tel/Fax: +353 44 43229/+353 44 43533

Macra Na Feirme
The Arts Officer
Irish Farm Centre
Bluebell
Dublin 12

Tel/Fax: +353 1 4508000/+353 1 4514908
Email: macra@macra.ie

Macra Na Feirme is a national, voluntary, non-sectarian organisation with the objectives of agricultural and rural development, and the personal development, social and cultural education and leadership training of all its members, which number 10,000. The Arts Officer aims to develop new and innovative projects in the arts, and support the existing cultural work of the organisation. The position is co-funded by the Arts Council and Macra na Feirme, and supported by the Calouste Gulbenkian Foundation.

National Maternity Hospital
Tove O'Flanagan
Part Time Arts Co-ordinator
Holles Street
Dublin 2

Tel/Fax: +353 1 6610277 Ext. 2131/
+353 1 6766623

The National Maternity Hospital introduced an arts programme during its Centenary celebrations in 1994. The
success of site specific art works, drama and music in
the wards strengthened the hospital's determination to
include the arts as an integral strategy in the overall
programme of healthcare. The priorities for 2000 are to
introduce more art forms and include more music.
There is also the intention to develop the visual art environment further to generate a more relaxed atmosphere
to benefit patients, staff and visitors alike.

South Kerry Development Partnership Ltd
Sarah O'Brien
Cultural Development Officer
An tSean Scoil
Sun Hill
Killorglin
Co. Kerry

Tel/Fax:+353 66 9761615/+353 66 9762059
Other key staff: Bill Thorne (General Manager),
Siobhán Griffin (Community Development Co-
ordinator)

The South Kerry Development Partnership Ltd, grew
from local recognition of the need to establish and ade-
quately resource an area based development company
to address social exclusion and the root problems in
South Kerry. The internal structure of the Partnership
has been able to integrate local initiative, State and
European measures (including the LEADER and Local
Development Programmes) very effectively, and to deliv-
er these at local level. Cultural animation is one of the
core elements of the partnership's community development strategy. The Cultural Officer aims to co-ordinate
and stimulate isolated and individual cultural activities
already existing in the region, and initiate new projects
that enhance the general cultural life of the region. The
Cultural Officer is also available to advise and facilitate
arts and community groups, and to encourage national
arts companies to include South Kerry in their tour
diaries. The newsletter 'Ar Agaidh Linn' is issued on a
quarterly basis.

National Youth Council of Ireland - National Youth Arts Programme
Monica Corcoran
Arts Officer
3 Montague Street
Dublin 2

Tel/Fax: +353 1 4784122/+353 1 4783974
Email: arts@nyci.ie

The National Youth Arts Programme is a partnership
initiative between the National Youth Council of Ireland,
the Arts Council, and the Youth Affairs Section of the
Department of Education and Science. It is dedicated to
the development and advancement of youth arts in
Ireland. Key activities include: advocacy, networking,
provision of resources, support and development. Runs
a youth arts forum, maintains a database/network facility, runs pilot projects and develops resource materials.
The newsletter 'In 2 - Youth Arts Participation' is issued
bi-annually.

CULTURAL INSTITUTIONS

Alliance Française
Marie-Christine Vandoorne
Director
1 Kildare Street
Dublin 2

Tel/Fax: +353 1 6761732/+353 1 6764077
Email: info@alliance-francaise.ie
Website: www.alliance-francaise.ie
Other key staff: Elizabeth Gilligan (Administrator)

The Alliance Française was founded in 1883 in Paris to
promote the French language and culture. It is now
established in more than 125 countries, with more than
1,000 autonomous centres. The Alliance Française offers
French classes to all age groups and levels, a library and
video library, and cultural events. There are nationwide
branches in Cork, Galway, Limerick, Athlone, Carlow,
Enniscorthy, Kildare, Kilkenny, Sligo and Waterford.

€

The British Council
Harold Fish
Director
Newmount House
22-24 Lower Mount Street
Dublin 2

Tel/Fax: +353 1 6764088 or +353 1 6766943/ +353 1 6766945
Email: firstname@bcdublin.iol.ie
Website: www.britishcouncil.org/ireland/index.htm
Other key staff: Helen Jones (PA to Director/ Administrator/Accountant), Angela Crean (Education Officer)

The British Council promotes Britain abroad. It provides access to British ideas, talents and experience in education and training, the arts, sciences, technology and the English language. It works to promote partnership between the UK and Ireland. The British Council has a small reference collection of educational information which is open form 2.30pm to 5.00pm.

The British Council in Northern Ireland
Peter Lyner
Director
1 Chlorine Gardens
Belfast BT9 5DJ
Northern Ireland

Tel/Fax: 048 9066 6770 or 048 9066 6706/ 048 9066 5242
Email: peter.lyner@britcounc.org
Other key staff: Lynda E.E. Wilson (Deputy Director), Paul Burrows (Head of Central Bureau), Bernie McAllister (Deputy Head of Council - Bureau Section)

The Council in Northern Ireland aims to ensure that the Province's unique expertise and experience are known and exploited in pursuit of the Council's corporate aims. Contributing to the Council's work in development, the office looks after students and visitors under Council auspices whose programmes bring them to the Province. The British Council organises international seminars on a range of topics usually drawing on the expertise and experience in the Province. Special programmes unique to Northern Ireland.

Goethe-Institut
Reinhard Schmidt-Supprian
Director
37 Merrion Square
Dublin 2

Tel/Fax: +353 1 6611155/+353 1 6611358
Email: goethe@iol.ie
Website: www.goethe.de/dublin
Other key staff: Barbara Deutschmann (Head of

Language Department), Barbara Ebert (Events Co-ordinator), Heidrun Rottke (Secretary/Film Co-ordinator)

The Goethe-Institut is a worldwide organisation promoting German language and culture and developing international cultural co-operation. The Dublin branch was established in 1962. The Goethe-Institut organises cultural events (music, theatre, film, literature, exhibitions), German language courses and runs a library and information service. A calendar of events is issued bi-monthly.

Instituto Cervantes
Ignacio Montes
Director
58 Northumberland Road
Dublin 4

Tel/Fax: +353 1 6682024/+353 1 6688416
Email: cendub@cervantes.es
Website: www.cervantes.es
Other key staff: Juan Robisco (Head of Studies), Isabel Lopez (Head Librarian), Ramona Marino (Administration Officer)

The Instituto Cervantes aims to promote the culture of the people of all Spanish speaking countries. It runs exhibitions, lectures, musical recitals, films, poetry readings and social events during the academic year. The Instituto Cervantes also provides language tuition, a library and reading room, a resource centre, video library and computer room. A newsletter is issued on a quarterly basis.

Instituto Italiano Di Cultura
Dr Laura Oliveti
Director
11 Fitzwilliam Square
Dublin 2

Tel/Fax: +353 1 6766662 or +353 1 6623208/ +353 1 6766716
Email: italcult@iol.ie
Website: www.iol.ie/-italcult

The Institute, founded in 1957, fosters the implementation of the 'Cultural Agreement' between Italy and Ireland signed in 1984 consisting of joined initiatives with Irish cultural institutions in the fields of education, culture and science. The Institute organises seminars, conferences, book presentations, exhibitions, concerts, theatre and cinema representations. It also provides library and audio-visual facilities as well as courses in Italian language and culture at all levels from October to the end of May.

MUSIC COLLECTIVES
REPUBLIC OF IRELAND

Federation of Music Collectives
Angela Dorgan
Director
Space 28
North Lotts
Dublin 1

Tel/Fax: +353 1 8782244 or +353 1 8721882/
+353 1 8726827
Email: fmc@imn.ie
Website: under construction
Other key staff: Tony Doherty (Project
Development Officer, Northern Ireland)

The Federation of Music Collectives (FMC), are a cross
border umbrella organisation who support, encourage
and develop the work of music collectives in Ireland.
This is achieved through education and masterclass
initiatives so that members can facilitate the grass roots
needs of musicians to the best standards. Key activities
include: to act as a contact point for music collectives/
resource centres; to provide training opportunities to
member collectives; to assist in the set up of new
collectives; to facilitate the work of existing collectives;
to raise the profile of the FMC and its members; to
provide information and advice resource for members
and to act as a conduit form the industry/arts to grass
roots musicians. The newsletter 'The Fed' is issued on a
quarterly basis (see advert page 14).

Alternative Entertainments
Liam Morissey
Administrator
Tymonstown Community Centre
Firhouse Road West
Tallaght
Dublin 24

Tel: +353 1 4520611

This music collective specialises in traditional and folk
music. There are recording facilities and live gigs.

Athlone Music Collective
Bobby Hewitt
Director
The Docks
Athlone
Co. Westmeath

Tel: +353 902 92026

Mobile: +353 86 8207983
Other key staff: Louis Bourgoyne (Vice President)

Aims to set up a base for local talent. Operates a
recording facility.
(see also page - The Grove Studios)

City Arts Centre
John Lalor
23-25 Moss Street
Dublin 2

Tel: +353 1 6770643

Hold 'Music Map' which is a music industry training
programme for people with disabilities.

Cork Music Resource Centre
Ronan Spillane
c/o 2 Rutland Court
Douglas Street
Cork

Tel: +353 26 40234
Mobile: +353 87 2968442

This music collective is a voluntary organisation. Provides
an information and advisory service and also holds live
performances.

Fusebox Music Resource Centre Ltd
Moira Cassidy
Manager
Glenhill House
Glenhill
Finglas
Dublin 11

Tel/Fax: +353 1 8643354/+353 1 8642141
Other key staff: Ken Burke (Studio Manager),
Mark Burke (Education officer), Anne Marie
Walsh (P.R Officer)

Fusebox Music Resource Centre Ltd, was established in
1995. It is a community based initiative designed to
assist musicians and musically minded people in the
pursuit of education, employment, expression and creativity. Key activities and services include: a 32 track digital recording studio using pro tools, music workshops
and instrument tuition, evening courses in sound engineering, midi sequencing and sampling aimed at careers
within the music industry. There are also singer/song-
writer performances and regular electric performances
and information and graphics services related to music
(see advert page 14).

Kildare Performing Arts Group
Eddie O'Neill
Supervisor
Unit 2A
Cutlery Road
Newbridge
Co. Kildare

Tel: +353 45 431213
Email: kpag@eircom.net
Website: www.kildare.ie/kpag
Other key staff: Terri Moore (Bealtaine Co-ordinator and Information Officer,) Claire Noon (Youth Programmer), Sophie Costigan (Administrator)

This music collective provides information for musicians. There are workshops for singers and songwriters provided.

Marketown Music Collective
Fergus Egan
Supervisor/Development Manager
Space 28
North Lotts
Dublin 1

Tel/Fax: +353 1 8721882/+353 1 8726827
Email: fmc@imn.ie
Other key staff: Glenn Brady (Education Officer)

Marketown Music Collective (MMC) was established in 1995. It provides music education to children and young adults in the form of workshops in schools, festivals and specifically designed courses for small groups. MMC is the Dublin representative of music for the International Yehudi Menuhin Foundation. Key activities include school workshops, participation in festivals providing workshops, creating national and international links to create a broader education programme.

Mullingar Music Collective
Niall Masterson
82 Hillside Drive
Mullingar
Co. Westmeath

Mobile: +353 86 8437868

This music collective is working on a documentary about rock bands in the Mullingar area and they also hold live performances in the the locality.

Oifig An Cheoil - The Music Office
Aina Davis
Music Administrator

Dykegate Lane
Dingle
Co. Kerry

Tel/Fax: +353 66 9152772/+353 66 9152242
Email: oac@eircom.net
Website: http://homepage.eircom.net/~oac
Other key staff: Joan Maguire (Director), Eoin Duignan (Secretary)

This music collective is a contact and information centre for musicians. Its main aim is to promote creative expression and to encourage the composition of new music and the development of personal style. Facilities include: computers, photocopying, information book about the music industry and also advice given on the recording process and setting up tours.

Re: Sound
Rachel Butler
Mullinary
Carrickmacross
Co. Monaghan

Tel: +353 42 9664876

This music collective provides support for groups in Monaghan and groups travelling to Monaghan.

Singer, Songwriter Forum
John Palmer
Director
7 Georges Street
Waterford

Tel: +353 51 879333
Other key staff: Joe Whelan, Keith MacDonald, Liam Merriman

This music collective started in February 1998. The Songwriter Forum promotes original music. Key activities include showcase nights where musicians and songwriters perform original songs. Showcase nights run every second week on a Wednesday night and up to five acts perform. Full PA and professional engineer provided.

Sligo Music Collective
Deirdre Byron-Smith
26 Ashbury Lawn
Ballinode
Co Sligo

Tel: +353 71 47380

This music collective is a voluntary organisation providing an information and advisory service. Specialises in world music and offers support for Sligo groups.

Tipperary Music Collective

Johnny Dunne
Manager
Lower Glanbane
Holycross
Thurles
Co. Tipperary

Tel: +353 504 43349
Email: system7@eircom.net

This music collective has recording and production facilities. It aims to assist people with budget restrictions, works on a non-profit basis.

Masamba Samba School

Sarah Walker
Administrator
30 Bayview Avenue
North Strand
Dublin 3

Tel: +353 1 8551838
Mobile: +353 87 2363813
Email: simieon@connect.ie
Website: www.masamba.com

Masamba was formed in 1995 to promote access to the diverse rhythms of Brazil. The group numbers 17 members from a variety of cultural and artistic backgrounds. Participates in festivals/ performance as well as delivering workshops in Latin percussion to a broad range of target groups. Key activities include performances for parades, workshops with special needs groups, youth groups and schools.

MUSIC COLLECTIVES NORTHERN IRELAND

Federation of Music Collectives - Northern Ireland Office

Tony Doherty
Project Development
531 Falls Road
Belfast BT19 9AA
Northern Ireland

Tel: 048 9030 1033

Aims to support new start-up music collectives in Northern Ireland.

Andersonstown Music School

Maxi McElroy
Co-ordinator
531 Falls Road
Belfast BT11 9AA
Northern Ireland

Tel/Fax: 048 9061 1144
Email: admin@atcms.freeserve.co.uk

This music collective specialises in contemporary and traditional music. The 'Music Notes' newsletter is issued on a quarterly basis.

Armagh Musicians Collective

Chris Pattison
Divisional Youth Office
38 Scotch Street
Armagh
Co. Armagh BT61 7DY
Northern Ireland

Tel/Fax: 048 3752 7882
Other key staff: Richard Lavery

Set up in 1997 to provide practice space for new groups in the locality. Provides them with equipment. There are future plans to have a lending library and recording facilities.

Belfast Musicians Collective

Petesy Burns
Chairperson
1-5 Donegall Lane
Belfast BT1 2LZ
Co. Antrim
Northern Ireland

Tel/Fax: 048 9024 4640/048 9031 5629
Email: bycg@dial.pipex.com
Website: martinx-demon.co.uk
Other key staff: Cathy Summerville (Treasurer), Suzie Asperger (Venue Manager), Stuart Martin (Studio Manager)

The aim of the group is to encourage the creative development of young people. This is carried out through the method of delivering various goals, in particular the encouragement of collective work, accessibility and empowerment through self reliance. Key services include live music venue (capacity for 200) with in-house 4k PA & engineer, 16 track analogue/16 track digital recording studio with in-house engineer, fully equipped rehearsal space, screenprinting, photographic, computer design workshop, cafe, drop-in service, office, computer and internet services. The newsletter 'Warzine' is issued on a quarterly basis.

Bestcellars Music Collective
Dean Llewellyn
Project Officer
Ballybeen Activity Centre
Ballybeen Square
Dundonald
Belfast BT16 2QE
Northern Ireland

Tel/Fax: 048 9048 6290
Email: bestcellars@ukgateway.net
Website: www.bestcellars.ukgateway.net
Other key staff: Janice Gordon-Stockman (Development Officer)

Key services include recording and video facilities and an information & advisory service is available. The newsletter 'Cellar- News' is issued three times a year.

Musicians of Antrim District Development Group
Brian Burns
Music Co-Ordinator
Clotworthy Arts Centre
Antrim Castle Grounds
Ranalstown Road
Co. Antrim BT41 46H
Northern Ireland

Tel/Fax: 048 9442 8000/048 9446 0360
Email: clotworthy@antrim.gov.uk
Key staff: Catherine Gilchrist (Treasurer), Jim Gilchrist (Chairman), Donard Cushenan

Set up in 1996 to support young emerging musicians. Provides practice facilities and various music classes.

Newry & Mourne Arts Collective
Colette Ross
81a Hill Street
Newry
Co. Down
Northern Ireland

Tel/Fax: 048 3026 8132
Other key staff: Alan Wadforth (Chairman)

Newry & Mourne Arts Collective is a community based organisation which was set up in 1987 with the Northern Ireland Voluntary Trust as the initial funders. The Collective offers music lessons in guitar, bass drums, keyboard and piano, drama and art. Performances are held on a regular basis.

North West Musicians Collective
Mick O'Connell
The Nerve Centre
6-8 Magazine Street
Derry BT48 6HJ
Northern Ireland

Tel: 048 7126 0452 Ext. 27

This music collective is a new community employment pilot scheme which operates the 'New Deal'. This enables musicians to pursue a career in music. Rehearsal and recording facilities. Produces compilation CDs for Northern Ireland.

Planet Music
Deirdre Molloy
80-82 Rainey Street
Magherafelt
Co. Derry
Northern Ireland

Tel: 048 7930 0235

This music collective provides an information and advisory service, instrumental classes and training courses.

Portadown Music Collective
Eddie Creany
82 Ballynery North Road
Derrymacash
Craigavon BT66 6LQ
Northern Ireland

Tel: 048 3834 0469

This music collective provides an information and advisory service and holds performances and produces compilation CDs.

Roe Valley Musicians Collective
Damien Corr
Chairman
25 Church Street
Limavady

Co. Derry BT49 OBX
Northern Ireland

Tel/Fax: 048 7776 9160 or 048 7776 5438/
048 7776 2303
Other key staff: Fiona McGregor (Secretary),
Stephen Rodgers (Treasurer), Carl Allen (Shadow
Secretary)

Roe Valley Musicians Collective was established in
March 1999 as a result of public interest and support.
Established a committee and have recently secured a
premises and funding for courses and equipment. Key
activities will include exploration of different music
genres, purchase of new equipment for use to collective
members, to run courses e.g sound engineering, to
showcase new groups and to provide teaching facilities
and services.

Triangle Music Collective

Paul Clegg
49 Caherm Road
Broughshane
Co. Antrim BT42 4QA
Northern Ireland

Tel/Fax: 048 2586 1693/048 2586 2693
Other key staff: Paul Cullen (Chairman),
Johnnie Roger (Treasurer), Graham Baker

This music collective aims to nurture and encourage
local musicians at all levels of music. Provision of
rehearsal space and a PA system hire for all members.

Education

The following symbols are used within this section:

 Disabled access

 Partial disabled access

Instrument bank

HIGHER EDUCATION

Ballyfermot College of Further Education
Anna Brett
Ballyfermot Road
Ballyfermot
Dublin 10

Tel/Fax: +353 1 6269421/+353 1 6266754
Email: info@scb.cdvec.ie
Other key staff: Matt Kelleghan (Co-ordinator - Popular Music Performance), Larry O'Toole (Co-ordinator - Music Technology), Maureen Conway (Co-ordinator - Music Management and Production), Brian Ó hUiginn (Co-ordinator - Traditional Music Performance), Denis Murray (Co-ordinator - Media Production and Management)

Ballyfermot College of Further Education offers a Higher National Diploma in Music Management and Production (two years), BA (Hons) in Media Management and Production (top-up vocational degree for successful graduates of other media courses), Higher National Diploma in Music Technology and Multi-Media Applications (two years), National Diploma in Popular Music Performance (two years), and a Higher National Diploma in Traditional Music Performance (two years).

Ballyfermot College of Further Education Ceoltóir
Brian Ó hUiginn
Co-ordinator
Centre for Creative & Emerging Technologies
18-22 Dame Street
Dublin 2

Tel/Fax: +353 1 6704686/+353 1 6704684
Email: ceoltoir@iol.ie

Set up by Ballyfermot College of Further Education (BCFE), to provide structured training for traditional musicians at undergraduate level. Began in September 1994 with a Certificate in Progressive Traditional and Folk Music Performance. In 1996 ran a Certificate in Professional Traditional Music Performance and now runs a Higher National Diploma in same (2 year course). Diploma caters for people who have previous experience in the performance of traditional music and song. Key areas of the courses include: source material, arrangement and performance, music technology, music business and traditional music from other countries. Showcase performances are held frequently in well-known venues.

All students produce a CD of their material at the end of the second year. To apply to BCFE refer to prospectus for that year. BCFE is a constituent college of the City of Dublin Vocational Education Committee.

Comhaltas Ceoltóirí Éireann
Labhrás Ó Murchú
Director General
32 Belgrave Square
Monkstown
Co. Dublin

Tel/Fax: +353 1 2800295/+353 1 2803759
Email: enquiries@comhaltas.com
Website: www.comhaltas.com
Other key staff: Séamus MacMathúna (Timire Cheoil), Bernard O'Sullivan (Project Officer), CM Hodge (Rúnaí Oifige)

Founded in 1951 to promote Irish traditional music, song, dance and the Irish language, Comhaltas Ceoltóirí Éireann offers a diploma course for Irish traditional music teachers. To-date over 400 have already qualified.

Cork School of Music - A Constituent School of Cork Institute of Technology
Dr Geoffrey Spratt
Director
Union Quay
Cork

Tel/Fax: +353 21 4270076/+353 21 4276595
Email: gspratt@cit.ie
Website: www.cit.ie
Other key staff: Conor Ó Ceallacháin (Vice-Principal), Jan Cáp (Head of Keyboard Studies), Adrian Petcu (Head of String Studies), Bernard Casey (until 3/8/00 John O'Connor from 1/9/00 - Head of Wind, Percussion, Singing, Speech & Drama), Aiveen Kearney (Head of Musicianship & Academic Studies), Patricia McCarthy (Head of Suzuki Section within the Department of String Studies)

BMus (four years) - The first and second years are best described respectively as 'foundation' and 'transition' years. After acquiring a secure foundation in the elements of Performance Studies which are: principal & second instrument or voice, ensemble music-making (band, choir, opera workshop, orchestral), Applied Musicianship Studies (aural skills, keyboard skills, analysis, and compositional techniques), Historical Studies including (Irish traditional music and historical performance practice), Music & Technology (music origination, midi fundamentals, recording studio theory & practice and music industry studies), community music, conducting, music education, music therapy and orchestration, students choose to specialise in either Applied Musicianship Studies, Community Music, Music History, Music & Technology, Music Therapy, Pedagogic Studies (music education) or Performance in their third and fourth year.

Dublin Institute of Technology - Conservatory of Music & Drama
Vincent O'Hora
Admissions Officer
Fitzwilliam House
30 Upper Pembroke Street
Dublin 2

Tel/Fax: +353 1 4023000/+353 1 4023399
Other key staff: Dr Eibhlís Farrell (Head of Music), Dr Mary Lennon (Head of Keyboard Studies), Brighid Mooney (Head of Orchestral studies), Anne Marie O'Sullivan (Head of Vocal & Dramatic Studies), Victor Merriman (Course Chair Drama DT603), Roy Holmes (Course Chair FT602), Padhraic O'Cunneagain (Head of Musicianship), Margaret O'Sullivan-Farrell (Course Chair DT 602), Dr Bernadette Greevy (Artist in Residence)

The types of music courses include: a BMus in Music Performance, BMusEd in Music Education (conjoint course with TCD and RIAM), Diploma in Music Teaching, Certificate in Music Foundation, MPhil/PhD Postgraduate, MA in Music Technology and a Graduate Diploma in Music Technology. The application procedure is through the CAO for undergraduate courses or through the DIT Admissions office for postgraduate courses. Disabled access. (Chatham Row & Rathmines) (see ad. p.68).

Froebel College of Education
Sr Darina Hosey O.P
Principal
Sion Hill
Blackrock
Co. Dublin

Tel/Fax: +353 1 2888520 or 2885915/ +353 1 2880618
Email: admin@froebel.ie
Website: www.froebel.ie/

Other key staff: Brian Ó Dubhghaill (Head of Music)

The types of music courses offered are in preparatory and basic music programme which are designed to prepare primary school students/teachers for class use. The Degrees and Diplomas awarded are BEd. Higher Diploma in Primary Education and postgraduate Diploma in Froebel Education. The application procedure for school leavers is through the CAO. Mature students and students for the HDip should apply to the admissions office. Students for the postgraduate Diploma in Froebel Education should apply to the college's Admissions office also. Disabled facilities are currently being planned.

Irish World Music Centre - University of Limerick
Paula Dundon
Administrator
Foundation Building
University of Limerick
Limerick

Tel/Fax: +353 61 202590/+353 61 202589
Email: paula.dundon@ul.ie
Website: www.ul.ie/~iwmc
Other key staff: Prof Mícheál Ó Súilleabháin (Head of Music), Helen Phelan (Academic Co-ordinator), Olive Brennan (Assistant Administrator), Ellen Byrne (Public Relations)

The types of music courses include: an MA in Community Music, Irish Traditional Music Performance, Classical String Performance, Chant Performance, Dance Performance (traditional and contemporary), Ethnomusicology, MA Ethnochoreology, Music Therapy, Graduate Diploma in Music Education and Research degrees at Masters and Doctorate levels in all related areas. (see advert page 75).

Mary Immaculate College - University of Limerick
Dr Gareth Cox
Head of Music
South Circular Road
Limerick

Tel/Fax: +353 61 314588/+353 61 313632
Email: gareth.cox@mic.ul.ie
Website: www.mic.ul.ie

The types of music courses offered include: a BMus (in preparation), BEd in Primary Teaching with music, BA in Liberal Arts with music, Diploma in Music & Music

Education (part time) and an MA and PhD in Musicology & Music Education by research. The application procedure is through the CAO. Students have access to a choral society, chamber ensemble, traditional Irish group and instrumental lessons are available.

Mater Dei Institute of Education

Dr Anne Murphy
Head of Music
Mater Dei Institute of Education
Clonliffe Road
Dublin 3

Tel/Fax: +353 1 8376027/+353 1 8370776
Email: annemurphy@materdei.ie
Website: www.materdei.ie
Other key staff: Sr Marcellina O'Sullivan (Director of Studies), Donal Hurley (Music Lecturer), Eithne Donnelly (Music Lecturer)

The types of music courses offered include music to primary degree level (ie. arts elective subject in Bachelor of Religious Science) with Education and Religious Studies (Theology). Liturgical music module is offered in final year Degrees and Diplomas awarded are BA in Religious Studies, MA in Religious Science, Chaplaincy Studies and a Graduate Diploma in Religious Studies (GDRS). The application procedure is through the CAO with entrance tests in aural musicianship and performance, which are held in March/April. The music courses cover compositional skills (harmony/counter-point), historical and analytical studies, performance and keyboard studies for classroom practitioners. Traditional musicians may present one traditional piece of music in part fulfilment of the practical examination requirements at the end of each academic year. Students have access to Mater Dei Chorale.

National University of Ireland Galway - Arts Administration Studies

Joe Mahon
Course Director
Arts Administration Studies
National University of Ireland Galway
Galway

Tel: +353 91 524411
Other key staff: Dr Jane O'Leary (Music Tutor)

The Diploma in Arts Administration is for one year. It has three terms with the first term studies concentrating on the business aspects of the arts, the second term includes music, theatre and literature. The third term of studies involves a six week work placement with a professional cultural organisation. Application forms can be obtained from the admissions office at the University. Entries are advised to be made in April.

National University of Ireland Maynooth

Prof Gerard Gillen
Professor of Music & Head of Department
Department of Music
Maynooth
Co. Kildare

Tel/Fax: +353 1 7083733/+353 1 6289432
Email: musicsec@may.ie
Other key staff: Dr Barra Boydell (Senior Lecturer), Dr Patrick Devine (Lecturer), Dr Victor Lazzarini (Lecturer in Technology)

The types of music courses offered include: a BMus for three years, BA (two subjects, one of which is music for three years, MA for one year full-time or two years part-time taught courses in Performance and Musicology or Historical Studies or Composition, MA and PhD also awarded on pure research, HDip in Music Technology, Diploma in Arts in Church Music (one year full-time or two years part-time). The application procedure is through the CAO and direct interview for undergraduate degree courses. Postgraduate and Diploma students should apply directly to the Department of Music. Further information is available from the Music Secretary. (see advert p.82).

The Queen's University of Belfast

Caroline Fegan
School Secretary
School of Music
Belfast BT7 1NN
Northern Ireland

Tel/Fax: 048 9033 5105 or 048 9027 3081 (admissions office)/048 9023 8484
Email: c.fegan@qub.ac.uk
Website: www.music.qub.ac.uk
Other key staff: Prof Jan Smaczny (Head of Music), Michael Alcorn (Music Technology), Sarah McCleave (Postgraduate Admissions)

The types of music courses offered include: a BMus, BA, BSc in Music & Technology, Diploma and MA in Music Technology, Renaissance Music, Baroque Music and an MA in 20th Century Music. Postgraduate courses are taught or completed by research. Informal enquiries and application forms are available from the Admissions office or the School of Music (see advert p.89).

Royal Irish Academy of Music

Anthony Madigan
Registrar
36-38 Westland Row
Dublin 2

Tel/Fax: +353 1 6764412/+353 1 6622798
Email: riam@indigo.ie
Website: www.riam.ie
Other key staff: John O'Conor (Director), Patricia Kavanagh (Head of Keyboard Studies), Elizabeth Csibi (Head of Strings), James Cavanagh (Head of Woodwind, Brass and Percussion), Paul Deegan (Head of Vocal Studies), Pamela Flanagan (Head of Musicianship), Dorothy Sheil (Secretary)

The types of courses offered include: a BA in Music Performance for four years (validated by Dublin City University), BA in Music Education for four years (validated by Trinity College Dublin), Master of Music in Performance for two years (validated by Dublin City University), Access Course for one year duration, Diploma in Music (Performance and Teaching) for one year and a Certificate in Conducting for one year. The application procedure for the BA in Music Performance and the BMusEd is through the CAO. For all other listed courses students should apply directly to the RIAM (see advert p. 89).

St. Mary's University College

Patrick Bradley
Academic Registrar
191 Falls Road
Belfast BT12 6FE
Northern Ireland

Tel/Fax: 048 9032 7678/048 9033 3719
Email: p.downey@stmarys-belfast.ac.uk
Website: www.stmarys-belfast.ac.uk
Other key staff: Dr Peter Downey (Head of Music), Claire Connolly (Senior Lecturer)

The types of courses offered include: a BEd for four years, BA in Liberal Arts for three years (first teaching of this will begin in September 2000), and a PGCE in Irish Medium Education for one year. The application procedure is through the college in October for the Postgraduate course, December for the BEd and March

for the BA. The BEd focuses on primary teaching and includes music, other areas in the primary curriculum, education and school experience. The Postgraduate course includes music and other areas in the primary curriculum and is directed towards Irish Medium teaching. The new BA in Liberal Arts includes the study of Irish and European musical culture.

St Patrick's College Drumcondra

Therese Savage
Admissions Officer
St Patrick's College
Drumcondra
Dublin 9

Tel/Fax: +353 1 8376191/+353 1 8376197
Email: marion.doherty@spd.ie
Other key staff: Marion Doherty (Head of Music), Sean MacLiam (Senior Lecturer), Dr Patricia Flynn (Lecturer)

The types of music courses offered include a BEd with music as an academic subject for three years, BA with music as a two-subject arts degree, MEd with music as a specialist area and an MA is offered in research. Performance is 20% of each year of the BEd and BA, this includes solo, chamber music, ensemble and conducting. The application procedure is through the CAO with an interview for mature students.

Stranmillis University College - A College of The Queen's University of Belfast

M. Watson
Director of External Affairs
Academic Registry
Main Building
Stranmillis University College
Stranmillis Road
Belfast BT9 5DY
Northern Ireland

Tel/Fax: 048 9038 4263/048 9066 4423
Email: admissions@stran-ni.ac.uk
Website: www.stran-ni.ac.uk
Other key staff: Alex McKee (Head of Music), Dr Carol Dunbar (Postgraduate Co-ordinator)

The types of music courses offered include: a BEd for those specialising in teaching music at primary level, BEd/Postgraduate for non-specialists within BEd and Postgraduate programmes as part of curriculum studies, BA in Arts in the Community for specialist and non-specialists (music is an element of this). The application procedure is through the academic registry office at the college. Candidates are selected for interview.

Tralee Institute of Technology

Admissions Office
Institute of Technology
Clash
Tralee
Co. Kerry

Tel/Fax: +353 66 7145638/+353 66 7125711
Other key staff: Brian O'Connor (Head of Music, School of Business & Social Studies), Dr Oliver Murphy (Head of Department), Peter Sharpe (Head of Department)

The type of music course offered is a National Diploma in Humanities (Irish Folk Theatre Studies). The application procedure is through the CAO/CAS. This course is designed and implemented in co-operation with Siamsa Tire - The National Folk Theatre, and applicants are required to audition.

Trinity College Dublin

Michael Taylor
Head of Music
House 5
Dublin 2

Tel/Fax: +353 1 6081120/+353 1 6709509
Email: musicsec@tcd.ie
Website: www.tcd.ie/music

The types of music courses offered include: a BA Moderatorship in Music for four years, Two Subject Moderatorship including music as one subject for four years, BMusEd for four years, in conjunction with the Royal Irish Academy of Music and the Dublin Institute of Technology College of Music. The application procedure is through the CAO/CAS.

University College Cork

Prof David Harold Cox
Professor of Music
Music Department
Cork

Tel/Fax: +353 21 4904530/+353 21 4271595
Email: music@ucc.ie
Website: www.ucc.ie/ucc/depts/music

The types of music courses offered include: degree programmes relating to the study of western music, Irish traditional music and world music. Selected repertories are studied both academically and through performance. Degrees and Diplomas awarded include: a BMus for four years, BA Music Single Honours for three years, BA Music Joint Honours for three years, MA taught postgraduate programmes for two years, MPhil research degree for two years, MMus in performance/research for two years, PhD research or original composition for three years. The application procedure is through the CAO (see advert p. 100).

University College Dublin

Prof White
Head of Music
Music Department
Belfield
Dublin 4

Tel/Fax: +353 1 7068178/+353 1 2694409
Email: music.department@ucd.ie

The music courses offered include: a BA in Music for three years, BMus for four year, MA in Musicology (taught course for one year), MLitt by research for two years and a PhD in Musicology for three to five years.

University College Dublin - Arts Administration Studies

Anne Kelly
Director
530 Library Building
Belfield
Dublin 4

Tel/Fax: +353 1 7067632/+353 1 2691963
Email: artsadministration.studies@ucd.ie
Other key staff: Shirley Redmond (Executive Assistant)

The higher diploma in Arts Administration prepares students for a professional career as administrators in museums, galleries and the performing arts. Areas covered include contemporary practice in the arts and cultural policy (including music policy). First two terms are spent at UCD and the third on internship with a professional cultural organisation. Application is through the university and involves an interview.

University of Ulster at Coleraine

Barry Burgess
Head of Music
Cromore Road
Coleraine
Co. Derry BT52 1SA
Northern Ireland

Tel/Fax: 048 7032 4056/048 7032 4918
Email: br.burgess@ulst.ac.uk
Website: www.ulst.ac.uk
Other key staff: Dr Roger Austin (Campus Co-ordinator, PGCE)

The diploma awarded is a Postgraduate Certificate in Education (Music) for one year which qualifies students to teach pupils in the 11 - 18 year age range. This course runs for thirty-six weeks, including twenty-four weeks of school based work. The application procedure is through the Admissions office.

University of Ulster at Jordanstown

H.M Bracefield
Head of Music
University of Ulster at Jordanstown
Newtownabbey
Co. Antrim BT37 0QB
Northern Ireland

Tel/Fax: 048 9036 6955/048 9036 6810
Email: hm.bracefield@ulst.ac.uk

The types of music courses offered include: a Certificate in Foundation Studies in Music for one year part-time, a Bachelor of Music with Honours for three years full-time, a Postgraduate Certificate, Diploma and MA in Music for two years part-time, MPhil for two years full-time or four years part-time and a DPhil for three years full-time or five years part-time.

Waterford Institute of Technology

Admissions Officer
Music Department
Waterford Institute of Technology
Cork Road
Waterford

Tel/Fax: +353 51 302000/+353 51 378292
Other key staff: Dr Eric Sweeney (Head of Music), Malcolm Proud, Anne Woodworth, Paddy Butler, Theresa Costello

The types of music courses offered include: a BA Music, MA in Performance, MA and PhD in Music Editing, Music Composition, Contemporary Music History and analysis. Each student has the option of either studying two instruments to a high level of performance or one instrument and a subsidiary subject either English, French, Arts Administration, Dance or Music Therapy. The application procedure is through the CAO. For further information contact the admissions office. (see advert p.104).

SCHOOLS OF MUSIC

Abbey School of Music and Drama

Conor Farren
Director
96 Lower Abbey Street
Dublin 1

Tel: +353 1 8747908
Other key staff: Kevin Robinson (Guitar/Classical Guitar Tutor), Mary Fahy (Violin Tutor)

This privately funded music school offers tuition in piano and keyboard, clarinet, saxophone, flute, drama classes, guitar and classical guitar for adults and children, Junior and Leaving Cert theory. Trinity College London music diplomas offered.

Andersonstown Traditional & Contemporary Music School

Maxi McElroy
Co-ordinator
531 Falls Road
Belfast BT11 9AA
Co. Down
Northern Ireland

Tel/Fax: 048 9061 1144
Email: admin@atcms.freeserve.co.uk

Current student numbers are over 200. Tuition is offered in tin whistle, flute, guitar, mandolin, fiddle and bodhran. All levels taught. Courses in Irish traditional music are accredited by the London College of Music. Also organises concerts, cultural exchanges, school visits, nursing home visits, a songwriters network, various workshops and masterclasses as well as publishing a newsletter.

Belfast & District Set Dancing &Traditional Music Society

Mary Fox
Chairperson
38 Milltown Lane
Portadown
Co. Armagh BT62 ITB
Northern Ireland

Tel/Fax: 048 3885 2469
Other key staff: Peter Woods (Secretary),
Pauline Tarrens (Treasurer), Tom Clarke (Music
Co-ordinator)

Current student numbers are 150. Aims to promote traditional music to all age groups and to a wider audience. Tuition is offered for beginners and intermediate classes in flute, button accordion, guitar, uilleann pipes and bodhrán. Beginner, intermediate and advanced tuition in tin whistle and fiddle. Classes run from Sept-Dec, Jan-Mar, April-June.

Boyne School of Music

Marie Leddy
Administrator
North Quay
Drogheda
Co. Louth

Tel/Fax: +353 41 9831078/+353 41 9834977
Email: sndshop@indigo.ie

Current student numbers are 300. Tuition is offered in guitar, violin, drums, brass and piano/keyboard over five eight-week terms throughout the year, for all ages from 7 years upwards.

Bray Music Centre - Co. Wicklow VEC

Peter Power
Administrator
Florence Road
Bray
Co. Wicklow

Tel: +353 1 2866768
Other key staff: Mirette Dowling (Musical Director)

Current student numbers are 220. Tuition is offered in music for children and adults. Individual tuition in singing, piano, violin, viola, cello, flute, clarinet, saxophone, recorder, guitar and theory of music. Group

tuition in recorder theory, music initiation, Junior and Leaving Certificate. Classes for all ages from 4 years upwards. Performing groups include childrens opera, junior choir and string quartet.

Carlow College of Music

Majella Swan
Director and Teacher
1 Larkfield
Green Lane
Co. Carlow

Tel/Fax: +353 503 40676
Email: carlcol@eircom.net
Other key staff: Ann-Marie Wall (Piano/Flute Tutor), Catherine Hill (Flute/Recorder/Piano Tutor), Lisa Parker (Piano/Recorder/Keyboard Tutor), Aingeala de Burca (Violin/Viola Tutor), Eamonn Cahill (Clarinet/Saxophone/Piano Tutor), Ber Doyle (Guitar/Clarinet Tutor), Mary Gaskin (Violin Tutor)

Current student numbers are 176. Aims to provide a high standard of music tuition and to encourage performing in groups ie. youth choir and orchestra, quartets and small chamber groups. Tuition is offered in piano, keyboard, violin, viola, cello, flute, recorder, clarinet, saxophone, guitar, musicianship and theory, Junior and Leaving Cert music. All instruments are taught from beginners to senior and diploma levels. Music makers for 4 to 6 year olds. Carlow Youth Choir for ages 8 upwards. Youth orchestra for grade 2 upwards.

Carrickbeg School of Music

John Murphy
Coonamuck Road
Carrickbeg
Co. Waterford

Tel: +353 51 641108
Other key staff: Catherine Power (Secretary),
Catriona Power (Treasurer)

Current student numbers are 30. Aims to bring more music to the locality giving access to everyone. Tuition is offered in keyboards, tin whistle and guitar for 8 to 14 year olds.

Des Carty Music School
Linda Kelly
Administrator
Tymon Bawn Community Centre
Firhouse Road West
Tallaght
Dublin 24

Tel/Fax: +353 1 4621029 or +353 1 4520611/
+353 1 4520611
Mobile: +353 88 2152247
Email: dcarty@eircom.net
Other key staff: Liam Morrissey (Managing
Director), Niamh Ní Bheoláin (Administrator of
Des Carty Summer School)

Current student numbers are 240. Tuition is offered in
traditional and popular music in banjo, guitar, fiddle,
whistle/flute, mandolin, accordion and bodhrán.
Classes are offered at beginner, improver and advanced
levels. The school also runs a junior céilí band. Ten
scholarships are awarded through the school.
The school is open to all ages at affordable rates.
Enrollment takes place in January, April and September.
A summer school is also run annually.

Castlederg School of Music
Cladys McKinley
Enterprise Centre
Drumquin Road
Castlederg
Co. Tyrone
Northern Ireland

Tel: 048 8167 0414

Ceoláras Coleman Music School
John McGettrick
Manager
Gurteen
Co. Sligo

Tel/Fax: +353 71 82599/+353 71 82602
Email: cctrad@iol.ie
Website: www.colemanirishmusic.com
Other key staff: Marie Queenan (Secretary)

Tuition is offered in tin whistle, flute, fiddle, keyboard,
accordion and banjo for all ages and abilities
(see advert page 68).

Charleville School of Music
Colette Moloney
Director
Old Cork Road
Charleville
Co. Cork

Tel: +353 63 89343
Email: colettem@eircom.net

Current student numbers are 400. Aims to provide quality music tuition. Tuition is offered in violin, viola, cello,
piano, accordion, keyboard, guitar, recorder, flute, cornet,
trumpet as well as in most traditional music instruments.
Also Junior and Leaving Certificate music taught.

Chenta Music School
Chenta Ní Ríordáin
Music Teacher
2 French Church Street
Cork

Tel: + 353 21 4279353

Current student numbers are 80. This is a keyboard
school. Teaches groups of up to six pupils at a time, and
some privately. The main focus is to enjoy music as a
leisure activity but if pupils wish to pursue exams this is
also available to them. The school offers a wide range
of music to 5 to 14 year olds. Pupils perform in libraries,
hospitals, plazas and theatres. The school also offers a
limited number of piano lessons.

City of Belfast School of Music
Robin Hewitt
Principal Tutor
99 Donegall Pass
Belfast BT7 1DR
Northern Ireland

Tel/Fax: 048 9032 2435/048 9032 9201
Email: music.belb@btinternet.com
Other key staff: Stanley Foreman (Instrumental
Co-ordinator), Dr Elspeth Ellis (Primary
Curriculum Co-ordinator)

Current student numbers are 650. Aims provide a high
quality music service which is readily accessible and
affordable to the schools and the wider community
within its area. Tuition is offered in strings, woodwind,
brass, keyboard, guitar, percussion, recorder and voice.
Curriculum advice and support is offered to schools.
Performing groups include orchestras, bands, choirs and
junior groups. Includes Saturday morning junior department. The Term times are from Sept-Dec and Jan-June.

City Music College

Kay O'Sullivan
Director
Drinan Street
Cork

Tel: +353 21 4313211

Current student numbers are 600-650. Tuition is offered in piano, flute, violin, recorder, saxophone, clarinet, voice, cello and double bass. The school term is from Sept-Nov, Nov-Feb and Feb-June.

Clare Music Makers

Andrea Creech
Director
Nationwide House
Bank Place
Ennis
Co. Clare

Tel/Fax: +353 65 6842480/+353 65 7084405
Email: cmmacto@iol.ie
Website: www.iol.ie/~cmmacto
Other key staff: Anthony Ovenell (Head of Music)

Current student numbers are 200. Aims to advance and encourage the art of music in Co. Clare by providing classical music tuition and performance opportunities and by developing a classical music summer school and festival. Tuition is offered in violin, viola, cello, flute, recorder, trumpet, french horn and piano. Theory and aural training is taught to all grades. Preparation for London College and Associated Board examinations is taught. Activities include Kinder-Music-Maker (a music kindergarten for children 3 to 5 years). Performing groups include recorder groups, string orchestras (beginner, junior and senior), string quartets, flute choirs and childrens choir. (see also page youth orchestra, youth choir)

Clontarf School of Music

Paul McCabe
Head of Music
11 Marino Mart
Fairview
Dublin 3

Tel/Fax: +353 1 8330936/+353 1 8338651
Email: csmusic@iol.ie
Other key staff: Gerry Jago

Tuition in guitar, piano, keyboards, fiddle, tin whistle, bodhran, violin, flute and banjo. All levels of music is taught including introduction to Music for children of 3 to 6 years. Preparation for Royal Irish Academy exams.

Coláiste Stiofáin Naofa

Chris Ahern
Head of Music & Course Director
Tramore Road
Cork

Tel/Fax: +353 21 4961020/+353 21 4961320
Email: csn@iol.ie
Other key staff: Ursula O'Sullivan (Music Teacher), Johnny Campbell (Sound Engineering), Rob Craig (Vocal Training)

Current student numbers are 60. Aims to familiarise musicians with all aspects of the music industry, specifically music management and sound. Tuition is offered in keyboards, guitar, bass and drums. Preparation for Associated Board and NCVA exams. All age groups.

Coolmine Community School

Sean O'Beachain
Principal
Clonsilla
Dublin 15

Tel/Fax: +353 1 8214141/+353 1 8213374

Tuition is offered in guitar to all ages from 6 years upwards. Also offer a referral service to music teachers outside the school.

Cork Musicians Project - a constituent of Cork Academy of Music

Bob Seward
Hon. Secretary & Development Officer
Cork Academy of Music
Unit 32
Sunbeam Industrial Park
Mallow Road
Cork

Tel: +353 21 4210573

Current student numbers are 30. Tuition is offered in brass, piano to grade 2 and to grade 7 in theory, percussion to grade 4 and theory from grades 1 to 8. Each area of study takes place within the structure of a 46 week course (20 hours per week), primarily to the unemployed. There is also access to the choir and ensemble.

County Cork School of Music

John Fitzpatrick
Director
County Cork Vocational Education
Committee
Floor 9
County Hall
Cork

Tel/Fax: +353 21 4285347/+353 21 4273465
Email: fitzpatrick@cocorkvec.ie

Current student numbers are 1500 approximately. The County Cork Vocational Education Committee, under the umbrella of the County Cork School of Music, provides for the musical education of children through its music service. For almost 50 years this has played an important role in the cultural development of the county and also the community at large. Tuition is offered to groups and individuals in brass, wind, classical guitar, percussion, piano, recorder, strings, traditional and woodwind in twenty five centres throughout County Cork. Music is taught from 7 years upwards. There are two terms in the year from Sept-Jan and Feb-June. Students also avail of the junior and senior orchestra and bands classes in the larger centres who participate in a range of concerts during the year and are prepared for annual examination. A scholarship and prize scheme, based on examination results is in operation. The recently formed County Cork Youth Orchestra is open to all young musicians resident in the county. (see also page)

Cremona Violins School of Music

Mark Jeffares
Head of Music
56 George's Ave
Blackrock
Co. Dublin

Tel/Fax: +353 1 2833381
Mobile: +353 87 2416723

Tuition is offered in violin from beginners to diploma standard.

Dublin Institute of Technology - Conservatory of Music and Drama

Lisa Molloy
Senior Administrator
Adelaide Road
Dublin 2

Other key staff: Dr Eibhlis Farrell (Head of School), Dr Mary Lennon (Head of Keyboard Studies), Brighid Mooney-McCarthy (Head of Orchestral Studies), Anne-Marie O'Sullivan (Head of Vocal and Dramatic Studies), Padhraic O'Cunnegáin (Head of Musicianship)

Current student numbers are 1600. Tuition is offered in all instruments and theory. The term times are from Sept-Dec and Jan-June. Classes are taught to all age groups and levels. Performing groups include a concert band, swing band, junior, intermediate and senior orchestras, choral society and chamber choir. Entrance and continuation scholarships available. For further information refer to DIT course booklets.

 (Chatham Row and Rathmines) (see advert p.68).

The Dublin School of Guitar

Alan Grundy
Head of Music
26-27 Drury Street
Dublin 2

Tel/Fax: +353 1 6714732/+353 1 6796049
Other key staff: Patrick Fagan (Lecturer), Bernard Traynor (Lecturer)

Current student numbers are approximately 100. Aims to offer a complete range of tuition from beginner levels to professional standards. Tuition is offered in classical, folk, electric and jazz guitar. All examinations and grades catered for.

Dun Laoghaire Music Centre

Deirdre Collins
Administrator
130a Lower Georges Street
Dun Laoghaire
Co. Dublin

Tel: +353 1 2844178
Email: dlmc@eircom.net
Other key staff: John McCrea (Director & Head of Music), Catherine Madden (Director & Head of Music), Ann-Marie McNamee (Strings), Maeve Buckley (Strings), Mary Barnecutt (Woodwind),

Cathal Roche (Woodwind), Rachel Talbot (Voice), Drazen Derek (Guitar)

Current student numbers are 547. Aims to provide a sound music education for people of all ages and musical backgrounds through the medium of enjoyment and quality learning. Tuition is offered in all instruments including brass and percussion, up to diploma standard. Music awareness classes for children of 2-6 years Childrens' World of Music, wind and string ensembles are also part of the curriculum.

Essaness Music Keyboard School
Fionnuala Shaw
Joint Director
Kieran Street
Kilkenny

Tel/Fax: +353 56 65693
Other key staff: Frank Salmon (Joint Director), Margaret Patterson (Head of Music)

Tuition is offered in keyboards and guitar from beginners to advanced level from 7 years upwards.

The Flowing Tide
Bill McNamara
Director
Doughmore
Doonbeg
Co. Clare

Tel: +353 65 7087528
Email: theflowingtide@yahoo.com

Aims to preserve the regional style of traditional roots music. The Flowing Tide was set up in 1995. Students are resident in the school for short blocks, where they learn the original techniques of traditional roots music from teachers who are themselves national champions on their chosen instruments. The School also contains a library of books on customs and traditions, tape cassettes and videos as well as written interviews with leading traditional musicians (see advert p.68).

An Gaelacadamh
Caitríona Ní Oiuicín
Administrator
Cólaiste Connacht
An Spidéal
Co. Gallimhe

Tel: 053 91 553124

Provides lessons and teachers in accordion, tin whistle, keyboard, Sean-nós singing and dancing. Caters for all of Connemara and the Aran Islands.

The Galway School of Irish Traditional Music
Grace Dalton
Administrator/Director
98 College Road
Galway

Tel/Fax: +353 91 562099
Email: gsitm@indigo.ie
Other key staff: Mick Crehan (Executive Director), Colm Naughton (Secretary/Treasurer), Éamon Ó Bróithe (Director)

Current student numbers are 200. Aims to promote the learning, practice and performance of Irish traditional music, song and dance among local, national and international communities. Tuition is offered in fiddle, tin whistle, accordion, piano accordion, uilleann pipes, guitar, banjo, mandolin, concertina, piano, traditional singing in English and Sean-nós singing. It is open to all ages at beginner, intermediate and advanced level. There are a series of weekend workshops and masterclasses held each year for intermediate and advanced students, featuring experts in regional styles.

Kerry School of Music
Aidan O'Carroll
Director
Old Customs House
High Street
Tralee
Co. Kerry

Tel/Fax: +353 66 7125690/+353 66 7120079
Email: kerrymusicschool@eircom.net

Current student numbers are 1,500. Tuition is offered in piano, electric keyboard, organ, harpsichord, voice and traditional music instruments. Graded theory is taught to diploma and Junior/Leaving Certificate music courses. Term time is from Sept-Jan and Jan-June. Performing groups include: Kerry Chamber Orchestra, Kerry School of Music (KSM), Junior & Senior Orchestras, KSM Wind Band, KSM Flute Choir, KSM String Trio, KSM Piano Trio, KSM Flute trio, Kerry Chamber Choir and KSM Musical Society.

Kildare International School of Excellence for Young Musicians

Bernadette Hayden
Director
Herbert Lodge Arts Centre
The Curragh
Co. Kildare

Tel/Fax: +353 45 481598
Other key staff: Christian Tecklenborg (Principal), Vincent Hunt (cello), Majella Cahill (piano)

Current student numbers are 150. Aims to encourage music in Co. Kildare. Term times are from Sept-Dec, Jan-April and April-June.

Kilkenny School of Music

Philip Edmondson
Director
Ormonde Road
Kilkenny

Tel: +353 56 62969
Other key staff: Margaret Murran (Head of Woodwind), Fiona Warren (Head of Strings), Jean Corrie (Secretary)

Current student numbers are 256. Tuition is offered in a pre-instrumental foundation year, weekly theory class and instrumental lessons on violin, viola, cello, double bass, flute, oboe, clarinet, recorder, trumpet, tenor horn, French horn, euphonium, tuba and piano for first class (primary school) to Leaving Cert. Students have access to a junior choir, junior string orchestra (primary level), youth choir (secondary level), percussion ensemble, flute choir and string quartets.

Killarney School of Music

Aidan Lynch
Director
15 Hawthorn Avenue
Ballycasheen
Killarney
Co. Kerry

Tel/Fax: +353 64 33749

Aims to develop an understanding, appreciation and love for music through good teaching standards. Tuition is offered in brass and piano for beginners to diploma level, keyboards (midi computer assisted composition), aural training for beginners to diploma level, Junior Cert and Leaving Cert, summer theatre and musicianship training.

Kylemore College

Declan MacDaid
Principal
Kylemore College
Kylemore Road
Ballyfermot
Dublin 10

Tel/Fax: +353 1 6265901/+353 1 6234780
Other key staff: Declan MacDaid (Head of Music), Eileen McGrath (Piano Teacher) Irene Thompson (Voice Production Teacher), Connie Gardiner (Violin Teacher)

Current student numbers are 700. Tuition offered in accordion, piano, guitar, voice production, harp, cello, clarinet, saxophone, speech and drama, violin, flute and recorder. All students study music theory for Associated Board Exams. Students have access to an orchestra and band.

Leeson Park School of Music

Geraldine Moran
Administrator
Kensington Hall
Grove Park
Rathmines
Dublin 6

Tel/Fax: +353 1 4967890/+353 1 4967496
Email: leesonpark@eircom.net
Other key staff: Rhona Gouldson (Head of Piano), Emma Montonen (Head of Strings), Tom Toher (Head of Music)

Current student numbers are 900. Tuition is offered in piano, violin, cello, guitar and flute. There is also a Music Kindergarten for 3 months to 6 years using the internationally recognised 'Colourstrips' approach to music education based on the Kodaly principles.

The Leinster School of Music

Sheila Murphy
Secretary
Griffith College Campus
South Circular Road
Dublin 8

Tel/Fax: +353 1 4751532/+353 1 4549265
Email: leinster_school@gcd.ie
Website: www.gcd.ie
Other key staff: Gary Deaton (Administrator)

UNIVERSITY of LIMERICK

OLLSCOIL LUIMNIGH

IRISH WORLD MUSIC CENTRE

The Irish World Music Centre was established in 1994 to house postgraduate research and performance endeavours in music and dance. Since then, the centre has developed to include doctoral researchers as well as a suite of nine full-time, postgraduate programmes:

Master of Arts   Ethnochoreology

Master of Arts   Ethnomusicology

Master of Arts   Music Therapy

Master of Arts   Classical String Performance

Master of Arts   Chant Performance

Grad. Dip   Music Education

Master of Arts   Traditional Irish Music Performance

Master of Arts   Community Music

Master of Arts   Dance Performance

Further Information & application Forms: Ellen Byrne, PRO, Irish World Music Centre, Foundation Building, University of Limerick
Tel: + 353 61 202917   Fax: +353 61 202589   email: ellen.byrne@ul.ie

Current student numbers are 650. Aims to provide expert tuition by experienced and dedicated teachers and to provide individual and group classes for all ages and levels. Emphasis is on learning through enjoyment. Offers a diverse range of musical styles from classical to jazz, to popular and traditional. Term times are from Sept-Dec, Jan-March and March-June. (see advert p.82).

Lowney School of Music
P.J & Isabel Lowney
Peter Street
Co. Wexford

Tel: +353 53 22468

Current student numbers are 100. Tuition is offered in piano, saxophone, clarinet, flute, recorder, guitar, keyboard and theory of music. All levels taught from beginners to advanced.

Maoin Cheoil an Chláir
Tracey Smurthwaite
Director
College Road
Ennis
Co. Clare

Tel/Fax: +353 65 6841774

Current student numbers are 500. Tuition is offered in classical and traditional music in: cello, recorder, clarinet, saxophone, accordion, concertina, guitar, banjo, singing, piano, keyboard, tin-whistle, violin, viola, fiddle, flute (traditional and classical), cornet, trumpet, music theory for junior and leaving certificate students and kindermusic. Term times are from Sept-Jan and Feb-June. Performing groups include Clare Youth and Junior Orchestras, traditional groups and choirs.

Marino Music Studio
Declan Farrell
13 St. Declan Road
Marino
Dublin 3

Tel: +353 1 8531027
Email: marinomusic@eircom.net

Current student numbers are 50. Aims to teach music to as high a standard as possible and to encourage a love for music. Tuition is offered in voice, acoustic guitar, lead guitar, bass guitar, midi sequencing and hard

disk recording. All levels taught from beginners to advanced. Voice training is offered to those over 18 years.

Melody School of Music
Michael Heffernan
Administrator
178e Whitehall Road West
Perrystown
Dublin 12

Tel/Fax: +353 1 4650150/+353 1 4936023
Email: tumi@indigo.ie
Other key staff: Paul Heffernan (Head of Music), Tina Lawlor (Guitar), Sharon Davis (Piano & Keyboard), Joan Davis (Violin & Piano)

Tuition is offered in piano, keyboard, voice, drums, guitar, classical guitar and violin as well as theory. All levels taught from beginners to advanced. Open to all age groups. Closed during August.

Metropolitan College of Music
Eamonn O'Keeffe
Administrator
59 Lower Baggot Street
Dublin 2

Tel/Fax: +353 1 4540753
Mobile: +353 87 2534771
Email: eokeeffe@indigo.ie

Current student numbers are approximately 60. Tuition is offered in piano, drums, guitar, violin, flute, recorder, clarinet, saxophone, trumpet, singing and music theory. Term times are from Sept-May. Students have access to the school concert band.

Municipal School of Music
Eileen Hudson
Acting Principal
Mulgrave Street
Limerick

Tel/Fax: +353 61 417348/+353 61 417011
Other key staff: Moira Gray (Piano/Accompanist), David O'Connell (Violin/Viola/Senior Orchestra), Maria O'Brien (Flute/Early Music Consort)

Current student numbers are approximately 1,100. Aims to develop and nurture a love of music in its students. Tuition is offered in violin, viola, cello, double bass, piano, organ, recorder, clarinet, flute, saxophone, oboe, bassoon, trumpet, horn, trombone, voice, speech, music theory (including an adult class), Junior Certificate music and Leaving Certificate music. This school caters mainly for students from 6 years to Leaving Certificate level, and some adults. Preferred age for beginners is between 6-8 years. A part-time diploma course is available, which is offered in conjunction with a degree course at university level. Performing groups include junior string orchestra, middle string orchestra, senior orchestra (all instruments), wind band, brass ensemble, early music consort, junior choir, guitar choir, percussion ensemble and percussion bands (for age 10 and under).

Nature Art Centre

Thomas Wiegandt
Ballybane
Ballydehob
Co. Cork

Tel/Fax: +353 28 37323
Website: www.holistic.ie/nature-art
Other key staff: Annette Pätzold (Organiser)

The Nature Art Centre is dedicated to West-African drumming (Djembe) and to ethnic music. Aims to teach technique and feeling as well as the cultural and social context. The centre invites musicians from different traditions world-wide to perform and give workshops. Workshops and lessons in the centre and in other venues are by arrangement. Tuition is offered in: djembe -drum (playing technique); West-African polyrhythms; attitude and feeling; patterns and variations (solo); djun-djun bass-drums and small percussion; patterns and variation; guitar and lutes (West-African style and blues), structure (scales and chords) and improvisation. Activities cater for an age group of 9 years upwards. Drums and percussion instruments available for use. Instrument sales, repairs and performance are also available.

Newcastle West & District Pipe & Band School

Seamus Hunt
School Director & Head of Music
'Ard ne Gréine'
Dromin Deel
Newcastle West
Co. Limerick

Tel/Fax: +353 69 77545/+353 69 61125
Other key staff: Trevor Sexton (Drumming

Assistant), Patrick Hunt (Drumming Tutor), John Hunt (Piping Tutor)

Current student numbers are 50. Tuition is offered in pipes, drums and theory. Term times are from Oct-Dec and Jan-June. Performing groups include the Newcastle West & District Pipe Band. Open to all ages from 12-25 years.

Newpark Music Centre

Hilda Milner
Administrator & Head of Music
Newtownpark Avenue
Blackrock
Co. Dublin

Tel/Fax: +353 1 2883740/+353 1 2883989
Email: newparkmusic@eircom.net

Tuition is offered in all instruments. Jazz tuition and improvisation are also available. A 'Gateway to Music' introduction course is available for 4-7 year olds. The school provides theory tuition and diplomas in musicianship. Full-time professional music training course and Diploma in jazz studies is also available.

Nolan School of Music

Margaret Nolan
Administrator
3 Dean Street
Dublin 8

Tel: +353 1 4933730
Other key staff: James Nolan (Head of Music)

Current student numbers are 60/70. Aims to create and foster an understanding and appreciation of music in general, and to teach students to express themselves through their chosen instruments. Tuition is offered in button or piano accordion, keyboard, recorder, saxophone and clarinet as well as theory and Leaving and Junior Certificate music. All instruments participate in ensembles. Classes are open to students from 8 -18 years and private lessons are open to students of all ages. All levels taught, from beginners to advanced.

North Eastern Education & Library Board Music Service

Eric Boyd
Head of Music Services
17 Lough Road
Antrim BT41 4DH
Northern Ireland

Tel/Fax: 048 9448 2231/048 9446 0224
Other key staff: Paul McCrisken (Senior Instrumental Tutor)

Current student numbers are 3,400. Aims to develop the potential of all those involved in music education (staff and pupils) in the North-Eastern Education and Library Board, through the provision of high quality education services which are relevant to the needs of the schools. Tuition is based in schools and music centres and includes tuition in the full range of orchestral instruments, piano, guitar, vocal studies and theory. Performing groups include junior, intermediate and senior orchestras, junior, intermediate and senior wind bands, and four regional string orchestras. Curriculum support is offered to all schools with school based in-service training and centre-based courses. Terms times are from Sept-Dec, Jan-March and April-June.

John Palmer Music Centre
John Palmer
Manager
7 Georges Street
Waterford
Tel: +353 51 879333

Tuition is offered in keyboard and guitar.

Parnell School of Music & Performing Arts
Martin Merriman
14 Sackville Place
Dublin 1

Tel/Fax: +353 1 8786909

Current number of students is 150. Tuition is offered in guitar, keyboard, drums, piano, voice and dance and theory of music. All levels taught from beginners to advanced. All ages from 4 years upwards.

Riverstown Music Club
David Murray
Chairperson
37 Bayview
Riverstown
Tramore
Co. Waterford

Tel/Fax: +353 51 391080/+353 51 391364
Other key staff: June Kavanagh (Secretary)

Current student numbers are 30. Tuition is offered in keyboard and guitar.

Royal Irish Academy of Music
Anthony Madigan
Registrar
36-38 Westland Row
Dublin 2

Tel/Fax: +353 1 6764412/+353 1 6622798
Email: riam@indigo.ie
Website: www.riam.ie
Other key staff: John O'Conor (Director), Patricia Kavanagh (Head of Keyboard Studies), Elizabeth Csibi (Head of Strings), James Cavanagh (Head of Woodwind, Brass and Percussion), Paul Deegan (Head of Vocal Studies), Pamela Flanagan (Head of Musicianship), Dorothy Sheil (Secretary), Theresa Doyle (Local Centre Manager), Ciara Higgins (Public Relations/Concerts Manager), Philip Shields (Librarian)

Current student numbers are 1,000. Aims to foster, nurture and develop excellence in music and the performing arts. Also to provide a comprehensive range of teaching and learning opportunities for music and speech and drama for talented students at all levels and to set/monitor the highest standards of achievement through a reputable nationwide examination system. Founded in 1848, a number of musicians have received their training at the Academy, which offers a full range of musical studies, as well as speech and drama, from pre-instrumental to diploma level (Associate RIAM and Licentiate RIAM) and graduate level (Bachelor of Arts in Music Performance and Bachelor in Music Education). The Academy also conducts the following full-time courses: Diploma in Music (Performance and Teaching), an access course and a Master of Music in Performance. The RIAM performing groups include the RIAM Symphony Orchestra, the RIAM Chamber Orchestra, the RIAM Wind Ensemble, the RIAM Chamber Choir, the RIAM Intermediate Orchestra and the RIAM Junior String Group. For details about special age considerations contact the RIAM general office.
(see advert page 89)

Schola Cantorum
Shane Brennan
Director
St. Finian's College
Mullingar
Co. Westmeath

Tel: +353 44 42906
Mobile: +353 86 2528029
Email: schcan@eircom.net

Other key staff: Pádraic Ó Cuinneagáin (Piano Studies Tutor), Seamas O'Brien (Music Technology Tutor), Mary Mulligan (Woodwind Tutor), Sean Brennan (Organ/Composition/Choral Tutor)

Current student numbers are 17-20 second level students. Tuition is offered in piano, music technology, woodwind, organ, composition and voice. Specialised training in organ, piano and choral music. Term times are from Sept-Dec, Jan-Easter and Easter-June. 5 year scholarships are available for boys and girls. Boarding accommodation available for boys. Performing groups include various choirs and instrumental ensemblesj80 (see advert page 100).

Scoil Acla Traditional Music School
Alice McGinty
Chairperson
Tonragee East
Westport
Co. Mayo

Tel: +353 98 45584(h) or +353 98 47306(w)/ +353 98 47306
Other key staff: Eoin McNamara (Assistant Chairperson)

(see advert)

Scoráiocht Lann-Léire
Sean Ó Flanagaín
Uachtáran
Scioból Mór
Lann Léire
Co. Lú

Tel: +353 41 6861033

Current student numbers are 70. Aims to get young people interested in and playing traditional music. Tuition is offered in tin whistle, flute, bodhrán, fiddle, guitar, accordion, banjo and Irish dancing. Grades are taught and certificates are awarded.

Silver Sounds
Michael Fottrell
Honorary Music Director/Caretaker
69 Michael Street
New Ross
Co. Wexford

Tel/Fax: +353 51 425063 (w) or 422918 (h)/ +353 51 422326

Current student numbers are 34. Aims to provide opportunities to the community, in the spirit of volunteer bands dating to the middle 1700's, to learn a wind or percussion instrument and to be provided with a musical instrument, tuition, sheet music and rehearsal area free of charge. Tuition is offered in E flat and B flat cornet, flügel horn, tenor horn, baritone, euphonium, E flat and B flat bass, B flat and F trombone, bass trombone, timpani, kit-drums, glockenspiel, vibraphone, xylophone and up to grade 3 level piano (RIAM). Instrumental and percussion tuition is offered to performance level. The band regularly gives concerts and take part in community events. Age range from 4 years upwards.

Sligo Music Academy
Niamh Crowley
c/o The Arts Office
Sligo County Council Offices
Riverside
Sligo

Tel/Fax: +353 71 56629/+353 71 41119
Email: arts@2sligococo.ie

As part of the Vogler Quartet in Sligo 3 year residency programme until 2002, structured instrumental teaching will be achieved by the delivery of a contracted range of services to be offered by the recently formed Sligo Academy of Music. The Vogler Quartet will act as consultants in the design and delivery of the Instrumental Tuition Programme.

Sound Studio Music Keyboard School
Ciara Gibney
Head Teacher
6 Church Road
Malahide
Co. Dublin

Tel: +353 1 8456669
Email: ciarag@clubi.ie

Tuition is offered in keyboard classes, usually private and group lessons morning, afternoon and evenings on a Saturday. A limited number of lessons are given in piano and guitar.

South Eastern Education & Library Board Music Centre
Brian Agus
Director
Church Road
Ballynahinch
Co. Down BT24 8LP
Northern Ireland

Tel/Fax: 048 9756 3989 or 048 9756 2030/
048 9756 5120
Other key staff: Dolores McArdle (Head of
Strings), Lawrence Neill (Head of Keyboards and
Theory), Andrew Rowan (Head of Woodwind),
David English (Administrator and Head of
Percussion), Robert Dawson (Head of Brass)

Current student numbers are 2,000. Aims to introduce
talented and promising young people to music as a
potential life-long interest and activity. Tuition is offered
in all strings, wood-wind, brass and percussion instruments taught at advanced and lower grade levels in 126
schools per week and in four district music centres.
Tuition is normally restricted to students still in full-time
education. Selected students can play in senior, intermediate and training orchestras, bands at board level, in
junior orchestras and bands at district level.

Southern Education & Library Board
Eithne Benson
Assistant Education Music Officer
Bann House
Bridge Street
Portadown
Co. Armagh BT63 5AE
Northern Ireland

Tel/Fax: 048 3833 2371/048 3839 4525
Email: selbmusic@hotmail.com
Other key staff: Martin White (Head of
Performance), Nuala Tohill (Head of Strings &
Administration), Elaine Mills (Head of Woodwind
& Newry Centre), Seamus Dinsmore (Head of
Brass & Percussion)

Current student numbers are 2,600. Aims to foster a
love for and understanding of music by providing
tuition and wide-ranging performance opportunities for
young people. Tuition is offered in all orchestral instruments and recorder from beginner to diploma level.
Tuition is delivered mainly in schools with advanced lessons available at three music centres. Annual summer
school for 1 week in August. Over 20 performance
groups at junior, intermediate and senior levels involving
over 900 members.

Ulster College of Music
Paul McNulty
Director
13 Windsor Avenue
Belfast BT9 6EE
Co. Antrim
Northern Ireland

Tel: 048 9038 1314
Email: mcnulty.ucm@dnet.co.uk
Website: under construction
Other key staff: Bill Lloyd (Chairman of
Management Committee), Patricia King
(Honorary Treasurer)

Current student numbers are approximately 3,000. The
Ulster College of Music is a major cross-community
provider of high quality teaching in all instruments,
voice and theory for students of all ages, from beginners
to adults, including those preparing for the profession.
Tuition is offered in piano, voice, strings, brass, woodwind, guitar, harp (classical and traditional), A-level
harmony and Associated Board theory. The term time is
from Sept-Dec, Jan-Easter and April-June. The college
has a junior music programme for primary school
children, aged 5-7 years, including recorder tuition. The
college also has a large enrolment of adult students
and offers rooms for hire.

Waltons New School of Music
John Mardirosian
Director
69 South Great Georges Street
Dublin 2

Tel/Fax: +353 1 4781884/+353 1 4751346
Email: waltons@indigo.ie
Other key staff: Josephine Boyle

Current student numbers are 1,500. Tuition is offered in
a wide range of instruments and styles (classical, traditional, jazz, world, popular) in: piano/keyboard, voice,
strings (violin, viola, cello), brass and wind (clarinet, concert flute, recorder, saxophone, trumpet), guitar (classical, acoustic, electric, jazz, traditional), traditional instruments (button and piano accordion, banjo, bodhrán,
bouzouki, fiddle, wooden flute, harmonica, Irish harp,
mandolin, tin and low whistle, uilleann pipes), percussion (jazz and rock drum kit, African, Latin and world
percussion), music theory and music technology.
Students range in age from 4-80 years of age. Waltons
welcome beginners who choose to study music purely
for enjoyment and also provide training to diploma
standard and beyond for those who want to make a
career of music. Courses include adult beginners
groups, pre-instrumental courses for children, theory
and musicianship courses, listening and appreciation

courses, courses for primary and post-primary teachers and courses in music technology. Workshops scheduled throughout the year offer specific topics of interest to intermediate and advanced students as well as training in specialised styles and techniques. Term times are from Sept-Dec, Jan-March/April, April-June/July and the summer term is in July. Performing groups include Cantoiri (adult mixed choir), Young Cantoiri, New School String Ensemble, New School Wind Ensemble, Friday Night Sessions (traditional music). The New School offers rehearsal facilities for singers, pianists, instrumentalists and small ensembles. Amplified instruments are not allowed. Opening hours of rehearsal space are Monday-Thursday 10am-10pm, Fri 10am-8pm and Sat 10am-6pm. (see advert page 104)

Wards School of Music

Patrick Ward
Director
Castle Street
Donegal Town
Co. Donegal

Tel/Fax: +353 73 21313/+353 73 22326
Other key staff: Caroline Morrow (Teacher of Keyboard/Piano)

Tuition is offered in keyboard to grade 8 students. Specially equipped school for all ages. Group tuition. Exams taken through the Victoria College of Music London.

Western Education & Library Board Music School

Donal Doherty
Head of Music Services
1 Spillars Place
Omagh
Co. Tyrone BT78 IHL
Northern Ireland

Tel/Fax: 048 8224 4821/048 8224 1443
Email: mairead-gallagher@welbni.org
Other key staff: Melanie Quick (Regional Manager Omagh), Robert Quick (Regional Manager Fermanagh), Ann Bergin (Regional Manager Derry)

Current student numbers are 3,000. Tuition is offered in graded instruments to all levels from a team of brass, woodwind and string tutors and also from six peripatetic teachers. Tuition is offered to 6-17 year olds.

Wexford School of Music

Eileen Herlihy
Managing Director
St. Mary's
Summerhill
Co. Wexford

Tel/Fax: +353 53 41284
Other key staff: Alan Cutts (Head of Strings), Sue Furlong (Conductor Youth Orchestra)

Aims to provide a high quality musical education at all levels, in all instruments, and to encourage ensemble playing. Tuition is offered in all orchestral instruments, piano, organ, recorder and voice. There are beginners classes and aural awareness classes offered. Term times are from Sept-Jan and Feb-June. Performing groups include Wexford Youth Orchestra and Junior Strings, Wexford Youth Choir, Wexford Recorder Consort and Wexford Wind Ensemble.

Wilson's Hospital School

Ken Cowley
Head of Music
Multyfarnham
Co. Westmeath

Tel/Fax: +353 44 71115/+353 44 71563
Other key staff: S. Graham (Choir Mistress)

Current student numbers are 330. Tuition is offered in piano and guitar. There are Junior Certificate music classes per week and five forty minute Leaving Certificate classes per week. Students have access to the school choir which is accompanied by the church organ. Transition year pupils are introduced to music during two forty minute classes per week. The school caters for 12-18 year olds.

The Wright Music Centre

Pat Corcoran
Music Teacher
9 Castle Street
Cork

Tel: +353 21 4277328
Other key staff: Pat Corcoran (Head of Music), Michael Bradley (Music Teacher)

Tuition is offered in guitar, classical guitar, bass guitar, drumming and saxophone. All grades up to diploma are taught in guitar and classical guitar. All grades are taught in drumming and saxophone.

Established 1904

Tel: 01-4150 467 / 4150 400
Fax: 01-4549 265
Email: leinster_school@gcd.ie

The Leinster School of Music & Drama
Griffith College Campus
South Circular Road, Dublin 8

The Leinster School of Music and Drama offers expert tuition by experienced and dedicated teachers and provides individual and group classes for all ages and all levels. The emphasis is on learning through enjoyment, and while exams are encouraged they are not compulsory. Diverse ranges of styles are also on offer from classical to modern through to popular and traditional.

The Leinster School of Music & Drama is located at Griffith College Dublin, a seven-acre campus within a mile of St. Stephen's Green on the South Circular Road.

Facilities provided on the Griffith College Campus by the Leinster School of Music & Drama include recording studios, recital rooms, an opera studio, and a restaurant and free car parking.

NUI MAYNOOTH
Ollscoil na hÉireann Má Nuad

Music Department

Full undergraduate courses in music offered to **B.A. Honours Degree**
(Students have the option of taking music on its own or combined with another Arts subject)

M.A. Degrees are offered in the following areas:
Performance Studies (taught course)
Historical Studies (taught course)
Composition (taught course)

New Postgraduate Courses
Higher Diploma in Music Technology
M.A. Degree in Music Technology

For further information contact: **Music Department Secretary** / **Tel:** (01) 7083733
Fax: (01) 6289432 • **Email:** musicsec@may.ie • **www:** http://www.may.ie

Young European Strings School of Music

Maria Kelemen
Director
21 The Close
Cypress Downs
Templeogue
Dublin 6w

Tel/Fax: +353 1 4905263/+353 1 4920355
Email: yes@iol.ie
Other key staff: Ronald Masin (Guest Teacher - Violin), Deborah Kelleher (Piano Teacher), Sonja Ruys (Cello Teacher)

Aims to cater for young children with an above average musical potential. The acceptance criteria is by assessment. Performance and examination oriented teaching based on the development of the inner ear. The Kodály approach to music appreciation is taught from the age of 2 and a half years. Tuition is offered in violin, viola, piano and cello to the level of Associated Board grade 8 and individually from the age of 2 years. Musical literacy can be achieved by the age of 3 and a half years. Theory classes are available to grade 8 level. Orchestra membership from the age of 5 years. Senior orchestra caters for 5-9 year olds and chamber orchestra for 7-16 year olds.

YAMAHA SCHOOLS OF MUSIC

CO. CORK

Yamaha Music School

Dunmanway
Máiréad Higgins
Head of Music
The Square Shopping Centre
Dunmanway
Co. Cork

Tel: +353 23 45532
Mobile: +353 86 8161478

Tuition is offered in keyboard and theory to Leaving Certificate standard. Term times are from Sept-Dec, Jan-April and April-June.

CO. DUBLIN

Danfay Yamaha Music School

Joan Coleman
Head of Music
75 Aungier Street
Dublin 2

Tel: +353 1 4751248

Aims to give access to music to everyone. Tuition is offered in keyboard, electronic organ and electric piano for all ages for all examining boards and the Leaving Certificate.

Mangan Keyboard & Guitar Centre Coolmine

Jacqui Smith
School Manager/Head of Music
Coolmine Community School
Coolmine
Dublin 15

Tel/Fax: +353 1 8370244
Email: mkgc@oceanfree.net
Other key staff: Tommy Mangan (Director), Jerry Foy (Guitar School Manager)

Current student numbers are 110. Tuition is offered for grades 1-8 using the Yamaha method. Also Junior and Leaving Certificate practical tuition. Open to all age groups.

Mangan Keyboard & Guitar Centre Dundrum

Jacqui Smith
Head of Music
5 Ashgrove Terrace
Dundrum
Dublin 14

Tel/Fax: +353 1 2965211/+353 1 8370244
Email: mkgc@oceanfree.net
Other key staff: Tommy Mangan (Director), Jerry Foy (Guitar School Manager)

Current student numbers are 120 students. Tuition is offered in keyboard for grades 1-8 using the Yamaha method, guitar tuition in rock, ballad, country, pop and blues music. Also Junior and Leaving Certificate practical tuition. Open to all age groups.

Mangan Keyboard and Guitar Centre Glasnevin

Glasnevin
Jacqui Smith
School Manager/Head of Music
210 Botanic Avenue
Glasnevin
Dublin 9

Tel/Fax: +353 1 8370244
Email: mkgc@oceanfree.net

Other key staff: Tommy Mangan (Director), Jerry Foy (Guitar School Manager)

Current student numbers are 185 students. Tuition is offered in guitar in rock, ballad, country, pop and blues for grades 1-8 using the Yamaha method. Also Junior and Leaving Certificate practical tuition. Open to all age groups.

CO. KILDARE

Naas Yamaha Music School
John Forde
Director
7 North Main Street
Naas
Co. Kildare

Tel/Fax: +353 45 879297

Tuition is offered in the Yamaha Music Course in keyboards steps 1 to 7 which is acceptable by the Department of Education and Science for Junior and Leaving Certificate music.

CO. LIMERICK

Ger Keane's Limerick Yamaha Music School
Ger Keane
60 William Street
Limerick

Tel: +353 61 410104

Aims to teach students to enjoy the skills of music from an early stage to a more advanced level. Tuition is offered in keyboard and theory which is taught to second level. Special adult only classes.

CO. WEXFORD

Cloke's Yamaha School of Music
Deirdre Murphy
Administrator and Head of Music
10a Weafer Street
Enniscorthy
Co. Wexford

Tel/Fax: +353 54 33988/+353 54 34614

Current student numbers are 70. Tuition for all ages up to Grade 8.

CO. WICKLOW

Yamaha Music School Delgany
Henry Kennedy
20 Glenbrook Park
Delgany
Co. Wicklow
Tel: +353 1 2872862

Tuition is offered in keyboard and piano for students aged from 8 years upwards.

SUMMER SCHOOLS, WINTER SCHOOLS & SHORT COURSES

Annaghmakerrig International Summer School
Regina Doyle
Acting Director
Tyrone Guthrie Centre
Annaghmakerrig
Newbliss
Co. Monaghan

Tel/Fax: +353 47 54003/+353 47 54380
Email: thetgc@indigo.ie
Website: www.tyroneguthrie.ie

Aimed at recent music graduates of stringed instruments and trainee conductors, who are outstanding students from Ireland, both North and South, Britain and Eastern Europe. A variety of baroque, contemporary, Irish and traditional Irish music performed. This course constitutes ten days of workshops and performances at Annaghmakerrig and around the country in July. (see also page)

Blas International Summer School
Sandra Joyce
Director
Irish World Music Centre
Foundation Building
University of Limerick
Limerick

Tel/Fax: +353 61 202565/+353 61 202589
Email: sandra.joyce@ul.ie
Website: www.ul.ie/~iwmc
Other key staff: Niall Keegan (Co-director), Ellen Byrne (PRO)

Aimed at the international market. It is a two-week intensive summer school in Irish traditional music, song and dance. Performance tutorials are offered in all main instruments, voice and dance, by internationally acclaimed visiting lecturers and performers. The school is residential and includes recitals, concerts and field trips. Will be held in July 2000, 2001 and 2002.

Boghill Centre

Sonja O'Brien
Manager
Boghill
Kilfenora
Co. Clare

Tel/Fax: +353 65 7074644
Email: boghill@eircom.net
Website: www.homepage.eircom.net/~boghill

Aimed at adults who are interested in learning more about traditional Irish music and want to improve their playing skills. The workshops cater for mixed instruments. Local musicians are involved in teaching. The workshops are held in a very relaxed and friendly session atmosphere and participants are encouraged to play at sessions held locally. Participants can stay at the centre on a full-board basis. Vegetarian meals are provided.

Ceol na Locha

Síle Ní Thuathail
Riarthóir/Rúnaí
Tuarmhicéadaigh
Co. Mhaigh Eo

Tel/Fax: +353 92 44229/+353 92 44183
Email: ceolnalocha@tourmakeady.com
Website: www.tourmakeady.com/ceolnalocha.htm
Other key staff: Siobhan ní Eanacháin (Cisteoir), Sean Ó Conghaile (Cathairleach)

Aimed at all age groups from 10 years to adults who are willing to learn about traditional music. Course is held in Coláiste Muire, Tourmakeady. Tuition is offered in flute, fiddle, bodhrán, banjo, mandolin, tin whistle, guitar, button accordion, Irish conversation and Sean nós singing. Will be held from the 14th August 2000, and the second Monday in August 2001 and 2002.

An Chúirt Chruitireachta - Irish Harp Summer School

Aibhlin McCrann
Director
50 Wyvern
Killiney
Co. Dublin

Tel/Fax: +353 1 2856345/+353 1 6768007
Email: mccranna@indigo.ie or cruit@harp.net
Website: www.harp.net/cnac/cnac.htm
Other key staff: Joe Joyce (Treasurer), Ann Jones Walsh (Membership Secretary and Editor of newsletter)

Aimed at students of all nationalities of all ages and standards. Tutors are drawn from Ireland's most experienced performers. There is a particular emphasis on interpretation of Irish traditional music as well as all aspects of harp music. Oral, aural and sheet music methods used. The programme includes morning classes, afternoon workshops and evening concerts. The location for this summer school is An Grianán, Termonfeckin, Co. Louth. Will be held from 25-30 June 2000 and the last week in June 2001.

Des Carty Summer School

Liam Morrisey
Alternative Entertainments
Tymon Bawn Community Centre
Firhouse Road
Tallaght
Dublin 24

Tel/Fax: +353 1 4621029 or +353 1 4520611/ +353 1 4520611
Email: dcarty@eircom.net

Aimed at children and adults. The School commemorates Des Carty who spent most of his life teaching fiddle, whistle, banjo and mandolin, making a major contribution to traditional music in Tallaght and outlying districts. Includes workshops, classes, recitals, sessions and ceilí. Tutors have included Martin Nolan, Joe Burke, Maire O'Keefe and Fintan Vallely. Will be held in July 2000, 2001 and 2002.

Comhaltas Ceoltóirí Éireann

Labhrás Ó Murchú
Director General
32 Belgrave Square
Monkstown
Co. Dublin

Tel/Fax: +353 1 2800295/+353 1 2803759
Email: enquiries@comhaltas.com
Website: www.comhaltas.com
Séamus MacMathúna (Timire Cheoil), Bernard O'Sullivan (Project Officer), C.M. Hodge (Rúnaí Oifige)

Comhaltas Ceoltóirí Éireann, was founded in 1951 to promote Irish traditional music, song, dance and the Irish language. It organises Scoil Éigse which is an annual summer school attended by up to 600 eligible students each year, mostly on scholarships.

Cumann Merriman
Úna Uí Chuinn
Rúnaí - Secretary
28 Páirc an Fhia Thoir
Cathair na Mart
Co. Mhaigh Eo

Tel: +353 98 27758
Email: unaquinn@esatclear.ie
Other key staff: Mary O'Sullivan-Long
(Treasurer), Colette Ní Mhoitleigh (Rúnaí
Ballraíochta - Membership Secretary)

Aimed at national and international adults. Covers the following areas: Irish heritage, history, archaeology, literature, folklore, music, politics, religion, European countries and Irish nationalism/traditions and poetry. Lectures are presented in Irish and English and are given by those who are experts in the given subject areas. The winter school will be held on the last weekend of January 2001 and 2002. The summer school will be held on the last week in August 2000, 2001 and 2002.

Cumann Náisiúnta na gCór - Assoc of Irish Choir's Annual Summer School for Choral Conductors and Teachers
Margaret O'Sullivan
Acting Chief Executive Officer
Cumann Náisiúnta na gCór
Drinan Street
Cork

Tel/Fax: +353 21 4312296/+353 21 4962457
Email: cnc@iol.ie

Aimed at conductors, choristers, teachers (primary and post-primary) and students. These courses include: basic, intermediate and advanced choral conducting, tutorials, workshops, lectures, vocal training sessions, masterclasses with experienced choir, recitals and a course on music in the classroom for primary teachers. All courses are sanctioned by the Department of Education & Science for extra personal leave. Will be held from 3-7 July 2000, the first week in July 2001 and 2002 (see advert page 7).

Disability Arts Training Course
Louise Foott
Disability Arts Course Tutor
Art Therapy Department
Crawford College of Art & Design
Sharman Crawford Street
Cork

Tel: +353 21 4966777
Email: lfoott@cit.ie

Aims to facilitate the participation of people with and without disabilities, who have an interest and commitment to the development of their leadership skills in creative group work. This course is a community arts training programme, involving training in visual arts, drama, movement, music, group facilitation skills and disability equality. It explores the potential of creativity in a group setting, within the context of disability equality and self-advocacy training. It is run over ten weekends, including four long weekends, from September to June (Saturday and Sunday 10-4.30pm). Participants will also carry out approximately 10 hours of work practice in their own time. Entry to this course is by interview.

Donegal Fiddlers Summer School
Caomhin Mac Aoidh
Registrar
Tullymorkey
Ballyshannon
Co. Donegal

Tel: +353 72 52144
Email: dldclk1@iol.ie
Other key staff: Rab Cherry (Chairman), Paul Ó Shaughnessy (PRO)

Aimed at students of the fiddle at all levels, primarily those living in Donegal but students from elsewhere are also welcome. Ten classes are taught by experienced teachers from the Donegal fiddle tradition. 90-100 students usually attend. Those who are interested should register in advance to secure a place. Course includes private recitals with seminal players from the tradition. Will be held 1-6 August 2000, 2001 and 2002.

Doyle Instruments Since 1890
Paul Doyle
Director
38a Dominic Street
Galway

Tel/Fax: +353 91 566948
Email: paul.doyle@ireland.com
Website: //members.tripod.com/doyle_instrum
Other key staff: Markus Laughlin (Violin Maker), Marielle Florio (Harp Maker)

Aimed at people with wood working experience who wish to make instruments. This is a short course of up to 12 weeks in the manufacture of harps, guitars, violins, violas, cellos, double basses, mandolins, mandocellos and bouzoukis. Certificate on completion of instrument. Contact shop for course date details (see advert p. 282).

Droichead Arts Centre Summer School

Tony Conaghy
Acting Director
Stockwell Lane
Drogheda
Co. Louth

Tel/Fax: +353 41 9833946/+353 41 9842055
Email: droichead@indigo.ie
Other key staff: Kathleen O'Brien (Financial Manager)

Aimed at children aged 8-18 years old. Provides weekly sessions in art, music and drama throughout the summer months, with the emphasis on storytelling, fantasy and fun, lively workshops leading to colourful performances and displays. Will be held July and August 2000, 2001 and 2002.

Dublin Chamber Music Group - Termonfechin Course

Brian McBryan
Course Director
19 Brooklawn Wood
Blackrock
Co. Dublin

Tel/Fax: +353 1 2883627/+353 1 6793919
Email: dcmg@altavista.net
Website: www.geocities.com/vienna/1905/

Aimed at adult chamber musicians, including students, aged 18 or over. Groups already formed may apply and also individuals who would like to join a group during the course. Groups may include strings, wind, brass and piano. In addition to receiving coaching within groups, the weekends offer opportunities for informal playing with other groups and in the chamber orchestra. The emphasis is on enjoyment. Coaching is provided by professionals with extensive chamber music experience including such names as Constantin Zanidache, Helmut Seeber and Adele O'Dwyer.

Dublin Youth Orchestra Summer Courses

Michéle O'Brien
24 Barnhill Avenue
Dalkey
Co. Dublin

Tel/Fax: +353 1 2352233
Email: mobadmin@gofree.indigo.ie

Other key staff: Vanessa Sweeney (Musical Director), Robert Pierce (Asst. Musical Director)

Aimed at young string/wind/brass musicians aged 10-20 years approximately, from all parts of Ireland. International visitors are also welcome and chamber music at all levels is played. String/wind/brass players are all catered for and are formed in quartets, quintets, wind ensembles and brass ensembles. The groups are encouraged to enjoy music-making while being guided by their tutors towards the highest possible standards of musical awareness and performance. Will be held from 28/6-7/7 2000, 4-13 July 2001 and 3-12 July 2002.

Ennis IMRO Composition Summer School

Eithne Egan
Administrator
C/o IMRO
Copyright House
Pembroke Row
Dublin 2

Tel: +353 1 6283454
Email: info@imro.ie
Website: www.imro.ie
Other key staff: James Wilson (Senior Course Director), Michael Alcorn (Course Director), Martin O'Leary (Course Director)

Aimed at third level music students who want to intensify their work on composition, and at people outside third level education who would like to discuss their work in a more focussed atmosphere. The course is not necessarily aimed at complete beginners, but rather those with a certain amount of knowledge and experience. Two guest composers are invited to take part in the Summer School, one from Ireland and the other from abroad. The composers give lectures and individual tutorials to the students, who compose works for an invited group of guest composers. Will be held in Colaiste Mhuire, Ennis, and will run from 10-22 July 2000, July 2001, July 2001.

Séamus Ennis Summer School

Mary McDermott
Chairperson
Finglas Arts Centre
Artsquad
Unit 14b Main Shopping Centre
Finglas
Dublin 11

Tel/Fax: +353 1 8343950/+353 1 8348115

Email: finart@eircom.net
Other key staff: Sylvia McGill (Secretary)

ESB Music Education Programme
c/o The Arts Office
Sligo County Council Offices
Riverside
Sligo

Tel/Fax: +353 71 56629/+353 71 41119
Email: arts@sligococo.ie

This is a new initiative operating at primary, secondary
and third level in County Sligo, as part of the Vogler
Quartet in Sligo 3 year residency programme until 2002.
This education programme includes concert workshops,
chamber music masterclasses for advanced students, a
music for fun course and a training programme for primary
teachers and transition co-ordinators.

ESB West Clare Jazz School
Jim Connolly
Secretary
Kilbaha
Kilaush
Co. Clare

Tel/Fax: +353 65 9058229/+353 65 9058242

Aimed at jazz students and enthusiasts. This school is a
community centred event with an emphasis on the
highest musical standards in an atmosphere of creativity,
inclusion and enjoyment. Non-musicians and jazz lovers
are welcome to the event. The Jazz School is located at
the mouth of the Shannon, south of the popular sea-
side resort of Kilkee where the loophead peninsula of
Kilbaha lies. Previous tutors on the course have been
Louis Stewart, Myles Drennan, Stephen Keogh and
Michael Coady. Will be held 17-23 June 2000 and in
June of 2001 and 2002.

Fiddlers Green International Festival
Kate Murphy
Chairman
2 Cherryhall
Rostrevor
Co. Down BT34 3KM
Northern Ireland

Tel/Fax: 048 4173 8738/048 4173 9819
Other key staff: Sheila McKeown (Treasurer),

Tommy Sands (President), Maureen McConville
(Secretary)

Takes part as part of the Fiddlers Green International
Festival. Tuition is offered in harp (traditional and classical), percussion, bodhrán, guitar and songwriting.
Will be held 23-30 July 2000 and last week in July
2001.

Film Scoring Program - Screen Training Ireland
Brendan Hayes
Course Administrator
P.O. Box 4716
c/o Ceoil Productions
Dublin 1

Tel/Fax: +353 1 6235744
Email: ceoilpro@indigo.ie
Website: www.ceoilproductions.com
Other key staff: Gavin O'Sullivan (Orchestra
Contractor)

Aimed at composers from classical, rock and commercial
music backgrounds who aspire to become composers of
film television music. Tuition is offered in the form of an
8 module programme including the mechanics of film
scoring, instrumentation, studio consulting, 20th
Century harmony I and II, studio consultancy II, music
technology for film and television and a master class in
scoring.

Fonn Traditional Music Summer School-Galway
Grace Dalton
Administrator/Director
98 College Road
Galway

Tel/Fax: +353 91 562099
Email: gsitm@indigo.ie
Website: www.fonntradmus.ie.nu
Other key staff: Mick Crehan (Executive Director)

Aimed at international and national students who are
interested in Irish traditional music, song, dance and its
associated folklore, history and heritage. The summer
school, which is held for a week, is hosted by Galway
School of Irish Traditional Music. It is a celebration and
exploration of Ireland's musical heritage, placing special
emphasis on the traditions of Galway and surrounding
counties. It incorporates workshops and masterclasses in
traditional music, song and dance, There are lectures on
various aspects of the tradition and cultural and historical trails. Also includes a special 'Hall of Fame' awards
honouring lifelong contributions of an individual/group

to the Irish tradition. Recipients for 1999 were Rita and Sarah Keane. Will be held 13th-19th August 2000, August 2001 and 2002.

Group Creative Musicmaking - A Therapeutic Approach

H.M. Bracefield
Head of Music
University of Ulster at Jordanstown
Newtownabbey
Co. Antrim BT37 0QB
Northern Ireland

Tel/Fax: 048 9036 6955/048 9036 6870
Email: hm.bracefield@ulst.ac.uk

Aimed at those who use music with adults or children with mental, physical or profound handicap or other communication difficulties. Aims to develop existing musical skills and explore various musical approaches.

Dr Douglas Hyde Summer School of Traditional Irish Music & Dance

M. Devine-O'Callaghan
Co-ordinator
Ballaghaderreen
Co. Roscommon

Tel/Fax: +353 907 60013 or +353 907 60136/ +353 907 60765
Email: ocall@iol.ie
Other key staff: Paddy McGarry (Co-ordinator), Joe Smyth (Co-ordinator)

Instrumental workshops are held each morning with a lecture in the afternoon and recitals and seisiúns in pubs at night. In addition there is one afternoon concert, an opening concert, and a céilí on three nights. Planning takes place six to eight months in advance of the event. Will be held 2/7 2000, 3/7 2001 and 4/7 2002.

Inishowen Traditional Singers Circle-International Folk Song & Ballad Seminar

Jimmy McBride
'Dun Emir'
Shore Road
Buncrana
Co. Donegal

Tel: +353 77 61210
Email: jimmymcb@iol.ie
Other key staff: Pat McGonigle (Chairperson)

Aimed at singers and listeners of traditional songs and ballads worldwide. The theme of the 2000 weekend was 'Songs about Work' and featured traditional unaccompanied folk song and ballads in the form of lectures, workshops, discussion, singing sessions and a concert. Planning decisions are made in the Summer/Autumn. Preliminary arrangements for the 2001 event will be made eighteen months in advance. Held on the last weekend in March 2001 and 2002.

International Jazz Summer School

Brian Carson
Director
7 University Road
Belfast BT7 INA
Northern Ireland

Tel/Fax: 048 9024 8818
Email: movingltd@aol.com

Aimed at young improvisers of jazz. Acclaimed international faculty. Will be held in August 2000.

Introduction to Music Course

Colin McKenzie
Director
49 Martello Court
Portmarnock
Co. Dublin

Tel: +353 1 8462320

Current student numbers are 60. Aimed at children aged 4-11 years as an introduction course to music. The course takes place in Mount Temple School, Malahide Road, Dublin 3 on Saturday mornings from September.

Kerry School of Music Summer School

Aidan O'Carroll
Artistic Director
Old Customs House
High Street
Tralee
Co. Kerry

Tel/Fax: +353 66 7125690/+353 66 7120077
Email: kerrymusicschool@eircom.net

Aimed at first time music, dance and theatre students and intending students, instrumentalists, vocalists, actors and dancers at the early stages of training, more advanced performers, people with creative potential (budding composers, writers, choreographers). There are approximately 250 students. The course emphasises the interdisciplinary ethos of the school. Students work in rotation on creative dance, movement, mime, costume, set, mask and make up design and making music, improvisation, script (situational) improvisation and realisation, which are all linked to a central narrative line. Will be held in July each year in the form of 3 separate courses each lasting a week.

Kylemore Music Centre Summer School
Gerard Flanagan
Director/Conductor
Ballyfermot
Dublin10

Tel/Fax: +353 1 6265901/+353 1 6234780

Magh Ena Fiddle School
Caoimhín Mac Aoidh
Registrar
Tullymorkey
Ballyshannon
Co. Donegal

Tel: +353 72 52144
Email: dldclk1@iol.ie
Other key staff: Catherine Nic Aoidh (Co-ordinator)

Aimed at fiddle players of all levels interested in Donegal fiddling. Classes include private recitals with seminal players plus an evening field trip. Weekend courses targeted at specific playing levels are held throughout autumn, winter and spring. Runs weekly throughout the summer months with the exception of the first week in August.

Maoin Cheoil an Chláir Summer School
Dr Tracey Smurthwaite
Director
College Road
Ennis
Co. Clare

Tel/Fax: +353 65 6841774

Aimed at primary and post-primary students. The music summer school is for both traditional and classical music. This course will be held in July 2000, 2001 and 2002.

The Joe Mooney Summer School of Traditional Music, Song & Dance
Nancy Woods
Secretary
Drumshanbo
Co. Leitrim

Tel: +353 78 41213
Email: nwoods@iol.ie
Other key staff: Mary Doyle (Assistant Secretary), Michael Smyth (Treasurer)

Aimed at students wishing to improve their traditional music skills and styles, and students who wish to learn set-dancing and traditional singing. The school offers daily workshops in flute, fiddle, tin whistle, button accordion, uilleann pipes, concertina, harp, banjo, mandolin, bodhrán, piano accordion, traditional singing, Sean-nós singing and set dancing. Evening lectures and recitals, concerts, céilí and impromptu sessions. Will be held from 16-24 July 2000, 3rd week in July 2001 and 2002.

Michael J. Murphy Folklore School
Crónán Devlin
Archive Co-ordinator
Tí Chulainn
An Múllach Bán
Co. Armagh
Northern Ireland

Tel/Fax: 048 3088 8828/048 3088 8821
Email: tculainn@dial.pipex.com
Website: www.tichulainn.ie
Other key staff: Kieran Murphy, Ursula Mhic an tSaor (Educational Officer)

Aimed at those who have a general interest in folklore, folklife and song. Guided tours given based on Michael J. Murphy's folklore. Will be held 26th May 2000, May 2001 and 2002.

Northern Lights Festival
Cathal Newcombe
Chairman
45a Drumavoley Road
Ballycastle
Co. Antrim
Northern Ireland

Tel: 048 2076 3352 (evenings)
Other key staff: Dick Glasgow (Music Co-ordinator)

Traditional music workshops in tin whistle, fiddle and bodhrán (playing and making), intended to develop learning and enhance skills. Childrens session on the last day of festival. Will be held May 2000, 2001 and 2002.

O'Carolan Summer School

Paraic Noone
Secretary
Keadue
Co. Roscommon

Tel/Fax: +353 78 47204/+353 78 47511
Email: ocarolan@oceanfree.net
Other key staff: Margaret Grimes (Chairperson)

Aimed at adults and young people who are interested in learning Irish traditional music. Tuition is offered in harp, flute, tin whistle, fiddle, banjo, button accordion, piano accordion, uilleann pipes, concertina, bodhrán, traditional singing and set dancing. Will be held 31/7-4/8 2000, 30/7-3/8 2001 and 29/7-2/8 2002.

Opera Summer School

Philip Hammond
Performing Arts Director
Arts Council of Northern Ireland
Macneice House
77 Malone Road
Belfast BT9 6AQ
Northern Ireland

Tel/Fax: 048 9038 5200/048 9066 1715
Email: performance@artscouncil-ni.org

Aimed at students who are serious about singing and opera in particular between the ages of 20-35 years. Priority is given to students from Ireland both North and South. Approximately 20 places are available with possible places for repetiteurs interested in expanding their pianistic and accompanying skills. The course content varies from year to year but may include individual coaching, group sessions, special masterclasses, language work, movement classes, repertoire development and role preparation. The course is fully resident and is organised by the Arts Council of Northern Ireland in association with An Comhairle Ealaíon / The Arts Council. Will be held early July 2000.

Na Píobairí Uilleann Teoranta

Liam McNulty
Administrator
15 Henrietta Street
Dublin 1

Tel/Fax: +353 1 8730093/+353 1 8723161

Email: npupipes@iol.ie
Website: www.iol.ie/~npupipes/npuhome.htm
Other key staff: Paula Roche (Administrative Assistant)

Scoil Acla Traditional Music School Summer School

Alice McGinty
Chairperson
Tonragee East
Westport
Co. Mayo

Tel/Fax: +353 98 45584(h) or +353 98 47306(w)/ +353 98 47306
Other key staff: Eoin McNamara (Assistant Chairperson)

Aimed at all persons regardless of age. Tuition is offered in tin whistle, accordian, fiddle, flute, concertina, banjo, uilleann pipes and harp. Will be held in August 2000, 2001 and 2002. (see advert)

Scoil Samhraidh Willie Clancy

Muiris Ó Rócháin
Director
Miltown Malbay
Co. Clare

Tel: +353 65 7084148 or +353 65 7084281
Other key staff: Harry Hughes (Administrative Director), Eamon McGivney (Music Liaison)

Aimed at people of all ages who wish to learn more about Irish music and culture. Every morning, in excess of 100 workshops are held at several different venues. Tuition is offered in tin whistle, flute, pipes, concertina, accordion and fiddle. Other activities include set dancing workshops, music lectures, singing lectures and special music workshops. Will be held in July 2000, 2001 and 2002.

Share Music External Course

Dawn Latimer
Director
Share Holiday Village
Smiths Strand
Lisnaskea
Co. Fermanagh BT92 0EQ
Northern Ireland

Tel/Fax: 048 6772 2122/048 6772 1893

Email: share@dnet.co.uk
Website: www.sharevillage.org

Aimed at anyone with a disability or sensory impairment aged 17-40 years. Share Music is an annual week-long music programme held in four locations, the Share Centre is the only Irish venue. Share Music aims to provide facilities and encourage young people with physical disabilities to take part in a variety of musical activities, often with elements of theatre and visual arts in the company of other musicians and volunteers. Guidance is provided from professional tutors, which in 1999 included producer Stephen Langridge and designer Conor Murphy who were both involved with Northern Ireland Opera's 'Magic Flute'. Beverly White, dancer David Toole from 'Can Do Co' company and composer Nigel Osbourne were also involved. Will be held in August 2000, 2001 and 2002.

Slieve Gullion Winter School
Ursula Mhic and tSaoir
Education Officer
Tí Chulainn
An Mullach Bán
Newry BT35 9TT
Co. Armagh
Northern Ireland

Tel/Fax: 048 3088 8828/048 3088 8821
Email: tculainn@dial.pipex.com
Website: www.tculainn.ie
Other key staff: Sean O'Coinn (Manager), Crónán Devlin (Archive Officer)

Aimed at those who are interested in history, current affairs, cultural heritage and music. Social, political and cultural issues are examined and debated by a wide range of invited guest speakers. Over the weekend there are lectures, films and evenings of traditional music. Will be held 3-5 November 2000 and first weekend in November 2001 and 2002.

Songlines
Sean Nolan
Arts office
County Hall
John Street
Kilkenny

Tel: +353 56 52699

Aimed at professional and amateur songwriters. Provides a songwriting workshop in which creative and business aspects of song writing are explained. Will take place May 2000.

Sound Training Centre
Eithne Mooney
Course Co-ordinator
Temple Bar Music Centre
Curved Street
Temple Bar
Dublin 2

Tel/Fax: +353 1 6709033/+353 1 6709042
Website: www.soundtraining.com
Other key staff: Dave Christophers (Head Lecturer), Paul Lacey (Research & Development)

Aimed at those who wish to pursue a career in the technical side of the music industry such as: sound engineering, lighting & stage production, music technology & recording techniques, sequencing, sampling & synthesis. These courses are accredited to London City & Guilds (City of Westminister College). For further details contact the above centre.

South Sligo Summer School
Rita Flannery
Director
Tubbercurry
Co. Sligo

Tel: +353 71 85010
Other key staff: Marie Flannery, Geraldine Murtagh

Aimed at everyone who plays or is interested in Irish traditional music and dance. Classes are held daily in fiddle, piano and button accordions, flute, guitar (flat-picking), banjo, concertina, uilleann pipes, traditional singing, bodhrán, tin whistle, harp and set dancing. The week's activities include classes each morning from 10-1pm, a lecture is held on some aspect of traditional music or dance each afternoon and a recital is held every evening. All ages, nationalities and abilities are welcome. There is also a nightly céilí accompanied by céilí bands. Will be held from the 9 July 2000, from the second Sunday of July 2001 and 2002.

Summer Music on the Shannon
Anthony Ovenell/Andrea Creech
Artistic Directors
Clare Music Makers
Nationwide House
Bank Place
Ennis
Co. Clare

Tel/Fax: +353 65 6842480/+353 65 7084405

Email: cmmacto@iol.ie
Website: www.iol.ie/~cmmacto
Other key staff: Bob Creech (Administrator),
Nancy Creech (Administrator)

Aimed at young musicians aged 9 upwards. Is located at the University Concert Hall, Limerick which has concert halls, recital halls, music studios, cafés, bars and recreational facilities. The course features string orchestras, a wind band, a flute choir, masterclasses, chamber music and a community choir. There is a special option of taking part in a percussion ensemble, Irish dancing, choir or art classes. Will be held from 24/7-4/8 2000, last two weeks in July 2001 and 2002.

Suzuki Education Institute of Ireland
Sheila Benny
13 Cois Sleibhe
Southern Cross
Bray
Co. Wicklow

Tel: +353 1 2829798
Other key staff: Magsi Goor, Annacrivey House, Enniskerry, Co. Wicklow.
Tel/Fax: +353 1 2868297/ +353 1 2864355

Aimed at very young children throughout Ireland. Provides holiday courses, national days and local workshops.

Tailor Made Arts Programmes at Share's Arts Arena
Dawn Latimer
Director
Share Holiday Village
Smiths Strand, Lisnakea
Co. Fermanagh BT92 0EQ
Northern Ireland

Tel/Fax: 048 6772 2122/048 6772 1893
Email: share@dnet.co.uk
Website: www.sharevillage.org
Other key staff: Aine Weir (Arts Development Officer), Declan Campbell (Arts Development Officer)

Aimed at everyone. The arena is available for external hire or residential use to organisations wishing to use the arts or conference facilities to host their own courses. The arts team are available to design and co-ordinate arts and music courses tailor-made to suit your needs. Share's purpose built arts arena is ideal for running your own arts programmes or hosting external arts courses.

The dedicated arts development workers are available not only to advise and assist with your arts programmes but to design and co-ordinate arts sessions specific in individual or group needs. The current artist in residence specialise in visual and creative arts as well as performance arts and drama. Programmes available include youth arts and drama, ceramics and sculpture, print making and batik. Specialist courses include puppetry, mosaic and mask making. The arena also offers a professional pottery suite and craft workshop. Dance and music studios are available and summer courses include carnival and festival drama workshops.

Traditional Music, Cultural Heritage and Irish Language
Kieran Murphy
Events Manager
Tí Chulainn
An Mullach Bán
Newry
Co. Antrim BT35 9TT
Northern Ireland

Tel/Fax: 048 3088 8828/048 3088 8821
Email: tculainn@dial.pipex.com
Website: www.tculainn.ie
Other key staff: Sean O'Coinn (Manager)

Aimed at those who wish to learn or improve Irish language, Irish music, Irish heritage, culture and activities. There are 3-5 day courses available in Irish language or cultural heritage and intensive short courses for beginners and more advanced learners of Irish traditional music. The courses can be combined with a wide range of cultural and recreational activities and entertainment. Will be held June, July, August and September 2000, 2001 and 2002.

Ulster Folk and Transport Museum
Robbie Hannan
Curator of Musicology
Cultra
Holywood
Co. Down
Northern Ireland

Tel/Fax: 048 9042 8428
Other key staff: Dr J. Bell (Head of Curatorial Division)

Aimed at all those interested in learning to play the uilleann pipes, fiddle, tin whistle or flute. Classes are graded to suit everyone from beginners to advanced level. The fiddle classes are held in February, the uilleann pipes in September and the tin whistle and flute in November. Classes conclude with a recital featuring the tutors.

Ulster Youth Choir Short Course
Majella Hollywood
Choral Organiser
Chamber of Commerce House
22 Great Victoria Street
Belfast BT2 7LX
Northern Ireland

Tel/Fax: 048 9023 1414/048 9033 3845
Email: uyc@ukgateway.net
Other key staff: Christopher Bell (Artistic Director)

Aimed at all those who are interested in singing between 16-24 years of age. Approximately 120 people take part each year. This course is held once a year and is a residential course open to all. It consists of individual singing lessons, group vocal coaching, sight singing and vocal workshops. There are five productions held over the course and concert weekend. Will be held from 4-12 Aug 2000 (with a concert held from 15-17 Sept), Aug 2001 and 2002. (see also pages)

Ulster Youth Jazz Summer Course
Ken Jordan
Director
29 Glendarragh
Belfast BT4 2WB
Co. Antrim
Northern Ireland

Tel/Fax: 048 9076 0403
Email: kenjordan@connectfree.co.uk
Other key staff: Gerard McAtasney (Wind Tutor)

Aimed at any young musician from grade 3 standard upward who plays saxophone, clarinet, trumpet, cornet, trombone, piano, bass, drums or guitar. The course is held at the Crescent Arts Centre, University Road, Belfast, and runs from Monday to Friday, 10-1pm in July. A jazz orchestra is formed for each course and a short programme is learned, which is performed on the last day of the course, for parents and friends. A large part of the course is spent introducing the students to improvisation. (see also pages)

Waterford Festival of New Music
Eric Sweeney
Head of Music Department

Waterford Institute of Technology
Cork Road
Waterford

Tel/Fax: +353 51 302000/+353 51 378292

Aimed at composers and instrumentalists. The Resident Ensemble, Black Hair Contemporary Music Ensemble, give masterclasses, workshops, concerts and lectures in piano, violin, trombone, percussion and clarinet.

West Cork Arts Centre Short Courses
Justine Foster
Education Officer
North Street
Skibbereen
Co. Cork

Tel/Fax: +353 28 22090/+353 28 22084

Aimed at children (including Junior and Leaving Certificate students) and adults. Tuition is offered to Grade 8 level in guitar, classical guitar, piano accordion and keyboard. Also classical music appreciation classes. Courses are held in autumn, winter and spring.

The Charles Wood Summer School
Aubrey McClintock
Community Relations Officer
Tourist Information Centre
40 English Street
Armagh BT61 7BA
Northern Ireland

Tel/Fax: 048 3752 9600/048 3752 9601
Email: crdo@armagh.gov.uk

Aimed at all abilities and ages. A celebration of music in in the form of singing, choir training, choral conducting, organ playing and composition. Consists of workshops. masterclasses, concerts and choral services. Based in the two cathedrals. Takes place on last Monday in August each year and lasts for one week.

Yeats International Summer & Winter School
Miriam Quinn
Enterprise Development Director
Yeats Society Sligo
Yeats Memorial Building
Hyde Bridge
Sligo

Tel/Fax: +353 71 42693 or +353 71 47264/ +353 71 42780
Email: yeatsoity@eircom.net
Website: www.itsligo.ie/yeats/yeats.html
Other key staff: Sheila McCabe (Secretary), Anne Currid (Secretary)

Aimed at those who are interested in literature and the work of W.B. Yeats, in particular. Consists of morning lectures, evening seminars, tours, poetry workshops, drama workshops and social get-togethers, occasional lunch-time recitals and other music events as part of the summer school and associated festival.

Young European Strings Masterclasses

Maria Kelemen
Director
21 The Close
Cypress Downs
Templeogue
Dublin 6w

Tel/Fax: +353 1 4905263/+353 1 4920355
Email: yes@iol.ie
Other key staff: Galina Turchaninova (Guest Teacher), Ronald Masin (Guest Teacher)

Aimed at music students preparing for a professional career which includes public performances. Masterclasses are organised during the Summer holidays and Autumn school holidays. They are open to a number of very talented Irish musicians residing abroad, together with Irish and non-Irish musicians. Tape audition. In 2000, teachers are invited from Russia and the Netherlands. Will be held in October 2000, 2001 and 2002.

EXAMINING INSTITUTIONS

Associated Board of the Royal Schools of Music

Richard Morris
Chief Executive
14 Bedford Square
London WC1B 3JG
England

Tel/Fax: +44 20 7636 5400/+44 20 7637 0234
Email: abrsm@abrsm.ac.uk
Website: www.abrsm.ac.uk
Other key staff: Miriam Halpin (Irish Co-ordinator)
Tel/Fax: +353 1 2350752/+353 1 2350775
Email: musexam@iol.ie

This institution offers preparatory test, theory and practical graded exams, professional diplomas and a performance assessment scheme for adults. Syllabuses are available for over 30 instruments, jazz piano and jazz ensembles, singing, choral singing, practical musicianship and theory. The CT ABRSM is a 1 year part time professional development course for instrumental and singing teachers held at various regional locations. For application procedure contact Miriam Halpin. ABRSM (Publishing) Ltd is known for its extensive keyboard and instrumental catalogues. Also publishes music for its exams, which are available in Ireland (see advert page 97).

Dublin Institute of Technology - Conservatory of Music & Drama

Dr Eibhlis Farrell
Head of School
Dublin Institute of Technology
Adelaide Road
Dublin 2

Tel/Fax: +353 1 4023000/+353 1 4023555

This institution offers an internal examination system from grades 1-8 and DIT examinations: BMus (FT 601), BMus Ed (TR 009/FT 602), Diploma in Music Teaching (DT 602), Diploma in Speech and Drama Studies (DT 603) and a Music Foundation Course (DT 604), postgraduate studies by research at masters/doctorate levels and a Postgraduate Diploma in Music Technology. There is an internal application system for grade examinations. Application procedure for the degree and diploma courses is through the CAO and applicants for postgraduate studies apply to the DIT Admissions Office. (See advert page 68).

Guildhall School of Music and Drama

Eric Hollis
Director of Initial Studies
Examinations Service
3 Lauderdale Place
Barbican, London EC2Y 8EN
England

Tel/Fax: +44 20 7382 7167/+44 20 7382 7212
Email: exams@gsmd.ac.uk
Website: www.gsmd.ac.uk
Other key staff: Regional centre contacts: A. Moroney (Dublin Representative), 388 Orwell Park Drive, Templeogue, Dublin.
Tel/Fax: +353 1 4505980
J. McLaren (Belfast Representative), 1 Ballysillan Road, Belfast, BT14 7QP, Northern Ireland.

A|B|R|S|M
PUBLISHING

The Associated Board of the Royal Schools of Music (Publishing) Limited

The Associated Board of the Royal Schools of Music is the leading international music examining body with over 500,000 candidates every year in more than 80 countries.

ABRSM (Publishing) Limited is renowned for:
- an extensive keyboard catalogue
- a wide-ranging catalogue of instrumental albums
- authoritative performing editions of classical works
- innovative jazz publications

Recent publications that have received critical acclaim include:

The Well-Tempered Clavier PART 1   J. S. Bach
(edited by Dr Richard Jones)
'Best Standard Publication' award MUSIC RETAILERS ASSOCIATION

Baroque Violin Pieces
Four-volume graded anthology of baroque music for solo violin and continuo
'a pleasing introduction to the Italian baroque style... so much to enjoy and much to learn from playing these pieces' ESTA NEWS

Spectrum 2   30 contemporary works for solo piano
(compiled by Thalia Myers)
'The breadth and depth of contemporary thought is quite astonishing... this is truly a must-have!' PIANO

Jazz Piano from Scratch   Charles Beale
'brilliant, lucid and thorough-going' PIANO
'intensely practical and contains many excellent activities' MUSIC TEACHER

Associated Board Irish co-ordinator · MISS MIRIAM HALPIN
31 Sefton Rochestown Avenue Dun Laoghaire Co. Dublin Ireland
Telephone +353 1 235 0752 *Fax* +353 1 235 0775 *E-mail* musexam@iol.ie

ABRSM (Publishing) Limited
14 Bedford Square London WC1B 3JG United Kingdom
Telephone +44 20 7636 5400 *Fax* +44 20 7637 0234 *E-mail* publishing@abrsm.ac.uk
Website www.abrsmpublishing.co.uk

Tel/Fax: 048 9071 8256
A. Bachelor (Omagh Representative), Woodlands,
12 Retreat Close, Omagh, Co. Tyrone BT79 0HW,
Northern Ireland.
Tel/Fax: 048 8224 4599

This institution offers syllabuses of graded exams, recital
and drama certificate and LGSM performance diploma
in piano, violin, viola, cello, double bass, singing, flute,
clarinet (classical and jazz), saxophone (classical and jazz),
oboe, bassoon, recorder, orchestral brass and brass band
instruments, single keyboard, electronic organ, guitar
(classical and plectrum), orchestral percussion and drum
kit. Specialist examiners for all instruments at every level.
Application procedure can be obtained by contacting the
Area Representatives or the Examinations Service directly.

The Leinster School of Music
Sheila Murphy
Secretary
Griffith College Campus
South Circular Road
Dublin 8

Tel/Fax: +353 1 4751532/+353 1 4549265
Email: leinster_school@gcd.ie
Website: www.gcd.ie

This institution offers graded exams, Music Proficiency,
Licentiate, Fellowship, Diploma and Teaching Diploma.
To apply contact direct. (see advert p.82).

London College of Music Examinations
Gillian Patch
Examinations Manager
Thames Valley University
St. Mary's Road
London W5 5RF
England

Tel/Fax: +44 20 8231 2364/+44 20 8231 2433
Email: lcm.exams@tvu.ac.uk
Website: www.elgar.tvu.ac.uk
Other key staff: Regional centre contacts:
K. Briggs (Portadown Contact), 21 Irwin
Gardens, Lurgan BT66 7DP, Northern Ireland,
Tel: 048 3832 1256
P. Barry (Dublin Contact), 7 Kenilworth Square,
Rathmines, Dublin 6
Tel: +353 1 4978026
G. Meighan (Cork Contact), 38 Tracton Avenue,
Montenotte, Co. Cork,
Tel/Fax: +353 21 4503832

This institution offers introductory steps exams, grades
1-8, and the following diplomas: ALCM, LLCM (Teachers
and Performers), FLCM, AMusLCM and LMusLCM, all
instruments, singing, music theatre, speech and drama,
and Irish traditional music are catered for. Application
procedure is through the regional centre contacts with
regard to the following centres throughout the North
and South of Ireland: Armagh, Ballymena, Bangor,
Belfast, Castlederg, Dromore, Dungannon, Enniskillen,
Lislap, Londonderry, Portadown, Portstewart,
Rathfriland, Strabane, Bunclody, Celbridge, Charleville,
Clones, Cootehill, Cork, Dublin, Dundalk, Dunmanway,
Galway, Kanturk, Lanesboro, Limerick, Listowel,
Monaghan, Ramelton, Tipperary, Tralee and Waterford.

Royal Irish Academy of Music
Theresa Doyle
Local Centre Manager
36-38 Westland Row
Dublin 2

Tel/Fax: +353 1 6764412/+353 1 6622798
Email: riam@indigo.ie
Website: www.riam.ie
Other key staff: Frances Hogan (General Office
Supervisor)

This institute provides a wide-ranging local centre
examinations system. Founded in 1894, this system is
designed to improve and develop music and drama
performance and teaching in Ireland. The local centre
examinations system examines all musical disciplines
from grades elementary to senior certificate. This examination system has grown to serve every county in
Ireland, examining over 30,000 students annually. The
system also has a comprehensive speech and drama
syllabus and has published its own poetry anthology.
The 'Irish Permanent High Achiever Awards' (launched
December 1999) recognises the achievements of students who gain exceptional results in this examination
system. In December 1998 the Royal Irish Academy of
Music, in association with Comhaltas Ceoltóirí Éireann
and supported by PMPA Insurance, introduced traditional Irish music examinations from elementary to senior
cycle. The RIAM also offers an Associate Diploma
(Teachers and Performers) and Licentiate Diploma
(Teachers and Performers) in all musical disciplines and
speech and drama. Applications procedure: three examination sessions are held every year (spring, summer and
winter). Contact the local centre office of the RIAM for
further details (see advert page 89).

Trinity College London
Nicholas King
Chief Examiner in Music
89 Albert Embankment

London SE1 7TP
England

Tel/Fax: +44 20 7820 6100/+44 20 7820 6161
Email: info@trinitycollege.co.uk
Website: www.trinitycollege.co.uk
Other key staff: Regional centre contacts:
Luke Tobin (Dublin Contact)
Tel: +353 1 8390347,
Eileen Madden (Cork Contact)
Tel: +353 21 4271659,
Betty Drennan (Belfast Contact)
Tel: 048 9048 2759

This institution offers graded examinations in all instruments and voice from grades 1-8, Performers Certificate, ATCL (Performers), LTCL (Performance or Instrumental/Vocal Teaching or Compositional Techniques), FTCL (Performers or Composition). The College also offers Certificate, ATCL, LTCL and FMusEd in Music Education, theory examinations for grades 1-8, AMusTCL, LMusTCL and ensemble and choral assessment examinations at three levels. The First Concert Certificate is being introduced progressively in all instruments and voice. For external examinations, apply to local contacts.

YOUTH ORCHESTRAS

Irish Association of Youth Orchestras
Agnes O'Kane
Honorary Administrator
6 Alexandra Place
Wellington Road
Cork

Tel/Fax: +353 21 4507412
Email: agnesokane@eircom.net
(see advert page 7).

The following orchestras are members of the IAYO:

Alexandra College Orchestras
Brenda Wilkes
Head of Music
Alexandra College
Milltown
Dublin 6

Tel/Fax: +353 1 4977571/+353 1 4974873
Email: alexadm@iol.ie
Other key staff: Ron Cooney (Wind Band

Director), Vanessa Sweeney (Intermediate Strings), Evelyn Hearns (Choral Director)

There are two orchestras, The College Orchestra 15-18 years and The Intermediate Orchestra 12-15 years. Have participated in the Irish Association of Youth Orchestras (IAYO) Festival, winning awards for artistic achievement. Four productions per year. Rehearsal from 4-5pm at school.

Belfast Training Orchestra
Paul McBride
37 Croft Hill
Four Winds
Belfast BT8 4GX
Northern Ireland

Tel: 048 9040 1548

Blackrock College Orchestra
Una O'Kane
Director
Blackrock College
Blackrock
Co. Dublin

Tel/Fax: +353 1 2888681/+353 1 2834267
Email: blrockc@iol.ie

There are 40 members, aged 12-18 years, including pupils of Mount Anville School. Annual concert in the National Concert Hall for the orchestra, choirs, bands and solo items. 3-4 concerts are held annually, masses, shows, opera and plays. Rehearsal Wednesday morning.

Borris National School Orchestra
Michael Perkins
Borris National School
Borris
Co. Carlow

Tel: +353 503 73402

City Music College Orchestra
Kay O'Sullivan
Director
City Music College
Drinan Street
Cork

Tel: +353 21 4313211

This orchestra holds 1 main production per year. They meet every third Saturday from 2-5.30pm

The aims of Scoil Acla are to:
- Promote and develop Traditional Irish Music
- Caomhna agus forbairt na teanga - "Gaeilge Acla"
- Summer school of Music, Painting, Set Dance and Writing
- Organise seminars on the historical, geological and archaeological features of the locality
- Promote local songs and poetry writing
- Study the social development of the locality
- Drama

Scoil Acla, An Chaiseal, Acaill, Co. Mhaigh Eo, Éire

Tel: (098) 47306 • **Fax:** (098) 47306
Email: teangai@anu.ie

Music Scholarships at The Music School (SCHOLA CANTORUM)
St. Finians College, Mullingar

A unique range of music scholarships for both boys and girls is now on offer at St. Finians College in Mullingar.

This special music school, known as the Schola Cantorum, which now approaches the thirtieth anniversary of its institution, has already produced dozens of well known professional musicians, now working in influential musical positions, both at home and abroad.

The generous five year scholarship scheme, which has been funded since 1970 by the Irish Catholic Hierarchy, covers all specialisesd tuition fees in Organ, Piano, Voice, Choral Singing, Liturgical Music, Composition and a second instrument.

For male candidates there is the added advantage of free boarding at St. Finians College.

Our Specialised Music Staff includes:

Shane Brennan, MA BMus HDE LTCL - Director of Organ, Choral Work, Composition and General Studies

Pádraic Ó Cuinneagáin, MA BA BMus HDE LRAM - Director of Piano Studies

Seamus O'Brien, MA BA BMus LTCL - Assistant Director of Piano Studies and Director of Music Technology

Mary Daly Mulligan, BA BMus LTCL - Director of Woodwind Studies.

For further information, or to apply, please write to:

Shane Brennan
Director, Schola Cantorum, St. Finians College, Mullingar, Co. Westmeath.
Tel: 044-42906 086-2528029
E-mail: schcan@eircom.net

University College Cork

Department of Music
A lively and rapidly expanding department offering

- Three undergraduate degrees:
  BMus; BA Single Honours; BA Joint Honours

- Course structures that promote an exciting and productive interchange between musicology and performance, encouraging each to support the other.

- Academic and practical courses in:
  Western Art Music from 900AD to the present day, a wealth of musicological disciplines, Irish Traditional Music, World Music, Music Technology, Composition, Conducting and Analysis.
  The department's unique musical life includes the only Javanese Gamelan in Ireland, a busy schedule of concerts, sessions and talks, two choirs, an orchestra, a fiddle group, a New Music Ensemble, African Dance and Drumming, a carillon, the Capriccio Jazz and Classical Music Society, the Irish Traditional Music Society and UCC's artists-in-residence the RTÉ Vanbrugh String Quartet.

- A wide choice of postgraduate degrees:
  Taught MA programmes including Composition, and Music Before 1800; MPhil by research in many areas including Irish Traditional Music, Ethnomusicology and all periods of Western Art Music; MMus in performance; PhD by research or composition.

Further details of all courses from:
The Secretary, Department of Music, National University of Ireland, Cork - Tel: 021 4904530
or from our website at http://www.ucc.ie/ucc/depts/music

Clare Youth Orchestra
Cheoil an Chláir
College Road
Ennis
Co. Clare

Tel/Fax: +353 65 6841774

There are 40 members. Special interest in youth orchestra repertoire. Participated in Edinburgh Music Festival 1998. Rehearsal is every second Saturday.

Clongowes Wood College Orchestra
Philip Thomas
Conductor
Clongowes Wood College
Clane
Co. Kildare

Tel/Fax: +353 45 868202/+353 45 861042

There are 50 members aged 12-18 years. Special interest in the music of T.C. Kelly (founder of the orchestra). Participated in Irish Association of Youth Orchestras (IAYO) Festival 1998. Holds two productions annually. Rehearsal Mon 6-7pm and Thurs 1.30-2pm.

Coláiste an Chroise Naofa
Catherine Buckley
Ceolfhoirn An Chroise Naofa
Carraig na bhFear
Co. Corcaigh

Tel: +353 21 4884104

Cork School of Music Orchestras
Adrian Pectu
Head of Strings
Cork School of Music
Union Quay
Cork

Tel/Fax: +353 21 4270076/+353 21 4276595
Email: apectu@mail.cit.ie
Other key staff: Tomás McCarthy, Conor Ó Ceallacháin, Geoffrey Spratt, Declan Townsend (Conductors)

The principle orchestra within the Cork School of Music is The Cork School of Music Symphony Orchestra. Founded over 20 years ago and has over 100 members. Regularly performs at City Hall, Cork and throughout Ireland. Areas of special interest include classical, romantic and 20th Century works. Recently commissioned and premiered John Kinsella's Symphony No 7.

Participated in the 3rd and 9th International Festival of Youth Orchestras, Valencia, Spain, 1985 and 1989. Provides a platform for talented soloists. Other orchestras include The Sinfonietta, Junior Chamber Orchestra and The Chamber Orchestra. There are also three junior and one intermediate orchestras, each with 40 members.

Cork Youth Orchestra
Thomás McCarthy
Musical Director
30 Manor Hill
Paulavone
Carrigrohane
Co. Cork

Tel: +353 21 4872982
Mobile: +353 88 2136277
Other key staff: Hugo O'Rahilly-Drew (Manager)

There are 145 members - 35 junior orchestra, 110 senior orchestra, aged 10-13 years and 13-21 years. Areas of special interest are concert orchestral material, overtures, show music and platforms for soloists in the orchestra. Works with various professional soloists. Toured Wales in 1998, have performed in the National Concert Hall. Founded over 41 years ago. Large music library containing over 400 works. Hold seven productions annually. Rehearsal Sat 7-9.30pm at Fr O'Leary Hall, Bandon, Co. Cork.

County Cork Youth Orchestra
Carol Daly
Conductor
Glanmire Community College
Glanmire
Cork

Tel/Fax: +353 21 4822377
Other key staff: John Fitzpatrick (Director),
County Cork V.E.C, County Hall Cork,
Tel/Fax: +353 21 4285347

There are 79 members, aged 13-18 years. Formed in 1998. Have performed at the National Festival of Youth Orchestras 1999. Over five productions annually. Rehearsal every third Sat 10.30-2.30pm at Glanmire Community College.

County Donegal Youth Orchestras
Sr Concepta Murphy
Convent of Mary
Ballyshannon
Co. Donegal

Tel/Fax: +353 72 51268 (convent) or
+353 72 51369 (school)/+353 72 51369

Senior orchestra has 70 members, aged 12-19 years
and the Training Orchestra has 30 members, aged 7-12
years. Areas of special interest are chamber music workshops and masterclasses for the various sections of the
orchestra. Have performed at the National Concert Hall
in the Festival of Youth Orchestras. Rehearsal is every
two weeks in Abbey Vocational School, Donegal Town.
Christmas carol service, annual concert and a concert
with a visiting youth orchestra produced each year.
Working to achieve a higher standard of orchestral
playing by encouraging all members to study for the
various grades of instrumental examinations and to
attend courses organised by other orchestral groups.

County Wexford Youth Orchestras

Eileen Herlihy
Director
Wexford School of Music
St. Marys
Summerhill
Wexford

Tel/Fax: +353 53 41284

Have participated in many festivals including Arklow
Festival, Feis Ceoil and the Irish Association of Youth
Orchestras festival.

Crescent College Comprehensive School Orchestra

Helen Molony
Music Director
Crescent College Comprehensive
Dooradoyle
Limerick

Tel: +353 61 229655

Members aged 13-18 years. Aims to promote good
ensemble playing with Irish music and pieces written for
the school orchestra. Has participated in the Feis Ceoil
and came joint first in the Feis Ceoil 1995, winners
1996 and third in 1999. Two productions held each
year. Rehearsal every Friday.

The Cross Border Orchestra

Sharon Treacy-Dunne
Director
St Louis Secondary School
Dundalk
Co. Louth

Tel/Fax: +353 42 9335536 or +353 42 9334474/
+353 42 9335536
Email: dunlughaidh.ias@eircom.net

Members aged 12-18 years. Areas of special interest are
popular music, and classical genres. Have participated in
Warwick Music Festival and cross border festivals.
Winners of Feis Ceol 1996, 1997, 1998 and 1999.
Winners of Portadown Music Festival 1996 and 1997.
Winners of Newry Music Festival 1999. Concert tours to
England, Czech Republic and Finland. Performed in the
National Concert Hall 1998 and 1999. Eight productions
per year.

Dublin Youth Orchestras

Carmel Ryan
Administrator
12 Wesley Heights
Sandyford
Dublin 16
Co. Dublin

Tel/Fax: +353 1 2954206 or 2952100/
+353 1 2954206 or 2952100

There are 330 members, divided into four orchestras,
junior strings, intermediate, transitional and symphony
orchestras. Aged from 9-21 years. Areas of special interest are symphonic repertoire and chamber music.
Auditions are held annually and applications open on
January 1st each year. Hold an annual chamber music
day and organise an annual residential chamber music
summer course in July. Have travelled to Germany, Italy,
Belgium, the Netherlands, France, England and Canada.
They also make regular appearances at the National
Concert Hall. Perform a total of twelve productions per
year. Rehearsals take place every Sunday from 2.30-5.30
pm in Sancta Maria College, Dublin 16.

Dunlavin Youth Orchestra

Dorly O'Sullivan
Conductor
Newtown House
Grangebeg
Dunlavin
Co. Wicklow

Tel/Fax: +353 45 401483/+353 45 865758

There are 43 members in the group, aged 10-18 years.
Areas of special interest is promoting music in rural
areas where children can develop their musical talents.
Have participated in the Dunlavin Arts Festival yearly
since 1989, The Festival of Youth Orchestras 1996 -
1999. Achievements include a trip to North Wales in
March 1999, performing 2 concerts and the orchestra

received a grant of £4,720 from Wicklow Rural Partnership which represents 50% of an investment into a new instrumental bank. The orchestra rehearses 3 separate programmes each year and plays between 4-5 performances per programme. Rehearses on Wednesday evenings from 6.30-8.30 pm.

Galway Youth Orchestra
Carmel Garrett
Honorary Administrator
'Rustic Gables'
Knocknacarra Village
Co. Galway

Tel: +353 91 521324

Members aged from 9-24 years. Areas of special interest are public concerts, participating in masterclasses and organising concerts with visiting orchestras. Have participated in The Festival of Youth Orchestras 1996 and 1998, Winner of West Challenge Cup in Feis Ceoil 1995. Achievements include participation in Feis Ceoil by both the senior and intermediate orchestras and three exchange visits with École de Musique et de Danse in Lorient, Brittany, France. Performs three concerts per year.

Glenstal Abbey Orchestra
Albert Llussa Torra
Glenstal Abbey
Murroe
Co. Limerick

Tel: +353 61 386099

Greystones Youth Orchestra
Artemis Kent
Director
6 Silverpines
Bray
Co. Wicklow

Tel: +353 1 2829594
Email: kentai@tcd.ie

55 members, aged 9-18 years. Special interest in 20th Century music. Participated in the Festival of Youth Orchestras, winning the award for artistic achievement 1999. Six productions per year. Rehearsal time Tuesday 5.30-7pm, during term time at St Patrick's School Hall, Church Rd, Bray.

Kerry School of Music Orchestras
Aidan O'Carroll
Director
Old Customs House
High Street
Tralee
Co. Kerry

Tel/Fax: +353 66 7125690/+353 66 7120077
Email: kerrymusicschool@eircom.net

Participants are aged from 12-18 years. There are three orchestras attached to Kerry School of Music, Kerry School of Music Senior Orchestra and Junior Orchestras and Kerry School of Music Chamber Orchestra.

Kildare Youth Orchestras
Bernadette Hayden
Herbert Lodge Arts Centre
The Curragh
Co. Kildare

Tel/Fax: +353 45 481598

Kilkenny Youth Orchestra
Philip Edmondson
Conductor
Kilkenny School of Music
Ormonde Road
Kilkenny

Tel: +353 56 62969

The orchestra is for players of grade 3 standard and over, and performs between two and three concerts per year. Have performed throughout Ireland, tours of Wales, Cambridge and France. Area of special interest is the full classical repertoire. The orchestra has played on television and radio, in the National Concert Hall, Dublin, and has featured in Kilkenny Arts Week. Rehearsal time is Saturdays from 2.30-4.30 pm in St. Kieran's College, Kilkenny.

Kylemore College Orchestra
Mona McMahon
Kylemore College
Kylemore Road
Ballyfermot
Dublin 10

Tel/Fax: +353 1 6265901/+353 1 6234780

Liffey Valley Orchestra

Pat McDonnell
Secretary
22 Weston Drive
Lucan
Co. Dublin

Tel/Fax: +353 1 6282264/+353 1 6234537

There are 70 members, aged 8-18 years. Have participated in the Rostrevor Festival and Fiddlers Green International Festival. Two to three productions annually. Rehearsal time every second Saturday 2.30-5.30pm at Salesian College, Maynooth Road, Celbridge, Co. Kildare.

Loreto Primary School Gorey Orchestra

Aileen Kennedy
Musical Director
Loreto Primary School
Gorey
Co. Wexford

Tel/Fax: +353 55 21827/+353 55 20881

Loreto School Kilkenny Orchestra

Jacinta Cantwell
Musical Director
Loreto School
Granges Road
Kilkenny

Tel/Fax: +353 56 65132/+353 56 65131

There are 56 members, aged 12-18 years. Participated in Feis Ceol and the Arklow Festival. Performed in school musicals and Lions Club benefit concerts.

Maynooth University Orchestra

Trini Armstrong
Conductor
Music Department
Logic House
NUI Maynooth
Co. Kildare

Tel/Fax: +353 1 7084636/+353 1 6289432

There are 45 members, aged 18-65 years. Have participated in the Irish Association of Youth Orchestras Festival of Youth Orchestras in the NCH, Dublin. Membership is open to students and staff of NUI Maynooth and St. Patricks College Maynooth and to the residents of Maynooth Town. Have performed works by Irish composers, Martin O'Leary and Rachel Holstead. Rehearsal time is Wednesday 7.30- 9.45pm Music Dept, NUI Maynooth. Two productions per year.

Mayo Concert & Youth Orchestra

Pauline Rodgers
Spencer Street
Castlebar
Co. Mayo

Tel: +353 94 21794

Municipal School of Music Orchestras

Eileen Hudson
Acting Principal
Mulgrave Street
Limerick

Tel/Fax: +353 61 417348/+353 61 417011
Other key staff: David O'Connell (Violin/Viola/ Senior Orchestra)

There is a junior strings, middle orchestra, senior orchestra, wind band, brass ensemble and early music consort. Performed at the National Concert Hall during the Festival of Youth Orchestras in February 1999.

National Youth Orchestra of Ireland

Joanna Crooks
General Manager
37 Molesworth Street
Dublin 2

Tel/Fax: +353 1 6613642
Email: joanna@iol.ie
Website: //homepage.eircom.net/~nyoi

The National Youth Orchestra of Ireland (NYOI), has 200 members in 2 ensembles, one ensemble is for members aged 12-17 years and the other for those aged 18-23 years. Orchestra was established in 1970. Have participated in many festivals including Galway Arts Festival, Kilkenny Arts Festival and The Festival of British Youth Orchestras. Offers orchestral training and experience to the most talented young musicians in Ireland, throughout the period of their secondary and third level education. Annual auditions take place in Dublin, Cork, Sligo and Dundalk in October and November for the following season. The NYOI works under guest conductors. Concerts are regularly broadcast on RTÉ. The orchestras appear regularly at national venues including the National Concert Hall. Have appeared in Belfast's

Waterfront Hall in 1999 with Julian Lloyd Webber (cellist) who performed Elgar's Cello Concerto with the orchestra. Toured in the United States in 1998. Major works of symphonic repertoire are performed, sometimes involving choirs. Conductors booked to work with the orchestra include Albert Rosen, Roland Kieft, Alexander Anissimov, Roberto Benzi, En Shao and Andrey Boreyko. NYOI has commissioned a new work by Dr. Séoirse Bodley for the millennium. NYOI is an active member of the European Federation of National Youth Orchestras and will perform in August 2000 in the Konzerthaus, Berlin, in the ENFYO 2000 Festival as part of an extensive European tour. Fifteen productions per year. The orchestras meet in various locations throughout Ireland for intensive residential rehearsal periods.

Newpark Junior Orchestra
Hilda Milner
Administrator
Newtownpark Avenue
Blackrock
Co. Dublin

Tel/Fax: +353 1 2883740/+353 1 2883989
Email: newparkmusic@eircom.net
Other key staff: Nick Milne

There are 20-25 members, aged from 7-12 years. Area of special interest is classical music. Rehearsal time is Thursdays at 6.00 pm in Newpark Music Centre. Have performed in the National Concert Hall. Three productions per year.

RIAM Chamber Orchestra
Elizabeth Csibi
Director
Royal Irish Academy of Music
36-38 Westland Row
Dublin 2

Tel/Fax: +353 1 6764412/+353 1 6622798
Email: riam@indigo.ie
Website: www.riam.ie

There are 18 members. This chamber orchestra evolved from the RIAM Baroque Ensemble. Areas of special interest range from Bach, Vivaldi, Mozart, Tchaikovsky, Britten and into the 1990's with John Kinsella. Have performed at Kilkenny Arts Week, the Bank of Ireland Arts Centre, the National Gallery of Ireland and the National Concert Hall. The orchestra usually performs without a conductor which develops the musical awareness and musicianship of the players. Six productions per year. Rehearsal time is Friday evenings in the Royal Irish Academy of Music. (see advert)

RIAM Intermediate Orchestra
James Cavanagh
Conductor
Royal Irish Academy of Music
36-38 Westland Row
Dublin 2

Tel/Fax: +353 1 6764412/+353 1 6622798
Website: riam@indigo.ie
Website: www.riam.ie
Other key staff: Paddy McElwee (Manager)

There are 50-60 members, aged from 9-15 years. The orchestra produces approximately 6 performances per year. Have performed regularly throughout Ireland, most recently in the educational programmes 'Meet the Orchestra' at The Ark Children's Cultural Centre and 'Children Playing for Children' at the Royal Irish Academy of Music, also the National Concert Hall, the Watergate Theatre in Kilkenny and in various schools around the country. Have broadcast for RTÉ television and radio. Achievements include being presented with an award at the Irish Association of Youth Orchestra's Festival 1998, for its work with The Ark Children's Cultural Centre. Rehearsal time is Saturday mornings in the Royal Irish Academy of Music. (see advert)

RIAM Symphony Orchestra
James Cavanagh
Conductor
Royal Irish Academy of Music
36-38 Westland Row
Dublin 2

Tel/Fax: +353 1 6764412/+353 1 6622798
Email: riam@indigo.ie
Website: www.riam.ie
Other key staff: Paddy McElwee (Manager)

There are 80 members, aged between 16-23 years. Its members are from both the North and South of Ireland. Aims to provide a platform for RIAM students to perform as concerto soloists. Have performed regularly at the National Concert Hall. Rehearses a widely varying repertoire, which is performed regularly nationwide. Have made several radio and television appearances on such programmes as the Gay Byrne Show and 'Songs of Praise' for the BBC. Have performed at the Symphony Hall, Birmingham, as part of a collaboration with Birmingham Conservatoire. Participates in a concert/lecture programme. Distinguished students who have performed with the orchestra include cellist Gerald Peregrine, flautist Riona Ó Duinnín, and RTÉ's 1994 'Musician of the Future' pianist, Finghin Collins. Rehearsal time is Saturday afternoons in the Royal Irish Academy of Music.

St Canice's National School Orchestras

Regina O'Leary
Director
Maigh Eala
St Maul's
Kilkenny

Tel/Fax: +353 56 61479/+353 56 70552

There are 400 members in three orchestras, aged 4-12 years. Instruments that are played include all string instruments, trumpet, trombone, saxophone (alto and tenor), flutes, clarinet and guitar (electric and acoustic). Have participated in the Feis Ceoil Open Day at the National Concert Hall 1999. The main orchestra performs over seven times a year.

St Malachy's College Orchestra

Fr Gerry Magee
St Malachy's College
36 Antrim Road
Belfast BT15 2AE
Northern Ireland

Tel/Fax: 048 9074 8285/048 9074 1066
Email: gmagee@stmalachys.belfast.sch.uk

There are 70 members, aged 12-18 years. Areas of special interest are classical and romantic period repertoire. Have participated in Belfast Music Festival 1999, School Prom for Youth 1999, Irish Association of Youth Orchestra's Festival 1996, City of Belfast Schools of Music - Music Extravaganza 1999 and Celebration of Schools Music 1999. Have commissioned work by past pupil John Fitzpatrick. Two productions annually. Rehearsal time is Mon 3.30-4.45pm.

St Mary's Secondary School

Maura McAuliffe
Mallow
Co. Cork

Tel: +353 22 21998

There are 15 members (1st-6th years). Have participated in Feis Maitiu - Cork, Slógadh, Ringaskiddy Youth Festival, Voices of the World, Cork Choral Festival, Feile Luimní and Cor Fheile Corcaigh. Areas of special interest include orchestral and chamber music for strings and traditional arrangements for chamber groups. Achievements include winners of Slógadh, Feile Luimní and Ringaskiddy Youth Festival, Second place at Feis Maitiu.

Sacred Heart School Orchestra

Concepta Casserly
Sacred Heart Secondary School
Tullamore
Co. Offaly

Tel: +353 506 21747

Scoil Bhride Orchestra

Margaret Kelly
St Brigid's School
Athgarvan
The Curragh
Co. Kildare

Tel: +353 45 436852

South Eastern Music Centre Senior Youth Orchestra

Brian Agus
Director of Music Centre
South Eastern Music Centre
Church Road
Ballynahinch
Co. Down BT24 8LP
Northern Ireland

Tel/Fax: 048 9756 2989 or 048 9756 2030/ 048 9756 5120

There are 85 members, aged between 16-20 years. Have participated in the Irish Association of Youth Orchestras Festival in the National Concert Hall, Dublin. Areas of special interest include serious and light music, classical and romantic period music and contemporary music. Achievements include tours in Europe every second summer and performing in venues such as The Waterfront Hall Belfast, and the National Concert Hall, Dublin. Three productions per year. Rehearsal time is Saturday mornings from 10.00-12.30 pm at the South Eastern Music Centre, Ballynahinch.

Ulster Youth Orchestra

Paula McHugh
General Manager
Chamber of Commerce House
22 Great Victoria Street
Belfast BT2 7LX
Northern Ireland

Tel/Fax: 048 9027 8287/048 9033 3845

There are 100 members, aged between 14-21 years who are in full-time education. Special areas of interest include performing new works by Irish composers. Have participated in the Festival of British Youth Orchestras 1995 and the European Youth Orchestra Festival 1997. Performed a joint concert with the Ulster Orchestra in the Waterfront Hall, Belfast which was broadcast on BBC Northern Ireland television and was also broadcast on BBC Radio 3, Classic FM and BBC Radio Ulster. There is a residential course each August at the University of Ulster for 10 days with its staff and tutors. They perform in 2-4 productions per year.

University College Cork Orchestra
Dr John Godfrey
Music Department
University College Cork
Cork

Tel/Fax: +353 21 4904530/+353 21 4271595

Ursuline Convent Orchestra
Sr Rita Condon
Ursuline Convent
Thurles
Co. Tipperary

Tel: +353 504 21340

Wesley College Orchestra
Paula Dowzard
Wesley College
Ballinteer
Dublin 16

Tel/Fax: +353 1 2987066/+353 1 2987406
Email: admin@wesleycollege.ie

There are 30 members, aged between 12-18 years. Special areas of interest are classical and romantic music and music for strings. Have participated in the Irish Association of Youth Orchestras Festival 1998, Newpark Music Festival 1997 and the Wesley College Inter School which takes place annually in late February early March. Rehearsal time is each Wednesday for 40 minutes.

West Dublin Youth Orchestra
Angela Corr
53 The Paddock
Astown Gate
Dublin 15

Tel: +353 1 8681356

WIT Junior Strings
Deirdre Scanlon
Waterford Institute of Technology
College Street
Waterford

Tel: +353 51 878581

Young Dublin Symphonia
Dorothy Conaghan
Musical Director
190 Seapark
Malahide
Co. Dublin

Tel/Fax: +353 1 8451666
There are 30-35 members, aged from 13 -20 years. Have participated in the Feis Ceoil and the Irish Association of Youth Orchestras Festival. The group is a chamber orchestra comprising of strings and woodwind instruments. Areas of interest are Baroque and other string orchestra music, including jazz and traditional Irish music. Achievements include being winners at the Feis Ceoil, gaining the Pennys' Youth Orchestra Award for joint ventures in 1999, broadcasting live on both RTÉ radio and television. Produces 9 performances per year. Rehearsal is in the Presbyterian Church Hall in Malahide.

OTHER ORCHESTRAS

Ceoltóirí Óga Mobhí
Adele O'Dwyer
Music Director
Silver River Studios
Acontha, Durrow
Tullamore
Co. Offaly

Tel/Fax: +353 506 24044
Email: silverrivermusic@eircom.net

There are 60 members, aged 6-13 years. Participated in Cór Fhéile na Scoileanna, Dublin Feis Ceoil and Newpark Festival. Feis Ceoil winners in orchestra 'c' category. Five productions annually.

City of Belfast School of Music Training Orchestra
Paul McBride
Conductor
36 Antrim Road
Belfast

Co. Antrim BT15 2AE
Northern Ireland

Tel/Fax: 048 9074 8285/048 9074 1066
Email: correspondent@stmalachys.belfast.ni.sch.uk

There are 80 members, aged 12-19 years. Have partici-
pated in the festival of the Irish Association of Youth
Orchestras 1999 and 'Musical Extravaganza', 1999
Ulster Hall, Belfast. Area of special interest is classical
music. Recent programmes have included the 'Overture
to Ruslan and Ludmila' (Glinka), 'Montagues and
Capulets' (Prokofiev), 'Egmont Overture' (Beethoven),
Symphonies nos. 1 and 5 (Beethoven) and the 'Karelia
Suite' (Sibelius).

Clare Music Makers Performing Groups

Andrea Creech
Director
Nationwide House
Bank Place
Ennis
Co. Clare

Tel/Fax: +353 65 6842480/+353 65 7084905
Email: cmmacto@iol.ie
Website: www.iol.ie/~cmmacto

There are two groups, the first of which is the Clare
Music Makers (CMM), Strings with 25 members, aged
8-18 years. Areas of special interest are original repertoire for full string orchestra and effective arrangement
of popular classics. Have participated in Galway Arts
Festival, Feile Luimní and Summer Music in Clare
Festival. There are five productions per year. Rehearsal
time is Saturdays at Clare Music Makers. CMM also has
a flute choir with a maximum number of 20 members,
aged 12 years upwards. Areas of special interest in the
arrangement of standard and popular classics for flutes
of all sizes. Have participated in Feile Luimní, Galway
Arts Fringe and Summer Music in Clare Festival. There
are five productions per year. Rehearsal time is
Saturdays at CMM.

Irish Youth Wind Ensemble

Pat Mullen
Administrator
12 Strand Road
Portmarnock
Co. Dublin

Tel/Fax: +353 1 8557481/+353 1 8557508
Email: gywe@eircom.net

There are 55 members, aged 16-25 years. Special interest in performance of original and quality wind music
composed for wind ensembles. Have participated in the
British Association of Symphonic Bands & Wind
Ensembles Festival 1987, Aberdeen Festival of Music
1995, 1996 and 1997, Kilkenny Arts Festival 1985 and
1999. Two productions held each year. Meet in August
in Dublin each year.

Iveragh Youth Orchestra

Adolf Packeiser
Clahane
Cahirciveen
Co. Kerry

Tel/Fax: +353 66 9472571

There are 12 members, aged 8-15 years. Special interest
in traditional music and early baroque music.
Participated in the Celtic Music Festival, Cahircaiveen
1997, 1998 and 1999. Perform various concerts in the
locality. Also runs the Kerry Orchestra for those aged
15-65 and older. Kerry Orchestra have toured in Europe
and have produced a tape of their performances.
Rehearsal time Wednesdays, 8pm, at Scoile na Skellige.

Kildare International School of Excellence for Young Musicians Youth Orchestras

Christian Tecklenborg
Principal
Herbert Lodge Arts Centre
The Curragh
Co. Kildare

Tel/Fax: +353 45 481598

There are two orchestras, Junior and Senior. Members
are aged from 9-16 years. Participated at the Brigidine
Festival and Millennium Gardens opening 1999. Past
pupils involved in Co. Kildare Orchestra. Four productions annually. Rehearsal Mon 5-6pm for the Junior
Orchestra) and Thurs 6-8pm for the Senior Orchestra.

Laurel Hill Coláiste FCJ Senior Orchestra

Orla Colgan-Ahern
Director
South Circular Road
Limerick

Tel/Fax: +353 61 313636/+353 61 315373

There are 25-30 members aged 14-18 years. Winners of
Feis Ceoil, Sligo Feis Ceoil and Slógadh. Three productions annually. Rehearsal once a week at school.

Leinster Orchestra
Sarah Lane
Conductor
Leinster School of Music
Griffith College
South Circular Road
Dublin 8

Tel/Fax: +353 1 4751532/+353 1 4549265
Email: leinster_school@gcd.ie
Website: www.gcd.ie

The number of members varies from year to year and there is no age limit. Areas of special interest include playing for patients in various hospitals. Performs a minimum of two but usually five concerts per year. Rehearsal time is Wednesdays from 7.00-9.30 pm at Griffith College.

Music Matters Orchestra/Ensembles
Máire Ní Dhuibhir
Director
New Inn
Béal Átha na Slua
Co. Na Gaillimhe

Tel/Fax: +353 905 75880/+353 905 75773
Email: tommaire@eircom.net

Junior, intermediate string ensembles, senior ensembles and orchestra meet on a project basis for workshops. The ensembles and orchestra perform at an annual concert in February and participate in other concerts when invited. The ensembles and orchestra cater for all age groups the youngest member being 8 years of age. The baroque string group plays at weddings and the orchestra has played in the National Concert Hall, Dublin.

North Eastern Education & Library Board Music Service
Eric Boyd
Head of Music Services
Antrim Board Centre
17 Lough Road
Co. Antrim BT41 4DH
Northern Ireland

Tel/Fax: 048 9448 2231 or 048 9448 2233/
048 9446 0224

There are 700 members in the various groups, aged between 9-19 years. The music service supports 4 regional string orchestras, 3 symphony orchestras, 3 wind bands, a harp ensemble and a percussion group. Each group produces 2 productions per year, in addition

to a summer school and tour. Rehearsal time for regional groups is on weekday evenings, while centre-based groups meet on Saturday morning.

Scoil Mhuire Orchestra
Ashlyn Carter
Rath Stewart
Athy
Co. Kildare

Tel: +353 507 38215

There are 25-35 members. Areas of special interest are classical and traditional music. Have Participated in Telethon 1999 and various local events including carol services. Eight productions annually.

Southern Education & Library Board Music Service
Youth Orchestra
Martin White
Head of Performance
Bann House, Bridge Street
Portadown
Co. Armagh BT63 5AE
Northern Ireland

Tel/Fax: 048 3833 2371/048 3839 4525
Email: selbmusic@hotmail.com

There are 20 groups with a total of 900 students, aged between 8-21 years. The groups are non-competitive. Have performed in Atlanta, Georgia, summer 1999 and Paris, summer 1997. The youth orchestra and youth band undertake a concert tour every two years.

St Vincents Secondary School Orchestra
Ita Mc Mahon
Director
St Mary's Road
Cork

Tel/Fax: +353 21 4307730/+353 21 4367252
Email: vincentsoffice@eircom.net

Members aged 12-18 years.

Tutti Con Belto Youth Orchestra
Hugh Kelly
Director

1 Oaklands
Salthill
Co. Galway

Tel: +353 91 526394

Ulster Youth Jazz Orchestra
Ken Jordan
Director
29 Glendarragh
Belfast BT4 2WB
Northern Ireland

Tel/Fax: 048 9076 0403
Email: kenjordan@connectfree.co.uk

There are 30 members, aged from 15-21 years. Have participated in the Music For Youth National Jazz Festival. The aims of the orchestra are to entertain audiences with performances all over Ireland and beyond and to educate its members in the idiom of jazz through rehearsals and courses. The orchestra is available for hire. Achievements include winning the Bass Arts Award in 1997, tour of Austria 1998 and Holland 1999, winning the regional section of the Daily Telegraph Young Jazz Competition. Client partners of the Arts Council of Northern Ireland. Perform 40 concerts per year. Rehearsal time is from 2-5.00 pm on Saturdays during the months of September-April in the Music Department of the Methodist College, Belfast.

Young European Strings Chamber Orchestra
Maria Kelemen
Director
21 The Close
Cypress Downs
Templeogue
Dublin 6w

Tel/Fax: +353 1 4905263/+353 1 4920355
Email: yes@iol.ie

There are 25 members, aged from 7-16 years. Special areas of interest include classical string orchestra repertoire from the 18th to the 20th centuries, contemporary and crossover music. Have participated in the Autumn Sound Fest, the Summer Sound Fest, Feis Ceoil (Category A cupwinners in 1999), and have appeared in one of Michaels Barrymore's television shows. Achievements include an invitation to perform in St. Petersburg, Russia, in April 2000. The orchestra perform between 10-15 concerts per year. Rehearsal time is Saturdays from 12.00-1.00 pm in Zion National School, Dublin 6.

YOUTH CHOIRS

Cumann Náisiúnta na gCór - Association of Irish Choirs
Margaret O'Sullivan
Acting Chief Executive Officer
Administrator
Drinan Street
Cork City

Tel/Fax: +353 21 4312296/+353 21 4962457
Email: cnc@iol.ie   (see advert page 7).

Alexandra College Choirs
Brenda Wilkes
Head of Music
Alexandra College
Milltown
Dublin 6

Tel/Fax: +353 1 4977571/+353 1 4974873
Email: alexadm@iol.ie
Other key staff: Ron Cooney (Wind Band Director), Vanessa Sweeney (Intermediate Strings)

There are two choirs, College Choir 15-18 years, Intermediate Choir 12-15 years. Feis Ceoil winners. Four productions per year. Rehearsal is from 4-5pm at school.

Bray Music Centre Junior Choir
Patricia McCarry
Florence Road
Bray
Co. Wicklow

Tel: +353 1 2866768

Members are aged 8-15 years. Areas of special interest include Irish music and songs both in Irish and English, French, Italian and German with a particular emphasis on French song. This choir are Feis Ceoil winners, Arklow Music Festival winners and Rosebowl winners. Rehearsal time is Tuesday from 4.15-5.15pm. Perform end of term concerts three times a year.

Camerata
Anne Grennan
Director
Balgatheran
Tullyallen

Drogheda
Co. Louth

Tel: +353 41 9837843
Email: agrennan@eircom.net

There are 22 members, aged 18 years and upwards. It is a 4-part mixed choir who perform sacred works at Mass each month. Have participated in Navan, Dundalk and Carrickmacross Choral Festivals in the past and North Wales Stenna Choral Festival in Llandudno, Wales. Areas of special interest include participation at choral festivals, performances of short works such as Vivaldi's 'Gloria' and Fauré's Requiem, encouraging and supporting young singers in the performance of contemporary works. Most members also sing with the Irish Youth Choir. Achievements include second place in its 2 most recent competitions. Rehearsal time is on Tuesdays 8-9.30 pm at Val Halla, Friar Street, Drogheda.

Cór na nÓg RTÉ
Blánaid Murphy
Musical Director
16 Westgate St
Augustine Street
Dublin 8

Tel/Fax: +353 1 6773712 +353 1 6773712
Email: blanaidm@gofree.indigo.ie

There are 80 members, aged 8-14 years. Areas of special interest in performing skills and vocal training for children. Have performed at the RTÉ Proms, Cork International Choral Festival, National Concert Hall and the Point Theatre. Have featured on several CDs, 'Songs of Praise' for BBC, RTÉ TV and Radio. Six to nine productions every year. Rehearsal time is Wed 5.30-7pm and Sat 10-12.30pm. Contact for new applicants is Catherine Kennedy Tel: +353 1 2082480.

Irish Youth Choir
Margaret O'Sullivan
Acting Chief Executive Officer
Cumann Náisiúnta na gCór
Drinan Street
Cork

Tel/Fax: +353 21 4312296/+353 21 4962457
Email: iyc@cnc.iol.ie

There are 120 members (mixed voice), aged 17-29 years. Performs large scale works from the choral repertory, with orchestral or organ accompaniment. Commissioned works includes de Barra's 'Canticum in Laudibus' 1988 and Gerard Victory's 'The Everlasting Voices' 1993. Have participated in Kilkenny Arts Week, Cork International Choral Festival, Ennis Arts, Music for

Wexford, Sense of Cork Arts Festival, Celtic Connections (South Wales). Two to four productions per year. Annual week long residential rehearsal course (usually at the beginning of July or the end of August).

Kerry School of Music Choirs
Aidan O'Carroll
Director
Old Customs House
High Street
Tralee

Tel/Fax: +353 66 7125690/+353 66 7120077
Email: kerrymusicschool@eircom.net

Contact Kerry School of Music for details.

Kildare International School of Excellence for Young Musicians Youth Choirs
Christian Tecklenborg
Principal
Herbert Lodge Arts Centre
The Curragh
Co. Kildare

Tel/Fax: +353 45 481598
Other key staff: Ita O'Donovan (Choral Director)

There are two choirs, the Young Kildare Singers and the New Kildare Chorale. Members aged 5-9 years and 9-16 years. Have participated at the Brigidine Festival and Millennium Gardens opening 1999. Four productions annually. Rehearsal time is Wednesday 5-5.30pm (Young Kildare Singers) and 5.30-6.30pm (New Kildare Chorale).

Kilkenny Youth Choir
Philip Edmondson
Conductor
Kilkenny School of Music
Ormonde Road
Kilkenny

Tel: +353 56 62969

This choir meets on Saturdays from 11-1 pm in Kilkenny School of Music. The choir is for girls of secondary school age only, and performs between two and three concerts per year. The choir has performed in most towns and cities throughout Ireland, and has completed concert tours to Wales, Cambridge and France. The choir has also participated in exchange visits. Area of special interest is classical repertoire. The choir has performed on television and radio, in the National Concert Hall, Dublin, and has featured in Kilkenny Arts Week. (see also orchestras)

Laurel Hill Coláiste FCJ Senior Choir

Orla Colgan-Ahern
Director
Laurel Hill Coláiste FCJ
South Circular Road
Limerick

Tel/Fax: +353 61 313636/+353 61 315373

There are 130 members, aged 12-18 years. Areas of special interest include contemporary Irish Music. Have Participated in Cork Choral Festival, Telecom Eireann Schools Choir Competition and Church Music International. Winners of Cork Choral Festival and Telecom Eireann Schools Choir Competition. Four productions annually. Rehearsal twice a week at school.

The National Childrens Choir - Cór na nÓg

Colette Hussey
Organiser
Roth Rua Lodge
Kilgobbin Road
Sandyford
Dublin 18

Tel: +353 1 2941806

Founded in 1985 by Seán Creamer. Aims to foster a love of choral singing among primary school pupils. An average of 8,500 children participate in the choir bi-annually. Membership of this choir is open to pupils of 5th and 6th classes of any primary school in Ireland. The participating children are taught a common repertoire of songs in their own schools. The success of the choir is teacher involvement. Area rehearsals are school based throughout the year (approx 4). Each area (groups of 300 -500 children) hosts a local concert where all children who have learned the repertoire perform in public. This bi-annual event culminates in 1,000 children, representing all affiliated schools, being selected to perform in the National Concert Hall in a three-night event. The choir is sponsored by the ESB.

Pontana Childrens Choir

Anne Grennan
Balgatheran
Tullyallen
Drogheda
Co. Louth

Tel: +353 41 9837843
Email: agrennan@eircom.net

There are 54 members. Special areas of interest include the performance of contemporary works, and have performed Seamas Heaney's 'Poetry to Music'. Have participated in national and international festivals, the Festival of Song, RTÉ Late Late Show and on RTÉ Radio One. Have travelled abroad in 1988 to represent Ireland in the opening ceremony of the European Cup Final, to Holland for the 24th Maastricht Convention, have hosted visits from America, Italian and German choirs in the past.

St. Mary's Secondary School Youth Choir

Maura McAuliffe
Mallow
Co. Cork

Tel: +353 22 21998

St. Patrick's Cathedral Choir

John Dexter
Organist and Master of the Choristers
St. Patricks Cathedral Choir School
St. Patricks Close
Dublin 8

Tel/Fax: +353 1 4531867/+353 1 4539472
Email: stpcath@iol.ie
Website: www.stpatrickscathedral.ie

There are approximately 20 boys aged, 9-13 years and approximately 3 prosationers aged 8-9 years. Area of special interest is church music. Have participated in festivals such as the Dublin International Organ and Choral Festival. Have CD recordings and RTÉ and BBC broadcasts, TV documentaries, backed pop groups (Erasure and The Cranberries), have sung at national services and special events. The Choir sing services everyday except on Saturday when the boys attend choir school.

St Vincents Secondary School Choir

Ita McMahon
Director
St Mary's Road
Cork

Tel/Fax: +353 21 4307730/+353 21 4367252
Email: vincentsoffice@eircom.net

Members aged 12-18 years.

Young Cantoiri
Mary O'Donnell
Music Director
Waltons New School of Music
69 South Great George's Street
Dublin 2

Tel/Fax: +353 1 4781884/+353 1 4751346

Children's mixed choir, aged 9-12 years. Rehearsal is at
Waltons New School of Music. (see advert)

Music Educationalists/ Community Musicians

MUSIC EDUCATIONALISTS / COMMUNITY MUSICIANS

Rory Adams

Castleruddery
Dondard
Co. Wicklow

Tel: +353 45 404929
Mobile: +353 87 2397473

Areas of special interest includes the use of rhythm through African drums and percussion instruments and melody making through use of SOLFA. Has worked with creches, pre-schools, primary schools, post-primary institutions, gives private tuition, community groups and summer camps. Examples of activities offered within projects includes percussion and vocal workshops, composition based activity with story/music link, performance orientated tuition, recording composition on cassette tape and instrument making projects. Available for work in the Dublin, Wicklow, Carlow and Kildare areas. Qualifications include a Diploma in Classical Guitar.

Elaine Agnew

17 Deerpark Road
Killwaughter
Larne
Co. Antrim BT40 2PW
Northern Ireland

Tel: 048 2827 7566

Areas of special interest includes work in education and community environments with a special emphasis on healthcare environments, children with special needs, young children aged 4-7 years and adults out of the education framework. Has worked in primary/secondary/grammar schools, specialist music schools, projects with professional ensembles e.g Irish Chamber Orchestra, Ulster Orchestra, and arts centres and County Councils. Work experience in community based settings includes remand centres (Ards Peninsula), prisons (HMP Maze), psychiatric hospital (Knockbracken), St. Annes Youth & Community Centre, ethnic minority groups (Chinese and Asian communities) in Glasgow. Examples of activities offered within projects include composition, use of percussion, body percussion, voice workshops and participatory workshops. Is a member of the Arts Council of Northern Irelands Artists in Schools programme 1999/2000. Qualifications include: BMus from The Queen's University Belfast, Postgraduate Certificate in Composition from the Royal Scottish Academy of Music and Drama.

Joy Beattie

6 Upper Celtic Park
Enniskillen BT47 6JA
Northern Ireland

Tel: 048 6632 2753

Plays the viola. Has worked with Belfast School of Music and a Turkish summer camp. Is a member of the Arts Council of Northern Irelands Artists in Schools programme 1999/2000. Graduate of The Queen's University Belfast and the Royal Scottish Academy of Music and Drama, Glasgow.

Libby Bennett

23 Middle Braniel Road
Belfast BT5 7TU
Northern Ireland

Tel: 048 9079 1937

Has worked in schools under the 'Adopt A Player' scheme, is a member of the Ulster Orchestra, has written and performed in childrens radio programmes for BBC Northern Ireland and is a member of the Phoenix Duo and the Belfast Wind Quintet. Examples of activities offered within projects are sound stories, i.e music to 'The Pied Piper', creative music making by looking at childrens outside environments e.g the weather or painting a picture. Is a member of the Arts Council of Northern Irelands Artists in Schools programme 1999/2000.

Colin Blakey

The Crock
Ballyakenny
Drogheda
Co. Louth

Tel: +353 41 9822944
Email: ainecol@gofree.indigo.ie
Website: http://gofree.indigo.ie/~ainecol/recap

Areas of special interest includes collective music making through percussion e.g samba, use of computer technology to explore creativity, teaching classical guitar and composition. Has worked with City Arts Centre Dublin, Mela Festival Edinburgh, Droichead Arts Centre Drogheda, Drogheda Samba School, Upstate Theatre Project and Drogheda School of Performing Arts. Work experience in community based settings includes FÁS projects, adult groups engaged in personal development, youth theatre and samba groups in Ireland and Scotland. Examples of activities offered within projects includes: collective music making with percussion, based on Afro Brazilian and Afro Cuban traditions, workshops with the use of computer software recording technology and the composition of new pieces of music. Qualifications include: a Diploma in Community Arts and Community Development (CAFE accredited by NUI Maynooth).

Yvonne Blythe
72 Downview Gardens
Belfast BT15 4GH
Northern Ireland

Tel/Fax: 048 9028 9051

Areas of special interest includes music for disabled people, those with learning difficulties, world and ethnic music, classical/jazz and choral music. Has worked with the Drake Music Project, Share Music and Beechwood Special School. Work experience in community based settings includes work with Belfast Community Drum Circle and 'Voca Loca' which is a Womens singing collective. Qualifications include a BMus.

David Boyd
2 Claremont Villas
Adelaide Road
Glenageary
Co. Dublin

Tel/Fax: +353 1 2841819
Email: daveb@irishmusicians.com

Areas of special interest includes music technology, percussion and personal/group development. Has worked with The Ark Childrens' Cultural Centre, Opera Northern Ireland, Combat Poverty Agency, RTÉ, TG4, Department of Education and Skyros Holistic Holidays. Instruments include piano, guitar, percussion, didjereedoo and bodhrán. Examples of activities offered within projects includes percussion/vocal workshops, improvisation, composition workshops and technology/recording. Qualifications include a BA in Performing Arts/ Psychology in Interpersonal Behaviour.

Paul Boyd
13 Briarwood Park
Belfast BT5 7H2
Northern Ireland

Tel: 048 9079 0755

Areas of special interest include work with students from primary to third level education and those with special needs. Is a member of the Arts Council of Northern Irelands Artists in Schools programme 1999/2000.

Nico Brown
'Fenit'
Strand Road
Bray
Co. Wicklow

Tel: +353 1 2862566
Email: nicobrown41@yahoo.co.uk

Areas of special interest includes work with children to make music for family audiences and groups. Has worked with The Ark Childrens' Cultural Centre as the musician-in-residence.

John Buckley
4 Ayrefield Grove
Malahide Road
Dublin 13

Tel: +353 1 8475042
Email: jbuck@indigo.ie
Website: www.cmc.ie/composers/buckley.html

Areas of special interest includes musical creativity and compositional workshops for primary students to adults. Has worked with the National Concert Hall, The Arts Council, The Ark Childrens' Cultural Centre, Music Association of Ireland, Department of Education, Music Network, National Chamber Choir, National University of Ireland, Maynooth, Samhlaíocht Chiarraí and others. Examples of activities offered within projects includes composition based activity and curriculum based activity both interactive and participatory. Has produced education based composition suitable for student performance. Full time composer, member of Aosdána and the Association of Irish Composers.

Brian Burns
Clotworthy Arts Centre
Randalstown Road
Antrim BT41 4LH
Northern Ireland

Tel/Fax: 048 9442 8000/048 9446 0366

Area of special interest is community music development. Has worked with schools and colleges, third level institutions, adult education centres, those with special needs, youth groups and older people. At present is co-ordinator of a 3 year music development programme aimed at the local community. Examples of activities offered within projects includes percussion/vocal workshops, composition based activities and curriculum based activities.

Bill Campbell
20 Abbots Road
Newtownabbey
Co. Antrim BT37 9RB
Northern Ireland

Tel: 048 9036 4569

Has worked with special needs groups, Opera Northern Ireland and the Arts Council of Northern Ireland. Examples of work experience in community based settings includes CAFE Dublin. Examples of activities offered within projects includes vocal/percussion workshops and the use of multi-media. Qualifications include: BMus and an MPhil in Music Composition.

Tom Clarke
9 Ardmore Avenue
Belfast BT7 3HD
Northern Ireland

Tel: 048 9020 8909
Email: tom.jean@cableol.co.uk

Is director of the 'Jigtime Programme', which gives a knowledge and appreciation of Irish music and song to school children. Is a member of the Arts Council of Northern Irelands Artists in Schools programme 1999/2000.

Shane Constable
Incheese
Kilgarvan
Killarney
Co. Kerry

Tel/Fax: +353 64 85506/+353 64 31748

Area of special interest is samba music. Has worked with the Kerry Diocesan Youth Service in Killarney. Examples of activities are ten week projects leading to a level of performance on completion.

Julie Craig
24 Castlewood
Enniskillen
Co. Fermanagh BT74 6BF
Northern Ireland

Mobile: 048 7788 440300
Email: juliecraig10@hotmail.com

Areas of special interest are teaching, performing and workshop work. Has worked with schools and colleges and is Musical Director at Dee Street Community Centre Belfast. Examples of activities offered within projects includes percussion/vocal workshops particularly with children aged 5-12 years. Is a member of the Arts Council of Northern Irelands Artists in Schools programme 1999/2000. Qualifications include: BMus, PGCE and a Certificate in Community Development.

Dr. Cliona Doris
35 The Meadows
Strangford Road
Downpatrick BT30 6LN
Northern Ireland

Tel/Fax: 048 4461 3856/048 4461 7740

Works with students from lower primary to further education following the music curriculum guidelines. Is a member of the Arts Council of Northern Irelands Artists in Schools programme 1999/2000.

Ewan Easton
39 Ballyhome Road
Bangor BT20 5JR
Northern Ireland

Tel/Fax: 048 9145 2644/048 9127 5355

Areas of special interest includes working with children of all abilities, working with those from lower primary education to further education. Examples of activities offered within projects includes introducing students to composition and performance within the curriculum guidelines. Is a member of the Ulster Orchestra and is a member of the Arts Council of Northern Irelands Artists in Schools programme 1999/2000.

Ray Fahy
Knocknakilla
Kilflynn
Tralee
Co. Kerry

Tel: +353 66 7132681
Email: randbfahy@fsmail.net

Area of special interest is work with children and youth groups. Has worked in primary and secondary schools, youth groups, Kerry Travellers Development Project and with Cardiff County Council. Facilitates workshops and offers staff training on the use of music to children and youth groups. Examples of activities offered within projects includes the use of percussion instruments, scrap instrument making, 'Rock School' project, composition (lyric writing, rap and techno). Also teaches banjo, guitar and keyboards. Qualifications include a Certificate in Teaching Skills (Community Music Wales/Dartington College of Arts).

Stephen Gardner
10 Royal Terrace West
Dun Laoghaire
Co. Dublin

Tel: +353 1 2842136

Has worked with community groups and was composer in residence with Dun Laoghaire/Rathdown Council. Examples of activities offered within projects are composition and vocal workshops. (see also page composer/arranger)

Len Graham

4 Glendesha Road
Mullaghbawn
Newry
Co. Down BT35 9XN
Northern Ireland

Tel: 048 3088 8135

Area of special interest is Irish traditional folksong. Works with those aged 7-14 years. Has recorded a collection of traditional songs in English for young people (Gael-Linn records). Is a member of the Arts Council of Northern Irelands Artists in Schools programme 1999/2000.

Hayley Howe

63 Surrey Street
Belfast BT9 7FR
Northern Ireland

Tel: 048 9020 9784

Areas of special interest include violin tuition and workshops to introduce string instruments to primary school children and offers masterclasses for students of the violin in secondary schools. Examples of activities offered within projects include an introduction and demonstration of string instruments to children, study of the violin and an interactive workshop. Is a member of the Arts Council of Northern Irelands Artists in Schools programme 1999/2000. Qualifications include: MMus, PGCE and LTCL Teaching Diploma.

Fergus Johnston

16 Trader's Wharf
40-43 Usher's Quay
Dublin 8

Tel/Fax: +353 1 6728864
Email: fergusjohnston@eircom.net
Website: www.cmc.ie/composers/johnston.html

Areas of special interest are contemporary music, composition in schools, music technology and community music projects. Has worked with the National Concert Hall 'In Tune Music Residencies', Opera Theatre Company schools projects with the 'Four Note Opera', National Symphony Orchestra of Ireland, Irish Chamber Orchestra, Young European Strings and the Project Arts Centre. Work experience with community based projects includes the Eastern Health Board Arts Projects with 'Soilse' for recovering drug addicts. Examples of activities offered within projects are composition based activity for children, which to date has principally been with children aged 7-12 years with some elements directed at the Leaving Certificate syllabus, in the areas of interactive music and algorithmic composition. Is a member of Iream's Forum and Aosdána. Qualifications include: LTCL, BA Moderatorship in Music from Trinity College, Dublin and MPhil from Trinity College, Dublin.

Hilda Leader

Rahaniskey
Whitechurch
Co. Cork

Mobile: +353 87 6247901
Email: hilda@esatclear.ie

Areas of special interest are in community music and cross-arts work with music and drama. Has worked with the Irish Chamber Orchestra, National Symphony of Ireland, primary schools mainly in Cork City, Opera Theatre Company (viola work performance), Cork School of Music, Cork VEC and primary schools in London. Examples of activities offered within projects includes percussion/vocal workshops, composition based activity and instrumental workshops. Qualifications include: a Dip CSM, ALCM, LGSMO, BMus from Guildhall School of Music and Drama.

Michelle McCormack

68 Annsville
Rathfriland Road
Newry
Co. Down BT34 1AB
Northern Ireland

Tel: 048 3025 2944 (h) or 048 3025 7502 (w)

Has worked in Amsterdam and Vancouver for composition residencies. Areas of special interest include community music that involves talks and demonstrations with the audience and the use of music technology equipment. Works with all age groups. Founder of the Drake Music Project which specialises in providing access to music making for people with disabilities. Qualifications include: BMus from University of Ulster, MSc in Music Technology and a PhD from City University London.

Iain McCurdy

14 Ebor Drive
Belfast BT12 6NR
Northern Ireland

Tel: 048 9059 2416
Email: i_mccurdy@hotmail.com

Areas of special interest includes music technology, composition and improvisation. Works with those who have learning or physical disabilities, older people and primary/secondary schools. Examples of activities offered within projects includes percussion, Javanese gamelan, music creation and performance using all aspects of Midi. Qualifications include: BMus and an MA in Music Technology.

Paul McGuirk

c/o Galway City Partnership
Kiltartan House
Forster Street
Galway

Tel/Fax: +353 91 566617/+353 91 566618
Email: services@gcg.iol.ie

Areas of special interest includes using music to helpl with social exclusion. Has worked with Foróige, Sound People, Cerebral Palsy Ireland, the Gulbenkian Foundation, youth organisations, schools, traveller organisations, nursing homes, mens' groups and after-schools programmes. Examples of activities offered within projects are percussion/vocal workshops, instrument making, songwriting, music games, cross-arts and composition. Qualifications include: one year Community Training Programme.

Deirdre McKay

21 Hall Road
Ballynahinch
Co. Down BT24 8XY
Northern Ireland

Tel: 048 9756 2640
Email: d.t.mckay@qub.ac.uk

Areas of special interest include composition projects involving collaboration with other performing art forms and with professional orchestras/ensembles. Has worked with Opera Northern Ireland, Irish Chamber Orchestra, Sonorities Contemporary Music Festival and Ulster Orchestras education project and vocal composition with music for dance/theatre project in Bangor. Examples of activities offered within projects includes percussion/voice workshops and composition based activity. Qualifications include: BMus, Mus.M (Composition).

Kevin McNicholas

Co-ordinator
Access Music Project
St. Patricks Bandhall
c/o Galway City Partnership
Forster Street
Galway

Mobile/Fax: +353 86 8595366/+353 91 566618
Email: kevinmac@iol.ie

Paul Marshall

32 Rugby Avenue
Bangor BT20 3PZ
Northern Ireland

Tel/Fax: 048 9145 5737
Email: paul@drumtec.com
Website: www.drumtec.com

Areas of special interest includes work with visual artists and children using multi-media. Has worked with the Old Museum Arts Centre and Belfast Community Drum Circle. Qualifications include: MBA and DMS.

Ricky Matson

27 Orange Lane
Magheralin
Craigavon BT67 ORG
Northern Ireland

Tel: 048 9261 3060

Area of special interest is those with special needs. Examples of activities offered within projects includes working with children on all aspects of music, performance and composition. Is a member of the Arts Council of Northern Irelands Artists in Schools programme 1999/ 2000. Qualifications include: AGSM in performance and teaching from Guildhall School of Music and Drama.

Tony Maude

c/o Teresa Larkin
Cusack Road
Ennis
Co. Clare

Tel: +353 65 6841519
Email: teresalar.ennis@eircom.net

Areas of special interest includes performance of poems and verse. Examples of activities offered within projects include workshops with music and rhythm/riddle writing. Produces a performance by using established literature and the use of percussion instruments.

Gabriela Mayer

56 Pembroke Road
Dublin 4

Tel: +353 1 6683223
Email: mayerga@esat.clear.ie

Has worked with the National Concerts Hall Outreach Programme. Examples of activities includes music appreciation workshops. Qualifications include: MMus and DMA.

Brian Morrissey

Benedine
Nenagh
Co. Tipperary

Mobile: +353 87 2038823
Email: morrissey@hotmail.com

Qualified with BA with music and HDip. Has worked with Music Network and UCC. Examples of activities include traditional music and percussion musical appreciation workshops.

Phil Mullen

27 Cavendish Mansions
Clerkenwell Road
London EC1R 5DO
England

Tel: +44 20 7833 2433
Email: phil.mullen@ul.ie

Areas of special interest includes community music with young people, work in healthcare environments and with those who are socially excluded. Has worked in primary/secondary/third level education, The Ark Childrens Cultural Centre, CAFE Dublin, Irish World Music Centre and Cork School of Music. Examples of activities offered within projects are composition work, songwriting, world music, rhythm based workshops, cross-arts and project development. At present is Director of the MA in Community Music course at the Irish World Music Centre and is also the Director of Sound People who organise special music education projects.

Michèle Murphy

19 Riverwood Crescent
Castleknock
Dublin 15

Tel/Fax: +353 1 8226541

Qualified with BMus, Diploma in Music Therapy from the Guildhall School of Music and Drama and the University of York. Also BSc in Physiotherapy.

Martin O'Dwyer

Windmill House
Cashel
Co. Tipperary

Tel/Fax: +353 62 62193

Area of special interest is traditional guitar. Has worked in primary and secondary schools.

Anne Marie O'Farrell

28 Grange Manor Drive
Rathfarnham
Dublin 6w

Tel/Fax: +353 1 493 1873
Email: amofharp@iol.ie

Has worked with Music Network and Camphill Communities. Activities include illustrated recitals. Qualifications include: MA, LRSM, LLCL, LLCM, ARIAM and ALCM.

Miriam O'Sullivan

c/o The Ark Childrens' Cultural Centre
11a Eustace Street
Temple Bar
Dublin 2

Tel/Fax: +353 1 6707788/+353 1 6707758
Email: miriam@ark.ie
Website: www.ark.ie

Areas of special interest includes flute performance, directing and organising courses in music for primary teachers and directing childrens choral and recorder groups. Has worked with primary schools through her work at The Ark. Is working collaboratively with the National Concert Hall, Contemporary Music Centre, Opera Theatre Company and Improvised Music Company, youth groups, outreach groups and other venues e.g childrens' hospitals. Examples of activities offered within projects include courses for children in composition, choral, percussion and technology, family concerts, organising the annual 'MusicFest' Festival in The Ark in spring each year. Is the founder member of FUAIM - The Association for the Promotion of Primary Level Music and Secretary of this association from 1997-1998. Qualifications include: BEd and ALCM (flute).

Steve Pickett

2 Clonaver Crescent North
Belfast BT4 2FD
Northern Ireland

Tel: 048 9067 3115

Area of special interest is composing music for school orchestras both at primary and secondary levels. Member of the Ulster Orchestra and founder member of the Belfast Wind Quartet. Is a member of the Arts Council of Northern Irelands Artists in Schools programme 1999/2000.

Brendan Popplestone
136 Haypark Avenue
Belfast BT7 3FG
Northern Ireland

Tel: 048 9029 0468

Areas of special interest includes songwriting and performance, use of percussion, singing, recording, arranging and use of multimedia. Has worked with Opera Northern Ireland, Down Arts Centre and Belfast Musicians Collective, Open Arts, Wheelworks, Association for Mental Health and Extern in Bulgaria. Examples of activities offered within projects are percussion/vocal workshops, songwriting and composition, curriculum based music, use of technology, drum making and cross-art form collaborations. Is a member of the Arts Council of Northern Irelands Artists in Schools programme 1999/2000. Qualifications include a Certificate in Music from Ulster University at Jordanstown.

Possibilities Network
Ruth Walsh and David Stewart
111 Drumbo Road
Lisburn
Co. Antrim BT27 5TX
Northern Ireland

Tel: 048 9082 6932

Paul Roe
227 Grace Park Heights
Drumcondra
Dublin 9

Tel: +353 1 8376884
Mobile: +353 87 2393173
Email: pproe@eircom.net

Has worked with the National Concert Hall Outreach Programme, Concorde Ensemble and Music Network. Qualifications include: LTCL and FTCL.

Colin Stark
41 Somerton Park
Belfast BT15 4DP
Northern Ireland

Tel: 048 9077 2325 (h) or 048 9066 4535 (w)
Email: colin.stark@ukgateway.net

Areas of special interest include work with students from upper primary to higher education. Examples of activities offered within projects includes all aspects of music in education from performing to preparing for a career in music. Is a member of the Arts Council of Northern Ireland's Artists in Schools programme 1999/2000. Qualifications include a BMus.

Edel Sullivan
'St. Josephs'
Scart Hill
Donnbrook
Douglas
Cork

Tel: +353 21 4361267
Email: edelfiddle@postmark.net

Areas of special interest includes early intervention through music with pre-school children who have special needs, creative music making through improvisation/composition, tuition in violin and piano. Has worked with primary and secondary schools, The National Concert Hall, Irish World Music Centre, Cork School of Music, Cork County VEC and the Camden Secondary Learning Support Service for young people with emotional and behavioural difficulties. Examples of activities offered within projects include composition and recording workshops, workshops in improvisation and folk styles and workshops aimed to encourage physical, emotional and intellectual development. Qualifications include: RMTH (Registered Music Therapist), BMus, Dip CSM, LTCL and MTTC (Community Music Ltd).

Stuart Tanner
24 Windsor Gardens
Bangor BT20 3DD
Northern Ireland

Tel/Fax: 048 9146 7052
Mobile: +44 1159 602614
Email: stuarttanner@compuserve.com

Areas of special interest includes tuition and performance in conducting, arranging, composing and piano. Has worked in many primary, secondary and third level institutions and church youth groups. Examples of activities offered within projects are piano/brass/composition workshops, computer based work and preparation for exams. Works with all age groups. Qualifications include: BMus (Hons), LRAM and LTCL.

Joe Thoma

Gorthamullin
Kenmare
Co. Kerry

Tel: +353 64 41212

Area of special interest is work with youth groups. Has worked with local youth groups in Kenmare.

Beverley Whyte

21b Ballinderry Road
Lisburn BT28 2SA
Northern Ireland

Tel/Fax: 048 9260 3485/048 9266 3814
Email: openarts@aol.com

Areas of special interest include gamelan tuition and visual art. Has worked in primary and secondary schools giving flute tuition, gamelon tuition and composition projects with Belfast Education & Library Board. At present is working in Queen's University Belfast as the Gamelon tutor for Ethnomusicology students and those with learning disabilities. Also works with Open Arts involving work with arts centres, day centres, hospitals, older people, people with mental health difficulties and children with behavioural problems. Examples of activities offered within projects are the use of the gamelan instrument to perform a traditional Javanese piece after one hour of tuition, the use of hand chimes and singing and 'A World of Song' project which is a ten week project focusing on songs from around the world. Also works with Live Music Now giving one hour concerts to people in hospitals, day centres and prisons. Qualifications include: MA in (20th century music) and BMus.

Desi Wilkinson

19 Oaklawns
Castletroy
Limerick

Tel: +353 61 335403 or +353 61 202960
Email: desi.wilkinson@ul.ie
Website: www.cran.net

Areas of special interest includes music of Ireland, Scotland, the Francophone diaspora, the world of professional music and contemporary Celticism, music in its cultural context (aesthetics and socio-political). Has worked with the Irish World Music Centre, Willie Clancy Summer School, Queen's University, Quartz Theatre Complex France, The Arts Council of Northern Ireland and Music Network. Has performed music and been engaged in fusion music projects throughout Western Europe. Examples of activities offered within projects includes the use of Irish traditional music performance, Breton music and dance, European folk music survey and study, American folk music survey and study. Qualifications include a BED and a PhD in Ethnomusicology/ Cultural studies.

Caroline Wynne

Director
Artscope
Abbeytown
Boyle
Co. Roscommon

Tel/Fax: +353 79 62963
Email: artscope@eircom.net

Areas of special interest includes music education through interactive workshops in a wide variety of musical genres, cross-arts involving dance/movement and drama and facilitating interaction between musicians and a wider public audience. Has worked with primary and secondary schools nationwide, CDVEC Curriculum Development Unit, North Western Health Board, Institute of Technology Sligo and TG4. Examples of community based settings include Balor Development Community Group, neighbourhood youth projects nationwide, Baboró International Arts Festival For Children, Westport Arts Festival and Clifden Arts Festival. Examples of activities offered in projects includes workshops in percussion, jazz, traditional music, classical music, world music, guitar, piano, stage dance, latin/modern dance, contemporary music and rock music and the co-ordination of musical productions. Director of Artscope, which uses the arts as a means of education and personal development. Qualifications include: ALCM Diploma in Music Education, Diploma in Psychology and Diploma in Drama.

Libraries

The following symbols are used within this section:

 Disabled access

 Partial disabled access

PUBLIC LIBRARIES

Belfast Public Library
Jill E. Stewart
Senior Librarian
Central Library
Royal Avenue
Belfast BT1 IEA
Northern Ireland

Tel/Fax: 048 9024 3233/048 9033 2819
Email: info@libraries.belfast-elb.gov.uk
Other key staff: Tom Watson (Chief Llibrarian)

Opening hours: Monday, 9.30-8.00pm, Tuesday and Wednesday, 9.30-5.30pm, Thursday, 9.30-8.00pm, Friday, 9.30-5.30pm and Saturday, 9.30-1.00pm.
Lending services: Loan of books, scores, CDs, cassettes, videos, records. Reference collection of collected works, dictionaries, encyclopedias, year books, periodicals. Free postal service to visually disabled people. Special collections include books on Irish music and Irish music scores.

Carlow County Library
Carmel Flahavan
Assistant Librarian
Tullow Street
Carlow

Tel/Fax: +353 503 70094/+353 503 40548
Other key staff: Thomas King (Chief Librarian)

Opening hours: Monday, 10-1pm/2-5.30pm, Tuesday, 10-1pm/2-5.30pm/6.30-8.30pm, Wednesday, 10-1pm/2-5.30pm, Thursday, 10-1pm/2-5.30pm/6.30-8.30pm, Friday, 10-1pm/2-5.30pm, closed Saturday and Sunday.
Services offered: CDs - classical, books (all topics), tapes - Irish dance music, scores of opera, operetta, musicals (e.g Oliver, Salad Days etc), music for individual instruments - piano scores, guitar music.
Other district libraries: Muinegheag - Books, tapes.

Cavan County Library
Tom Sullivan
Assistant Librarian
Cavan Co. Library
Farnham Street
Cavan

Tel/Fax: +353 49 31799/+353 49 31384
Email: cavancountylibrary@eircom.net
Other key staff: Josephine Brady (Chief Librarian)

Opening hours: Monday, 11-1pm/2-5pm/6-8.30pm, Tuesday and Wednesday, 11am-5pm, Thursday, 11-1pm/2-5pm/6-8.30pm, Friday, 11-1pm/2-5pm, closed Saturday and Sunday.
Services offered: Sheet music, small selection of tapes. Lending services free.
Other district libraries: Bailieborough branch library, listening facility available.

Clare County Library
Noel Crowley
Chief Librarian
Library Head Quarters
Mill Road
Ennis
Co. Clare

Tel/Fax: +353 65 6821616 or +353 65 6842461/ +353 65 6842462
Email: clarelib@iol.ie
Website: www.iol.ie/~clarelib

Opening hours: Contact individual libraries.
Lending services: Music books available in all libraries. Traditional music collection, tapes and CDs in Miltown Malbay library. 15 branch libraries in County Clare, 7 full-time and 8 part-time.

Cork City Library
Kitty Buckley
Music Librarian
Grand Parade
Cork

Tel/Fax: +353 21 4277110/+353 21 4275684
Email: corkcitylibrary@indigo.ie
Other key staff: Hanna O'Sullivan (Chief Librarian)

Lending services: Sheet music, books, CDs, cassettes and LPs of classical, traditional, world, jazz, blues, rock and country music. Membership costs £25 per annum, and there is free membership for visually impaired persons. Members are entitled to borrow up to four CDs and two books at a time.

Cork County Library

Christine Daly
Farranlea Road
Cork

Tel/Fax: +353 21 4546499/+353 21 4343254

Opening hours: Monday-Friday, 9-1pm/2-5pm, closed Saturday and Sunday.
Lending services: The sheet music collection was initiated in 1976. Has stocks of over 13,000 pieces, a choral music lending service is offered. The collection houses sheet music of classical, traditional, folk, spiritual, popular songs and anthologies of sacred, traditional, country, rock, etc. A childrens/schools section is also included. Cork County Library co-operates with Cumann Naisiunta na gCór (The Association of Irish Choirs) to provide a nationwide service to members of that association. It co-operates also with 'The Cork International Choral Festival' and stocks music received by the Festival through the years, much of which is original and/or previously unpublished. It also holds collections donated by private individuals which, again, may contain unpublished material.

Donegal Central Library & Arts Centre

Geraldine McHugh
Assistant Librarian
Oliver Plunkett Road
Letterkenny
Co. Donegal

Tel/Fax: +353 74 24950
Email: dglcolib@iol.ie
Website: www.donegal.ie
Other key staff: Liam Ronayne (Chief Librarian)

Opening hours: Monday, 10.30-5.30pm, Tuesday, 10.30-8.00pm, Wednesday, 10.30-5.30pm, Thursday, 10.30-8.00pm, Friday, 10.30-5.30pm, Saturday 10.30-1.00pm, closed Sunday.
Lending services: books, CDs, cassettes, videos of classical, traditional, folk, world, country, jazz, rock & pop. Listening services. Consultation offered for information about scores/sheet music (classical). £10 annual charge for audio-visual membership.
Other district libraries: Leabharlann Phobail na Rosann.

Dublin Corporation Public Libraries

Eithne Boyd
Senior Librarian
Central Library
ILAC Centre
Henry St
Dublin 1

Tel/Fax: +353 1 8734333/ +353 1 8721451
Email: cicelib@iol.ie
Website: www.dublincorp.ie
Other key staff: Deirdre Ellis-King (Chief Librarian)

Opening hours: Mon-Thursday, 10-8pm, Friday and Saturday 10-5pm, closed Sundays.
The music library forms an integral part of Dublin Public Library Service. Primary function is to provide a music information service through a network of library resources.
Reference services: Contains major reference works such as Grove, catalogue of printed music, the British Music Yearbook, a music database, recording organisations and associations, audio facilities, including music sampling; a continuous programme of music recitals, workshops and a music appreciation lecture series, and a syllabus and prospectus of graded diploma courses at home and abroad
Lending services: Sheet music, vocal scores (block loan facilities for musical societies), CDs, LPs, tapes of classical, jazz, blues, rock, pop, traditional, country, world, folk, film soundtracks and big band music. Membership is open to all those living and working in the Dublin area and gives entitlement to borrow eight items at one time, except in the case of CDs and LPs which are restricted to three at one time. There is an annual subscription fee of £5 to borrow CDs and LPs.

Dun Laoghaire/Rathdown County Library Service

Muiris O'Raghaill
County Librarian
Headquarters
Duncairn House
14 Carysfort Avenue
Blackrock
Co. Dublin

Tel/Fax: +353 1 2781789/90/91/+353 1 2781792
Email: dlrlibs@iol.ie
Librarian)

Opening hours: Open to the public 6 days a week.
Lending services: In 10 branches including music

books, tapes, CDs of traditional, folk, classical, jazz and pop. Piano room and harp room available for use by the public at Dalkey Library. Sheet music available at Dun Laoghaire Library. No charge for membership.
Other district libraries: Blackrock, Cabinteely, Deansgrange, Dalkey, Dundrum, Dun Laoghaire, Sallynoggin, Shankhill, Stillorgan, Glencullen.

Galway County Library
Pat McMahon
County Librarian
Island House
Cathedral Square
Galway

Tel/Fax: +353 91 562471/+353 91 565039
Email: gallibr@indigo.ie

Opening hours: Monday, 2-5.00pm, Tuesday-Thursday, 11-8pm, Friday, 11-5pm, Saturday, 11-1pm/2-5pm.
Lending services: Tapes, CDs, scores and books on classical, traditional and jazz.
Other district libraries: Galway City, Tuam, Portumna and Clifden. Also has a mobile library service.

Kerry County Library
Kathleen Browne
Chief Librarian
Tralee
Co. Kerry

Tel/Fax: +353 66 7121200/+353 66 7129202
Email: traleelibrary@eircom.net

Lending services: Sheet music, books, records, tapes and CDs of traditional, folk and classical music.
Other district libraries: Killarney and Listowel.

Kildare County Libraries
Athgarvan Road
Newbridge
Co. Kildare

Tel: +353 45 431215/+353 45 432490

Kilkenny County Library
Dorothy O'Reilly
Assistant Librarian
County Library
6 Johns Quay
Kilkenny

Tel/Fax: +353 56 22606 or +353 56 22021/ +353 56 70233
Email: katlibs@iol.ie
Other key staff: James Fogarty (Chief Librarian)

Opening hours: At headquarters: Monday-Friday, 9-1pm/2pm-5pm, closed Saturday and Sunday.
Lending services: Books, videos, CDs and tapes of classical, traditional, jazz, world, blues, rock & pop music. Five full-time and two part-time branches, a mobile library service and schools library service.
Other district libraries: Loughboy Library +353 56 22021, Callan Library +353 56 25040, Thomastown Library +353 56 24911, Graiguenamanagh Library +353 503 24224, Uringford Library +353 56 31655. Mobile library enquiries to +353 56 22606. Six out of seven branches have disabled access (mobile library incorporates a lift).

Laois County Library
Patrick Macken
Dunamase House
Portlaoise
Co. Laois

Tel: +353 502 22333
Other key staff: Edwin Phelan (Chief Librarian)

Opening hours: Tuesday, 10-5pm, Wednesday, 10-7pm, Thursday, 10-7pm, Friday, 10-5pm, Saturday, 10am-1pm.
Lending services: Sheet music for traditional, folk, jazz, country, rock & pop. Books and tapes of classical, traditional, folk, jazz, country, rock & pop. Listening facility available.

Leitrim County Library
Geraldine Flynn
Assistant Librarian
County Library
Ballinamore
Co. Leitrim

Tel/Fax: +353 78 44012/+353 78 44425
Email: leitrimlibrary@eircom.net
Other key staff: Séan Ó Suilleabháin (Chief Librarian)

Opening hours: Monday, 10-5pm, Tuesday, 10-8pm, Wednesday-Friday, 10-5pm, closed Saturday and Sunday.
Lending Services: Books and tapes of traditional, folk, country, and classical music in some branch libraries. Sizeable indexed collection of songs and ballads from various sources that is indexed.

Limerick City Library
Dolores Doyle
City Librarian
The Granary
Michael Street
Limerick

Tel/Fax: +353 61 314668 or +353 61 415799/
+353 61 415266
Email: ddoyle@citylib.limerickcorp.ie
Website: www.limerickcorp.ie
Other key staff: Dolores Doyle (Chief Librarian), Mary King (Music Librarian)

Opening hours: Monday and Tuesday, 10-5.30pm, Wednesday-Friday, 10-8pm, Saturday 10-1pm, closed Sundays.
Lending services: Music books, sheet music, records, tapes, CDs of classical, traditional, folk, world, jazz, rock and pop, country, blues, band/military, musicals, opera, TV music, music reference books. Listening facilities for records, CDs and tapes.

Limerick County Library Service
Helen Walsh
Executive Librarian
58 O'Connell Street
Limerick

Tel/Fax: +353 61 318477/+353 61 318478
Email: hwalsh@limerickcoco.ie
Other key staff: Damien Brady (Chief Librarian)

Opening hours: Closed Monday, Tuesday and Wednesday, 11-1pm/2-5.30pm, Thursday and Friday, 11-1pm/2-8.30pm, Saturday, 11-1pm/2-5.30pm
Lending services: Books on classical, traditional, jazz, blues, rock and pop.

Longford County Library
Mary Carleton Reynolds
County Librarian
County Library Headquarters
Town Centre
Longford

Tel/Fax: +353 43 41124/5/+353 43 41124
Email: longlib@iol.ie
Other key staff: Mary Carleton Reynolds (Chief Librarian)

Opening hours: Monday-Thursday, 9.30-1pm/2-5.30pm, Friday 9.30-1pm/2-5.15pm, closed Saturday and Sunday
Lending services: Music tapes and books about music.

Louth County Library
Ann Ward
County Librarian
Roden Place
Dundalk
Co. Louth

Tel/Fax: +353 42 9335457/+353 42 9337635

Opening hours: Closed Monday, Tuesday, 9-5pm/
6-8pm, Wednesday, 9-5pm, Thursday, 9-5pm/6-8pm, Friday and Saturday, 9-5pm, closed Sunday.
Lending services: Tapes, CDs, videos, classical, traditional, jazz, blues, rock & pop. Listening and viewing facilities. All tastes catered for.
Other district libraries: With music facilities: Drogheda, Ardee, Dunleer.

Mayo County Library
Austin Vaughan
Chief Librarian
Castlebar
Co. Mayo

Tel/Fax: +353 94 24444/+353 94 24774
Other key staff: Richard Hickey (Assistant Librarian)

Lending services: Books of classical, traditional, folk, world, jazz, country, rock and pop music.

Meath County Library

Olive Falsey
Assistant Librarian
Railway Street
Navan
Co. Westmeath

Tel/Fax: +353 46 21134 or +353 46 21451/
+353 46 21563
Email: meathlib@indigo.ie
Other key staff: Geraldine Donnelly (Acting
Chief Librarian)

Opening hours: Monday, 1.30-5pm, Tuesday 1.30-
5pm/7-8.30pm, Wednesday 10.30-6.30pm, Thursday,
1.30-5pm/7-8.30pm, Friday 10.30-4pm, Saturday 10-
12.30pm, closed Sunday.
Lending services: Musical scores, tapes, CDs, videos,
CD-ROMs. Genres include classical, traditional, musical
theatre and popular.
Other district libraries: Dunshaughlin, Duleek, Kells
and Trim.

Monaghan County Library

Joe McElvaney
County Librarian
County Library Headquarters
The Diamond
Clones
Co. Monaghan

Tel/Fax: +353 47 51143/+353 47 58163
Other key staff: Joe McElvaney (Chief Librarian).

National Library of Ireland

Duty Librarian
Kildare Street
Dublin 2

Tel/Fax: +353 1 6030200/+353 1 6766690
Email: info@nli.ie
Website: www.heanet.ie/natlib/
Other key staff: Brendan O'Donoghue (Director)

Opening hours: Monday-Wednesday, 10-9.00pm,
Thursday and Friday, 10-5.00pm, Saturday 10-1pm,
closed Sunday
Lending services: Classical, traditional and jazz sheet
music and books.

North Eastern Education & Library Board Library Service

Assistant Librarian
Ballymena Library
Demesne Avenue
Ballymena
Co. Antrim BT43 7BG
Northern Ireland

Tel: 048 2566 4110
Other key staff: P. Valentine (Chief Librarian)

Opening hours: Monday, 10-8.30pm, Tuesday and
Wednesday, 10-5.30pm, Thursday and Friday 10-8pm,
Saturday 10-5pm, closed Sunday
Lending services: Sheet music, books, CDs, records,
tapes of classical, jazz, traditional, folk, world, country,
rock and pop music.

Offaly County Council

Anne Coughlan
County Librarian
County Library Headquarters
O'Connor Square
Tullamore
Co. Offaly

Tel/Fax: +353 506 46833/+353 506 52769
Email: colibrar@offalycoco.ie
Website: www.offaly.ie

Libraries: Banagher +353 509 51471, Birr +353 509
20961, Clara +353 506 31389, Daingean +353 506
53005, Edenderry +353 405 31028, Ferbane +353 902
54259, Kilcormac +353 509 35086, Shinrone, Tullamore
+353 506 46832.

Roscommon County Library

Helen Kilcline
County Librarian
Abbey Street
Roscommon

Tel/Fax: +353 903 37271/+353 903 25474
Email: roslib@iol.ie
Website: www.ireland.iol.ie/~roslib

Opening hours: Closed Monday, Tuesday, 1-8pm,
Wednesday, 1-5pm, Thursday, 1-8pm, Friday and
Saturday, 10-1pm/2-5pm
Lending facilities: Songbooks, tapes, CDs. Books and
tapes include classical, traditional, folk, jazz, country, rock
& pop, and popular music. Listening facilities available.

Sligo County Library

Fran Hegarty
Assistant Librarian
Westward Centre
Bridge Street
Co. Sligo

Tel/Fax: +353 71 47190/+353 71 46798
Email: sligolib@iol.ie
Other key staff: Donal Tinney (Chief Librarian)

Lending services: Sheet music and books only. Plan to expand to tapes and CDs with emphasis on traditional music or the music of the Sligo region. Reference facility free.

South Eastern Education & Library Board Library Service

J.W Glenn
Library Headquarters
Windmill Lane
Ballynahinch
Co. Down BT24 8DH
Northern Ireland

Tel/Fax: 048 9756 6420/048 9756 5072
Other key staff: B. Porter (Chief Librarian)

Lending services: Books, sheet music, scores, song-books, CDs and cassettes of classical music, folk and traditional, country, world, jazz, rock & pop music. Music reference and information service. Listening facilities available in some branches. Loan of vocal and orchestral sets. All public service points carry stocks of music, CDs, cassettes and books (26 branches, 5 mobiles).

Southern Education & Library Board Library Service

Janet Blair
Public Services Co-ordinator
Library Headquarters
1 Markethill Road
Armagh BT60 1NR
Northern Ireland

Tel/Fax: 048 3752 5353/048 3752 6879

Lending services: CDs and tapes of classical, traditional, jazz, blues and rock and pop. There are 23 branch libraries and 7 mobile libraries.

Tipperary Libraries

Gerard Flannery
Assistant Librarian
Castle Avenue
Thurles
Co. Tipperary

Tel/Fax: +353 504 21555/+353 504 23442
Email: tipplibs@iol.ie
Website: www.iol.ie/~tipplibs
Other key staff: Martin Maher (Chief Librarian)

Opening hours: Monday-Friday 9.30-1pm/2-5.30pm, closed Saturday and Sunday.
Lending services: Clonmel library contains cassettes of a range of musical genres. Nenagh library contains CDs of same.

Waterford City Library

Richard Fennessy
Chief Librarian
Lady Lane
Waterford

Other key staff: Kathleen Moran (Assistant Librarian/Music Librarian)

Opening hours: Closed Monday, Tuesday 11-1pm/2.30-5pm, Wednesday, 2-8pm, Thursday, 11-1pm/2.30-5pm, Friday, 2-8pm, Saturday, 11-1pm/2.30-5pm.
Lending services: Books, CDs, records, tapes of classical, traditional, folk, world, jazz, country, rock & pop.

Waterford County Libraries

Donal Brady
Chief Librarian
County Library
Lismore
Co. Waterford

Tel/Fax: +353 58 54128/+353 58 54877
Email: ebhqcirc@iol.ie

Lending services: Offer books, CDs, records and tapes of classical, traditional, folk, world , jazz, country and rock and pop music.
Other district libraries: Dungarvan, Tramore and Lismore.

Western Education & Library Board Library Service

Library Headquarters
1 Spillars Place
Omagh
Co. Tyrone BT78 1HL
Northern Ireland

Tel/Fax: 048 8224 4821/048 8224 6716
Email: librarian@omalib.demon.co.uk

Opening hours: Monday, 9.15-5.30pm, Tuesday, 9.15-8pm, Wednesday, 9.15-5.30pm, Thursday, 9.15-8pm, Friday 9.15-5.30pm, Saturday, 9-1pm/2-5pm, closed Sunday.
Lending services: CDs and tapes.
Reference service: Sheet music. Mobile library service.
Other district libraries: Fermanagh, Tyrone and part of Derry.

Westmeath County Library

Tom Cox
Assistant Librarian
Dublin Road
Mullingar
Co. Westmeath

Tel/Fax: +353 44 40781/2/3/+353 44 41322
Other key staff: Mary Farrell (Chief Librarian)

Opening hours: Monday-Friday 9.30-1/2-5pm, closed Saturday and Sunday.
Lending services: Sheet music of classical, traditional, folk, CDs and tapes of classical, traditional, folk, rock, jazz, pop, country and books.
Other district libraries: Athlone library +353 902 92166, Mullingar Library +353 902 44 48278.

Wexford Public Library

Fionnuala Hanrahan
County Librarian

Tel/Fax: +353 53 21637
Email: library.wexford @eircom.net
Other key staff: Rita O'Brien (Schools Librarian)

Opening hours: Closed Monday, Tuesday, 1-5.30pm, Wednesday, 10-4.30pm/6-8pm, Thursday and Friday, 10-5.30pm, Saturday, 10-1pm.
Lending services: Books and CDs for loan. CD collec-

tion strengths: classical, traditional and jazz. Sheet music for childrens choirs. Journals for reference reading in library. Schools librarian supports the new primary school curriculum and choirs throughout the county.

Wicklow County Library

Gerry Maher
County Librarian
Library Headquarters
UDC offices
Boghall Road
Co. Wicklow

Tel/Fax: +353 1 2866566/+353 1 2865811

Opening hours: Monday to Friday 9-5pm. Closed Saturday and Sunday.

SPECIALIST LIBRARIES

BBC Northern Ireland Music Library

Andrea Rea
Acting Music Librarian
Music and Arts
BBC Northern Ireland
4th Floor Broadcasting House
Ormeau Avenue
Belfast BT2 8HQ
Northern Ireland

Tel/Fax: 048 9033 8295/048 9033 8807
Email: andrea.rea@bbc.co.uk
Other key staff: Ruth Gregory (Music Librarian)

Opening hours: Open Mon-Fri by appointment only. Small specialist collection of Irish scores and parts.
Areas of special interest: Manuscript collections of orchestral music from late 1930s-1950s, Ulster Airs, Irish rhythms and miscellaneous arrangements.

BBC Northern Ireland Research Centre

Mark Cox
Librarian
BBC Northern Ireland
Broadcasting House
Ormeau Avenue
Belfast BT2 8HQ
Northern Ireland

Tel/Fax: 048 9033 8324/048 9033 8329

Areas of special interest: Specialises in research for sound effects, mood music, classical music, contemporary and Irish music.

The Chester Beatty Library

Dr Michael Ryan
Director
The Clock Tower Building
Dublin Castle
Dublin 2

Tel/Fax: +353 1 2692386/+353 1 2830983
Email: mryan@cbl.ie
Website: www.cbl.ie

Special collections: There are some musical items, including instruments and manuscripts from around the world.

CAFE Community Arts Library

Margaret Smith
Administrator
143 Townsend Street
Dublin 2

Tel/Fax: +353 1 6770330/+353 1 6713268
Email: cafe@connect.ie

Opening hours: Contact office to make an appointment.
Areas of special interest: Books, journals, magazines about community arts.

Central Catholic Library

Teresa Whitington
Librarian
74 Merrion Square
Dublin 4

Tel/Fax: +353 1 6761264/+353 1 6787618

Opening hours: Monday-Friday, 11-7pm, Saturday, 11-5pm
Areas of special interest: Christian and Western cultures, includes some traditional and non-Western cultures, anthropology and humanities. Science and technology are not included.
Special collections: Include Irish history, culture, art and culture.
Services offered: Sheet music and tapes of medieval music, church and liturgical music, gregorian chant, Irish church music, Irish traditional music, hymns and hymnology, sacred music and hymns.

The Contemporary Music Centre

Jonathan Grimes
Information & Outreach Manager
19 Fishamble Street
Temple Bar
Dublin 8

Tel/Fax: +353 1 6731922/+353 1 6489100
Email: info@cmc.ie
Website: www.cmc.ie

Opening hours: Monday-Friday, 10-1pm/2-5pm, closed Saturday and Sunday.
Special collections: Score library and sound archive of contemporary Irish classical music.
Services offered: Scores available for reference or sale, sound archive for reference only. Information materials, periodicals and books for reference.

Goethe-Institut

Monika Schlenger
Deputy Librarian
37 Merrion Square
Dublin 2

Tel/Fax: +353 1 6611155/+353 1 6611358
Email: library@goethe.iol.ie
Website: www.goethe.de/dublin

Opening hours: Closed Monday, Tuesday-Thursday, 10-1pm/2-7pm, Wednesday, 1-7pm, Friday, 10-1pm, Saturday, 10-1pm, closed Sunday.
Areas of special interest: Books, videos, magazines, audio tapes and CDs about Germany for lending and reference in German and English.
Services offered: Approximately 220 CDs, mainly classical (German composers only). Printed stock list available on request.

Instituto Cervantes Library

Mabel Lopez
Chief Librarian
58 Northumberland Road
Ballsbridge
Dublin 4

Tel/Fax: +353 1 6682024/+353 1 6688416
Email: bibdub@cervantes.es
Website: www.cervantes.es

Opening hours: Monday-Thursday, 11-7.45 pm, Friday, 10-2pm, closed Saturday and Sunday.
Areas of special interest: Specialises in Spanish music, contains CDs of classical, traditional, folk, opera, rock and pop, Spanish Zarzuela and Flamenco music etc. Listening facilities and lending facilities are available.

Irish Traditional Music Archive

The Secretary
63 Merrion Square
Dublin 2

Tel/Fax: +353 1 6619699/+353 1 6624585
Website: www.itma.ie

Opening hours: Monday-Friday, 10-1pm/2-5pm throughout the year.
Areas of special interest: Listening facilities to sound recordings of all formats, viewing facilities for photographs and video tapes, access to computerised catalogues and indexes, photocopying and other copying services.
Special collections: Sound recordings (over 10,000 hours), 1890s to present - commercial 78s, SPs, EPs, LPs, audio cassettes, CDs, field sound recordings (on cylinders, reel-to-reel tapes, audio cassettes, DAT tapes, mini-discs and CDs) include the Breathnach, Shields, Hamilton, Ó Conluain, Carroll-Mackenzie, MacWeeney, De Buitléar, RTÉ and BBC radio collections. Printed matter (over 13,000 items excluding ephemeral): works of reference, serials, song and instrumental collections, studies, sheet music, ballad sheets, ephemeral including posters, flyers and newspaper cuttings, dating from the 18th century to present. Photographs and other images (over 3,000 items), 18th century to present, music manuscripts, theses and other unpublished typescripts (over 500 items excluding manuscript archives), dating from the 18th century to present, video recordings (over 500 items). Publications include guides published by the archive, an information leaflet, which is available on request, and Nicholas Carolan's 'Irish Traditional Music Archive/Taisce Cheol Dúchais Éireann: The First Ten Years/Na Chéad Deich mBliana' (1997), Hugh Shields' 'Tunes of the Munster Pipers: Irish Traditional Music from the James Goodman Collections' Volume 1 (1998), and Colette Moloney's 'The Irish Music Manuscripts of Edward Bunting (1773 - 1843): An Introduction and Catalogue' (1999).

Irish World Music Centre

Paula Dundon
Administrator
Foundation Building
University of Limerick
Limerick

Tel/Fax: +353 61 202590/+353 61 202589
Email: paula.dundon@ul.ie
Website: www.ul.ie/~iwmc

Areas of interest: Irish music and dance.
Special collections: Chant studies and liturgical music, Irish music and dance archive. (see advert p.75).

Kerry School of Music

Marie Thiere
Chief Librarian
Old Customs House
High Street
Tralee
Co. Kerry

Tel/Fax: +353 66 7125690/+353 66 7120077
Email: kerrymusicschool@eircom.net

Opening hours: Drop-in/phone enquiries, Monday-Friday, 9-5pm. Lending materials offered.
Special collections: Piano, vocal and orchestral music form Drishane Convent and Dick Edwards collections. Other specialist services include a large collection of LPs donated and available for students use, and a collection of choral and orchestral works for Kerry Chamber Orchestra and Choir. Sheet music, scores, commentaries and books.

Linen Hall Library

Gerry Healey
Irish and Reference Librarian
17 Donegall Square North
Belfast BT1 5GB
Northern Ireland

Tel/Fax: 048 9032 1707/048 9043 8586
Email: info@linenhall.com
Other key staff: John Gray

Opening hours: Monday-Friday, 9.30-5.30pm, Saturday, 9.30-4pm, closed Sunday.
Areas of special interest: Irish and Scottish Music. There are published collections of Irish and Scottish music from the 18th and 19th Century.
Special collections: Published works of Edward Bunting.

Marsh's Library

Ann Simmons
Assistant to Keeper
St. Patrick's Close
Dublin 8

Tel/Fax: +353 1 4543511
Email: marshlib@iol.ie
Website: www.kst.dit.ie/marsh
Other key staff: Dr Muriel McCarthy (Keeper)

Opening hours: Monday, 10-12.45pm/2-5pm, closed Tuesday, Wednesday-Friday, 10-12.45pm/2-5pm, Saturday, 10.30-12.45pm, closed Sunday.
Areas of special interest: Collection of early printed books, mainly from 17th Century.

Special collections: Music books and manuscripts, including 17th Century part books.

National Archives of Ireland
Aideen Ireland
Archivist
Bishop Street
Dublin 8

Tel/Fax: +353 1 4072300/+353 1 4072333
Email: mail@nationalarchives.ie
Website: www.nationalarchives.ie

Opening hours: Monday-Friday 10-5pm, closed Saturday and Sunday.
Special collections: Includes a small amount of sheet music and ballads that were of a subversive nature. 1120 Royal Irish Academy of Music - this is a special collection including ledger books, scholarships etc. Consultation service provided.

Royal Dublin Society
Mary Kelleher
Librarian
Ballsbridge
Dublin 4

Tel/Fax: +353 1 6680866 Ext. 368/ +353 1 6604014

Opening hours: Monday, closed (except for reading area), Tuesday, 10-5pm, Wednesday and Thursday, 10-7pm, Friday, 10-5pm, Saturday, 11-5pm, closed Sunday.
Services offered: Sheet music, including parts for chamber music trio/quartet/quintet. Tapes, CDs, listening and video facilities. Basic collection of operas on video.

Royal Irish Academy of Music - Monteagle Library
Philip Shields
Music Librarian
36-38 Westland Row
Dublin 2

Tel/Fax: +353 1 6764412/+353 1 6622798
Website: www.riam.ie

Opening hours: Monday and Tuesday, 2-6pm, Wednesday, 10-1pm/2-6pm, Thursday and Friday, 10-1pm/2-6pm, Saturday, 11-2pm, closed Sunday.
Areas of special interest: Music education and music performance.

Special collections: Hudleston Collection (19th Century guitar music), Antient Concerts Society, Anacreontic Society, Monteagle Bequest.

Royal Irish Academy
Siobhán O'Rafferty
Chief Librarian
19 Dawson Street
Dublin 2

Tel/Fax: +353 1 6762570 or +353 1 6764222/+353 1 6762346
Email: s.orafferty@ria.ie
Website: www.ria.ie

Opening hours: Monday-Friday, 10.30-5.30pm, closed Saturday and Sunday.
Areas of interest: The Academy is a learned society which promotes the sciences and humanities in Ireland. The library holds major Irish manuscript, book and pamphlet collections, together with substantial holdings of international journals.
Special collections: Forde-Pigot Music Collection: Mss.24.0.19-34 (mainly Irish airs)
Services offered: Printouts from microfilms and photocopying of journal articles.

RTÉ Programme Library
Donnybrook
Dublin 4

Tel/Fax: +353 1 2082502/+353 1 2083031

RTÉ Sound Library
Majella Breen
Chief Librarian
Donnybrook
Dublin 4

Tel: +353 1 2082430

Area of special interest: Recorded music
Special collections: Traditional music and recorded works of Irish composers. This service is provided to RTÉ programmes only. There is a tape copying service for the public.

Trinity College Dublin Library
Roy Stanley
Music Librarian
College Street
Dublin 2

Tel/Fax: +353 1 6081460/+353 1 6719003
Email: rstanley@tcd.ie
Website: www.tcd.ie/library
Other key staff: William G. Simpson (Chief
Librarian)

Opening hours: (Term-time) Monday-Friday, 9am-
10pm, Saturday, 9.30-1p.m. (Vacation) Monday-Friday
9.30-5pm, Saturday 9.30-1pm.
Areas of special interest: All aspects of the academic
discipline of music. Sheet music, tapes, CDs, listening
facilities and enquiry service.

Ulster Orchestra Society Ltd Library
Paul McKinley
Librarian
Elmwood Hall at Queen's
89 University Road
Belfast
BT7 1NF

Tel/Fax: 048 9066 4535/048 9066 2761

Opening hours: Monday-Friday, 9-5pm, closed
Saturday and Sunday.
Services offered: Information about repertoire and
related areas. Orchestral sets are not available for
external use.

Health

MUSIC THERAPISTS

Irish Association of Creative Arts Therapists
Jim Cosgrove
Training Officer
PO Box 4176
Dublin 1

Tel: +353 1 8386171
Other key staff: Gerri Geoghegan
(Chairperson), Pauline Sweeney (Secretary),
Denise Burke (Treasurer)

The Irish Association of Creative Arts Therapists (IACAT)
was formally launched in 1994. Aims to promote and
protect the practice of the creative arts therapies in
Ireland. Acts as the professional registration body for
therapists practising music therapy, drama therapy, art
therapy and dance movement therapy. IACAT offers
associate membership which is open to all interested in
creative arts therapy. Workshops and presentations are
held throughout the year (minimum twice a year).
IACAT is working on gaining statutory recognition for
creative arts therapists and to monitor training and
work practices in Ireland. Newsletter 'IACAT News' is
issued on a quarterly basis.

Judith Brereton
Cork Music Therapy Centre
28b McCurtain Street
Cork

Tel: +353 21 4502777

Qualified with a BMus and Postgraduate Diploma in
Music Therapy from Bristol University. Areas of special
interest includes those with learning disability and the
area of child abuse. Has worked with Cork Association
for Autism and the Southern Health Board. Has an
interest in the further development of music therapy in
Ireland.

Trudi Carberry
44 Leopardstown Avenue
Blackrock
Co. Dublin

Tel: +353 1 2885498

Qualified with BSocSC, Dip Psych, LRAM
(Accompaniment), LRSM (Performance) and DipMTh
from The University of Bristol. Areas of special interest
include music therapy, vocal work with young professional and third level singers. Has worked with DIT
Conservatory of Music and Drama, Young People's

Theatre Group, Irish National Opera, RTÉ, ESB Veronica
Dunne Vocal Bursary, Kinsale Opera and West Belfast
Bursary. Currently répetiteur/accompanist in DIT
Conservatory of Music & Drama. Also works privately as
a music therapist for children with communication/
language difficulties, children with autism and children
with behaviour and learning difficulties.

John Clarke
Camphill Community
Ballytobin
Callan
Co. Kilkenny

Tel: +353 56 25576/+353 56 25849
Email: ballytobin@camphill.ie
Website: www.camphill.ie

Qualified with curative education, specialising in Music
Therapy in Curative Education. Areas of special interest
include music therapy for children who have special
needs and the development of new instruments for use
in therapy. Has worked with the Camphill Movement,
Arion Association of Lyre Players and the Naked Piano
Lyre Ensemble. Also contributor to the Groves
Dictionary, new edition 2000. Member of Irish
Association of Creative Arts Therapists.

Jim Cosgrove
15 Carnew Street
Dublin 7

Tel: +353 1 8386171

Qualified with a BMus from UCD and a DipMTh from
The University of York. Areas of special interest include
work in hospices, work with children who have emo-
tional/behavioural problems and adult mental health.
Has worked in inner city schools, Cerebral Palsy Ireland,
Cheeverstown House (those with learning difficulties),
Our Lady's Hospice and St. Brendan's Hospital. Is available for workshops/presentations on music therapy and
for session work with a client/group. Lectures in music
therapy training in The Irish World Music Centre (2 year
MA in Music Therapy).

Aingeala De Búrca
20 Kerrymount Rise
Cornelscourt
Dublin 18
or
Knockeens
Guleen
Skibbereen
Co. Cork

Tel: +353 1 2893304 or +353 28 35152

Qualified with BA Moderator in Music and Dip Mth ffrom Welsh College of Music and Drama. Areas of special interest include work with children who have autism, emotional or behavioural problems.

Karen Diamond
NIMTT
Graham House
Knockbracken Healthcare Park
Saintfield Road
Belfast BT8 8BH
Northern Ireland

Tel/Fax: 048 9070 5854

Qualified with BMus from The Queen's University Belfast, DipMTh from The Guildhall School of Music and Drama, London and The University of York and RMTh. Areas of special interest includes learning disabilities in children and adults, mental health and speech and language difficulties. Has worked with health and social services trusts, education boards, voluntary organisations including Barnardos, NSF and Early Years.

Keith Medash
4 Priory Walk
St. Raphael's Manor
Celbridge
Co. Kildare

Tel: +353 1 6276320
Mobile: +353 86 8166577

Qualified with BMus from Marywood University, Scranton Pa, USA. Certified as a music therapist by the National Certificate Board for Music Therapists. Areas of special interest include improvisational music therapy and jazz bass. Has worked with Taconic Developmental Disabilities Service Office, New York, which is dedicated to the care and treatment of learning disabled persons. Currently employed as an instructor with the Order of St. John of God's, Islandbridge, Dublin.

Michèle Murphy
19 Riverwood Crescent
Castleknock
Dublin 15

Tel: +353 1 8226541

Qualified with BMus, Diploma in Music Therapy from the Guildhall School of Music & Drama and The University of York, also BSc in Physiotherapy. Areas of special interest includes Paediatrics, especially

learning/physical disability, autism and oncology, work with adult neurology and care of the elderly. Has worked with Cerebral Palsy Ireland, Royal Hospital Brain Injury Unit, London, St. Charles' Hospital, St. Mary's Adult Psychiatry, London and St. James' Hospital, Dublin. Interested in working with other therapists especially art and drama therapists. Designs music, movement and relaxation groups for adults.

Nuala Murray
NIMTT
Graham House
Knockbracken Healthcare Park
Saintfield Road
Belfast BT8 8BH
Northern Ireland

Tel/Fax: 048 9070 5854

Qualified with BMus from Queen's University Belfast, MA in Performance from Queen's University Belfast, Diploma in Music Therapy from The Guildhall School of Music and Drama London and The University of York, PPRNCM and PG Dip RNCM. Areas of special interest include work with those who have been bereaved, those with autism, and with children. Has worked with The National Society for the Prevention of Cruelty to Children, North and West Trust and education boards.

Danusia Oslizlok
4 Thornhill Road
Mount Merrion
Co. Dublin

Tel: +353 1 2888075

Qualified with Postgraduate Diploma in Music Therapy from The University of Bristol, PP from The Royal Northern College of Music Manchester, Diploma in Supervisor for Piano and Chamber Music from Conservatoire Royal de Musique Bruxelles. Areas of special interest includes music therapy, dance and movement, piano performance and chamber music. Has worked with Our Lady's Hospital for Sick Children Dublin, Lucena Child Care Clinic Dublin, Cork School of Music, Dublin Institute of Education - Social Science Department and various closed workshops in various settings.

Possibilities Network
Ruth Walsh and David Stewart
111 Drumbo Road
Lisburn
Co. Antrim BT27 5TX
Northern Ireland

Tel: 048 9082 6932

Promotes positive strategies for health and well-being through innovative programmes in music and other arts. Possibilities Network is a voluntary organisation, currently seeking charitable status. Ruth Walsh is qualified with a BA in Music and Psychology and a Diploma in Music Therapy, David Stewart is qualified with a BMus, Masters in Music Therapy, and a Masters in Social Work. Areas of special interest include clinical music therapy and music psychotherapy, community performance projects, training and consultancy, carer/staff support and personal development. Has worked with Our Lady's Hospital for Sick Children Dublin, various day-centres, schools, therapeutic communities in Northern Ireland, City Arts Centre Dublin, Crescent Arts Centre Belfast, Derry Arts Centre, Ulster Orchestra, Opera Northern Ireland, Very Special Arts, Open Arts, teachers, social workers, psychologists, care-workers, carers, The Queen's University Belfast, University of Ulster, Department of Education and the Department of Health and Social Services Northern Ireland.

Stephen Sandford
NIMTT
Graham House
Knockbracken Healthcare Park
Saintfield Road
Belfast BT8 8BH
Northern Ireland

Tel/Fax: 048 9070 5854

Qualified with BMus from Queen's University Belfast, DipMTh from The Guildhall School of Music and Drama, London and The University of York. Areas of special interest include learning disabilities and psychiatry. Has worked with health, social services and education boards.

Edel Sullivan
'St. Joseph's'
Scart Hill
Donnybrook
Douglas
Cork

Tel: +353 21 4361267
Email: edelfiddle@postmark.net

Qualified with BMus, RMTh (Dip. Nordoff-Robbins), Dip CSM, LTCL and MTTC (Community Music Ltd). Areas of special interest include early intervention with pre-school children with special needs, exploring creative emotional expression particularly with adolescents who have behavioural difficulties. Has worked with The Nordoff-Robbins Music Therapy Centre, London and

Open Dorr (a parent-run music therapy charity for pre-school children with special needs).

HEALTH & MUSICIANS

Lesley Bishop
Massage Therapist
30 The Crescent
Woodpark
Ballinteer
Dublin 16

Tel: +353 1 2987441
Email: lbishop@indigo.ie

Qualified with an ITEC Diploma in Massage Therapy and is a member of The Irish Massage Therapy Association. Areas of special interest include muscle strain, repetitive strain injury and performance stress in classical musicians. Services available include deep tissue massage, aromatherapy massage, repetitive strain injury advice and treatment for stress. Has worked with musicians from The National Symphony of Ireland and other freelance musicians. Principal Horn player with the National Symphony of Ireland.

Richard Brennan
Alexander Technique Teacher
Kirkullen Lodge
Tooreeny
Moycullen
Co. Galway

Tel/Fax: +353 91 555800
Email: rickbrennan@eircom.net
Website: www.homepage.eircom.net/~alexandertechnique

Qualified teacher from the Society of Teachers of the Alexander Technique, member of Alexander Technique International and member of the Back Pain Association. Services available include advice and treatment of repetitive strain injury, back pain, neck, voice, postural and breathing problems advice. Area of special interest is the education of Alexander Technique through workshops and lectures. Has worked with various classical and jazz musicians, workshops for musicians and Dartington College of Music England. Is the author of four books about Alexander Technique: The Alexander Technique Manuel, Stress Relief with The Alexander Technique, Alexander Technique - A Practical Introduction and The Alexander Technique - Natural Poise for Health.

Leonard Condren

GP/Medical Advisor
232 Kylemore Road
Ballyfermot
Dublin 10

Tel/Fax: +353 1 6260748/+353 1 6234156
Email: condren@indigo.ie

Qualified with MA/MB, FRCGP and MICGP. Area of special interest is difficulties encountered by musicians who play brass instruments. Has worked with a number of musicians but does not have a formal association with any group or orchestra. Has attended meetings organised by the British Performing Arts Medical Trust.

Dr. Pádraigín Cooney

GP/Medical Advisor
'Heather'
Brookfield
Rochestown Road
Co. Cork

Tel: +353 21 4362095
Email: pcooney@indigo.ie

Qualified with MB, BCh, BAO, DCH, DO, DFP, MICGP. Areas of special interest include work with instrumentalists and singers. Has worked as an advisor and referral doctor for students of the Cork School of Music. Will organise 'fast track' referral to consultants for musicians.

Thomas Donnelly

Occupational Medical Advisor
10 Hogan Place
Dublin 2

Tel: +353 1 6147091
Email: tomd@hsa.ie
Website: www.hsa.ie

Qualified with MB, MFOM(I). Services available include health and safety advice. Area of special interest is occupational medicine.

David Fitzgerald

Physiotherapist
Dublin Physiotherapy Clinic
Swiss Cottage House
Swords Road
Santry
Dublin 9

Tel/Fax: +353 1 8622161/+353 1 8622161
Email: dublinphysio@yahoo.com

Qualified with Dip Eng, MISCP, Grad Dip Manipulative Therapy. Services available include manipulative therapy, severe injury rehabilitation and exercise facility. Areas of special interest include occupational over use injury, muscle re-education and manual therapy. Has worked with opera singers, guitarists, drummers, pianists and dancers.

Theresa Fitzmaurice

Chartered Physiotherapist
Manor Physiotherapy
6 Manor Street
Dublin 7

Tel/Fax: +353 1 6710222

Qualified as a member of the Irish Society of Chartered Physiotherapists and is a member of the Chartered Society of Physiotherapists (UK). Areas of special interest include spinal and peri-natal problems.

Frank Kennedy

Alexander Technique Teacher
35 Callary Road
Mount Merrion
Co. Dublin

Tel/Fax: +353 1 2882446/+353 1 2882721
Email: frankkennedy@eircom.net

Qualified teacher of the Alexander Technique and is a member of the Society of Teachers of Alexander Technique. Services available include private teaching practice dealing with a full range of ailments, where tension and loss of poise are contributory factors. Gives lectures and conducts workshops. Areas of special interest include correcting tension habits and restoring natural poise in everyday activity, using the Alexander Technique. Has worked with students of The Dublin Institute of Technology Conservatory of Music & Drama College teaching the Alexander Technique.

Rosemary Moone

Alexander Technique Teacher
8 Knockrea Drive
Ballinlough
Cork

Tel: +353 21 4311411

Qualified as a member of Society of Teachers of Alexander Technique. Services available include help with posture, breathing, repetitive strain injury, vocal difficulties, back and neck pain and stage fright. Has worked with Cork School of Music, Nordoff-Robbins Music Therapy Centre London and the Guildhall School of Music and Drama London.

Michèle Murphy
Chartered Physiotherapist
19 Riverwood Crescent
Castleknock
Dublin 15

Tel: +353 1 8226541

Qualified with BMus, Diploma in Music Therapy from
the Guildhall School of Music and Drama and The
University of York, also BSc in Physiotherapy. Services
available include musculoskeletal assessment and treatment. Areas of special interest include stress-related
chronic pain syndrome.

Karin O'Flanagan
Alexander Technique Teacher
54 Mountjoy Square West
Dublin 1

Tel/Fax: +353 1 8787778
Email: oflanaga@indigo.ie

Qualified as graduate of Alexander Technique from the
Alexander Training Institute San Francisco, member of
The Society of Teachers of Alexander Technique. Services
available include the teaching of the Alexander
Technique. Areas of special interest include postural
re-education for overall improved functioning. Has
worked with individual singers, string players and other
musicians.

Brian O'Rourke
Human Resource Department
RTÉ Performing Groups
RTÉ
Donnybrook
Dublin 4

Tel: +353 1 4907328
Email: orourkeb@rte.ie

Referral contact for advice with regard to health problems and injuries of musicians with a specific emphasis
on work related injuries. Particular interest in neurologi-
cal problems with contacts abroad.

Jeralyn Scott
Alexander Technique Teacher
'Pigges Eye'
South Schull
Schull
Co. Cork

Tel/Fax: +353 28 28429
Email: piggesi@gofree.indigo.ie

Qualified as member of The Society of Teachers of the
Alexander Technique. Area of special interest is process
oriented psychology.

Tom Wilson
21 Mount Merrion Avenue
Blackrock
Co. Dublin

Tel: +353 1 2887977
Email: tdwilson@eircom.net

Retired Ear and Throat surgeon. Area of special interest
is voice protection training. Services available include
voice training for all genres of music, music workshop
and 'Studio 21' which is a workshop held on the 21st
of each month.

Promoters & Venues

The following symbols are used within the
Venues section:

 Disabled access

 Parking

 Limited parking

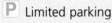 Dressing room(s)

 Kitchen facilities

Laundry facilities

Shower facilities

Security provided

 Restaurant

 Bar

 Piano available

 Shop

 Café

 Hearing aid loop

Catering

 Sound Engineer

 Book shop

PROMOTERS
REP. OF IRELAND

CO. CARLOW

Carlow County Council
Caoimhín Corrigan
Arts Officer
Athy Road
Carlow

Tel/Fax: +353 503 70300/+353 503 41503
Email: art@carlowcoco.ie

Local authority promoter. Promotes orchestral, choral, opera, blues, crossover, chamber, jazz/improv, trad/folk, world and rock/pop music. Music is promoted throughout the year. The programme is planned 3 months in advance. Grand piano is available for performances.

CO. CAVAN

Cavan County Council
Catriona O'Reilly
Arts Officer
17 Farnham Street
Cavan

Tel/Fax: +353 49 4331799 Ext. 7350/
+353 49 62127
Other key staff: Mary Hanley (Museum Curator), Josephine Brady (County Librarian)

Local authority promoter. The programme is planned 3 months in advance.

CO. CLARE

Clare County Council
Siobhán Mulcahy
Arts Officer
Library Headquarters
Harmony Row
Co. Clare

Tel/Fax: +353 65 6821616/+353 65 6842462

Local Authority promoter. Promotes orchestral, choral, opera, blues, crossover, chamber, jazz/improv, trad/folk,

world and rock/pop music. Music is promoted throughout the year. The programme is planned 6 months in advance. Grand piano is available for performers.

CO. CORK

Beara Community Arts Committee
Pat Farrell
Bank Place
Castletownbere
Co. Cork

Tel/Fax: +353 27 70765/+353 27 70964

Voluntary arts organisation. Promotes orchestral, choral, opera, chamber, jazz/improv, traditional and folk music. Musical events are promoted all year round. The programme is planned up to one year in advance.

Cloyne Community Enterprises
Patricia Lyons
Lisanley
Cloyne
Midleton
Co. Cork

Tel/Fax: +353 21 4652479/+353 21 4631918

Programme is planned 6-8 months in advance. Music events are promoted in July and August, but would be interested in promoting music at other times of the year also.

Cork Arts Festival
Tricia Harrington
Arts Officer
Cork Institute of Technology
Rossa Avenue
Bishopstown
Co. Cork

Tel/Fax: +353 21 4326100/+353 21 4545343
Email: artsfest@cit.ie

Promotes orchestral, crossover, chamber, jazz/improv, trad/folk and world music.

Cork Corporation
Mark Mulqueen
Arts Officer
City Hall
Cork

Tel/Fax: +353 21 4924298/+353 21 4314238
Email: arts@corkcorp.ie
Website: www.corkcorp.ie

Local authority promoter. Promotes orchestral, choral, opera, jazz/improv, traditional and folk music. Piano available for performers.

Cork County Council
Ian McDonagh
County Arts Officer
County Hall
Cork

Tel/Fax: +353 21 4346210/+353 21 4343254
Email: cosec@corkcoco.com
Website: www.corkcoco.com

Local authority promoter. Promotes choral, chamber and trad/folk music. 6 events are promoted during the year. The programme is planned 6 months in advance.

Cork Orchestral Society
Dr. Geoffrey Spratt
Chairman
Minneville
Old Blackrock Road
Cork

Tel/Fax: +353 21 4270076/+353 21 4276595
Email: gspratt@cit.ie

Voluntary arts organisation. Promotes orchestral, choral and chamber music. 20-30 events are promoted during the year. Musical events are promoted from September to June. Steinway piano is available for performers.

Cork Pops Ltd
Gerard Kelly
Managing Director
11 Summerhill South
Cork

Tel: +353 21 4316088
Email: grantkelly@eircom.net
Other key staff: Evelyn Grant (Musical Director)

Promotes orchestral, chamber music, childrens concerts and outdoor events. 20 music events are promoted throughout the year. The programme is planned up to one year in advance.

Irish Writers Union
Charles Miller
Crookhaven
Goleen
Skibbereen
Co. Cork

Tel: +353 27 35461

Voluntary arts organisation. Promotes all types of music for and with narration. 2 music events are promoted throughout the year. Events are promoted from February-June and September-November. The programme is planned 6-9 months in advance.

Barra O'Tuama
Operatic Impresario
Lane Office Centre
Monahan Road
Cork

Tel/Fax: +353 21 4963811/+353 21 4963541
Email: botuama@eircom.net
Other key staff: Deirdre O'Tuama (Operations Manager)

Promotes choral music and popular opera. The programme is planned 6-9 months in advance. 12-15 events are promoted throughout the year. Musical events are promoted from September to April.

Opera Cork
Frank Buckley
'Rossetti House'
Tisaxon Beg
Kinsale
Co. Cork

Tel/Fax: +353 21 4774483
Email: operacork@eircom.net

Promotes opera events. At present promotes two operas, one each in autumn and spring. Also promotes operatic concerts.

St. Barrahane's Church
Angela Eborall
Tally Ho House
Castletownshend
Co. Cork

Tel/Fax: +353 28 36193/+353 28 36339
Other key staff: Jacquiline Weit (Assistant Secretary & PRO), Susan Hosford (Treasurer)

Festival promoter. Promotes chamber and baroque music. The programme is planned 10-12 months in advance. 5-6 events are promoted throughout the year. Yamaha grand or Steinway grand piano is hired as required.

Sirius Arts Centre
Cobh
Co. Cork

Tel/Fax: +353 21 4813790
Email: cobharts@iol.ie
Website: www.iol.ie/~cobharts

Arts centre promoter. Promotes choral, trad/folk, chamber and blues music. 12 music events are promoted during the year. The programme is planned 6 months in advance.

Triskel Arts Centre
Deirdre Enright
Director
Tobin Street
Cork

Tel: +353 21 4272022/+353 21 4272592
Email: triskel@iol.ie

Promotes choral, chamber, jazz/improv, trad/folk and also experimental and multi-media events involving music. Events are promoted throughout the year. There is a piano available for performers.

University College Cork
Prof David Harold Cox
Professor of Music
Department of Music
University College Cork
Cork

Tel/Fax: +353 21 4904530/+353 21 4271595
Email: music@ucc.ie

Promotes orchestral, chamber, choral, jazz/improv, trad/folk and world music. 100 music events are promoted during the year. The programme is planned one year in advance for the January to May and October to December seasons. Kawai grand piano is available for performers (see advert p.100).

The Village Arts Centre
Liam Howard
Chairman
c/o Avondhu Press Ltd

18 Lower Cork Street
Mitchelstown
Co. Cork

Tel/Fax: +353 25 24451/+353 25 84463
Email: info@avondhupress.ie
Other key staff: Jerry O'Leary (Secretary), Maureen Howard (Committee Member)

Promotes orchestral, choral, chamber, trad/folk, world, crossover, rock/pop and bluegrass music. 40 music events promoted during the year. The programme is planned 3 months in advance. Akai Upright piano is available for performers.

West Cork Arts Centre
Jackie Butler
Executive Director
The Sutherland Centre
North Street
Skibbereen
Co. Cork

Tel/Fax: +353 28 22090/+353 28 23237
Other key staff: Ita Freeney (Visual Arts Officer), Justine Foster (Community & Education Officer), Teresa O'Sullivan (PR & Development Officer)

West Cork Music
Francis Humphrys
Director
1 Bridge Street
Bantry
Co. Cork

Tel/Fax: +353 27 52789 or +353 27 52788 (box office)/+353 27 52797
Email: westcorkmusic@eircom.net
Website: www.westcorkmusic.ie
Other key staff: Roisin McGuigan (Administrator), Rudolf Kuper (Manager), Martin Greenwood (IT Specialist)

Promotes orchestral, choral, trad/folk and chamber music. 12 music events are promoted during the year as well as the West Cork Chamber Music Festival and school concerts. The programme is planned 6-18 months in advance.

Youghal Festival of the Arts
Kathleen Greer
Treasurer
63-64 North Main Street

Youghal
Co. Cork

Tel/Fax: +353 24 92762
Other key staff: Mrs Warren (Secretary),
Winston Greer (Chairman)

Promotes orchestral, choral and chamber music. 6 music events are promoted from May-September. Programme is planned 6 months in advance.

CO. DONEGAL

Donegal County Council
Traolach Ó Fionnáin
Arts Officer
c/o Donegal County Library
Rosemount
Letterkenny
Co. Donegal

Tel/Fax: +353 74 21968/+353 74 26402

Promotes orchestral, choral, opera, chamber, trad/folk, world and jazz/improv music. 20 music events are promoted throughout the year. The programme is planned 2-6 months in advance. Petrov 11 grand piano available for performers.

Tionscnamh Lugh
Debbie McGarvey
Teach 22 Carraig A tSeascain
Doirí Beaga
Co. Dun Na NGall

Tel/Fax: +353 74 32127
Email: tlugh@iol.ie
Website: www.iol.ie/~tlugh

Promotes traditional and folk music. 40-50 music events are promoted throughout the year.

DUBLIN

Alternative Entertainments
Liam Morrisey
Arts Director
Tymon Bawn Community Centre
Fairhouse Road West
Tallaght
Dublin 24

Tel/Fax: +353 1 4520611/+353 1 4521028
Email: altents@eircom.net

Voluntary arts group. Promotes jazz/improv, trad/folk, crossover and rock/pop music. 10-15 events per year. The programme is planned in October each year for the January to December schedule. Events are promoted throughout the year.

Áras Chrónáin - Irish Cultural Centre
Brian O'Gáibhin
Director Development Worker
Orchard Road
Clondalkin
Dublin 22

Tel/Fax: +353 1 4574847
Mobile: +353 87 2844195

Promotes jazz/improv, trad/folk and classical music.

Bank of Ireland Arts Centre
Barry O'Kelly
Social and Cultural Affairs
Bank of Ireland
Lower Baggot Street
Co.Dublin
Tel/Fax: +353 1 6615933/+353 1 6615695

Promotes chamber, choral, jazz/improv, trad and folk music. 50 music events are promoted throughout the year. (see advert p.150).

Christ Church Baroque
Liz Powell
2 Ingram Road
Dublin 8

Tel/Fax: +353 1 4539197
Email: lizpowell@eircom.net
Other key staff: Mark Duley (Co-Artistic Director), Thérèse Timoney (Co-Artistic Director)

Promotes baroque music on period instruments. 8-12 music events promoted throughout the year. Programme is planned up to six month in advance.

Christ Church Cathedral
Christopher Shiell
Administrator
The Chapter House
Christ Church Place
Dublin 8

Tel/Fax: +353 1 6778099/+353 1 6798991
Email: cccdub@indigo.ie
Website: www.indigo.ie/~cccdub
Other key staff: Helen Roycroft (Cathedral Arts PRO), Stuart Kinsella (Web & E-mail Editor)

Promotes orchestral, choral, chamber, organ and general cathedral music. Approximately 200 music events are promoted throughout the year. Programme is planned 1-4 months in advance.

Dalkey Castle & Heritage Centre
Vanessa Butler
Manager
Castle Street
Dalkey
Co. Dublin

Tel/Fax: +353 1 2858366/+353 1 2843141
Email: diht@indigo.ie

Promotes orchestral, choral, jazz/improv, trad/folk, world and rock music throughout the year.

Drawing Room Opera Company
Ray Twyford
Director
120 Sweetmount Avenue
Dundrum
Dublin 14

Tel/Fax: +353 1 2982219
Email: dr-opera@clubi.ie
Website: www.clubi.ie/dr-opera
Other key staff: Elizabeth Ryan (Producer)

Promotes opera and operetta. Forty music events are promoted throughout the year.

Dublin Corporation
Jack Gilligan
Arts Officer
20 Parnell Square North
Dublin 1

Tel/Fax: +353 1 8722816/+353 1 8722933
Email: arts@dubc.iol.ie

Dublin Corporation - Music in the Parks
Martina Halpin
Environment & Cultural Department
Civic Offices

Wood Quay
Dublin 8

Tel/Fax: +353 1 6722222/+353 1 6707334

Promotes jazz and other band performances in a number of parks, including Merrion Square, Fairview Park, Markievicz Park and Herbert Park. Music is promoted from June-August.

Dublin Jazz Society
Ralph O'Callaghan
Secretary
4 Knocknacree Park
Dalkey
Co. Dublin

Tel: +353 1 2851114
Other key staff: John Holmes (Chairman)

Promotes jazz/improv music. 12 music events are promoted throughout the year. The programme is planned 4-5 months in advance.

Dúchas-The Heritage Service
Historic Properties Division
51 St. Stephen's Green
Dublin 2

Tel/Fax: +353 1 6473000/+353 1 6621767

Lunchtime concerts in St. Stephen's Green and Sunday concerts in The Phoenix Park and St. Enda's National Historic Park take place during June, July and August. The programme is planned in February each year.

Dun Laoghaire - Rathdown County Council
Clíodhna Shaffrey
Arts Officer
County Hall
Marine Road
Dun Laoghaire
Co. Dublin

Tel/Fax: +353 1 2054749/+353 1 2054719
Email: arts@dlrcoco.ie
Website: www.dlrcoco.ie
Other key staff: Aisling Sheridan (Assistant Arts Officer)

Promotes chamber, crossover, jazz/improv and trad/folk music. 6-8 music events promoted throughout the year. The programme is planned nine months in advance.

Kawai grand or upright is hired if requested by the artist(s).

Fingal Arts Centre
James McGreer
Venue Manager
Chapel Green
Rush
Co. Dublin

Tel/Fax: +353 1 8437567 or +353 1 8432020/
+353 1 8432021
Email: jmcgreer@tms.iol.ie
Other key staff: Melissa Monks (Administrator)

Promotes orchestral, chamber, choral, opera, jazz/improv and trad/folk music. One music event per month throughout the year. The programme is planned 6 months to one year in advance.

Fingal County Council
Rory O'Byrne
County Arts Officer
2-3 Parnell Square
Dublin 1

Tel/Fax: +353 1 8727777 Ext. 2244/
+353 1 8727914
Email: fincoart@club.ie

Music events are promoted from May to October.

Improvised Music Company
Gerry Godley
Chief Executive
50 South William Street
Dublin 2

Tel/Fax: +353 1 6703885/+353 1 6703890
Email: imcadmin@eircom.net

Promotes jazz/improv and world music. 150 music events are promoted throughout the year. Promotes ESB Dublin Jazz Week.

Instituto Cervantes
Ignacio Montes
Director
58 Northumberland Road
Dublin 4

Tel/Fax: +353 1 6682024/+353 1 6688416
Email: cendub@cervantes.es

Website: www.cervantes.es
Other key staff: Juan Dobisco (Head of Studies), Isabel Lopez (Head Librarian)

Promotes chamber, jazz/improv and trad/folk music. 25-30 music events are promoted from September to June.

International Concert Management/ ICM Artists & Tours
Ashley Pringle
Director
23 Farmleigh Avenue
Stillorgan
Co. Dublin

Tel/Fax: +353 1 2886251
Email: icmtours@esatclear.ie

Promotes orchestral, choral, opera, chamber and trad/folk music throughout the year. Programme is planned 6-9 months in advance (see ad. p309, agents).

Irish Museum of Modern Art
Philomena Byrne
Head of Public Affairs
Royal Hospital
Military Road
Kilmainham
Dublin 8

Tel/Fax: +353 1 6129900/+353 1 6129999
Email: info@modernart.ie
Website: www.modernart.ie
Other key staff: Rowena Neville (Public Affairs Executive)

Promotes orchestral and chamber music. 10 music events are promoted throughout the year. Bernadette Greevy Masterclasses take place in January. Programme is planned 18 months-2 years in advance. Kawai piano is hired from Piano Plus.

Jazz on the Terrace
Allen Smith
Director
44 Belgrave Square West
Dublin 6

Tel/Fax: +353 1 4979562
Email: jazzontheterrace@ireland.com

Promotes jazz/improv music from February-June and September-November (see advert p.150).

Hugh Lane Municipal Gallery of Modern Art

Gavin O'Sullivan
Music Programmer
Charlemont House
Parnell Square North
Dublin 1

Tel/Fax: +353 1 8741903/+353 1 8722183
Email: hughlane@iol.ie

Promotes chamber, crossover, jazz/improv, trad/folk and world music. 40 music events are promoted from September to June. The programme is planned 6-12 months in advance. Kawai RXA piano is available.

Larkin Concert Series

Marie-Louise O'Donnell
Events/Promotions
Dublin City University
Glasnevin
Dublin 9

Tel/Fax: +353 1 7045216/+353 1 7045567
Email: marie-louise.donnell@dcu.ie
Website: www.dcu.ie

Promotes chamber, choral and instrumental music.

Limerick Music Association

John A. Ruddock
Director
48 Ulverton Road
Dalkey
Co. Dublin

Tel/Fax: +353 1 2804676/+353 1 2302265

Promotes orchestral and chamber music. 20-25 music events are promoted throughout the year. Programme is planned two years in advance. Steinway piano is available for performers.

The Machine

Avril Ryan
Executive Director
SFX City Theatre
23 Upper Sherrard Street
Dublin 1

Tel/Fax: +353 1 8554090
Email: scottart@eircom.net
Website: www.homepage.eircom.net/~sfa
Other key staff: Michael Scott (Artistic Director)

Promotes choral, opera, chamber, trad/folk, world and pop/rock music. 4-6 music events are promoted throughout the year. Programme is planned 3-6 months in advance.

Des McMahon

Director
Abbot Press
6 St. Agnes Road
Crumlin
Dublin 12

Tel/Fax: +353 1 4554551/+353 1 4559850

Promotes blues, jazz/improv and world music in Renards, Mother Redcaps and Whelans. 20 music events are promoted throughout the year. Programme is planned 2-3 months in advance. Kawai baby grand is available for performers.

National Concert Hall

Judith Woodworth
Director
2 Earlsfort Terrace
Dublin 2

Tel/Fax: +353 1 4751666/+353 1 4783797
Email: info@nch.ie
Website: www.nch.ie
Other key staff: Karen Thompson (Events & Operations Manager), Jacqui Mahon (PR/Marketing Manager)

Promote orchestral, choral, opera, crossover, chamber, jazz/improv, trad/folk, world, ballet, rock and pop music. Over 300 music events are promoted throughout the year. Programme is planned up to two years in advance. Steinway Model D is available for performers.

Robert Nolan

36 Castleknock Way
Laurel Lodge
Castleknock
Dublin 15

Tel/Fax: +353 1 8204559/+353 1 8210302
Other key staff: Miriam Reid (Secretary)

Promotes orchestral, jazz/improv and rock and pop music. 12-20 music events are promoted throughout the year. Steinway Concert Grand available for performers.

Note Productions
Ben Jackson
Director
108 Rathmines Town Centre
Dublin 6

Tel/Fax: +353 1 4970450
Email: ben@note.ie
Website: www.note.ie

Promotes jazz/improv music. 10 music events are promoted throughout the year. Programme is planned six months in advance. Steinway model D piano is available for performers. Promotes the ESB Jazz Series.

Opera Theatre Company
Gemma Murray
Administrator
Temple Bar Music Centre
Curved Street
Dublin 2

Tel/Fax: +353 1 6794962/+353 1 6794963
Email: info@operatheatreco.com
Website: www.imn.ie/otc
Other key staff: James Conway (Director), Nick Costello (Marketing/Education), Jan Duffy (PRO), Sadhbh O'Connor (Administrative Assistant)

Promotes opera and chamber music. 3-4 opera production tours are promoted from January-February, May or July and October-November. Programme is planned 6-18 months in advance.

Pim Street Productions
Gavin O'Sullivan
10 Pim Street
Dublin 8

Tel: +353 1 4531303
Email: gavinosu@indigo.ie

Promotes classical music and music for film and television.

Project Arts Centre
Tom Coghlan
General Manager
39 East Essex Street
Temple Bar
Dublin 2

Tel/Fax: +353 1 6796622/+353 1 6369151
Email: info@project.ie

Website: www.project.ie
Other key staff: Kathy McArdle (Artistic Director), Janice McAdam (Director of Public Affairs)

Promotes blues, crossover, chamber, jazz/improv, trad/folk, world, rock/pop and contemporary music. Music events are promoted throughout the year. Programme is planned four to six months in advance.

Royal Dublin Society
Adrienne Dunne
Development Executive - Arts
Ballsbridge
Dublin 4

Tel/Fax: +353 1 6680866 Ext. 211/
+353 1 6604014
Email: adrienne.dunne@rds.ie
Website: www.rds.ie

RTÉ Music Department
Niall Doyle
Director of Music
Donnybrook
Dublin 4

Tel/Fax: +353 1 2083143/+353 1 2082511
Email: doylen@rte.ie
Website: www.rte.ie/music/index.html
Other key staff: Miriam McDonald (General Manager, Marketing & Communications), Martyn Westermann (General Manager, National Symphony Orchestra of Ireland), Gareth Hudson (Executive Producer, RTÉ Concert Orchestra)

Promotes orchestral, choral, opera, chamber and jazz/improv music. 50 music events promoted throughout the year. Programme is planned 18 months to two years in advance (see advert p. 37).

South Dublin County Council
Emily Jane Kirwan
Arts Officer
Town Centre
Tallaght
Dublin 24

Tel/Fax: +353 1 4149000 Ext. 3314 or 3345/
+353 1 4149106
Email: artsofficer@sdublincoco.ie
Website: www.sdcc.ie

Promotes crossover, jazz/improv, trad/folk and rock/pop music. 8-10 music events are planned throughout the year. Programme is planned twelve months in advance.

Tallaght Community Arts Centre
Mary Grehan
Director
Virginia House
Old Blessington Road
Tallaght
Dublin 24

Tel/Fax: +353 1 4621501/+353 1 4621640
Email: tcacart@itw.ie
Website: www.tallaghtcommunityartscentre.ie

Promotes orchestral, blues, crossover, jazz/improv, trad/folk, rock/pop and world music. Music events are promoted throughout the year. Programme is planned 5 months in advance.

CO. GALWAY

Clifden Community Arts Week
Brendan Flynn
Clifden
Co. Galway

Tel/Fax: +353 95 21644/+353 95 21481
Email: artsweek@indigo.ie
Other key staff: Brendan O'Scannaill (Secretary), Eamon McLaughlin (Chairman)

Promotes orchestral, choral, blues, chamber, jazz/trad and jazz/improv music. 10 music events are promoted throughout the year. Programme is planned 6-8 months in advance. (see also pages)

An Gaelacadamh
Caitríona Ní Oibicín
Cólaiste Connacht
An Spidéal
Co. Gallimhe

Tel: +353 91 553124

Promotes traditional and folk music. 6 music events are promoted throughout the year. Programme is planned 3 months in advance.

Galway Arts Centre
Paul Fahy
47 Dominick Street
Galway

Tel/Fax: +353 91 565886/+353 91 568642
Email: gac@indigo.ie
Website: www.galwayartscentre.ie

Promotes chamber music. 6 music events promoted in Spring/Autumn. Programme is planned 2 months in advance.

Galway Corporation/ Galway County Council
James Harrold
Arts Officer
Wood Quay Court
Wood Quay
Galway

Tel/Fax: +353 91 563841/+353 91 361328
Email: jcharrold@hotmail.com

Promotes orchestral, choral, opera, blues, crossover, chamber, jazz/improv, trad/folk, rock/pop and world music. 20-30 music events are promoted throughout the year. Programme is planned three months in advance. Pianos can be hired according to the artist's requirements.

The Mall Theatre & Cinema Co. Ltd
Jarlath P. Canney
Director
Stable Lane
Tuam
Co. Galway

Tel/Fax: +353 93 24463
Other key staff: Teresa Hopkins (Office Manager)

Promotes choral, opera, jazz/improv and trad/folk music. Programme is planned 3-6 months in advance.

Music For Galway
Madeleine Flanagan
Administrator
9 Lakeview
Claregalway
Co. Galway

Tel/Fax: +353 91 798140
Email: mfg@iol.ie
Other key staff: Jane O'Leary (Programme Director)

Promotes orchestral, chamber music and song recitals. 25 music events are promoted from September-April and during the Galway Arts Festival in July. Programme is planned 2 years in advance. Steinway Model B piano available for performers.

CO. KERRY

Ceol Uíbh Ráthaigh
Sarah O'Brien
South Kerry Development Partnership
An Sean Scoil
Killorglin
Co. Kerry

Tel/Fax: +353 66 9761615/+353 66 9762059

Promotes classical, trad/folk, jazz, world, crossover and blues music. 5-6 music events are promoted throughout the year.

Kenmare Folk Club
Joe Thoma
Kenmare
Co. Kerry

Tel: +353 64 41212

Promotes blues, chamber, jazz/improv, trad/folk and world Music. 6 music events are promoted in spring and summer. Programmes are planned three months in advance.

Kerry County Council
Kate Kennelly
Arts Officer
Kerry County Council
Rathass
Tralee
Co. Kerry

Tel/Fax: +353 66 7121111/+353 66 7122466
Email: kcc@kerrycoco.ie
Website: www.kerrycoco.ie

Promotes orchestral, choral, crossover, chamber, jazz/improv, rock/pop and trad/folk music. 6-10 music events are promoted throughout the year.

St. Johns Arts Centre
Joe Murphy
Administrator
The Square
Listowel
Co. Kerry

Tel/Fax: +353 68 22566/+353 68 23485
Website: www.listowel.com

Promotes orchestral, choral, opera, blues, crossover, chamber, jazz/improv, trad/folk, rock/pop and world music. 70 music events are promoted throughout the year. Programme is planned 1-12 months in advance. Yamaha E108 OS/UR is available for performers.

Sessions from the Hearth
Benny O'Carroll
Director
'Fortlands'
Ballyard
Tralee
Co. Kerry

Tel/Fax: +353 66 7126952
Email: benny@sfh.ie.nu
Other key staff: Yvonne McMahon (Personal Assistant/PR)
Tel/Fax: +353 1 6674171/+353 1 6673920

Promotes trad/folk music throughout the year. Provides package tours whereby those interested go to fireside or pub sessions. Traditional music sessions consist of music, song and dance.

Siamsa Tíre
Martin Whelan
General Manager
Town Park
Tralee
Co. Kerry

Tel/Fax: +353 66 7123055/+353 66 7127276
Other key staff: Anne Kennelly (Public Relations), Jimmy McDonnell (Technical)

Promotes orchestral, choral, opera, crossover, chamber, jazz/improv, trad/folk, rock/pop and world music. 12-15 music events are promoted from January-May and October-December. Programmes are planned 6 months in advance. Steinway Model C grand piano available for performers.

CO. KILDARE

County Kildare Arts Centre
Maeve O'Brien
County Arts Centre Manager
Kildare County Library
Athgarvan Road
Newbridge
Co. Kildare

Tel/Fax: +353 45 433480/+353 45 432490
Email: colibrary@kildarecoco.ie
Other key staff: Mary Linehan (County Arts Officer)

From September 2000 intends to promote blues, chamber, jazz/improv, trad/folk, rock/pop, world and contemporary music. 12 music events will be promoted throughout the year. Programme is planned 6-12 months in advance. Petrof Upright Model 125 piano available for performers.

Dunshane Camphill Community
Michiel Brave
Senior Co-Worker
Dunshane House
Brannockstown
Naas
Co. Kildare

Tel/Fax: +353 45 483628/+353 45 483833
Other key staff: Claudia Brave (Senior Co-Worker), Veronica Van Duin (Senior Co-Worker)

Promotes chamber, jazz/improv, trad/folk, world, blues, crossover and a limited amount of orchestral and choral music. 4-5 music events are promoted throughout the year, except June, July and August. Programme is planned 5-6 months in advance. August Forster baby grand piano available for performers.

Kildare County Council
Mary Linehan
Arts Officer
County Library
Athgarvan Road
Newbridge
Co. Kildare

Tel/Fax: +353 45 431215/+353 45 432490
Email: kap@eircom.net
Website: www.kildare.ie/arts

Promotes orchestral, choral, crossover, chamber, jazz/improv, trad/folk and rock/pop music. 6-10 music events are promoted throughout the year. Programme is planned 4 months in advance.

Kildare Performing Arts Group
Eddie O'Neill
Unit 2a Cutlery Road
Newbridge
Co. Kildare

Tel: +353 45 431213
Email: kpag@eircom.net
Website: www.kildare.ie/kpag
Other key staff: Terry Moore (Information Officer), Claire Noons (Music Performance Youth Programmer), Sophie Costigan (Administrator)

The Red Hot Music Club promotes contemporary music.

CO. KILKENNY

Duiske Concerts Ltd
Dr. Marian Tierney
Treasurer
The Rectory
Graignamanagh
Co. Kilkenny

Tel/Fax: +353 503 24277 or +353 503 24495/+353 503 24495
Email: ahayden@iol.ie
Other key staff: Ann Hayden (Assistant Treasurer), Margaret Cosgrave (PRO)

Promotes orchestral, choral, opera, organ, chamber and trad/folk music. 8-10 music events are promoted at certain time during the year. Programme is planned 6-12 months in advance. Steinway piano available for performers.

Kilkenny Music Club/ Kilkenny County Council
Margaret Cosgrave
Arts Organiser
County Hall
John Street
Kilkenny

Tel/Fax: +353 56 52699/+353 56 63384
Email: mcosgrav@kilkennycoco.ie
Website: www.kilkennycoco.ie
Other key staff: Susan Proud (Music Development), Fiona Kelly (Supervisor)

Promotes orchestral, choral, chamber, jazz/improv, trad/folk and world music. 12 music events are promoted from September-May. Programme is planned 6-9 months in advance. Steinway D grand piano is available for performers.

CO. LAOIS

Dunamaise Theatre
Louise Donlon
Manager
Portlaoise
Co. Laois

Tel/Fax: +353 50263355 or +353 502 63356/
+353 502 63357

Promotes chamber, orchestral, choral, opera, jazz, traditional and folk music.

Laois County Council
Muireann Ní Chonaill
Arts Officer
Laois Arts Office
Áras an Chontae
Portlaoise
Co. Laois

Tel/Fax: +353 502 22044/+353 502 22313
Email: artsoff@laoiscoco.ie

Promotes orchestral, choral, opera, blues, crossover, chamber, jazz/improv, trad/folk and world music. 6 music events are promoted throughout the year. Programme is planned four months in advance.

CO. LEITRIM

The Cornmill Theatre
Del Thorogood
General Manager
Main Street
Carrigallen
Co. Leitrim

Tel/Fax: +353 49 4339612
Email: delthoro@gofree.indigo.ie

Promotes choral, jazz/improv, trad/folk and world music. 12 music events are promoted throughout the year. Programme is planned 3-6 months in advance.

Leitrim County Council
Terre Duffy
Arts Officer
Park Lane House
Carrick-on-Shannon
Co. Leitrim

Tel/Fax: +353 78 20005/+353 78 20925
Email: artsoff@leitrimcoco.ie

Promotes orchestral, choral, jazz/improv, trad/folk, rock/pop and world music. 3-4 music events are promoted throughout the year. Programme is planned 3-6 months in advance.

North Leitrim Glens Centre
Liz Culloty
Project Manager
New Line
Manorhamilton
Co. Leitrim

Tel/Fax: +353 72 55833/+353 72 56063
Email: nlgdc@eircom.net
Other key staff: Nora McTiernan
(Administrator), Betty Duignan (Committee Member)

Promotes choral, blues, chamber, jazz/improv, trad/folk and would be interested in promoting all types of music. 12 music events are promoted throughout the year. Programme is planned 6 months in advance. Upright piano is available for performers (see ad p.159).

CO. LIMERICK

Belltable Arts Centre
Mary Coll
Director
69 O'Connell Street
Limerick

Tel/Fax: +353 61 319866/+353 61 418552
Email: belltabl@iol.ie
Website: www.commerce.ie/belltable

Promotes choral, opera, crossover, chamber, jazz/improv and trad/folk music. Music events are promoted throughout the year. Programme is planned 6 months in advance.

Friars Gate Theatre & Arts
John Brazill
Manager
Sarsfield Street
Kilmallock
Co. Limerick

Tel/Fax: +353 63 98727/+353 63 20180

Promotes orchestral, opera, ballet, crossover and trad/folk music.

CO. LONGFORD

Limerick Corporation
Sheila Deegan
Arts Officer
City Hall
Merchants Quay
Limerick

Tel/Fax: +353 61 415799/+353 61 415266
Email: artsoff@limerickcorp.ie

Promotes jazz/improv and trad/folk music. 3-4 music events are promoted in spring and autumn. Programme is planned 3 months in advance.

Limerick County Council
Joan MacKernan
County Arts Officer
County Buildings
79-84 O'Connell Street
Limerick

Tel/Fax: +353 61 318477/+353 61 317280
Email: artsoffice@limerickcoco.ie
Other key staff: Elaine Hill (Assistant County Arts Officer)

Promotes choral, chamber, jazz/improv, trad/folk and world music. 8-10 music events are promoted in autumn, spring and early summer. Programme is planned 3-6 months in advance.

Limerick Jazz
Evan Morrissey
President
Mary Immaculate College
South Circular Road
Limerick

Tel/Fax: +353 61 204389/+353 61 313632
Email: evan.morrissey@mic.ul.ie
Other key staff: Tony Rodgers (Secretary), Finbar Dowling (Treasurer)

Promotes jazz/improv music. 8 music events are promoted from January-April and October-December. Programme is planned 1-3 months in advance. A piano is hired as needed.

Backstage Theatre & Centre for the Arts
Jane Hughes
Development & Promotions Executive
Farneyhoogan
Longford

Tel/Fax: +353 43 47888 or +353 43 47889/ +353 43 47890
Email: backstage@eircom.net
Other key staff: Mona Considine (Theatre Operations Manager), Sean Mulroy (Stage Manager)

Promotes orchestral, choral, opera, blues, chamber, jazz/improv, trad/folk, world and rock/pop music. 10-12 music events are promoted from September-April. Programme is planned 3 months in advance. Events are programmed 3 months in advance, and all events take place within the theatre itself.

Longford County Council
Fergus Kennedy
Arts Officer
Áras An Chontae
Great Water Street
Longford

Tel/Fax: +353 43 48376/+353 43 41125
Email: longfordcoco@eircom.net

Lough Ree Development Association
Carmel Fallon
Main Street
Lanesborough
Co. Longford

Tel/Fax: +353 43 27070/+353 43 27042
Email: loughree@esatclear.ie
Website: www.lough-ree.com

Promotes traditional and classical music. 4 music events are promoted throughout the year.

CO. LOUTH

CO. MEATH

Carlingford Lough Heritage Trust
Teach Eolas
Old Quay Lane
Carlingford
Co. Louth

Tel/Fax: +353 42 9373888/+353 42 9373882

Promotes choral, trad/folk and chamber music. 6 music events are promoted throughout the year. Programme is planned 3-6 months in advance. Yamaha baby grand piano is available for performers (see advert p.150).

Droichead Arts Centre
Tony Conaghy
Acting Director
Stockwell Lane
Drogheda
Co. Louth

Tel/Fax: +353 41 9833946/+353 41 9842055
Email: droiched@indigo.ie
Other key staff: Kathleen O'Brien (Financial Manager)

Promotes orchestral, choral, opera, blues, crossover, chamber, jazz/improv, trad/folk, rock/pop and world music. 26 music events are promoted throughout the year. Programme is planned six months in advance. A Yamaha baby grand piano is available for performers.

Dundalk Urban District Council
Brian Harten
Arts Officer
Market Square
Dundalk
Co. Louth

Tel/Fax: +353 42 9332276/+353 42 9336761
Email: dunarts@eircom.net
Other key staff: Mary O'Sullivan (Assistant Arts Officer), Carl Dearey (CE Supervisor)

Promotes orchestral, choral, opera, blues, crossover, chamber, jazz/improv, trad/folk, rock/pop and world music. 10-15 music events are promoted throughout the year. Programme is planned 6-9 months in advance. Both a Yamaha grand and a Yamaha upright piano are available for performers.

Meath County Council
Gerardette Bailey
Arts Officer
Dunshaughlin Library
Main Street
Dunshaughlin
Co. Meath

Tel/Fax: +353 1 8240000/+353 46 21463
Email: gbailey@meathcoco.ie

Promotes choral, crossover, chamber, trad/folk and world music. 6-10 music events are promoted throughout the year. Programme is planned 3 months in advance.

Music Hibernia
Anne Farrelly
Director
Cúl Cuana
Balrathboyne Glebe
Cortown
Kells
Co. Meath

Tel/Fax: +353 46 34019
Mobile: +353 87 2394090
Email: hibernia@eircom.net

Promotes orchestral and choral music. Approximately 30 music events are promoted throughout the year.

CO. MAYO

Ballina Arts Events
Teeling Street
Ballina
Co. Mayo

Tel/Fax: +353 96 73593/+353 96 71238

Promotes choral, chamber, jazz/improv, trad/folk and world music. 2 music events are promoted throughout the year. Programme is planned 6 months in advance. Bechstein Grand piano available for performers.

Charlestown Regional Arts
Gerry Murray
Chairman

Your community working for you!

NORTH LEITRIM Glens

Development Co. Ltd.

New Line,
Manorhamilton,
Co. Leitrim

Tel: **072 55833**
Fax: **072 56063**
E-mail: **nlgdc@eircom.net**

TIPPERARY EXCEL LIMITED
MITCHELL STREET, TIPPERARY, Co. TIPPERARY
TEL: 062-33466
e-mail: info@Tipperary-excel.com

Modern 380 seat Theatre, fly tower, 4 dressing rooms. Facilities include light and sound to the highest standard. Also 2 other smaller audio visuals/cinemas of 160 and 120 seats. Dedicated Art Gallery and workshop area. Interpretative area for tourism purposes.

UNIVERSITY
CONCERT HALL
Limerick

Ph: 061 331549
Fax: 061 331585
www.uch.ie

1038 Seat Venue

Concerts, Opera, Drama, Classical, Recitals, Comedy, Dance A/V Recordings

Full details available on website:
www.uch.ie

The design and print professionals

Design
Print
Internet

Ferbane, Co. Offaly
Tel: **0902 54327**
Fax: **0902 54609**
Email: **brosna@iol.ie**
www.brosnapress.ie

The Square
Charlestown
Co. Mayo

Tel: +353 94 54736
Email: murrayg@eircom.net

Promotes choral, blue, crossover, chamber, jazz/improv, trad/folk, rock/pop and world music. 5-6 music events are promoted mostly in summer with the intention to be year round. Programme is planned 6 weeks in advance.

Linenhall Arts Centre
Marie Farrell
Director
Linenhall Street
Castlebar
Co. Mayo

Tel: +353 94 23733/+353 94 26162
Email: linenhall@anu.ie

Promotes orchestral, opera, blues, chamber, jazz/improv, trad/folk and world music. 20 music events are promoted throughout the year.

Mayo County Council
The Arts Officer
Arts Office
Áras An Chontae
Castlebar
Co. Mayo

Tel/Fax: +353 94 24444 Ext. 577/+353 94 24774
Email: mayococoarts@hotmail.com

Promotes choral, crossover, jazz/improv and trad/folk music. Programme is planned at least three months in advance.

CO. MONAGHAN

The Garage Theatre
Eileen Costello
PRO
Mifit Buildings
St. Davnet's Complex
Armagh Road
Monaghan

Tel/Fax: +353 47 81597/+353 47 81564

Email: garagetheatre@eircom.net
Website: under construction
Other key staff: Kathleen O'Dowd (Financial Officer), Tony McKenna (Technician)

Promotes orchestral, opera, blues, chamber, jazz/improv and trad/folk music. 6 music events are promoted throughout the year. Programme is planned three months in advance.

Monaghan County Council
Somhairle MacConghail
Arts Officer
The Glen
Monaghan

Tel/Fax: +353 47 82928/+353 47 71189

Promotes choral, trad/folk, jazz/improv, blues, rock, world and crossover music. 30 music events are promoted from February-June and September-December. Programme is planned 2-5 months in advance.

Re: Sound
Brendan McCahey
Chairperson
Staying Alive Centre
32c Main Street
Carrickmacross
Co. Monaghan

Tel: +353 42 9664191
Email: stayingalivecentre@eircom.net

Promote chamber, classical and rock/pop music. 10 music events are promoted throughout the year. Will hire piano if necessary.

Ulster Canal Stores
Jim Kerr
Supervisor
c/o Clones Development Society
Ulster Canal Stores
Clones
Co. Monaghan

Tel/Fax: +353 47 52125 or +353 47 51718/
+353 47 51720 .
Email: callcare@eircom.net
Website: www.cluaineois.demon.co.uk
Other key staff: Paddy Boylan (Projects Manager)

Promotes chamber, jazz/improv and trad/folk music. 12-14 music events are promoted in spring, autumn and winter. Programme is planned one month in advance. Upright piano is available for performers.

CO. OFFALY

Offaly Community Arts Group
Ed Cunningham
Chairman
'Carraig Dún'
Daingean Road
Tullamore
Co. Offaly

Tel: +353 504 51365
Mobile: +353 86 8761495
Other key staff: Catherine Roche (Secretary), Helen Wilson (PRO)

Promotes orchestral, choral, blues, crossover, chamber, jazz/improv, trad/folk and world music. 4-6 music events are promoted from winter-spring. Programme is planned 3-6 months in advance.

Offaly County Council
Noreen O'Hare
Arts Officer
The Arts Office
The Courthouse
Tullamore
Co. Offaly

Tel/Fax: +353 506 46830/+353 506 46868
Email: artsoff@offalycoco.ie

Promotes orchestral, choral, opera, blues, crossover, chamber, jazz/improv, trad/folk, world, rock/pop and contemporary music. 9 music events are promoted throughout the year. Programme is planned 3-12 months in advance.

CO. ROSCOMMON

Fr. Shane Fitzgerald
Donamon Castle
Roscommon

Tel/Fax: +353 903 62222/+353 93 62511
Email: castlemusic@indigo.ie

Promotes chamber music. 9 music events promoted throughout the year.

Roscommon County Council
The Arts Officer
Roscommon County Council
Abbey Street
Roscommon

Tel/Fax: +353 903 26100/+353 903 25477

CO. SLIGO

Con Brio - Sligo Music Association
Luisa MacConville
Co-ordinator
c/o Atlas Language Services
Business Innovation Centre
Institute of Technology
Sligo

Tel/Fax: +353 71 44131 (day) or +353 71 60180/ +353 71 44500
Email: mcconville.luisa@sligo.ie
Other key staff: John Buckley (Committee Member), Brendan Canning (Committee Member), Seamus Concannon (Committee Member)

Promotes orchestral, chamber, opera, song recitals and jazz music. 5-8 music events are promoted from September-April. Con Brio - Sligo Music Association work with the Vogler Quartet in Sligo Residency Programme. Will co-promote the Vogler Quartet Winter Subscription Series, which will run from autumn through to spring in each year of the residency until 2002. Con Brio aims to employ mostly young musicians and professional local talent.

Hawk's Well Theatre
Denis Clifford
Executive Director
Hawk's Well Theatre
Temple Street
Sligo

Tel/Fax: +353 71 61526/+353 71 71737
Email: hawkswell@eircom.net
Other key staff: Averyl Dooher (Assistant Director), Barry McKinney (Technical Manager)

Promotes orchestral, choral, opera, blues, chamber, jazz/improv, trad/folk, rock/pop and world music. 20 music events are promoted throughout the year. Programme is planned 3-6 months in advance. Yamaha Upright piano is available for performers.

Model and Niland Arts Centre
Una McCarthy
Director
The Mall
Sligo

Tel/Fax: +353 71 41405/+353 71 43694
Email: modelart@iol.ie
Website: www.iol.ie/~modelart/
Other key staff: Ann O'Dea (Education), Paul Cunningham (Music)

Promotes orchestral, chamber, jazz/improv, world, trad/folk music. Programme is planned 8-9 months in advance (see advert p.150).

Sligo County Council & Corporation
Mary McAuliffe
Arts Officer
County Council Offices
Riverside
Co. Sligo

Tel/Fax: +353 71 56629/+353 71 41119
Email: arts@sligococo.ie
Other key staff: Lorraine Mulligan (Clerical Assistant)

Sligo County Council & Corporation, in collaboration with Music Network and the Arts Council, have developed the Vogler Quartet in Sligo Residency Programme. This programme runs from September 1999 - August 2002.

Traditional Music Society - Institute of Technology Sligo
Seán Moloney
Organiser
Institute of Technology
Balllinode
Sligo

Tel/Fax: +353 71 55222/+353 71 44096
Email: moloney.sean@itsligo.ie
Website: www.itsligo.ie/students/tradsoc/tradsoc.html
Other key staff: Maria Keaney (Organiser)

Promotes trad/folk music. 6 music events are promoted from December-May. Programme is planned 1-3 months in advance. Upright piano available for performers.

CO. TIPPERARY

Cahir Castle Arts Society
Maureen Ahern
New Haven
Cahir
Co. Tipperary

Tel/Fax: +353 52 41508
Mobile: +353 87 2319639

Promotes orchestral, choral, crossover, chamber, jazz/improv and trad/folk music. Over 12 music events are promoted from January-June and September-December. Programme is planned 3-4 months in advance.

South Tipperary Arts Centre
Siobhan Mulcahy
Artistic Director
Nelson Street
Clonmel
Co. Tipperary

Tel/Fax: +353 52 27877/+353 52 27866
Email: stac@eircom.net
Other key staff: Frank Taylor (Music Officer), Ronnie Fitzgerald (Education Co-ordinator)

Promotes blues, crossover, chamber, jazz/improv and trad/folk music. 5-10 music events are promoted in spring and autumn. Programme is planned 6 months in advance.

Tipperary North County Council
Melanie Scott
Arts Officer
The Courthouse
Nenagh
Co. Tipperary

Tel/Fax: +353 67 31771/+353 67 33134
Email: artsoffice@northtippcoco.ie

Promotes a variety of music throughout the year.

CO. WATERFORD

Garter Lane Arts Centre
Caroline Senior
Artistic Director
22a O'Connell Street
Waterford

Tel/Fax: +353 51 855038/+353 51 871570
Email: admin@garterlane.ie
Other key staff: Lilly O'Reilly (General Manager)

Promotes orchestral (occasionally), choral, opera, blues, crossover, chamber, jazz/improv, trad/folk, world and rock/pop music. 25 music events are promoted throughout the year. Programme is planned 6-9 months in advance.

Symphony Club of Waterford
Vanessa Sadlier
Music Department
Waterford Institute of Technology
Cork Road
Waterford

Tel/Fax: +353 51 302277/+353 51 302293

Promotes orchestral music. 8 music events are promoted from September-August. Programme is planned one year in advance. Yamaha grand piano available.

Waterford Corporation
Derek Verso
Arts Officer
City Hall
The Mall
Waterford

Tel/Fax: +353 51 309983/+353 51 879124
Email: art@waterfordcorp.ie

Promotes orchestral, choral, opera, blues, crossover, chamber, jazz/improv, trad/folk, world and rock/pop music. 50 music events are promoted throughout the year. Programme is planned 3-12 months in advance. 1995 Steinway Baby Grand is available for performers.

Waterford County Council
Margaret Fleming
Arts Officer
Civic Offices
Davitt's Quay
Dungarvan
Co. Waterford

Tel/Fax: +353 58 41416/+353 58 42911

Waterford Music Club
Evelyne O'Riordan
Honorary Secretary
14 Grange Park Avenue
Waterford

Tel/Fax: +353 51 874405/+353 51 874912
Other key staff: Patrick Grogan (Chairman), James Walsh (Treasurer)

Promotes choral and chamber music. 8 music events are promoted from Autumn to April. Steinway Model C baby grand piano available for performers. Programme is planned one year in advance.

West Waterford Music
Jan Van Putten
Bridane Cottage
Lismore
Co. Waterford

Tel/Fax: +353 58 54416/+353 58 54137

Promotes orchestral, chamber, choral and jazz/improv music. At least 6 music events are promoted throughout the year.

CO. WESTMEATH

Derravaragh Music Association
David Taylor
Chairman
Lough Bawn
Collinstown
Co. Westmeath

Tel.: +353 44 66344/+353 44 66245
Email: loughbawn@eircom.net
Other key staff: Bill Butler (Vice-Chairman/Promotion), Mary O'Neill (Secretary/Bookings)

Promotes chamber music. 5-6 music events are promoted from September-April. Programme is planned approximately twelve months in advance. A piano is hired if necessary needed, this is usually a Kawai.

Mullingar Arts Centre
Patricia Gibney
Centre Director
Mount Street
Mullingar
Co. Westmeath

Tel/Fax: +353 44 47777/+353 44 47783
Email: patriciagibney@eircom.net
Other key staff: Seán Lynch (Programme Director)

Promotes orchestral, opera, blues, chamber, jazz/improv, trad/folk and rock/pop music. 12 music events are promoted throughout the year. Programme is planned months in advance.

Tuar Ard Arts Centre

Maura Farrell
Manager
Church Street
Moate
Co. Westmeath

Tel: +353 902 82042
Other key staff: Peter Dolan (PRO)

Promotes orchestral, chamber, jazz/improv and trad/folk music. 12 music events are promoted throughout the year.

CO. WEXFORD

Camphill Community

Thomas Meyer-Hündorf
Cultural Events Co-ordinator
Duffcarrig
Gorey
Co. Wexford

Tel/Fax: +353 55 25911/+353 55 25910
Email: duffcarrig1@eircom.net
Website: www.camphill.ie
Other key staff: Clare Goodman (Assistant Cultural Events Co-ordinator), Christian Thurm (Technical Supervisor)

Promotes choral, chamber and trad/folk music. 10 music events are promoted throughout the year. Programme is planned 2-6 months in advance. Yamaha baby grand piano available.

Des Mahon

Ballyfinogue
Killinick
Co. Wexford

Tel: +353 53 58986
Mobile: +353 87 2907151

Promotes blues, crossover, jazz/improv, trad/folk, world, rock/pop music. Programme is planned at least 6 weeks in advance.

Music For Wexford

Bernie Lloyd
Chairperson
17 Davitt Road North
Wexford

Tel/Fax: +353 53 23923
Email: quaynote@esatclear.ie

Promotes choral and chamber music. 10 music events are promoted from November-March (evening concerts) and lunchtime concerts in July. Programme is planned 3-6 months in advance. Kawai Boudoir 6' piano available for performers.

Connie Tantrum

Festival Administrator
Cross Street
New Ross
Co. Wexford

Tel: +353 51 421766

Promotes choral, blues, chamber, jazz/improv and trad/folk music. 10 music events are promoted from September-June and the AIMS Choral Festival takes place in May. Programme is planned about nine months in advance. Piano can be hired if necessary.

Wexford Arts Centre

Denis Collins
Artistic Director
Cornmarket
Wexford

Tel/Fax: +353 53 23764/+353 53 24544
Other key staff: Johanna Murphy (Publicity Officer), Anne Heffernan (Community Artist)

Promotes blues, crossover, trad/folk, world and rock/pop music. 30 music events are promoted throughout the year. Programme is planned 4 weeks in advance of the event. Yamaha Upright piano available for performers.

Wexford County Council

Lorraine Comer
County Arts Officer
Wexford

Tel/Fax: +353 53 42211 Ext. 369/+353 53 43532
Email: lcomer@wexfordcoco.ie
Website: www.wexford.ie
Other key staff: Anita Rossiter (Clerical Officer)

Promotes orchestral, choral, blues, crossover, chamber, jazz/improv and trad/folk music. 10-12 music events are promoted throughout the year. Programme is planned one year in advance.

CO. WICKLOW

Tinahely Courthouse Centre

Sharon Corcoran
Director
Courthouse Centre
Main Street
Tinahely
Co. Wicklow

Tel/Fax: +353 402 38529/+353 402 38440
Email: tinahely@iol.ie
Website: www.tinahely-courthouse.ie
Other key staff: Magret Gallagher (Productions Manager)

Promotes blues, crossover, chamber, jazz/improv, trad/folk and world music. 10-12 music events are promoted in autumn, winter and spring. Programme is planned 6 months in advance.

Wicklow County Council Arts Office

Leah Coyne
Arts Officer
St. Manntan's House
Kilmantin Hill
Wicklow

Tel/Fax: +353 404 20155/+353 404 66057
Email: wao@eircom.net
Website: www.wicklow.ie/arts/

Promotes all types of music. Programme is planned six weeks in advance.

PROMOTERS NORTHERN IRELAND

CO. ANTRIM

Antrim Borough Council

Gary Shaw
Arts & Heritage Development Officer
Randalstown Road
Co. Antrim BT41 4LH
Northern Ireland

Tel/Fax: 048 9442 8000/048 9446 0360
Other key staff: Brian Burns (Community Music Development Officer), Cathy McNally (Assistant Arts & Heritage Officer)

Promotes blues, chamber, jazz/improv, trad/folk, world

and rock/pop music. 16 music events are promoted throughout the year. Programme is planned approximately 3 months in advance.

Arts Council of Northern Ireland

Pam Smith
MacNeice House
77 Malone Road
Belfast BT9 6AQ
Northern Ireland

Tel/Fax: 048 9038 5200/048 9066 1715
Email: psmith@artscouncil-ni.org

Promotes chamber, jazz/improv and trad/folk music. 36 music events are promoted each year. Programme is planned 2-4 months in advance. Steinway Model D 500710 (1988) piano is available for performers.

Arts and Disability Forum

Avril Crawford
Development Officer
73-75 Great Victoria Street
Belfast BT2 7AF
Northern Ireland

Tel/Fax: 048 9023 9450/048 9024 7770
Email: adf.dforum@dnet.co.uk

A networking and co-ordinating agency, showcasing the best examples of disability arts practice; on a regional, national and international basis.

Ballymena Borough Council

William Young
Aldeevin
80 Galgorm Road
Ballymena
Co. Antrim BT42 1AB
Northern Ireland

Tel/Fax: 048 2566 0320
Email: william.young/ballymenabc@ballymena.gov.uk

Promotes orchestral, choral, chamber, jazz/improv, trad/folk, world and rock/pop music. 30 music events are promoted throughout the year. Programme is planned up to 1 year in advance. Yamaha grand piano is available for performers.

Ballymoney Borough Arts Committee

Margaret Higgins
Cultural Services Officer
Riada House
14 Charles Street
Ballymoney
Co. Antrim BT53 6DZ
Northern Ireland

Tel/Fax: 048 2766 2280/048 2766 7659
Email: ballymoneybc@psilink.co.uk
Website: www.ballymoney.gov.uk

Promotes orchestral, choral, crossover, opera, chamber, jazz/improv, trad/folk music. 6-10 music events are promoted from September-May. Programme is planned 6-12 months in advance. Yamaha Upright piano is available for performers.

BBC Music & Arts

David Byers
Chief Producer of Music & Arts
Room 419 BBC Broadcasting House
Ormeau Avenue
Belfast BT2 8HQ
Northern Ireland

Tel/Fax: 048 9033 8291/048 9033 8807
Email: stephanie.mckee@bbc.co.uk
Website: www.bbc.co.uk/northernireland/tvr-music-arts.shtml
Other key staff: Stephanie McKee (Radio Production Assistant), Declan McGovern (Producer of Music & Arts), Bill Lloyd (Producer of Music & Arts)

Promotes orchestra and chamber music. 50 music events are promoted throughout the year excluding July. Programme is planned 6 months to one year in advance. Steinway grand piano is available for performers.

Belfast City Council

Chris Bailey
Arts & Heritage Manager
Belfast City Council
Cecil Ward Building
4-10 Linenhall Street
Belfast BT2 8BP
Northern Ireland

Tel/Fax: 048 9032 0202/048 9027 0325

Email: baileyc@belfasteity.gov.uk
Other key staff: Angela McCloskey (Arts Officer)

Belfast Music Society

Margaret Langhammer
Concerts Manager
7 Highgrove Avenue
Ballyclare
Co. Antrim BT39 9XL
Northern Ireland

Tel: 048 9335 2912
Other key staff: Elizabeth Bicker (Chairperson), Seamas Hunt (Honorary Treasurer)

Promote chamber music. 7-8 music events are promoted from October-December and June-May. Programme is planned 1-2 years in advance. Steinway Model D piano is available for performers.

Belfast Waterfront Hall

Tim Husbands
General Manager
2 Lanyon Place
Belfast BT2 3LP
Northern Ireland

Tel/Fax: 048 9033 4400/048 9024 9862
Email: lynchm@belfastcity.gov.uk
Website: www.waterfront.co.uk
Other key staff: Fiona McKeown (Entertainments Co-ordinator), Martin Murray (Arts & Community Co-ordinator)

Promotes orchestral, choral, opera, blues, crossover, chamber, jazz/improv, trad/folk, world, rock/pop music. 50 music events are promoted throughout the year. Programme is planned 3 months to 2 years in advance. Steinway Grand Model D piano is available for performers.

Carrickfergus Borough Council

Colin Ellis
Community Relations Officer
Heritage Plaza
Antrim Street
Carrickfergus
Co. Antrim BT38 7DG
Northern Ireland

Tel/Fax: 048 9336 6455/048 9335 0350

Email: cellis@carrickfergus.org

Promotes orchestral, choral, crossover, jazz/improv and trad/folk music. 10 music events are promoted throughout the year.

Causeway Coast Arts

Malcolm Murchison
Chairman
c/o Flowerfield Arts Centre
185 Coleraine Road
Portstewart
Co. Antrim BT55 7HU
Northern Ireland

Tel/Fax: 048 7083 3959/048 7083 5042
Email: flowerfield@dnet.co.uk
Website: under construction
Other key staff: Margaret Higgins (Hon. Secretary)

Promotes orchestral, opera, chamber, jazz/improv, trad/folk and world music. 6-10 music events are promoted throughout the year. Programme is planned 9 months to 1 year in advance.

Craigavon Borough Council

Rosaleen McMullan
Arts Development Officer
Pinebank Arts & Resource Centre
Tullygally Road
Craigavon BT65 5BV
Northern Ireland

Tel/Fax: 048 3834 1618/048 3834 2402

Promotes orchestral, opera and trad/folk music. 2 music events are promoted in autumn. Programme is planned 9 months to 1 year in advance. Boudoir and upright piano available for performers.

Crescent Arts Centre

Louise Emerson
Manager
2-4 University Road
Belfast BT7 1NH
Northern Ireland

Tel/Fax: 048 9024 2338/048 9024 6748
Email: info@crescentarts.org
Website: www.crescentarts.org

Promotes blues, jazz/improv, world and rock/pop music. 30 music events are promoted throughout the year

excluding November. Programme is planned 2 months in advance. Upright piano is available for performers.

Flowerfield Arts Centre

Malcolm Murchison
Arts Centre Manager
185 Coleraine Road
Portstewart
Co. Antrim BT55 7HU
Northern Ireland

Tel/Fax: 048 7083 3959/048 7083 5042
Email: flowerfield@dnet.co.uk
Website: under construction

Promotes chamber, jazz/improv, trad/folk and world music. Programme is planned six months to 1 year in advance. Yamaha upright piano available for performers.

Larne Borough Council

H.G Francis
Tourism & Community Development Manager
Smiley Buildings
Victoria Road
Larne BT40 1RU
Northern Ireland

Tel/Fax: 048 2827 2313/048 2826 0660
Email: mail@larne-bt.com

Promotes orchestral, choral, crossover, chamber, jazz/improv and trad/folk music. 20 music events are promoted from January-June and September-November.

Live Music Now! Ireland

Rober A. Wilson
Director
22 Brooklands Park
Whitehead
Carrickfergus BT38 9SN
Northern Ireland

Tel/Fax: 048 9337 3942/048 9337 8836
Email: livemusicireland@btconnect.com
Other key staff: David Openshaw (Music Advisor), Dr. Michael Swallow (Music Advisor)

Organise concerts in hospitals, schools, hospices, disability centres and prisons.

Moving On Music Limited

Brian Carson
Director
7 University Road
Belfast BT7 1NA
Northern Ireland

Tel/Fax: 048 9024 8818
Email: movingltd@aol.com
Other key staff: Paul Brown (Production & Promotions Manager)

Promotes blues, crossover, chamber, jazz/improv, trad/folk, world and rock/pop music. Approximately 60 music events are promoted throughout the year. Programme is planned 3-12 months in advance.

Moyle District Council

Arts Co-ordinator
Sheskburn House
7 Mary Street
Ballycastle BT54 6QH
Northern Ireland

Tel/Fax: 048 2076 2225/048 2076 2515
Email: dev@moyle-council.org
Website: www.moyle-council.org
Other key staff: Pauline Russell (Community Relations Officer)

Promotes orchestral, choral, opera, blues, crossover, chamber, jazz/improv, trad/folk, world and rock/pop music.

The Music Company

Malcolm Neale
Chairman
6 Pembroke Court
Belfast BT4 2RW
Northern Ireland

Tel/Fax: 048 9047 3394 or 048 9086 7980/ 048 9047 3394
Email: camerata@globalnet.co.uk
Other key staff: Barry Douglas (Artistic Director)

Promotes orchestral, chamber, jazz/trad music tailored to suit personal and corporate requirements.

Newtownabbey Borough Council

Cathy Cole
Development Officer for the Arts
Department of Leisure & Technical Services
49 Church Road
Newtownabbey BT36 7LG
Northern Ireland

Tel/Fax: 048 9086 8751/048 9036 5407

10-12 music events are promoted from September-May. Programme is planned 4-6 months in advance. Baby grand piano is available for performers.

Old Museum Arts Centre

Anne McReynolds
Director
7 College Square North
Belfast BT1 6AR
Northern Ireland

Tel/Fax: 048 9023 5053/048 9032 2912
Email: info@oldmuseumartscentre.freeserve.co.uk
Other key staff: Elaine Gaston (Development Officer)

Promotes choral, crossover, jazz/improv and trad/folk music. 10 music events are promoted throughout the year. Upright piano is available for performers.

Pinebank House Arts Centre

Rosaleen McMullan
Tullygally Road
Craigavon BT65 5BY
Northern Ireland

Tel/Fax: 048 3834 1618/048 3834 2402
Email: rosaleenmcmullan@gov.uk

Promotes orchestral and jazz/improv music. Programme is planned 6 months in advance.

Ulster Museum

Angela Reid
Public Relations Officer
Botanic Gardens
Belfast BT9 5AB
Northern Ireland

Tel/Fax: 048 9038 3000/048 9038 3103

Promotes orchestral, chamber, jazz/improv and trad/folk music. 6 music events are promoted in October and March. Programme is planned 6 months in advance.

University of Ulster

H.M. Bracefield
Music Department
University of Ulster at Jordanstown
Newtownabbey BT37 0QB
Northern Ireland

Tel/Fax: 048 9036 6955/048 9036 6870
Email: hm.bracefield@ulst.ac.uk

Promotes orchestral, chamber, choral and jazz/improv music. 4 music events are promoted from January-May and October-December and lunch-time concerts.

CO. ARMAGH

Armagh City Folk Club

John Butler
Secretary/Treasurer
1 St. Marys Place
Armagh BT61 9BH
Northern Ireland

Tel/Fax: 048 3752 4418 (h) or 048 3752 2928/ 048 3752 7174
Email: cjb@star.avm.ac.uk

Promotes 6-10 music events from January-April and September-December. Programme is planned 1-3 months in advance.

The Market Place - Armagh Theatre & Arts Centre

Vincent McCann
Administrator
Market Street
Armagh BT61 7AT
Northern Ireland

Tel: 048 3752 1821 or 048 3752 1820
Email: armagh.arts@dnet.co.uk
Website: www.marketplacearmagh.com
Other key staff: Sharon Kerr (Arts Assistant), Lenny Mullan (Arts Officer (Development))

Promotes orchestral, choral, opera, blues, crossover, chamber, jazz/improv, trad/folk, world, rock/pop and country music. Programme is usually planned 4-6 months in advance, depending on the size of the event.

The Stray Leaf Folk Club

Gerry O'Hanlon
Secretary
6 Glendesha Road
Mullaghbawn BT35 9XN
Northern Ireland

Tel/Fax: 048 3088 8565/048 3026 1360
Email: gerry.ohanlon@btinternet.com
Other key staff: Mick Quinn (Chairperson), Patricia Flynn (Treasurer)

Promotes traditional music. 20 music events are promoted from February-June and September-November. Programme is planned six months in advance.

CO. DERRY

Classical Music Society

Kevin Murphy
Audience Development Manager
Foyle Arts Centre
Lawrence Hill
Derry BT48 7NJ
Northern Ireland

Tel/Fax: 048 7126 1449/048 7130 9091
Email: classical.music.society@talk21.com
Other key staff: Fidelis Doran (Chairperson), Angela Liston (Vice-Chairperson)

Promotes orchestral, chamber and opera music. 7-10 music events are promoted on a monthly basis between September and May. Programme is planned 2 years in advance. Steinway concert grand piano is available for performers.

Derry City Council

David McLaughlin
Arts Officer
Rialto Entertainment Centre
5 Market Street
Derry City BT48 6EF
Northern Ireland

Tel/Fax: 048 7126 4177/048 7126 0688
Email: derrytheatre@yahoo.com
Website: www.derrytheatre.com

Promotes orchestral, choral, opera, crossover, chamber, trad/folk, world and rock/pop music. 50 or more music events are promoted from January-May and September-December. Programme is planned 8 months in advance. Steinway piano is available for performers.

Limavady Borough Council
S. Bell
Community Relations Officer
7 Connell Street
Limavady
Northern Ireland

Tel/Fax: 048 7776 0304 or 048 7772 2226/
048 7772 2010

14 music events are promoted throughout the year.
Programme is planned from six months to one year in
advance.

Magherafelt District Council
Sean Henry
Community Relations Officer
50 Ballyronan Road
Magherafelt BT45 6EN
Northern Ireland

Tel/Fax: 048 7963 2151/048 7963 1240
Email: mdc@magherafelt.demon.co.uk
Website: www.magherafelt.demon.co.uk

Riverside Theatre
Janet Mackie
Theatre Manager
University of Ulster
Cromore Road
Coleraine BT52 1SA
Northern Ireland

Tel/Fax: 048 7032 4683/048 7032 4924

Promotes choral, opera, blues, chamber, jazz/improv
and rock/pop music. 6-10 music events are promoted
from January-June and August-November. Programme is
planned 3-6 months in advance. Baby grand piano is
available for performers.

CO. DOWN

Ards Borough Council - Ards Arts Centre
Eilis O'Baoill
Arts officer
Town Hall
Conways Square
Newtownards
Northern Ireland

Tel/Fax: 048 9181 0803/048 9182 3131
Email: angelahaley@ards.council.gov.uk
Other key staff: Kate Wimpress (Community
Arts Development Officer), Angela Haley (Arts
Centre Co-ordinator)

Promotes choral, blues, chamber and trad/folk music.
3-6 music events are promoted from September-June.
Programme is planned up to 6 months in advance.
Yamaha upright available for performers.

Banbridge District Arts Committee
Leah Duncan
Arts & Events Officer
Civic Building
Downshire Road
Banbridge
Northern Ireland

Tel/Fax: 048 4066 0605/048 4066 0601
Email: info@banbridgedc.gov.uk
Website: www.banbridgedc.gov.uk

Promotes all types of music. 20 music events are promoted mostly in October. Programme is planned 3
months in advance.

Castlereagh Borough Council
James Rose
Director of Leisure & Community Services
111 Old Dundonald Road
Dundonald BT16 1XT
Northern Ireland

Tel/Fax: 048 9048 2611/048 9048 9604
Email: leisure@castlereagh.gov.uk

Promotes orchestral, chamber and jazz/improv music. 6
music events are promoted from October-May.

Down District Council
Jill Holmes
Arts Officer
Down County Museum
The Mall
Downpatrick
Co. Down BT30 6AM
Northern Ireland

Tel/Fax: 048 4461 5218/048 4461 5590
Email: jholmes@downdc.gov.uk

Promotes orchestral, choral, opera, blues, crossover,
chamber, jazz/improv, trad/folk, world and rock/pop

music. 6-8 music events are promoted from September-June. Programme is planned 4-8 months in advance. Upright piano is available for performers.

Lisburn Borough Council
Siobhán Stewart
Arts Development Officer
Harmony Hill Arts Centre
54 Harmony Hill
Lisburn BT27 4ES
Northern Ireland

Tel/Fax: 048 9267 8219/048 9266 2679
Email: manager.hhac@lisburn.gov.uk

Promotes orchestral, blues, jazz/improv, trad/folk, world and rock/pop music. 10 music events are promoted from September-December and January-June. Upright baby grand and grand pianos available. Programme is planned 4-6 months in advance.

The National Trust
Mike Gatson
Castle Ward
Strangford BT30 7LS
Northern Ireland

Tel/Fax: 048 4488 1204/048 4488 1729

4 music events are promoted in June, July, August and September. Programme is planned 3-12 months in advance.

Newry & Mourne District Council
Mark Hughes
Arts Administrator/Facilitator
Newry and Mourne Arts Centre
1a Bank Parade
Newry BT35 6HP
Northern Ireland

Tel/Fax: 048 3026 6232/048 3026 6839
Other key staff: Jacqueline Turley (Administrative Assistant)

Promote orchestral, choral, blues, crossover, trad/folk and rock/pop music. Programme is planned 4-6 months in advance. 8-10 music events are promoted throughout the year. Two baby grand pianos and two upright pianos are available for performers.

North Down Borough Council
Lorna Hastings
Arts Officer
Tower House
34 Quay Street
Bangor BT20 5ED
Northern Ireland

Tel/Fax: 048 9127 8032/048 9146 7744
Other key staff: Phil Allely (Marketing), Carol McErlean (Arts Administration Officer)

Promotes orchestral, choral, blues, jazz/improv and trad/folk music. 6-8 music events are promoted throughout the year. Programme is planned 2-6 months in advance.

CO. FERMANAGH

Ardhowen Theatre
Pamela Scrayfield
Assistant Manager
Dublin Road
Enniskillen BT74 6BR
Northern Ireland

Tel/Fax: 048 6632 3233/048 6632 7102
Other key staff: Eamonn Bradley (Manager), Thomas Sharkey (Technician)

Promotes orchestral, choral, opera and chamber music. 6-10 music events are promoted from September-May. Programme is planned at least 6 months and sometimes up to two years in advance. Yamaha upright piano is available for performers.

Fermanagh District Council
Geraldine O'Reilly
Arts Officer
Town Hall
Enniskillen BT74 7BA
Northern Ireland

Tel/Fax: 048 6632 5050/048 6632 2024
Website: www.fermanagh-online.com

Promotes orchestral, choral, opera, blues, crossover, chamber, jazz/improv, trad/folk, world and rock/pop music throughout the year.

CO. TYRONE

Coalisland Folk Club
Donal Quinn
266 Coalisland Road
Dungannon Road
Tyrone BT71 GEP
Northern Ireland

Tel/Fax: 048 8774 0539/048 8774 8904

Promotes jazz/improv, rock, trad/folk and crossover music. 15-20 music events are promoted from September-June.

Cookstown District Council
Linda McGarvey
Secretary
Council Offices
Burn Road
Cookstown BT80 8DT
Northern Ireland

Tel/Fax: 048 8676 2205 Ext. 219/
048 8676 4360
Email: econdev@cookstown.gov.uk
Website: www.cookstown.gov.uk
Other key staff: Adrian McCreesh
(Development Manager), Tony McCance
(Development Officer)

Promotes orchestral, choral, blues, jazz/improv and trad/folk music. 3-4 music events are promoted throughout the year. Programme is planned 3 months in advance.

Dungannon District Council
Theresa McNicholl
Arts Officer
Circular Road
Dungannon BT71 6DT
Co. Tyrone
Northern Ireland

Tel/Fax: 048 8772 0300/048 8772 0368
Email: theresa.mcnicholl@dungannon.gov.uk

Omagh District Council
Jean Brennan
Arts Development Officer
The Grange
Mountjoy Road
Omagh BT79 7BL
Northern Ireland

Tel/Fax: 048 8224 5321/048 8224 3888
Email: jean.brennan@omagh.gov.uk
Website: www.omagh.gov.uk

Promotes orchestral, opera, blues, crossover, chamber, jazz/improv, trad/folk and world music. 6 music events are promoted in October and from January-May. Programme is planned 2-6 months in advance.

Strabane District Council
Karen McFarland
Community Services Officer
47 Derry Road
Strabane
Northern Ireland

Tel/Fax: 048 7138 2204/048 7138 2264
Other key staff: Roisin Bradley (Community Relations Officer)

Promotes orchestral, opera, trad/folk and rock/pop music. 4 music events are promoted in spring and autumn. Programme is planned 6 months in advance.

VENUES

The address given for the venue refers to the contact details for that venue, which may not be the actual venue address. All initial enquiries should therefore be made to the contact person, at the telephone or fax number given.

Further information about venues in Ireland, North and South, can be obtained from the relevant local county arts officer.

VENUES - REP. OF IRELAND

CO. CAVAN

Church of Ireland Virginia
Derek Johnston
Archdeacon
Virginia
Co. Cavan

Tel: +353 49 8548465

Venue type: Church located in the centre of Virginia town.
Facilities: Small organ is available. Fixed church seating.
Policy: Music promoted includes orchestral, chamber and choral. Available for hire Monday-Friday.

Drumlin House
Breege O'Reilly
Administrator
Cooney's Row
Cootehill
Co. Cavan

Tel/Fax: +353 49 5552605/+353 49 5556058
Other key staff: Hugh B. O'Brien (Chairperson), Arlette Howell (Centre Manager)

Venue type: Training centre with one room available for hire.
Facilities: Capacity for 120, seating is fixed and tiered.
Policy: Available for hire from Monday-Sunday. One months notice is required for booking. Theatre productions are also catered for.
Technical details: Stage is 37 ft x 18 ft and is at floor level. Loading equipment is at street level.

Ramor Theatre
Catriona O'Reilly
Arts Officer
Cavan County Council
The Courthouse
Cavan

Tel/Fax: +353 49 4331799 or +353 49 8547074/ +353 49 4362127 or +353 49 8547074
Other key staff: Tony Routers (Caretaker Attendant), Marian Smith (PRO), Maria Nolan (Administrator)

Venue type: Gallery/theatre - converted old Catholic church.
Facilities: Capacity for 182 in large auditorium and 20 in meeting room. Fold-up seating with cushions.
Policy: Available for hire from Monday-Sunday. Booking notice is required. Theatre productions, poetry and dance are also catered for. Music promoted includes choral, opera, traditional and world.
Technical details: Stage is 5 metres x 7 metres x 9 metres. Canvas staging. Size of loading doors are 1.5 metres x 1.75 metres. Speaker system available.

The Seven Horse Shoes
Francis Cahill
Belturbet
Co. Cavan

Tel/Fax: +353 49 22166/+353 49 22118

Venue type: Pub with function room.
Facilities: Capacity for 400.
Policy: Music promoted includes jazz, traditional, world, folk and blues.

CO. CLARE

Dánlann An Chláir
Mary Bradshaw
Principal
Colaiste Muire
Harmony Row
Ennis
Co. Clare

Tel/Fax: +353 65 6829497/+353 65 6828605
Email: colaistemuire@scm.emus.eircom.net

Venue type: School/college was built in 1980.

Facilities: Capacity for 400. Baby grand piano available.
Policy: Available for hire from Monday-Sunday. Music promoted includes chamber, orchestral, choral, opera, jazz, traditional, rock, folk and world. Booking notice is required.
Technical detail: Stage size is 21 metres x 10.5 metres.

International Folk Music Centre of Ireland Ltd
Josephine Cotter Coughlan
Clare County Council
Waterpark House
Ennis
Co. Clare

Tel/Fax: +353 65 6828040/+353 65 8258182
Email: jcoughlan@clarecoco.ie

Venue type: Cultural centre for music and the performing arts, scheduled to open in June 2001.
Facilities: Capacity for 500. Audio visual room. Storage space.

Maoin Cheoil an Chláir
Tracey Smurthwaite
Director
College Road
Ennis
Co. Clare

Tel/Fax: +353 65 6841774

Venue type: Converted chapel built in 1950, which is now used as an auditorium.
Facilities: Capacity for 200.
Policy: Music promoted includes chamber, orchestral, choral, jazz, traditional and world.

Old Ground Hotel
Marion Kelly
Sales Manager
O'Connell Street
Ennis
Co. Clare

Tel/Fax: +353 65 6828127/+353 65 6828112
Email: oghotel@iol.ie

Website: www.ennis.ie/hotels/oldground.html
Other key staff: Mary Gleeson (General Manager), Raymond Foudy (Assistant Manager)

Venue type: Hotel.
Facilities: Function room with capacity for 300 seated and 500 standing. Conference chair type seating.
Policy: Music promoted includes chamber, orchestral, choral, opera, jazz, traditional, folk, pop, dance, country and western and world. Booking notice is required.
Technical detail: Loading is at street level.

St. Columba's Church
Rev. Bob Hanna
Rector
The Rectory
Bindon St
Ennis
Co. Clare

Tel: +353 65 6820109
Email: rchanna.ennis@eircom.net

Venue type: Victorian church with intimate atmosphere.
Facilities: Capacity for 200. Church seating. Mini grand piano and 1873 large pipe organ available.
Policy: Available for hire from Monday-Sunday. Two months booking notice is required. Music promoted includes orchestral, choral and opera.

West County Conference & Leisure Hotel
Brian Harrington
Executive General Manager
Clare Road
Ennis
Co. Clare

Tel/Fax: +353 65 6828421/+353 65 6828801
Email: info@lynchotels.com
Website: www.lynchotels.com

Venue type: Hotel, bar and restaurant
Policy: Available for hire from Monday-Saturday. Up to six months booking notice is required. Music promoted includes traditional, dance and world.

CO. CORK

Aula Maxima - University College Cork

Prof. David Cox
University College Cork
Cork

Tel/Fax: +353 21 4904530/+353 21 4271595

Venue type: University.
Facilities: Capacity for 300. Kawai grand piano is available.
Policy: Music promoted includes orchestral, choral, jazz, traditional and world.

Church of the Ascension Timoleague

Robert Travers
Trustee
The Fleming Trust
Timoleague House
Bandon
Co. Cork

Tel/Fax: +353 23 46116/+353 23 46523
Email: robert@tdi.iol.ie
Other key staff: Rev. Ian Jones (Rector)

Venue type: Small Anglican church with the interior decorated with multicoloured mosaics.
Facilities: Capacity for 130.
Policy: Available for hire from Monday-Sunday. Two weeks booking notice is required. Music promoted includes chamber, orchestral, choral, opera, jazz and traditional.
Technical details: Equipment is loaded at street level.

City Hall Cork

Cork Corporation
Cork

Tel/Fax: +353 21 4966222/+353 21 4314238

Venue type: City hall.
Facilities: Capacity for 1,300.
Policy: Music promoted includes chamber, orchestral, choral, jazz, traditional, country, folk, rock, blues, dance and pop.

Connolly Hall

John Smyth
Lapps Quay
Cork

Tel/Fax: +353 21 4277466/+353 21 4273868

Venue type: Purpose built auditorium.
Facilities: Capacity for 600.

Connollys of Leap

Paddy McNickell
Leap
Co. Cork

Tel/Fax: +353 28 33215

Email: connollys@eircom.net
Venue type: Rural bar, 250 years old, built on a natural rockface.
Facilities: Capacity for 250-300. Moveable seating. Roland RD1000 piano available.
Policy: Available for hire from Monday-Sunday. Music promoted includes choral, jazz, trad, rock, pop, dance, alternative, world and country & western. Two to three months booking notice is required.
Technical details: Street loading. Wood and stone, medium sized stage.

Cork Opera House

Gerry Barnes
Executive Director
Emmet Place
Cork

Tel/Fax: +353 21 4274308 or +353 21 4270022 (box office)/+353 21 276357
Email: operahousecork@eircom.net
Other key staff: Aileen Sweeney (Financial Controller), Miriam Hurley (Marketing Manager)

Venue type: Modern theatre building overlooking the River Lee.
Facilities: Capacity for 1,000 (Cork Opera House), 125 (seated - Half Moon Theatre), 200 (standing - Half Moon Theatre).
Policy: Available for hire from Monday-Sunday. Music promoted include opera, jazz and all musical types.
Technical details: Full technical specification available on request.

Everyman Palace Theatre

Geoff Gould
Artistic Director
15 Macurtain Street
Cork

Tel/Fax: +353 21 4503077/+353 21 4502820
Mobile: +353 86 8199800
Other key staff: Patricia O'Sullivan (Administrator),
Tom Feehily (Technical Manager)

Venue type: Purpose built performance venue, which was recently refurbished.
Facilities: Capacity for 600 (auditorium). Cinema style seating.
Policy: Available for hire from Monday-Sunday. Music promoted includes choral, opera, jazz, trad and dance. Three months booking notice is required.
Technical details: Stage size is 20 ft x 56 ft x 26 feet. Loading equipment is at street level. Full technical specification available on request.

Firkin Crane

Ger O'Riordan
Marketing Manager
Shandon
Cork

Tel/Fax: +353 21 4507487/+353 21 4501124
Other key staff: Mary Brady (Director), Sharon Sheehan (Administrator)

Venue type: Purpose built performance venue.
Facilities: Capacity for 240 (Smurfit Theatre), 77 (Musgrave Theatre). The Smurfit Theatre has moveable seating. Upright piano available.
Policy: Available for hire from Monday-Sunday. Six months booking notice is required.
Technical details: Stage size is 15 ft x 31 ft x 20 ft. Stage is maple covered with hardboard. Loading equipment is at street level.

Glen Theatre

John Flynn
Duinc
Banteer
Co. Cork

Tel/Fax: +353 29 56115
Other key staff: Kathleen Buckley (Administrator)

Venue type: Old school building built in 1841, converted into a gallery/theatre.
Facilities: Capacity for 104. Tiered moveable seating.
Policy: Available for hire from Monday-Sunday. Music promoted includes chamber, orchestral, choral, opera, jazz, traditional, pop, dance, alternative and country & western. Two months booking notice is required.
Technical details: Stage is 13 ft x 20 ft x 17 ft.

Jurys Hotel

Julia Crowley
Sales Manager
Western Road
Cork

Tel/Fax: +353 21 4276622/+353 21 4274477

Venue type: Hotel, bar and restaurant.
Facilities: Capacity for 500-700. Upright and grand piano available.
Policy: Available for hire from Monday-Sunday. Music promoted includes jazz, traditional, rock and blues.

The Lobby Bar

Pat Conway
Director
1 Union Quay
Cork

Tel/Fax: +353 21 4311113/+353 21 4318202
Email: enquiries@lobby.ie
Website: www.lobby.ie
Other key staff: Ann Marie Ryan (PR/Production), Breeda Conway (Bar Manager)

Venue type: City centre bar.
Facilities: Capacity for 80.
Policy: Available for hire from Monday-Sunday. Music promoted includes jazz, traditional, folk, world, alternative and dance. One month's booking notice is required.

The Metropole Hotel

Joan Kenny
Sales Manager
MacCurtain Street
Cork

Tel/Fax: +353 21 4508122/+353 21 4506450
Email: enq@metropoleh.com
Website: www.metropoleh.com
Other key staff: Edel Drinan (Conference &
Banqueting), Hugh Coyle (General Manager)

Venue type: Hotel/Bar.
Facilities: Capacity for 400. Upright piano is available.
Policy: Available for hire from Monday-Sunday. Music
promoted includes opera, jazz, traditional, alternative,
and country & western. One month's booking notice is
required.

Nature Art Centre
Thomas Wiegandt
Manager
Ballybane
Ballydehob
Co. Cork

Tel/Fax: +353 28 37323
Website: www.holistic.ie/natureart
Other key staff: Annette Pätzold

Venue type: Workshop centre in a rural centre.
Facilities: Capacity for groups of 20 (with seating) or
30 (without seating). Instruments include djembe drums
and other hand drums, percussion, tibetan singing
bowls and plucked instruments.
Policy: Available for hire from Monday-Sunday. Two
weeks minimum booking notice required. Music promoted includes jazz, reggae, world, traditional and
ethnic. Acoustic music making only.

North Cathedral
Fr. Young
Roman Street
Cork

Tel/Fax: +353 21 4304325/+353 21 4304204
Email: fold@corkandross.org

Venue type: Cathedral.
Facilities: Capacity for 1,000. Church organ available.
Policy: Available for hire by arrangement only. Music
promoted includes choral and opera.

St. Fachtna's Cathedral
Rev. Christopher Peters
The Deanery
Rosscarbery
Co. Cork

Tel: +353 23 48166
Email: peters@esatclear.ie

Venue type: Cathedral.
Facilities: Capacity for up to 180. Organ available.
Policy: Available for hire from Monday-Saturday. Music
promoted includes chamber, choral and opera.

Triskel Arts Centre
Deirdre Enright
Director
Tobin Street
Cork

Tel/Fax: +353 21 4272022/+353 21 4272592
Email: triskel@iol.ie

Venue type: Multi-purpose arts centre.
Facilities: Capacity for 100 (Auditorium), 75 (cafe/bar,
standing). Contains two galleries and education workshop facility. Kawai CS40 baby grand piano available.
Policy: Available for hire from Monday-Saturday. Music
promoted includes chamber, opera, jazz, traditional,
rock, folk alternative and world. Two months booking
notice is required.
Technical details: Stage is 17 ft x 14 ft. Loading of
equipment is at street level.

Village Arts Centre
Liam Howard
Chairman
c/o Avondhu Press Ltd
18 Lower Cork Street
Mitchelstown
Co. Cork

Tel/Fax: +353 25 24451/+353 25 84463
Email: info@avondhupress.ie
Other key staff: Jerry O'Leary (Secretary),
Maureen Howard (Committee)

Venue type: Old church, converted into an arts centre.
Facilities: Capacity for 100. Tiered seating.
Policy: Available for hire from Monday-Sunday. Three
months booking notice is required.
Technical details: Stage size is 19 ft x 12 ft. Loading
equipment is at street level.

CO. DONEGAL

Abbey Centre
Barney McLaughlin
Tirconnell Street
Ballyshannon
Co. Donegal

Tel/Fax: +353 72 51375/+353 72 52832
Email: bmcl@iol.ie

Venue type: Old cinema, converted into an arts centre.
Facilities: Capacity for 294 and 60 (standing). Music promoted includes orchestral, choral, traditional, country and folk. Boston baby grand piano available.

Balor Theatre
Mark McCollum
Community Arts Section
Ballybofey
Co. Donegal

Tel: +353 74 31840
Other key staff: Kieran Quinn, Kathleen McGowan (Secretary)

Venue type: Converted cinema with two theatre spaces.
Facilities: Capacity for 162 (theatre 1), 150 (theatre 2), 30 (meeting room). Raked seating in both theatres.
Policy: Available for hire from Monday-Sunday. Music promoted includes chamber, jazz, traditional and world.

Glenveagh Castle & Visitor Centre
Joe Gatins
Regional Manager
Church Hill
Co. Donegal

Tel/Fax: +353 74 37090/+353 74 37072

Venue type: Drawing room at Glenveagh Castle.
Facilities: Capacity for 80. Grand piano available.
Policy: Music promoted includes chamber and choral.

An Grianán Theatre
Patricia McBride
Director
Port Road
Letterkenny
Co. Donegal

Tel/Fax: +353 74 23288 or +353 74 20777(box office)/+353 74 20665
Email: patriciamcbride@eircom.net
Website: www.angrianan.com
Other key staff: Helene McMenamin (Administrator), Niall Cranney (Technical Stage Manager)

Venue type: Purpose built theatre venue.
Facilities: Capacity for 345 and 7 disabled persons (large auditorium), 20-30 small conference room. Multimedia facilities. Grand piano available.
Policy: Available for hire from Monday-Sunday. Booking notice is required. All types of music promoted.
Technical details: Stage is 17 metres x 10.7 metres. Full technical specification available on request.

Ionad Cois Locha
Dún Luiche
Leitri Ceanainn
Co. Donegal

Tel: +353 75 32127

Venue type: Interpretive centre built around an old farmhouse.
Facilities: Capacity for 200.
Policy: Music promoted includes traditional, folk and world.

Letterkenny Arts Centre
Sean Hannigan
Letterkenny
Co. Donegal

Tel/Fax: +353 74 21968/+353 74 23276
Email: lkarts@indigo.ie

Venue type: Library and arts centre, which is a multi-purpose space.
Facilities: Capacity for 100.
Policy: Music promoted includes chamber, choral, jazz, traditional, world and folk.

DUBLIN CITY & COUNTY

Adam & Eve's Church

Paul Mckeever
Director of Music
Franciscan Friary
Merchants Quay
Dublin 8

Tel/Fax: +353 1 6771128/+353 1 6771000

Venue type: Church.
Facilities: Capacity for 1,200. Capacity in choir room for 100 and the Sacristy (warm-up room) for 50. Seating is rows of long wood bench seats. Upright piano available. Other instruments include a pipe organ and 2 harmonicas.
Policy: Music promoted includes chamber, orchestral and opera. Two-four months booking notice is required.
Technical details: Loading equipment is at street level and a private side laneway. Stage is 40 ft x 30 ft. Raised stage.

Áras Chrónáin - Irish Cultural Centre

Brian O'Gáibhín
Director Development Officer
Clondalkin
Dublin 22

Tel/Fax: +353 1 4574847
Mobile: +353 87 2844195
Email: info@araschronain.com
Website: www.araschronain.com
Other key staff: Bernadine Ni Ghiolla Phádraig (Director of Muintir Chrónáin)

Venue type: 19th Century house set in 3 acres of land converted into a cultural centre. Established by Muintir Chrónáin, a group set up to promote Irish culture.
Facilities: Capacity for 200. Moveable seating.
Policy: Available for hire from Monday-Sunday. Three-six months booking notice is required. Music promoted includes classical, jazz and traditional.

The Ark - A Cultural Centre for Children

Clodagh O'Brien
General Manager
Eustace Street
Dublin 2

Tel/Fax: +353 1 6707788/+353 1 6707758
Email: info@ark.ie
Website: www.ark.ie
Other key staff: Martin Drury (Director), Phill McCaughey (Administrator), Miriam O'Sullivan (Music Programmer)

Venue type: 16,000 sq. ft arts centre, housed on four floors, containing a theatre, gallery and workshop space. It is designed specifically with children in mind.
Facilities: Capacity for 150 (theatre), 50 (gallery), 50-80 (workshop). Arena-style seating in theatre, elsewhere individual seating. Upright piano available.
Policy: Six months booking notice is required. All types of music are promoted.

Bank of Ireland Arts Centre

Barry O'Kelly
Social & Cultural Co-ordinator
Foster Place
Dublin 2

Tel/Fax: +353 6615933 Ext. 3837 or +353 6711488/ +353 1 6615675 or +353 6707556
Other key staff: Billy Buckley (Tours Administrator), Pat Rowe (Services Porter)

Venue type: Arts centre, housed in a historical building.
Facilities: Capacity for 200. Seating is fold up chairs. Two Petrof grand pianos available.
Policy: Available for hire from Tuesday-Sunday. Six months booking notice is required. Music promoted includes chamber, choral, opera, jazz, traditional, rock, folk, dance and world.
Technical details: Stage is 19 ft x 9 ft. Fixed staging with removable extensions (see advert p.150).

Samuel Beckett Theatre

Francis Thackaberry
General Manager
Trinity College
Dublin 2

Tel/Fax: +353 1 6081334/+353 1 6793488
Email: fthackab@tcd.ie
Website: www.tcd.ie/drama
Other key staff: Ann Mulligan (Front of House), Kieran Murphy (Technical Manager)

Venue type: Modern black box theatre space, housed in the grounds of Trinity College.
Facilities: Capacity for 208. Seating is retractable and raked.
Policy: Available for hire from Monday-Sunday. Booking notice is required.
Technical details: Stage is 13 metres x 13 metres.

The Issac Butt

Mick Lennox
Venues Manager
Store Street
Dublin 1

Tel: +353 1 8555021

Venue type: Purpose built performance venue, which is attached to the Issac Butt Youth Hostel. This venue is modelled on 'The Cavern' venue in Liverpool, where the Beatles performed.
Facilities: Capacity for 300 standing and 150 seated. Seating is fixed.
Policy: Two months booking notice is required. Music promoted includes choral, jazz, chamber, traditional, world, cajun and rock.

Ceol

Harry Bradshaw
Chief O'Neills
Smithfield
Dublin 7

Tel: +353 1 8173800 or +353 1 8173820
Other key staff: Mark Lancaster-Purnell (Managing Director), Sorcha Potts (Assistant Manager)

Venue type: Purpose built performance venue, gallery/theatre and hotel/bar and restaurant.
Facilities: Capacity for 100 (white room - multi purpose room used for performances, art exhibitions, music sessions and small conferences), capacity for 120 (main auditorium). White room has moveable seating and the main auditorium has raked seating.
Policy: Music promoted includes traditional and cajun music.

Christ Church Cathedral

The Administrator
Christ Church Place
Dublin 8

Tel/Fax: +353 1 6778099/+353 6798991
Email: cccdub@indigo.ie
Website: www.indigo.ie/~cccdub
Other key staff: Mark Duley (Director of Music)

Venue type: Cathedral with crypt and music room.
Facilities: Capacity for 600 seated (main area), 200 seated (crypt), 80 seated (music room). Grand piano available in music room. Organ also available.
Policy: Available for hire from Monday-Sunday. Three months booking notice is required. Music promoted includes chamber, orchestral, choral and opera.

Church of Ireland Monkstown

Rev. Kevin D'Alton
Monkstown Road
Monkstown Village
Co. Dublin

Tel/Fax: +353 2806596

Venue type: Large church designed by George Semple.
Facilities: Capacity for 800-1,000. Seating is fixed. Organ is available.

Civic Theatre

Bríd Dukes
Director
Tallaght
Dublin 24

Tel/Fax: +353 1 4627460/+353 1 4627478
Email: civictheatre@eircom.net
Other key staff: John Mallon (Administrator), Mick Doyle (Technical Manager)

Venue type: Purpose built performance venue and gallery/theatre. Contains a main auditorium and studio space.
Facilities: Capacity for 320 (main auditorium), 60-80 (studio). Raked seating which can be moved back to create an open space in the auditorium.
Policy: Six months booking notice is required. Music promoted includes chamber, opera, traditional, rock, folk and dance.
Technical details: Stage size is 10 metres x 7.37 metres. Stage is a ground level. Equipment is loaded at street level.

Clasac

Jim McAllister
Chairman
PO Box 5681
Alfie Byrne Road
Fairview
Dublin 3

Venue type: Proposed centre for the Clontarf branch of Comhaltas Ceoltóirí Éireann. Will be a centre for teaching and performing excellence in Irish traditional music. The venue will have a 300 seated theatre. Due to open in June/August 2001.

The Coach House

Denis McCarthy
Conference Centre
Dublin Castle
Dublin 2

Tel/Fax: +353 1 6793713 or +353 1 6796433/ +353 1 6797831
Email: dublincastle@eircom.net

Venue type: Historical building, situated within the grounds of Dublin Castle. Two room venue.
Facilities: Capacity for 125.
Policy: Booking notice is required. Music promoted includes chamber, vocal, traditional and jazz.

The Cobblestone Bar

Paul Lee
Music Venue Manager
7 North King Street
Smithfield
Dublin 7

Tel: +353 1 8721799
Mobile: +353 87 6825306
Email: reelbeer@indigo.ie
Other key staff: Tom Mulligan

Venue type: Bar situated in the heart of Dublin City. Two downstairs bars catering for top traditional music artists seven nights a week. The upstairs bar is a listening venue and popular with singers and songwriters.
Facilities: Capacity for 150 seated and 180 standing (upstairs bar).
Policy: Available for hire from Monday-Sunday. Three-four weeks booking notice is required. Types of music promoted includes choral, jazz, traditional, rock, folk, cajun, pop and world.

Technical details: Stage size is 15 ft x 15 ft. Stage is raised and wooden.

Crypt Arts Centre

Dublin Castle
Dublin 2

Tel/Fax: +353 1 6713387/+353 6713370

Venue type: Theatre
Facilities: Capacity for 90.
Policy: Available for hire from Monday-Saturday.
Technical details: Stage size is 20 ft x 40 ft.

Dalkey Castle & Heritage Centre

Vanessa Butler
Manager
Castle Street
Dalkey
Co. Dublin

Tel/Fax: +353 1 2858366/+353 1 2843141
Email: diht@indigo.ie
Other key staff: Eileen Mills (Project Co-ordinator), Alberto Palop (Assistant Project Co-ordinator)

Venue type: Recently refurbished centre, suitable for theatre, concerts, exhibitions and small conferences.
Facilities: Capacity for 220 (hall), 40 (green room). Fixed seating in hall, moveable seating in conference room.
Policy: Available for hire from Tuesday-Saturday. One months booking notice is required. Music promoted include chamber, orchestral, choral, opera, jazz, traditional, rock and world.
Technical details: Stage size is 4.4 metres x 11 metres. Equipment is loaded at street level or bay level.

Fingal Arts Centre

James McGreer
Venue Manager
Chapel Green
Rush
Co. Dublin

Tel/Fax: +353 1 8437567 or +3531 8432020/ +353 1 8432021
Email: jmcgreer@tms.iol.ie

Venue type: 5,000 sq. ft restored Norman church, which was built in 1760. Arts centre and auditorium.
Facilities: Capacity for 300. Interlocking individual seats.
Policy: Available for hire from Monday-Saturday (except second Sunday and fourth Sunday of month). Booking notice is required. Music promoted includes chamber, orchestral, opera, jazz, traditional, cajun and country and western.
Technical details: Stage size is 37 ft x 22 ft.

The Gaiety Theatre

John Costigan
Executive Director
South King Street
Dublin 2

Tel/Fax: +353 1 6795622/+353 1 6771921
Email: johncostigan@gaietytheatre.com
Website: www.gaietytheatre.com
Other key staff: Gail Wroth (Technical Manager)

Venue type: Theatre.
Facilities: Fixed seating.
Policy: Available for hire from Monday-Sunday.
Technical details: Stage is black wood. Sound equipment is hired form a local hire company. Technical specification is available on request.

Rupert Guinness Theatre

Steven Cahill
Venue Manager
Watling Street
Dublin 8

Tel: +353 1 4089668

Venue type: Purpose built performance venue built in 1959. Originally was used for staff shows and performances, it is now used for local community groups, music groups and the Guinness choir.
Facilities: Capacity for 460. Electronic piano available.

Harcourt Hotel

Mary Cashin
General Manager
60 Harcourt Street
Dublin 2

Tel/Fax: +353 1 4783677/+353 1 4752013
Email: reservations@harcourthotel.ie

Venue type: Hotel.
Facilities: Fixed and loose bar stools.
Policy: Available for hire form Monday-Sunday. Two months booking notice is required. Music promoted includes traditional and folk.
Technical details: Stage size is 10 metres x 4 metres.

HQ - At the Irish Music Hall of Fame

Alan Townsend
General Manager
57 Middle Abbey Street
Dublin 1

Tel/Fax: +353 1 8783345/+353 1 8782225
Website: www.irishmusichof.com
Other key staff: Barry Walsh (Operations Manager), Marion McCormick (Assistant to General Manager)

Venue type: Purpose built performance venue housed in the Hot Press Irish Music Hall of Fame.
Facilities: Capacity for 500. Type of seating includes banquette, campus chairs and stools.
Policy: Available for hire from Monday-Sunday. Music promoted includes jazz, traditional, rock, cajun, pop, country and western and world.
Technical details: Stage is beech wood with synthetic cover.

James Joyce Centre

Ken Monaghan
35 North Great Georges Street
Dublin 1

Tel/Fax: +353 1 8788547/+353 1 8788488
Email: joycecen@iol.ie
Website: www.jamesjoyce.ie

Venue type: Restored Georgian townhouse built in 1784, which was originally the townhouse of the Earl of Kenmare.
Facilities: Capacity for 80. Upright piano available.
Policy: Music promoted includes chamber, choral, jazz and traditional.

Lambert Puppet Theatre

Miriam Lambert
Clifton Lane
Monkstown
Co. Dublin

Tel/Fax: +353 1 2800974/+353 1 2804772
Email: puppet@iol.ie

Venue type: Theatre
Facilities: Capacity for 200. Fixed seating. Mobile stage unit.
Policy: One month's booking notice is required.

Larkin Theatre - Dublin City University

Marie-Louise O'Donnell
Dublin City University
Glasnevin
Dublin 9

Tel/Fax: +353 1 7045216/+353 1 7045567
Email: marie-louise.odonnell@dcu.ie
Website: www.dcu.ie

Venue type: Theatre.
Facilities: Capacity for 380-400.
Policy: Music promoted includes instrumental, chamber and vocal recitals.

The Lutheran Church in Ireland

Rev. Fritz-Gert Mayer
24 Adelaide Road
Dublin 2

Tel/Fax: +353 1 6766548

Venue type: Church.
Facilities: Capacity for 150.
Policy: Available for hire from Monday-Sunday. Promotes chamber music. Organ available.

Mean Fiddler

Desi Balmer
Assistant Manager
Liberty Lane
Dublin 2

Tel/Fax: +353 1 4758555/+353 1 4751060
Other key staff: Philomena Whyte

Facilities: Capacity for 600. Production office.
Policy: Music promoted includes world, folk, rock, blues, dance and alternative.

Mother Redcaps

Kevin Ryan
Manager
Back Lane
Christchurch
Dublin 8

Tel/Fax: +353 1 4538306/+353 1 4533960

Venue type: Hotel/Bar/Restaurant.
Facilities: Capacity for 500.
Policy: Available for hire from Monday-Sunday. Music promoted includes rock, folk, cajun, pop, traditional and alternative.

National Concert Hall

Judith Woodworth
Director
Earlsfort Terrace
Dublin 2

Tel/Fax: +353 1 4751666/+353 1 4783797
Email: info@nch.ie
Website: www.nch.ie
Other key staff: Anne Fitzpatrick (Contracts Manager)

Venue type: Purpose built performance venue. Designed in the classical style for the Great Exhibition of 1865.
Facilities: Capacity for 250 (John Field Room), 1,200 (main auditorium). Free seating (John Field Room), fixed seating (main auditorium). Steinway Model D x 2 piano available. Continuo organ in main auditorium.
Policy: Available for hire from Monday-Sunday (except Friday). Music promoted includes chamber, orchestral, choral, opera, jazz, traditional, cajun, dance, country and western and world.
Technical details: Stage size is 47 ft x 34 ft. Type of staging is steeldeck. Equipment is loaded at street level.

National Gallery of Ireland

Tina Roche
Head of Development
Merrion Square West
Dublin 2

Tel/Fax: +353 1 6615133/+353 1 6615372
Email: artgall@eircom.net
Website: www.nationalgallery.ie
Other key staff: Maureen Ryan (Administrator - Friends of The National Gallery)

Venue type: 19th Century building, which houses the National Art Collection.
Facilities: Capacity for 320-500 (Shaw Room), 300-500 (Baroque Gallery), 100-200 (Atrium). Type of seating is concert or round table.
Policy: Available for hire from Monday-Sunday. Two weeks booking notice is required. Music promoted includes chamber, orchestral, choral, opera, jazz, traditional and world.
Technical details: Stage size is 23 ft x 18 ft. Stage is a permanent raised platform. Loading of equipment is at street level.

National Museum of Ireland - Collins Barracks

Amanda Gregan
Marketing Executive
Collins Barracks
Benburb Street
Dublin 7

Tel/Fax: +353 1 6777444/+353 1 6707533
Other key staff: Bernadette O'Neill (Head of Marketing)

Venue type: Ireland's museum of decorative arts and the economic, social, political and military history of the country.
Policy: Available for hire from Monday-Sunday. One month's booking notice is required. The spaces available for hire are Collins Barracks Foyer, The Riding School (capacity for 300 seating), Audiovisual Room (60-90) and Meeting Room (40).

National Museum of Ireland - Kildare Street

Amanda Gregan
Marketing Executive
Kildare Street
Dublin 2

Tel/Fax: +353 1 6777444/+353 1 6707533
Other key staff: Bernadette O'Neill (Head of Marketing)

Venue type: Officially opened in 1890, designed by Thomas Newman Deane and Thomas Manly Deane in the Victorian Palladian style.
Policy: Available for hire from Monday-Sunday.

The New Theatre

Thèrése Kelly
43 East Essex Street
Temple Bar
Dublin 2

Tel/Fax: +353 1 6703361/+353 1 4968388

Venue type: Purpose built performance space converted from a private meeting room/club in 1995.
Facilities: Capacity for 71.
Policy: Promotes acoustic music.

O'Reilly Hall - University College Dublin

Anita Blake
Belfield Campus
Belfield
Dublin 4

Tel/Fax: +353 1 7062827/+353 1 7062188

Venue type: Flexible purpose built auditorium, suitable for performances, receptions and large events.
Facilities: Capacity for 1,000.
Policy: Music promoted includes chamber, orchestral and choral.

The Pavilion Theatre - Dun Laoghaire

Peter Corcoran
Administrative Officer
Dun Laoghaire-Rathdown County Council
County Hall
Marine Road
Dun Laoghaire
Co. Dublin

Tel/Fax: +353 1 2054700/+353 1 2806969
Website: www.dlrcoco.ie

Venue type: Purpose built arts venue.
Facilities: Capacity for 360 (main theatre), 50 (small studio theatre).
Policy: Music promoted includes chamber, choral, rock, jazz, traditional and world.

The Pillar Room

Ann-Marie Ryan
Rotunda Hospital
Parnell Street
Dublin 1

Tel/Fax: +353 1 8730700 or 8722729/ +353 1 8722926
Email: friends@rotunda.ie
Website: www.rotunda.ie

Venue type: Purpose built performance venue, built in the 1800's by Bartholomew Moss to aid hospital fundraising.
Facilities: Capacity for 250.
Policy: Music promoted includes orchestral, chamber, vocal, jazz, world, traditional and pop.

The Point

Cormac Rennick
General Manager
North Wall Quay
Dublin 1

Tel/Fax: +353 1 8366777/+353 1 8366422
Email: management@thepoint.ie
Other key staff: Paddy Soper (Technical Manager), Phil Rogers (Deputy Manager)

Venue type: Purpose built performance venue.
Facilities: Capacity for 5,500 (standing - main auditorium), 3,000 (seating - main auditorium). Combination of flat and tiered seats.
Policy: Available for hire from Monday-Sunday. Booking notice is required. Music promoted includes opera, rock, jazz, traditional, pop, dance, alternative and world.

The Presidents Hall

The Secretary
Law Society of Ireland
Blackhall Place
Dublin 7

Tel/Fax: +353 1 6724800/+353 1 6724801
Email: general@lawsociety.ie

Facilities: Capacity for 300. Upright piano available.
Policy: Booking notice is required. Music promoted includes chamber, orchestral and opera.

Project Arts Centre

Cathy McArdle
Artistic Director
39 East Essex Street
Temple Bar
Dublin 2

Tel/Fax: +353 1 6796622 or +353 1850 260027 (box office)/+353 1 6369151
Email: info@project.ie
Website: www.project.ie
Other key staff: Thomas Coghlan (General Manager), Janice McAdam (Director of Public Affairs)

Venue type: Arts centre and purpose built performance venue.
Facilities: Capacity for 250 (seated - large space), 400 (standing - large space). 75 (seated - small space).
Policy: Available for hire from Monday-Sunday. Six months booking notice is required. Music promoted includes opera, jazz, traditional, rock, folk, cajun, pop, dance, alternative and world.

Renards

Des McMahon
35 South Frederick Street
Dublin 1

Tel: +353 1 6775876
Mobile: +353 87 2511755
Other key staff: Terry Fox (Manager)

Venue type: Basement jazz club.
Facilities: Capacity for 150. Kawai - baby grand is available.
Policy: Available for hire from Monday-Sunday. One-two months booking notice is required. Music promoted includes jazz, cajun and world.

RHA Gallagher Gallery

Patricia Moriarty
Administrator
15 Ely Place
Dublin 2

Tel/Fax: +353 1 6612558/+353 1 6610762
Email: rhagallery@eircom.net
Other key staff: Patrick T. Murphy (Director)

Venue type: City centre art gallery.
Facilities: Capacity for 100-600.
Policy: Available from Monday-Sunday. One month's booking notice is required. Music promoted includes chamber, orchestral, choral, opera, jazz, traditional, rock, folk, cajun, pop, reggae, alternative and world.

Royal College of Physicians
Conference Administrator
6 Kildare Street
Dublin 2

Tel/Fax: +353 1 6616677/+353 1 6763989
Email: lindastubbs@rcpi.ie

Venue type: This venue has been the home of the Royal College of Physicians of Ireland since 1860.
Facilities: Capacity for 200. Music promoted includes chamber, orchestral and choral.

Royal Dublin Society
Adrienne Dunne
Development Executive -
Arts & Membership Services
Ballsbridge
Dublin 4

Tel/Fax: +353 1 6680866 Ext. 211/
+353 1 6604014
Email: adrienne.dunne@rds.ie
Website: www.rds.ie
Other key staff: Niamh Kelly (Marketing Manager), Eddie McCarron (Booking Enquiries)

Venue type: Both an open air and indoor facility.
Facilities: Capacity for up to 1,000 (Concert Hall), 3,000 (Shelbourne Hall), 3,000-5,000 (Main Hall), 7,000 (Simmonscourt Pavilion), 35,000 (RDS Stadium). Flexible stage and seating layout.
Policy: Booking notice is required.

St. Ann's Church
Suzanne Campbell
Dawson Street
Dublin 2

Tel: +353 1 4733648

Venue type: Church.
Facilities: Capacity for 640. Upright Petrov piano and organ available.
Policy: Available for hire from Monday-Sunday. Two weeks booking notice is required.
Music promoted includes chamber, choral, opera, jazz, traditional and world.

St. Patrick's Cathedral
Kate Manning
St. Patrick's Close
Dublin 8

Tel/Fax: +353 1 4539472/+353 1 4546374
Email: stpcath@iol.ie
Website: www.stpatrickscathedral.ie
Other key staff: Kerry Houston (Administrator), Jennifer Hickey (Dean's Secretary)

Venue type: Cathedral, which was founded in 1191.
Facilities: Capacity for up to 1,000. Fixed seating and space for moveable seating available. 1902 Willis organ, which was restored by J.Walker & Sons in 1963 and in 1995 by Harrison & Harrison.
Policy: Available for hire from Monday-Sunday.
Two months booking notice is required. Music promoted includes chamber, orchestral, choral and opera.

St. Stephen's -
The Peppercanister Church
Peter Evans
Administrator
Mount Street Crescent
Dublin 2

Tel: +353 1 6681958

Venue type: Church.
Facilities: Capacity for 475. Upright Petrov piano and organ available.
Policy: At least two weeks booking notice required. Music promoted includes chamber, choral, opera, jazz, traditional and world.

SFX City Theatre
Michael Scott
Artistic Director
23 Upper Sherrard Street
Dublin 1

Tel/Fax: +353 1 8554090
Email: scottart@eircom.net
Website: www.homepage.eircom.net/~sfx
Other key staff: Avril Ryan (Executive Director)

Venue type: Centre for excellence in the performing arts and arts training in Dublin's Inner City.
Facilities: Capacity for up to 600 (auditorium - seated), 1,200 (auditorium - standing). Seating is raked.
Policy: Available for hire from Monday-Sunday. Booking notice is required. Music promoted includes chamber, orchestral, choral, opera, jazz, traditional, rock, pop and dance.
Technical details: Stage can be reversed and used as an auditorium with capacity for 50. Synthesizers, drum machines and effects units available. Equipment is loaded at street level.

J.J Smyth's
Brian Smyth
Manager
12 Aungier Street
Dublin 2

Tel: +353 1 4752565
Other key staff: J.J Smyth (Proprietor)

Venue type: Bar.
Policy: Music promoted includes jazz and blues.

Tallaght Community Arts Centre
Mary Grehan
Director
Virginia House
Old Blessington Road
Tallaght
Dublin 24

Tel/Fax: +353 1 4621501/+353 4621640

Venue type: Arts centre.
Facilities: Capacity for 40 (seated).
Policy: Available for hire Tuesday, Thursday and Saturday. Hire fees available on request.

Temple Bar Music Centre
Aoife Woodlock
Event Co-ordinator
Curved Street
Temple Bar
Dublin 2

Tel/Fax: +353 1 6709202/+353 1 6709042
Email: ruairi@tbmc.ie
Website: www.tbmc.ie
Other key staff: Ruairi O'Scanaill (Event Co-ordinator)

Venue type: Multi purpose theatre and venue, with a fully equipped 24 track recording studio.
Facilities: Capacity for 600 (standing) and 315 (seated). Tiered theatre style seating. Upright Yamaha piano available.
Policy: Available for hire from Monday-Sunday. Preferably six weeks booking notice is required. Music promoted includes choral, rock, cajun, folk, country and western, pop, opera, jazz, reggae, world, traditional, dance and alternative.
Technical details: Stage is 30 ft x 15 ft.
(see advert page 309)

Vicar St
Bren Berry
Aiken Promotions
59 Thomas St
Dublin 8

Tel/Fax: +353 1 4546656/+353 1 4546787
Email: office@aikenpromotions.ie
Website: www.vicarstreet.com

Venue type: Purpose built performance venue.
Facilities: Capacity for 750 (seated) and 900 (standing-removable seating).
Policy: Promotes all kinds of music.
Technical details: Stage size is 45 ft x 16 ft.

Whelans
David Allen
25 Wexford Street
Dublin 2

Tel/Fax: +353 1 4780766
Email: whelanswex@eircom.net
Website: www.whelans.net

Venue type: Music venue and bar.
Facilities: Capacity for 330 (standing)

Policy: Available for hire from Monday-Sunday. Two months booking notice is required. Music promoted includes rock, cajun, folk, alternative, pop, country and western, reggae, world and traditional.

CO. GALWAY

Alcock & Brown Hotel
Deirdre Keogh
Clifden
Co. Galway

Tel: +353 95 21842
Other key staff: Mary Vaughan (Manager).

Venue type: Hotel, bar and restaurant, used by Clifden Community Arts Group for live music performances.
Facilities: Capacity for 60-140.

Augustinian Church Galway
Augustus Street
Galway

Tel/Fax: +353 91 562524/+353 91 564378

Venue type: Church.
Facilities: Capacity for 400. Music promoted includes chamber, orchestral and choral. Organ available.

Aula Maxima
Ann Duggan
Conference Manager
Conference Office
NUI Galway

Tel/Fax: +353 91 524411 Ext. 2264/
+353 91 750512
Email: a.duggan@mis.nuigalway.ie

Facilities: Capacity for 100 upstairs and 100 downstairs.

Christ Church Clifden
Archdeacon A.M.A Previté
The Rectory
Church Hill
Clifden
Co. Galway

Tel/Fax: +353 95 21147
Email: previte@anu.ie

Venue type: Church.
Facilities: Capacity for 150 (seated). Upright piano available. Pipe organ available.
Policy: Available for hire from Monday-Saturday. Four weeks booking notice is required. Music promoted includes chamber, orchestral, choral, opera and traditional.

Galway Arts Centre
Paul Fahy
Programmer
47 Dominick Street
Galway

Tel/Fax: +353 91 565886/+353 91 568642
Email: gac@indigo.ie
Website: www.galwayartscentre.ie

Venue type: Arts centre housed in a converted church.
Facilities: Capacity for 110. Raked seating.

Leisureland
Paddy Martin
Manager
Salthill
Galway

Tel/Fax: +353 91 521455/+353 91 521093

Venue type: Recently refurbished modern venue with concert hall and exhibition space.
Facilities: Capacity for 1,020 (seated), 1,250 (standing).
Policy: Available for hire from Monday-Sunday. Booking notice is required.
Technical details: Stage size is 51 ft x 36 ft. Type of staging is sprung maple which is suitable for dancing.

The Mall Theatre & Cinema
Jarlath Canney
Director
Stable Lane
Tuam
Co. Galway

Tel/Fax: +353 93 24463 or +353 93 24141/
+353 93 24141

Venue type: Refurbished cinema converted into a multi purpose venue.
Facilities: Capacity for 215.
Policy: Three months booking notice is required.

Station House Hotel

Cian Landers
General Manager
Clifden
Connemara
Co. Galway

Tel/Fax: +353 95 21699/+353 21677
Email: station@eircom.net
Website: www.station-house.com

Venue type: Restored railway station, converted into a hotel and museum.
Facilities: Capacity for 200 (Omey Suite). Theatre style seating.
Policy: Available for hire from Monday-Sunday. One-two months booking notice is required. Music promoted includes cajun, jazz and traditional.
Technical details: Mobile stage units.

Town Hall Theatre

Michael Diskin
Manager
Courthouse Square
Galway

Tel/Fax: +353 91 569777/+353 91 569664
Email: tht@eircom.net
Other key staff: Peter Ashton (Technical Manager), Anne Mannion (Box Office).

Venue type: Municipal theatre.
Facilities: Capacity for 393 (main auditorium), 80 (studio).
Policy: Booking notice is required.

St. Nicholas' Collegiate Church

The Rectory
Taylors Hill
Galway

Tel: +353 91 521914 or +353 91 522998

Venue type: Medieval parish church.
Facilities: Capacity for 300 (seated). Organ available.
Policy: One weeks booking notice is required. Music promoted includes chamber, choral and opera.

CO. KERRY

Derrynane House

James O'Shea
Caherdaniel
Co. Kerry

Tel/Fax: +353 66 9475387/+353 66 9475432
Other key staff: Evelyn Breen

Venue type: Has a chapel which is suitable for concerts.
Facilities: Capacity for 60. Music promoted includes chamber, orchestral, choral and jazz.

Ionad an Bhlascaoid Mhóir - The Blasket Centre

Michéal de Mórdha
Dún Chaoin
Tralee
Co. Kerry

Tel/Fax: +353 66 9156444/+353 66 9156446
Email: demordha@indigo.ie
Website: www. dingle-peninsula.ie

Venue type: Duchas heritage service centre, with an interpretive centre, relating the story of the now abandoned Great Blasket Island.
Facilities: Capacity for 135 (standing).
Policy: Music promoted includes chamber, choral, folk, world.

St. Johns Arts Centre

Joe Murphy
Administrator
The Square
Listowel
Co. Kerry

Tel/Fax: +353 68 22566/+353 68 23485

Venue type: Former Gothic Church of Ireland built in 1819.
Facilities: Capacity for 134. Seating is both raked and moveable. Yamaha E108 Upright piano available.
Policy: Available for hire from Monday-Sunday. Six weeks booking notice is required. Music promoted includes chamber, orchestral, choral, opera, jazz, traditional, rock, folk, cajun, pop, reggae, dance, alternative, country and western and world.

Technical details: Stage is 18 ft x 18 ft. Loading of equipment is at street level.

Siamsa Tíre Theatre & Arts Centre

Martin Whelan
General Manager
Tralee
Co. Kerry

Tel/Fax: +353 66 7123055/+353 66 7127276
Website: www.skypages.com
Other key staff: Anne Kennelly (Administrative Assistant).

Venue type: Purpose built theatre and arts centre, catering for all aspects of the arts in the South West region.
Facilities: Capacity for 355 (main auditorium), 50 (Round Gallery) or 80 (standing). Steinway grand model C piano available.
Policy: Available for hire from Monday-Sunday. Two-three months booking notice is required. Music promoted includes chamber, orchestral, choral, opera, cajun, pop, jazz, traditional and world.
Technical details: Stage size is 10.5 metres x 11.2 metres. Loading of equipment is at street level.

Athy Community Library

Josephine Coyne
Librarian
Town Hall
Emily Square
Athy
Co. Kildare

Tel: +353 507 31144
Email: athylib@eircom.net
Website: www.kildare.ie

Venue type: Purpose built library containing an exhibition and performance space.
Facilities: Capacity for 50-70 (The Gallery - standing).
Policy: Available for hire from Tuesday-Friday. Two months booking notice required. Music promoted includes chamber, orchestral, choral, opera, jazz, traditional, cajun, pop, reggae, country and western and world.

Aula Maxima - National University of Ireland Maynooth

Maynooth
Co. Kildare

Tel: +353 1 7083726 (Bill Tinley - June-Sept) or +353 1 6285222 Ext. 3046 (Aula Maxima Committee - Oct-May)
Email: guest.rooms@may.ie

Venue type: Purpose built auditorium for concerts, film and theatre productions, located on the college campus.
Facilities: Capacity for 600.

Castletown House

Joanna Cramsie
Manager
Celbridge
Co. Kildare

Tel/Fax: +353 1 6288252/+353 1 6271811
Other key staff: Josephine Higgins (Administrator)

Venue type: Palladian style country house, built c. 1722 for the Speaker of the Irish House of Commons, William Conolly.
Facilities: Capacity 252 (Long Gallery - seating).
Policy: Available for hire from Monday-Sunday. At least two months booking notice is required. Music promoted includes chamber, orchestral, choral, opera, jazz and traditional.

Celbridge Library

Mary Coughlan
St. Patrick's Park
Main Street
Celbridge
Co. Kildare

Tel: +353 1 6272207

Venue type: Modern Purpose built library, built in 1983, which houses an exhibition and performance space.
Facilities: Capacity for 50.

Coire Na Soilse

Michiel Brave
Camphill Community
Dunshane

Naas
Co. Kildare

Tel/Fax: +353 45 483628/+353 45 483833

Venue type: Purpose built performance venue.
Facilities: Capacity for 150. August Föster baby grand available.
Policy: Available for hire from Monday-Sunday. Three months booking notice is required. Music promoted includes chamber, opera, cajun, jazz and world.

County Kildare Arts Centre
Maeve O'Brien
County Arts Centre Manager
Kildare County Library
Athgarvan Road
Newbridge
Co. Kildare

Tel/Fax: +353 45 433480/+353 45 432490
Email: colibrary@kildarecoco.ie
Other key staff: Mary Linehan (County Arts Officer)

Venue type: Arts centre with flexible theatre space, which is due to open in September 2000.
Facilities: Capacity for 194 (seated - theatre), 250 (standing - theatre). Outdoor amphitheatre. Petrof Upright model 125 available.
Policy: Available for hire from Tuesday-Sunday. Six months booking notice is required. Music promoted includes chamber, orchestral, jazz, traditional, rock, folk, cajun, pop, dance, country and western and world.
Technical details: Loading equipment is at street level.

Goffs Conference Centre
Rosemary Carroll
Projects Manager
Kildare Paddocks
Kill
Co. Kildare

Tel/Fax: +353 45 886600/+353 45 877080
Email: sales@goffs.ie
Website: www.goffs.com
Other key staff: Leo Powell (Sales & Admin Manager)

Venue type: Multi purpose amphitheatre.

Policy: Available for hire from Monday-Sunday. Music promoted includes chamber, orchestral, choral, opera, jazz, traditional, rock, folk, cajun, pop, reggae, dance and country and western.

Herbert Lodge Arts Centre
Bernadette Hayden
Director
The Curragh
Co. Kildare

Tel/Fax: +353 45 481598

Venue type: Old RIC barracks/stables converted into small theatre rooms.
Facilities: Capacity for 30 and 50 (standing). Music promoted includes chamber, orchestral, choral, jazz, traditional, country and folk.

Naas Public Library
Caroline Collins
Assistant Librarian
Basin Street
Naas
Co. Kildare

Tel: +353 45 879111

Venue type: Library with an exhibition and performance space on the upper floor.
Facilities: Capacity for 70 and 100 (standing).
Policy: Available for hire from Tuesday-Friday. Two months booking notice required. Music promoted includes chamber, folk, jazz, traditional and world.

CO. KILKENNY

Cleere's Theatre
John Cleere
28 Parliment Street
Kilkenny

Tel: +353 56 62573
Email: sperlonga@eircom.net
Other key staff: Phyl Cleere

Venue type: Situated within an old stonewalled yard which was converted in to a theatre in 1990.

Facilities: Capacity for 90 and 100 (standing).
Policy: Music promoted includes jazz, traditional, world, country, folk, cajun, rock, blues and alternative.

Graiguenamanagh Branch Library
Brenda Ward
Librarian
Convent Road
Graiguenamanagh
Co. Kilkenny

Tel: +353 503 24224

Venue type: Purpose built library.
Facilities: Capacity for 70 and 90 (standing).
Policy: Available for hire from Tuesday-Friday. Two weeks booking notice is required. Music promoted includes chamber, folk, jazz, world and traditional.

Hotel Kilkenny
Richard Butler
General Manager
College Road
Kilkenny

Tel/Fax: +353 56 62000/+353 56 65989
Email: kilkenny@griffingroup.ie
Website: www.griffingroup.ie

Venue type: Hotel, bar and restaurant.
Facilities: Upright piano available.
Policy: Music promoted includes chamber, orchestral, choral, opera, jazz, traditional, rock, folk, cajun, reggae, alternative, country and western and world.

Kilkenny Castle
Patricia Friel
Curator
Kilkenny
Co. Kilkenny

Tel/Fax: +353 56 21450/+353 56 63488

Venue type: 3 venue spaces - The Billard Room, The Drawing Room and The Long Gallery, housed within Kilkenny Castle.
Facilities: Capacity for 60-250. Music promoted includes chamber, orchestral, choral, jazz and traditional.

St. Canices Cathedral
George Bell
Cathedral Verger
Kilkenny

Tel/Fax: +353 56 64971/+353 56 23646

Venue type: Cathedral.
Facilities: Capacity for 600-850. 1854 Bevingon organ available.
Policy: Music promoted includes chamber, choral, opera and traditional.

Watergate Theatre
Ger Coady
Parliament Street
Kilkenny
Co. Kilkenny

Tel/Fax: +353 56 61674/+353 56 51780
Website: www.watergatetheatre.homepage.com

Venue type: Purpose built theatre, catering for all aspects of the arts.
Facilities: Capacity for 330.
Policy: Music promoted includes chamber, orchestral, choral, jazz, traditional, world, country and folk.

CO. LAOIS

Dunamaise Theatre
Louise Donlon
Manager
Portlaoise
Co. Laois

Tel/Fax: +353 502 63355 or +353 502 63356/ +353 502 63357
Mobile: +353 87 6836142
Email: dunamaise@eircom.net

Venue type: Arts Centre.
Facilities: Capacity for 250. Upright Petrof piano available.
Policy: Available for hire from Monday-Sunday. Two months booking notice required. Music promoted includes chamber, orchestral, choral, opera, jazz, traditional, rock, folk and cajun.

Egan's Hostelry
John Egan
24-25 Main Street
Portlaoise
Co. Laois

Tel/Fax: +353 502 21106

Venue type: Bar and restaurant.
Facilities: Capacity for 200-300.
Policy: Music promoted includes traditional, jazz, rock, folk, cajun, pop and reggae.

Laois County Hall
Muireann Ní Chonaill
Arts Officer
Portlaoise County Council
Portlaoise

Tel/Fax: +353 502 22044/+353 502 22313
Email: artsoff@laoiscoco.ie

Facilities: Capacity for 100.
Policy: Music promoted includes chamber, orchestral, choral, jazz, traditional, folk, blues and dance.

CO. LEITRIM

The Cornmill Theatre & Arts Centre
Del Thorogood
General Manager
Main Street
Carrigallen
Co. Leitrim

Tel/Fax: +353 49 4339612
Email: delthoro@gofree.indigo.ie

Venue type: Old community hall fitted with a purpose built auditorium.
Facilities: Capacity for 180.
Policy: Available for hire from Monday-Saturday. Music promoted includes choral, jazz, traditional and world.
Technical details: Stage size is 40 ft x 25 ft.

North Leitrim Glens Centre
Liz Culloty
Manager
New Line
Manorhamilton
Co. Leitrim

Tel/Fax: +353 72 55833/+353 72 56063
Email: nlgdc@eircom.net
Other key staff: Nora McTiernan (Administrator)

Venue type: Multi purpose venue for community education, community arts, performances, exhibitions and conference facility.
Facilities: Capacity for 120 and 200 (standing). Upright piano available.
Policy: Available for hire from Friday-Sunday. Two months booking notice required. Music promoted includes chamber, opera, jazz, traditional, cajun, pop, country and western and world (see advert p.159).

CO. LIMERICK

Belltable Arts Centre
Mary Coll
Director
69 O'Connell Street
Limerick

Tel/Fax: +353 61 319866/+353 61 418552
Email: belltabl@iol.ie
Website: www.commerce.ie/belltable

Venue type: Traditional theatre.
Facilities: Capacity for 257.
Policy: Music promoted includes chamber, choral, jazz, traditional, world, country and folk.

Friars' Gate Theatre for Arts
John Brazill
Manager
Sarsfield Street
Kilmallock
Co. Limerick

Tel/Fax: +353 63 98727/+353 63 20180

Venue type: Theatre and arts centre.
Facilities: Capacity for 60 (main auditorium)

Policy: Available for hire from Monday-Sunday. Three months booking notice is required. Music promoted includes choral, opera, traditional, pop, dance and alternative.
Technical details: Stage size is 23 ft x 20 ft.

Venue type: Lecture theatre within the university complex.
Facilities: Capacity for 350. Piano available.
Policy: Music promoted includes chamber, orchestral, choral, jazz, traditional, world, country, folk and cajun.

Hunt Museum
Naomi O'Nolan
Administrator
Custom House
Rutland Street
Limerick

Tel/Fax: +353 61 312833/+353 61 312834
Email: naomi@huntmuseum.com
Other key staff: Ciarán MacGonigal (Director)

Venue type: Museum.
Facilities: Capacity for 150.
Policy: Two months booking notice is required. Music promoted includes chamber, orchestral, opera, jazz, traditional and world.

Limerick City Gallery of Art
Paul O'Reilly
Carnegie Building
Pery Square
Limerick

Tel/Fax: +353 61 310633 or +353 61 415266/
+353 61 311345
Email: lcgartzz@iol.ie
Website: www.limerickcorp.ie

Venue type: Romanesque building which was originally a library, and converted for use as a city gallery in 1985.
Facilities: Capacity for 100.
Policy: Music promoted includes choral, jazz and traditional.

Jean Monnet Theatre
Emily Spencer
University of Limerick
Castletroy
Co. Limerick

Tel/Fax: +353 61 202133/+353 61 202946
Email: emily.spencer@ul.ie

Stables Club - University of Limerick
Donal Fagan
University of Limerick
Limerick

Tel/Fax: +353 61 202368/+353 61 330516

Venue type: Music area within the university complex.
Facilities: Capacity for 400.
Policy: Music promoted includes jazz, traditional, world, country, folk, cajun, rock, blues, reggae, dance, pop and alternative.

Student Centre - University of Limerick
Ents Officer
Student Union
University of Limerick
Limerick

Tel/Fax: +353 61 202324/+353 61 335033
Email: ceo@ubu.iol.ie

Venue type: Lively venue within a busy college campus.
Facilities: Capacity for 250 (standing).

University Concert Hall
Michael J. Murphy
Director
University of Limerick
Limerick

Tel/Fax: +353 61 331549/+353 61 331585
Email: billf@eircom.net
Website: www.uch@ul.ie
Other key staff: Bill Flynn (Artistic/Technical Liaison)

Venue type: Purpose built performance venue.
Facilities: Capacity for 1,038. Grand Steinway piano available.
Policy: Available for hire from Monday-Sunday. Four weeks booking notice required. Music promoted

includes chamber, orchestral, choral, opera, jazz, traditional, rock, folk, cajun, pop, reggae, dance, alternative, country and western and world.
Technical details: Stage size is 18 metres x 11 metres. Loading of equipment is at street level (see advert p.159).

CO. LONGFORD

Backstage Theatre & Centre for the Arts
Jane Hughes
Promotions & Development Executive
Farneyhoogan
Longford

Tel/Fax: +353 43 47888 or +353 43 47889/ +353 43 47890
Email: backstage@eircom.net
Other key staff: Mona Considine (Theatre Operations Manager), Sean Mulroy (Stage Manager)

Venue type: Purpose built theatre.
Facilities: Capacity for 214 (main auditorium - seated), 40 (gallery - seated).
Policy: Available for hire from Monday-Sunday. Booking notice is required. Music promoted includes chamber, orchestral, opera, jazz, traditional, rock, folk, cajun, pop, dance and country and western.
Technical details: Stage size is 15.5 metres x 7.6 metres. Loading of equipment is at street level.

CO. LOUTH

Droichead Arts Centre
Tony Conaghy
Acting Director
Stockwell Lane
Drogheda
Co. Louth

Tel/Fax: +353 41 9833946/+353 41 984205
Email: droichead@indigo.ie
Other key staff: Kathleen O'Brien (Financial Manager)

Venue type: Arts centre, committed to social and cultural development by promoting artistic activity and facilitating active involvement in all the arts.
Facilities: Capacity for 178. Yamaha baby grand piano available.
Policy: Available for hire from Monday-Saturday. Six months booking notice is required. Music promoted includes chamber, orchestral, choral, opera, jazz, traditional, rock, folk, cajun, pop, reggae, dance, alternative and world.
Technical details: Stage size is 10.7 metres x 7.5 metres. Loading equipment is at first floor level.

Dundalk Institute of Technology
Multi Purpose Centre
Conor Lait
Buildings Officer
Dublin Road
Dundalk
Co. Louth

Tel/Fax: +353 42 9370408/+353 42 9351412
Email: conor.lait@dkit.ie
Website: www.dkit.ie

Venue type: Multi purpose hall.
Facilities: Capacity for 700 with orchestra.
Policy: Available for hire from Friday-Sunday. Music promoted includes chamber, orchestral, choral and opera.

Holy Trinity Heritage Centre
The Secretary
Carlingford Lough Heritage Trust
Teach Eolais
Old Quay Lane
Carlingford
Co. Louth

Tel/Fax: +353 42 9373888/+353 42 9373882

Venue type: Restored medieval church, nestled in the Cooley Mountains.
Facilities: Capacity for 200. Individual seating. Yamaha baby grand piano available.
Policy: Available for hire from Monday-Sunday. One month's booking notice is required. Music promoted includes chamber, orchestral, choral, traditional and cajun.

Louth County Museum

Susan O'Connor
Curator
Jocelyn Street
Dundalk
Co. Louth

Tel/Fax: +353 42 9327056 or +353 42 9327057/
+353 42 9327058
Other key staff: Martin Clarke (Technician),
Jimmy Marron (Maintenance/Caretaker)

Venue type: Audio visual theatre within the museum,
in the centre of Dundalk.
Facilities: Capacity for 72. Fixed seating.
Policy: Available for hire from Monday-Sunday. One
month's booking notice is required. Music promoted
includes chamber, orchestral, choral, opera, jazz, traditional, rock, reggae, country and western and world.

St. Nicholas' Church

Rev. Mark Wilson
Church Street
Dundalk
Co. Louth

Tel: +353 42 9321402
Email: stnicholas@eircom.net

Venue type: Church, known as 'The Green Church'.
Facilities: Capacity for 400-500. Baby grand piano and
organ available.
Policy: Six-eight weeks booking notice is required.
Music promoted includes chamber, orchestral and choral.

Spirit Store

Mark Deary
Co-owner
George's Quay
Dundalk
Co. Louth
Tel: +353 42 30712

Email: markmulh@indigo.ie
Other key staff: Mark Mulholland (Co-owner)

Venue type: Bar situated on the harbour, overlooking
the Cooley Mountains.
Facilities: Capacity for 70-80 seated (upstairs performance room). Intend to supply a piano and a quality
sound system. Internet access available. Will assist in

promoting events. Performance room is also suitable for
film societies, drama groups and comedy shows.
Policy: Available for hire from Monday-Sunday. Music
promoted includes rock, folk, alternative, jazz, traditional,
reggae and world.

Táin Theatre

Rosie O'Reilly
Town Clerk's Office
Town Hall
Dundalk
Co. Louth

Tel/Fax: +353 42 9332276/+353 42 9336761
Email: dundarts@eircom.net
Other key staff: Cormac Greene (Caretaker),
Brian Harten (Arts Officer)

Venue type: Concert hall venue, housed within
Dundalk Town Hall.
Facilities: Capacity for 693 (seated). Amharclann an
Chú, which is a smaller hall within the Town Hall,
accommodates 80-100. Yamaha upright and Yamaha
grand piano available. New sound and lighting system
recently installed.
Policy: Available for hire from Monday-Sunday. Booking
notice is three-six months in advance. Music promoted
includes chamber, orchestral, choral, opera, jazz, traditional, rock, folk, pop, reggae, dance and world.
Technical details: Stage size is 26 ft x 24 ft. Loading of
equipment is at street level.

CO. MAYO

Estoria Arts Centre

Ballina Arts Events
Estoria Building
Teeling Street
Ballina
Co. Mayo

Tel/Fax: +353 96 73593

Venue type: The Estoria building is the venue for the
future arts centre. It will house facilities such as a theatre, gallery and workshop space. It aims to provide a
centre for the production and promotion of community
arts events and to provide facilities for touring exhibitions and performances.

Foxford Woollen Mills Visitor Centre

Frank Devaney
Foxford
Co. Mayo

Tel/Fax: +353 94 56756/+353 94 56794
Email: foxfordresourcesltd@eircom.net
Other key staff: Bernie Joyce, Mary Conlon

Venue type: Working woollen mill, which houses a theatre and restaurant.
Facilities: Capacity for 53 (theatre).
Policy: Music promoted includes choral, jazz, traditional, world and folk.

Linenhall Arts Centre

Marie Farrell
Director
Linenhall Street
Castlebar
Co. Mayo

Tel/Fax: +353 94 23733/+353 94 26162
Email: linenhall@anu.ie
Other key staff: Maura Connolly (Administrator), Cass McCarthy (Arts Outreach)

Venue type: Arts centre, containing a gallery and auditorium.
Facilities: Capacity for 80 (gallery), 220 (auditorium).
Policy: Two months booking notice is required. Music promoted includes chamber, orchestral, choral, opera, jazz, traditional, folk, pop, alternative and world.

T. F. Theatre

Pat Jennings
Westport Road
Castlebar
Co. Mayo

Tel/Fax: +353 94 23111/+353 94 21919
Email: patj@anu.ie

Venue type: Theatre which houses three purpose built performance spaces, located within a hotel.
Facilities: Capacity for 100-1,000 and 150-2,500 (standing). Upright piano available.
Policy: Music promoted includes chamber, orchestral, choral, jazz, traditional, world, folk, country, rock, blues, reggae and pop.

CO. MEATH

Cultúrlann na Cille

Eibhlín Pléamonn
Company Director
Ashbourne
Co. Meath

Tel/Fax: +353 1 8351600/+353 1 8352585
Other key staff: Antóin MacGabhann (Chairperson), Cormac Lawless (Treasurer)

Venue type: Purpose built performance venue, housed within Gaelscoil na Cille.
Facilities: Capacity for 250 (seated).
Policy: Available for hire from Tuesday-Sunday. Two weeks booking notice is required. Music promoted includes chamber, orchestral, choral, opera, jazz, traditional, dance and world.
Technical details: Stage size is 12 metres x 10 metres. Loading of equipment is at street level.

St. Mary's Church

Rev. John Clarke
The Rectory
Boyle Road
Navan
Co. Meath

Tel/Fax: +353 46 21172
Email: johndmclarke@eircom.net

Venue type: Church.
Facilities: Capacity for 270. Organ available.
Policy: Available for hire from Monday-Saturday. Music promoted includes chamber, orchestral, choral and opera.

CO. MONAGHAN

Ulster Canal Stores

Jim Kerr
Supervisor/Manager
Cara Street
Clones
Co. Monaghan

Tel/Fax: +353 47 52125 or +353 47 51718/ +353 47 51720
Other key staff: Paddy Boylan (Projects Officer)

Venue type: Heritage centre. Cutstone 1840's warehouse, built on the banks of the Ulster Canal.
Facilities: Capacity for 80. Types of music promoted includes chamber, orchestral, choral, jazz, traditional, folk, cajun and blues.
Policy: Available for hire from Monday-Sunday. One weeks notice is required. Music promoted includes chamber, jazz, traditional, cajun, country and western and world.

CO. OFFALY

Bridge House Hotel
Colm McCabe
Manager
Tullamore
Co. Offaly

Tel/Fax: +353 506 22000/+353 506 41338
Email: bhouse@iol.ie
Other key staff: Christy Maye (Managing Director)

Venue type: Hotel, bar and restaurant.
Facilities: Capacity for 150-1,000.
Policy: Available for hire from Monday-Sunday. One month's booking notice is required. Music promoted includes chamber, orchestral, choral, rock, folk, jazz, traditional and world.

Church of the Assumption Tullamore
Fr. Oliver Skelly
Parochial House
Tullamore
Co. Offaly

Tel/Fax: +353 506 21587 or +353 506 22244 or +353 506 22415/+353 506 51510
Other key staff: Michael Moore (Organist)

Venue type: Church.
Facilities: Capacity for 1,500 (seated). Organ available.
Policy: Available for hire from Monday-Sunday (except Saturdays). Six weeks booking notice is required. Types of music promoted includes organ, chamber, orchestral, choral and opera.

Offaly Exhibition & Research Centre
Michael Byrne
Bury Quay
Tullamore
Co. Offaly

Tel/Fax: +353 506 21421
Email: ohas@iol.ie
Website: www.offalyhistory.com

Venue type: Gallery/theatre.
Facilities: Capacity for 60-100 (seated).
Policy: Available for hire from Monday-Sunday. One month's booking notice is required. Promotes chamber music.

Pat's Function Room
John Kilroe
Carraigdún
Dangan Road
Tullamore

Tel/Fax: +353 506 41345

Facilities: Capacity for 480.
Policy: Music promoted includes chamber, orchestral, choral, jazz, trad and rock/pop.

Shinrone Community Centre
Francis J. Bergin
Shinrone
Birr
Co. Offaly

Tel: +353 505 47133

Venue type: Large hall and function room.
Facilities: Capacity for 800-900 (large hall), 150 (seated - function room).
Policy: Available for hire from Monday-Sunday. Music promoted includes choral, rock, folk, alternative, pop, traditional and dance.

Tullamore Dew Heritage Centre
Amanda Pedlow
Project Manager
Bury Quay
Tullamore
Co. Offaly

Tel/Fax: +353 506 25015/+353 506 25016
Email: tullamoredhc@eircom.net
Website: www.tullamoredew.com

Venue type: Heritage centre.
Facilities: Capacity for 50 (lower ground floor).

Policy: Available for hire from Monday-Sunday. Booking notice is required.

Clonalis House
Marguerite O'Conor Nash
Castlerea
Co. Roscommon

Tel: +353 907 20014

Venue type: 19th Century Victorian Italianate mansion, which is the ancestral home of the O'Conor's of Connaght.
Facilities: Capacity for 90.

Donamon Castle
Fr. Shane Fitzgerald
Roscomon

Tel/Fax: +353 903 62222/+353 903 62511
Email: castlemusic @indigo.ie

Facilities: Capacity for 100. Kawai baby grand piano available.

Keadue Venues
Paraic Noone
Keadue
Co. Roscommon

Tel/Fax: +353 78 47204/+353 78 47511
Email: carolan@oceanfree.net
Other key staff: Berna Gibbons (PRO)

Venue type: There are three venues: Community hall, Credit Union House and Keadue Church.
Facilities: Capacity for 300-350, 75-100 and 500-600, respectively.
Policy: Music promoted includes chamber, traditional and folk.

King House
Regina Finn
Secretary
Boyle
Co. Roscommon

Tel/Fax: +353 79 63242/+353 79 63243
Email: kinghouseboyle@hotmail.com
Other key staff: Tommy Egan (Caretaker)

Venue type: 18th Century restored mansion in the centre of Boyle town.
Facilities: Capacity for 100 (Main Salon), 100 (Long Gallery). 25 (Room No 20). Steinway grand piano available.
Policy: Available for hire from Monday-Sunday. One week's booking notice is required. Music promoted includes chamber and jazz.

Ceoláras Coleman
John McGettrick
Manager
Gurteen
Co. Sligo

Tel/Fax: +353 71 82599/+353 71 82602
Email: cctrad@iol.ie
Website: www.colemanirishmusic.com

Venue type: Purpose built performance venue, visitor and teaching centre for traditional Irish music.
Facilities: Capacity for 120 (theatre).
Policy: Promotes traditional music (see advert p.68).

Drumcliffe Church
Canon Ian Gallagher
Drumcliffe
Co. Sligo

Tel/Fax: +353 71 63125

Venue type: Church built in 1809.
Facilities: Capacity for 220.
Policy: Music promoted includes chamber and choral.

Hawk's Well Theatre
Denis Clifford
Executive Director
Temple Street
Sligo

Tel/Fax: +353 71 61526/+353 71 71737
Email: hawkswell@eircom.net
Other key staff: Averyl Dooher (Assistant Director), Barry McKinney (Stage Manager)

Venue type: Gallery/theatre.
Facilities: Capacity for 348 (auditorium). Upright piano available.
Policy: Available for hire from Monday-Sunday. Two-four months booking notice is required. Music promoted includes chamber, orchestral, choral, opera, jazz, traditional, alternative and world.
Technical details: Stage size is 11.2 metres x 8.25 metres. Loading of equipment is at street level.

Model and Niland Centre
Una McCarthy
Director
The Mall
Sligo

Tel/Fax: +353 71 41405/+353 71 43694
Email: modelart@iol.ie
Website: www.iol.ie/~modelart/
Other key staff: Ann O'Dea (Education), Paul Cunningham (Music)

Venue type: Purpose built arts centre and gallery. At present the sympathetic refurbishment of the adjoining 150 year old school building is underway. This will become the Niland Centre which will house the Niland art collection.
Facilities: Capacity for 100 (auditorium), space available in gallery.
Policy: Available for hire from Monday-Sunday. Booking notice is required. Music promoted includes orchestral, chamber, jazz, world, traditional and folk.

 (see advert p.150).

Yeats Memorial Buildings
Marian Quinn
Enterprise Development Officer
Sligo

Tel/Fax: +353 71 42693/+353 91 42780
Email: info@yeats-sligo.com
Website: www.yeats-sligo.com

Facilities: Capacity for 110.
Policy: Music promoted includes recitals, chamber and solo performances.

Abymill Theatre
Austin O'Flynn
Burke Street
Fethard
Co. Tipperary

Tel/Fax: +353 52 31254/+353 52 31817

Venue type: Converted mill, built in 1847 and used as a working mill. The Abymill Trust is made up of a local committee, which established the theatre in 1988.
Facilities: Capacity for 161 (seated).
Policy: Available for hire Monday-Sunday (except Thursdays). Music promoted includes chamber, orchestral, choral, opera, jazz, traditional and world.

Brewery Lane Arts Centre
Tom Nealon
Artistic Director
Carrick-on-Suir
Co. Tipperary

Tel: +353 51 640312
Other key staff: Walter Dunphy (Chairman), Regi Power (Artistic Director)

Venue type: Arts centre.
Facilities: Capacity for 75.
Policy: Music promoted includes chamber, jazz and traditional.

Brú Ború Centre
Una O'Murchú
Director
Rock of Cashel
Cashel
Co. Tipperary

Tel/Fax: +353 62 61122 or +353 62 61779/ +353 62 32700
Email: bruboru@comhaltas.com

Venue type: Purpose built performance venue, built in 1990, situated beneath the Rock of Cashel.
Facilities: Capacity for 200.
Policy: Available for hire from Monday-Sunday.

Cahir Castle
Eleanor Morrissey
Castle Street
Co. Tipperary

Tel: +353 52 41011
Other key staff: Maureen Ahern (Cahir Castle Arts Society.
Tel/Fax: +353 52 41508
Mobile: +353 87 2619639

Venue Type: Medieval banqueting hall with a stone structure.
Facilities: Capacity for 100.
Policy: Music promoted includes chamber, orchestral, choral, jazz, crossover and traditional.

Carrick-on-Suir Heritage Centre
Patrick Fitzgerald
Administrator
Main Street
Carrick-on-Suir
Co. Tipperary

Tel: +353 51 640200
Email: cosda@iol.ie

Venue Type: Heritage Centre, which was the former Church of Ireland.
Facilities: Capacity for 120 (main hall).
Policy: Available for hire from Monday-Sunday. One months booking notice is required. Types of music promoted includes chamber and traditional.

Cashel Heritage Centre
Hannah Looby-Coates
City Hall
Main Street
Cashel
Co. Tipperary

Tel/Fax: +353 62 62511/+353 62 62068
Email: cashelhc@iol.ie
Website: www.iol.ie/tipp/

Venue Type: Heritage centre with museum.
Facilities: Capacity for 50-100.
Policy: Available for hire from Monday-Sunday. Music promoted includes choral, rock, folk, jazz, traditional and country and western.

County Museum
Pat Holland
Curator
Borstal Square
Emmet St
Clonmel
Co. Tipperary

Tel: +353 52 25399

Venue Type: Museum with two galleries.

Roscrea Castle & Damer House
Des Walsh
Roscrea Heritage Society
Roscrea
Co. Tipperary

Tel/Fax: +353 505 21322/+353 505 21976

Facilities: Capacity for up to 100 in each of these venues. Roscrea Castle is not suitable for piano recitals.
Policy: Music promoted includes chamber, opera, jazz and traditional.

St. Mary's Church of Ireland
Rev. Patrick Towers
Church Road
Nenagh
Co. Tipperary

Tel/Fax: +353 67 32598

Venue Type: Church built in 1864.
Facilities: Capacity for 300. Organ is available.
Policy: Music promoted includes chamber, choral and orchestral.

South Tipperary Arts Centre
Siobhán Mulcahy
Artistic Director
Nelson Street
Clonmel
Co. Tipperary

Tel/Fax: +353 52 27877/+353 52 27866
Email: stac@eircom.net
Website: under construction
Other key staff: Naomi Burke

Venue type: Arts centre with gallery space and workshop.

Facilities: Capacity for 30 (seated), 40 (standing).
Policy: Available for hire from Monday-Sunday. Eight weeks booking notice is required. Music promoted includes chamber, choral and traditional.

Strand Theatre

Alice Hennessy
Manager
Main Street
Carrick-on-Suir
Co. Tipperary

Tel/Fax: +353 51 640421/+353 51 640118
Other key staff: Liam Butler (Director)

Venue type: Theatre/cinema.
Facilities: Capacity for 360.
Policy: Available for hire from Monday-Wednesday. One months booking notice is required.

Tipperary Excel Centre

Paul Grisewood
Project Manager
Enterprise Centre
Tipperary Town

Tel/Fax: +353 62 52011 or +353 62 33466/
+353 62 31067

Venue type: Cultural and Interpretive centre with a cinema, theatre and workshop space, which is due to open in December 2000.
Facilities: Capacity for 100 (cinema no 1), 90 (cinema no 2).
Technical details: Stage size is 10 metres x 8.3 metres.

(see advert p.159).

CO. WATERFORD

The Bridge Hotel

Rosemary Drinan
1 The Quay
Waterford

Tel/Fax: +353 51 877222/+353 51 877229
Email: bridgehotel@treacyhotelsgroup.com
Website: www.treacyhotelsgroup.com

Venue type: Hotel, bar and restaurant.
Facilities: Capacity for 350-500 (The Wallace Suite), 275-350 (The O'Casey Room).
Policy: Available to hire from Monday-Sunday. One month's booking notice is required. Music promoted includes chamber, orchestral, choral, opera, jazz, traditional, rock, folk, pop, alternative and world.

Christ Church Waterford

Saphne Stewart-Liberty
Co-ordinator & Administrator
PO Box 2000
Cathedral Street
Waterford

Tel/Fax: +353 51 858958
Mobile: +353 86 8183165
Other key staff: Dean Barret (Dean of Cathedral)

Venue type: Restored cathedral built in the Georgian period.
Facilities: Capacity for 400, also provide extra folding chairs. Intend to make Thomas Elliot organ available, after the 'Conservation 2000' renovation scheme is completed.
Policy: Booking notice is required. Music (suitable for church) promoted includes chamber and orchestral.

City Hall

Joe O'Sullivan
Senior Staff Officer
The Mall
Waterford

Tel/Fax: +353 51 309915/+353 51 879124
Email: jsullivan@waterfordcorp.ie
Website: www.waterfordcorp.ie

Venue type: Public building.
Facilities: Capacity for up to 250 (The Large Room). Grand piano available.
Policy: Two weeks booking notice is required. Music promoted includes chamber, orchestral, choral, opera, jazz, traditional and world.

Courthouse Theatre
Edward Lynch
South Mall
Lismore
Co. Waterford

Tel/Fax: +353 58 54227 or +353 58 54041/ +353 58 54041
Mobile: +353 88 2757466

Venue type: Heritage centre.
Facilities: Capacity for 165 (theatre). Upright piano available.
Policy: Music promoted includes light opera, traditional and dance.
Technical details: Stage size is 60 ft x 30 ft.

Dungarvan Arts Centre
c/o Margaret Fleming
Arts Officer
Civic Offices
Davitts Quay
Dungarvan
Co. Waterford

Tel/Fax: +353 58 41416/+353 58 42911

Venue type: Arts Centre situated within the Old Market House, Dungarvan.

The Forum Theatre
Ciaran O'Neill
Managing Director
The Glen
Waterford

Tel/Fax: +353 51 871111/+353 51 871122
Email: fourmtheatre@eircom.net
Website: under construction
Other key staff: Ken Crangle (Manager)

Venue type: Gallery/theatre.
Facilities: Capacity for 300-900 (auditorium).
Policy: Available for hire on Monday, Wednesday, Friday and Saturday. Music promoted includes chamber, orchestral, choral, opera, jazz, traditional, folk and rock.

Garter Lane Arts Centre
Caroline Senior
Artistic Director
22a O'Connell Street
Waterford

Tel/Fax: +353 51 871573 (Admin) or +353 51 855038 (box office)/ +353 51 871570
Email: admin@garter.lane.ie
Other key staff: Lilly O'Reilly (General Manager)

Venue type: Arts centre, housed in two Georgian buildings. Multi-disciplinary space, containing a theatre, gallery, cinema, office and rehearsal space.
Facilities: Capacity for 176 (theatre), 100-150 (gallery).
Policy: Available for hire from Monday-Saturday. Six-nine months booking notice is required. Music promoted includes chamber, orchestral, choral, opera, jazz, traditional, rock, folk and world.
Technical details: Stage size is 32 ft x 22 ft. Loading of equipment is at street level.

Lismore Cathedral
Jan Van Putten
Bridane Cottage
Lismore
Co. Waterford

Tel/Fax: +353 58 54416/+353 58 54137

Venue type: 17th Century Church of Ireland Cathedral.
Facilities: Capacity for 300-400. Organ and harpsichord are available.
Policy: Music promoted includes chamber, orchestral and choral.

St. Carthaghs Cathedral
Tom Gailey
Churchwarden
Castle Estate
Lismore
Co. Waterford

Tel/Fax: +353 58 53285/+353 58 56763
Email: dianadungan@esatclear.ie
Other key staff: Diana Dungan (Churchwarden), Dr. Jan Van Putten (Organist)

Venue type: 800 year old cathedral in a heritage town.

Facilities: Capacity for 90 (Chancel), 300 (Nave) Organ is available.
Policy: Available for hire from Monday-Sunday. Three months booking notice is required. Music promoted includes chamber, orchestral, choral, opera, jazz and traditional.

Theatre Royal
Richard Seager
Theatre Manager
The Mall
Waterford

Tel/Fax: +353 51 853626 or +353 51 874402 (box office)/ +353 51 8536900
Email: theatreroyalwaterford@eircom.net

Venue type: Victorian theatre with three levels.
Facilities: Capacity for 592.
Policy: Available for hire from Monday-Sunday. Three months booking notice is required. Music promoted includes choral, opera, jazz, rock, folk, pop and world.
Technical details: Available on request.

Victoria House
Derek Barry
Manager
Queen Street
Tramore
Co. Waterford

Tel: +353 51 390338
Email: thevic@indigo.ie

Venue type: Bar.
Facilities: Capacity for 90.
Policy: Available for hire from Monday-Sunday. Music promoted includes jazz, folk and world.
Technical details: Stage size is 20 ft x 6 ft.

Tuar Ard Arts Centre
Maura Farrell
Manager
Church Street
Moate
Co. Westmeath

Tel: +353 902 81733
Other key staff: Peter Dolan (PRO)

Venue type: Arts Centre and purpose built performance venue.
Facilities: Capacity for 176 (fixed seating). Exhibition area.
Policy: Available for hire from Monday-Sunday

Tullynally Castle
David Taylor
Lough Bawn
Collinstown
Co. Westmeath

Tel/Fax: +353 44 66344/+353 44 66245
Email: loughbawn@eircom.net
Other key staff: Valerie Pakenham (President), Mary O'Neill (Secretary)

Venue type: 18th Century castle, which was the seat of the Earls of Longford.
Facilities: Capacity for 200 (Great Hall).
Policy: Available for hire from Monday-Sunday, October-March. Music promoted includes chamber, orchestral and jazz.

John F. Kennedy Arboretum
Geoff Michael
Assistant Superintendent
New Ross
Co. Wexford

Tel/Fax: +353 52 388171
Other key staff: Chris Kelly (Director)

Venue type: Built in 1968, opened by President de Valera, to commemorate John F. Kennedy.
Facilities: Capacity for 60.

The Old Rectory Hotel
Dee Cooney
Manager
Rosbercon
New Ross
Co. Wexford

Tel/Fax: +353 51 421719/+353 51 422974

Venue type: Hotel, bar and restaurant.
Facilities: Capacity for 100 and 200 (standing).

St. Iberius Church

Chancellor N.Ruddock
The Rectory
Wexford

Tel/Fax: +353 53 43013

Venue type: Georgian church.
Facilities: Kawai grand piano available.
Policy: Available for hire from Monday-Sunday.
One month's booking notice is required.

St. Michael's Theatre

Geraldine Ronan
Supervisor
South Street
New Ross
Co. Wexford

Tel/Fax: +353 51 421255/+353 51 420346
Other key staff: Suzane Sinnott (Administrator),
Deirdre Newport (Secretary)

Venue type: Gallery/theatre.
Facilities: Capacity for 329.
Policy: Available for hire from Monday-Sunday. Two-
three weeks booking notice is required. Music promoted
includes chamber, orchestral, choral, opera, jazz, traditional, rock and folk.
Technical details: Available on request.

Stella Maris Centre

Mary Bates
Manager
Stella Maris Community Centre
Kilmore Quay
Co. Wexford

Tel/Fax: +353 53 29922
Other key staff: Caroline Power

Venue type: Community centre.
Facilities: Capacity for 80-100 (meeting room),
180-200 (sports hall).
Policy: One month's booking notice is required.

Wexford Arts Centre

Denis Collins
Artistic Director
Cornmarket
Wexford

Tel/Fax: +353 53 23764
Other key staff: Johanna Murphy (PRO),
Bill Butler (House Manager)

Venue type: Arts centre.
Facilities: Capacity for 122-135 (Ballroom), 80 (Pillar
Room), 40 (Cellar Bistro). Yamaha upright piano available.
Policy: Available for hire from Monday-Sunday. Four
weeks booking notice is required. Music promoted
includes chamber, orchestral, traditional, rock, folk, pop
and world.
Technical details: Stage size is 24 ft x 16 ft.

CO. WICKLOW

Craft Framing Gallery

Jean Colohan
3 Dublin Road
Bray
Co. Wicklow

Tel: +353 1 2866728

Venue type: Gallery.
Facilities: Capacity for 100 (standing).
Policy: Available for hire from Monday-Sunday. One
months booking notice is required. Music promoted
includes chamber, jazz, traditional and world.

Tinahely Courthouse Centre

Sharon Corcoran
Director
Main Street
Tinahely
Co. Wicklow

Tel/Fax: +353 402 38529/+353 402 38440
Email: tinahely@iol.ie
Website: www.tinahely-courthouse.ie

Venue type: Arts centre.
Facilities: Capacity for 150.
Policy: Six months booking notice is required. Music
promoted includes chamber, orchestral, jazz, traditional,
pop and world.

VENUES - NORTHERN IRELAND

CO. ANTRIM

Balloo House

Martin Wolsey
1 Comber Road
Killinchy
Co. Antrim BT23 6PA
Northern Ireland

Tel: 048 9754 1210

Venue type: Hotel.
Facilities: Capacity for 100.
Policy: Music promoted includes traditional and easy listening.

Ballymena Town Hall

Rosalind Lowry
Arts Officer
80 Galgorm Road
Ballymena
Co. Antrim BT42 1AB
Northern Ireland

Tel/Fax: 048 2566 0319/048 2566 0400
Website: www.ballymean.gov.uk
Other key staff: Ken McGookin (Superintendent), Chris Warden (Assistant Superintendent)

Venue type: Public building.
Facilities: Capacity for 700 (main hall), 100 (minor hall). Yamaha grand and upright piano available.
Policy: Available for hire from Monday-Saturday. One month's booking notice is required. Music promoted includes chamber, orchestral, choral, opera, jazz, traditional, rock, folk, cajun, pop, reggae, dance, alternative, country and western and world.

Ballymoney Town Hall

R. J. Graham
Amenities Officer
Riada House
14 Charles Street
Ballymoney
Co. Antrim BT53 6OZ
Northern Ireland

Tel/Fax: 048 2766 2280/048 2766 7659
Email: ballymoneybc@psilink.co.uk
Website: www.ballymoney.gov.uk
Other key staff: Margaret Higgins (Cultural Services Officer)

Venue type: Public building.
Facilities: Capacity for 250 (town hall), 100 (balcony), 90 (minor hall).
Policy: Available for hire from Monday-Saturday. Three-six months booking notice is required. Music promoted includes chamber, orchestral, choral, opera, jazz, traditional, folk, dance and world.

BBC Studio One

Anne Cormican
Production Executive
BBC Resources
Third Floor, Broadcasting House
Ormeau Avenue
Belfast BT2 8HQ
Northern Ireland

Tel: 048 9033 8723

Venue type: Music recording studio.
Facilities: Capacity for 100. Steinway grand piano and harpsichord available. Frequently used for chamber music recitals.
Policy: Availability by negotiation.

Belfast Waterfront Hall

Tim Husbands
General Manager
2 Lanyon Place
Belfast BT1 3WH
Northern Ireland

Tel/Fax: 048 9033 4400/048 9024 9862
Email: husbands@waterfront.co.uk
Website: www.waterfront.co.uk
Other key staff: Mark McBride (Finance & Admin Manager), Andrew Kyle (Sales & Marketing Manager)

Venue type: Purpose built concert hall with two auditoriums.
Facilities: Capacity for 2,235-2,800 (Waterfront Hall), 380-650 (BT Studio). Steinway grand - Model D.
Policy: Available for hire from Monday-Sunday. Booking notice is required. Music promoted includes chamber, orchestral, choral, opera, jazz, traditional, rock, folk, pop, reggae, dance, alternative, country and western and world.

Technical details: Stage size is 20 metres x 20 metres x11.5-14 metres.

Venue type: Hotel.
Facilities: Capacity for 350.

Carrickfergus Castle

Campbell Ferris
Castle Manager
Marine Highway
Carrickfergus
Co. Antrim BT38 7BG
Northern Ireland

Tel/Fax: 048 9335 1273/048 9336 5190
Website: www.touristnetuk.com/ni/carrickcastle
Other key staff: Blaina White (Custodian)

Venue type: 12th Century Medieval castle.
Facilities: Capacity for 60.
Policy: Available for hire from Monday-Saturday. Three weeks booking notice is required.

Carrickfergus Town Hall

George Gibson
Community Services Officer
Joymount
Carrickfergus
Co. Antrim
Northern Ireland

Tel/Fax: 048 9335 1604/048 9336 6676
Email: cservices1@carrickfergus.org

Venue type: Public building.
Facilities: Capacity for 300 (Jubilee Hall), 60 (Dobbs Room). Upright piano available.
Policy: Available for hire from Monday-Sunday. Two weeks booking notice is required.

Causeway Coast Hotel

Mary O'Neill
Marketing Manager
36 Ballyreagh Road
Portrush
Co. Antrim
Northern Ireland

Tel: 048 7082 2435
Email: info@causewaycoast.com
Website: www.causewaycoast.com

Clotworthy Arts Centre

Gary Shaw
Arts & Heritage Development Officer
Antrim Castle Gardens
Randalstown Road
Co. Antrim BT41 4LH
Northern Ireland

Tel/Fax: 048 9442 8000/048 9446 0360
Other key staff: Cathy McNally (Assistant Arts & Heritage Officer), Michael McLaughlin (Technician/Caretaker)

Venue type: Arts centre, containing three exhibition spaces.
Facilities: Capacity for 96.
Policy: Available for hire from Monday-Saturday. Music promoted includes chamber, orchestral, opera, jazz, traditional, rock, dance and world.
Technical details: Stage size is 17 ft x 20 ft.

Courtyard Theatre

Cathy Cole
Development Arts Officer
Development Department
49 Church Road
Newtownabbey
Co. Antrim BT36 7LG
Northern Ireland

Tel/Fax: 048 9086 8751/048 9036 5407
Other key staff: Paula Donaghy (Community Relations Officer), Ursula Fay (Leisure Centres Manager)

Venue type: Arts centre and theatre.
Facilities: Capacity for 180. Baby grand piano available.
Policy: Available for hire from Monday-Sunday. Booking notice is required. Music promoted includes choral, cajun, opera, jazz, traditional, dance and world.

Crescent Arts Centre

Louise Emerson
Director
2-4 University Road
Belfast BT7 2NH
Northern Ireland

Tel/Fax: 048 9024 2338/048 9024 6748
Email: info@crescentarts.org
Website: www.crescentarts.org
Other key staff: Liz Donnan (Accounts/
Programme Office), Hazel McAnally (Administrator)

Venue type: Multidisciplinary arts centre including the Fenderesky Gallery. Upright piano available.
Facilities: Capacity for 230 (gym), 150 (dance studio)
Policy: Available for hire from Thursday-Sunday. Three month's booking notice is required. Music promoted is jazz, traditional, rock, folk, cajun, country and western and world.

Elmwood Hall at Queen's

Barbara McKinley
89 University Road
Belfast BT7 1NF
Northern Ireland

Tel: 048 9066 4535

Venue type: Former church.
Facilities: Capacity for 518.
Policy: Music promoted includes chamber, orchestral, choral, jazz, traditional, country, folk and dance.

Fisherwick Presbyterian Church

Derek McKelvey
2-4 Chlorine Gardens
Malone Road
Belfast
Northern Ireland

Tel/Fax: 048 9066 7667 or 048 9066 6683/
048 9038 1435

Venue type: Traditional church with pew seating in the centre.
Facilities: Capacity for 1,200. Upright piano.
Policy: Music promoted includes chamber, orchestral and choral.

Galgorm Manor Hotel

Stephanie Bloomfield
Operations Manager
136 Fenaghy Road
Cullybackey
Ballymena
Co. Antrim BT42 1EA
Northern Ireland

Tel/Fax: 048 2588 1001/048 2588 0080
Email: galgorm.manor@galgorm.com
Website: www.galgorm.com
Other key staff: David Cadwallader (General Manager), Lucie Wright (PR & Sales Manager)

Venue type: Former 19th Century gentlemans residence, situated on an 85 acre estate, by the River Maine.
Facilities: Capacity for 500. Upright piano available.
Policy: Available for hire from Monday-Sunday. One month's booking notice is required. All types of music are promoted.
Technical details: Full technical specification available on request.

Grand Opera House

Derek Nicholls
Theatre Director
Great Victoria Street
Belfast BT2 7HR
Northern Ireland

Tel/Fax: 048 9024 0411 or 048 9024 1919 (box office)/048 9023 6842
Email: dnicholls@gohbelfast.com
Website: www.gohbelfast.com
Other key staff: Hary Trainor (Marketing Manager), Patricia Doyle (Ticket Shop Manager)

Venue type: Gallery/Theatre.
Facilities: Capacity for 1,000 (auditorium). Theatre style seating.
Policy: Booking notice is required. Music promoted includes orchestral, choral, opera, jazz, pop, country and western and world.

Harty Room at Queen's

Elizabeth Moore
Estates and Building Office
The Queen's University
Belfast BT7 1NN
Northern Ireland

Tel: 048 9024 5133 Ext. 3075
Email: elizabeth.moore@qub.ac.uk

Venue type: Located in the University Square.
Facilities: Capacity for 170. Steinway concert grand and Steinway boudoir pianos, a Grant, Deglens and Bradbeer organ available.
Policy: Music promoted includes chamber and choral.

Hastings Stormont Hotel

Roslyn Wilson
Events Co-Ordinator
587 Upper Newtownards Road
Belfast BT4 3LP
Northern Ireland

Tel/Fax: 048 9065 8621/048 9048 0240
Email: conf@stor.hastingshotels.com
Website: www.hastingshotels.com
Other key staff: Donna Wilson (Events Co-Ordinator)

Venue type: Situated opposite the Stormont Parliament buildings.
Facilities: Capacity for 400. Hyundai baby grand piano available.
Policy: Available for hire from Monday-Sunday. One-two weeks booking notice is required.

King's Hall Exhibition & Conference Centre

Philip M. Rees
Director
Balmoral
Belfast BT9 6GW
Northern Ireland

Tel/Fax: 048 9066 5225/048 9066 1264
Email: prees@kingshall.co.uk
Website: www.kingshall.co.uk
Other key staff: Tommy Deane (Showgrounds Manager), Oliver Egan (Health & Safety Officer)

Venue: Purpose built performance venue, containing exhibition halls and a conference centre.
Facilities: Capacity for 8,000.
Policy: Available for hire from Monday-Sunday. Music promoted includes rock, cajun, pop and country and western.

Larne Grammar School

Sylvia Restrick
Bursar
4-6 Lower Cairncastle Road
Larne
Co. Antrim BT40 1PQ
Northern Ireland

Tel/Fax: 048 2827 2791
Email: hmorrow@larnegrammar.larne.ni.sch.uk
Other key staff: H. Morrow (Headmaster)

Venue type: School/college.
Facilities: Capacity 350 (assembly hall), 86 (theatre). Yamaha clavenova and Knight upright piano available.
Policy: Available for hire from Monday-Sunday. Music promoted includes chamber, orchestral, choral, opera, jazz and traditional.

Lyric Theatre

Les McClean
Director of Administration & Resources
55 Ridgeway Street
Stranmillis Embankment
Belfast BT9 5FB
Northern Ireland

Tel/Fax: 048 9066 9660/048 9038 1395
Email: admin@lyrictheatre.co.uk
Website: www.lyrictheatre.co.uk

Venue type: Producing theatre.
Facilities: Capacity for 304. Sign performing for blind people, through use of audio described performance.
Policy: Music promoted includes chamber, choral, jazz and traditional.

McNeill Theatre

Herbie Francis
Tourism & Community Relations Manager
Smiley Buildings
Victoria Road
Larne
Co. Antrim
Northern Ireland

Tel: 048 2827 2313
Email: mail@larne.bc.com
Other key staff: Ronnie Blair (Director of Leisure

& Technical Services), Anne Thompson (Leisure Services Manager)

Venue type: Gallery/theatre.
Facilities: Capacity for 200.
Policy: Available for hire from Monday-Saturday. Eight months booking notice is required. Music promoted includes orchestral, traditional and world.
Technical details: Stage size is 6.1 metres x 13.7 metres. Type of staging is PVC on top of plastic.

Old Museum Arts Centre

Elaine Gaston
7 College Square North
Belfast BT1 6AR
Northern Ireland

Tel/Fax: 048 9023 5053 or 048 9023 3332 (box office)/048 9032 2912
Other key staff: Anne McReynolds (Director)

Venue type: Arts centre.
Facilities: Capacity for 90 (theatre), 60 (gallery). Marshall & Rose upright piano available.
Policy: Available for hire from Monday-Sunday. Six months booking notice is required. Music promoted includes orchestral, jazz, new rock and alternative.
Technical details: Stage size is 25 ft x 21 ft.

St. Anne's Cathedral

David Drinkell
Organist & Master of Choristers
Lower Donegall Street
Belfast BT1 2HB
Northern Ireland

Tel/Fax: 048 9032 8332/048 9023 8855
Email: belfast.cathedral@dial.pipex.com

Venue type: Cathedral.
Facilities: Capacity for 1,200. Harrison & Harrison organ available.
Policy: Music promoted includes chamber, orchestral and choral.

St. George's Parish Church

D.A.R Chillingworth
Secretary
Select Vestry
65 Whitehouse Park

Newtownabbey
Co. Antrim BT37 9SH
Northern Ireland

Tel: 048 9085 2615
Other key staff: Walter Banks (Caretaker)

Venue type: Parish church dating from 1816.
Facilities: Capacity for 300 (seated). Upright piano available.
Policy: Available for hire from Monday-Sunday. Three months booking notice is required. Music promoted includes chamber, orchestral, choral and opera.

Sheskburn Recreation Centre

Damian McAfee
Recreation Sports Officer
7 Mary Street
Ballycastle
Co. Antrim BT54 6QH
Northern Ireland

Tel/Fax: 048 2076 3225/048 2076 2515

Venue type: Leisure centre.
Facilities: Capacity for 375.

Ulster Museum Lecture Theatre

Angela Reid
Botanic Gardens
Belfast BT9 5AB
Northern Ireland

Venue type: Located within the Ulster Museum and is used for arts events.
Facilities: Capacity for 150. Grand piano available.
Policy: Music promoted includes chamber, choral, jazz, traditional, world.

Whitla Hall at Queen's

Elizabeth Moore
Estates & Buildings Office
The Queen's University
Belfast BT7 1NN
Northern Ireland

Tel: 048 9024 5133 Ext. 3075
Email: elizabeth.moore@qub.ac.uk

Venue type: Located on the campus of The Queen's University, and is used by festival and university organisations.
Facilities: Capacity for 250. Steinway/Chappell piano and pipe organ available.
Policy: Music promoted includes chamber, orchestral and choral.

Charlemont Arms Hotel
Mr. Foster
Upper English Street
Armagh
Northern Ireland

Tel: 048 3752 2028

Venue type: Hotel function room.

Craigavon Civic Centre
Iann Bann
Facilities Manager
P.O Box 66
Lakeview Road
Craigavon
Co. Armagh BT64 1AL
Northern Ireland

Tel/Fax: 048 3831 2400
Email: info@craigavon.gov.uk
Other key staff: June Guy (Administration Assistant)

Venue type: Multipurpose venue.
Facilities: Capacity for 640. Upright and baby grand piano available.
Policy: Available for hire from Monday-Saturday. Booking notice is required. Music promoted includes chamber, orchestral, choral, opera, jazz, traditional, rock, folk, cajun, pop, reggae, dance and world.

Crozier Hall
The Mall
Armagh
Northern Ireland

Tel: 048 3752 1800

Venue type: Church hall.
Facilities: Capacity for 220.

Lurgan Town Hall
Kate Freeburn
Manager
2-6 Union Street
Lurgan
Craigavon BT66 8DY
Northern Ireland

Tel/Fax: 048 3832 2422/048 3834 8298
Website: www.craigavon.gov.uk
Other key staff: Shirley Taylor (Caretaker), Molly Livingston (Caretaker), Aubrey McShane (Stage Technician)

Venue type: Victorian listed building, built in 1868. Community arts and resource centre.
Facilities: Capacity for 220 (first floor area), 300 (auditorium). Upright Yamaha piano available.
Policy: Available for hire from Monday-Sunday. Two weeks booking notice is required. All types of music promoted.
Technical details: Stage size is 9 metres x 7 metres.

The Market Place - Armagh Theatre & Arts Centre
Vincent McCann
Administrator
Market Street
Armagh BT61 7AT
Northern Ireland

Tel/Fax: 048 3752 1820/048 3752 1822
Email: armagh.arts@dnet.co.uk
Website: www.marketplacearmagh.com

Venue type: Arts centre/purpose built fully-equipped theatre.
Facilities: Capacity for 150 (studio theatre), 400 (main auditorium), 20-40 (workshop rooms), 70-80 (bar areas).
Policy: Available for hire from Monday-Sunday. Music promoted includes chamber, orchestral, choral, opera, jazz, traditional, rock, folk, reggae and world.
Technical details: Technical specifications on request.

Navan Centre
Anne Hart
Education Officer
81 Killylea Road
Armagh
Northern Ireland

Tel/Fax: 048 3752 5550/048 3752 2323
Email: navan@enterprise.com

Venue type: Heritage centre.
Facilities: Capacity for 120.
Policy: Booking notice is required. Music promoted includes choral, opera, traditional, folk and world.

Portadown Town Hall
Violet Johnston
Manager
15-17 Edward Street
Portadown
Co. Armagh BT62 3LX
Northern Ireland

Tel/Fax: 048 3833 5264/048 3836 1987
Other key staff: Diane Robb (Principal Officer)

Venue type: Multipurpose building.
Facilities: Capacity for 265 (main auditorium), 320 (flat), 100 (minor hall), 40 (committee room). Kawai upright and Yamaha upright piano available.
Policy: Available for hire from Monday-Sunday. Booking notice is required. Music promoted includes orchestral, opera and jazz.

St. Patrick's Cathedral
Rev. H. Cassidy
The Library
Abbey Street
Armagh BT61 7DY
Northern Ireland

Tel/Fax: 048 3752 3142/048 3752 4177
Email: armroblib@aol.com

Venue type: Cathedral.
Policy: Available for hire from Monday-Friday. One month's booking notice is required. Music promoted includes orchestral and opera.

St. Patrick's Hall
Marissa Foye
Parochial Hall
42 Abbey Street
Armagh BT6 17D2
Northern Ireland

Tel/Fax: 048 3752 2802/048 3752 2245

Venue type: Public building.
Facilities: Capacity for 600.
Policy: One month's booking notice is required.

Tí Chulainn
Kieran Murphy
Events Manager
An Mullach Bán
Co. Armagh BT35 9TT
Northern Ireland

Tel/Fax: 048 3088 8828/048 3088 8821
Email: tculainn@dial.pipex.com
Website: www.tculainn.ie
Other key staff: Seán Ó Coinn (Manager), Crónán Devlin (Archivist)

Venue type: Purpose built performance venue, dedicated to the development of the cultural heritage of the Ring of Gullion.
Facilities: Capacity for 75 (auditorium), 180-200 (performance area). Upright piano available for hire.
Policy: Available for hire from Monday-Sunday. One month's booking notice is required. Music promoted includes rock and traditional.

CO. DERRY

Edgewater Hotel
Linda McKee
Manager
88 Strand Road
Portstewart
Co. Derry BT55 7LZ
Northern Ireland

Tel/Fax: 048 7083 3688/048 7083 2224
Email: edgewater.hotel@virgin.net
Website: www.freespace.virgin.net/edgewater.hotel/index.htm

Venue type: Hotel.
Facilities: Capacity for 200.
Policy: Available for hire on a Saturday. Music promoted includes chamber, orchestral, choral, traditional, folk, alternative and country and western.

Flowerfield Arts Centre

Malcolm Murchison
Centre Manager
185 Coleraine Road
Portstewart
Co. Derry BT55 7HU
Northern Ireland

Tel/Fax: 048 7083 3959/048 7083 5042
Email: flowerfield@dnet.co.uk
Website: under construction

Venue type: Listed Georgian residence, which has been converted into a local authority arts centre.
Facilities: Capacity for 70 (gallery). Yamaha upright piano available.
Policy: Available for hire Friday and Saturday. One years booking notice is required. Music promoted includes chamber, jazz, traditional, folk, pop and world.

Foyle Arts Centre

Paddy Casey
Lawrence Hill
Derry City BT48 7NJ
Northern Ireland

Tel/Fax: 048 7126 6657/048 7136 3166

Venue type: Renovated school.
Facilities: Capacity for 80, 80 and 90 (three separate spaces). Upright piano available.
Policy: Music promoted includes chamber, jazz, traditional, folk.

Magee College - University of Ulster

Northland Road
Derry BT48 7DL
c/o Dr. Irene Adams
University of Ulster at Coleraine
Coleraine BT52 15A
Northern Ireland

Tel/Fax: 048 7032 4449/048 7032 4160
Email: izadams@ulst.ac.uk

Venue type: Situated on the first floor of the college.
Facilities: Capacity for 200. Baby grand piano.

The Millennium Complex

David McLaughlin
Venues Manager
Rialto Centre
5 Market Street
Derry BT48 6EF
Northern Ireland

Tel/Fax: 048 7126 4177/048 7126 0516

Venue type: Theatre, which will open in 2001 replacing the Rialto Centre.

Rialto Centre

David McLaughlin
Venues Manager
5 Market Street
Derry BT48 6EF
Northern Ireland

Tel/Fax: 048 7126 4177/048 7126 0516
Other key staff: Jim Nelis (Technician)

Venue type: Arts centre.
Facilities: Upright piano available.
Policy: Available for hire from Monday-Sunday. Booking notice is required. Music promoted includes chamber, orchestral, choral, opera, jazz, traditional, rock, folk, cajun, pop, reggae, dance, alternative, country and western, world (Millennium Complex, see above, will replace this in January 2001)

Riverside Theatre

Janet Mackle
Theatre Manager
University of Ulster
Cromore Road
Coleraine
Co. Derry BT52 1SA
Northern Ireland

Tel/Fax: 048 7032 4683/048 7032 4924
Other key staff: David Coyle (Technical Supervisor)

Venue type: Gallery/theatre, situated on the campus of the University of Ulster.
Facilities: Capacity 274-358 (auditorium). Yamaha baby grand piano available.
Policy: Available for hire from Monday-Sunday. Three-six months booking notice is required. Music promoted

includes chamber, orchestral, choral, jazz, traditional, rock, folk, cajun, pop and alternative.
Technical details: Stage size is 36 ft x 22 ft.

St. Columb's Church of Ireland Cathedral
Timothy Allen
Bishop Street
Derry City BT48 6PP
Northern Ireland

Tel/Fax: 048 7126 2412
Email: e.allen@lineone.net

Venue type: Cathedral built in 1633.
Facilities: Capacity for 800. Organ is available.
Policy: Music promoted includes chamber and choral.

University of Ulster at Coleraine
Dr. Irene Adams
University of Ulster at Coleraine
Coleraine BT52 15A
Co. Derry
Northern Ireland

Tel/Fax: 048 7032 4449/048 7032 4160
Email: izadams@ulst.ac.uk

Venue type: Two theatres - The Diamond and The Octagon, housed within the University of Ulster at Coleraine.
Facilities: Capacity for 1,300 (The Diamond), 500 (The Octagon).

CO. DOWN

Ards Arts Centre
Eilis O'Baoill
Arts Officer
Townhall
Conway Square
Newtownards
Co. Down

Tel/Fax: 048 9181 0803/048 9182 3131

Email: ards@ards-council.gov.uk
Other key staff: Kate Wimpress (Community Arts Dev. Officer), Angela Hayley (Arts Centre Co-ordinator)

Venue type: Arts centre based in old town hall.
Facilities: Capacity for 100 (The Londonderry Room). Yamaha upright piano available.
Policy: Available for hire from Monday-Saturday. One month's booking notice is required. Types of music promoted includes chamber, opera, jazz and world.

Banbridge Town Hall
Vanessa Miller
Arts & Events Officer
Banbridge District Council
Civic Building
Downshire Road
Banbridge
Co. Down
Northern Ireland

Tel/Fax: 048 4066 2991/048 4066 2959
Email: info@banbridgedc.gov.uk
Website: www.banbridge.com

Venue type: Multi purpose venue.
Facilities: Capacity for 150.
Policy: Available for hire from Monday-Saturday. Booking notice is required. Music promoted includes choral, traditional, pop and country and western.

Down Arts Centre
Jill Holmes
2-6 Irish Street
Downpatrick
Co. Down BT30 6BN
Northern Ireland

Tel/Fax: 048 4461 5283/048 4461 6621

Venue type: Arts centre.
Facilities: Capacity for 200.

Down Leisure Centre

Macartan Bryce
1-4 Market Street
Downpatrick
Co. Down BT30 6LZ
Northern Ireland

Tel/Fax: 048 4461 3426/048 4461 6905

Venue type: Leisure centre.
Facilities: Capacity for 600.

Bangor Heritage Centre

Ian Wilson
Castle Grounds
Bangor
Co. Down
Northern Ireland

Tel/Fax: 048 9127 1200/048 9147 8906

Facilities: Capacity for 120.

Lough Moss Centre

Ron McKnight
Duty Manager
Hillsborough Road
Carryduff
Co. Down BT8 8HR
Northern Ireland

Tel/Fax: 048 9081 4884/048 9081 5316
Other key staff: Lea Booth (Duty Manager),
George Doherty (Area Manager)

Venue type: Arts and leisure centre.
Facilities: Capacity for 800 (main hall), 375 (minor hall),
110 (arts & crafts room).
Policy: Music promoted includes traditional, rock, cajun
and pop.

Newcastle Centre

Willie McCullough
10-14 Central Promenade
Newcastle
Co. Down
Northern Ireland

Tel/Fax: 048 4372 5034/048 4372 2400

Facilities: Capacity for 300. Yamaha piano available.
Policy: Music promoted includes chamber, traditional,
alternative and country and western.

Newry Arts Centre

Mark Hughes
Arts Administrator
1a Bank Parade
Newry
Co. Down BT35 6HP
Northern Ireland

Tel/Fax: 048 3026 6232/048 3026 6839
Other key staff: Pat Duffy (Caretaker)

Venue type: Arts centre.
Facilities: Capacity for 150 (auditorium). Baby grand
and upright piano available.
Policy: Available for hire from Monday-Sunday. Booking
notice is required. Music promoted includes chamber,
orchestral, choral, opera, jazz, traditional, rock, folk,
cajun, pop, reggae, dance, alternative and world.

Newry Town Hall

Mark Hughes
Arts Administrator
1a Bank Parade
Newry
Co. Down BT35 6HP
Northern Ireland

Tel/Fax: 048 3026 6232/048 3026 6839
Other key staff: Jacqueline Turley
(Administration Assistant)

Venue type: Public building and purpose built venue.
Facilities: Capacity for 500 (main hall), 100 (minor hall).
Steinway grand and upright piano available.
Policy: Available for hire from Monday-Sunday. Two
weeks booking notice is required. Music promoted
includes chamber, orchestral, choral, opera, jazz, traditional and rock.

Queen's Hall

Town Hall Arts Centre
Conway Square
Newtownards

Co. Down BT20 4RG
Northern Ireland

Tel/Fax: 048 9181 0803/048 9182 3131
Email: ards@ards_council.gov.uk

Venue type: Community hall.
Policy: Two-three months booking notice is required.
Music promoted includes chamber, opera, jazz and
traditional.

Queen's Hall-Holywood

c/o Lorna Hastings
Arts Officer
Tower House
34 Quay Street
Bangor BT20 5ED
Co. Down
Northern Ireland

Tel/Fax: 048 9127 8032/+44 2891 467744

Facilities: Capacity for 250.

Ulster Folk & Transport Museum

Robbie Hannan
Curator of Musicology
Cultra
Holywood
Co. Down

Tel/Fax: 048 9042 8428
Other key staff: Jonathan Bell (Head of
Curatorial Division)

Venue type: Museum. There are a number of venues
within the museum site. The Parochial Hall and The
Church of St. John The Baptist provide ideal concert
venues. Cafe, shop facilities.
Policy: Promotes traditional music.

CO. FERMANAGH

Ardhowen Theatre

Pamela Scrayfield
Assistant Manager
Dublin Road
Enniskillen
Co. Fermanagh BT74 6BR
Northern Ireland

Tel/Fax: 048 6632 3233/048 6632 7102

Venue type: Fully equipped theatre and arts centre,
which was opened in 1986.
Facilities: Capacity for 290.
Policy: Music promoted includes chamber, orchestral,
choral, rock, jazz, traditional, world, country, folk, blues,
dance and pop.

Bawnacre Centre

George Beacon
Centre Manager
Irvinestown
Co. Fermanagh BT94 1EE
Northern Ireland

Tel/Fax: 048 6862 1177/048 6862 8082
Email: georgebeacom@fermanagh.gov.uk

Venue type: Community centre.
Facilities: Capacity for 900 (main hall), minor hall (300).
Policy: Booking notice is required. Music promoted
includes chamber, orchestral, choral, traditional, rock,
pop and world.

Share Arts Arena & Conference Venue

Dawn Latimer
Director
Share Holiday Village
Smiths Strand
Lisnaskea
Co. Fermanagh BT92 0EQ
Northern Ireland

Tel/Fax: 048 6722 2122/048 6772 1893
Email: share@dnet.co.uk
Website: www.sharevillage.org
Other key staff: Declan Campbell (Arts
Development Worker), Aine Weir (Arts
Development Worker)

Venue type: Arts centre and purpose built performance
venue.
Facilities: Capacity for 100-300 (Trannish Suite), 30-60
(Shanaghy and Innishmore Suites). Equipped conference
and arts rooms. Photography darkroom suite will be
available by 2001. Pottery and craft suites. Yamaha
Synthesiser available.
Policy: Available for hire from Monday-Sunday. Booking
notice is required. All types of music promoted.

South West Divisional Library Headquarters

Desmond Preston
Divisional Librarian
Hall's Lane
Enniskillen
Co. Fermanagh BT74 7DR
Northern Ireland

Tel/Fax: 048 6632 2886/048 6632 4685

Venue type: Library.
Facilities: Capacity for 250. Grand piano available.
Policy: Available for hire from Monday-Friday. One months booking notice is required. All types of music promoted.

CO. TYRONE

Burnavon Arts & Cultural Centre

Tony McCance
Acting Manager
Burn Road
Cookstown
Co. Tyrone BT80 8DN
Northern Ireland

Tel/Fax: 048 8676 9949/048 8676 5853
Email: econdev@cookstown.gov.uk

Venue type: Arts centre.
Facilities: Capacity for 351 (auditorium).
Policy: Available for hire from Monday-Sunday. One months booking notice is required. Music promoted includes chamber, orchestral, choral, opera, jazz, traditional, rock, folk, cajun, pop, dance, country and western and world.

An Creagan Visitor Centre

John Donaghy
Manager
Creggan
Omagh
Co. Tyrone BT79 9AR
Northern Ireland

Tel/Fax: 048 8076 1112/048 8076 1116

Venue type: Heritage centre.
Facilities: Capacity for 30 (room no. 1), 60-80 (room no. 2).

Policy: Available for hire from Monday-Friday. Two-three months booking notice is required. Music promoted includes traditional and folk.
Technical details: Loading of equipment is at street level.

Melmount Centre

Elizabeth O'Hare
37 Melmount Road
Strabane
Co. Tyrone BT82 9EF
Northern Ireland

Tel/Fax: 048 7138 3777/048 7188 6469

Facilities: Capacity for 500.
Policy: Two months booking notice is required. All types of music promoted.

Omagh Library

R. Farrow
Chief Librarian
1 Spillers Place
Omagh
Co. Tyrone
Northern Ireland

Tel/Fax: 048 8224 4821/048 8224 0905
Email: librarian@omalib.demon.co. uk
Other key staff: May Magee (Personal Assistant)

Venue type: Public building.
Facilities: Capacity for 150 (lecture room - seated).
Policy: Available for hire from Monday-Sunday. Booking notice is required.

St. Patrick's Hall

Raymond Kirk
Entertainment Manager
Barrack Street
Strabane
Co. Tyrone BT82 8HS
Northern Ireland

Tel/Fax: 048 7188 2483

Venue type: Community/parish hall.

Facilities: Capacity for 400 (main hall). Yamaha upright piano available.

Policy: Available for hire from Monday-Sunday. Three-four weeks booking notice is required. Music promoted includes chamber, orchestral, choral, opera, traditional, rock, folk, pop, reggae, dance, country and western and world.

Festivals

FESTIVALS - REP. OF IRELAND

Africa Festival
Adekunle Gómez
Director
Ulster Bank Chambers
4 Lower O'Connell Street
Dublin 1

Tel/Fax: +353 1 8780613/+353 1 8780615

Festival will be held late October to early November in the year 2000, 2001 and 2002. Music promoted includes African traditional and urban music. Three different groups feature within the festival. Festival is planned 10-12 months in advance. Events range from formal sit-down evening concerts (National Concert Hall, churches and arts Centres) to pub venues (Whelan's, Vicar Street etc), workshops are also available to promoters and organisers.

AIMS Choral Festival
Connie Tantrum
Administrator
Cross Street
New Ross
Co. Wexford

Tel/Fax: +353 51 421766

Festival will be held 20/21 May 2000, late May 2001 and 2002. Promotes choral music. Format of festival includes one day of choir competitions in 11 separate categories, a main concert and workshops (open to all choirs). Festival is planned 10 months in advance.

Aisling Childrens' Arts Festival
Maeve Curtin
Public Relations Officer
Harbour House
Harbour Row
Longford

Tel: +353 43 47455
Other key staff: Jean Healy (Chairman). Tony Headon (Treasurer), Eddie Ward (Secretary)

Festival will be held in October 2000, 2001 and 2002. Music promoted includes chamber, traditional/folk, world and crossover. 3-4 musical events take place within the festival. There are workshops and performances during this festival. In 1999 there was National Concert Hall workshops for post-primary schools. Festival is planned 9 months in advance.

The Anna Livia International Opera Festival
Brian Raythorn
Festival Manager
St. Stephen's Green House
3rd Floor
Earlsfort Terrace
Dublin 2

Tel/Fax: +353 1 6617544/+353 1 6617548
Email: operaannalivia@eircom.net
Other key staff: Dr. Bernadette Greevy (Founder/Artistic Director)

The inaugural festival will be held from 16-25 June 2000. This festival will be an annual summer event. Promotes opera. During the festival there are 2 operas, celebrity recitals, a gala opera concert and fringe events. Examples of venues used will be The Gaiety Theatre, The Pro-Cathedral, The Irish Film Centre and The Botanic Gardens.

Aonach Paddy O'Brien Traditional Music & Arts Festival
Deirdre McSherry
Honorary Secretary
45 Hawthorns
Summerhill
Nenagh
Co. Tipperary

Tel/Fax: +353 67 34927/+353 67 34217
Mobile: +353 87 2445848
Email: aonach@iol.ie
Website: www.iol.ie/~aonach
Other key staff: Eileen O'Brien (Chairperson), Michael Scanlan (Treasurer), Bridget O'Neill (Public Relations Officer)

Festival will be held 18th August 2000, 17th August 2001 and 16th August 2002. Music promoted includes traditional and folk. Format of festival includes formal sit-down concerts, workshops, song and dance, street theatre, open-air concert, pub sessions, busking, art and photographic exhibitions, céilís, lectures and a musical boat trip with traditional/folk music. During the festival there are 50 events - concerts, sessions and workshops. Festival is planned in September/October each year.

Arklow Seabreeze Festival
Jo Walker
Secretary
14 Pearse Terrace

Arklow
Co. Wicklow

Tel: +353 402 31338
Other key staff: Gerry McMahon (Chairperson), Rosa O'Farrell (Treasurer)

Music promoted includes world, jazz/trad and rock/pop. Format of musical events includes open air concerts and band competitions. Planning takes place 10 months in advance.

Arts Festival
Joseph A. O'Dwyer
Intermediate School
Killorglin
Co. Kerry

Tel/Fax: +353 66 9761246/+353 66 9761954

Festival takes place in November each year. Music promoted includes orchestral, chamber, choral and jazz/improv. Format of festival includes formal concerts in an intimate setting. During the festival there are 3 musical events. Planning takes place up to early autumn.

Autumn Sound Fest
Maria Kelemen
Director
21 The Close
Cypress Downs
Templeogue
Dublin 6W

Tel/Fax: +353 1 4905263/+353 1 4220355
Email: yes@iol.ie
Website: www.cybermusician.com
Other key staff: Deborah Kelleher (Pianist), Brian MacKay (Pianist & Conductor), Ronald Masin (Conductor)

Festival will be held in October 2000, 2001 and 2002. Music promoted includes orchestral, chamber and classical, which is played by children aged 8-15 years. 7-10 public performances are given during this festival. The festival includes formal sit-down concerts, workshops, lunchtime concerts and open-air concerts. The festival is planned 12 months in advance.

Baboró International Children's Festival
Emer McGowan
Executive Director
Black Box

Dyke Road
Galway

Tel/Fax: +353 91 509705 or +353 91 562655
Email: baboro@gaf.iol.ie
Website: www.barboro.ie

Festival will be held in mid October 2000, October 2001 and 2002. This festival's musical programming varies from year to year, to include different music genres. Format of musical events includes daytime/evening concerts and workshops for children. The festival is planned 6-12 months in advance.

Ballinode Heritage Festival
Bill Hayden
8 Cappog
Ballinode
Co. Monaghan

Tel: +353 47 89757
Other key staff: Patrick Boylan (Treasurer). Peter Deary (PRO), Amy McKeever (Secretary)

Festival will be held 10th July 2000, 9th July 2001 and 8th July 2002. Music promoted includes trad/folk, rock/pop and crossover. There are band recitals and marching bands also. During the festival there are 4-5 musical events. Planning takes place 6 months in advance.

Ballintogher Traditional Music Festival
Teresa McCormack
Secretary
Altvelid
Ballintogher
Co. Sligo

Tel: +353 71 64250
Other key staff: Francis Taaffe (Chairman)

Festival will be held 3-5 November 2000. Format of festival includes one formal sit-down concert, traditional music workshops/masterclasses céilís. Planning takes place one year in advance.

Ballyshannon Folk & Traditional Music Festival
Ray Gaughan
Director
East Port
Ballyshannon
Co. Donegal

Tel/Fax: +353 72 51088/+353 72 52832
Other key staff: Fidelma Gaughan (Secretary), Billy Grimes (Treasurer), Brendan Travers (PRO)

Festival is held on the August bank holiday weekend each year. Format of musical events includes workshops, open air concerts, busking in the street, music sessions and live concerts in the marquee every night. Planning takes place 11 months in advance.

Bank of Ireland Mostly Modern Series

Brian Farrell
Administration Officer
4 Luttrellstown Park
Castleknock
Dublin 15

Tel/Fax: +353 1 8216620/+353 1 8216620
Email: mostly.modern@indigo.ie
Other key staff: Benjamin Dwyer (Director & Artistic Director)

This music series is held from November to May, each year. Promotes contemporary music. Format of musical event includes sit-down, lunchtime concerts and workshops. Free admission. Planning takes place approximately 10 months in advance.

Bealtaine Community Arts Festival

Terry Moore
Co-ordinator
Unit 20
Cutlery Road
Newbridge
Co. Kildare

Tel: +353 45 431213
Other key staff: Noel Heavey (Chairperson), Tom Poole (Treasurer), Fiona O'Loughlin (PRO), Mary Linehan (Arts Officer)

Music promoted includes orchestral, trad/folk, choral, world, jazz/improv, rock/pop, opera and band recitals. Format of musical events includes formal sit-down evening concerts, workshops, lunchtime concerts, sessions, open-air recitals by pipe and community bands and busking on the street. Planning takes place throughout the year.

Beara Community Arts Festival

Pat Farrell
Bank Place
Castletownbere
Co. Cork

Tel/Fax: +353 27 70765/+353 27 70964

Music promoted includes orchestral, trad/folk, chamber, blues, choral, world, jazz/improv and opera. During the festival there are 10-12 musical events. Format of musical events includes lunchtime concerts, drumming workshops, open-air concerts and formal sit-down concerts. Planning takes place up to 1 year in advance.

Blackstairs Blues Festival

Sharon Heffernan
Chairperson
14 Slaney Street
Enniscorthy
Co. Wexford

Tel/Fax: +353 54 35364/+353 54 35392
Email: sheff@indigo.ie
Other key staff: Bobby Rackard (Vice Chairperson), Lorraine Comer (Arts Officer)

Festival will be held September 2001 and 2002. Promotes blues music. During the festival there are 25-30 music events. Planning takes place 7-8 months in advance.

Blas International Summer School Festival

Sandra Joyce/Niall Keegan
Festival Directors
Irish World Music Centre
University of Limerick
Limerick

Tel/Fax: +353 61 202565/+353 61 202589
Email: sandra.joyce@ul.ie
Website: www.ul.ie/~iwmc/blas/
Other key staff: Ellen Byrne (PRO), Paula Dundon (Administrator), Olive Brennan (Administrator)

Festival will be held from the 10th July 2000, 7th July 2001 and 8th July 2002. During the festival 53 musical events take place. Format of musical events includes 2 formal sit-down evening concerts, 2 evening céilís, 9 lunchtime concert, 19 workshops in each instrument, 5 sessions and 16 lectures. Planning takes place 10 months in advance.

Bloomsday

Helen Monaghan
Administrator
35 North Great Georges Street
Dublin 1

Tel/Fax: +353 1 8788547/+353 1 8788488
Website: www.jamesjoyce.ie
Other key staff: Samantha Creane (Marketing Assistant)

Festival will be held 10-20 June 2000 and 9-23 June 2001. Music promoted includes chamber, choral and trad/folk. Music features as part of events surrounding this festival. Planning takes place 6-7 months in advance.

Boyle Arts Festival

Regina Finn
Secretary
King House
Boyle
Co. Roscommon

Tel/Fax: +353 79 63242 or +353 79 63085 or +353 79 62215/+353 79 63242
Email: kinghouseboyle@hotmail.com
Other key staff: Gerry Kielty (Treasurer), Fergus Ahern

Festival will be held 20-30 July 2000 and July 2001. Music promoted includes orchestral, trad/folk, chamber, choral, jazz/improv and opera. During the festival there are 10-12 musical events. Format of musical events includes evening and lunchtime concert, busking and workshops. Planning takes place 6 months in advance.

Bray International Festival of Dance & Music

Patrick Murphy
Chairman
3 Roselawn Park
Bray
Co.Wicklow

Tel: +353 1 2860080
Email: sparksmurphy@eircom.ie

Festival will be held 9-12 August 2000, weekend after August bank holiday 2001 and 2002. Promotes trad/folk music. Format of musical events is workshops and open air concerts. Planning takes place 7-8 months in advance.

Bray Millennium Jazz Festival

George Jacob
Ballydonagh Cottage
Glen of the Downs
Delgany
Co. Wicklow

Tel/Fax: +353 1 2873992
Email: gjacob@indigo.ie

It is hoped that this festival will be held in April/May 2001 and 2002. Music promoted includes blues, world and jazz/improv.

Bridge House Irish Festival

Colm McCabe
Manager
Bridge Street
Tullamore
Co. Offaly

Tel/Fax: +353 506 21704 or +353 506 22000/ +353 506 41338
Email: bhouse@iol.ie
Website: www.bridgehouse.com

Festival will be held 9-19 March 2001. Promotes trad/folk music.

Burtonport Summer Festival

Eugene McGarvey
Director
Meenmore
Dungloe
Co. Donegal

Tel/Fax: +353 75 22282/+353 75 21807
Other key staff: Noreen McGarvey (Co-Director), David Alcorn (PRO), Gerard O'Donnell (Chairperson)

Festival will be held 17 July 2000, 18 July 2001 and 19 July 2002. Music promoted includes trad/folk and rock/pop. Format of musical events includes sit-down concerts, lunchtime concerts and sessions.

Caherciveen Celtic Music Festival

John O'Connor
Public Relations Officer
4 O'Connell Street
Caherciveen
Co. Kerry

Tel/Fax: +353 66 9472973/+353 66 9473262
Other key staff: Shane O'Driscoll
(Entertainments Officer), Angela O'Neill
(Secretary), Paudie Dineen (Treasurer)

Festival will be held August bank holiday 2000, 2001 and 2002. Music promoted includes trad/folk and samba. During the festival there are 25-30 musical events. Format of musical events includes busking, workshops and open-air concerts. Planning takes place 11 months in advance.

Cape Clear Island International Storytelling Festival

Chuck Kruger
Director
Cape Clear Island
Co. Cork

Tel/Fax: +353 28 39157
Email: ckstory@indigo.ie
Website: www.indigo.ie/~ckstory/

Festival will be held from 1-3 September 2000 and 31/8-2/9 2001. Promotes traditional music. Approximately 6 musical events take place. Planning takes place 10-18 months in advance.

Mick & Miceal Carr Memorial Traditional Music Weekend

Rory O'Donnell
Public Relations Officer
Meenaneary
Carrick
Co. Donegal

Tel/Fax: +353 73 39009 or +353 73 39299/
+353 73 39009

Format of musical events includes sessions and workshops. Planning takes place six months in advance.

Cashel Cultural Festival

Hannah Looby-Coates
Administrator
Cashel Heritage Centre
City Hall
Main Street
Cashel
Co. Tipperary

Tel/Fax: +353 62 62511/+353 62 62068
Email: cashelhc@iol.ie

Festival will be held in July 2000, 2001 and 2002. Format of musical events includes open air concerts, formal sit-down concerts and sessions. Planning takes place 8-10 months in advance.

Castlegregory Summer Festival

Mike Cahillane
Festival Co-ordinator
Tailors Row
Castlegregory
Co. Kerry

Tel/Fax: +353 66 7139422
Other key staff: Helen Besseling (Secretary),
Elayne O'Halloran (PRO)

Format of musical events includes dances, concerts, open-air musical displays and parades. Planning takes place approximately 6-8 months in advance.

Cavan Percy French Festival

Patrick O'Brien
Executive Officer
Musicians House
Main Street
Cavan

Tel: +353 49 4361477

Festival will held 3-7 August 2000, 1st weekend in August 2001 and 2002. Types of music promoted includes trad/folk, blues, choral, jazz/improv, rock/pop and crossover. During the festival 5-10 musical events take place. Format of musical events includes lunchtime and evening concerts. Planning takes place 7 months in advance.

Chamber Music in Retreat Lodges

Juliet Jopling
Director
7 Chamberlain Street
London NW1 8XB
England
or
Retreat Lodges
Rossbeigh (near Glenbeigh)
Co. Kerry

Tel/Fax: +44 20 7586 1728/+44 20 7722 3959
Email: julietjopling@julietjopling.screaming.net

Festival will take place in May 2000. Promotes chamber music. Format of musical events includes 5 formal concerts in Kerry, masterclasses and 2 workshops with music students.

Le Chéile - Oldcastle Arts & Music Festival

Derek Finnegan
Public Relations Officer
Thomastown
Crossakiel
Kells
Co. Meath

Tel/Fax: +353 46 43920/+353 44 66461
Email: derekf@dromore.ie
Website: www.lecheile.com
Other key staff: Noel Finnegan (Chairman), Vera Larkin (Secretary), Barry Fanning (Vice Chairman)

Festival will be held in August 2000, 2001 and 2002. Music promoted includes trad/folk and rock/pop. Planning takes place 10 months in advance.

An Chúirt Chruitireachta

Aibhlín McCrann
Director
50 Wyvern
Killiney
Co. Dublin

Tel/Fax: +353 1 2856345/+353 1 6768007
Email: cruit@harp.net
Website: www.harp.net/cnac/cnac.htm
Other key staff: Joe Joyce (Treasurer)

Will be held 25-30 June 2000. Music promoted includes trad/folk, music of harpers, singing and singing with the harp. Format of musical events includes formal evening concerts, lunchtime concerts, afternoon workshops and morning classes. Planning takes place 10 months in advance.

Church Music International Choral Festival

Fergus Quinlivan
Director
Limerick Corporation
City Hall
Limerick

Tel/Fax: +353 61 415799 (w) or +353 61 229914 (h)/+353 61 418601 or +353 61 415266
Mobile: +353 87 2212168
Email: fquinlivan@limerickcorp.ie
Website: www.limerickcorp.ie

Festival will be held 24-26 March 2000, 23-25 March 2001 and 22-24 March 2002. Promotes choral music. Festival is held in the 800 year old St. Mary's Cathedral, Limerick. Planning takes place 3 years in advance. (see ad. p.226)

City of Tuam Festival

John Cahill
Secretary
Church View
Tuam
Co. Galway

Tel/Fax: +353 93 25001 or +353 93 26534
Other key staff: Tom Reilly (Chairperson), Midie O'Grady (Treasurer), Mary Higgens (Office Administrator)

Festival will take place June/July 2000, 2001 and 2002. Music promoted includes trad/folk and rock/pop. Format of musical events includes evening concerts and open-air concerts. Planning takes place 6-7 months in advance.

Clare Festival of Traditional Singing

Tim Munnelly
Administrator
Fintra Beg
Miltown Malbay
Co. Clare

Tel: +353 65 7084365
Email: munnelly@eircom.net
Website: www.iol.ie/~clarelib
Other key staff: Róisín White (Chairperson), Frances Madigan (Secretary), Maureen Rynne (Treasurer)

Festival will be held 2-4 June 2000, 1-3 June 2001 and 31/5-2/6 2002. Promotes traditional music. During the festival 2 concerts, recitals, 2 lectures and sessions take place.

Clifden Community Arts Week

Brendan Flynn
Director
Clifden
Co. Galway

Tel/Fax: +353 95 21644 or +353 95 21295/ +353 95 21481
Email: artsweek@indigo.ie
Website: www.clifden-artsweek.com
Other key staff: Brendan O'Scannell (Secretary), Eamon Mcloughlin (Chairman)

ARKLOW

MUSIC FESTIVAL
(estd. 1970)

Runs annually on the 1st Sunday in March:
2000 March 5th - 12th
2001 March 4th - 11th
Syllabus available end of
September annually.
For syllabus and information contact:
Arklow Music Festival Office,
1 Upper Main St.
Arklow, Co. Wicklow
Tel: 0402-32732 • Fax: 0402-91030

R O A

Roundstone Open Arts Week, Errisbeg House,
Roundstone, Connemara, Co. Galway.
Tel: 095-35834
Fax: 095-35715
E-mail: marquis@eircom.net
Website: www.connemara.net/
roundstone-open-arts

Director: Richard de Stacpoole

Roundstone Millennium Open Arts Week
1 - 9 July 2000

IRELAND

Church Music International
Choral Festival
St. Mary's Cathedral, Limerick, Ireland

23 - 25 March 2001
22 - 24 March 2002
21 - 23 March 2003

This Festival is established as one of Ireland's leading musical events and provides an ideal opportunity for choirs and choral groups to participate in a competitive festival which embraces both the traditional and modern aspects of church music.

Enquiries should be sent to:
Fergus Quinlivan, Director/Co-ordinator, Limerick Civic Week,
Festival Office, City Hall, Limerick, Ireland.
Telephone: 00-353-61-415799 (0);
00-353-61-229914 (H)
Fax: 00-353-61-410401/418601

Festival will be held 20-30 September 2000. Music promoted includes orchestral, trad/folk, blues and rock/pop. During the festival there are over 70 events. Format of musical events includes sit-down evening concerts, traditional concerts in pubs, poetry readings and exhibitions. Planning takes place one year in advance.

Clonakilty August Festival

Joseph Hodnett
No 2 The Mews
McCurtain Hill
Clonakilty
Co. Cork

Tel: +353 23 34952
Mobile: +353 86 2454823
Other key staff: Dave Sheehan (Co-ordinator), Una Jennings (Administrator)

Festival will be held 24-27 August 2000 and last weekend of August 2001 and 2002. Music promoted includes trad/folk and bluegrass. During the festival there are over 30 musical events. Format of musical events changes each year.

Cobh Carillon Recitals

Adrian P. Gebruers
Springfield
Cobh
Co. Cork

Tel/Fax: +353 21 4811219 or +353 21 4813222/+353 21 427212 or +353 21 4813488
Email: agebruers@eircom.net
Website: www.eircom.net/~adriangebruers
Other key staff: Rev. Gerard Casey

Recitals will be held on Sundays from May-September 2000, 2001 and 2002. Format of musical events includes open-air concerts and occasional guest recitals. The 2002 season will include the 13th Congress of the World Carillon Federation.

Coleman Traditional Festival

Marie Queenan
Secretary
Ceoláras Coleman
Gurteen
Co. Sligo

Tel/Fax: +353 71 82599/+353 71 82602
Email: cctrad@iol.ie
Website: www.colemanirishmusic.com

Festival will be held 1-6 September 2000, first weekend of September 2001 and 2002. Promotes traditional music. Format of musical events includes concerts, sessions, competitions and céilís.

Comhaltas Ceoltóirí Éireann

Labhrás Ó Murchú
Director General
32 Belgrave Square
Monkstown
Co. Dublin

Tel/Fax: +353 1 2800295/+353 1 2803759
Email: enquiries@comhaltas.com
Website: www.comhaltas.com

Founded in 1951 to promote Irish traditional music, song, dance and the Irish language. 400 branches worldwide and 600 classes. There are 44 Fleadhanna Cheoil each year attracting 20,000 competitors.

Cootehill Arts Festival

Ann Tully
Chairperson
Cavan Road
Co. Cavan

Tel: +353 49 5552241
Other key staff: Roisin Lyons (Secretary)

The festival will be held 12-24 October 2000 and the two last weeks in October 2001 and 2002. Music promoted includes orchestral, chamber, choral, jazz/improv, rock, trad/folk and crossover. Format of musical events includes formal concerts and sessions.

Cork Arts Festival

Tricia Harrington
Arts Officer
Cork Institute of Technology
Rossa Avenue
Bishopstown
Cork

Tel/Fax: +353 21 4326445/+353 21 4545343
Email: artsfest@cit.ie
Website: www.cit.ie
Other key staff: Larry Poland (Chairperson), Vicky O'Sullivan (Administrator - Students Union), Peter Somers (Accounts Department)

Festival will be held 12-19 November 2000, November 2001 and 2002. Music promoted includes orchestral, trad/folk, chamber, blues, world, jazz/improv, rock/pop and crossover. During the festival there are 12 musical events. Format of musical events includes sit-down evening concerts, workshops, lunchtime concerts, bands competition, club venue gigs, stand-up public concert in large indoor area. Planning for the event is ongoing from year to year.

Cork Folk Festival
William Hammond
17 Victoria Avenue
Cork

Mobile: +353 87 2759311
Fax: +353 21 317271
Email: whammond@ocean.net
Website: aardvark.ie
Other key staff: Jim Walsh (Chairman), Anne Brennan (Secretary), Mary O'Reilly (Treasurer)

Festival will be held 1/9 2000, 2/9 2001 and 3/9 2002. Promotes traditional music. During the festival there are 30 musical events. Format of musical events includes formal sit-down concerts, workshops and sessions. Planning takes place 4 months in advance.

Cork International Choral Festival
John Fitzpatrick
Festival Director
PO Box 68
Cork

Tel/Fax: +353 21 4308308/+353 21 4308309
Email: chorfest@iol.ie
Website: www.musweb.com/corkchoral.htm
Other key staff: Belinda Quirke (Festival Administrator)

Festival will be held from 27-30 April 2000, 3-6 May 2001 and 2-5 May 2002. Promotes choral music. During the festival there are over 100 musical musical events. Format of musical events includes evening concert performances, lunchtime concerts, public concerts (some open-air), seminars, fringe series, daytime concert performances and church performances. Planning takes place 9 months in advance.

County Wicklow Gardens Festival
Charlet Whitmore
Chairperson
Wicklow County Tourism
St. Manntan's House

Kilmartin Hill
Wicklow

Tel/Fax: +353 404 66058/+353 404 66057
Email: wctr@iol.ie
Website: www.wicklow.ie
Other key staff: Vibeke Dykman (Marketing Manager), Bairbre Curley (Marketing Executive)

Festival will be held 12/5 - 9/7 2000. Music promoted includes jazz/improv and salsa. This is a gardens festival, with over thirty private gardens open to the public on selected days throughout the festival. There are also a number of special events each year, such as a jazz concert outdoors. Planning takes place 9 months in advance.

Donegal Fiddlers Weekend
Caoimhin MacAodh
Registrar
Tullyhorkey
Ballyshannon
Co. Donegal

Tel: +353 72 52144
Email: dldclk1@iol.ie
Other key staff: Rab Cherry (Chairman), Paul Ó Shaughnessy (PRO), Roisin Harrigan (Co-ordinator)

Festival will be held 1-3 October 2000, 2001 and 2002. The Festival features Donegal fiddle music with special guests from related traditions. Free fiddle workshops are provided. There is one main concert of fiddle playing and many informal fiddle sessions. Planning takes place 9 months in advance.

Donegal Town Summer Festival
Pauric O'Neill
Director
Millbrook
Donegal Town

Mobile: +353 86 8293994
Website: www.donegaltown.ie
Other key staff: Zack Gallagher (Committee Member)

Festival will be held from the 30th June 2000, July 2001 and 2002. Music promoted includes trad/folk, blues, rock/pop and crossover. Format of musical events includes open-air concerts. Planning takes place 5 in advance.

Drogheda Samba Festival

Tony Conaghy
Acting Director
Droichead Arts Centre
Stockwell Lane
Drogheda
Co. Louth

Tel/Fax: +353 41 9833946/+353 41 9842055
Email: droiched@indigo.ie
Other key staff: Brain & Phil Conyngham
(Festival Committee), Kathleen O'Brien (Financial
Manager)

Festival will be held 7-9 July 2000, 10-12 July 2001 and
2002. Music promoted includes world and Latin
American. During the festival there are 12 musical
events.The format of this festival is a three day intensive
weekend, celebrating Latin music and Brazillian inspired
samba. Planning takes place 1 year in advance.

Dublin Corporation Music in the Parks

Martina Halpin
Clerical Officer
Environment & Culture Department
Block 4, Ground floor
Civic Offices, Wood Quay
Dublin 8

Tel/Fax: +353 1 6723145/+353 1 6707334
Email: martina.halpin@dublincorp.ie

Will take place from June to August 2000, 2001 and
2002. It is hoped that orchestral, chamber, choral,
jazz/Improv, blues and world music will feature in this
series. During this musical series 30 events take place.
The format is open-air concerts held in city centre parks
including Merrion Square Park, Wolftone Park, Civic
Offices Park, Herbert park there are also family days
held in Fairview Park, St. Anns Park Raheny and Bushy
Park. Planning takes place 1 year in advance.

Dublin 15 Community Arts Festival

Richie Farrell
Vice Chairperson/Secretary
Blanchardstown Library
Roselawn Shopping Centre
Dublin 15

Tel/Fax: +353 1 8212701/+353 1 8205066

Email: cskills/@aol.com
Other key staff: Bill Hughes (Chairperson),
Nora Cumiskey (Treasurer), Marie Meehan (Arts
Co-ordinator)

Festival will be held on the third and fourth week of
May 2000, 2001 and 2002. Music promoted includes
trad/folk, blues, choral, jazz/improv, rock/pop and
crossover. During the festival there are 10-12 musical
events. Format of musical events includes youth service
workshops, musical societies performances, brass band
performances and open-air concerts. Planning takes
place 6-8 months in advance of the festival.

Dublin Guitar Week

Ignacio Montes
Director
Instituto Cervantes
58 Northumberland Road
Dublin 4

Tel/Fax: +353 1 6682024/+353 1 6688416
Email: cendub@cervantes.es
Website: www.cervantes.es

Festival takes place February/March each year. Promotes
trad/folk guitar music. During the festival there are 16-
18 musical events. Format of musical events includes
evening and lunch time concerts. Planning takes place 1
year in advance.

Dublin International Organ & Choral Festival

Eoin Garrett
Festival Administrator
Liffey House
Tara Street
Dublin 2

Tel/Fax: +353 1 6773066 Ext. 416/
+353 1 6727279
Email: organs@diocf.iol.ie
Website: www.iol.ie/~orga1/diocf
Other key staff: Gerard Gillen (Artistic Director),
Lewis Clohessy (Chairman)

Music promoted includes orchestral, choral and organ.
During the festival there are approximately 20 musical
events. Format of musical events includes lunchtime and
evening concerts, masterclasses, special cathedral
services and an international organ playing competition.
Planning for the event takes place 2 years in advance.

Dúchas Chill Dara - Kildare International Folk Arts Festival

Susan Feery
Secretary
Enterprise Centre
Melitta Road
Kildare

Tel/Fax: +353 45 521190/+353 45 521198
Email: mdassociates@eircom.net
Website: www.members.theglobe.com/mdassociates/duchas.html
Other key staff: Martin Dempsey (Director), Pat Sweeney (Chairman), Robin Dempsey (Sales & Marketing)

Festival will be held 24-27 August 2000 and 23-26 August 2001. Promotes trad/folk music. During the festival there are 20 musical events. Format of musical events includes formal sit-down concerts, workshops, sessions, open-air concerts, parades, recitals and seminars. Planning takes place 8 months in advance.

Dundalk International Maytime Festival

Kevin Hall
Secretary
c/o Festival Office
3 Jocelyn Street
Dundalk
Co. Louth

Tel/Fax: +353 42 9335253/+353 42 9326317
Email: dundalkfestival@eircom.net
Other key staff: Gerry Murphy (President), Angela McQuaid (Vice President & PRO)

Festival will be held 26/5 - 4/6 2000. Music promoted includes rock and traditional music in pubs, open-air concerts and a Festival club. Planning takes place from February onwards.

Dunlavin Festival of Arts - Kildare

Mairead Connellan
Secretary
Ard Augline
Kilgowan
Kilcullen
Co. Kildrare

Tel: +353 45 485283
Other key staff: Kathleen Owens (Arts Officer), Dorly O'Sullivan (Dunlavin Youth Orchestra),

Mary Deering (Musical Director - Milltown Singers)

Festival will be held 17-19 June 2000, third week in June 2001 and 2002. Music promoted includes orchestral, trad/folk, chamber, choral and rock/pop. During the festival there are 5 musical events. Format of musical events includes formal sit-down evening concerts (classical), open-air, lunchtime concerts (string quartet), choral concerts in one of the local churches, musicals, workshops, sessions and an army band concert. Planning takes place in September.

Dunlavin Festival of Arts - Wicklow

Margaret Lynott
Co-ordinator
Grangebeg
Dunlavin
Co. Wicklow

Tel/Fax: +353 45 401459
Email: the lynotts@hotmail.com

Festival will be held 16-18 June 2000, 2001 and 2002. Music promoted includes orchestral, chamber, choral, rock/pop and world. Format of musical events includes evening concerts and open-air concerts. Planning takes place 6 months in advance.

The Durrow Carnival

Imelda Foyle
The Square
Durrow
Co. Laois

Tel: +353 502 36423

This festival will be held in August each year. Music promoted includes traditional/folk, rock/pop and crossover. During this carnival 3-4 musical events take place. Planning takes place 10 months in advance.

Michael Dwyer Memorial Festival

Anne Goulding
Secretary
Reentrisk
Allihes
Bera
Co. Cork

Tel: +353 27 73042
Other key staff: Deirdre Ní Donnachadha (Chairperson), Joe Hanley (Treasurer)

Festival will be held 9-11 June 2000, 2001 and 2002. Promotes trad/folk music. Format of musical events includes sit-down evening concerts, workshops, lunchtime concerts and busking in the streets. Planning takes place 6 months in advance.

Earagail Arts Festival

Traolach Ó Fionnáin
Arts Officer
Donegal County Library
Letterkenny
Co. Donegal

Tel/Fax: +353 74 21968 or +353 74 29186/ +353 74 26402
Other key staff: Shaun Hannigan (Director of Letterkenny Arts Centre)

Festival will be held 10-23 July 2000, the second week of July 2001 and 2002. Music promoted includes orchestral, chamber, jazz/improv, trad/folk, world and rock/pop. During the festival there are 20 musical events. Format of musical events includes evening and lunchtime concerts, open-air concerts and a festival club. Planning takes place 3-12 months in advance.

Éigse Na Brídeoige

Pádraig De Buis
Cathaoirleach
Bóthar na Faille
An Coireán
Co. Chiarraí

Tel/Fax: +353 66 9474123/+353 66 9474836
Email: pd@buis@eircom.net
Other key staff: Michéal Ó Leidhinn (Secretary)

Promotes traditional music. Format of musical events is poetry reading with music sessions.

Éigse Carlow Arts Festival

Thérèse Jackman
Office Administrator
Festival Support Office
Bridewell Lane
Carlow

Tel/Fax: +353 503 40491/+353 503 30065
Email: eigsecarlo@eircom.ie

Festival will be held in June 2000, 2001 and 2002. Music promoted includes orchestral, trad/folk, choral, world, jazz/improv and rock/pop. Format of musical events includes lunchtime concerts, open-air, work-

shops, busking and sessions. Planning takes place 1-2 years in advance.

Éigse Mrs Crotty Traditional Music Festival

Rebecca Brew
Chairperson
Crotty's
Kilrush
Co. Clare

Tel/Fax: +353 65 52470/+353 65 51228
Other key staff: Lisa Walsh (Secretary), Marie Nolan (Treasurer), Áine Hensey (Musical Director), Maire O'Leary (PRO)

Promotes trad/folk music. During the festival there are 10 formal musical events and many informal events. Format of musical events includes concerts, lectures, pub sessions, open-air céilís, concertina classes, workshops. Planning takes place 10 months in advance. (see advert)

Éigse An Spidéal

Caitríona Ní Oibicín
Administrator
Cólaiste Connacht
An Spidéal
Co. Gallimhe

Tel: +353 91 553124

Festival will be held April 2001 and 2002. Promotes traditional music. Format of musical events includes lectures, sessions and workshops in singing and dancing. Planning takes place 3 months in advance.

Ennis Arts Festival - October Arts In Ennis

Mary Cashin
Chairperson
3 Francis Street
Ennis
Co. Clare

Tel/Fax: +353 65 6840060/+353 65 6840034
Email: cashsolreiol.ie or lynn_guiney@hotmail.com
Website: www.octoberarts.ennis.ie
Other key staff: Lynn Guiney (PRO)

Festival will be held in October 2000, 2001 and 2002. Music promoted includes orchestral, chamber, choral, jazz/improv, trad/folk, blues, and world. During the festival there are 12-14 musical events. Format of musical events includes workshops, concerts and sessions. Planning tales place 1 year in advance.

ESB Environmental Summer School & Arts Festival

Ciaran Mullooly
Chairperson
Lough Ree
Development Association
Main Street
Lanesborough
Co. Longford

Tel/Fax: +353 43 27070
Email: loughree@esatclear.ie
Website: www.lough-ree.com
Other key staff: Margaret Cullen (Secretary), Carmel Fallon (Chairperson of Arts Festival)

Festival will take place in July 2000, 2001 and 2002. Music promoted includes orchestral, traditional, chamber and choral. Format of musical events includes formal evening concerts, sessions in lounge and river boat settings, open-air concerts. Planning takes place 6 months in advance.

ESB Lough Ree Environmental Winter School Festival

Ciaran Mullooly
Chairperson
Lough Ree Development Association
Main Street
Lanesborough
Co. Longford

Tel/Fax: +353 43 27070/+353 43 27070
Email: loughree@esatclear.ie
Website: www.lough-ree.com
Other key staff: Margaret Cullen (Secretary), Carmel Fallon (Festival Chairperson)

Festival will be held in February 2001 and 2002. Music promoted includes orchestral, traditional, chamber and choral. During the festival there are 3 musical events. Format of musical events includes formal evening concerts and sessions on board the river boat.

ESB Vogler Spring Festival

c/o Mary McAuliffe
Arts Officer
Arts Office

Sligo County Council Offices
Riverside
Sligo

Tel/Fax: +353 71 56629/+353 71 41119
Email: arts@sligococo.ie
Other key staff: Caroline Wynne (Festival Administrator)

Festival will be held on the May bank holiday weekend 2001 and 2002. Promotes chamber music. This festival is produced under the artistic direction of the Vogler Quartet, in collaboration with a series of invited guest musicians. Each year a new work from a significant Irish composer will be premiered. This festival is part of the Vogler Quartet in Sligo three year residency programme. Format of festival includes morning, afternoon and evening concerts, held in St. Columba's Church, Drumcliffe, Sligo.

Expo Limerick

Dave O'Hora
Chairman
Southern Advertising
Killoran House
Catherine Place
Limerick

Tel/Fax: +353 61 310286/+353 61 313013
Other key staff: Patricia Prendergast (Festival Organiser), Fergal Deegan and Pat Daly

Festival will be held 5/5 2000, May 2001 and 2002. Music promoted includes orchestral, trad/folk, chamber, jazz/improv and rock/pop. During the festival there are 6-10 musical events. Format of musical events includes sit-down evening concerts, open-air concerts, busking and sessions. Planning takes place 6 months in advance.

Joe Fallon Traditional Music Weekend

Michael Connolly
Main Street
Collooney
Co. Sligo

Tel: +353 71 67377

Festival will be held on the second weekend of August 2000, 2001 and 2002. This trad/folk festival was established in 1992, the weekend consists of a 'Golden Voice' competition, tin whistle and button accordion competitions. The weekend takes place in local pubs and outdoors.

Feakle International Traditional Music Festival

Gary Pepper
Public Relations Officer
Feakle
Co. Clare

Tel/Fax: +353 61 924322/+353 61 924288
Other key staff: Pat Hayes (Chairperson), Tina Nelson (Secretary), Seamus Bohan (Treasurer)

Festival will be held 10-14 August 2000. Promotes traditional music. Format of musical events is formal concerts, céilís, workshops, lectures and sessions. Planning takes place 6-12 months in advance.

Féile Na Bealtaine

Dr. Michéal Fanning
Director
The Wood
An Daingean
Co. Chiarraí

Tel: +353 66 9151465
Other key staff: Míchéal Ó Coileáin, Joan Rohan

Types of music promoted includes chamber, trad/folk, choral, world, jazz/improv and rock/pop. During the festival there are 15 events. Format of musical events includes sessions, workshops and street theatre.

Feile na nDéise

John Foley
Chairperson
Kilrush Service Station
Dungarvan
Co. Waterford

Tel/Fax: +353 58 42998/ +353 58 43262
Other key staff: Nicky Power (Vice Chairperson), Áine O Riordan (Hon. Treasurer), Mella Fahey (Assistant Honorary Secretary)

Festival will be held May bank holiday 2000, 2001 and 2002. Promotes trad/folk music. During the festival 35 musical events take place. Format of musical events includes sit-down concerts, sessions, busking, workshops, street theatre, open air dancing and open air concerts. Each year an event other than traditional/folk music is introduced. In 1999 Ronan Tynan performed. Planning takes place 8 months in advance.

Féile Chulutir Chiarraí

Toddy Doyle
Farms Manager
Muckross Traditional Farms
Muckross House
Killarney
Co. Kerry

Tel/Fax: +353 64 31440/+353 64 33926
Mobile: +353 87 2531625
Email: mucross@iol.ie
Website: www.muckross-house.ie

Festival is held in May each year. Promotes trad/folk music. During the festival there are 6 musical events. Celebrates the various musical traditions from Co. Kerry.

Féile Chomórtha Joe Éinniú

Micheál Ó Cuaig
Cill Chiaráin
Conamara
Co. Na Gaillimhe

Tel: +353 95 33599

Festival will be held 1/5 2000, 2001 and 2002. Promotes trad/folk music. During the festival 5 musical events take place. Format of musical events includes workshops, childrens Sean-nós singing competition, lectures, presentations, set dancing, céilís formal and informal sessions. Planning takes place 4 months in advance.

Féile Seamus Ennis

Mary McDermott
Chairperson
Finglas Arts Centre
Artsquad
Unit 14b, Main Centre
Finglas
Dublin 11

Tel/Fax: +353 1 8343950/+353 1 8348115
Email: finart@eircom.net
Other key staff: Mary McDermott (Chairperson), Sylvia McGill (Secretary)

Festival will be held in October 2000, 2001 and 2002. Music promoted includes orchestral and trad/folk. Format of musical events includes sessions, lunchtime concerts and busking. Planning takes place 6 months in advance.

Féile Shamhna na gCrann - Samhain Festival of Trees

John Lawlor
Co-ordinator
Crann Head Office
Crank House
Main Street
Banagher
Co. Offaly

Tel/Fax: +353 509 51718/+353 509 51938
Other key staff: Emma Perry (Co-ordinator)

Festival will be held in October 2000, 2001 and 2002. Planning takes place 4 months in advance.

Féile na Sraide

Annette Caine
Secretary
5 Radharc na Mara
Achill Sound
Co. Mayo

Tel: +353 98 45199
Other key staff: Ann Fadden (Treasurer), Peggy Cattigan (Chairperson)

Festival will be held early July 2000, 2001 and 2002. Music promoted includes traditional/folk and choral music. The main event is an open-air concert with seating provided. Planning takes place 4 months in advance.

Feis Maitiú Corciagh

Timothy McCarthy
Administrator
Feis Maitiú
Fr. Matthew Hall
Fr. Matthew Street
Cork

Tel/Fax: +353 21 4273347
Email: feismaitiu@eircom.net

Music promoted includes chamber, choral and opera. During this feis 132 musical events take place. Planning takes place 2 years in advance.

Festival of the Arts Balbriggan

Anne Gallen
Secretary
Rockley
Balbriggan
Co. Dublin

Tel: +353 1 8412516
Other key staff: Barry Cassin (Chairman), Tom Monaghan (PRO)

Festival is held on the October bank holiday weekend each year. Music promoted includes orchestral, choral and rock/pop. During the festival there are 4 musical events. Planning takes place up to 1 year in advance.

Festival of the Carbaries, Leap & Glandore

Emily O'Sullivan
Secretary
Dromm
Leap
Co. Cork

Tel: +353 28 33371
Other key staff: Paddy Collins (Chairperson)

Festival will be held 30/7-8/8 2000. Music promoted is trad/folk. During the festival there are 3 musical events. Format of musical events includes open-air concerts and sessions. Planning takes place 8 months in advance.

Festival Francais dé Portarlington

Mary Foy
Chairperson
The Barrow Lodge
French Church Street
Portarlington
Co. Laois

Tel: +353 502 23651
Other key staff: Carmel Dunne (Secretary), Treasa Briody (Treasurer)

Festival takes place in July. Types of music promoted includes trad/folk, jazz/improv and rock/pop. Format of musical events includes open-air concerts and busking. Planning takes place 6 months in advance of the festival.

Fête de la Musique

Francoise Brung
Cultural Officer
Alliance Francaise
1 Kildare Street
Dublin 2

Tel/Fax: +353 1 6767116/+353 1 67674077
Website: www.alliancefrancaise.ie

Festival will be held 21-22 June 2000, 2001 and 2002. One day music event in France, French speaking countries and countries which have French cultural representation. Music promoted includes orchestral, trad/folk, chamber, blues, world and jazz/ improv.

Promotes trad/folk music. During this festival over 140 competitive events take place.

Fethard Street Party
Mary Trehin
Chairperson
Fethard-on-Sea
New Ross
Co. Wexford

Tel/Fax: +353 51 397611 or +353 51 397502/ +353 51 397502
Other key staff: Nicholas Tweedy, John Neville, Maureen Molloy

Open air concerts, busking, sessions, dance and cabaret. Planning takes place 8-10 months in advance of the festival.

Fleadh Nua
Frank Whelan
Secretary
Fleadh Nua International Centre
Ennis Chamber of Commerce
54 O'Connell Street
Ennis
Co. Clare

Tel/Fax: +353 65 6842988/+353 65 6824783
Email: ceoltrad@iol.ie
Website: www.ctr.com/fleadh
Other key staff: Labhrás Ó Murchú (Ard-Stiúrthóir - Comhaltas Ceoltóirí Éireann)

Promotes trad/folk music. During the festival there are 45-50 musical events. Format of musical events includes sessions, fleadh club, singing and set dancing workshops, street entertainment and competitions.

Fleadh Ceoil Na hÉireann
Labhrás Ó Murchú
Director General
32 Belgrave Square
Monkstown
Co. Dublin

Tel/Fax: +353 1 2800295/+353 1 2803759
Email: enquiries@comhaltas.com
Website: www.comhaltas.com
Other key staff: Séamus MacMathúna (Timire Cheoil), Bernard O'Sullivan (Project Officer), C.M. Hodge (Rúnaí Oifige)

Forum for Arts Ballymun
Edith Poole
Office Co-ordinator
c/o Glór na nGael
187 Coultry Road
Ballymun
Dublin 11

Mobile: +353 88 2101971
Other key staff: Seán Cooke, Ollie McGlinchey (Chairperson), Anton McGiolla Rua (Secretary)

Music promoted includes trad/folk, blues, world and rock/pop. Format of musical events includes open-air concerts, busking and workshops. Planning takes place 3 months in advance.

4th of July Festival
Breasal Ó Caollaí
Chairperson
Northumberland Chambers
Northumberland Avenue
Dun Laoghaire
Co. Dublin

Tel/Fax: +353 1 2302311 or +353 1 2841864/ +353 1 2301656
Website: www.dun-laoghaire.com
Other key staff: Liam Plunkett (Events Director), Pat Houlihan (Parade Organiser), Colonel Saltness (Representative of the American Embassy)

Festival takes place on the 4th of July each year. Music promoted includes orchestral, trad/folk, jazz/improv and American bluegrass. Format of musical events includes evening concerts, afternoon concerts and busking.

Galway Arts Festival
Fergal McGrath
Festival Manager
Black Box Theatre
Dyke Road
Woodquay
Galway

Tel/Fax: +353 91 509700/+353 91 562655
Email: info@gaf.iol.ie
Website: www.galwayartsfestival.ie

Festival will take place from the 15th July 2000, July 2001 and July 2002. Music promoted includes orchestral, chamber, trad/folk, blues, choral, world, jazz/improv, opera and crossover. During the festival there are 60-70 musical events. Format of musical events includes seated concerts, evening concerts, lunchtime concerts and open-air concerts. Planning takes place 1 year in advance.

Galway Early Music Festival

Janet Vinnell
Secretary
11 Presentation Road
Galway

Tel: +353 91 564654
Other key staff: Ann McDonagh (Chairperson), Justina McElligott (Treasurer)

Festival will be held from 11-14 May 2000. Promotes early music (12th-17th Century). Format of musical events includes formal and informal concerts, schools and adult workshops, street music, dance and historical re-enactment. Planning takes place 10 months in advance.

Gaol Arts Week

Leah Coyne
Arts Officer
St. Manntan's House
Kilmantin Hill
Wicklow

Tel/Fax: +353 404 20155/+353 404 66057 or +353 404 20078
Email: wao@eircom.net
Website: www.wicklow.ie/arts

Festival will be held in July 2000. Music promoted includes trad/folk, chamber, world and jazz/improv. During the festival there are 6-7 musical events. Planning takes place 6-8 months in advance.

Glen River Summer Festival

Rory O'Donnell
Public Relations Officer
Meenaneary
Carrick
Co. Donegal

Tel/Fax: +353 73 39009 or +353 73 39297/ +353 73 39009

Festival will be held in August 2000 and 2001. Promotes trad/folk music. Format of musical events includes sessions and open-air concerts. Planning takes place 6 months in advance.

Glengarriff Festival

Donal Deasey
Chairman
Caseys Hotel
Glengarriff
Co. Cork

Tel/Fax: +353 27 63010

Festival will be held on the first weekend in June 2000. Music promoted includes trad/folk, blues and jazz/folk. Format of musical events includes open air concerts and sessions. Planning takes place 6 months in advance.

Greystones Summer Arts Festival

Gráinne McLoughlin
Arts Co-ordinator
170 Heathervue
Greystones
Co. Wicklow

Tel/Fax: +353 1 2877308/ +353 402 31065
Email: gronia@indigo.ie
Other key staff: Peter Donnelly (Chairperson), John Stanley (Assistant Chairperson) Elaine Willis (Secretary)

Festival will be held 30/7-3/8 2000, 3-6 August 2001 and 2-5 August 2002. Format of musical events includes formal concerts, outdoor concerts, free indoor concerts, busking and workshops. Planning takes place 10 months in advance.

Guinness Cork Jazz Festival

Jack McGouran
Festival Programme Director
18 Stephens Lane
Upper Mount Street
Dublin 2

Tel/Fax: +353 1 6765091/+353 1 6765803
Email: questcom.iol.ie
Website: www.corkjazzfestival.com
Other key staff: Deirdre Smith (Administrator), Mary Browne (Secretary)

Festival will be held 27-30 October 2000, late October 2001 and 2002. Music promoted includes blues, world, jazz/improv and crossover. Format of musical events includes formal concerts and sessions. There is also a fringe element to this festival, which is comprised of workshops and masterclasses. Planning takes place 15 months in advance.

Guinness International Dunmore East Bluegrass Festival

Mick Daly
Director
The Anchor Bar
Dunmore East
Co. Waterford

Tel/Fax: +353 51 383133/+353 51 870991
Email: crosslane@eircom.net

Festival will be held 24-27 August 2000. Music promoted includes trad/folk, jazz/improv, crossover and bluegrass. During the festival there are over 50 musical events. Format of musical events includes lunchtime concerts, evening concerts, sessions and busking. Planning takes place the previous September.

Harvest Time Blues Festival

Somhairle MacConghail
Festival Organiser
c/o Monaghan County Museum
1-2 The Hill
Monaghan

Tel/Fax: +353 47 82928/+353 47 71189
Email: harvestblues@eircom.net
Website: www.harvestblues.net
Other key staff: Donna Macklin (Festival Administrator)

Festival will be held 7-10 September 2000, first weekend in September 2001 and 2002. Music promoted includes blues, soul, gospel, zydeco and cajun. During the festival over 50 musical events take place. Planning takes place 6-10 months in advance.

Iniscealtra Festival of Arts

Val Balance
Chairperson
Bodyke
Co. Clare

Tel/Fax: +353 61 921600/+353 61 927276
Email: iniscealtra@hotmail.com
Other key staff: Nicola Harvey, Kevin Cressea

Festival will be held June 2000, 2001 and 2002. Music promoted includes trad/folk, chamber, jazz/improv and crossover. During the festival there are 7 musical events. Format of musical events includes sit-down concerts, sessions and workshops. Planning takes place 1 year in advance.

Inishowen Traditional Singers Circle Seminar on Folk Song & Ballads

Jimmy McBride
Director/Secretary
'Dun Emir'
Shore Road
Buncrana
Co. Donegal

Tel: +353 77 61210
Email: jimmymcb@iol.ie
Other key staff: Pat McGonigle (Chairperson), Sal Lichfield (Registrar)

Will be held the last weekend in March 2001. Format of musical events includes 5 lectures, 1 formal recital, and 1 formal concert. The seminar also promotes unaccompanied folk and ballad singing. Planning takes place 18 months in advance of the seminar and bookings are confirmed in the Autumn prior to the event.

Irish Association of Youth Orchestras Festival of Youth Orchestras

Michèle O'Brien
Festival Director
24 Barnhill Avenue
Dalkey
Co. Dublin

Tel/Fax: +353 1 2352233
Other key staff: Agnes O'Kane (IAYO Administration), Vanessa Sweeney (Festival Director), Trish Casey (IAYO Executive)

Festival will be held 17/2 2001 and February 2002. Promotes orchestral music. During the festival there are 2 concerts in the National Concert Hall, with 4 youth orchestras participating in each. Planning takes place 15 months in advance. This festival is sponsored by Penneys.

International Choir Festival

Thomas Molnar
MWS Festivals
Vikingagatan 39-41
S-113 42 Stokholm
Sweden

Tel/Fax: +46 8 7360565/+46 8 307515
Email: mwsfestivals@tmresor.se

or

Anne Farrelly
Music Hibernia
Cúl Cuana
Balrathboyne Glebe
Kells
Co. Meath

Tel/Fax: +353 46 34019
Mobile: +353 87 2394090
Email: hibernia@eircom.net

Festival will be held 9-12 August 2001 and 8-11 August 2002. Music promoted includes choral, orchestral, trad/folk, chamber, blues and jazz/improv. During the festival there are 30 musical events. Format of musical events includes evening concerts, lunchtime concerts, open-air concerts and busking. Planning is taking place at present.

Kilkenny Arts Festival

Maureen Kennelly
Administrator
92 High Street
Kilkenny

Tel/Fax: +353 56 63663/+353 56 57704
Email: info@kilkennyarts.ie
Website: www.kilkennyarts.ie
Other key staff: Susan Proud (Music Director)

Festival will be held from 11-20 August 2000, August 2001 and August 2002. Music promoted includes orchestral, chamber, choral, jazz/ improv, opera, trad/folk, blues, world, rock and pop and crossover. During this festival approximately 50 musical events take place. Format of musical events includes open air concerts, workshops, lunchtime/evening concerts and busking in the streets. Planning takes place 6-12 months in advance.

Killaloe Music Festival

John Kelly
Chief Executive
Irish Chamber Orchestra
Foundation Building
University of Limerick
Limerick

Tel/Fax: +353 61 202620/+353 61 202617
Email: ico@ul.ie
Other key staff: Fionnuala Hunt (Artistic Director), Imelda Dervin (Administrator/PRO), Margaret McConnell (Friends/Advertising Co-ordinator)

Festival will be held 21-25 July 2000, July 2001 and July 2002. Music promoted includes orchestral, trad/folk, chamber, choral and jazz/improv. During the festival there are approximately 10-12 musical events. Format of musical events includes lunchtime concerts, workshops, formal concerts, open-air concerts and sessions. Planning takes place 1 year in advance.

Killarney Roaring 1920's Festival

Mary Susan MacMonagle
Mac PR
Ivy Cottage
6 Port Road
Killarney
Co. Kerry

Tel/Fax: +353 64 32833/+353 64 33883
Email: macmon@iol.ie
Other key staff: Catherine Duggan (Co-ordinator), Teresa Irwin (Assistant Chairperson), Steve Newby (Accounts/Treasurer)

Festival will be held March 2001 and March 2002. Music promoted includes choral, trad/folk, jazz/improv and barbershop. During the festival there is a 1920's Gatzby Ball featuring the Pasedena Roof Orchestra and also sit-down barbershop concerts, workshops, sessions, lunchtime concerts and busking. Planning takes place approximately 10 months in advance.

Kilmallock Arts Festival

John Brazill
Director
Friars Gate Theatre
Sarsfield Street
Kilmallock
Co. Limerick

Tel/Fax: +353 63 98727/+353 63 20180
Other key staff: Grace Bailey (Office Secretary)

This festival will be held in October 2000, 2001 and 2002. Music promoted includes orchestral, chamber, choral, trad/folk and classical. During the festival there are 3-5 musical events. Format of musical events includes sit-down concerts. The 1999 programme of events included the Binneas Singers, Limerick and Kilmallock Church Choir and Hilary Reynolds accompanied by Jacco Lamfers, Ballet Ireland, poetry reading and Kilmallock Drama Society Drama Festival. Also featured was Fuinneogea art exhibition, which included works of 20 artists.

Kinsale Arts Festival

Tom O'Hare
Artistic Director
The Gallery
The Glen
Kinsale
Co. Cork

Tel/Fax: +353 21 4774558 or +353 21 4774990/ +353 21 4774958
Email: maritime@indigo.ie
Other key staff: Eddie McCarthy (Co-ordinator), Philip McEvoy (Fundraiser)

Festival will be held 20/9-1/10 2000, September 2001 and September 2002. Music promoted includes orchestral, chamber, trad/folk, choral, world, jazz/improv and opera. During the festival there are 4 main music events and 5 smaller events. Format of musical events includes formal sit-down concerts, school workshops, open-air concerts and sessions. Planning takes place 6 months in advance.

Lá na nAmhrán

Dr. Lillis Ó Laoire
Festival Director
Irish World Music Centre
Foundation Building
University of Limerick
Limerick

Tel/Fax: +353 61 202590/+353 61 202589
Email: lillis.olaoire@ul.ie
Website: www.ul.ie/~iwmc
Other key staff: Ellen Byrne (Publicity Officer)

Festival will be held in March 2001 and 2002. During this Sean-nós singing festival there are workshops, concerts and sessions. Planning takes place 6 months in advance.

Lá na gCos

Dr. Catherine Foley
Festival Director
Irish World Music Centre
Foundation Building
University of Limerick
Limerick

Tel/Fax: +353 61 202922/+353 61 202589
Email: catherine.e.foley@ul.ie
Website: www.ul.ie/~iwmc
Other key staff: Ellen Byrne (Publicity Officer)

Festival will be held in April 2000, 2001 and 2002. During this Sean-nós dance and related music festival, there are workshops, concerts and sessions.

Lennon Festival

Kathleen Duffy
Secretary
Meeting House Street
Ramelton
Co. Donegal

Tel: +353 74 51258

Festival will be held 1-12 July 2000. Music promoted includes trad/folk and rock/pop. Format of musical events includes street music. Planning takes place in October of each year.

Let's All Sing - Choral Festival for School Children

Anne Woodworth
Administrator
Music Department
Waterford Institute of Technology
College Street
Waterford

Tel: +353 51 302277
Email: awoodworth@wit.ie
Other key staff: Catherine O'Neill (Secretary)

Promotes choral music. Up to 400 children participate over a two day period (one day in February and one day in November). Format of festival is Lunchtime concerts and workshops.

Liberties Festival

Louise O'Hanrahan
Director
SICCDA Heritage Centre
10-11 South Earl Street
Dublin 8

Tel/Fax: +353 1 4541465/+353 1 4543021
Email: siccda@iol.ie

Festival will be held in June 2000, 2001 and 2002. Music promoted includes trad/folk, choral and rock/pop. During the festival there are 5-6 musical events. Format of musical events includes a combination of indoor and outdoor concerts and sessions. Also many drumming acts take part in the festival.

Limerick Civic Week Festival

Fergus Quinlivan
Director
Limerick Corporation
City Hall
Limerick

Tel/Fax: +353 61 415799 (w) or +353 61 229914 (h)/ +353 61 418601 or +353 61 410401
Email: fquinlivan@limerickcorp.ie
Website: www.limerickcorp.ie

Festival will take place 17-25 March 2001 and 2002. Music promoted includes orchestral, chamber, trad/folk, choral, jazz/improv, rock/pop and opera. During the festival there are over 40 musical events. Format of musical events includes formal sit-down evening concerts, lunchtime concerts, sessions, open-air concerts, busking and workshops. Planning takes place 2 years in advance. (see also advert)

Limerick International Band Festival

Caroline Nolan-Diffley
Director
Shannon Development
The Granary
Michael Street
Limerick

Tel/Fax: +353 61 410777/ +353 61 315634
Email: bandfest@shannon-dev.ie
Website:www.shannon-dev.ie/bandfest
Other key staff: Elenora Hogan (Project Executive), Mary Guiry (Administrator)

Festival will be held 18-19 March 2001 and 2002. Promotes concert band music. Format of festival includes drill and dance competitions (indoor, sit-down) in the morning, a marching band parade outdoors during the daytime, and a band recital competition (indoor, sit-down) in the evening. Planning takes place 2 years in advance.

Josie McDermott Memorial Festival

Anne Healy
Secretary
Ballyfarnon
Boyle
Co. Roscommon

Tel: +353 78 47096
Other key staff: Mary Shivnan (Chairperson), Sean Lavin (Treasurer), Martin Lavin (PRO)

Festival will be held May bank holiday 2001 and 2002. Promotes trad/folk music. During the festival there are 5 musical events. Format of musical events includes céilis, concerts, competitions and sessions. Planning takes place 10 months in advance.

Mary from Dungloe International Festival

Anne Marie Doherty
Festival Office
Main Street
Dungloe
Co. Donegal

Tel/Fax: +353 75 21254/+353 75 22120
Other key staff: Pat Connaghan, Judy Lea, Fionnuala Sweeney

Festival will be held in July/August each year. Music promoted includes trad/folk and rock/pop. Format of festival includes concerts in festival dome and street entertainment.

Mayfest

Fergal Gough
Public Relations Officer
Clonmel
Co. Tipperary

Fax: +353 52 26378
Email: clonmel350@eircom.net
Other key staff: John Higgins (Chairman)

Festival will be held May bank holiday 2001 and 2002. Music promoted includes trad/folk, world and rock/pop. During the festival there are 15-20 musical events. Planning takes place 12 months in advance.

Milford Busking Festival

Elaine McFadden
General Manager
IRD Milford Limited
Main St
Milford
Co. Donegal

Tel/Fax: +353 74 53736 or +353 74 53682/ +353 74 53736
Email: ird_milford@eircom.net
Other key staff: Declan Williams (Projects & IT Assistant), Padraig O'Dwyer (Development Manager)

Festival will take place in August 2000, 2001 and 2002. Music promoted includes orchestral, trad/folk, blues, jazz/improv, rock/pop and crossover. Format of musical events includes busking in the street and open-air concerts. Planning is 10 months in advance.

Millennium Bach Festival

Blánaid Murphy
Director
16 Westgate
St. Augustine Street
Dublin 8

Tel/Fax: +353 1 6773712
Email: blanaidm@gofree.indigo.ie
Other key staff: Michael Conroy (Canzona
Chairman), Tanya Sewell (Canzona Secretary),
Lindsay Armstrong (Orchestral Co-ordinator)

Festival will be held from November to April 2001 and
2002. Music promoted is choral with orchestra and
soloists. During the festival there are 4 musical events.
Format of musical events includes sit-down concerts,
with the performance of the 3 Bach major choral works
to commemorate the 250th anniversary of his death.
Planning takes place 9 months in advance.

Joe Mooney Summer School of Traditional Music, Song & Dance Festival

Nancy Woods
Secretary
Drumshanbo
Co. Leitrim

Tel: +353 78 41213
Email: nwoods@iol.ie
Website: www.indigo.ie/~davebird/joemooney/
Other key staff: Mary Doyle (Assistant
Secretary), Michael Smyth (Treasurer)

Festival will be held third week in 2001 and 2002.
Promotes traditional music. Format of musical events
includes workshops in traditional instruments, Sean-nós,
set dancing, evening lectures, céilís and sessions.
Planning takes place 10 months in advance.

Paddy Morrissey Memorial Weekend

John Flynn
Public Relations Officer
Duinch
Banteer
Co. Cork

Tel/Fax: +353 29 56115/+353 29 56115
Other key staff: Kathleen Buckley (Administrator)

Promotes trad/folk music. During the festival there are 3
musical events. Format of musical events includes concerts, sessions and workshops. Planning takes place 8
months in advance.

James Morrison Traditional Music Weekend

Martin Enright
Co-ordinator
Kilmacowen
Co. Sligo

Tel/Fax: +353 71 67560
Email: martinenright.ias@eircom.net

Festival will be held from 28-30 July 2000, last weekend
of July 2001 and 2002. Promotes trad/folk music.
Format of musical events includes evening concerts,
sessions, lectures, workshops and masterclasses.

Moyvane Village Festival

Bobby Stack
Secretary
Church Road
Moyvane
Co. Kerry

Tel/Fax: +353 68 49298/+353 68 49298
Other key staff: Denis O'Flaherty
(Chairperson), Brenda Cahill (Assistant Secretary),
Tom Roche & Mike O'Sullivan (Joint Treasurers)

Festival will be held October 2000, 2001 and 2002.

Denis Murphy Memorial Weekend

Máiread Kiely
Dan O'Donnells Traditional Pub
Knocknagree
Mallow
Co. Cork

Tel: +353 64 56014

Festival will be held on the June bank holiday weekend
2000, 2001 and 2002. Promotes trad/folk music.
Format of this festival includes a gathering of Sliabh
Luachra musicians in Dan O'Connells pub.

Music Amongst The Mosaics

Robert Travers
Trustee
The Fleming Trust

Timoleague House
Timoleague
Bandon
Co. Cork

Tel/Fax: +353 23 46116/+353 23 46523
Email: robert@tdi.iol.ie

Festival will be held July 2000, 2001 and 2002. Music promoted includes chamber, trad/folk, choral and opera. During the festival there are 5 musical events. Format of musical events includes formal afternoon and evening concerts and picnics in Timoleague Castle Gardens. Planning takes place 6 months in advance.

Music @ Drumcliffe
Daragh Morgan
Artistic Director
Flat 2
Raisbeck Court
26 Rosendale Road
West Dulwich
London SE21 8DR

Tel/Fax: +44 956 916510/+44 20 8761 6039
Email: darraghm@hotmail.com
Other key staff: Jessamye Boyd (Administrator)

This music series will be held July/August 2000, 2001 and 2002. Music promoted includes orchestral, trad/folk, chamber, choral and crossover. During the festival there are 6 evening recitals. Format of event includes pre-concert talks before recitals. Planning takes place 10 months in advance.

The Music Festival in Great Irish Houses
Crawford Tipping
Festival Administrator
First Floor, Blackrock Post Office
Blackrock
Co. Dublin

Tel/Fax: +353 1 2781528/+353 1 2781529
Other key staff: Judith Woodworth (Artistic Director), Ciara Higgins (PRO)

Festival is held in June each year. Promotes chamber music. During the festival there are 9-12 musical events. Format of musical events includes formal sit-down evening concerts. Planning takes place 9-10 months in advance.

National Heritage Week
Anne Grady
Education & Marketing Officer
Dúchas - The Heritage Service
51 St. Stephen's Green
Dublin 2

Tel/Fax: +353 1 6472455/+353 1 6616764
Email: visits@indigo.ie
Website: www.heritageireland.ie
Other key staff: Aisling McMahon (Heritage Card Officer), Úna McDermot (Education & Interpretation Officer), Gráinne Ní Allúin (Assistant Marketing Officer)

Festival will be held in September 2000, 2001 and 2002. Music promoted includes trad/folk, chamber and rock/pop. Format of musical events includes open-air concerts and formal sit-down events. Planning takes place 1 year in advance.

Newcastlewest Arts Festival
Carmel Mhic Dhomhnaill
Public Relations Officer
Dúchas
Gortboy
Newcastlewest
Co. Limerick

Tel: +353 69 61974
Email: mikemacd@eircom.net
Other key staff: Vicki Nash (Chairperson)

Festival will be held on the second weekend of April each year. Music promoted includes orchestral, chamber, trad/folk, blues, world, jazz/improv, rock/pop and crossover. Format of festival includes evening concerts, open-air concerts and busking. Planning takes place 5-6 months in advance.

O'Carolan Harp Cultural & Heritage Festival
Ann Finnegan
Public Relations Officer
Altmush
Kilmainhamwood
Kells
Co. Meath

Tel: +353 46 52113
Website: www.nobber.harp.net
Other key staff: Tony Finnegan (Chairman), Helen Fagan (Secretary), Teresa Kelly (Treasurer)

Festival will be held 29/9-1/10 2000. Promotes traditional music. Format of musical events includes sit-down evening concerts, workshops, lunchtime concerts and sessions.

O'Carolan Harp & Traditional Music Festival

Paraic Noone
Secretary
Keadue
Co. Roscommon

Tel/Fax: +353 78 47204/+353 78 47511
Email: ocarolan@oceanfree.net
Other key staff: Margaret Grimes (Chairperson), Berna Gibbons (PRO)

Festival will be held 4-7 August 2000, 3-6 August 2001 and 2-5 August 2002. Promotes traditional harp music. During the festival there are 20 musical events. Format of musical events includes sit-down concerts, workshops and open-air sessions.

Oideas Gael Festival

Liam O'Cuinneagain
Director
Gleann Cholm Cille
Co. Donegal

Tel/Fax: +353 73 30248
Email: oidsgael@iol.ie
Website: www.oideasga/gael.com
Other key staff: Siobhan Ní Churraighín (Office Manager)

Promotes trad/folk music. Format of musical events is workshops for bohdran, flute and whistles. Planning takes place 1 year in advance. (see advert p.89).

An tOireachtas

Liam Ó Maolaodha
Director
6 Harcourt St
Dublin 2

Tel/Fax: +353 1 4753857/+353 1 4781947
Email: oireacht@indigo.ie
Website: www.indigo.ie/egt/ighlin/oireachtas/
(new website currently under construction)

Takes place on two different weekend each year, usually in May and November. Music promoted includes trad/folk, choral and Sean-nós singing. An tOireachtas comprises of some 150 literary, sheet music and stage competitions, a major art exhibition and many fringe activities including concerts, traditional music sessions, musical workshops, Sean-nós competition (featuring Corn Uí Riada - traditional singing competition). Planning takes place 2 years in advance.

Old Fair Festival

John Gillespie
Chairperson
Teeling Street
Tubbercurry
Co. Sligo

Tel: +353 71 86210
Other key staff: Mary Henry, Roger McCarrick, Derek Sherlock

Festival will be held 9 August 2000. Music promoted includes trad/folk and crossover. During the festival there are 10-15 musical events. Format of musical events includes evening concerts, sessions and open-air concerts.

The Other World Festival

Festival Co-ordinator
Ballymun Partnership
North Wall
Ballymun
Dublin 11

Tel/Fax: +353 1 8423612/+353 1 8427004
Email: bmunpart@indigo.ie

Festival is held in October each year. Music promoted includes samba and world. Format of musical events includes open-air concerts and sessions.

Pan Celtic International Festival

Margaret Maunsell
Secretary

Tel: +353 66 7180050
Email: panceltic.eircom.net
Website: www.panceltic.com
Other key staff: Fiona Friel (Public Relations Officer), Caitlin De Ris (Treasurer), Caitlin Uí Chaoimh (President - Tralee Festival)

Festival is held in April each year. Music promoted includes choral, trad/folk and rock/ pop. Format of musical events includes formal sit-down evening concerts (Irish, Breton, Cornish, Welsh, Scottish nights).

Powers Irish Coffee Festival
Margaret O'Shaughnessy
Director
Foynes
Co. Limerick

Tel/Fax: +353 69 65416
Email: famm@eircom.net
Website: www.webforge.net
Other key staff: Helena McMahon (Artist &
Designer), Marie Rohan (Director)

Festival will be held 17-20 August 2000. Music promoted includes trad/folk, jazz/improv and rock/pop. During the festival there are 10-15 musical events. Format of musical events includes open-air concerts. Planning takes place 9 months in advance.

Rose of Tralee International Festival
Noreen Cassidy
Chief Executive
Ashe Memorial Hall
Denny Street
Tralee
Co. Kerry

Tel/Fax: +353 66 7121322/+353 66 7122654
Email: info@roseoftralee.ie
Website: www.roseoftralee.ie
Other key staff: Eileen Kenny (Secretary),
Eleanor Carrick (Secretary)

Festival will be held in August 2000, 2001 and 2002. Wide selection of music promoted. Format of musical events includes formal concerts, sessions and open-air concerts. Planning is takes place 10 months in advance.

Roundstone Open Arts Week
Richard de Stacpoole
Director
Errisbeg House
Roundstone
Connemara
Co. Galway

Tel/Fax: +353 95 35834/+353 95 35715
Email: marquis@eircom.net
Website: www.connemara.net
Other key staff: Penny Perrick (Secretary),
Paddy Browne (Treasurer), Ann Conneelly (PRO)

Festival will be held 26/6-4/7 2000, 2001 and 2002. Music promoted includes trad/folk, choral and

jazz/improv. Format of musical events includes workshops, formal sit-down concerts and busking. Planning takes place 9-10 months in advance. (see advert p.226)

RTÉ Millennium Musician of the Future Festival
Jane Carty
Festival Director
RTÉ
Donnybrook
Dublin 4

Tel/Fax: +353 1 2082048/+353 2082511
Email: cartyj@rte.ie
Other key staff: Deborah Kelleher (Assistant to the Director), Ciara Higgins (Events Manager)

This festival takes place every two years and consists of five competitions, masterclasses and concerts. All events are sponsored by RTÉ.

St. Barrahane's Church Festival of Classical Music
Angela Eborall
Secretary
Tally Ho House
Castletownshend
Co. Cork

Tel/Fax: +353 28 36193/+353 28 36339
Other key staff: Jacqueline Weij (PRO), Susan Hosford (Treasurer)

Festival will be held last two Thursday's in July and first three Thursdays in August. Music promoted includes chamber, choral and baroque. Format of musical events includes formal evening concerts in the church. Planning takes place 10 months in advance.

St. Michael's Dun Laoghaire Summer Organ Series
Anne Leahy
Director
94 Gresham House
Cathal Brugha Street
Dublin 1

Tel: +353 1 8786926
Email: amleahy@esatclear.ie

Series will be held 11/6-3/9 2000 and each year starting on the second Sunday in June and ending on the first Sunday in September. Promotes organ music. During this series there are 13 musical events. Format of musical events includes concerts held every Sunday at 8.30pm in St. Michael's Church, Dun Laoghaire, Co. Dublin.

St. Patrick's Festival

Grainne Walker
Festival Co-ordinator
St. Stephen's Green House
Earlsfort Terrace
Dublin 2

Tel/Fax: +353 1 6763205/+353 1 6763208
Email: info@paddyfest.ie
Website: www.stpatricksday.ie
Other key staff: Rupert Murray (Festival Director), Marie Claire Sweeney (Executive Director), Louise McLoughlin (Hospitality Manager)

Festival is held in March each year. Music promoted includes trad/folk, world and crossover. Format of musical events includes open-air concerts, street entertainment and busking. Planning takes place 10 months in advance.

Samhlaíocht Chiarraí

Maggie Fitzsimons
Artistic Director
Tralee
Co. Kerry

Tel/Fax: +353 66 7129934/+353 66 7120934
Other key staff: Noel King (Ceannaire Ealaíon), Maurice Galway (Ceannaire Ealaíon)

Festival is held on the Easter weekend each year. Music promoted includes orchestral, trad/folk, chamber, choral, jazz/improv, rock/pop and opera. Format of musical events includes exhibitions, recitals, seminars and workshops. Planned from September-November of the previous year.

Michael Shanley Traditional Weekend

Frank Fox
Chairperson
Glenfarne Road
Kiltyclogher
Co. Leitrim

Tel/Fax: +353 72 54222/+353 72 54044
Mobile: +353 87 2653927
Email: frankfox@acnielsen.iol.ie
Other key staff: Pat Fox (PRO), Stella McGriskine (Treasurer), Olive Gallagher (Secretary)

Festival will be held on the third weekend of August 2000, 2001 and 2002. Promotes trad/folk music. Format of musical events includes workshops, concerts and sessions. Planning takes place 6 months in advance.

Sean-nós Cois Life

Pádraig Ó Cearbhaill
Secretary
88 Céide Windsor
Baile Na Manach
Co. Bhaile Átha Cliath

Tel: +353 1 2804023
Other key staff: Antaine Ó Faracháin

Festival will be held the last weekend of March to early April 2001 and 2002. Promotes trad/ folk music. Format of musical events includes workshops, informal sessions, lectures, Sean-nós singing classes for adults and children and story telling workshops. Planning takes place 1 year in advance.

Síamsa Sráide

Bríd O'Connell
Co-ordinator
Main Street
Swinford
Co. Mayo

Mobile: +353 86 8453118
Fax: +353 94 51401
Other key staff: Francis Brennan, Liam Campbell, Jacqui Campbell

Festival will be held 5-9 August. Music promoted includes trad/folk and jazz/improv.

Siemens Feis Ceoil

Carmel Byrne
Administrator
37 Molesworth Street
Dublin 2

Tel/Fax: +353 1 6767365/+353 1 6767429
Other key staff: Joan Cowle (Honorary Music Secretary), T.A Buckley (Honorary Treasurer), E.F Ryan (Honorary Treasurer)

Siemens Feis Ceol will be held 19/3-1/4 2001. Music promoted includes orchestral, chamber, choral, opera and instrumental. There are 161 competitions, junior and senior prizewinner concerts. Planning takes place 2 years in advance.

Singer Songwriter Festival
John Plamer
Director
7 Georges Street
Waterford

Tel: +353 51 879333

Festival is held mid April each year. Music promoted includes trad/folk, rock/pop and crossover. Planning takes place 8 months in advance.

Slatequarries Festival of Art & Culture
Thérèse Walsh
Secretary
Tullahought
Piltown
Co. Kilkenny

Tel: +353 51 648366
Other key staff: Mary Cummins (Chairperson), James Power (Vice-Chairperson), John Delaney (Treasurer), Martin Riches (Secretary)

Festival is held in July each year. Promotes trad/folk Music. Format of musical events includes sessions. Planning takes place 6 months in advance.

Sligo Arts Festival
Danny Kinnane
Festival Manager
Model and Niland Centre
The Mall
Sligo

Tel/Fax: +353 71 69802 or +353 71 69813/ +353 71 69802
Email: artsfestival@eircom.net
Website: www.homepage.eircom.net
Other key staff: Tim Newell (Fás Supervisor)

Festival will be held from the 27 May 2000, 26 May 2001 and 25 May 2002. Music promoted includes trad/folk, world, jazz/improv, rock/pop, opera and crossover. During the festival there are 30-40 musical events. Planning takes place 6 months in advance.

Sligo Contemporary Music Festival
Una McCarthy
Director
Model & Niland Centre

The Mall
Sligo

Tel/Fax: +353 71 41405/+353 71 43694
Email: modelart@iol.ie
Website: www.iol.ie/~modelart/
Other key staff: Ann O'Dea (Education), Paul Cunningham (Music)

Festival is held in November each year. Promotes contemporary music.

Sligo Early Music Festival
Rod Alston
Eden
Rossinver
Co. Leitrim

Tel/Fax: +353 72 54122/+353 72 54122 or +353 71 43694
Email: modelart@iol.ie
Other key staff: Paul Cunningham (Music Co-ordinator, Model & Niland Centre), Roland Blennerhassett (Treasurer)

Festival is held in October each year. Promotes period and baroque music. During the festival there are 15-20 musical events. Format of musical events includes lunchtime concerts, evening concerts, workshops, masterclasses, cafe music and school visits.

Sligo International Choral Festival
Rev. J.J Gannon
Chairperson
c/o Summerhill College
Sligo

Tel/Fax: +353 71 70733/+353 71 62048
Email: cicsummerhill@bigfoot.com
Other key staff: Joe Kelly (Honorary Treasurer), Anne Hylland (PRO)

Festival is held in October/November each year. Music promoted includes orchestral, choral and barbershop. Format of festival includes competitions, concerts and church services. Planning takes place 12 months in advance.

South Dublin County Council Family Days
Billy Conran
South Dublin County Council
Town Centre

Tallaght
Dublin 24

Tel/Fax: +353 1 4149000 Ext. 3302/
+353 1 4149106
Other key staff: Esther Walsh (Staff Officer)

Family days are held in July each year. Music promoted includes orchestral, jazz/improv and rock/pop. Family days are held each Sunday in selected parks.

South Roscommon Celtic Festival

Declan Coyne
Culleenirwin
Dysart
Ballinasloe
Co. Roscommon

Tel/Fax: +353 903 22827/+353 902 88046
Email: dhalonprom@eircom.net
Other key staff: Peter O'Brien (PRO), Charlie Finnegan (Financial Director)

Festival will be held 28-31 July 2000, 27-30 July 2001 and 26-29 July 2002. Music promoted includes trad/folk, celtic (Scottish, Welsh, Breton and Irish), cajun, bluegrass and appalachian. Format of musical events includes sit-down concerts, céilí dances, workshops, masterclasses, open-air concerts, sessions and exhibitions. Planning takes place 1 year in advance.

Summer Sound Fest

Maria Kelemen
Director
21 The Close
Cypress Downs
Dublin 6W

Tel/Fax: +353 1 4905263/+353 1 4920355
Email: yes@iol.ie
Website: www.cybermusician.com.ireland
Other key staff: Brian MacKay (Conductor), Ronald Masin (Conductor), Deborah Kelleher (Pianist)

Festival will be held in August 2000, 2001 and 2002. Music promoted includes orchestral and chamber. Format of musical events includes sit-down evening concerts, workshops, lunchtime concerts, open-air concerts, with performances by children aged 8-15 years. Planning takes place 12 months in advance.

Swords Heritage Festival

Bernadette Marks
Chairperson
Mountgorry
Swords
Co. Dublin

Tel/Fax: +353 1 8403629 or +353 1 8400080/
+353 1 8400080
Other key staff: Pauline Archbold (Treasurer/PRO), Michael McDonagh (Carnival Co-ordinator), Pat O'Brien (Auditor)

Festival will held 4-10 September 2000, 3-9 September 2001 and 2-8 September 2002. Music promoted includes trad/folk, blues, choral, jazz/improv and crossover. Format of musical events includes evening concerts, sessions and open-air concerts. Planning takes place 6 months in advance.

Taghmon Mardi Gras

Vonnie Roche
Secretary
Old Mill
Main Street
Taghmon
Co. Wexford

Tel/Fax: +353 53 34319 or +353 53 34901/
+353 53 34901

Festival is held in August each year. Music promoted includes trad/folk, jazz/improv and crossover. Format of musical events includes evening concerts, sessions, busking, singing, dancing and mummers.

Trá Festival

Martin Murphy
The Old Vic
Queen Street
Tramore
Co. Waterford

Tel/Fax: +353 51 390338/+353 51 386626

Festival is held on the first weekend in July each year. Music promoted includes trad/folk and rock/pop. Format of musical events includes workshops. Planning takes place 3 months in advance.

Virginia Street Fair & Vintage Display

Steve Toman
Chairman
Virginia Heritage Group
Virginia
Co. Cavan

Tel: +353 49 8547700

Fair is held in June each year. Promotes traditional music. Planning takes place 10 months in advance.

The Warriors Festival

Michael Murray
Public Relations Officer
The Bridge
Strandhill
Co. Sligo

Tel/Fax: +353 71 68339 or +353 71 69967/ +353 71 44511
Email: mhunt@iol.ie
Other key staff: Fergal Conway (Secretary), Jennifer Barrins (Chairperson), Enda Horan (Treasurer)

Festival will be held in August 2000, 2001 and 2002. Music promoted includes blues and rock/pop. Format of musical events includes open-air concerts and sessions. Planning takes place 8-10 months in advance.

Waterford International Festival of Light Opera

Sean Dower
General Secretary
60 Morrissons Ave
Waterford

Tel: +353 51 375437
Other key staff: Patrick Giles (Chairperson), Maurice Cummins (Vice Chairperson), Kevin Kavanagh (Musical Director)

Festival will be held 13/9-8/10 2000, 21/9-6/10 2001 and 20/9-5/10 2002. Promotes light opera music. During this festival there are 14-16 musical events. Format is evening performances in the Theatre Royal, Waterford. Planning takes place 10 months in advance.

Waterford New Music Festival

Marion Ingolsby
Administrator
Waterford Institute of Technology

Music Department
College Street Campus
Cork Road
Waterford

Tel/Fax: +353 51 302809 or +353 51 855038 (box office - Garter Lane Arts Centre)/ +353 51 302293

Music promoted includes new music/contemporary music. During the festival there are 10 musical events. Format of musical events includes sit-down evening concerts, composition workshops, lecture demonstrations and masterclasses. Planning takes place 6 months in advance.

Waterford Spraoi

Miriam Dunne
Programme Director
The Glen
Waterford

Tel/Fax: +353 51 841808/+353 51 858023
Email: spraoi@eircom.net
Website: www.spraoi.com
Other key staff: Sarah Clancy (Administrator)

Held in August each year. Music promoted includes orchestral, chamber, trad/folk, blues, chamber, choral, world, jazz/improv and rock/pop. During the festival there are 200-300 musical events. Format of musical events includes open-air concerts and sessions.

West Cork Chamber Music Festival

Francis Humphries
Festival Director
1 Bridge Street
Bantry
Co. Cork

Tel/Fax: +353 27 52789 or +353 27 52788 (box office)/+353 27 52797
Email: westcorkmusic@eircom.net
Website: www.westcorkmusic.ie
Other key staff: Roisin McGuigan (Administrator), Rudolf Kuper (Manager), Martin Greenwood (IT Specialist)

Festival will be held 25/6-2/7 2000, 24/6-1/7 2001 and 30/6-7/7 2002. Promotes chamber music. Format of festival includes coffee concerts, lunchtime concerts (in satellite venues), masterclasses, 1 hour recital at 5pm, late evening concert at 8.30pm, full concert with interval and late night one-work concerts at 11.30pm. Planning takes place 8 months-2 years in advance.

Westport Arts Festival

Sinéad Wall
Secretary
The Resource Centre
Mill Street
Westport
Co. Mayo

Tel/Fax: +353 98 26787
Email: rcwestport@eircom.net
Other key staff: Stephen Walsh (Chairman)

Festival will be held 15-24 September 2000, September 2001 and 2002. Music promoted includes orchestral, trad/folk, chamber, blues, choral, world, jazz/improv, opera and crossover. During the festival 14 musical events take place. Format of musical events includes lunchtime concerts, evening concerts and late night performances.

Wexford Celtic Community Festivals

Noel Ferguson
Supervisor
Festival Centre
Westgate Heritage Centre
Wexford

Tel/Fax: +353 53 42939 or +353 53 46506/ +353 53 24646
Other key staff: Susan O'Connor (Chairperson), Harvey Hillis (Co-ordinator), Helen Corish-Wylde (President)

This festival committee organise the following festivals: Wexford in Bloom (July each year), Wexford Children's Community Christmas Festival (December-January each year), Wexford Viking Festival (May bank holiday each year), Wexford Family Sports & Fun Festival (August each year) and Wexford St. Patrick's Day Festival (March each year). All of these festivals promote trad/folk, choral, world, jazz/improv and rock/pop music.

Wexford Festival Opera

Jerome Hynes
Chief Executive
Theatre Royal
High Street
Wexford

Tel/Fax: +353 53 22400/+353 53 24289
Email: info@wexfordopera.com

Website: www.wexfordopera.com
Other key staff: Philomena Keeling (Administrator), Luigi Ferrari (Artistic Director), Ted Howlin (Chairperson)

Festival will be held 19/10-5/11 2000, 18/10-4/11 2001 and 17/10-3/11 2002. Music promoted includes opera, orchestral, chamber and choral. During the festival there are over 60 musical events. Format of musical events includes lunchtime concerts, operas in Theatre Royal and orchestral events in churches. Planning takes place 1-2 years in advance.

Wicklow Regatta Festival

Anne Hollingsworth
Secretary
3 Lakeview Crescent
St. Patricks Road
Wicklow Town

Tel/Fax: +353 404 68354/+353 404 44838
Other key staff: Thomas Byrne (Chairperson), Robert Hollingsworth (Committee Member)

Festival will be held on the last week in July and first week in August 2000. Music promoted includes trad/folk, chamber, choral and rock/pop. Format of musical events includes sit-down concerts and open-air concerts.

Wicklow Uilleann Pipes Festival

Chairman
Kevin Street
Tinahely
Co. Wicklow

Tel/Fax: +353 402 38477/+353 402 38533
Email: pan-euro@iol.ie
Other key staff: Denis Quigley (Co-organiser)

Festival will be held February 2001 and 2002. Promotes trad/folk music on uilleann pipes. Format of musical events includes workshops, sessions, concert and lunchtime/afternoon events.

Winding Banks of Erne Fiddler's Weekend

Caoimhin MacAoidh
Tullyhorkey
Ballyshannon
Co. Donegal

Tel: +353 72 52144
Email: dldclk1@iol.ie
Other key staff: Catherine NicAoidh (Co-ordinator)

Festival will be held 1-3 March 2001 and 2002. Promotes trad/folk music. Features the fiddle music of South Donegal with special guests from fiddle traditions, workshops and concerts. Planning takes place 9 months in advance.

Woodford Mummers Festival

Marie McMahon
Secretary
Woodford
Co. Galway

Tel: +353 509 49248
Other key staff: Michael Moran (Chairman)

Festival will be held in December each year. Mummer Féile groups compete in each public house in Woodford on the first day of the festival and in the local hall on the second day. Planning decisions are made in September.

Youghal Festival of the Arts

Winston Greer
Chairman
63-64 North Main Street
Youghal
Co. Cork

Tel/Fax: +353 24 92762

Festival will take place in July 2000. Music promoted includes orchestral, chamber, choral, world and crossover. During the festival there are 8-10 musical events. Format of musical events includes formal sit-down concerts. Planning takes place up to 10 months in advance.

FESTIVALS - NORTHERN IRELAND

Ardoyne Fleadh Cheoil Project

Philip McTaggart
43 Herbert Street
Belfast BT14 7FE
Northern Ireland

Tel/Fax: 048 9075 1056/048 9075 1055
Email: info.ardoynefleadh@cinni.org
Other key staff: Gerard McGuigan (Development Officer), Kevin McVeagh (Chairperson), Joe Stewarts (Treasurer)

Festival will be held 23-30 July 2000. Music promoted includes trad/folk and rock/pop. Format of musical events is evening concert, workshops, lunchtime concerts, sessions and open-air concerts and busking. Planning takes place 12 months in advance.

Ards International Guitar Festival

Eilís O'Baoill
Arts Officer
Ards Arts Centre, Town Hall
Conway Square
Newtownards
Co. Down
Northern Ireland

Tel/Fax: 048 9181 0803/048 9182 3131
Email: eilisobaoill/leisser/abc@ardscouncil.gov.uk
Other key staff: Nigel Martin (Committee Consultant), George Lowden (Music Consultant), Angela Haley (Arts Centre Co-ordinator)

Festival will be held on the second weekend in October 2000, October 2001 and 2002. Music promoted includes trad/folk, chamber, blues, world, jazz/ improv, rock/pop, crossover, acoustic guitar. Format of musical events includes evening concerts, chamber concert, workshops, open sessions and visits to a guitar factory. Planning takes place 9 months in advance.

Armagh Arts Festival

Lenny Mullan
Arts Officer (Development)
The Market Place
Armagh Theatre & Arts Centre
Market Street
Armagh BT61 7AT
Northern Ireland

Tel/Fax: 048 3752 1820/048 3752 1822
Email: armagh.arts@duet.co.uk

Festival will be held May 2000, 2001 and 2002. Music promoted includes orchestral, trad/folk, chamber, blues, choral, world, jazz/improv, rock/pop and opera. During the festival there are 4-10 musical events. Format of musical events includes sit-down concerts, sessions, open-air performances and workshops. Planning takes place 7-8 months in advance.

Ballyclare Musical Festival Association

Alice Turner
General Secretary
56 Ballyeaston Road
Ballyclare BT39 9BP
Co. Antrim
Northern Ireland

Tel: 048 9334 0498
Other key staff: Barbara Acheson (Music Secretary), Carol Maxwell (Speech and Drama Secretary), Dymphna Howe (Irish Dancing Secretary)

Festival is held in May/April 2000, 2001 and 2002. Music promoted includes orchestral and choral. Format of music events includes competitions.

Ballymena Arts Festival
Rosalind Lowry
Arts Officer
80 Galgorm Road
Ballymena
Co. Antrim
Northern Ireland

Tel/Fax: 048 2566 0318/048 2566 0400
Website: www.ballymena.gov.uk

Festival will be held 1-16 October 2000, 2001 and 2002. Music promoted includes orchestral, chamber, choral, trad/folk, blues, world and rock/pop. During the festival there are approximately 10 musical events. Format of musical events includes workshops, seminars, open-air concerts and busking. Planning takes place 10 months in advance.

Banbridge District Arts Committee
Vanessa Miller
Arts & Events Officer
Banbridge District Council
Civic Building
Downshire Road
Banbridge
Co. Down
Northern Ireland

Tel/Fax: 048 4066 2991/048 4066 2592
Email: info@banbridgedc.gov.uk
Website: www.banbridge.com
Other key staff: John Dobson (Honorary Chairman)

Festival will be held October 2000, 2001 and 2002. Music promoted includes orchestral, trad/folk, choral, jazz/improv and rock/pop. Format of musical events includes evening concerts and open-air concerts. Planning takes place 4 months in advance.

Bangor Choral Festival
Joan Houston
Festival Co-ordinator
71 Bryansford Meadow
Bangor West
Co. Down BT20 3NX
Northern Ireland

Tel/Fax: 048 9145 6851/048 9127 1370
Other key staff: Roberta Dunlop (Treasurer), Pat McNally (Chairperson)

Promotes choral music. Format of musical events includes competitions, gala evening and workshops. Planning takes place 12 months in advance.

Banks of the Foyle Halloween Carnival
Nuala McGee
Festivals Officer
Council Offices
98 Strand Road
Derry BT48 7NN
Northern Ireland

Tel/Fax: 048 7136 5151/048 7137 0080
Email: festivals.dcc@btinternet.com
Other key staff: Claire Lundy (Press Officer)

Festival will be held 29-31 October 2000, 2001 and 2002. Music promoted includes trad/folk, blues, jazz/improv and rock/pop. Format of musical events includes open air concerts and sessions.

BBC Music Live 2000
Jim Sheridan
Co-ordinator
BBC Ormeau Avenue
Belfast BT2 8HQ
Northern Ireland

Tel/Fax: 048 9033 8322/048 9033 8431
Email: jim.sheridan@bbc.co.uk
Website: www.bbc.co.uk/musiclive

Festival will be held 25-29 May 2000. All musical genres promoted. During the festival there are over 1,000 musical events in Northern Ireland and many thousand across the UK. Format of musical events includes events in schools, community halls, village greens, sports grounds, shopping centres, offices, bus & train stations and air & sea ports and many more. Planning takes place 1 year in advance.

Belfast Carnival
David Boyd
Community & Carnival Director
Beat Initiative
183a Albertbridge Rd
Belfast
Northern Ireland

Tel/Fax: 048 9046 0863/048 9046 0865
Email: beat@appleonline.net

Other key staff: Geoff Ingram (Publicity Officer), Glynis Rolston (Administration Manager), Helen Davies (Training Officer)

Festival will be held 24 June 2000, 23 June 2001 and 22 June 2002. Music promoted includes world, rock/pop, crossover, samba, salsa and ethnic. During the festival there are 4 musical events. Format of musical events includes street parade and mobile stage performances. Planning takes place 6 months in advance.

Belfast City Summerfest
Cormac McCann
Leisure Development Manager
The Cecil Ward Building
410 Linenhall Street
Belfast BT2 8BD
Northern Ireland

Tel/Fax: 048 9027 0345/048 9024 4301
Email: mccannc@belfastcity.gov.uk
Website: www.belfastcity.gov.uk/summerfest
Other key staff: Heather Horner (Events Co-ordinator)

Festival will be held in May/June 2000, 2001 and 2002. During the festival 35 musical events take place. Format of musical events includes formal sit-down concerts. Planning takes place January/February.

Belfast Festival at Queen's
Robert Agnew
Executive Director
25 College Gardens
Belfast BT9 6BS
Northern Ireland

Tel/Fax: 048 9066 7687/048 9066 3733
Email: festival@qub.ac.uk
Website: www.qub.ac.uk/festival
Other key staff: Rosie Turner (Assistant Executive Director), Margaret McKee (Marketing Manager)

Festival will be held 27/10-12/11 2000, 2001 and 2002. Music promoted includes orchestral, trad/folk, chamber, blues, choral, world, jazz/improv, rock/pop, opera and crossover. During the festival there are approximately 30 musical events. Format of musical events includes concerts in the Waterfront Hall, Whitla Hall, Ulster Hall and Elmwood Hall at Queen's. Planning takes place 6 months-2 years in advance.

Carrickfergus Music Festival Association
W.P Howard
Honorary Administrator
1 Downshire Avenue
Carrickfergus BT38 7EL
Co. Antrim
Northern Ireland

Tel: 048 9336 1310
Other key staff: D.D Graham (Chairman), A. Stewart (Music Secretary), M. Muir (Speech & Drama Secretary)

Festival will be held on the last week in April 2001 and the first week in May 2002. Music promoted includes orchestral and choral. Planning takes place 1 year in advance.

Carrickfergus Waterfront Festival
Colin Ellis
Community Relations Officer
Tourism Information Office
Heritage Plaza
Antrim Street
Carrickfergus BT38 7QG
Northern Ireland

Tel/Fax: 048 9336 6455/048 9335 0350
Email: tic.tourism@carrickfergus.org

Festival will be held in June 2000, 2001 and 2002. Music promoted includes trad/folk and rock/pop. Format of musical events includes open-air concerts and a marquee. Planning takes place 9 months in advance.

Castleward Opera Festival
Hilda Logan
General Manager
737 Lisburn Road
Belfast BT9 7GU
Co. Antrim
Northern Ireland

Tel/Fax: 048 9066 1090/048 9068 7081
Other key staff: Ian Urwin (Joint Artistic Director), Jack Smith (Joint Artistic Director), Michael McGuffin (Musical Director)

Festival will be held in June 2000, 2001 and 2002. Promotes opera music. Format of musical events includes formal sit-down evening concerts. Planning takes place 9 months in advance.

Ceol na gCeilteach - Celtic Music Festival
Kieran Murphy
Manager
Tí Chulainn
An Mullach Bán
Co. Armagh BT35 9TT
Northern Ireland

Tel/Fax: 048 3088 8828/048 3088 8821
Email: tculainn@dial.piper.com
Website: www.tculainn.ie

Festival will be held 15-17 September 2000. Music promoted includes trad/folk and world. Format of musical events includes formal sit-down evening concerts, workshops, lunchtime concerts, sessions. Planning takes place 6 months in advance.

Coalisland International Music Festival
Donal Quinn
Honorary Treasurer
266 Coalisland Road
Dungannon
Co. Tyrone
Northern Ireland

Tel/Fax: 048 8774 0539 or 048 8774 8904
Other key staff: Oliver Corr (Fundraiser)

Festival will take place on the first weekend of July. Music promoted includes trad/folk, rock and crossover. Planning takes place 6 months in advance.

Coleraine Music Festival
Josephine Carter
Honorary General Secretary
34 Grange Road
Coleraine
Co. Derry
Northern Ireland

Tel/Fax: 048 7034 2314
Other key staff: Brian Simpson (Chairman), Mary Riddell (Speech & Drama Secretary), Mary Ellard (Music Secretary)

Festival will be held March 2001 and 2002. Music promoted includes orchestral and choral. Format of musical events includes competitions in several classes.

Community & Arts Festival for the Borough of Coleraine
Malcolm Murchison
Arts Centre Manager
Flowerfield Arts Centre
185 Coleraine Road
Portstewart
Co. Antrim BT55 7HU
Northern Ireland

Tel/Fax: 048 7083 3959/048 7083 5042
Email: flowerfield@dnet.co.uk
Website: under construction

Festival will be held in October 2000, 2001 and 2002. Music promoted includes orchestral, trad/folk, chamber, blues, choral, world, jazz/improv, rock/pop, opera and crossover. During the festival 20-30 musical events take place.

County Antrim Fleadh Cheoil
Tony Connery
Chairperson
29 Finlaystown Rd
Portglenone
Ballymena
Co. Antrim BT44 8EA
Northern Ireland

Tel: 048 2582 2736
Email: kieran@convery.freeserve.co.uk
Other key staff: N. Graham (Secretary), G. Donnelly (Treasurer), E. Graham (Vice Chairperson)

Festival takes place May/June 2000. Format of festival includes open-air concerts, sessions, and competitions. Planning takes place 8 months in advance.

The Eddie Duffy Memorial Traditional Music Festival
John Corrigan
Treasurer
23 Newtown Road
Derrygonnelly
Co. Fermanagh BT93 6JP
Northern Ireland

Tel: 048 6864 1679
Other key staff: Ann Gallagher (Secretary), Joe Corrigan (Chairman), Lena McGurn (Assistant Secretary)

Festival takes place on the second weekend in October each year. Promotes traditional music. Format of musical events includes formal sit down, workshops and open-air concerts. Planning takes place 7 months in advance.

Dungannon Music & Drama Festival
Naomi Doran
Joint Honorary Secretary
Castlecaulfield
Dungannon
Co. Tyrone BT70 3TG
Northern Ireland

Tel: 048 8776 1481
Other key staff: P. Dowd (Chairman). W. Robinson (President), J. Little (Treasurer)

Types of music promoted includes trad/folk and choral. Festival features bands and music making for disabled children from special schools.

Early Music Festival at Queen's
Dr Ian Woodfield
Festival Director
School of Music
The Queen's University of Belfast
Belfast BT7 INN
Northern Ireland

Tel/Fax: 048 9033 5105/048 9023 8484
Website: www.music.qub.ac.uk
Other key staff: Dr. Anthony Carver (Senior Lecturer)

The festival aims to promote early music in Northern Ireland by presenting good quality concerts from recognised artist, and by encouraging the development of promising local talent.

Feile Camloch
Des Murphy
Chairperson
Crann Mor
17 Quarter Rd
Camlough, Newry
Co. Down
Northern Ireland

Tel/Fax: 048 3083 8292/048 3026 1071
Other key staff: Martin McCone (PRO), Catherine Murphy (Secretary), Terry Conlon (Treasurer)

Festival will be held on the second weekend of August

2000 and 2001. Music promoted includes trad/folk and rock/pop. Format of musical events includes sessions, celtic rock night and concerts. Planning takes place 10 months in advance.

Féile An Phobail - West Belfast Community Festival
Caitríona Ruane
Director
473 Falls Road
Belfast BT12 6DD
Northern Ireland

Tel/Fax: 048 9031 3440/048 9031 9150
Email: feile@irish-culture.com
Website: www.irish-culture.com
Other key staff: Carol Moore (Childrens Arts), Anthony McGraton (Marketing), Donna McGarry (Administrator)

Festival will held in August 2000, 2001 and 2002. Types of music promoted includes trad/folk, blues, world and rock/pop. Format of musical events includes sit-down concerts, open air concerts and sessions. Planning takes place 10 months in advance.

Féile Na Samhna
Caoimhghin Ó Murchadha
Stiúrtaóir
An Gael Áras
34 Mórshráid Shéamais
Dorie BT48 7DB
Northern Ireland

Tel/Fax: 048 7126 4132/048 7126 9292
Email: gaelaras@iol.ie

Music promoted includes trad/folk, blues, choral, jazz/improv and sean-nós singing. Format of musical event includes informal sit-down concerts, workshops, sessions and lunchtime concerts.

Féis Dhoire Cholmcille
Father Francis Bradley
Secretary
St. Joseph's
Fairview Road
Galliagh
Derry BT48 8NU
Northern Ireland

Tel/Fax: 048 7135 7979 or 048 7135 2351/ 048 7135 0458
Email: francis@fbradley.freeserve.co.uk

Music promoted includes orchestral, trad/folk, choral, jazz/improv and opera. Format of musical events includes competitions and formal sit-down adjudicated sessions.

Féis na nGleann

Patrick J. Clerkin
Vice-Chairman
61 Coast Road
Cushendall
Ballymena
Co. Antrim BT44 0RX
Northern Ireland

Tel: 048 2177 1349
Other key staff: Marie McAllister (Secretary), Nuala McSparran (Music Secretary), Seamus Clarke (Chairman)

Held in June each year. Format of musical events includes music, singing and choral competitions for different age groups. Planning takes place approximately nine months in advance.

Fiddlers' Green Festival of Arts

Kate Murphy
Chairperson
2 Cherryhill
Rostrevor
Co. Down BT34 3KM
Northern Ireland

Tel/Fax: 048 4173 8738/048 4173 9819
Other key staff: Sheila McKeown (Treasurer), Tommy Sands (President), Maureen McConville (Secretary)

Festival is held on the last week in July. Music promoted includes trad/folk and world. During the festival 30 musical events take place. Format of musical events includes sit-down evening concerts, lunchtime concerts and sessions.

Fleá Cheoil Thí Chulainn

Kieran Murphy
Events Manager
Tí Chulainn
An Mullach Bán
Co. Armagh BT35 9TT
Northern Ireland

Tel/Fax: 048 3088 8828/048 3088 8821
Email: tculainn@dial.pipex.com

Website: www.tculainn.ie
Other key staff: Seán Ó Coinn (Manager), Crónán Devlin (Archivist), Ursula Mhic an tSaoir (Education Officer)

Fleá will be held in June each year. Promotes trad/folk music. Planning takes place 3-4 months in advance.

Fleadh Amhrán agus Rince

Padraig McCaughan
Chairperson
5 Atlantic Avenue
Ballycastle
Co. Antrim
Northern Ireland

Tel/Fax: 048 2076 3703
Other key staff: Paddy McShane (Vice Chairperson), Jeannie McGrath (Secretary), Noel O'Neill (Treasurer)

Festival takes place on the third weekend in June. Promotes trad/folk music. Format of musical events is sessions and open air concerts.

The Percy French Society Festival

Gladys O'Neill
Honorary Secretary
14 Sydenham Ave
Belfast BT4 2DR
Northern Ireland

Tel: 048 9065 6091
Email: doublejay@clara.net
Website: www.dmc-ni.co.uk/PercyFrench
Other key staff: Jack Johnston (Secretary)

Music promoted includes trad/folk and crossover. Format of musical events includes evening concerts. Planning takes place 6 months in advance.

Greater Shankhill Community Festival

Adam Turkington
Festival Development Worker
250a Shankill Road
Belfast BT13 2BL
Northern Ireland

Tel: 048 9031 1333/048 9031 1413

Festival will be held in July 2000. Music promoted includes trad/folk, blues and rock/pop.

Guth an Earraigh

Caoimhghin Ó Murchadha
Stiúrthóir
An Gaeláras
34 Mórshráid Shéamais
Dóire BT48 7DB
Northern Ireland

Tel/Fax: 048 7126 4132/048 7126 9292
Email: gaelaras@iol.ie
Other key staff: Deirdre Doherty

Festival is held in March each year. Format of musical events includes informal sit-down evening concerts, lunchtime concerts, open-air performances, sessions and workshops. Concert venues include pubs and the cathedral. The festival also promotes Sean-nós and Scots Gaelic traditional music. Planning takes place 9 months in advance.

Heart of the Glens Festival Committee

Maria Lavery
Development Officer
Old School House
25 Mill Street
Cushendall
Co. Antrim BT44 ORR
Northern Ireland

Tel/Fax: 048 2177 1378
Email: cushendall@nacn.org
Website: www.nacn.org
Other key staff: Kieran Dempsey (Chairman), Andrew McAlister (Committee Member)

Festival will be held from the 5 August 2000 and the second weekend in August each year. Music promoted includes trad/folk and rock/pop. During the festival there are 3 musical events. Format of festival includes open-air concerts, workshops and informal sessions. Planning takes place 9 months in advance.

Holywood International Jazz Festival

George Chambers
Partner - Ulster Jazz Events
18 Lyndhurst Drive
Belfast BT13 3PA
Co. Antrim
Northern Ireland

Tel/Fax: 048 9071 0793
Other key staff: Walter Love (Partner/ Organiser), Brian Dempster (Partner/ Organiser)

Festival takes place in June each year. Music promoted includes jazz/improv and blues. Festival includes mardi gras, jazz/blues afternoon pub trail, evening concerts and Sunday brunch.

William Kennedy Piping Festival

Brian Vallely
Director
14 Victoria Street
Armagh BT61 9DT
Northern Ireland

Tel/Fax: 048 3751 1248
Email: jbv@ukgateway.net
Other key staff: Eithne Vallely (Director of Music), Brian Vallely/Eamonn Curran (Uilleann-pipes Tutors) Eamon Curran (Uilleann-pipes maker & reed maker)

Festival is held November/December each year. Format of musical events includes 7 informal sessions, 4 formal sit-down concerts, 6 schools recitals, 10 workshops, 2 formal lectures, 2 informal discussion groups, an open public foyer concert and an exhibition. The events illustrate all forms of pipes in Ireland, England, Scotland and Wales. Planning takes place 8-10 months in advance of the festival (see advert p.260).

Tommy Makem International Song School

Kieran Murphy
c/o Tí Chulainn
An Mullach Bán
Co. Armagh BT35 9TT
Northern Ireland

Tel/Fax: 048 3088 8828/048 3088 8821
Email: tculainn@dial.pipex.com
Website: www.tculainn.ie

Festival takes place 5-10 June 2000, June 2001 and June 2002. Format of musical events includes concerts, workshops, classes and singing sessions. The school promotes traditional and folk singing. Planning takes place 1 year in advance.

Master Mcgrath Lurgan Community Festival

Bill Grant
Co-ordinator
10 Union Street
Lurgan BTGG 8DY
Northern Ireland

Tel/Fax: 048 3834 9149/048 3834 8612
Other key staff: Sean Hughes (Chairperson)

Festival will be held 16-20 August 2000, August 2001 and 2002. Music promoted includes trad/folk, blues and rock/pop. Format of musical events includes lunchtime concerts and evening concerts.

Moving on 00
Brian Carson
Director
Moving On Music
7 University Road
Belfast BT7 INA
Northern Ireland

Tel/Fax: 048 9024 8818
Email: movingltd@aol.com

Festival will be held 16-23 September 2000, mid September 2001 and 2002. Music promoted includes orchestral, trad/folk, chamber, blues, world, jazz/improv, rock/pop and crossover. During the festival there are 7-8 musical events. Format of musical events includes formal sit-down evening concerts, workshops, sessions, and multimedia events.

Music at Castle Coole
Anne Kelly
Property Manager
The National Trust
Castle Coole
Enniskillen
Co. Fermanagh BT74 6JY
Northern Ireland

Tel/Fax: 048 6632 2690/048 6632 5665
Email: casco@smtp.ntrust.org.uk
Other key staff: Siobhan Scullion (House Steward)

Festival will be held in June 2000. Music promoted includes chamber, choral, opera and crossover. During the festival there are 4-5 musical events. Format of musical events includes formal sit-down concert in the Grand Entrance Hall followed by a wine reception in the Morning Room. Planning takes place 6-10 months in advance.

Newry & Mourne Arts Feile
Mark Hughes
Arts Administrator
Newry & Mourne Arts Centre
1a Bank Parade
Newry

Co. Down BT35 6HP
Northern Ireland

Tel/Fax: 048 3026 6232/048 3026 6839
Other key staff: Jacqueline Turley (Arts Assistant)

Festival will be held 10-18 March 2000 and 2001. Music promoted includes trad/folk and rock/pop. Format of musical events includes open-air, evening concerts, parades and sessions. The festival is planned 6 months in advance.

Newtownabbey Arts Festival
Cathy Cole
Arts Development Officer
49 Church Road
Newtownabbey
Co. Antrim

Tel/Fax: 048 9086 8751/048 9036 5407
Other key staff: Paula Donaghy (Community Relations Officer)

Festival will be held in February 2001 and 2002. Music promoted includes trad/folk, chamber, choral and jazz/improv. During the festival there are 5-8 musical events. Format of musical events includes formal sit-down concerts, lunchtime recitals and concerts in the Courtyard Theatre and jazz in the parks. Planning takes place 8-10 months in advance.

Ninth World Harp Congress 2005
Dr. Clíona Doris
Chairman
35 The Meadows
Strangford Road
Downpatrick
Co. Down BT30 6LN
Northern Ireland

Tel/Fax: 048 4461 3856/048 4461 7740
Email: doris@unite.co.uk
Other key staff: Andreja Malir (Vice President), Sheila Larchet-Cuthbert (Secretary), Denise Kelly McDonnell (Treasurer), Aibhlín McCrann (Officer), Áine Ní Dhubhghaill (Officer), Ann Marie O'Farrell (Officer), Ann Jone Walsh (Officer), Gráinne Yeats (Advisor)

Festival will be held in July 2005. Music promoted includes orchestra, trad/folk, chamber, world and jazz/Improv. Format of festival includes eight days of recitals, 'Focus on Youth' performances, chamber music, orchestral concerts, jazz concerts, exhibitions, lectures, workshops and discussions.

Northern Lights Festival

Cathal Newcombe
Chairman
45a Drumavoley Road
Ballycastle
Co. Antrim
Northern Ireland

Tel: 048 2076 3352
Other key staff: Dick Glasgow (Music Co-ordinator)

Festival is held May 2000, 2001 and 2002. Promotes trad/folk music. During the festival there are 30 musical events. Format of musical events includes concerts, workshops, instrument making, poetry and songwriting. Planning takes place 12 months in advance.

Ó Bhéal Go Béal

Padraigín Ní Uallacháin
Tí Chulainn
An Mullach Bán
Co. Armagh BT35 9TT
Northern Ireland

Tel/Fax: 048 3088 8828/048 3088 8821
Email: tculainn@dial.pipex.com
Website: www.tculainn.ie

Music promoted includes trad/folk, singing and poetry. Format of musical events includes formal sit-down evening concerts. Planning takes place 6 months in advance.

Omagh Arts Festival

Jean Brennan
Arts Development Officer
Omagh District Council
The Grange
Mountjoy Rd
Omagh
Co. Tyrone BT79 7BL
Northern Ireland

Tel/Fax: 048 8224 5321/048 8224 3888
Email: jeanbrennan@omagh.gov.uk

Festival will be held in October 2000, 2001 and 2002. Music promoted includes trad/folk, chamber, blues, world, jazz/improv, rock/pop and opera. Format of musical events includes formal sit-down evening concerts, sessions and open air concerts. Planning takes place 6 months in advance.

Portglenone Fleadh Ceoil

Tony Connery
Chairperson
29 Finlaystown Road
Portglenone
Co. Antrim BT44 8EA
Northern Ireland

Tel: 048 2582 2736
Other key staff: E. Graham (Vice Chairperson), N.Graham (Secretary), G. Donnelly (Treasurer)

Promotes trad/folk music. Format of musical events includes sessions, open-air concerts and street entertainments.

Roe Valley International Folk Festival

George Murphy
Musical Director
34 Greenhaven
Curragh Road
Dungiven
Co. Derry BT47 4RW
Northern Ireland

Tel: 048 7774 1197
Other key staff: Paul Canning (Secretary), Cyril Roulston (Chairperson), Canice Heaveron (Co-ordinator)

Festival will be held 1-3 October 2000, 6-8 October 2001 and 4-6 October 2002. Music promoted includes trad/folk, blues and cajun. The festival has between 30-40 musical events. Format of musical events includes formal sit-down evening concerts, sessions and busking. Planning takes place 6 months in advance.

St. Patrick's Carnival

Catríona Ruane
Chairperson
Ashton Centre
5 Churchill Street
Belfast BT15 2BP
Northern Ireland

Tel/Fax: 048 9074 3331/048 9035 1326
Email: feile@irish-culture.com
Website: www.irish-culture.com
Other key staff: Irene Sherry, Philip Mac Taggart

Festival is held 17 March each year. Music promoted includes trad/folk, world and rock/pop. Format of musical events includes open-air concerts and parades. Planning takes place 8 months in advance.

Seachtain Chara Tóchair - Carntogher Festival

Patrick McAllister
Youth Development Officer
41-43 Glen Road
Maghera
Co. Derry BT46 5AP
Northern Ireland

Tel/Fax: 048 7964 5353/048 7964 5013
Email: patmcallister1@hotmail.com
Other key staff: Helena McGlane (Secretary), Stephen Murtagh (Music Advisor)

Festival will be held on the third week of July 2000, 2001 and 2002. Promotes trad/folk music. Planning takes place 5 months in advance.

Slieve Gullion Festival of Traditional Singing

Gerry O'Hanlon
Secretary
6 Glendeshea Rd
Mullaghbawn
Newry
Co. Down BT35 9XN
Northern Ireland

Tel/Fax: 048 3088 8565/048 3026 1360
Email: gerry.ohanlon@btinternet.com
Mick Quinn (Chairperson), Patricia Flynn (Treasurer)

Festival will be held 6-8 October 2000, 5-7 October 2001 and 4-6 October 2002. Promotes trad/folk music. During the festival there are 8 musical events. Format of musical events includes concerts, lectures and informal sessions. Planning takes place 4 months in advance.

Sonorities Festival of Contemporary Music

Dr. Michael Alcorn
Chairman
School of Music
The Queen's University of Belfast
Belfast BT7 INN
Northern Ireland

Tel/Fax: 048 9033 5403/048 9023 8484
Email: m.alcorn@qub.ac.uk
Website: //buzz.music.qub.ac.uk/sonorities
Other key staff: Piers Hellawell (Composer/ Treasurer)

Festival will be held 11-16 May 2000, May 2001 and 2002. Music promoted includes orchestral, jazz/improv, crossover and electroacoustic. During the festival there are 10-20 musical events. Format of musical events includes concerts, workshops and lectures. Features many UK, Irish and world premiers. Planning takes place 1-2 years in advance.

Tí Chulainn Sean-nós Festival

Seán Ó Coinn
Manager
Tí Chulainn
An Mullach Bán
Co. Armagh BT35 9TT
Northern Ireland

Tel/Fax: 048 3088 8828/048 3088 8821
Email: tculainn@dial.pipex.com
Website: www.tculainn.ie

Festival will be held in August 2000. Promotes Sean-nós singing. During the festival there are 6-8 musical events. Format of musical events includes formal sit-down evening concerts, workshops, lunchtime concerts and sessions. Planning takes place 6-8 months in advance.

Two Cathedrals Festival

Tim Allen
Co-Artistic Director
2 St. Columb's Court
Derry BT48 6PT
Northern Ireland

Tel/Fax: 048 7126 2412/048 7126 2412
Email: t.allen@lineone.net
Other key staff: Donal Doherty (Co-Artistic Director), Dermot Carlin (Secretary), Pauline Lusby (Administrator)

Festival will be held 8-10 October 2000, October 2001 and 2002. Music promoted includes orchestral, chamber, choral and jazz/improv. Format of musical events includes concerts, lunchtime recitals, workshops and fringe events. Planning takes place 14 months in advance.

Upstarts - A Festival of Arts for Young People

Jill Holmes
Arts Officer
Down County Museum
The Mall
Downpatrick

Co. Down
Northern Ireland

Tel/Fax: 048 4461 5218/048 4461 5590
Email: museum@downdc.gov.uk
Other key staff: Caroline Huey (Assistant Arts
Officer)

Festival will be held in October 2000, 2001 and 2002.
Music promoted includes orchestral, trad/folk, chamber,
blues, choral, world, jazz/improv, rock/pop, opera and
crossover. Format of musical events is performances and
workshops. Planning takes place 8 months in advance.

**The Walled City Festival
incorporating the Civic Parade**
Nuala McGee
Festivals Officer
Council Offices
98 Strand Road
Derry BT48 7NN
Northern Ireland

Tel/Fax: 048 3036 5151/048 3037 0080
Email: festivals.dcc@btinternet.com

Festival will be held 9-11 June 2000 and 8-10 June
2001. Promotes world music. Planning takes place 6
months in advance.

The William Kennedy
Piping Festival

14-20 November 2000

"The World of Piping"

Armagh Pipers Club presents an International Festival of piping with
pipers from Ireland, England, Scotland, Wales, France, Hungary, Italy,
Spain, Estonia, Latvia, Sweden and Bulgaria

Enquiries to:
Brian Vallely, 14 Victoria Street, Armagh BT61 9DT, Ireland
Tel/Fax: **(048) 3751 1248**
Email: **jbv@ukgateway.net**

Suppliers & Services

The following symbols are used within the Instrument Makers & Repairers and Instrument Sales sections:

 Hire

 Tuition offered

 Mail order service

 Instrument repair service

 Piano tuning service

The following symbols are used within the Recording & Practice section:

 Disabled access

 Parking

 Tea/coffee facilities

 Kitchen facilities

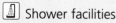 Shower facilities

 Accommodation

 Tuition offered

INSTRUMENT MAKERS & REPAIRERS - STRINGS

Peter Boardman

33a Hogstown Road
Donaghadee
Co. Down BT21 ONH
Northern Ireland

Tel: 048 9188 3474

Full time instrument maker. Violins, violas and cellos made to commission.
(see advert p.275)

Bow Makers

Paul Chartan
Bow Maker
18 St. Francis Terrace
Athlone
Co. Westmeath

Mobile: +353 87 2414130

Full time instrument maker. Fine bows for stringed instruments custom made, restored, repaired and re-haired. Hours of business are from 10-5pm. Phone for appointment.

Noel Burke Violin Bows

Noel Burke
Knockrooskey
Westport
Co. Mayo

Tel/Fax: +353 98 35394/+353 98 35229

Makes bows for violins, viola and cello in the french style method. Orders taken by phone, fax or letter. By appointment only.

Mick Cadec

Foley's Cottage
Clonmoyle
Kilmichael
Macroom
Co. Cork

Tel: +353 26 46385

Full time instrument maker. Repair and restoration of all woodwind instruments, violin fitting up and bow repair service. Fully equipped workshop for all woodwind repairs.

Cafferky Harps

Paddy Cafferky
Lisduff
Craughwell
Co. Galway

Tel/Fax: +353 91 846265
Other key staff: Toni Cafferky (Harpmaker's Assistant/Secretary)

Hours of business are from Monday to Friday, 10-6pm. Makes, repairs and restores harps. By appointment only (see advert p.275).

Rab Cherry Violins

Rab Cherry
185 Donegall Street
Belfast BT1 2FJ
Co. Antrim
Northern Ireland

Tel: 048 9024 7395

Makes violins and violas. Violins, violas, cellos and basses repaired and restored. Bows repaired and restored. A wide range of new and old instruments for sale as well as bows, strings, cases and accessories. By appointment only (Mostly in Belfast mid-week and some Saturdays, and Dublin at weekends) (see advert p.275).

Clareen Banjos

Tom Cussen
Slieveaun
Clarinbridge
Co. Galway

Tel/Fax: +353 91 796156/+353 91 796931
Email: tomcussen@eircom.net
Website: www.clareenbanjos.com

Business hours are from Monday to Saturday, Sunday by appointment. Custom made banjos available. Repairs to all fretted instruments. Mandolas also made to order. All banjo accessories available. Technician available.

Danvel Musical Instruments

Derrick Nelson
Marlay Park Craft Centre
Grange Road
Rathfarnham
Dublin 16

Tel: +353 1 4942741
Other key staff: Dorothy (Secretary)

Hand made steel string, classic, jazz and bass guitars, all custom designed. Full repair service for all stringed instruments. By appointment where possible.

Michiel De Hoog Violins
Michiel De Hoog
Unit 65 IDA Tower Design Centre
Pearse Street
Dublin 2

Tel/Fax: +353 1 6705245/+353 1 6775655

Makes violins, violas and cellos.

Doolin Bodhráns
Martin Murphy
Kilshanny Lodge
Kilshanny
Co. Cork

Tel/Fax: +353 65 7071888
Mobile: +353 86 9171888

Fiddle maker, repairer and bows re-haired. Also makes and repairs bodhráns.

Doyle Instruments Since 1890
Paul Doyle
38a Dominick Street
Galway

Tel/Fax: +353 91 566948
Email: paul.doyle@ireland.com
Website: //members.tripod.com/doyle_instrum
Other key staff: Markus Laughlin (Violin Maker), Marielle Florio (Harp Maker)

Maker of harps, guitars, violins, violas, cells, double bass, mandolin, mandola, mandocello, bouzouki, hurdy-gurdies and electric solid body instruments. Sells raw wood for instruments manufacturing. Runs 12 week courses on the making of the above instruments. (see advert p.282)

Laurence Egar Harps
Laurence Egar
Ard Mhuire
Herbert Park
Gardiners Hill
Cork

Tel: +353 21 4504832

Business hours are from Monday to Friday by appointment. Irish harps manufactured, repaired and restored. Pedal harps restored and regulated. Sale of harps.

Richard Ennis
Gransha Upper
Castlemaine
Co. Kerry

Maker and repairer of fretted stringed, stringed and percussion instruments to order. These instruments are also repaired and restored. Brass and woodwind instruments repaired and restored. Please contact by post only.

Martin Faherty
Unit 3 Shandon Craft Centre
Cork

Tel/Fax: +353 21 4302368/+353 21 4397686

Violin, cello, guitar, viola, bouzouki, mandolins, jazz archtop guitars made to order and repairs, restoration and bows re-haired.

Joe Foley
4 Braemor Road
Churchtown
Dublin 14

Tel/Fax: +353 1 4931614/+353 1 2982537

Manufacture, repair and restoration of bouzoukis, mandolas, citterns, mandolins and guitars.

Francois Violins
Jeremie Legrand
4 Lavitt's Quay
Cork

Tel/Fax: +353 21 4274885

Repair and restoration of cello, double bass, violin and viola. Bows re-haired. Violins, violas and cellos made. Accessories and cases for sale.

Chris Larkin Custom Guitars
Chris Larkin
Castlegregory
Co. Kerry

Tel/Fax: +353 66 71393300
Email: chris@clc.ie
Website: www.clc.ie

Handmaking of guitar family instruments. Full design, customisation and consultancy service. Occasional limited amount of repair work may be undertaken if time permits. Instruments made include acoustic and electric guitars, mandolins and electric upright basses. Almost everything is made to order and there is a waiting time of at least five months. 90% of the instruments made are exported. Works in a purpose built humidity controlled workshop. Visitors welcome by appointment.

Lughnasa Music
Gerry O'Connor
Ballymakellet
Ravensdale
Co. Louth

Tel/Fax: +353 42 9371538/+353 42 9380307
Email: oconnorg@iol.ie

Business hours are from Monday to Friday, 9-1pm. Works with violins, cellos and bows.

Kieran Moloney Musical Instruments
Kieran Moloney
Director
17 High Street
Old Malt Arcade
Galway

Tel/Fax: +353 91 566488/+353 91 565045

Repair and restoration of stringed instruments. Adjustments, tonal improvements made, re-fretting and bow re-hairing.

Eamonn Murray
10 Shandon Drive
Phibsboro
Dublin 7

Tel: +353 1 8388481
Email: gamba@gofree.indigo.ie

Makes, restores and repairs viols, violins, violas and cellos. Specialises in baroque and period instruments.

Phillip Murray
17 Idrone Close
Knocklyon
Dublin 16

Tel/Fax: +353 1 4941269 /+353 1 4941269
Email: phillip@clubi.ie
Other key staff: Gina Allen-Murray (Accounts Secretary).

Builder and repairer of stringed musical instruments. Many specialist services available, from minor repairs and modifications to full design, and manufacture. 22 string wire harp now being built to order. 30 and 34 string wire harp to follow in near future. Phone or email for details. By appointment.

Jan Muyllaert
Ardbraccan
Navan
Co. Meath

Tel: +353 46 29722

Design, manufacture and repair of all stringed instruments, except the piano. Exports approximately 70%. At present the order list is up to 9 months.

Nixon Guitars
Stephen Nixon
Unit 12
Thompson House
McCurtain Street
Cork

Tel: +353 21 4551644
Mobile: +353 86 2451760

Provides a repair service for most stringed instruments, particularly electric and acoustic guitar. Has a range of custom built electrics coming out soon.

James O'Halloran
Tigh Na Coradh
Ballea
Carrigaline
Co. Cork

Tel: +353 21 373270

Business hours are from Monday to Friday. All stringed orchestral instruments repaired and restored. Also sells violins.

Ogham Bodhráns

Eamon Maguire
Unit D31
Brookfield Mill
333 Crumlin Road
Belfast BT14 7EA
Northern Ireland

Tel/Fax: 048 9075 1366 (w) or 048 9080 3241 (h)
Email: eamon@omaguire.freeserve.co.uk

Manufactures, repairs, re-skinning, and painting of bodhráns and banjos. Also makes tunable bodhráns, by using a sliding wedge system.

Colm O'Meachair

The Harp Workshop
The Crafts Courtyard
Marlay Park
Grange Road
Rathfarnham
Dublin 16

Tel/Fax: +353 1 4942806
Mobile: +353 86 2463460

Hours of business are from Monday to Saturday, 9.30-6.30pm. Harp manufacture, sales and re-stringing. Makes 34 string, 28 string and 22 string harps. Extra commission works also undertaken.

Gerard O'Neill

Drumeen
Clonlara
Co. Clare

Tel/Fax: +353 61 354412

Violins, violas, cellos and bows made, repaired, tuned and restored. Sells violins. Teaches violin making at Limerick School of Music.

Douglas Patience Instruments

Meenross
Scarriff
Co. Clare

Tel: +353 61 921623

Business hours are from Monday to Saturday, 9-6 pm. Manufacture and repair of bouzouki, mandola, mandolin, cittern and guitar.

William D. Patterson

Camden House
Camden Quay
Cork

Tel/Fax: +353 21 506868

Business hours are from Monday to Saturday, 9-1 pm/2-5 pm. Manufactures violins. Accessories available and bows re-haired. New and old violins, violas, violoncellos and double basses available.

Pizzicato

Carsten Boettger
Manager
Kilcoran
Cahir
Co. Tipperary

Tel/Fax: +353 52 41906/+353 52 42630
Email: carsten@iol.ie
Website: www.pizzicato.de
Other key staff: Wolfgang Uebel (Master Instrument Maker), Franke Uebel-Derigs (Journeyman Instrument Maker)

Contact any time (appointment is recommended). Manufacture, repair, restoration and trade of baroque string instruments. Certified evaluation and estimation of instruments. Arrangement of finance. Stringed instruments include viola da gamba, viola d'amore, violin, viola, double bass, lute and acoustic guitar. Bows, cases and other instruments are also available. Uebel-made instruments are exhibited in Rheinische Landesmuseum, Bonn, Germany.

Anthony Quinn

Greenogue Industrial Estate
Rathcoole
Co. Dublin

Tel/Fax: +353 1 4589620

Handcrafted violincellos, violins and violas made.

Seán Radford

c/o Minstrel Music
Unit B Wexford Enterprise Centre
Kerlogue Industrial Estate
Rosslare Road
Wexford

Tel: +353 53 44105

Manufacture and repair of violins and associated stringed instruments. Bow repairs carried out.

William V. Rickerby

Kildermot
Ballymoney
Gorey
Co. Wexford

Tel: +353 55 25215

Business hours are from Monday to Friday, 9-6pm. Handmade violins and violas handcrafted to specification of the customer. Copies of Guarnerius and Stradivarius instruments made. Bow re-hairing carried out.

Conchobhar Ruiséal

The Cottage
Woodville House
Ballymurrin Lower
Kilbride
Co. Wicklow

Tel/Fax: +353 404 48388
Email: ruisealviolinmaker@eircom.net
Other key staff: Anne Marie Twomey

Makes, repairs and restores violins, violas and cellos. Bows repaired and re-haired. Sales of old violins, violas and cellos. Insurance valuations. Member of Entente Internationale des Maitres Luthiers et Archetiers d'Art.

Tony Ryan

20 McCurtain Street
Cork

Tel: +353 21 4503553

Business hours are from Monday-Saturday, 11-5.30 pm. Makes guitars, especially steel string guitars. Also manufactures bouzoukis and mandolins. Repair work is also carried out.

Michael Patrick Shannon

235 Castrom Point
Sligo

Tel: +353 71 43362

Violins and cases made. Repairs to all stringed instruments including violins, guitars, cellos and bows.

Kevin Sykes

Killeen
Ballyvary
Castlebar
Co. Mayo

Tel/Fax: +353 94 31019
Email: ksykes@eircom.net

Manufacture, restoration and repairs of violins, violas and cellos. Bow re-hairing, string accessories. Violins old and new handmade, bought and sold. By appointment.

Tara Harps

David Burke
Coolmore
Knocktopher
Co. Kilkenny

Tel/Fax: +353 56 68157
Email: harpo@gofree.indigo.ie
Other key staff: Jacky Burke

Business hours are from Monday to Sunday. Manufactures 18, 22, 30 and 34 string harps. Repairs on harps carried out.

INSTRUMENT MAKERS & REPAIRERS - WOODWIND

Mick Cadec

Foley's Cottage
Clonmoyle
Kilmichael
Macroom
Co. Cork

Tel: +353 26 46385

Repair and restoration of all woodwind instruments, violin fitting up and bow repair service. Fully equipped workshop for all woodwind repairs.

John Cronin Woodwind & Brass

The Castle Cottage
Kilcolgan
Co. Galway

Tel: +353 91 796795

Woodwind and brass repairs carried out.

Richard Ennis

Gransha Upper
Castlemaine
Co. Kerry

Maker and repairer of fretted stringed, stringed and percussion instruments to order. These instruments are also repaired and restored. Brass and woodwind instruments repaired and restored. Please contact by post only.

Feadóg Teoranta

Aidan McCullough
Director
8 The Westway Centre
Ballymount Avenue
Dublin 12

Tel/Fax: +353 1 4569533/+353 1 4569535
Email: whistles@feadog.ie
Website: www. feadog.ie
Other key staff: Lynette McCullough (Director)

Manufactures the Feadóg Irish whistle, in the key of C and D. Sold in a range of finishes - brass, nickel and colour. Also manufacture the 'Musical' - teaching slide guitar (an Irish invention which is patented in the EU and USA).

David Grant Woodwind Specialist

Ahenny
Carrick-on-Suir
Co. Tipperary

Tel: +353 51 648331

Repair of all woodwind instruments. Keywork making and alterations carried out to suit requirements. Restoration of period instruments.

Colin Hamilton

Coolea
Macroom
Co. Cork

Tel/Fax: +353 26 45209/+353 26 45578
Email: hammie@eircom.net
Website: www.homepage.eircom.net/~hammie

Repair and manufacture of traditional flutes. Most business is conducted by post.

Irish Wooden Flutes Ltd

Tom Ganley
Loughglynn
Castlerea
Co. Roscommon

Tel/Fax: +353 907 80115
Other key staff: Anne Ganley (Assistant)

Manufacture of wooden concert flutes, fifes and wood whistles. Supplied to home and overseas markets.

Eugene Lambe

Ballybranagan
Kinvara
Co. Galway

Tel/Fax: +353 91 638111
Email: elambe@indigo.ie
Website: www.homepage.eircom.net/~mirian/elambe

Manufacture of uilleann pipes and concert flutes for traditional music.

David Le Bas Manufacturing Co. Ltd

David Le Bas
26 Vernon Grove
Rathgar
Dublin 6

Tel/Fax: +353 1 4910366/+353 1 4910367
Email: dlebas@dna.ie
Website: //ourworld.compuserve.com/ homepages/lebasdavid/claretin.htm

Manufacture of the Clare tin whistle. The Clare whistle is one of the oldest instruments of Ireland.

M & E Flutes

Michael Cronnolly
Knockmullen View
Killasser
Swinford
Co. Mayo

Tel: +353 71 81336
Email: polymer@eircom.net
Website: //homepage.eircom.net/~mandeflutes

Flute maker of Irish T.D 5 piece blackwood flutes in D (also in polymer). Makes E Flat and F flutes in polymer. 6 keyed flutes made to order. Also flute restoration and repairs.

Donal McMahon
Ennistymon Road
Miltown Malbay
Co. Clare

Tel: +353 65 7084828

Business hours are from Monday to Saturday, 10-6pm. Traditional flutes manufactured and repaired. Keyless flutes and 6 keyed flutes are made from African Blackwood and Cocuswood. Keys and rings are made from sterling silver.

Paul Ryan Woodwind & Brass
Paul Ryan
Friends Meeting House
4 Eustace Street
Temple Bar
Dublin 2

Tel/Fax: +353 1 6798571/+353 1 6790464
Email: ryanpaul@iol.ie
Other key staff: Shay Cantwell (Financial Controller)

Sales of woodwind and brass musical instruments and accessories. Repair and restoration of woodwind instruments. Manufacture of early clarinets. Rental programme for student instruments. Main dealer for Arbiter and Yanagisawa saxophones. Also suppliers for Buffet, BG, Bam, Glotin, Keilwerth, Leblanc, Selmer, Vandoren and Yamaha.
(see advert p.299)

[H]

Seery Woodwind
Natasha Geraghty
Grallagh
Loughrea
Co. Galway

Tel/Fax: +353 91 841992

Business hours are from Monday to Saturday (except Thursdays), 9-9pm. Keyless, synthetic and timber flutes and whistles manufacture.

INSTRUMENTS MAKERS & REPAIRERS - BRASS

John Cronin Woodwind & Brass
The Castle Cottage
Kilcolgan
Co. Galway

Tel: +353 91 796795

Woodwind and brass repairs carried out.

Richard Ennis
Gransha Upper
Castlemaine
Co. Kerry

Brass and woodwind instruments repaired and restored. Please contact by post only.

Just Brass
Catríona O'Connor
36 Walsh Road
Drumcondra
Dublin 9

Mobile: +353 87 2373430

Repair and restoration of brass instruments specialising in dent removal. A call out service is available for bands throughout the country. All repairs are carried out by a fully qualified repairer.

Paul Ryan Woodwind & Brass
Paul Ryan
Friends Meeting House
4 Eustace Street
Temple Bar
Dublin 2

Tel/Fax: +353 1 6798571/+353 1 6790464
Email: ryanpaul@iol.ie
Other key staff: Shay Cantwell (Financial Controller)

Sales of woodwind and brass musical instruments and accessories.
(see advert)

INSTRUMENT MAKERS & REPAIRERS - PERCUSSION

The Bodhrán Maker
Paraic McNeela
137 Baldoyle Industrial Estate
Baldoyle
Dublin 13

Tel/Fax: +353 1 8322432/+353 1 8366212
Mobile: +353 87 2569672

Manufacture, restoration and repair of bodhráns. Area of special interest is tunable bodhráns.

Claddagh Musical Instruments
Michael Vignoles
69 Fairhill Road
Galway

Tel: +353 91 589094

Instrument repair and manufacture of Irish uilleann pipes, and tuneable bodhráns made, repaired and restored, and other traditional instruments repaired.

Doolin Bodhráns
Martin Murphy
Kilshanny Lodge
Kilshanny
Co. Clare

Tel/Fax: +353 65 7071888

Fiddle maker, repairer and bows re-haired. Also makes and repairs bodhrán.

Richard Ennis
Gransha Upper
Castlemaine
Co. Kerry

Maker and repairer of fretted stringed, stringed and percussion instruments to order. These instruments are also repaired and restored. Brass and woodwind instruments repaired and restored. Please contact by post only.

Mac Bodhrán
Aidan MacRory
Dublin 3

Tel/Fax: +353 1 8338816
Mobile: +353 87 2508708
Other key staff: Joan Mac Rory (Secretary)

Manufacture of 15', 18' and 20' bodhráns. Also makes tunable bodhráns.

Nature Art Centre
Thomas Wiegandt
Ballybane
Ballydehob
Co. Cork

Tel/Fax: +353 28 37323
Website: www.holistic.ie/nature-art
Other key staff: Annette Patzold

By appointment. Manufacture, repair, sales and hire of professional drums e.g djembe-drums, djun-djun, goumbe, bougarabon, sabar, talking drums, brekete, darbouka, bodhrán, tibetan singing bowls, tongue-drums, slit-drums. Other percussion instruments include balafon (xylophone), cow-bells, agogo-bells, shakers and gongs. All instruments can be sent by mail, through the mail order service.

Ogham Bodhráns
Eamon Maguire
Unit D31
Brookfield Mill
333 Crumlin Road
Belfast BT14 7EA
Northern Ireland

Tel/Fax: 048 9075 1366 (w) or 048 9080 3241 (h)
Email: eamon@omaguire.freeserve.co.uk

Manufactures, repairs, re-skinning, and painting of bodhráns and banjos. Also makes tunable bodhráns, by using a sliding wedge system.

Roundstone Musical Instruments Ltd
Malachy Kearns
The Monastery
Roundstone

Connemara
Co. Galway

Tel/Fax: +353 95 35808/+353 95 35980
Email: bodhran@iol.ie
Website: www.bodhran.com
Other key staff: Bridie Conroy (Sales), Mary
Woods (Sales), Martha Linnane (Secretary)

Business hours are from Monday to Saturday, 9.30-6pm
and Sundays April to November. Bodhrán makers. Music
shop with CDs and a range of world folk instruments
available. Mail order service worldwide. Instruments
sales of whistles, flutes, low whistles, bodhráns, uilleann
pipes, harps, concertinas, occarinas, chimes (tuned),
ocean drums, rainsticks, dulcimers and wooden bones.

✉

INSTRUMENTS MAKERS & REPAIRERS - KEYBOARDS

Cairdin
Michael Searson
Rathkeale Enterprise Centre
Bank Place
Rathkeale
Co. Limerick

Tel/Fax: +353 69 63255/+353 69 63233
Email: cairdin@iol.ie
Website: www.cairdin.com
Other key staff: Paddy Clancy (Partner)

Business hours are from Monday to Saturday. Manufactures
handmade accordions in factory and showroom.

✉

Seán Garvey
Rear of 35 Hughes Road North
Walkinstown
Dublin 12

Tel/Fax: +353 1 4502189

Business hours are from Monday to Friday. Accordion maker
and repairer. Accordions converted and re-conditioned.

Kenneth Jones Pipe Organs Ltd
Managing Director
Church Terrace
Bray
Co. Wicklow

Tel/Fax: +353 1 2868930/+353 1 2867664

Other key staff: David Maybury, Stephen
Adams (Directors)

Hours of business are Monday to Friday, 8.30-5pm.
Manufacture of handcrafted classical pipe organs, continued organs, practice organs. Engineer and technician
available. Restoration and maintenance service offered.

Dermot Locke Ltd
Dermot Locke
Camlin
Mitchelsfort
Watergrasshill
Co. Cork

Tel/Fax: +353 21 889183
Other key staff: Valda Locke (Secretary)

Business hours are from Monday to Friday, 9-5pm.
Church pipe organs, harmoniums and American organs
tuned, repaired and restored. By appointment.

R.E Meates & Son Ltd
Richard Meates
41 Foxrock Park
Foxrock
Dublin 18

Tel: +353 1 2893186

Restoration and servicing of pipe organs.

Paul Neiland & Associates
Paul Neiland
Unit 6
Kerlogue Industrial Estate
Rosslare Road
Wexford

Tel/Fax: +353 53 41784

Hours of business are from Monday to Friday, 8.30-5.30
pm. Manufacture, restoration, maintenance and tuning
of pipe organs for churches.

Noel Tuohy Accordion Repairs & Tuning
Noel Tuohy
11 Chancel Drive
Raheen
Limerick

Tel: +353 61 227460
Mobile: +353 87 2906842

Accordion repairs, tuning and advice.

Wells-Kennedy Partnership Ltd

David McElderry
Director
85-87 Gregg Street
Lisburn
Co. Antrim BT27 5AW
Northern Ireland

Tel/Fax: 048 9266 4257/048 9260 3722
Email: wellskennedy@dnet.co.uk
Website: www.d-n-a.net/users/wk/
Other key staff: Roberta Irwin (Administrator),
Jim Stewart (Contracts Manager)

Business hours are from Monday to Friday, 8.15-
5.15pm. All aspects of pipe organ design, building,
restoration, tuning and repair.

INSTRUMENT MAKERS & REPAIRERS - OTHER

Claddagh Musical Instruments

Michael Vignoles
69 Fairhill Road
Galway

Tel: +353 91 589094

Maker of uilleann pipes and bodhráns.

Hughes & McCledd Ltd

R.J Hughes
Chairman
Owlswood Lodge
5 Black Causeway Road
Strangford
Co. Down BT30 7LX
Northern Ireland

Tel/Fax: 048 4488 1880
Email: www.info@bagpipers.co.uk
Website: www.info@bagpipers.co.uk

Hours of business are from Monday to Friday.
Manufacturers of the 'Clanrye' synthetic highland chanter
reed and the 'Highland' synthetic drone reed. Uilleann
pipe makers and pipe band supplies. Price lists available.

Eugene Lambe

Ballybranagan
Kinvara
Co. Galway

Tel/Fax: +353 91 638111/+353 91 638111
Email: elambe@indigo.ie
Website: www.homepage.eircom.net/~mirian/elambe

Manufacture of uilleann pipes and concert flutes for
traditional music.

The Pipers Cave

Evelyn Kelso
Managing Director
138 Dungannon Road
Cookstown
Co. Tyrone BT80 9BD
Northern Ireland

Tel/Fax: 048 8676 3615/048 8676 2983

Business hours are from Monday to Friday, 8.30-5.30pm.
Manufactures Scottish bagpipes. Trade name is 'War-
Mac'. Repair and refurbishment of Scottish bagpipes.

Pre-historic Music

Marie Cullen O'Dwyer
Crimlin
Corr na Móna
Co. Galway

Tel/Fax: +353 92 48396
Email: bronzehorns@eircom.net
Website: www.eircom.net/~bronzehorns
Other key staff: Simon O'Dwyer (Manufacturer/
Researcher)

Reproduction of bronze horns from Kerry, Clare,
Limerick, Tyrone, Argyle in Scotland and Sussex in
England. Explore music and explore and investigate
instruments from around the world, these include, Iron
Age trumpets, silver pipes from Ur, sea shell trumpets,
animal horn and stone and bone flutes. Hand bells from
Offaly. Also available is their research to date into pre-
historic musical instruments and cultures.

Charles Roberts

IDA Craft Village
Donegal Town
Co. Donegal

Tel: +353 73 23311
Email: robertscharles@eircom.net
Other key staff: Alan Roberts

Manufacture of uilleann pipes and Northumbrian small
pipes. Concert D and flat pitch C, C sharp and B.
Practice sets, half sets and full sets available. Repairs to
flute. Piping tuition also available.

Kevin Rowsome

5 Hazelwood Park
Artane
Dublin 5

Tel: +353 1 8510031
Email: kevin-rowsome@esatclear.ie
Website: www.esatclear.ie/~rowsome

Uilleann pipes specialist. Works on a part time basis.

Siopa An Phíobaire

Cillian Ó Brianin
Ceardlann Na Coille
Dingle
Co. Kerry

Tel/Fax: +353 66 9151778/+353 66 9151918
Other key staff: Mauric Reviol, Greg Mac Sheáin

Business hours are from Monday to Saturday. Manufacture concert pitch uilleann pipe chanters to order. Stock and manufacture uillean pipes, bags and bellows and individually voiced tin whistles in the key of D.

INSTRUMENT SALES

AA Music

Anna Murphy
40 Nettlehill Road
Lisburn
Co. Antrim BT28 3HA
Northern Ireland

Tel/Fax: 048 9260 7155/048 9266 6844

Business hours are from Monday-Wednesday, 9-530pm Thursday, 9-8.30pm, Friday, 9-5.30pm and Saturday 9.30-4.30pm. Instruments brands available include pianos, digital pianos, keyboards, Steinbach, kemble, bechstein and all known brands, both new and old.

Acoustagraph Electronics Ltd

S. McEvoy
Ballyleague
Lanesboro
Co. Roscommon

Tel/Fax: +353 43 21304

Business hours are from Monday to Saturday, 10-6pm. Areas of special interest include electronic equipment and sound equipment. Instruments available include Solton and Yamaha keyboards.

Back 2 Music

Pat Cunningham
30 Upper Abbey Gate Street
Galway

Tel/Fax: +353 91 565272

Business hours are from Monday to Saturday, 9.30-5.30pm. Instrument brands available include Marshall, Laney, Carlsbro, Pearl, Maxtone, Premier, guitars by Lowden, Martin, Arai, Vintage and keyboards by Roland and Yamaha.

Tom Baylor Music

3 Newmarket Street
Fermoy
Co. Cork

Tel: +353 25 31012

Business hours are from Monday to Saturday, 11-6pm. Instrument available include keyboards, guitars, accordions, drums, accessories and PA systems.

Beat It Music

Conor Hughes
Manager
Main Street
Blackrock
Dundalk
Co. Louth

Tel/Fax: +353 42 9321700
Other key staff: Gene Berrill (Drum Department), Jim McReynolds (PA Department)

Business hours are from Monday to Saturday, 10-6pm. Areas of special interest includes vintage instruments from the 60's, 70's and 80's. Brands available include Fender, Gibson, Pearl, Sabian, Marshall and Yamaha.

Belfast Music Supplies

Linden Mack
Manager
283 Upper Newtownards Road
Belfast BT4 3GE
Northern Ireland

Tel/Fax: 048 9047 2555/048 9067 3434
Other key staff: Ronni Mack (Director)
Email: linden@belfastmusicsupplies.freeserve.co.uk
Website: www.belfastmusicsupplies.com

Business hours are from Monday to Saturday, 9.30-5.30pm. Instruments available include flutes, trumpets, cornets, violins, violas, cellos, double bass, guitars, accessories, sheetmusic and songbooks.

Charles Byrne Musik Instrumente

Geraldine Byrne
Manager
21-22 Lower Stephen Street
Dublin 2

Tel/Fax: +353 1 4781773/+353 1 4781904
Other key staff: Charles Byrne (Owner, Luthier)

Business hours are from Tuesday to Friday, 9-5.30pm and Saturday 9-5pm. Instruments available include violins, cellos, violas, double basses, bows, guitars, banjos, bozoukis, mandolins, mandolas, metronomes, cases, bodhráns and accessories, session books and tutor books. Brands include Thomastik, Amastro and Jargar.

C.G Electronics Service 2000

Martin Ryan
118 Tullow Street
Carlow

Tel/Fax: +353 503 31600
Other key staff: Jack Sheehan (Service Music), Martin Ryan (Audio & Video Service Manager)

Hours of business are from Monday to Saturday, 9.30-6pm. Instruments available include accordions, guitars, violins (new and secondhand). Brands available include Yamaha, Matrix, Martin, Celestion, Pioneer and JVC. Amplifiers and Mixers available.

Rab Cherry Violins

Rab Cherry
185 Donegall Street
Belfast BT 2FJ
Northern Ireland

Tel: 048 9024 7395

A wide range of new and old instruments for sale as well as bows, strings, cases and accessories. By appointment only (Mostly in Belfast mid-week and some Saturdays, and Dublin at weekends) (see also strings) (see advert p.275).

Clareen Banjos

Tom Cussen
Slieveaun
Clarinbridge
Co. Galway

Tel/Fax: +353 91 796156/+353 91 796931
Email: tomcussen@eircom.net
Website: www.clareenbanjos.com

Business hours are from Monday to Saturday, Sunday by appointment. Banjo accessories available. Engineer and technician available.

Richard Clarke Sport & Leisure

Richard Clarke
Director
Brendan Street
Portumna
Co. Galway

Tel/Fax: +353 509 41049

Business hours are from Tuesday to Saturday, 9.30-6pm. Instruments available include whistles, accordions, keyboards, guitars, flute, banjos, mouth organs, bodhráns, mandolins, recorders and fiddles.

Crehan Musical Instruments Ltd

Niall & Kieran Crehan
Directors
6 Carberry Road
Drumcondra
Dublin 9

Tel/Fax: +353 1 8372351/+353 1 8376135
Mobile: +353 86 2481933

Business hours are from Tuesday to Friday, 9-4pm, Saturday, 10-5pm. Instruments available include violins, violas, cellos, bass, bows, concertinas, bodhráns and strings. Brands available include Gremlin, Jeffers, Clareman, Roundstone, AMR, Thomastick, Jargar, D'Addario, Pirastor, Martin, Hill, Dorfler, Klier, Knoll, Penzl, Neudorfer, Kiel and Richter. Older instruments are also in stock. Bow re-hairing service.

Cremona Violins

Mark Jeffers
Director
56 George's Avenue
Blackrock
Co. Dublin

Tel/Fax: +353 1 2833381
Mobile: +353 87 2416723

Business hours are from Monday to Saturday, 10-10pm by appointment only. Instruments available include violins, violas, cellos - 18th, 19th and 20th Century German, English, Irish, French and Italian schools. German, English and French bows available.

Crowley's Music Centre Ltd

Sheena Crowley
29 MacCurtain Street
Cork

Tel/Fax: +353 21 4503426/+353 21 4503795
Other key staff: Michael Crowley (Director), Noel Curran (String Instrument Sales)

Business hours are from Monday to Saturday, 9-5.30pm. Large variety of musical instruments, amplifiers and PA sound equipment.

John Cumiskey & Sons Ltd

42-43 Clanbrassil Street
Dundalk
Co. Louth

Tel/Fax: +353 42 9334174/+353 42 9338275
Email: johncumiskey@eircom.net
Other key staff: Michael Cumiskey (Director)

Business hours are from Monday to Saturday. Instruments available include guitars, keyboards, accordions, bodhráns, banjos, mandolins, violins, cellos, flutes (concert and traditional), drums, bass instruments, drum units and amplifiers. Areas of special interest are acoustic and electric guitars and bodhráns.

Custys Music Shop

Frances Custy
2 Francis Street
Ennis
Co. Clare

Tel/Fax: +353 65 6821727
Email: custys.ennis@eircom.net
Website: www.custysmusic.com
Other key staff: Eoin Ó Neill

Business hours are from Monday to Friday, 10-6pm and Saturday 9.30-6pm. Areas of special interest include concertinas and locally produced tapes and CDs. Instruments and brands include French, English, German hand made fiddles and Lachenal, Crabb and Wheatstone concertinas.

Danfay Yamaha Ltd

Robbie Preston
Manager
75 Aungier Street
Dublin 2

Tel/Fax: +353 1 4754248/+353 1 4754785
Other key staff: John Dawson (Sales)

Business hours are from Monday to Friday, 9-5.30pm and Saturday, 9.30-5pm. Closed each day 1.30-2pm. Area of special interest is all Yamaha instruments except acoustic violins. (see advert p.282)

Deady Pianos

David Deady
John Player House
285 South Circular Road
Dublin 8

Tel/Fax: +353 1 4732673/+353 1 4732653
Email: dea@eircom.net

Business hours are from Mondy to Friday 9.30-5pm, Saturday and Sunday by appointment. Instruments available include new, pre-owned, re-conditioned pianos. Full written 10 year guarantee given with all purchases. Brands available include Steinway, Bechstein, Kawai and Yamaha. Hire service is available and delivery is nationwide.

Dempseys Music Salon

Brendan Dempsey
218 Parnell Street
Dublin 1

Tel: +353 1 8732044

Business hours are from Monday-Saturday 10-5.30pm, closed Wednesday and Sunday. Second hand instruments available, dating back to the the 1950's and 1960's.

Doyle Instruments Since 1890

Paul Doyle
38a Dominick Street
Galway

Tel/Fax: +353 91 566948
Email: paul.doyle@ireland.com
Website: //members.tripod.com/doyle_instrum
Other key staff: Mark McLaughlin (Violin
Maker), Marielle Florio (Harp Maker)

Business hours are from Monday to Friday, 10-7pm,
Saturday, 11-7pm and Sunday, 2-6pm. Instruments
available include acoustic guitars, bass (acoustic/electric),
violin, viola, cello, string bass, mandolin, mandola,
mandocello, bouzouke, banjo, ancient Irish/European
harps, modern harps, hurdy-gurdies, medieval, baroque
and renaissance instruments (see advert p.282).

Driftwood Music

Steve Pawsy
Kilkeran
Castlefreke
Clonakilty
Co. Cork

Tel: +353 23 40861

Instruments available include all stringed instruments,
jazz guitars, harps (headless fretless 5 string basses),
experimental noise making machines. Left-handed
instruments are a speciality.

Educational Music Services

Sarah Dowdall
Manager
22 Mountjoy Square East
Dublin 1

Tel/Fax: +353 1 8742310/+353 1 8725292
Email: emsltd@eircom.net

Business hours are from Monday to Friday, 9.30-6pm
and Saturday 9.30-5.30pm. Instruments available
include wind and brass, school percussion instruments
and recorders, sheet music.

H

Essaness Music

Frank Salmon
Managing Director
1 Kieran Street
Kilkenny

Tel/Fax: +353 56 65693

Hours of business are from Monday to Friday, 10-1pm/
2-6pm and Saturday, 10-6pm. Instruments available
include brass, guitars, keyboards, drums, percussion,
traditional instruments, bodhráns, violins, mandolins,
banjos.

Everest Music

Paul Ryan
Manager
Unit 1 Everest Centre
Castle Street
Bray
Co. Wicklow

Tel/Fax: +353 1 2861933/+353 1 2761127
Email: everestmusic@eircom.net
Website: www.everestmusic.com
Other key staff: Shay Ryan (PA & Advertising),
Kevin Doyle (Drums)

Business hours are from Monday to Saturday, 10-5.30pm.
Instruments available include acoustic and electric
guitars, drums and keyboards. Full range of accessories
and music books.

Flanagans of Buncrana Ltd

Peter Flanagan
Director
Deerpark Road
Mount Merrion
Co. Dublin

Tel/Fax: +353 1 2880218/+353 1 2881336
Email: flan@iol.ie
Website: www.theflanagan.com
Other key staff: Paul Houihan, Al Walsh and
Damian Kerins

Business hours are from Monday to Wednesday, 10-
6pm, Thursday 10-9pm, Friday and Saturday, 10-6 p.m.
Area of special interest is the sale of pianos (upright and
grand). Brands available include Kemble, Steinback,
Waldstein and secondhand Yamaha, Kawai, Chappel
and Steinway.

Keith Gibbons Music Services

Kenneth Gibbons
Gateside Road
Portrush

Co. Antrim BT56 8AE
Northern Ireland

Tel/Fax: 048 7082 3472/048 7082 3917
Email: cinema2@compuserve.com

Instruments available include church and classical organs. Church organs built and restored and reed organs and harmoniums re-built. Engineer available.

Goodwins Ltd
Liam Carroll
Managing Director
134 Capel Street
Dublin 1

Tel: +353 1 8730846

Business hours are from Monday to Saturday, 10-6pm. Areas of special interest include acoustic and electric acoustic guitars. Instruments available include guitars (acoustic and electric), violins, mandolins, banjos, harmonicas, whistles, effects processors, amplifiers, tuners and accessories. Brands available include Taylor, Takamine, Yamaha, Epiphone, Fender, Rodriguez, Marshall, Boss, Korg, Arai and Zoom.

Grehans
Eileen Grehan
Manager
Main Street
Boyle
Co. Rosommon

Tel/Fax: +353 79 62133
Other key staff: Bernard Flaherty

Hours of business are from Monday to Friday, 9-5pm and Saturday 9-1pm. Instruments available include a large range of traditional instruments, guitars (both electric and acoustic), music books and manuscript paper. Range of accessories available.

Griffin Pianos
William Griffin
Manager
Showrooms
Greenwood Estate
Togher
Cork

Tel/Fax: +353 21 4964773/+353 21 4313700
Other key staff: Conor Griffin (Concert Tuner), Barry Scannell (Consultant Technician)

Business hours are from Monday to Friday, 9-5pm and Saturday, 9-1pm. Pianos available include uprights and grands, which are of concert quality.

William Hofmann
'Way Cottage'
Kilpedder
Co. Wicklow

Tel: +353 1 2819614

By appointment only. Instruments available include violins, violas, bows and strings.

Holland Pianos Ltd
Alex Holland
Director
29 Monacurragh
Carlow

Tel: +353 503 31177
Other key staff: Sandra Holland, Liam Quinn

Hours of business are from Monday to Saturday, 10-8pm, by appointment. Area of special interest is the sale of pianos (new and secondhand). All brands of vertical and overstrung pianos (upright and baby grands). Hire, delivery and evaluation service available.

Jeffers of Bandon
Alex Jeffers
Director
2 Cloughmacsimon Industrial Estate
Bandon
Co. Cork

Tel/Fax: +353 23 44332/+353 23 44870
Email: pianos@jeffersmusic.ie
Website: www.jeffersmusic.ie
Other key staff: Johnathan Smyth (Piano Technician/Tuner), Gillian Smith (Information Department)

Hours of business are from Monday to Saturday, 9-6pm. Area of special interest is pianos. Instruments available include new and secondhand upright and grand pianos. Hire and delivery service available (see advert p.282).

Jeffers Music Company

Brian Calnan
Manager
First Floor
9 Parnell Place
Cork

Tel/Fax: +353 21 4277720/+353 21 4277724
Email: djeffers@indigo.ie
Other key staff: Yvonne Crowley (Accounts & Sales Assistant), David Jeffers (Director)

Business hours are from Monday to Saturday, 9.30-5.30pm. Areas of special interest include drums and percussion, keyboards and wind, church organs and pianos. Other instruments available include accordions, guitars, combo amplifiers, PA systems, and musical accessories. Brands available include Allen, Boss, Hohner, Sabian, Yamaha and Pearl.

Kellys Music Store

Noelle Kelly
Managing Director
15 Grand Parade
Cork

Tel/Fax: +353 21 4272355
Email: kelmus@iol.ie

Business hours are from Monday to Saturday, 9-5.30pm. Areas of special interest is traditional Irish music books, cassettes, CDs and a variety of handmade bodhráns. Instruments available include whistles, traditional flutes, violins, guitars and uilleann pipes.

Keynote Music Sales Ltd

Aidan McCullough
Director
8 The Westway Centre
Ballymount Avenue
Harolds Cross
Dublin 6W

Tel/Fax: +353 1 4569533/+353 1 4569535
Email: keynote@feadog.ie
Other key staff: Lynette McCullough (Director)

Business hours are from Monday to Friday, 9-5.30pm. Areas of special interest includes the Martin range of American handmade acoustic guitars. Instruments available include drums, whistles and violins. (see also page instrument makers)

Killeen Piano Services

Patrick Killeen
Liberty Stream
Ballygarvan
Co. Cork

Tel: +353 21 888445
Email: organs@indigo.ie

Digital computer organs sold. Pipe organs rebuilt and relocated. Upright and grand pianos tuned, repaired and rebuilt.

Kleiser Pianos

Karl Kleiser
General Manager
24 Thomas Street
Limerick

Tel: +353 61 416665

Hours of business are from Monday to Saturday, 9-5.30pm. Instruments available include upright and concert grand pianos. Engineer and technician available. Hire service provided (see advert p.289).

Litton Lane Studios

Lorcan Hughes
35a Barrow Street
Dublin 4

Tel/Fax: +353 1 6684103/+353 1 6683525
Email: littonlane@eircom.net

Instruments available for hire include "backline" (guitars, drums etc).

H

Joe Lynch Musical Instruments Ltd

Joe Lynch
Manager
25 Suffolk Street
Dublin 2

Tel/Fax: +353 1 6712410 or +353 1 6773138/ +353 6712410
Other key staff: Trish Lynch, Emmet Downey

Hours of business are from Monday to Saturday, 9-5.30pm. Areas of special interest include brass and woodwind. Instruments available include guitars, violins, cellos, bodhráns and harmonicas. Engineer/technician available.

McCullough Piggot
Joe Lynch
Manager
25 Suffolk Street
Dublin 2

Tel/Fax: +353 1 6712410
Email: joelynchmusic@eircom.net

Business hours are from Monday to Saturday, 9-5.30pm. Instruments available include clarinets, flutes, trumpets, saxophones, trombones, oboes, guitars, harmonicas and violins. Engineer and technician available. Accessories and music books available.

John McNeill Music
Stephen Chambers
Owner
140 Capel Street
Dublin 1

Tel/Fax: +353 1 8722159/+353 1 8725631

Business hours are from Monday to Saturday, 10-6pm. Areas of special interest include traditional Irish music instruments, acoustic instruments and new/secondhand, antique and craftsman-made instruments. Instruments available include accordions, banjos, bodhráns, bones, bouzoukis, concertinas, mandolins, timber flutes and uilleann pipes.

McQuaids Traditional Music Shop
Noel McQuaid
Owner
38 Pearse Street
Nenagh
Co. Tipperary

Tel/Fax: +353 67 34166
Other key staff: J. Conway, T. Lawlor

Business hours are from Monday to Saturday, 10-6pm,

closed Wednesday. Instruments available include guitars, bouzoukis, mandolins, accordions, fiddles, banjos, flutes, drums and bodhrán. Brands available include Buchaman, Conway, Martin, Yari, Gibson and Palatino. Re-fretting service. Range of traditional/contemporary Irish CDs and tapes.

Mangan Keyboard & Guitar Centre
Tommy Mangan
Director
210 Botanic Avenue
Glasnevin
Dublin 9

Tel/Fax: +353 1 8370244
Email: mkgc@oceanfree.net

Business hours are from Monday to Sunday, 10-6pm. Brands available include Yamaha, Casio, Gibson and Elliot.

Marching Band Shop
J. Crowley
Cappry
Ballybofey
Co. Donegal

Tel/Fax: +353 74 31454/+353 74 32787

Area of special interest is the supply of instruments to marching bands. Instruments available includes accordions, flutes, maces, drums and dom doms.

Marcus Musical Instruments Ltd
John McKernan
Managing Director
125 Royal Avenue
Belfast BT1 1FF
Northern Ireland

Tel/Fax: 048 9032 2871/048 9043 9955
Email: musicman@marcus.dnet.couk
Other key staff: Jeff Nelson, Paul Mills

Business hours are from Monday to Saturday, 9.30-5.30pm. Instruments available include guitars, keyboards, acoustic and digital pianos, brass, woodwind, strings, percussion, synthesisers and accessories. Engineer/technician and catalogue for educational market/ordering facility available.

Matchetts Music

Derek Crowther
Managing Director
6 Wellington Place
Belfast BT1 6GE
Northern Ireland

Tel/Fax: 048 9032 6695/048 9057 2133
Email: matchetts@dnet.uk
Website: www.matchettsmusic.com
Other key staff: Richard McCleary (Shop Manager), Mark Stewart (Sales)

Business hours are from Monday to Wednesday, 9-5.30pm, Thursday, 9-8.30pm, Friday and Saturday, 9-5.30pm. Areas of special interest include printed music, brass and woodwind instruments, orchestral string, folk, acoustic and classical, guitars and musical accessories. Brands available include Vintage, King, Pearl, Lauren and Sandiner (see advert p.289).

Matchetts Music

Neil Crowther
Managing Director
38 Wellington Place
Belfast BT1 6GE
Northern Ireland

Tel/Fax: 048 9057 2142/048 9057 2133
Email: matchetts@dnet.uk
Website: www.matchettsmusic.com
Other key staff: Paul Calvert (Manager), John Moorehead (PA & Recording)

Business hours are from Monday to Wednesday, 9-5.30pm, Thursday, 9-8.30pm, Friday and Saturday, 9-5.30pm. Areas of special interest includes electric and bass guitars, amplifiers, keyboards, drums, percussion and acoustic guitars. Brands include Fender, Warick, Casio, Seagull and Fostex.

Minstrel Music

John Roche
Unit B Wexford Enterprise Centre
Rosslare Road
Wexford

Tel/Fax: +353 53 44105/+353 53 43113

Business hours are from Monday to Wednesday, 2-5.30pm, Friday and Saturday, 11-5pm. Areas of special interest include folk music and bowed instruments. Suppliers of wood and tools for instrument making. Instruments available include the violin family, bows, guitars, mandolins, banjos, harps and accordions. Brands available include Stentro, Antoni, Klier, Johnson, Vega, Ozark, Wildwood and Steiner.

Modern Music

Michael McMahon
Unit 9 Cornstore
Middle Street
Galway

Tel/Fax: +353 91 563113

Business hours are from Monday to Saturday, 10-6pm. Instruments available include guitars, keyboards, drums, PA systems and traditional instruments.

Moloney Musical Instruments

Kieran Moloney
Director
17 High Street
Old Malt Arcade
Galway

Tel/Fax: +353 91 566488/+353 91 565045

Hours of business are from Wednesday to Friday, 10-30-6.30pm and Saturday 10.30-6pm. Instruments available include new and secondhand violins, violas, cellos, bouzoukis, dobros and mandolins. Small range of wind instruments available.

Music Centre

P.J McCreanor
Owner
Midland Cout
Longford

Tel: +353 43 46579
Other key staff: Irene Guckian (Manager)

Business hours are from Monday to Saturday, 10-6.30pm. Instruments available include guitars, keyboards and pianos. Accessories and music books available.

Music Centres

Gary Harvey
Manager
2 Main Street
Letterkenny
Co. Donegal

Tel/Fax: +353 74 23062/+353 74 23126
Website: www.music-centres.com

Business hours are from Monday to Thursday, 10-6pm, Friday, 10-8pm and Saturday, 10-6pm. Instruments available include guitars, bodhráns, books, CDs, tapes and accessories.

Music Express

Colette Casey
Manager
Inishfallen Shopping Mall
Killarney
Co. Kerry

Tel/Fax: +353 64 33077

Business hours are from Monday to Sunday 9am-10.30pm. Instruments available include guitars, violins, accordions, banjos, flutes, pipes, mandolins and bodhráns. Accessories, music books, CDs, tapes, videos also available.

Music Lane Ltd

Dave Lane
Director
Unit 21 Parkway Shopping Centre
Dublin Road
Limerick

Tel/Fax: +353 61 419950
Email: musiclan@iol,ie
Other key staff: Jason Lane (Manager/Buyer)

Business hours are from Monday to wednesday, 9.30-6pm, Thursday and Friday, 9.30am-9.30pm, Saturday, 9.30-6pm and Sunday, 2-6 p.m. Instruments available include guitars, keyboards, drums, bodhráns, tin whistles, harmonicas, books, CDs and tapes, music stands and amplifiers.

Music Maker

Lesley Kane
Manager
29 Exchequer Street
Dublin 2

Tel/Fax: +353 1 6779004/+353 1 6779281
Email: lesley@musicmaker.ie
Website: www.musicmaker.ie
Other key staff: Maeve Duane (Manager), Mark Walsh (Music Maker Express/ Promotion)

Business hours are from Monday to Saturday, 10-6pm. Areas of special interest include electric guitars, keyboards, drums and percussion instruments. Brands available include Pro-Mark, Taylor, Korg and Status.

The Music Room

Fergus Mannion
Manager
Harmony Hill
Sligo

Tel/Fax: +353 71 44765
Email: music@iol.ie

Business hours are from Monday to Saturday, 9.30-6.30pm. Instruments available include keyboards, guitars, percussion, music books, accessories and amplifiers.

The Music Stand

Patrick Farrell
Manager
23 Offaly Street
Athy
Co. Kildare

Tel: +353 507 32265

Business hours are from Monday to Saturday, 10-6pm. Instruments available include guitars, drums, keyboards and whistles. Full range of accessories include music books and microphones. Brands include Marshall and Yamaha.

The Music Store

John Gibbons
Manager
Bridge Street
Castlebar
Co. Mayo

Tel/Fax: +353 94 26166
Other key staff: Pat Gibbons

Business hours are from Monday to Thursday, 10.30-6pm, Friday, 10.30-7pm and Saturday 10.30-6pm. Instruments available include guitars, percussion, keyboards, whistles, bodhráns. Range of accessories and and music books available. Brands available include Marshall, Fender, Gibson and HK Audio.

Music World

Enda McCusker
24 Abbey Lane
Armagh BT61 7DW
Northern Ireland

Tel/Fax: 048 3752 7882
Email: info@musicworldarmagh.com
Website: www.musicworldarmagh.com
Other key staff: Chris Pattison

Business hours are from Monday to Saturday, 9-5.30pm. Instruments and accessories available. Hiring facility.

Musician Inc

Eugene Kavanagh
General Manager
26/27 Drury Street
Dublin 2

Tel/Fax: +353 1 6796048/+353 1 6796049
Email: info@musicianinc.ie
Website: www.clubi.ie/musicianinc
Other key staff: Colin Sullivan (Manager)

Business hours are from Monday to Saturday, 10-6pm. Areas of special interest include guitars and home recording equipment. Instruments available include guitars. Brands available include Fender, Gibson and Lowden. Engineer and technician available. Musical accessories available.

Musician Inc

Colin Little
Manager
56 Lower George's Street
Dun Laoghaire
Co. Dublin

Tel/Fax: +353 1 2300626/+353 1 6796049
Email: info@musicianinc.ie
Website: www.clubi.ie/musicianinc

Business hours are from Monday to Saturday, 10-6pm. All musical instruments for sale. Music books available. Supply to schools.

Navan Music Store

Mark Cahill
Manager
Kennedy Road
Navan
Co. Meath

Tel: +353 46 73173

Business hours are from Monday to Thursday, 9.30-6pm, Friday, 9.30-7.30 and Saturday, 9.30-6pm. Instruments include guitars, keyboards, drums and traditional instruments (accordion, flute and whistle). Amplifiers and PA systems also available. Accessories and music books available.

Onstage Music

Derek Fay
Manager
20 Upper Abbey Street
Dublin 1

Tel: +353 1 8727500

Business hours are from Monday to Saturday, 10-5pm. Instruments available include acoustic and electric guitars, drums and keyboards. Accessories, CDs, tapes and videos available.

Opus II

Michael Nichols
Director
24 South Great Georges Street
Dublin 2

Tel/Fax: +353 1 6778571/+353 1 6798733
Email: opus2@eircom.net
Other key staff: Patricia Nichols (Managing Director), Darren Walsh (Shop Manager)

Business hours are from Monday to Saturday, 9-6pm. Areas of special interest include sheet music, examination music, choral music, popular album and scores, recorders, tin whistles and musical accessories. Provide a selected concert ticket sales service.

John Palmer Music Centre

7 Georges Street
Waterford

Tel: +353 51 879333
Other key staff: Keith McDonald

Business hours are from Monday to Saturday, 10-5.30pm. Instruments available include guitars. Amplifiers and PA systems available. Brands available include Marshall, Laney, Seagull, Martin, Roland and Fender. Hiring facility.

Perfect Pitch

Gerry Crowe
35 Exchequer Street
Dublin 2

Tel/Fax: +353 1 6771553

Business hours are from Monday to Saturday, 10-6pm. Instruments available include guitars, violins and bodhráns. Brands available include Martin, Gibson, Yamaha, Godin, Vintage and Palatino. Bodhráns are by Brendan White, Malachy Kearns. Amplifiers are also sold.

Piano Service Roscommon

Castle Street
Rosommon

Tel: +353 903 26124
Mobile: +353 87 2597414

By appointment. New and secondhand pianos available. Yamaha and Woodchester brands available. Pianos re-conditioned, restored and French polished.

The Piano Studio

Gerry Black
Manager
Monaghan Road
Castleblaney
Co. Monaghan

Tel: +353 42 9746049
Mobile: +353 87 2724949
Other key staff: Paul Black, Michael Black

Business hours are from Monday to Friday, 9.30-6pm and Saturday, 10-6pm. Areas of special interest is pianos - old style, modern and new. Also manufacture church organs and digital pianos. Delivery service. Hiring facility and restoration.

Pianos Plus

Henry Gillanders
99a Rathgar Road
Rathgar
Dublin

Tel/Fax: +353 1 4920767
Email: pianos@pianosplus.ie
Website: www.pianosplus.ie
Other key staff: John Holland (Manager), David Holohan (Accounts)

Business hours are from Monday to Friday, 9.30-5.30 and Saturday, 10-5pm. Area of special interest is pianos. Brands available include Linden, Kawai, Yamaha, Boston, Seiler and Steinway. Hire and delivery service.

P. Powell & Sons

Colm Powell
The Four Corners
53 William Street
Galway

Tel/Fax: +353 91 562295/+353 91 568667
Other key staff: Ann Marie Kavanagh (Music Department Manager)

Business hours are from Monday to Thursday, 9-5.30pm, Friday 9-6pm and Saturday 9-5.30pm. Areas of special interest includes traditional Irish instruments and books. Instruments available include accordions, bagpipes, banjos, bodhráns, clarinets, concertinas, concert flutes, harps, low whistles, mandolins, trumpets and wooden flutes.

PR Music

Ian Bennett
Manager
Dominick Place
Mullingar
Co. Westmeath

Tel/Fax: +353 44 49003

Business hours are Monday and Tuesday, 10.30-6pm, Wednesday, 11-6pm, Thursday, 10.30-6pm, Friday and Saturday, 10.30-7pm. Instruments available include traditional instruments and a range of guitars. Brands available include Gibson, Fendor, Taylor and Squire.

PR Sound

Dorothy Percy
Main Street

Monasterevin
Co. Kildare

Tel: +353 45 525538

Business hours are from 10.30am-9pm. Instruments available include guitars and drums.

Pro Musica Ltd
Jim Madden
Director
20 Oliver Plunkett Street
Cork

Tel/Fax: +353 21 4271659/+353 21 4273780
Other key staff: Eileen Madden (Secretary), Eileen Dennehy (Manager)

Business hours are from Monday to Thursday, 9-5.30pm, Friday, 9-6pm and Saturday, 9-5.30pm. Areas of special interest includes the Suzuki method of education instruments, violins, violas, cellos, basses, brass and woodwind, percussion, keyboards, pianos, guitars also vintage instruments. Sheet music available. Ticketmaster agent.

Rea Sound
Sean Gallagher
Manager
87 Drum Road
Cookstown
Co. Tyrone BT80 8QS
Northern Ireland

Tel/Fax: 048 8676 4059/048 8676 4141
Other key staff: Rodney Stewart (Assistant Manager)

Business hours are from Monday to Saturday, 10-6pm. Instruments available include guitars. PA hire and lighting.

Rea Sound
Martin Bolger
Manager
7 Knockmitten Close
Western Industrial Estate
Naas Road
Dublin 12

Tel/Fax: +353 1 4601600/+353 1 4601604
Other key staff: David Burke

Business hours are from Monday to Saturday, 10-6pm. Instruments available include guitars. PA systems and amplifiers available.

Reynolds Music
Mike Reynolds
Manager
33-35 Castle Street
Omagh
Co. Tyrone BT78 1DD
Northern Ireland

Tel/Fax: 048 8224 5767/048 8225 0251
Email: reymusic@aol.com
Other key staff: John Reynolds (Sales Manager)

Business hours are from Monday to Friday, 9-5.30pm and Saturday, 10-5.30pm. Instruments available include guitars, keyboards, clavinovas and electric pianos. Specialists in band and orchestral instruments. Accessories and tutor books available.

Reynolds of Raphoe
Liam Reynolds
Raphoe
Co. Donegal

Tel/Fax: +353 74 45179/+353 74 45499
Email: ror@iol.ie
Other key staff: Liam Reynolds (Director), Declan Reynolds (Director)

Business hours are from Monday to Saturday (except Wednesdays), 9-6pm. Instruments available include guitars, keyboards, drums, accordions, violins and tin whistles. Music books and accessories available.

Rock Steady Music Ltd
David Callaghan
Managing Director
51 South William St
Dublin 2

Tel/Fax: +353 1 6794253/+353 1 6794257
Email: rocksteadymusic@hotmail.com
Other key staff: Colin Goodall (Sales Manager), Graham Bolger (Sales Manager)

Business hours are from Monday to Saturday, 10-6pm.

Instruments available include acoustic, electric and bass guitars, drums and percussion, keyboards, recording and studio equipment.

Roland Ireland
Enda Quealy
Internal Sales Manager
Audio House
No 2 Belmont Court
Dublin 4

Tel/Fax: +353 1 2603501/+353 1 2602026
Email: sfactor@rolandireland.com or info@rolandireland.co
Website: www.rolandireland.com
Other key staff: Gerry Forde (Managing Director), Ger Hughes (Service & Technical Support)

Trade suppliers of Roland, Datasonics and Boss throughout Ireland. Supplies recording and sequencing software.

Russell's Music
Bill Russell
27 Parnell Place
Cork

Tel/Fax: +353 21 4273912
Email: rusmusic@indigo.ie
Other key staff: P. McCarthy (Sales Manager), A. Russell (Accountant)

Business hours are from Monday to Saturday, 10-5.30pm. Areas of special interest includes guitars, amplifiers and accessories. Brands available include Fender, Korg, Yorkville and Marshall.

Ciarán Ryan Piano Services
Doise Lacháin Thior
Na Forbach
Co. Na Gallimhe

Tel/Fax: +353 91 553567

Business hours are by appointment from Monday to Sunday. Hire of grand pianos and piano restoration.

Paul Ryan Woodwind & Brass
Paul Ryan
Friends Meeting House
4 Eustace Street
Temple Bar
Dublin 2

Tel/Fax: +353 1 6798571/+353 1 6790464
Email: ryanpaul@iol.ie
Other key staff: Shay Cantwell (Financial Controller)

Sales of woodwind and brass musical instruments and accessories. Rental programme for student instruments. Main dealer for Arbiter and Yanagisawa saxophones. Also suppliers for Buffet, BG, Bam, Glotin, Keilwerth, Leblanc, Selmer, Vandoren and Yamaha. (see advert p.299).

Saltarelle Accordions
Sietske O'Connor
Annadown Pier
Annadown
Co. Galway

Tel/Fax: +353 91 791474
Email: moco@eircom.net

Area of special interest is accordion sales. Brands available include Bouebe, Connemara 2, Nuage and Tara.

Savins Music Centre
Brian O'Grady
Manager
111 O'Connell Street
Limerick

Tel/Fax: +353 61 414095/+353 61 412674

Business hours are from Monday to Saturday, 9-5.30pm. Instruments available include keyboards, guitars, violins, bodhráns, recorders, tin whistles and mouth organs.

Sensible Music
John Munnis
Director
8 Hanover Quay
Dublin 2

Tel/Fax: +353 1 6715530/+353 1 6793896

Email: info@sensiblemusic.ie
Website: www.sensiblemusic.ie
Other key staff: Mark Kennedy (Director), Greg Ryan (Hire Manager)

Business hours are from Monday to Saturday and Sunday (by appointment). Instruments available include drums, percussion, keyboards, hammond organs and recording equipment. Brands available include Otari, LA Audio Pro and Amek.

Session Music
Alan McGowan
Manager
155-157 Donegall Pass
Belfast BT7 1DT
Northern Ireland

Tel/Fax: 048 9023 8502/048 9031 1979

Business hours are from Monday to Saturday. Instruments available include guitars, PA, keyboards, drums and 'backline' instruments. Musical instruments and tutor books available.

Shellys Musical Instruments
Elizabeth Shelly
Unit 4 Hanover Street
Kennedy Avenue
Carlow

Tel/Fax: +353 503 42771

Business hours are from Monday to Thursday, 9-5.30pm, Friday, 9-6pm and Saturday, 9-6pm. Instruments available include keyboards, banjos, mandolins, violins, whistles and recorders. Music books and available.

Shortall Pianos
John Shortall
The Valley
Co. Tipperary

Tel: +353 52 31175
Mobile: +353 86 8582450

By appointment. Piano sales (upright and grand), repairs and restoration services.

Siopa An Phíobaire
Cillian Ó Brianin
Manager
Ceardlann Na Coille
Dingle
Co. Kerry

Tel/Fax: +353 66 9151778/+353 66 9151918
Other key staff: Mauric Reviol, Greg Mac Sheáin

Business hours are from Monday to Saturday. Stock and manufacture uillean pipes, bags and bellows and individually voiced tin whistles in the key of D.

Sound Shop
Tommy Leddy
Manager
11 Mayoralty House
North Quay
Drogheda
Co. Louth

Tel: +353 41 9831078/+353 41 9834977
Email: soundshop@indigo.ie
Website: www.soundshop.ie
Other key staff: Rhona Connor (Secretary)

Business hours are from Monday to Thursday, 9.30-6pm, Friday, 9.30-9pm and Saturday, 9.30-6pm. Instruments available include drums, guitars, violins and traditional instruments. Accessories, CDs, tapes and music books available. Agents for Gem keyboards. (see advert p.299)

Soundwaves
Ger Ryan
Shannon Town Centre
Shannon
Co. Clare

Tel: +353 61 362627

Business hours are from Monday to Wednesday, 9.30-6pm, Thursday, 10.15-7.30pm, Friday, 9.30-8pm and Saturday, 9.30-6pm Instruments available include bodhráns and guitars. PA hire service.

Sugrues Furniture & Pianos
Peter Sugrue
Managing Director
24 O'Brien Street

Mallow
Co. Cork

Tel/Fax: +353 22 22101/+353 22 21435

Business hours are from Monday to Sunday, 9.30-6pm. Instruments available includes pianos, tin whistles, guitars, harmonicas, recorders and accessories. Pianos repaired and restored.

Tallaght Music Centre
Unit 5 Village Green Centre
Tallaght Village
Dublin 24

Tel/Fax: +353 1 4610923

Business hours are from Monday to Sunday. Instruments available include electric, acoustic and bass guitars, keyboards, drums and wind instruments. Full range of accessories and music books. (see advert p.304)

Thornton Pianos
Adrian, Desmond & Jeffrey Thornton
7 Berkley Road
Phibsboro
Dublin 7

Tel/Fax: +353 1 8305223

Business hours are from Monday to Friday, 8-5pm and Saturday, 9-4pm. Established in 1968. Piano restoration service for upright and grand pianos - cabinet repairs, french polishing and mechanical overhaul. Piano evaluations. Delivery service available.

Tughan Crane Music Ltd
Noel Graham
Director
45 Fountain Street
Belfast BT1 5CU
Northern Ireland

Tel/Fax: 048 9032 9034/048 9023 8740

Areas of special interest includes church organs, sheet music, stringed instruments, keyboards, guitars, pianos and digital pianos. Brands available include Kawai, Yamaha, Roland and Lowrey.

Tullamore Sound & Music Centre
Carmel Cahill
Manager
Harbour Street
Tullamore
Co. Offaly

Tel/Fax: +353 506 51575/+353 506 54870
Other key staff: Darren Cahill (Proprietor)

Business hours are from Tuesday to Saturday, 10-6pm. Instruments include acoustic and electric guitars, violins, percussion, keyboards, tin whistles and bodhráns. Accessories and music books available. Amplifiers and lighting available.

Tuohy Pianos
Martin Tuohy
Unit 2 Addley Park
Liosbán
Tuam Road
Galway

Tel/Fax: +353 91 778266

Hours in business are from Monday to Friday, 9.30-5.30pm and Saturday, 9.30-5pm. Area of special interest is pianos, acoustic and digital pianos. Re-conditioning service offered.

Tynan Pianos
Andrew Tynan
Blackberry Lane
Lower Rathmines Road
Dublin 6

Tel/Fax: +353 1 4977807 or +353 1 4963587/ +353 1 4965369

Hours of business are from Monday to Saturday, 9-6pm. Sales of new and secondhand upright and grand pianos. Hiring and technical services available.

Variety Sounds
Pat & Breda O' Conor
7 College St
Killarney
Co. Kerry

Tel/Fax: +353 64 35755/+353 64 33155
Email: kerrypc@iol.ie

Other key staff: Tony O'Flaherty (Sales Manager)

Business hours are from Monday to Saturday, 9-6pm and Sunday, 12-6pm. Areas of special interest include Irish and Celtic instruments. Instruments available include guitars, banjos, keyboards, whistles, mandolins, bouzoukis, bodhráns, accordions, accordions, harmonicas, violins and celtic wooden spoons. Brands available include Yamaha, Tanglewood and Hohner.

Waltons World of Music

Fran Long
Manager
69-70 South Great George's Street
Dublin 2

Tel/Fax: +353 1 4750661/+353 1 4751346
Other key staff: Conor Long (Retail Sales Manager), David Burns (Assistant Manager)

Business hours are from Monday to Saturday, 9-5.30pm. Areas of special interest include pianos, digital pianos, keyboards, home recording, electric and acoustic guitars, amplifiers and percussion, folk instruments, brass and wind, accessories, music books and music education materials. Brands available include Yamaha, Roland and Gibson. Telesales service. (see advert)

Waltons World of Music

Andrew Radley
Manager
2-5 North Frederick Street
Dublin 1

Tel/Fax: +353 1 8747805/+353 1 8786065
Other key staff: Conor Long (Retail Sales Manager), Maurice Brennan (Assistant Manager)

Business hours are from Monday to Saturday, 9-5.30pm. Areas of special interest include pianos, digital pianos, keyboards, home recording, electric and acoustic guitars, amplifiers and percussion, folk instruments, brass and wind, accessories, music books and music education materials. Brands available include Yamaha, Roland and Gibson. Telesales service. (see advert)

Waltons World of Music
Head Office

Niall Walton
Managing Director

Units 6b-6c Rosemount Park Drive
Rosemount Business Park
Ballycoolin
Dublin 11

Tel/Fax: +353 1 8207425/+353 1 8207426
Email: waltons@indigo.ie
Other key staff: David Walton (Marketing Manager)

Business hours are from Monday to Friday, 9-6.30pm. Agents in Ireland for Gibson and Epiphone guitars, Premier percussion and Dunlop accessories. Retailers and musical instrument import and distribution.

Ward's Music Shop

Paddy Ward
Manager
Castle Street
Donegal

Tel: +353 73 21313/+353 73 21334

Business hours are from Monday to Friday, 10-6pm, closed Wednesday, Saturday, 10-7pm. Instruments available include bodhráns, guitars, violins, mandolins, banjos, accordions, harmonicas, drum kits, bouzoukis, recorders and concertinas. Brands available include Marshall, Tambo, Kimbara, Trace Elliot and Parrot. Large selection of traditional and modern music books. Accordion repairs, re-stringing and tuning of all string instruments.

Wilkinson Musical Instruments

Hugh Wilkinson
101 Main Street
Cullybackey
Co. Antrim BT42 1BW
Northern Ireland

Tel/Fax: 048 2825 881065

Business hours are from Monday to Friday, 9.30-5pm, closed Wednesday, Saturday, 9.30-4pm. Areas of special interest include accordions, drums and accessories, flutes, violins and recorders. Brands available include Hohner, Bugari, Guerrin and Dallape.

PIANO TUNERS

James Bevan
11 Brandon Terrace
Belfast BT4 1JF
Northern Ireland

Tel: 048 9065 0163

Pianos sold, tuned, repaired and restored.

Mark Cambell
26 Knockeden Park
Belfast BT6 OJF
Northern Ireland

Tel: 048 9064 1830

Tuning, repair and restoration (for the workings rather than the cabinet) on upright and grand pianos, fortepianos and harpsichords).

C. Cantwell
Pond Villas
Tramore
Co. Waterford

Tel: +353 51 381410

Pianos tuned and repaired.

Ronalo Cartin
15 Lower Drumcondra Road
Dublin 9

Tel: +353 87 2323602

Pianos tuned and minor repairs performed.

Deady Pianos
David Deady
John Player Houes
286 South Circular Road
Dublin 8

Tel/Fax: +353 1 4732673/+353 1 4732653
Email: dea@eircom.net

Grand and upright pianos tuned, repaired and re-built. Also provide a voicing and regulation service.

Griffin Pianos
William Griffin
Manager
Showrooms
Greenwood Estate
Togher
Co. Cork

Tel/Fax: +353 21 4964773/+353 21 4313700
Other key staff: Conor Griffin (Concert Tuner), Barry Scannell (Consultant Technician)

Pianos tuned, repaired and re-built.

Hance Piano Services
W. S Hance
Director
19 Westway Crescent
Belfast BT13 3NU
Northern Ireland

Tel: 048 9071 8324

Upright and grand pianos restored, tuned and keyboards re-covered. Also provides re-stringing for pianos.

Holland Piano Limited
Alex Holland
Director
29 Monacurragh
Carlow

Tel: +353 503 31177
Other key staff: Sandra Holland (Piano Tuner), Liam Quinn (Piano Technician)

Business hours are from Monday to Saturday, 10-8pm, Sundays by appointment only. Provides piano sales, tuning, hire, moving, restoration and evaluations.

Jeffers of Bandon Ltd
Alex Jeffers
Director
Unit 2
Cloughmacsimon
Bandon
Co. Cork

Tel/Fax: +353 23 44332/+353 23 44890
Email: pianos@jeffersmusic.ie
Website: www.jeffersmusic.ie

Other key staff: Johnathan Smyth (Piano Technician & Tuner), Gillian Smyth (Information Department)

Piano sales, tuning, re-conditioning, hire, moving, advisory service, re-polishing, piano stools and evaluations. (see advert p.282).

Killeen Piano Services

Patrick Killeen
Liberty Stream
Ballygarvan
Co. Cork

Tel: +353 21 888445
Email: organs@indigo.ie

Pipe organs rebuilt and relocated. Upright and grand pianos tuned, repaired and rebuilt.

Feena Lynch

296 South Circular Road
Dublin 8

Tel: +353 1 4530561
Mobile: +353 87 2251791

Piano tuning, evaluations and repairs service.

C. McGlade

Rear 14 St. Catherine's Avenue
South Circular Road
Dublin 8

Tel: +353 1 4542600

Services offered include tuning and repairs to upright and grand pianos, nationwide. Pianos supplied, new and fully reconditioned. Formerly employed by McCullough Piggotts.

Tim Manly Piano Tuning and Repairs

Tim Manly
7 Pineview Heights
Gilford
Co. Armagh BT63 6AX
Northern Ireland

Tel: 048 3883 1755
Email: tim.manly@tesco.net

Services offered include piano tuning, restoration, ivory keyboard repairs and piano sales advice.

Steven William Armstrong Maxwell

6 Helens Drive
Aghalee
Co. Armagh BT67 OHE
Northern Ireland

Tel: 048 9265 1530

Business hours are from Monday to Friday, 9-5pm, or by appointment. Pianos tuned and repaired.

Moloney Pianos

Peter Moloney
Manager
Unit 12 Midleton Enterprise Park
Dwyers Road
Midleton
Co. Cork

Tel: +353 21 4632633
Other key staff: Aíne Byrne (Technician), P. Coady (French Polisher)

Services offered include tuning, repairs, restoration, hire, moving, rebuilding and refinishing. Also offer and advisory service.

Jack O'Byrne

26 Hazelwood Park
Artane
Dublin 5

Tel: +353 1 8474215
Email: jackobyrne@oceanfree.net

Services available include tuning of pianos (upright and grand), American reed organs and harmoniums. Formerly employed by McCullough Pigotts. Areas covered includes Dublin and County Kildare, Louth, Meath, Monaghan, Cavan, Westmeath, Longford, North Offaly and East Leitrim and Roscommon.

Piano Service

Castle Street
Roscommon

Tel: +353 903 23124
Mobile: +353 87 2597414

By appointment. Services available include piano tuning, repairing, reconditioning, rebuilding, restoring and French polishing.

Pianos Plus
John Holland
Manager
99a Rathgar Road
Dublin 6

Tel/Fax: +353 1 4920767/+353 1 4920768
Email: pianos@pianosplus.ie
Website: www.pianosplus.ie
Other key staff: Martin Walsh (Piano Technician), Chris Jackson (Piano Technician)

Services available include piano tuning, voicing, regulation and repairing.

Brendan Prendergast
40 Heatherview Road
Aylesbury
Tallaght
Dublin 24

Tel: +353 1 4519184
Mobile: +353 87 2486933

Services available include piano tuning, repairing, sales, reconditioning. Evaluation service also offered.

R.J Piano Services
Rory Clements
Managing Director
12 Windsor Avenue
Limavady
Co. Derry BT49 0DA
Northern Ireland

Tel: 048 7776 2979 or 048 7776 4842

Services available include tuning, voicing and regulation. Pianos repaired, reconditioned, rebuilt, restored and polished.

John M. Redmond
208 Elm Mount Avenue
Beaumont
Dublin 9

Tel: +353 1 8311990

Business hours are from Monday to Saturday, 9-7pm. Pianos tuned, repaired and restored. Two tuners available at all times.

Kevin A. Redmond
72 Watson Drive
Killiney
Co. Dublin

Tel: +353 1 2853792

Pianos tuned, repaired and reconditioned.

Bernard Rosenberg
10 Bangor Road
Holywood
Co. Down

Tel: 048 9042 8796

Pianos prepared for professional recording, concerts, broadcasting and domestic use.

Ciarán Ryan Piano Services
Doise Locháin Thior
Na Forbacha
Co. Na Gallimhe

Tel/Fax: +353 91 553567

Services available include piano tuning, repairs, assessments, restoration and hire.

Shortall Pianos
The Valley
Fethard
Co. Tipperary

Tel: +353 52 31175

Upright and grand pianos tuned, repaired and restored.

Sugrues Furniture and Pianos
Richard Mulcahy
24 O'Brien Street
Mallow
Co. Cork

Tel/Fax: +353 22 22101/+353 22 21435

Services available include tuning, repairs and sales.

Thornburgh Piano Service

Rob Thornburgh
Carracanada
Swinford
Co. Mayo

Tel: +353 94 51955

Services available include piano tuning, repairs, reconditioning. Fully reconditioned pianos for sale.

Tuohy Pianos

Martin Tuohy
Unit 2 Addley Park
Liosraun Industrial Estate
Tuam Road
Galway

Tel/Fax: +353 91 778266

Upright and grand pianos tuned and repaired.

Paul Wade

64 Wyattville Park
Loughlinstown
Co. Dublin

Tel: +353 1 2826541
Mobile: +353 86 8115791

Services available include tuning, preparation of pianos for concerts, recitals, recording and technical advice in all areas of piano maintenance. Tuner for the National Concert Hall, National Symphony of Ireland, Windmill Lane Studios, Opera Theatre Company and Music for Galway.

Anthony and Fergus Woods

15 Parkhill Avenue
Kilnamanagh
Dublin 24

Tel: +353 1 4599556
Mobile: +353 87 2246398

Pianos repaired, reconditioned, polished and restored. Evaluations and estimations offered.

Waltons World of Music

Fergus Woods
69-70 South Georges Street
Dublin 2
or
2-5 North Frederick Street
Dublin 1

Tel: +353 1 4547684 or +353 1 4750661

Services available include piano tuning, repair and evaluation. (see advert)

RECORDING & PRACTICE FACILITIES

Denis Allen Studios

Denis Allen
Studio Manager
Mill Road
Ros Brien
Limerick

Tel: +353 61 229283
Email: denallen@eircom.net

Flexible opening hours. Facilities include a 16 track soundcraft console, linkable to 8 track on hard disk giving 24 tracks in total. Steinway piano and Yamaha QY700 sequencer linked into midi programme in computer.

Applerock Rehearsal Studios

Dermot Goggins
Managing Director
17-21 Foley Stret
Dublin 1

Tel/Fax: +353 1 8364400
Email: applerock@clubi.ie

Hours of business are from Monday to Sunday. Facilities include 6 sound treated rehearsal rooms with 1 drum room. Backline brands available, which include Marshall, Fender, Trace Elliott, Yamaha and Studiomaster. Equipment packages and block booking rates available on request.

The Barn

Andrew Malcolm
Manager
The Barn
Carrignagour
Lismore
Co. Waterford

Tel: +353 58 54610
Email: hepatitis@eircom.net

Hours of business are from Monday to Sunday, 10-10pm. Facilities include a Tasem 8 track Portastudio (488 MK 2), 8 track Guillemot 1515 computer, mastering onto CD-R or DAT, Shure SM588 and AKG C10005 microphones and Spirit Folio Life mixing desk.

Best Cellars Music Collective

Janice Gordon-Stockman
Development Officer
Ballybeen Activity Centre
Dundonald
Belfast BT16 2QE
Northern Ireland

Tel/Fax: 048 9048 6290
Email: bestcellars@ukgateway.net
Website: www.bestcellars.ukgateway.net
Other key staff: Margaret Chambers (Administrator), Dave McCullough (Recording Technician)

Hours of business are from Monday to Friday, 8.30-5pm, Saturday and Sunday as required. Facilities include a 24 track digital recording system (DC 2000 Soundcraft Desk) with effects units and cd writter, range of microphones, video suite which contains a digital camera and editing suite, PA hire and a rehearsal room with amplifiers and drum kit.

Blarney Recording Studio

David Murphy
'Dunleary'
Waterloo Road
Blarney
Co. Cork

Tel: +353 21 381457

Hours of business are flexible. Facilities include a 16 track digital studio, digital piano, Roland synthesizers, Alesis drum machines, Cubase computer system, Beringan desk with various effects. Producer/arranger available, mastering to DAT, CD and cassette.

Blast Furnace Studios

Rory Donaghy
Manager
Foyle Arts Centre
Lawrence Hill
Derry City
Northern Ireland

Tel/Fax: 048 7137 7870

Hours of business are from Monday to Sunday. Facilities include a DDA DUIR12 56 channel desk with 32 track of pro-tools/ logic audio and 24 tracks of ADAT, outboard by Lexicon and focusrite, Newman, Beyer and Rode microphones.

CEL Sound

Paddy Gilsenan
Production Manager
Radio Centre
RTÉ
Donnybrook
Dublin 4

Tel/Fax: +353 1 2082165/+353 1 2082793
Email: celstud@rte.ie
Website: www.rte.ie
Other key staff: Sean Cooney (Marketing &
Production Executive), John Grimes (Engineer)

Available on request. Facilities include a 24 track surround sound, all digital post-production, Beta SP and
Digi-Beta, Fairlight Fsme MFX Plus. Large music and
drama studio.

Ceol Puca Teo

Klaus Muller
Manager
Kingsriver Cottage
Co. Wicklow

Tel/Fax: +353 45 867364/+353 45 867374

By appointment only. Facilities include a 1 inch Doly S
24 track analogue desk.

City Arts Centre

John Lawlor
Studios Manager
23-25 Moss Street
Dublin 2

Tel/Fax: +353 1 6770643/+353 6770131

Disk Finder Studio

Joe Conway
Claremont Grove
Killiney
Co. Dublin

Tel/Fax: +353 1 2856392/+353 1 8454082

Hours of business are from Monday to Friday, 9-5.30pm.
Facilities include studio for narration, commercial and
editing, facility for media courses involving radio pro-

duction and studio operational techniques, library of
music and effects. Provides a wide range of music and
comedy programmes for radio stations.

Elecktra Studios

Oran Burns
Studio Manager
8 Crow Street
Temple Bar
Dublin 2

Tel/Fax: +353 1 6777134/+353 1 6791968
Other key staff: Canice Mills (Studio Engineer)

Business hours are from Monday to Sunday, 10am-
10.30pm. Facilities include a 16 track studio, Soundcraft
6000 24 channel console, Fostex 616 1/2 inch tape
machine (with dolby sound), live room, range of microphones, Steinberg and Cubase sequencer.

The Factory Studios

Terri Bones
Manager
35a Barrow Street
Dublin 4

Tel/Fax: +353 1 6684966/+353 1 6684859
Email: mail@thefactory.org
Website: www.thefactory.org
Other key staff: Eric Humphreys (Studio/
Technical Manager)

Hours of business are from Monday to Friday, 10-9pm
and Saturday and Sunday by request. Facilities include 3
daylight rehearsal rooms (70 ft x 40 ft), full PA and
monitor systems and 2 dance studios.

Firhouse Studios

Joseph Lahart
5 Carriglea View
Firhouse
Dublin 24

Tel/Fax: +353 1 4516748
Email: caruso@oceanfree.com

Hours of business are from Monday to Friday, 10-10pm
and Saturday and Sunday by appointment. Facilities
include 8 track digital recording or analogue, Cubase
VST or Logic Platinum sequencers for Midi producers
and sessions musicians and pre-production.

Green Dolphin Studios
Patrick Dalgety
Manager
7 Donegall Street Place
Belfast BT1 2FN
Northern Ireland

Tel/Fax: 048 9032 3767/048 9031 5055
Email: green.dolphin@dnet.co.uk
Other key staff: Alison Belshaw (Studio Administrator)

Business hours are flexible. Facilities include 2 control rooms, 2 live rooms and a vox box for overdubs .

Greenfields Studios
Gerald O'Donoghue
Claran
Ower
Co. Galway

Tel: +353 93 35440
Email: geraldod@boinet.ie

Hours of business are from Monday to Friday, Saturday and Sunday by appointment. Facilities include a 32 track digital tudio with Pro-tools, new mastering suite, Focusrite equipment, compressors, Lexicons, Yamaha and Alesis and full range of TDM plug-ins.

The Grove Studio
Louis Bourgoyne
Baylough
Athlone
Co. Westmeath

Tel: +353 902 75431
Other key staff: Bobby Hewitt

Hours of business are flexible. Facilities include a 16 track digital recording studio and rehearsal space. All backline instruments provided (PA, bass, guitars and keyboards).

High Nellie Studios
Steve Pawsey
Director
Kilkeran
Catlefreke
Clonakilty
Co. Cork

Tel: +353 23 40861
Website: www.aardvark.ie/zeitgeist

Hours of business are from Tuesday to Sunday. Facilities include sound and vision production company, digital recording and experimental recording equipment. Record company name is Eirenicon.

The House of Music Ltd
John Christie Willot
Chief Producer
3 Easons Avenue
Cork

Tel/Fax: +353 21 4509612
Email: homusic@eircom.net
Website: www.homusic.com

Facilities include studio and mobile recording for digital recording from chamber music to opera, 24 bit digital recording for CD, DVD and broadcasting, digital editing and mastering and CD manufacturing.

Keystone Studios
Brendan Hayes
Rear 22
St. Stephens Green
Dublin 2

Tel/Fax: +353 1 6761503/+353 1 6613948
Email: keystonestudio@eircom.net
Other key staff: Ken Kieran (Producer), Debbie Smyth (Engineer)

Hours of business are from Monday to Saturday, 9-11pm. Facilities include 2 studios. Studio 1 contains a 24 track digital Pro-tools recording system and studio 2 contains a 24 track digital recording system.

Lake Recording Studio and Mobile Recording Studio Unit

Liam Cunningham
Manager
Drumsillagh
Cootehill
Boyle
Co. Roscommon

Tel/Fax: +353 79 67055
Mobile: +353 86 8367055
Email: lake@esatclear.ie

Hours of business are from Monday to Sunday. Facilities include 24 track analogue, 8 track digital recording facility, acoustic room, live rooms, vocal booth and control room, equipment includes: Neuman U87, microphone plus AKGs, Beyers and Shures, Sony B7 Multi-fx and Quadra-verb, art Multi-fix and Drawmer compressors.

L G Studios

Larry Keogh
Director
Cahanagh
Longford

Tel/Fax: +353 43 47689
Email: lgstulk@iol.ie
Website: www.iol.ie/~lgstulk
Other key staff: Paul Gurney (Engineer)

Hours of business are from Monday to Sunday. Facilities include DDA QMR 12 desk, hard disk recording to Akai and Digital performer, mastering to Tascam DA30 11, monitors are Yamaha NS10 and JBL, outboards are from Focusrite, Drawmer, Alesis, Lexicon, Antares, Autotune, Behringer BBE and Midi set up includes Apple Mac running Digital performer with various sound modules.

Lightwater Studios

Des Mahon
Ballyfinogue
Killinick
Co. Wexford

Tel: +353 53 58986
Mobile: +353 87 2907151

Hours of business are from Monday to Sunday, 10-6pm. Facilities include Soundtracs Topez 24-8-2-24 desk, 24

track ADAT, Bose monitors, drum kit Pearl export, piano, CDR master and mini disc.

Lime Street Sound

Steve McGrath
Director
4 Windmill Lane
Dublin 2

Tel/Fax: +353 1 6717271/+353 1 6707639
Email: limesound@eircom.net
Website: www.limesound.com
Other key staff: Terry Cromer (Sound Designer)

Hours of business are from Monday to Friday, 10-7pm. Facilities include Pro-tools digital recording system, 4 studios with dolby surround sound, post-production sound design, sound restoration, Beta SP, DA88, Timecode DAT, Minidisc, ADAT, 1/4 inch Centre Timecode machines, CD pre-mastering and multi-media audio production.

New Mills Sound Studio

Percy Robinson
Glendooen
New Mills
Letterkenny
Co. Donegal

Tel: +353 74 24456
Email: glendoon@indigo.ie

Hours of business are from Monday to Sunday, 10-10pm. Facilities include 16 track analogue recording system, sound insulated playing areas, collection of Fender vintage amplifiers and digital sampled weighted action piano.

Nova Tech Studio

Gary Aiken
122 Hyde Park Road
Mallusk
Newtownabbey
Co. Antrim BT36 4PZ
Northern Ireland

Tel: 048 9083 8981
Email: gary_aiken@hotmail.com

Business hours are from Monday to Sunday. Facilities

include 32 track digital and automated Soundcraft console, Pro-tool 111, mastering onto DAT and CDR, large recording area, large midi set up, digital editing and mastering, 16 track analogue, collection of amplifiers, pop video production with digital video editing.

Ewan O'Doherty

Audio Engineer
35 Kenilworth Park
Harolds Cross
Dublin 6W

Tel: +353 1 4923616
Email: eodoherty@tcd.ie

Business hours are flexible. Location and live recording of orchestral, chamber, organ, vocal, choral, jazz, traditional anad other acoustic music. AKG C414, AKG C451, Neumann U87 microphones and Soundcraft Spirit Portfolio recording system.

OFI Recording Studio

Regal House
Fitzwilliam Street
Ringsend
Dublin 4

Tel/Fax: +353 1 6609628/+353 1 6609086

Hours of business are flexible. Facilities include a 24 track analogue and 32 track digital tape machine, television room.

Pats Tracks

Billy Donegan
Manager
Causeway
Co. Kerry

Tel/Fax: +353 66 7131170
Email: pats@esatclear.ie
Other key staff: Patrick Donegan (Producer/Engineer)

Hours of business are from Monday to Saturday. Facilities include 16 track Tascam analogue and 16 track digital system, DAT and CDR mastering, video facilities and music publishing and AKAI sampler.

Pine Valley Studio

Joe O'Dubhghaill
Manager
Ballyvalley
Killaloe
Co. Clare
Tel/Fax: +353 61 376459
Mobile: +353 87 2677523

Hours of business are by appointment. Facilities include location recording, digital recording, mastering and editing, sound effect library, audio post-production and tv/film soundtracks/jingles.

Salt Recording Studios

Frank Kearns
12a Dublin Road
Dublin 13

Tel/Fax: +353 1 8395969/+353 1 8324430
Mobile: +353 87 2765754
Email: frankkearns@hotmail.com

Hours of business are by appointment. Facilities include a 24 track analogue 2 inch recording studio. Also runs an introduction course and rock school for young bands.

Sensible Music

John Munnis
Director
Fortescue Lane
Mount Pleasant Avenue
Rathmines
Dublin 6

Tel/Fax: +353 1 4970661/+353 1 4970635
Email: info@sensiblemusic.ie
Website: //sensiblemusic.ie
Other key staff: Greg Ryan (Manager)

Hours of business are from Monday to Saturday. Location recording specialists. Facilities include 8-48 tracks on Adat, Tascam, Otari Radar Digital, Otari 24 track analogue, Pro-tools 24, Otari and Amek Consoles, Yamaha, Alesis and Meyer monitors, Focusrite reds and splitters available. Microphones by B&K, Neumann, AKG, Beyer and Audio Technica. Full crew and transport available.

Share Arts Arena

Dawn Latimer
Share Holiday Village
Co. Fermanagh BT92 0EQ
Northern Ireland

Email: share@dnet.co.uk
Website: www.sharevillage.org
Other key staff: Declan Campbell (Arts Development Worker), Aine Weir (Art Development Worker)

Hours of business are from Monday to Sunday. Facilities include a practice area which provides PA equipment, theatre lighting, large screen projection and a voice enhancement sound system, 10 channel mising desk, 5 x Byerdynamic misc and stands, Allen & Heath 10 mic input amplifier, Gooseneck microphone, VHF Tie clip radio mic, portable mic input Carlsboro amplifier, 2 x Motorolla radio communication handsets, Yamaha synthesiser, drum kit, general percussion instruments and piano also available.

Solitaire Recording Studio Ltd

Alan Whelan
Managing Director
45 Swiftbrook Drive
Tallaght
Dublin 24

Tel/Fax: +353 1 4625544/+353 1 4625545
Mobile: +353 86 2611655
Email: alanw@gofree.indigo.ie

Facilities include Yamaha 02R mixing console, 24 track of 20 Bit Adat digital recorders, Tl Audio valve mice, pre-amplifiers, Tl Audio valve compressors, Tl Audio valve parametric eq's, DBX compressors, Neumann, Earthworks and Audio technica microphones, 24 bit Dat mastering, performer sequencing, Akai S-2000 sampler, Korg Trinity and Fatar weighted keyboards.

The Songworks (formerly The Songwriters Workshop)

Tom Byrne
Director
Unit 6
3 Hanover Street East
Dublin 2

Tel/Fax: +353 1 6793880/+353 1 6793876

Email: songworks@esatclear.ie
Website: www.thesongworks.com
Other key staff: Colin Turner (Joint Managing Director)

Hours of business are from Monday to Friday, 10-5.30pm. Facilities include 24 track digital recording studio, Cubase VST, Wavelab, EMV audio production studio. selection of instruments, large control room, VOX booth, live room, mircrophones by AKG, Beyer and Shure and producer available.

Studio na Life

Fionnula MacAodha
Station Manager
Raidio na Life
Bord na Gaeilge
7 Cearnóg Mhurfean
Baile Átha Cliath

Tel/Fax: +353 1 6616333/+353 1 6763966
Website: www.rnl102@iol.ie

Facilities include a 32 track recording studio consisting of 24 track analogue and 8 track digital recording systems.

Studio 1

Dick Murphy
Lacken Road
Kilbarrow
Waterford

Tel/Fax: +353 51 372014/+353 51 372088
Email: murcowfd@eircom.net

Facilities include a Tascam 24 track desk, 16 track Tascam reel-to-reel to Dat or cassette, sound proof recording room, piano, keyboard, Fender precision bass, Gibson studion guitar, Fender Mustang electric guitar, hand made precision studio, Landole acoustic guitar, selection of microphones, effects units and session musicians available if requested.

Studio 8 Track

Manager
Lower Glenbane
Holycross
Thurles
Co.Tipperary

Tel: +353 504 43349
Email: system7@eircom.net
Other key staff: Jim Fanning (Engineer),
Brian Corbett (Engineer)

Hours of business are from Monday to Saturday.
Facilities include a large purpose built live room, full
backline system, PA system, drums, amplifiers and
effects, can produce demos from cassettes, multi-track
or live recording, cd recording, mastering, DAT and
session musicians available.

Studio Fiona Ltd
Brian O'Reilly
Allens Walk
Fermoy
Co. Cork

Tel/Fax: +353 25 31309
Email: stfiona@indigo.ie

Business hours are from Monday to Saturday, 10-10pm.
Facilities include a studio room, control room, drum
booth, vocal booth, automated digital desk with 48
track, Bechstein Budoir grand piano, 16 track 2 inch
analogue, 24 track digital live end dead end areas, 24
track midi and modules, CDR facility, digital editing,
effect and reverbs, AKG, Sennheiser and Geffel mics,
full production and arrangement available.

Sun Recording Studio
Denis Lovett
Studio Manager
8 Crow Street
Temple Bar
Dublin 2

Tel/Fax: +353 1 6777255/+353 1 6791968
Email: sun_studios@hotmail.com
Other key staff: Pat Downe (Producer/Engineer),
Denis Buckley (House Engineer)

Business hours are from Monday to Friday, 10-6pm.
Facilities include an Amek Einstein Supper E 40 channel
console, Saturn 824 2 inch tape machine, 24 track great
live rooms, vocal booth, upright piano, full backline for
hire, Neumann, Shure, Beyer and B&K microphones, Dat
mastering, editing on request, Focusrite and Neve pre
amplifiers.

Sun Street Studio
Ken Ralph
Engineer
Sun Street
Tuam
Co. Galway

Tel: +353 93 28296

Hours of business are flexible. Facilities include Yamaha
02R digital console with total recall and automated
mixing, 3 Adat x T's for 24 track digital recording, Neve
Vintage microphones amplifiers, UREI 1176's, outboard
by Drawmer, Lexicon, Allesis, Dynacord, digital mastering, Tascam DA 30 Mk 11 and Sony control room, 3
recording rooms.

Temple Bar Music Centre - Digi-8
Greg O'Hanlon
Studio Manager
Curved Street
Temple Bar
Dublin 2

Tel/Fax: +353 1 6709033/+353 1 6709042
Email: greg@tbmusic-centre.ie
Website: www.tbmusic-centre.ie

Facilities include digi-8 recording system, digital editing,
pc based facility with Souncard technology provided by
Event Electronics, Yamaha - 02r Version 2 including 8
tracks digital i/p and o/p to Alesis-ADAT, Tannoy-Reveal
and Yamaha-NS 10 monitos, Wavelab by Steinberg editing, AKai sampling, Drawner 1960 outboards, Roland
modules, Clavia synthesisers and Novation drum station.
(see advert)

Temple Lane Studios
Jenny Boland
Assistant Manager
Temple Bar Music Centre
Curved Street
Temple Bar
Dublin 2

Tel/Fax: +353 1 6709030/+353 6709042
Email: tbmusic@indigo.ie
Website: www.tbmc.ie

Hours of business are from Monday to Sunday, 10-
10.30pm. Facilities includes EV X200 Soundcraft Spirit,

Marshall JAM 900, JEM120 Roland, Trace Elliot GP7 SM130, Shure microphones and direct studio links to venue studios.

Totally Wired Ltd

Ivan O'Shea
Director
35a Barrow Street
Ringsend
Dublin 4

Tel/Fax: +353 1 6684918 or +353 1 6684966/ +353 1 6682383
Email: twired@indigo.ie
Website: www.fusio.ie/web1/twired
Other key staff: Tom Skerritt (Director)

Hours of business are from Monday to Sunday. Facilities include 24 bit hard disk recording and editing.

Variety Sounds

Tony O'Flaherty
7 College Street
Killarney
Co. Kerry

Mobile: +353 86 2611170
Fax: +353 1 6433155
Email: gliondur@hotmail.com
Other key staff: Ruairí O'Flaherty (Engineer)

Business hours are flexible. Facilities include ADAT digital recording facility, equipment by Neumann, Lexicon, Alesis, Audio Technica, Roland, Korg, Soundcraft and AKG. Sessions musicians available.

Westland Studios Ltd

Deirdre Costello
Manager
5-6 Lombard Street East
Dublin 2

Tel/Fax: +353 1 6774229/+353 1 6710421
Email: westland@indigo.ie
Website: www.westlandstudios.ie

Hours of business are from Monday to Sunday. Facilities include a Solid State Logic console with G series total recall recording system, 24 tracks of analogue recording

with Otari MTR 100 2 inch machine and 24 tracks of digital recording with Otari, range of outboards, Baldwin grand piano.

Windmill Lane Recording Studio

Catherine Rutter
Studio Manager
20 Ringsend Road
Dublin 4

Tel/Fax: +353 1 6685567/+353 1 6685352
Email: catherine@windmill.ie
Website: www.windmill.ie
Other key staff: Andrew Boland (Director/Head Engineer), Brian Masterson (Director/Head Engineer), Alister McMillan (Director)

Hours of business are from Monday to Friday 9.30-8.30pm. Studio One has a Neve VRP Legend 72 input with Flying Faders, analogue multitracks are 2 x Studer A827's locked by TLS 4000 int, outboard includes Tube Tech, Urei, GML, Lexicon and Neve, live area to facilitate an 85 piece orchestra and control room, 2 isolation booths. Studio Two has a Solid State Logic 4000 Series 48 Channel with Total Recall, multitacking s to Studer A827 or Tascam DA-88 x 1 Tascam, mastering to DAT or CR-R, 2 isolation booths and control room.

MUSIC COPYISTS AND TYPESETTERS

Killyan Bannister
65 Larkfield Gardens
Harolds Cross
Dublin 6W

Tel: +353 1 4922893

Works part-time, by hand. Flexible as to the kinds of work available. Has worked for RTÉ (National Symphony Orchestra of Ireland, RTÉ Concert Orchestra), the Irish Chamber Orchestra, Opera Theatre Company, for Irish composers including Gerard Victory and Raymond Deane. Has also worked on film scores.

Sarah M. Burn
'Tobar Ceoltóra'
PO Box 32
Greystones
Co. Wicklow

Tel/Fax: +353 1 2876370/+353 1 2876238

Works full-time, both by hand and computer (using 'Score' for IBM compatibles). Copies all kinds of orchestral parts and scores (own instrumental and orchestral playing helps here). Carries out transposition work and preparation of performance material for avant garde works. Has worked for most Irish composers, National Symphony Orchestra of Ireland and the RTÉ Concert Orchestra, choirs and string quartets and the Irish Chamber Orchestra, chamber ensembles including Concorde and Nua Nós, opera companies, military and brass bands. Writer of sleeve notes and has written several series of articles of Irish musical interest in NCH calendars. Has undertaken music copying work for song books, harp books and academic textbooks and has copied parts for incidental music for television and films for RTÉ, BBC, ITV and others. Also undertakes proof reading.

Irish Church Music Resources
Fr Paul Kenny
St. Nicholas of Myra
Francis Street
Dublin 8

Tel: +353 1 4542172
Email: pkenny@indigo.ie

Works part-time using 'Finale' for Macintosh computers. Area of special interest is church music. Has had liturgical music published by the Irish Church Music Association and the Irish Institute of Pastoral Liturgy (Jubilee Music Collection published by Columba Press).

Andrew Mackriell
1 Portobello Harbour
Dublin 8

Tel/Fax: +353 1 4781645
Email: amckrll@indigo.ie

Works full-time by computer, using 'Finale' for Macintosh. Copies parts and full scores. Covers all areas and holds the position of typesetter at the Contemporary Music Centre. Has also worked for Top Type Music Bureau.

Paul McKinley
5 Hightown Rise
Glengormley
Newtownabbey
Co. Antrim BT36 7XA
Northern Ireland

Tel/Fax: 048 9066 4535/048 9066 2761

Works by hand, transcribing orchestral repertoire e.g. the orchestral music of Stanford, by BBC and Chandos Records. Also works on commissioned works by local composers.

Debbie Metrustry
Managing Director
Top Type Music Bureau
76 St. Laurence Road
Chapelizod
Dublin 20

Tel/Fax: +353 1 6261409
Mobile: +353 86 2446256
Email: toptype@gofree.indigo.ie

Works by computer, using 'Finale' 98 for Macintosh and PC, PageMaker, Graphire Music Press, Adobe Illustrator and Acrobat Distiller programmes. Areas of special interest include contemporary music, full orchestral scores and parts, choral music (including plain chant) and text with music (DTP). Has worked with the Icelandic Music Information Centre, Veritas Publishing and RTÉ, Leaving Certificate - text and music for Curriculum Support Team, CUP and other Irish publishers. (see advert p.309)

Fergus O'Carroll
O'Carroll Music Publications
362 South Circular Road
Dublin 8

Tel: +353 1 4544122
Email: ocmp@clubi.ie
Website: www.clubi.ie/ocmp

Works by computer, using 'Finale' and 'Sibelius'. Areas of special interest include parts and scores for orchestral music, film, wind band and chamber music. Has worked with the National Symphony of Ireland, RTÉ Concert Orchestra, Irish Chamber Orchestra, Mícheál Ó Súilleabháin, Frank McNamara and others.

Playright Music Ltd

Daniel Walsh
Managing Director
95 Glasnevin Avenue
Dublin 11

Tel/Fax: +353 1 8422463
Email: danielwalsh@compuserve.com

Works by computer, using Score, Sibelius, Lime, Finale, Final Score, MidiScoreWrite, Beam, ScorEdit, CorelDRAW, Corel Ventura, Microsoft Word and Playright Music Utilities. Offers design and music type-setting, editing and score preparation services to composers and publishers. Engrave instrumental and choral music in any style. Provide parts and full scores for performance. Provide camera-ready artwork for paper, bromide or film for sheet music and books. Print on a 600/1200 dpi PostScript laser printer and offer Linotronic output. Has worked with Folens, RTÉ, Educational Company of Ireland, Bord na Gaeilge and Order of St. John of God. (see advert p.296).

Dennis Suttill

52 Meadowmount
Churchtown
Dublin 16

Tel: +353 1 2986355

Works by hand. Areas of special interest includes symphonic, pop, jazz, traditional, military and brass bands, choirs and church, parts, full scores, vocal scores and transpositions. Has worked with RTÉ Orchestras, private record companies, most prominent Irish composers and as Senior Recording Producer with RTÉ Music Department.

PROGRAMME NOTE WRITERS

Martin Adams

c/o Music Department
Trinity College
Dublin 2

Tel/Fax: +353 1 6081120/+353 1 6709509
Email: musicsec@tcd.ie
Website: www.tcd.ie/music

Works full-time. Area of special interest is 17th Century music, especially Purcell and 19th Century symphonic music. Has written programme notes for Leeds City Council, English National Opera North, Wexford Festival Opera and others.

John Allen

54 St. Columba's Rise
Swords
Co. Dublin

Tel/Fax: +353 1 8401637
Email: jamus@eircom.net

Areas of special interest include opera, operetta, music theatre and orchestral music. Has worked with Opera Ireland, RTÉ Orchestras and vocal concerts, Marco-Polo and Naxos CDs, scriptwriter for RTÉ broadcaster.

Rod Alston

Eden
Rossinver
Co. Leitrim

Tel/Fax: +353 72 54122/+353 54122 or +353 71 43684
Email: modelart@iol.ie

Area of special interest is baroque music. Writes programme notes for Sligo Early Music Ensemble concerts and for Tafel Musik concerts.

Sarah M. Burn

'Tobar Ceoltóra'
PO Box 32
Greystones
Co. Wicklow

Tel/Fax: +353 1 2876370/+353 1 2876238

Particularly interested in female composers and in researching and writing articles on Irish musicians, musical history and culture in Ireland, also standard orchestral and vocal concert repertory. Has worked for the National Concert Hall, RTÉ, Music Network and the Irish Chamber Orchestra. Writer of record sleeves notes and several series of articles of Irish musical interest in National Concert Hall calendars. Has written articles on Irish female composers for Grove's Dictionary of Music, New Grove Dictionary of Women Composers and Blackwell's Companion to Irish Culture. Also undertakes proof reading.

David Byers

425 Bearsbridge Road
Bloomfield
Belfast BT5 5DU
Northern Ireland

Tel/Fax: 048 9065 9706
Email: david.byers@btinternet.com
Website: www.btinternet.com/~david.byers/homepage.htm

Areas of special interest include a wide range of chamber and orchestral music from the 17th to the 20th Century. Has worked for BBC Invitation concerts and written sleeve notes for CDs (Unicorn-Kanchana: Lyrita).

Dr Anthony Carver

The Queen's University Belfast
School of Music
Belfast BT7 1NN
Northern Ireland

Tel: 048 9033 5496
Email: a.carver@qub.ac.uk

Areas of special interest include 19th Century orchestral music, renaissance, early baroque and chamber music. Has worked with the Ulster Orchestra and The Monteverdi Choir.

Michael Dervan

17 Upper Clanbrassil Street
Dublin 8

Tel: +353 1 4542574
Email: mjd@indigo.ie

Particularly interested in contemporary music (Irish and international), piano and chamber music. Music critic for the Irish Times, Irish correspondent for Opera Now. Classical music work has appeared in the Independent (London), the Guardian, BBC Music Magazine, Opera

News (New York) and The Radio Times. Has broadcast on BBC, RTÉ and researched and presented a 100 programme series called 'Countdown on the Music of the 20th Century' on Lyric FM.

Michael Dungan

1 The Park
Lutterell Hall
Dunboyne
Co. Meath

Tel/Fax: +353 1 8252847
Email: mdbs@iol.ie

Writes programme notes for classical concert programmes and CD sleeve notes. Programme editor for Wexford Festival Opera. Has written for the National Symphony Orchestra of Ireland, RTÉ Concert Orchestra, Music Network, The Contemporary Music Centre, Mostly Modern, The Guardian Dublin International Piano Competition and others. Works as the classical music columnist and critic for the Evening Herald and is a regular broadcaster on Lyric FM.

Ian Fox

62 Highfield Road
Dublin 6

Tel/Fax: +353 1 6765991 (day)/+353 1 4974355
Email: ian.fox@iapi.com

Writes programmes notes for the National Symphony Orchestra of Ireland since 1986. Has written for a wide range of concerts, recitals, festivals and opera. Holds a database of information. First wrote for the Irish Times in 1969, later Hibernia and the Sunday Independent. At present is the music critic for the Sunday Tribune and Irish correspondent for Opera Magazine. Has broadcast with RTÉ since 1968. Lectures on music, especially opera.

Dr Dermot Gault

4 Stormont Court
Belfast BT4 3LE
Northern Ireland

Tel/Fax: 048 9041 0584/048 9041 8980
Email: dermot@drmg.freeserve.co.uk

Areas of special interest include the music of Bruckner and 18th and 19th Century music. Writes for the Irish Times, The Bruckner Journal, the Ulster Orchestra, Arts Council of Northern Ireland and Kilkenny Arts Festival.

Francis Humphreys

Coomkeen
Durrus
Co. Cork

Tel/Fax: +353 27 61105/+353 27 61485
Email: coomkeen@eircom.net

Area of special interest is chamber music. Writes notes for all West Cork Chamber Music Festival programmes.

Paul McKinley

5 Hightown Rise
Glengormley
Newtownabbey
Co. Antrim BT36 7XA
Northern Ireland

Tel/Fax: 048 9066 4535/048 9066 2761

Area of special interest in British music from mid-19th century onwards. General interest in orchestral repertoire of the romantic era and the 20th Century.

Alec MacDonald

26 Cable Road
Whitehead
Co. Antrim BT38 9PX
Northern Ireland

Tel: 048 9337 3273

Areas of special interest includes the music of Haydn, 19th and 20th Century music (with a special interest in British and Russian composers). Works as a part-time lecturer at The Queen's University Belfast, music teacher/tutor, involved in church music with young people.

Sarah McQuaid

Apartment 6
63 Lower Clanbrassil Street
Dublin 8

Mobile: +353 86 8147523
Fax: +353 1 2960383
Email: smcquaid@indigo.ie

Areas of special interest include folk and traditional music. Regular columnist with the Evening Herald.

Róisín Maher

Apartment 4
Broc Hall
Beech Hill
Donnybrook
Dublin 4

Tel: +353 1 2603345
Email: roisinmaher@eircom.net

Areas of special interest include opera, contemporary music and women composers. Has worked with Opera Theatre Company, Crash Ensemble and the Contemporary Music Centre.

Alex Moffatt

29 Hazelwood
Shankill
Co. Dublin

Tel/Fax: +353 1 2822587
Mobile: +353 87 2842766
Email: amoffatt@eircom.net

Areas of special interest include classical guitar music, contemporary music and classical orchestral repertoire. Programme note writer with both RTÉ orchestras. Has worked for several years as a reviewer for the Irish Times, covering mainly traditional Irish music and jazz.

Declan O'Driscoll

Mill Road
Thurles
Co. Tipperary

Tel/Fax: +353 504 24385 (h) or +353 204 21636 (w)/+353 504 22740

Area of special interest is free improvised music. Has written for the Irish Times, the Wire, Rubbberneck and Kaden (American magazine). Recent reviews include the Mostly Modern Festival at the Bank of Ireland Arts Centre, Dublin, March 2000. Also writes liner notes for CDs.

ARTIST MANAGEMENT AGENCIES

Anseo Press and Publications

Amy Garvey
10 Adelaide Road
Dublin 2

Tel/Fax: +353 1 4783925/+353 1 4783926
Email: agarvey@indigo.ie

Types of music genres represented includes traditional, folk and crossover. Has worked with Martin Hayes, Dennis Cahill, Seán Tyrrell, Niamh Pasons, Feakle Festival and Green Linnet Records.

David Caren Management

David Caren
Managing Director
3rd Floor
9 Parliament Street
Dublin 2

Tel/Fax: +353 1 6719643 or +353 1 6719648/ +353 1 6719644
Email: dcm@eircom.net

A management company who represent classical, traditional, crossover and rock/pop artists. Examples of musicians represented are Iarla O'Lionaird, Terry Sutton, ORA and Aoife Nic Canna.

International Concert Management - ICM Artists and Tours

Ashley Pringle
Director
23 Farmleigh Avenue
Stillorgan
Co. Dublin

Tel/Fax: +353 1 2886251
Email: icmtours@esatclear.ie

ICM represents musicians and groups in classical, opera and folk music genres. Organise choral tours, cultural tours and artist representation worldwide. Deals with specific requirements of touring and performing arts groups (choirs, orchestras, ensembles, singers, dancers and folk bands). Also involved in concert promotion and occasionally present and produce international opera and musical evenings for corporate clients at the National Concert Hall, Dublin. International artist representation includes Gary Arbutnot (flute), Angela Lear (piano), Patricia Brady (soprano) (see advert p.309).

Jacob Promotions

George Jacob
Ballydowagh Cottage
Glen of the Downs
Delgany
Co. Wicklow

Tel/Fax: +353 1 2873992
Email: gjacob@indigo.ie

Represents jazz/blues, world and rock/pop music genres.

Jazz on the Terrace

Allen Smith
Director
44 Belgrave Square West
Rathmines
Dublin 6

Tel: +353 1 4979562
Email: jazzontheterrace@ireland.com

This agency represents jazz music. Examples of musicians and groups represented includes Dave Holland Quintet, Richie Buckley, Tommy Halferty, Dave Liebman, Oliver Jones Trio, Guilfoyle-Nielsen Trio, Oliver Jones Trio and Frank Tate Quintet (see advert p150).

Music Hibernia

Anne Farrelly
Director
Cúl Cuana
Balrathboyne Glebe
Cortown, Kells
Co. Meath

Tel/Fax: +353 46 34019
Mobile: +353 87 2394090
Email: hibernia@eircom.net

Represent ACFEA Tour Consultants (specialised travel Ltd in the UK and USA), International Festival and Tour Management UK, TM Resor Stockholm Sweden and The Royal Danish Embassy. Also organises concerts for charity events.

ARTS CONSULTANTS

Martin Barrett

7 Rose Lawn
Togher Road
Cork

Tel: +353 21 4311215
Email: martinb@musicnet.iol.ie

Areas of special interest includes arts management, audience development, arts education, community arts and artistic policy and programming. Commissioned reports for University Concert Hall, Limerick and has worked with the RDS, the Irish Peru Institute, Co-Operation

Ireland and the United Nations. Also freelance orchestral and choral conductor, producer, music director, a member of the International Society for Arts Managers, Sound Sense and the Incorporated Society of Musicians.

PJ Curtis
The Old Forge
Kilnaboy
Co. Clare

Tel: +353 65 6837117
Email: pjcurtis@eircom.net

Areas of special interest include world, ethnic, traditional and acoustic music. Has worked with RTÉ radio and television, BBC radio, Century radio, Clare FM, Lyric FM (as a presenter and producer), Irish Arts Foundation San Francisco, Music Network, Arts Council of Ireland, Hummingbird Films and various record companies. Has received many awards for radio, production and has published a book 'Notes From The Heart - A Celebration of Irish Traditional Music', Poolbeg 1994.

Prof. Gerard Gillen
Head of Music
National University of Ireland Maynooth
Co. Kildare

Tel/Fax: +353 1 7083733/+353 1 6289432
Email: gerard.gillen@may.ie

Graduate of University College Dublin, University of Oxford (was John Betts Fellow in 1992) and the Royal Conservatoire of Antwerp. Area of special interest is organ consultancy. Has worked with The National Concert Hall, Longford Cathedral, Letterkenny Cathedral, Rowe Street Church Wexford and Whitefriar Street Church Dublin.

Dr. Colin Hamilton
Cil-Aodh
Macroom
Co. Cork

Tel/Fax: +353 26 45209/+353 26 45778
Email: hammy@eircom.net

Qualified with MA and PhD. Area of special interest is traditional Irish music, with the emphasis on the history of Irish music, organology, music and identity. Has worked with the American Conference for Irish Studies, British Society for Ethnomusicology, Cork University Press, Ossian Publications, University College Cork and UCLA. Also works through French.

Liz Lennon
Apartment 2
Percy Court
7-9 Percy Place
Dublin 4

Tel: +353 1 6608815
Email: lippylala@yahoo.com

Qualified with BA Applied Science in Psychology, Graduate Diploma in Recreational Studies and part-completion of an MBA. Areas of special interest include organisational review, planning, evaluation, development, person to person business planning and lecturing. Has worked with Music Network, Irish World Music Centre, Sound Out, the Arts Council, Sligo Arts Office, Dublin Fringe Festival, Irish Museum of Modern Art and Temple Bar Galleries. Aims to work with people, organisations and communities, to create powerful, just and creative places to live and work. At present lectures on the MA in Community Music course at the Irish World Music Centre Limerick.

Debbie Metrustry
Top Type Music Bureau
78 St. Laurence Road
Chapelizod
Dublin 20

Tel/Fax: +353 1 6261409
Mobile: +353 86 2446256
Email: toptype@gofree.indigo.ie

Qualified with BA Mod in Music and Sociology from Trinity College Dublin and MPhil in Women's Studies from Trinity College Dublin. Areas of special interest include project management (project design, implementation, supervision and review), consultation process design (with special emphasis on the music industry in Ireland), research, database design, music software and hardware. Has worked with Music Network, RTÉ, various schools and colleges and the National Training and Development Institute. (see advert p.309)

EVENT MANAGEMENT COMPANIES

Arts and Noise Limited
Gerard Tannam
Managing Director
PO Box 6453
Dublin 14

Tel/Fax: +353 1 4953330/+353 1 4953331
Email: tannam@iol.ie
Website: www.excellentevents.com
Other key staff: Christine Tannam (Event Consultant)

Types of music genres represented includes traditional, folk, world, rock/pop, country and western and crossover. Has worked with De Dannan, Dervish, Martin Hayes and Dennis Cahill and has organised events for IBEC, ESB, The National Safety Council of Ireland and Hummingbird Records. Specialists in premium tailor-made events and corporate partnership events.

Camelot Corporation

Mark Shaughnessy
Church Buildings
Church Lane
Rathfarnham
Dublin 14

Tel/Fax: +353 1 4904348/+353 1 4920950
Email: poloco@iol/ie
Website: www.camelot-corp.ie

Represents all types of music genres. Organises themed evenings using a range of Irish and international performers.

Carpe Diem Productions

Una Johnston
Director
22 Belgrave Road
Garden Flat
Rathmines
Dublin 6

Tel/Fax: +353 1 4970381/+353 1 4910631
Email: production@carpediem.iol.ie
Other key staff: Lisa Tinley (Director)

Types of music genre represented includes jazz/blues, crossover, traditional, world and rock/pop. Has worked as the management company for the Guinness Blues Festival, consultants to the Guinness Humours of Bandon Traditional Music Festival and European management company for South by Southwest Music and Medial Conference Austin Texas. Carpe Diem are music programmers as well as production managers.

Ray Cawley

Director
2 Mahon Avenue
Douglas Road
Cork

Tel/Fax: +353 21 4295529/+353 1 21 4291522
Mobile: +353 86 2327691
Email: cawleymktingmedia@eircom.net

Has worked with Mícheál Ó Súilleabháin, Sharon Shannon and Cork Pops Orchestra and has organised the Mallow International Garden Festival, Irish Homecoming Festival and the Eurovision.

Chamber Opera Company

Kieran Nagle
Edgewood Productions
Industrial Yarns Complex
Bray
Co. Wicklow

Tel/Fax: +353 1 2864680/+353 1 2829209
Email: edgewood@indigo.ie
Website: under construction

Types of music genres represented includes jazz/improv and classical music. Provide custom made packages for theatre and corporate events.

Clara Clark Event Management Ltd

Clara Clark
Managing Director
17 Pine Lawn
Newtownpark Avenue
Blackrock
Co. Dublin

Tel/Fax: +353 1 2898533/+353 1 2898817
Email: cclark@indigo.ie
Other key staff: Simon Clarke (Technical Services Manager)

Types of music genres represented includes classical, traditional, folk, world and rock/pop. Has worked with Culwick Choral Society, Paddy Cole Orchestra, Carulli Trio and Gerry O'Connor.

Davelle Communications

3rd Floor
9 Parliament Street
Dublin 2

Tel/Fax: +353 1 6719643 or +353 1 6719648/ +353 1 6719644
Email: dcm@eircom.net

Has worked with Irish Music Magazine, Classical Ireland Magazine, Iarla O'Lionaird, Solas, Karen Casey, Cran and the Irish Music Magazine Awards. Areas of special interest include PR and promotion, design consultancy, retail marketing and music consultancy for overseas record companies.

Fifty Seventh Street Ltd

Maurice Cassidy
Managing Director
24 Upper Mount Street
Dublin 2

Tel/Fax: +353 1 6766751/+353 1 6766786
Email: street57@indigo.ie

Type of music genres promoted includes crossover, traditional and folk. Has worked with De Dannan, Clannad, Riverdance and Colm Wilkinson.

The Harrison Partnership

Simon Harrison
Managing Director
The Barracks
Annestown
Co. Waterford

Tel/Fax: +353 51 396270/+353 51 396341
Email: sharrison@eircom.net
Other key staff: Jane Harrison (Company Director), Julie Gold (Secretary)

Types of music genres represented includes classical, jazz/blues, traditional and rock/pop.

Lasrach Venue Agency

Sam Colbert
Managing Director
205 South Circular Road
Dublin 8

Tel/Fax: +353 1 4542508/+353 1 4734583

Represents classical, jazz/blues, opera, crossover, traditional, folk, world, country and western and rock/pop music genres.

Mac Teo

John Crumlish
Manager
The Black Box
Dyke Road
Galway

Tel/Fax: +353 91 561462/+353 1 563905
Email: macnos@iol.ie
Website: www.macnas.com

Types of music genres represented includes world, percussion and crossover music. Mac Teo is the commercial event management section of Macnas.

Lucette Murray and Associates

10 Beaumont Avenue
Ballintemple
Cork

Tel/Fax: +353 21 4293918/+353 21 4293930

Types of music genres represented includes classical and traditional. Has worked with classical trios including Orpheus Trio, Fiona O'Reilly (soprano) and traditional trios.

Senan O'Reilly Marketing and Event Management

Senan O'Reilly
Director
Ardara Annexe
Spawell Road
Wexford

Tel/Fax: +353 53 44634/+353 53 44498
Email: market@indigo.ie

Types of music genres represented includes jazz/blues, country and western, crossover, traditional, folk, world and rock/pop. Has worked with Wexford Festival Opera and bluegrass groups from the US.

Sapphire Promotions Ltd

Clyde Davidson
Managing Director
1 Fitzwilliam Street Upper
Dublin 2

Tel/Fax: +353 1 6789903/+353 1 6789905
Email: sapphirepro@eircom.net

Type of music genres represented includes jazz/blues, traditional and rock/pop.

Skymarch Production Management

Grainne Fitzpatrick
4 Georgian Hamlet
Baldoyle
Dublin 13

Tel/Fax: +353 1 8393154
Email: skymarch@iol.ie
Website: www.iol.ie/~skymarch/
Other key staff: Matt Kelleghan (Director)

Types of music genres represented includes jazz/blues and rock/pop. Has worked with the Arts Council, Aosdana, Guinness Blues Festival and St. Patricks Festival.

Young European String Ltd
Maria Kelemen
Director
21 The Close
Cypress Downs
Templeogue
Dublin 6W

Tel/Fax: +353 1 4905263/+353 1 4920355
Email: yes@iol.ie
Other key staff: Ronald Masin
(Conductor/Violinist), Deborah Kelleher (Pianist)

Types of music genres represented include classical,
jazz/blues, opera, crossover, traditional and folk. Has
worked with Siamsa Tire, Waterford International
Masterclasses Festival and Autumn Sound Festival.
Promotes festivals abroad and in Ireland.

Competitions, Scholarships and Bursaries

COMPETITIONS, SCHOLARSHIPS AND BURSARIES - REPUBLIC OF IRELAND AND NORTHERN IRELAND

AIMS Choral Festival
Connie Tantrum
Cross Street
New Ross
Co. Wexford

Tel: +353 51 421766

The choral festival includes a day-long set of competitions for choirs in 11 different categories, in 3 venues. The festival is usually held on the third weekend in May each year.

Arklow Music Festival
Michael McCarthy
Director
Arklow Music Festival Office
1 Upper Main Street
Arklow
Co. Wicklow

Tel/Fax: +353 402 32732/+353 402 91030
Email: ceca@eircom.net
Other key staff: Eileen Clandillon (Secretary), Elizabeth McLoughlin (Administrator), May Kavanagh (Treasurer)

Orchestral and choral festival. 120 separate competitions and 2 concerts. Indoor competition sessions at 2 venues daily. Held in March each year. (see advert p226)

Arts Council of Ireland Awards
Maeve Giles
Music Assistant
70 Merrion Square
Dublin 2

Tel/Fax: +353 1 6180200 or +353 1850 392492/
+353 1 6761302
Email: info@artscouncil.ie
Website: www.artscouncil.ie
Other key staff: Maura Eaton (Music Officer)

The following music awards are available from the Arts Council of Ireland:
Bursaries for advanced instrumentalists and singers: This scheme offers a small number of high-value awards

(maximum value c.£5,000) tenable for one or two years to facilitate high level development and training in performance in all forms of music. Successful applicants will demonstrate that they have completed formal performance studies to (at least) postgraduate level, or have attained a comparable standard in performance by other documented means.
Composers' Bursaries: The maximum sum for these awards is £7,500. They are primarily intended to assist an established composer in the development and growth of his/her work or professional skills. The aim of the bursary is to provide a period of sabbatical leave for those who wish to complete a specific composition project or undertake a particular course of study or development.
Composers' Apprenticeship Scheme: This scheme which can range in value from £600 to £2,200 (depending on the proposal), is intended for young composers who have completed, or are about to complete, their formal musical studies at postgraduate level. Apprenticeships may be used to fund short periods of study (1-3 months) with established composers.
Composers' Postgraduate Study Awards: These study awards (contributing an average sum of £2,500 to successful applicants), invite applications from composers wishing to pursue their composition studies at postgraduate level at either a recognised institution abroad, or one chosen in consultation with the Arts Council.
Conductors' Study Awards: These awards which range from £500-£4,500, (depending on the proposed project) are intended to assist and support Irish conductors who wish to pursue studies either in Ireland or abroad.
Doris Keogh Award: This award, established in 1993, is made every two years to assist the training and development of young flute and recorder players. Applicants must be under 23 years of age on 1st January 1999. The next award will be given in 2001.
Jazz Development Awards: Previous awards have ranged between £1,200 and £4,000. The Council will consider applications from jazz musicians wishing to develop their work.
Margaret Arnold Scholarship: This award of £2,000 is offered to facilitate high level development and training for instrumentalists and singers. The successful applicant will demonstrate that she/he has completed formal performance studies to an advanced level or have attained a comparable standard in performance by other required documented means.
Skidmore Jazz Award: The Council, in association with the Arts Council of Northern Ireland, offers a scholarship of £1,750 to enable a jazz musician to attend a summer course at Skidmore College in New York. The emphasis of this course is on ensemble or 'in combo' playing. (see Arts Council of Northern Ireland Awards below)
Opera Training Awards: A limited number of awards will be available to creative and/or technical personnel. other than singers, who wish to further their professional training in the area of opera either in Ireland or abroad.

Festivals Scheme: This is a new pilot funding scheme for multi-disciplinary arts festivals and events. Funding is not available for the entire cost of a festival/event, but is intended specifically to support the participation or involvement of professional artists or a professional arts group.

Music Workshops and Masterclasses: This scheme, valued at between £350 and £10,000 (depending on proposal) supports essential costs of events aimed at the transfer of skills, insights and understanding between established performers and others in all genres of music.

Arts Centres Commission Scheme: This scheme enables art centres to commission work in any medium for performance and/or exhibition. Proposals will be accepted from arts centres currently in receipt of Arts Council revenue funding.

Community Artist Development Fund: This scheme is intended to support development, critical reflection and evaluation in community arts practice.

Awards to individuals: Artsflight - The Arts Council and Aer Lingus collaborate in this scheme, which offers opportunities to people working in the arts to travel outside Ireland. 'Go See' Fund - This award has been created by the Arts Council and the British Council in Ireland. Its purpose is to enable arts managers, creative and interpretative artists to travel to Britain or Ireland, to develop professional contacts and explore touring, exchange or co-operative artistic ventures. (see also orgs)

Arts Council of Northern Ireland Awards

Awards Secretary
Macneice House
77 Malone Road
Belfast BT9 6AQ
Northern Ireland

Tel/Fax: 048 9038 5200/048 9066 1715
Email: performance@artscouncil-ni.org
Other key staff: Pamela Smith (Music & Opera Officer), Martin Dowling (Traditional Arts Officer)

ACNI administers a scheme for awards to creative and performing artists active in the fields of drama and dance, music and jazz, literature, traditional arts, community arts and visual arts, and to those engaged in the direction and presentation of artistic events. Applicants are invited to submit an official application form with a costed proposal which will be assessed by the Awards Panel, whose decisions in all matters concerning awards is final. Proposals may range in scope and scale from schemes requiring comparatively modest sums to schemes needing substantial financial support. It should be noted that awards are available for classical, jazz and traditional music. The awards are open to artists who contribute regularly to the artistic activities of the community, resident in Northern Ireland for at least one year. Previous award holders can also apply again. There are no stipulated age limits. Awards will not be available for prolonged study at centres of further education leading to professional qualifications, though this clause would not exclude attendance at specialist short courses and master classes (confirmation of acceptance must be provided). The Awards Panel reserves the right to invite applicants to consider modifying the proposal outlined in the application. Successful applicants will be required to enter into an agreement binding them to fulfilling the purpose for which they were given an award. In all aspects of its funding, the Arts Council bears in mind several criteria listed in 'To The Millennium - A Strategy for the Arts Council in Northern Ireland, September 1995'. These are excellence, effect, education, economic benefit, equity and efficiency. The next series of awards take place in 2000. Application forms are available from March 2000, and the deadline for applications is mid-April 2000.

Axa Dublin International Piano Competition

Ann Fuller
Administrator
Liffey House
Tara Street
Dublin 2

Tel/Fax: +353 1 6773066/+353 1 6711354
Email: pianos@iol.ie
Website: under construction
Other key staff: Rosemary Davies (Administration Assistant), Róisín Grimley (Administration Assistant), John O'Conor (Artistic Director)

This triennial competition will next take place during the first half of May 2003. Applicants should be professional pianists aged between 17 and 30 years. The total prize fund amounts to over £40,000. (see advert p.332)

Ballyclare Musical Festival Association

Alice Turner
General Secretary
56 Ballyeaston Road
Ballyclare
Co. Antrim BT39 9BP

Tel: 048 9334 0498
Other key staff: Barbara Acheston (Music Secretary), Carol Maxwell (Speech & Drama Secretary), Dymphna Howe (Irish Dancing Secretary)

Orchestral and choral festival. Competitions are held over 3 weeks, with 1 week for each section. Festival is held in March/April each year.

Bangor Choral Festival

Joan Houston
Festival Co-ordinator
71 Bryansford Meadow
Bangor West
Co. Down BT20 3NX
Northern Ireland

Tel/Fax: 048 9145 6851/048 9127 1370
Other key staff: Roberta Dunlop (Treasurer), Pat McNally (Chairperson)

Choral festival. Junior, intermediate and adult choir competitions with a Saturday gala evening. School choir competition for children with special educational needs. The festival will next take place from 28-31 March 2001 and March 2002. The Millennium Choral Weekend will be held in October 2000.

Bank of Ireland Millennium Scholars Trust

Eileen Punch
Project Manager
Trust Office
National College of Ireland
Sandford Road
Ranelagh
Dublin 6

Tel/Fax: +353 1 4060500/+353 1 4972200
Email: boischolars@ncirl.ie
Website: www.ncirl.ie

To mark the Millennium the Bank of Ireland is providing £10 million to establish the Bank of Ireland Millennium Scholars Trust. The trust will fund scholarships for people with talent and ability who because of economic circumstances or other barriers such as disability are prevented from reaching their full potential. The trust will operate over a 10 year period and will facilitate a broad range of third level educational opportunities for people from diverse backgrounds and who have in common the potential and motivation to succeed in their chosen field of study. The trust will also support further studies for people who wish to prepare themselves educationally to provide leadership in their communities. Advanced studies in the arts and postgraduate courses are also eligible. Candidates for scholarships will be nominated by nominating bodies. Organisations registered with the trust are from a wide range of educational, artistic and cultural fields. The nominating bodies will possess the

ability, resources and expertise to identify suitable candidates and to co-ordinate applications. The trust will fund some 60 scholarships each year. The average scholarship award is expected to be £5,000 per annum. The maximum scholarship to be awarded to any individual is capped at £30,000 for the designated period of study.

Bass Ireland Arts Awards - Arts Council of Northern Ireland

Awards Secretary
Macneice House
77 Malone Road
Belfast BT9 6AQ
Northern Ireland

Tel/Fax: 048 9038 5200/048 9066 1715
Email: performance@artscouncil-ni.org
Other key staff: Pamela Smith (Music & Opera Officer), Martin Dowling (Traditional Arts Officer)

The Bass Ireland Arts Award (£5,000 in 1999/2000) is open to individuals or groups in all branches of the arts. Applications are restricted to those born in Northern Ireland, or who have been resident there for at least one year. Bass Ireland instituted the arts award as a means of encouraging the enrichment of the cultural scene in Northern Ireland by providing financial assistance to aspiring creative individuals or groups in all branches of the arts. The award was last made in 1999 (closing date was the end of August). The award will next take place in the year 2000.

Blacktie National Piano Competition

Ann-Maire O'Farrell
Blacktie Head Office
Terenure Village Centre
Terenure
Dublin 6W

Tel/Fax: +353 1 4925410/+353 1 49205408
Email: info@blacktie.ie
Other key staff: Niall O'Farrell, Deirdre Doyle

The next competition takes place in 2001. The first prize is a Perpetual trophy, £5,000, a sponsored recital and complete evening wear presented by Blacktie. Second prize is £2,000 and evening wear presented by Blacktie. Third prize is £500 and evening wear presented by Blacktie. A special award of £500 will be made for the best performance of a work by a living Irish composer. Competitors should be under 28 years of age on 1st January 2001.

The British Council - Northern Ireland

Peter Lyner
Director
1 Chlorine Gardens
Belfast BT9 5DJ
Northern Ireland

Tel/Fax: 048 9066 6770 or 048 9066 6706/048 9066 5242
Email: peter.lyner@britcounc.org
Website: www.britishcouncil.org/nireland/
Key staff: Lynda E.E Wilson (Deputy Director), Paul Burrows (Head of Central Bureau), Bernie McAllister (Deputy Head of Council - Bureau Section)

The British Council organises special programmes unique to Northern Ireland promoting cultural exchange with various countries. It concentrates on civil society, human rights, governance, gender issues and cultural sector.

Carrickmacross Choral Festival

Seán O'Reilly
Liscastle
Lisanisk
Carrickmacross
Co. Monaghan

Tel: +353 42 9661422 (home)
Mobile: +353 87 2896811
Other key staff: Pat Cotter

The festival includes the following categories: solo singing (youth) - under 10 years, under 12 years, under 18 years and under 20 years; church choirs - 4 part or more, female voices - 3 or more parts, male voices - 4 or more parts; youth choirs unison - under 10 years, under 14 years, under 18 years; youth part choirs (3 or 4 parts) - under 12 years, under 16 years and under 18 years.

Heather Clarke Scholarship

Dr. Desmond Hunter
Music Department
University of Ulster Jordanstown
Newtownabbey
Co. Antrim BT37 0QB
Northern Ireland

Tel/Fax: 048 9036 6955/048 9036 6810

This scholarship was established in memory of Heather Clarke, a lecturer in music, who died in 1984. Normally awarded annually to a final year BMus student for the continuation of their music career. Money awarded is approximately £400.

Coleman Traditional Festival

Marie Queenan
Secretary
Ceolaras Coleman
Gurteen
Co. Sligo

Tel/Fax: +353 71 82599/+353 71 82602
Email: cctrad@iol.ie
Website: www.colemanirishmusic.com

This annual competition is open to fiddle players. There are 3 sections: senior (over 18), junior (under 18) and junior music feis. Entries for competitions are accepted both in advance and on the day. (see festivals)

Coleraine Music Festival

Josephine Carter
Honorary General Secretary
34 Grange Road
Coleraine
Co. Derry BT52 1NG
Northern Ireland

Tel/Fax: 048 7034 2314
Other key staff: Brian Simpson (Chairman), Mary Riddell (Speech & Drama Secretary), Mary Ellard (Music Secretary)

Orchestral and choral festival with several competitions. (see also festivals)

Comhaltas Ceoltóirí Éireann

Labhrás Ó Murchú
Director General
32 Belgrave Square
Monkstown
Co. Dublin

Tel/Fax: +353 1 2800295/+353 1 2803759
Email: enquiries@comhaltas.com
Website: www.comhaltas.com

Founded in 1951 to promote Irish traditional music, song, dance and the Irish language. 400 branches worldwide and 600 classes. There are 44 Fleadhanna Cheoil each year attracting 20,000 competitors. (see also page festivals)

Cork International Choral Festival

John Fitzpatrick
Festival Director
PO Box 68
Cork

Tel/Fax: +353 21 4308308/+353 21 4308309
Email: chorfest@iol.ie
Website: www.musicweb.com/corkchoral.htm

This annual competition will take place from 3-6 May 2001 and 2-5 May 2002. The choral festival has both international and national strands. The Fleischmann International Trophy Competition is open to applications from any amateur adult choir of international standing. A programme of A Capella music is required. First prize consists of a trophy, certificate and £2,000, second prize consists of a certificate and £1,500 and third prize consists of a certificate and £1,000. There are also national school choir and national adult choir competitions. These fall into several categories. Applications must be received before 31 January in the year of the competition.

Cork School of Music Scholarships

Dr. Geoffrey Spratt
Director
Union Quay
Cork

Tel/Fax: +353 21 4270076/+353 21 4276595
Email: gspratt@cit.ie
Website: www.cit.ie

The following scholarships are awarded by the Cork School of Music, applicable to students attending it: Tuition scholarships - all students who achieve a result of 90% or higher in any of the scholar's grade examination for any instrument/voice; The Barbara Harris Memorial Travelling Scholarship - in January of each academic year students who are registered for the full-time BMus degree course with guitar as their principle instrument, may apply for this scholarship to enable them to pursue an approved course of study during the summer vacation; Cork Youth Orchestra Scholarship - The Cork Youth Orchestra offers beginners scholarships in wind and percussion instruments.

Corn Séan Ó Riada

Liam Ó Maolaodha
6 Harcourt Street
Dublin 2

Tel/Fax: +353 1 4753857/+353 1 4758767
Email: oireacht@indigo.ie

This annual competition is open to winners of approximately 75 An tOireachtas. There are male and female Sean-nós singing competitions with three prizes - £750, £300 and £200, as well as the Ó Riada Cup. Held during the An tOireachtas festival each October/November. The closing date for entrants is mid September each year.

Department of Foreign Affairs Cultural Relations Committee

Secretary
Department of Foreign Affairs
69-71 St. Stephen's Green
Dublin 2

Tel/Fax: +353 1 4780822/+353 1 4082611

Grants may be made to organisations, groups or individuals which apply for assistance for participation in projects abroad, normally involving exhibition or performance. These grants are not available for study or training purposes.

Dublin Corporation Christy Brown Award

Jack Gilligan
Arts Officer
Dublin Corporation
20 Parnell Square North
Dublin 1

Tel/Fax: +353 1 8722816/+353 1 8722933
Email: arts@dubc.iol.ie
Other key staff: Derek McCauley (Arts Officer's Assistant)

This award is for an artist (in any discipline) with a disability, to enable the recipient to pursue further training, skills development or towards a special project. Applicants must be resident in Dublin City. The award is announced annually in January/February. The amount awarded is £1,500. Closing date for entries is the end of October each year.

Dublin Corporation Music Bursary

Jack Gilligan
Arts Officer
Dublin Corporation
20 Parnell Square North
Dublin 1

Tel/Fax: +353 1 8722816/+353 1 8722933
Email: arts@dubc.iol.ie
Other key staff: Derek McCauley

This bursary is usually awarded to go towards musicians' further education/training, but can also be made towards the development of a special project. Applicants must be resident in Dublin City. The bursary is awarded annually in January/February and currently amounts to £1,500 (to be reviewed). Closing date for entries is the end of October each year. The next award will be made in 2000.

Dublin Institute of Technology - Third Level Competitions and Scholarships

Lisa Molloy
DIT Conservatory of Music
Adelaide Road
Dublin 2

Tel/Fax: +353 1 4023000/+353 1 4023555
Email: lisa.molloy@dit.ie

There are a number of competitions opened to students of DIT Conservatory of Music. Entrance scholarships for part-time courses are awarded annually.

Dublin International Organ and Choral Festival

Eoin Garrett
Festival Administrator
Liffey House
Tara Street
Dublin 2

Tel/Fax: +353 1 6773066 Ext. 416/
+353 1 6727279
Email: organs@diocf.iol.ie
Website: www.iol.ie/~orga1/diocf
Other key staff: Gerard Gillen (Artistic Director), Lewis Clohessy (Chairman)

This competition takes place every 3 years. Applicants must submit a tape to qualify for round one and should be born in or after June 1967. The organ used for the competition is based at Christchurch Cathedral, Dublin, and accommodation is provided for those admitted to rounds 2 and 3. The next competition will take place in June 2002. The award amounts to £5,000.

Duhallow Pipe Band Championships

Con Hoy
Pipers Lodge
Cullen
Mallow
Co. Cork

Tel/Fax: +353 29 79003/+353 29 60024
Mobile: +353 87 6757676
Other key staff: Elaine Hickey (Chairperson), Catriona Hickey (Secretary)

Open-air pipe band competitions with a grand finale and street parade. The next competition will take place from the 18 June 2000.

Dundalk Urban District Council Music Awards

Mary O'Sullivan
Town Hall
Dundalk
Co. Louth

Tel/Fax: +353 42 9332276/+353 42 9351539
Email: dundarts@eircom.net

These music awards apply to residents of the Dundalk Urban District catchment area. Either classical or traditional musicians can apply. Must be aged 9-20 years. A total of 6 awards are presented. Applications must be received at the end of the previous November. Awards made in January each year.

ESB Veronica Dunne Singing Competition

Deirdre Kelleher
Friends of the Vocal Arts
Ben McArdle Ltd
42 Fitzwilliam Place
Dublin 2

Tel/Fax: +353 1 4784047
Email: dunnesingcomp@eircom.net

Applicants for this competition should be singers of Irish birth, citizenship, parentage or grandparentage. The competition is held every two years during the month of January, and will next take place in 2001. The total prize fund is £20,000 as well as the ESB trophy and a number of engagements.

Féile Luimní

Maeve Earlie
Co-ordinator
Ianthe
Ballinacurra
Limerick

Tel: +353 61 227082
Other key staff: Joe O'Connor (Vice President),
Padraig Ó Suilleabháin (Vice President)

The competitions (vocal, instrumental and choral) take place annually during February and March. There are 2 small bursaries and other trophies/awards. The closing date for entry is usually 1 December in the year preceding the competition.

Féis Maitiú

Timothy McCarthy
Administrator
Fr. Mathew Hall
Fr. Mathew Street
Cork

Tel/Fax: +353 21 4273347
Email: fesimaitiu@eircom.net

This is an annual competition. Award categories include: piano recital (£200 prize available), music repertoire (£500 prize available), music prizewinners (£100 prize available), vocal recital (£100 prize available), church choirs (£200 prize available), adult choirs (£200 prize available) and unison choirs under 13 years (£100 prize available).

Féis na nGleann - Roinn an Cheoil

Patrick J. Clerkin
Vice-Chairman
61 Coast Road
Cushendall
Ballymena
Co. Antrim BT44 ORX

Tel: 048 2177 1349
Other key staff: Marie McAllister (Honorary Secretary), Patrick J. Clerkin (Vice-Chairman), Nuala McSparran (Music Secretary)

Competitions are held in tin whistle, fiddle, flute, accordion and any other instrument. Age groups are under 8, 8-10, 10-12, 13-14, 14-16 and over 16. Solo singing competitions are held for the same age groups with songs chosen from a set list. Primary school, post-primary school and adult choirs can also compete. Awards are cups and medals. The competition will take place June 10th and 11th, 2000, June 2001 and June 2002.

Fleadh Ceoil na hÉireann

Comhaltas Ceoltóirí Éireann
Labhrás Ó Murchú
Director General
32 Belgrave Square
Monkstown
Co. Dublin

Tel/Fax: +353 1 2800295/+353 1 2803759
Email: enquiries@comhaltas.com
Website: www.comhaltas.com

Fleadh Ceoil na hÉireann will be held in Enniscorthy August 27-29 2000. There are over 140 competitive events held. This event takes place in different towns in Ireland every 1-2 years.

Fulbright Scholarship Programme

Executive Secretary
Cultural Section
Department of Foreign Affairs
79 St. Stephen's Green
Dublin 2

Tel/Fax: +353 1 4780822/+353 1 4082611
Website: www.ucd.ie/-fulbright/
Other key staff: Patrick Sammon (First Secretary)

Applicants for this scholarship to study in America must obtain their own placements. Grants are awarded by competition. Since the grantee must return to Ireland on completion of the grant period, no permanent visa (green card) or passport holders for the US are eligible to enter the programme. The grants are for sums of up to US$25,000 (academics) and US$10,000 (post graduates). The grants are awarded annually, and the number of scholarships varies slightly from year to year. In 1999 3 music scholarships were awarded. The scholarships are awarded in March, and the closing date for applications is the end of November.

Guinness Living Dublin Awards

Anne Burgun
Awards Co-ordinator
7 Clare Street
Dublin 2

Tel/Fax: +353 1 6612173/+353 1 6616043
Email: anne@dubchamber.ie

This award is given annually with a prize fund of £15,000. An additional £5,000 is available in the year 2000 for the best millennium project. The Guinness Living Dublin Awards recognises outstanding civic contributions and activities by groups, individuals and businesses. The purpose of the awards is to make Dublin a better place in which to visit, work or live. There are five categories: commercial, community development, entertainment/events, schools and residential. The £15,000 prize fund is to be divided among the category winners and the overall winner, at the judges discretion. A number of highly commended entries are also selected in each category. These awards were introduced in 1994 by Dublin Chamber of Commerce, Dublin Corporation and Guinness Ireland Group as an initiative designed to improve Dublin City and its environs. The closing date for the 2000 awards is the end of May 2000.

The Tyrone Guthrie Centre Subsidised Residencies

Regina Doyle
Acting Director
The Tyrone Guthrie Centre
Annaghmakerrig
Newbliss
Co. Monaghan

Tel/Fax: +353 47 54003/+353 47 54380
Email: thetgc@indigo.ie
Other key staff: Gráinne Millar (Administrator)

Applicants for these scholarships should be professional composers, or occasionally first rank performers in any musical medium. The amount of the awards are variable, and they take the form of subsidies where the artist must provide the balance. Twenty to forty of the awards are made every year to musicians. The awards are made throughout the year, and there is no closing date for entry.

Heineken Violin

Sharon McDonnell
Murray Consultants
35 Upper Mount Street
Dublin 2

Tel/Fax: +353 1 6614666/+353 1 6611932

The Heineken violin is presented on loan to an Irish professional musician for the duration of 4/5 years by Murphys Brewery Ireland.

The Ireland Funds Annual Grant Round

Grants Office
Oscar Wilde House
1 Merrion Square
Dublin 2

Tel/Fax: +353 1 6627878/+353 1 6627879
Email: ifdublin@iol.ie
Website: www.irlfunds.org
Other key staff: Kieran McLoughlin (Director)

The Ireland Funds support an annual grant round. In the 1998 grant round, the largest single grant was £20,000. The average disbursed was £5,000. There are four categories for Ireland Fund grants: arts and culture, community development, education and peace and reconciliation. The fund does not assist individuals. Within the area of the arts and culture, the Ireland Funds see the following as priorities: arts activities within the community; the arts and the education system; the inclusiveness and rehabilitative benefit of the arts, the arts and the economy; encouraging excellence, the arts and their impact; the arts, heritage and conservation and the promotion of culture.

Irish World Music Centre Scholarships

Ellen Byrne
Irish World Music Centre Foundation Studies
University of Limerick
Limerick

Tel/Fax: +353 61 202917/+353 61 202589
Email: ellen.byrne@ul.ie
Website: www.ul.ie/~iwmc/

Offer a limited number of scholarships for master level programmes. Scholarships currently available include the 100 Scholarship, the Fionnuala Hunt Scholarship, the Lyric FM Scholarship (all for MA in Classical String Performance Programme) and the Muckross House Scholarship for Irish Traditional Dance Performance. Candidates are evaluated according to funding availability, level of excellence and financial needs.

Kilcoole Music Festival

Clare Kilbride
Secretary
Windy Ridge
Kilquade
Greystones
Co. Wicklow

Tel: +353 1 2819217

50 competitions are held during this festival. Competitions for recorder, strings, brass, solo singing, duets and verse speaking. Held on the third weekend of May each year.

Limerick International Band Festival

Caroline Nolan-Diffley
Shannon Development
The Granary
Michael Street
Limerick

Tel/Fax: +353 61 410777/+353 61 315634
Email: bandfest@shannon-dev.ie
Website: www.shannon-dev.ie/bandfest
Other key staff: Eleanora Hogan (Project Executive), Mary Guiry (Administrator)

Drill and dance competitions and band recital competitions. The next competition will take place from 18-19 March 2001 and 17-18 March 2002.

John McCormack Golden Voice of Athlone

Siobhan Bigley
Executive Director
Athlone Chamber of Commerce
Jolly Mariner Marina
Coosan
Athlone
Co. Westmeath

Tel/Fax: +353 902 73173/+353 902 74386
Email: athcci@iol.ie
Other key staff: Mel O'Flynn (Secretary)

Classical singing competition with a prize fund of £8,000. The next competition will take place in March 2002.

Macardle Classical Music Scholarship

Mary O'Sullivan
Town Hall
Dundalk
Co. Louth

Tel/Fax: +353 42 9332276/+353 42 9351539
Email: dundarts@eircom.net

This scholarship is applicable to County Louth residents. £1,000 is awarded each year in January for players of classical instruments. Applicants from 12-16 years should apply in November of the previous year.

Elizabeth Maconchy Composition Fellowship

Eve O'Kelly
Contemporary Music Centre
19 Fishamble Street
Temple Bar
Dublin 8

Tel/Fax: +353 1 6731922/+353 1 6489100
Email: info@cmc.ie
Website: www.cmc.ie

This is a 3 year fellowship funded by the Arts Council/An Chomhairle Ealaíon, to enable a young Irish composer to undertake a DPhil in composition at the University of York in England. The fellowship will next be awarded in 2002, with an entry date in September 2001. Further details and application forms are available from the Contemporary Music Centre.

Mary Immaculate College - Postgraduate Assistantships

Dr Gareth Cox
Head of Music
South Circular Road
Limerick

Tel/Fax: +353 61 204904/+353 61 313632
Email: gareth.cox@mic.ul.ie
Website: www.mic.ul.ie

Award an organ scholarship and 3 graduate teaching scholarships to the value of £3,700 (including fee waiver) to suitable postgraduate students.

Thomas Moore Young Singers Competition

Anne McEvoy
Shalom
Newpark Drive
Kilkenny

Tel: +353 56 65063
Other key staff: Kay Sheehy (Secretary)

This bursary enables the winner to receive one year's voice training at DIT Conservatory of Music, Dublin. The aim of the competition is to foster an interest in Moore's melodies, which are so much a part of the Irish heritage. The competition has both a senior (for secondary school students) and junior section (for primary school students), and the scholarship/bursary is awarded to the winner of the senior section. Trophies are awarded to the second and third prizewinners in the senior section, and to the winner in the junior section.

National University of Ireland Maynooth - Organ Scholarship

Marie Breen
Department of Music
Maynooth
Co. Kildare

Tel/Fax: +353 1 7083730 or +353 1 7083733/ +353 1 6289432
Email: musicsec@may.ie
Other key staff: Prof. Gerard Gillen (Head of Department)

This scholarship is awarded in the first week of the first term to an organ student. The scholarship value is £1,200 and the scholar is required to perform certain duties in the college chapel.

Navan Choral Festival and Boyne Valley Honey National Choir of the Year Competition

Hugh Smyth
132 Ferndale
Navan
Co. Meath

Tel: +353 46 29163
Website: www.navanchoralfestival.com
Other key staff: Ernest McBride - mobile/fax: +353 87 2443739/+353 46 49637 (after 6pm)

Concerts and competitions featuring chamber and choral music.

New Music Commission Scheme

Eve O'Kelly
Contemporary Music Centre
19 Fishamble Street
Temple Bar
Dublin 8

Tel/Fax: +353 1 6731922/+353 1 6489100
Email: info@cmc.ie
Website: www.cmc.ie

The New Music Commission Scheme enables individuals or organisations based in Ireland or abroad to commission a new piece of music from a professional composer born, or permanently resident, in Ireland. The scheme is funded by the Arts Council/An Chomhairle Ealaíon, and administered by the Contemporary Music Centre. Applications are accepted twice per year, in February and September. Further details and application forms are available from the Contemporary Music Centre.

New Music for Sligo Composers Prize

Paul Cunningham
The Model & Niland Centre
The Mall
Sligo

Tel/Fax: +353 71 41405/+353 71 43694
Email: modelart@iol.ie
Website: www.iol.ie/~modelart/

Newpark Music Festival

Hilda Milner
Newpark Music Centre
Newtownpark Avenue
Blackrock
Co. Dublin

Tel/Fax: +353 1 2883740/+353 1 2883989
Other key staff: Noel Mason, Edel Devine (Festival Directors)

Orchestral, chamber, choral and jazz/improv are featured. Performances and competitions. 52 competitions are held in May each year.

Newry Musical Féis

Mary Goss
Honorary General Secretary
14 Windsor Hill
Newry
Co. Down BT34 1ER
Northern Ireland

Tel: 048 3026 2849
Email: a.m.goss@btinternet.com
Other key staff: Liam Quinn (Treasurer), Ethel Fitzpatrick (Chairperson)

An annual event with competitions in a wide variety of orchestral, chamber and choral categories. Choral work in English and Irish. Currently there are 113 competitions. Féis will take place in April 2001 and April 2002.

Northern Ireland Young Musician of the Year

R.D. Anderson
11 Holly Park Road
Killinchy
Co. Down BT23 6SN
Northern Ireland

Tel/Fax: 048 9754 1506

This annual competition is for solo instrumentalists and singers aged 12-16 years (18 years for singers). It takes place in the first week of March each year. The first prize is an engraved crystal bowl and £200.

The first prizewinners in the majority of classes receive either a cup or trophy. In the school choir section adult choral and adult vocal bursaries are awarded to the overall winners.

North of Ireland Bands Association

William J. Clements
28 Knockfergus Park
Greenisland
Carrickfergus
Co. Antrim BT38 8SN
Northern Ireland

Tel: 048 9086 6179
Other key staff: Douglas Gourley (Chairperson), George McFadden (Registration Secretary), John Patton (Treasurer)

The Association is the co-ordinating body for a number of separate leagues for different band types i.e accordions, brass concerts and flute, each with its own independent activity. The Association organises the Irish Band Championships and the individual leagues organise solo, quartet and other band concerts.

O'Carolan International Harp Competition

Padraic Noone
Keadue
Co. Roscommon

Tel/Fax: +353 78 47204/+353 78 47511
Email: ocarolan@oceanfree.net
Other key staff: Margaret Grimes (Chairperson), Berna Gibbons (PRO)

This competition is part of the O'Carolan Harp and Traditional Music Festival. The International Harp Competition has a prize fund of £2,000. The Senior Harp Competition has a first prize of £500 and a crystal trophy. Is held in August each year.

Portadown Music Festival

Carolyn McCabe
The Hollow
Bachelors Walk
Portadown
Co. Armagh BT63 5BQ
Northern Ireland

Tel/Fax: 048 3833 1046
Other key staff: T.N. Hutton (General Administrator)

The Queen's University of Belfast Scholarships

Caroline Fegan
School Secretary
School of Music
The Queen's University of Belfast
BT7 INN
Northern Ireland

Tel/Fax: 048 9033 5105/048 9023 8484
Email: c.fegan@qub.ac.uk
Website: www.music.qub.ac.uk
Other key staff: Professor Jan Smaczny (Head of Music)

The Queen's University of Belfast (QUB), offer the Harty-Brennan Scholarship, which is jointly funded by the School of Music at QUB and the Belfast Cathedral of St. Anne's. During university terms the scholar is expected to participate in the musical life of the cathedral. The scholar may also be required to assist in the University's choral activities as an accompanist or conductor. The scholar is entitled to free organ tuition from the cathedral organist, and to free practice on the cathedral's Harrison organ. This scholarship is opened to any student at QUB who is either an organist or singer. The closing date for applications is 1 March.

RTÉ Millennium Musician of the Future Festival

Jane Carty
Director
RTÉ
Donnybrook
Dublin 4

Tel/Fax: +353 1 2082048/+353 2082511
Email: cartyj@rte.ie
Other key staff: Deborah Kelleher (Assistant to the Director), Ciara Higgins (Events Manager)

This festival takes place every two years and consists of five competitions, masterclasses and concerts. The competitions are: The Musician of the Future, which has 5 sections including piano, keyboard, strings, wind and brass (age limit is 15-23 years; Singer of the Future (age limit is 17-30 years); Composer of the Future (age limit is 17-30 years); Poet of the Future - poems about music (age limit is 17-30 years); RTÉ Ensemble Prize (age limit is 15-30 years). The prize fund totals £24,000. The finals take place in the John Field Room at the National Concert Hall with the National Symphony of Ireland, broadcasted live on Network 2 television and Lyric FM. All events are sponsored by RTÉ.

Scór Sinsear and Scór na Nóg

Moria Graham
GAA Croke Park
Dublin 3

Tel/Fax: +353 1 8363222/+353 1 8366420

This competition is open to everybody. It is an annual competition with certificates and medals awarded. It comprises 8 categories: Instrumental music, novelty acts, question time, solo singing, ballad group singing, set dancing, recitation/story telling and figure dancing.

The Sibeal Sharkey Bursary

Fr Francis Bradley
St. Joseph's
Fairview Road
Galliagh
Derry
Northern Ireland

Tel/Fax: 048 7135 7979 or 048 7135 2351/ 048 7135 0458
Email: francis@fbradley.freeserve.co.uk
Other key staff: Giles Doherty (Chairman), Ursula Clifford (Registrar)

The bursary is awarded to those aged 16 years and over on or before 1st January immediately preceding the Feis. Opened to those who are resident in Counties Donegal, Derry or Tyrone. Open to candidates in instrumental music, vocal music (& Speech and Drama) who have outstanding potential and would benefit from advanced tuition. Normally paid out in installments to a school or teacher nominated by the winner. In addition to this bursary the following are also awarded: Ian Gow Memorial Fund (bursary to the Guildhall School of Music), Arts Council Bursary (normally £300), the Samuel Burke Award and the Edward Henry O'Doherty Shield.

Siemens Feis Ceoil

Carmel Byrne
Administrator
37 Molesworth Street
Dublin 2

Tel/Fax: +353 1 6767365/+353 1 6767429
Other key staff: Joan Cowle (Honorary Music Secretary), T.A Buckley (Honorary Treasurer), E.F Ryan (Honorary Treasurer)

Types of music promoted includes orchestral, chamber, choral, opera and instrumental. There are 161 competitions and junior and senior prizewinner concerts. Next held from 19/3 - 1/4 2001.

SIPTU Educational Scholarships Awards

Adelaide Waldron
Education & Training Department
SIPTU College
563 South Circular Road
Kilmainham
Dublin 8

Tel/Fax: +353 1 4530199/+353 1 4530194
Website: www.siptu.ie

The Services Industrial Professional and Technical Union (SIPTU), offers 2 specific scholarships for music studies. The first is a musical studies scholarship for members of SIPTU for at least 1 year, which is awarded each year and is valued at £4,000. Once it is granted it may be extended to successive years. The second musical scholarship is for daughters and sons of members of SIPTU for at least 5 years, which is awarded one a year. It is valued up to £4,000 per annum, depending on the place of residence. Application forms are available from 1 March each year. Closing date for applications is 1 January each year.

Skidmore Jazz Award

Awards Secretary
Arts Council of Northern Ireland
Macneice House
77 Malone Road
Belfast BT9 6AQ
Northern Ireland

Tel/Fax: 048 9038 5200/048 9066 1715
Email: performance@artscouncil-ni.org
Other key staff: Pamela Smith (Music & Opera Officer, Arts Council of Northern Ireland), Maura Eaton (Music Officer, Arts Council of Ireland)

The Arts Council of Northern Ireland and the Arts Council of Ireland jointly offer an award to enable a jazz musician to attend the summer jazz institute at Skidmore College, New York. One award is made each year, which covers travel expenses, fees and accommodation. Application forms are available from ACNI in March each year. Applicants should submit a tape with their application (specific details are on the application form).

Sligo International Choral Festival

Rev J.J Gannon
Chairperson
c/o Summerhill College
Sligo

Tel/Fax: +353 71 70733/+353 71 62048
Email: cicsummerhill@bigfoot.com
Other key staff: Joe Kelly (Honorary Treasurer), Anne Hylland (PRO)

The format of festival is competitions, concerts and church services. The festival takes place Oct/Nov each year.

The Songworks Song Competition

Tom Byrne
Director
Unit 63
Hanover Street East
Dublin 2

Tel/Fax: +353 1 6793880/+353 1 6793876
Email: songworks@esatclear.ie
Other key staff: Colin Turner (Creative Director)

This is an annual song competition for Irish and international songwriters, which received over 320 entries in its first year (1998). Prizes include the recording of 2 songs to a professional standard and a publishing deal for 3 years for the winning song. The entry fee is £10 per song.

South Dublin County Council Arts Bursary Scheme

Emily Jane Kirwan
Arts Officer
South Dublin County Council
Town Centre
Tallaght
Dublin 24

Tel/Fax: +353 1 4149000 Ext. 3314/
+353 1 4149106
Email: artsofficer@sdublincoco.ie
Website: www.sdcc.ie

This bursary scheme will provide support for artists to pursue residencies or develop a particular art project, either in Ireland or abroad at a location of their own determination. Applications are invited from artists working in the disciplines of music, photography, litera-

ture, painting and other art forms. Applicants must already have significant achievement to their credit, in the sense of having their work published, exhibited or performed in reputable places. Those applying should also have made a start on a particular project which might benefit from a stay at this workplace. Those applying for the bursary should have been born in or be living in the South Dublin administrative area.

TG4 National Traditional Music Awards/Gradam Ceoltóir Tradidsiúnta na Bliana

Gael Ocaidí Teo
29 Seacrest
Ballymoneen Road
Galway

Tel/Fax: +353 91 592700/+353 91 592723
Email: marymcp@eircom.net
Other key staff: Mary McPartlan (Director)

Gradam Ceoltóir Traidisiúnta na Bliana is an award and celebration of and in recognition of greatness in Irish traditional music. Teilifís na Gaeilge wishes to celebrate and give due recognition to the recordings, broadcasts and live performances of the awards' recipients. There are two awards: the main award and a special award to a young musician. The decision on recipients is taken on behalf of TG4 by six selected adjudicators. The awards are on an annual basis. Prizes include a cash bursary and a specially commissioned sculpture. The awards take place next in October 2000.

Trinity College School of Music Scholarships

Michael Taylor
Head of Music
House 5
Trinity College
Dublin 2

Tel/Fax: +353 1 6081120/+353 1 6709509
Email: musicsec@tcd.ie
Website: www.tcd.ie/music

The scholarships awarded include the Taylor Exhibition, which was founded in 1978. This scholarship is a gift from Mrs Eileen Taylor, to be awarded each year for a 2 year period at the discretion of the Professor of Music in consultation with the School of Music Committee. The Maffaffy Memorial Prize was founded in 1951 by a bequest from George Bell. It can be awarded to a Batchelor in Music or a Moderator in Music, for an original musical composition or for an essay on the theory of the history of music.

Waterford International Festival of Light Opera

Counsellor Sean M Dower
60 Morrisons Avenue
Waterford

Tel: +353 51 375437
Other key staff: Patrick Giles (Chairman),
Cllr Maurice Cummins (Vice-Chairman),
Kevin Kavanagh (Musical Director)

This is a competitive festival for amateur musical societies performing light opera and musicals. It will take place in Sept/Oct 2000, 2001 and 2002.

West Belfast Classical Music Bursary Awards

Una Downey
Administrator
56 Oakhurst Avenue
Blacks Road
Belfast BT10 0PE
Northern Ireland

Tel/Fax: 048 9062 6269
Other key staff: Angela Feeney (Artistic Director)

This is an annual event which takes place during the week following Easter. The seventh competition will take place from 18-21 April 2001 and the eighth will take place from 3-6 April 2002. The competition is open to all classical musicians born in the North or South of Ireland from 17-23 years (instrumentalists) or 18-28 years (vocalists). There is a chamber music section which is open to all nationalities, for trios, quartets and quintets aged 17-23 years. The total prize money is £9,500. In addition there are opportunities for BBC and RTÉ studio recordings, lunch-time concerts in Belfast, Munich and Brussels and appearances at a classical Christmas concert for past and present award winners.

University College Cork Undergraduate Scholarships

David Harold Cox
Music Department
University College Cork
Cork

Tel/Fax: +353 21 4904530/+353 21 4271595
Email: music@ucc.ie
Website: www.ucc.ie/ucc/depts/music

The following scholarships are awarded by UCC. 2 Comhaltas Ceoltóirí Éireann scholarships of £300 each are awarded annually to Irish traditional musicians who are studying music in the first year of BA or BMus studies. They are awarded on the basis of an audition. An organ scholarship of £500 is offered in association with St. Finbarres Cathedral. Duties include playing at services in the cathedral during term time. A choral scholarship of £500 is offered in association with St. Fin Barre's Cathedral. Duties include singing in the cathedral choir during term time. This is open to singers studying music in any year of the BA or BMus degree courses.

University College Dublin

Ms Maeve Mooney
Music Secretary
Belfield
Dublin 4

Tel/Fax: +353 1 7067632/+353 1 2691963

For the year 2000 an estimated 60 arts student scholarships worth £1,000 each, will be awarded. Awarded to every arts student who gets 520 points or above.

UTV School Choir of the Year

John Anderson
Ulster Television
Havelock House
Ormeau Road
Belfast BT7 1EB
Northern Ireland

Tel/Fax: 048 9032 8122/048 9024 6695
Email: schoolchoir@utvlive.com

The total prize fund for this award is £5,000 which is distributed between regional winners, section winners and the 'Choir of the Year'. The competition takes place in March and April each year. This competition is open to all primary, secondary and grammar schools in Northern Ireland. The closing date for entries is the end of January each year.

Michael Van Dessel Memorial Dundalk Choral Festival

Mary Mulligan
Secretary
72 Oakland Park
Dundalk
Co. Louth

Tel/Fax: +353 42 9338513/+353 42 9334639
Email: nmcgahon@eircom.net
Other key staff: Niall McGahon (Chairman),
Jan Van Dessel (Treasurer)

There are competitions in the following categories: adult mixed voice choirs (24 voices or more), adult mixed voice chamber choirs (24 voices or less), male voice choirs, female voice choirs, church choirs, sacred music for choirs, plain chant, junior choirs primary school age, junior choirs (intermediate school age and junior choirs senior school age).

Yamaha Music Foundation of Europe Scholarship

Kevin Farrell
General Manager
Danfay Ltd
61d Sallynoggin Road
Dun Laoghaire
Co. Dublin

Tel/Fax: +353 1 2859177/+353 1 2858810
Email: danfay@iol.ie

Applicants for this annual grant should be third level students born after 1 January 1976 (for 2001 scholarships). The instrumental discipline for which the award is made changes each year. The award of £2,000 sterling is made in January each year and the closing date for applications is November 20th of the previous year.

Young Traditional Musician of the Year Award

Donal Cassidy
Celtic Note Music Store
14-15 Nassau Street
Dublin 2

Tel/Fax: +353 1 6704157/+353 1 6704158
Email: sales@celticnote.ie
Website: www.celticnote.com

Applicants must be aged 18-25 years. The competition has a 1st prize of £10,000, which consist of £5,000 cash and a £5,000 recording deal with Celtic Note Records. The competition is sponsored by the Harcourt Hotel and Celtic Note Music Store in association with IMRO and Open House (RTÉ), Irish Music Magazine and local radio stations nationwide.

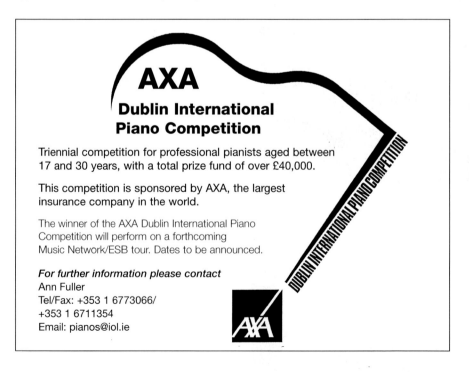

Composers

This section was compiled with the kind assistance of the following organisations:

Contemporary Music Centre

Jonathan Grimes
Information and Outreach Manager
19 Fishamble Street
Temple Bar
Dublin 8

Tel/Fax: +353 1 6731922/+353 1 6489100
Email: info@cmc.ie
Website: www.cmc.ie
Other key staff: Eve O'Kelly (Director),
Nicola Murphy (Promotions Officer)

Association of Irish Composers

John McLachlan
Executive Director
Copyright House
Pembroke Row
Dublin 2

Tel/Fax: +353 1 4961484
Email: aic@eircom.net

COMPOSERS & ARRANGERS

Elaine Agnew

17 Deerpark Road
Kilwaugher
Larne
Co. Antrim BT40 2PW
Northern Ireland

Tel: 048 2827 7566

Composes contemporary classical, classical and children's music. Qualified with BMus from The Queen's University Belfast, Postgraduate Diploma in Composition from the Royal Scottish Academy of Music and Drama. Has worked with the Irish Chamber Orchestra, Opera Theatre Company, ArtsCare and others.

Michael Alcorn

93 Scaddy Road
Crossgar
Co. Down BT30 9EU
Northern Ireland

Tel/Fax: 048 4483 1559
Email: alcorn@soundin.dnet.co.uk
Website: www.cmc.ie/composers/alcorn.htm

Composes contemporary classical and electro-acoustic music. Qualified with BMus and PhD. Has worked with the Ulster Orchestra, National Symphony of Ireland, the Smith String Quartet and others.

Mark Armstrong

25 Prospect Drive
Stocking Lane
Rathfarnham
Dublin 16

Tel/Fax: +353 1 4938786
Email: mja@indigo.ie

Composes and arranges film music and conducts Dun Laoghaire Choral Society. Qualified with BMus from Trinity College Dublin. Has worked with Shaun Davey, Ronan Hardiman, RTÉ Concert Orchestra and others.

Michael Ball

31 Sefton
Rochestown Avenue
Dun Laoghaire
Co. Dublin

Tel: +353 1 2350747

Composes contemporary classical, brass, wind, orchestral, choral and children's music. Qualified with BMus ARAM. Has worked with BBC Philharmonic Orchestra, BBC Singers, Royal Northern College of Music Wind Ensemble and others.

Stephen Barnett

3 Ashdale Crescent
Bangor
Co. Down BT20 4XL
Northern Ireland

Tel: 048 9145 2920
Email: sbar4660@aol.com

Composes and arranges classical, jazz, jingles, soundtracks and music for film/tv and music for children. Qualified graduate of music from the Royal Northern College of Music. Has worked with Ulster Orchestra and Ulster Brass.

Gerald Barry

2 Rosemount Terrace
Arbour Hill
Dublin 7

Tel/Fax: +353 1 6712899

Composes contemporary classical, opera, music for film/tv and theatre. Has worked with the BBC Symphony Orchestra, Frankfurt and Bavarian Radio Symphony Orchestras, the National Symphony of Ireland and others. Is a member of Aosdána.

Derek Bell

74 Bryansburn Road
Bangor
Co. Down BA20 3SB
Northern Ireland

Composes and arranges contemporary classical, opera, jazz, folk, celtic, soundtracks, jingles, church, classical, choral, world, traditional, background, theatre music and music for film/tv. Qualified with BMus from Trinity College Dublin, ARCM and LRAM. Has worked with BBC Symphony Orchestra, The Chieftains, the Belfast Philharmonic Chorus and others.

Seóirse Bodley

13 Cloister Green
Blackrock
Co. Dublin
Tel/Fax: +353 1 2781172
Email: seoirse.bodley@ucd.ie
Website: www.cmc.ie/composers/bodley.html

Composes contemporary classical, opera, church, choral music and music for children and film/tv. Qualified with DMus and LTCL. Emeritus Professor of Music UCD. Has worked with the National Symphony of Ireland, Irish National Youth Orchestra, University of Witten/Herdecke Choir and Orchestra and others. Is a member of Aosdána.

David Boyd

2 Claremont Villas
Glenageary
Co. Dublin

Tel/Fax: +353 1 2841819
Email: daveb@irishmusicians.com

Composes and arranges jazz, folk, soundtracks, rock, background, theatre music and music for film/tv and children. Qualified with BA in Performing Arts. Has worked with The Ark Childrens' Cultural Centre, The Royal Shakespeare Company, Opera Northern Ireland and others.

Paul Boyd

13 Briarwood Park
Belfast BT5 7HZ
Northern Ireland

Tel/Fax: 048 9079 0755
Email: paulboyd.music@dnet.co.uk
Website: www.paulboydmusic.co.uk

Composes and arranges theatre music. Has worked with Belfast Theatre Company, The Lyric Theatre Belfast, Kabosh Productions and others.

Brian Boydell

Derlamogue
Baily
Dublin 13

Tel: +353 1 8322021

Composes contemporary classical, choral and classical music. Qualified with DMus. Has worked with Dublin Orchestral Players and others and is founder of Dowland Consort. Is a member of Aosdána.

John Browne

31 Alconbury Road
London E5 8RG
England

Tel/Fax: +44 20 8806 9395

Composes contemporary classical, opera, theatre, dance, pop, music for children and film/tv. Qualified with BMus from University College Cork. Has worked with The Royal Opera House, The Ark Childrens' Cultural Centre, The Academy of St. Martin in the Fields London and others.

Melanie Brown

88 Bushy Park Road
Terenure
Dublin 6

Tel/Fax: +353 1 4903366/+353 1 4903251
Email: elaineb@eircom.net

Composes contemporary classical, opera, choral, church, theatre music, music for children and contemporary music of Jewish origin. Qualified with BAMod, MA from Trinity College Dublin, FTCL and ARIAM. Has worked with the Royal Irish Academy of Music, the National Concert Hall, RTÉ and others.

Ronan C. Browne

Mount Slaney
Stratford on Slaney
Co. Wicklow

Tel/Fax: +353 45 404873/+353 45 404015
Email: roro@esatclear.ie

Composes and arranges folk, celtic, soundtracks, jingles, traditional, background, theatre music and music for film/tv. Has worked with Donal Lunny, Riverdance, Peter Gabriel and others.

John Buckley

4 Ayrefield Grove
Malahide Road
Dublin 13

Tel: +353 1 8475042
Email: jbuck@indigo.ie

Composes contemporary classical music and music for film/tv and children. Qualified with MA in Composition from University College Cork. Has worked with Opera Theatre Company, National Symphony of Ireland, Hugh Tinney and others. Is a member of Aosdána.

David Byers

425 Beersbridge Road
Bloomfield
Belfast BT5 5DU
Northern Ireland

Tel/Fax: 048 9065 9706
Email: David.Byers@btinternet.com
Website: www.btinternet.com/~david.byers/homepage.htm

Composes contemporary classical, opera, classical, choral, church, theatre music and music for film/tv and children. Qualified with ARAM, GRSM, LRAM, ARCO and RAM Professional Certificate in Composition. Has worked with Ulster Orchestra, Belgian Radio Chamber Choir, Philip Martin and others.

Antonio Cafolla

40 Bolton Street
Dublin 1

Tel: +353 1 8733742
Email: cafolla@iol.ie

Composes and arranges contemporary classical, jazz, folk, celtic, soundtracks, jingles, theatre, traditional music and music for film/tv. Qualified with LTCL. Member of IMRO and Screen Training Ireland Film and TV.

Bill Campbell

1 Railway Cottages
Greenisland
Carrickfergus
Co. Antrim BT38 8RB
Northern Ireland

Tel: 048 9036 4569

Composes and arranges contemporary classical, jazz, soundtracks, choral, theatre music and music for film/tv and children. Qualified with BMus and MPhil in Music Composition. Has worked with the Scottish Chamber Orchestra, Ulster Orchestra and Sir Peter Maxwell.

David Catherwood

55 Schomberg Avenue
Belfast BT4 2JR
Northern Ireland

Tel/Fax: 048 9076 1610/048 9076 1156
Email: dwtcather@aol.com

Composes and arranges choral and church music and music for children. Qualified with BMus and PGCE. Has worked with Warner Brothers, Alfred Publishing Company and Hinshaw Music.

Rhona Clarke

Hillside
Strand Road
Sutton
Dublin 13

Tel/Fax: +353 1 8322450
Email: rhona@iol.ie
Website: www.cmc.ie/composers/clarke/html

Composes contemporary classical, opera, choral, theatre and music for film/tv and children. Qualified with BMus, Diploma in Music Teaching and PhD. Has worked with RTÉ, Music Network, The Arts Council and others.

Siobhan Cleary

20 Mount Temple Road
Stoneybatter
Dublin 7

Tel: +353 1 6715196
Email: siobhancleary@glebehse.iol.ie

Composes classical music and music for film/tv. Qualified with BA in Music and Irish and MA in Composition.

Denis Clohessy
150 Curlew Road
Drimnagh
Dublin 13

Tel: +353 1 4551429
Email: denis.clohessy@bigfoot.com

Composes and arranges choral, soundtrack, theatre and music for film/tv and children. Arranges music for rock groups. Qualified with BMus from the National University of Ireland Maynooth, Diploma in Arts Administration UCD and TV and Film Programme Certificate. Has worked with Dreamcatcher Productions, various primary and secondary schools, The Prayer Boat and others.

Aidan Coleman
28 Lisalea
Frascati Park
Blackrock
Co. Dublin

Tel: +353 1 2835117

Composes opera, jazz, folk, celtic, soundtrack, rock, pop, blues, reggae, jingles, church, choral, world, traditional, film/tv, background, theatre music and music for film/tv and children.

Frank Corcoran
Lenhartz Str. 8
20245 Hamburg
Germany

Tel/Fax: +49 40 463566

Composes contemporary classical, church music and music for children. Professor of music at the Hochschule für Musik, Hamburg, Germany. Has worked with the ORF Symphony Orchestra Vienna, National Symphony Orchestra of Ireland, RTÉ Chamber Orchestra and others. Is a member of Aosdána.

Anthony Costine
17 The Glen
Waterford

Tel: +353 51 850754

Composes and arranges soundtrack music and music for film/tv. Has worked with Waterford Youth Drama.

David Harold Cox
Department of Music
University College Cork
Cork

Tel/Fax: +353 21 4904530/+353 21 4271595

Composes contemporary classical music. Qualified with BMus, MA and PhD from the University of Birmingham.

Ellen Cranitch
33 Westfield Road
Harold's Cross
Dublin 6W

Tel/Fax: +353 1 4923486
Email: incran@indigo.ie

Composes jazz, world, theatre and music for film/tv. Qualified with BMus and ARIAM. Has worked with RTÉ Radio, Two Chairs Storytelling Company, Khanda and others.

Tom Cullivan
c/o The Contemporary Music Centre
19 Fishamble Street
Temple Bar
Dublin 8

Tel/Fax: +353 1 6731922/+353 1 6489100
Email: info@cmc.ie
Website: www.cmc.ie

Composes and arranges classical, choral and theatre music. Has worked with Cork School of Music Quintet, The Abbey Theatre, Choir of St. Audoens and others.

Shaun Davey
c/o Mick Barry

Tel/Fax: +353 1 2693821/+353 1 2693777
Email: mbe@clubi.ie

Composes music for theatre, film and tv.

Séamas de Barra
c/o Cork School of Music
Union Quay
Cork

Tel/Fax: +353 1 4270076/+353 1 4276595

Composes contemporary classical, choral, classical, church music and music for children. Has worked with the National Symphony of Ireland, RTÉ Concert Orchestra, Cork International Choral Festival and others.

Jerome de Bromhead

Martello Cottage
Strand Road
Killiney
Co. Dublin

Tel/Fax: +353 1 2825948

Composes contemporary classical music. Qualified with MA from Trinity College Dublin. Has worked with RTÉ, Culwick Choral Society, Emer Buckley and others. Is a member of Aosdána.

Raymond Deane

6 Haigh Terrace
Dun Laoghaire
Co. Dublin

Tel: +353 1 2841295
Email: rmdeane@eircom.net

Composes contemporary classical music. Is a member of Aosdána.

Stephen Deazley

Top Flat
57 Prince Regent Street
Edinburgh EH6 4AP
Scotland

Tel: +44 131 555 0586
Email: stephen@sco.org.uk

Composes contemporary classical, opera, improvised, theatre music and music for children. Qualified with BMus. Has worked with the Scottish Chamber Orchestra, Opera Northern Ireland, Edinburgh International Festival and others.

Donnacha Dennehy

24 Victoria Avenue
Donnybrook
Dublin 4
or
School of Music
5 Trinity College
Dublin 2

Tel: +353 1 6681131 or +353 1 6082503
Email: ddennehy@tcd.ie

Composes contemporary classical music. Qualified with BMus from Trinity College Dublin, MMus from the University of Illinois and also studied at IRCAM Paris. Has worked with London Brass, RTÉ Vanbrugh Quartet, Crash Ensemble and others.

Mark Dougherty

56 South Parade
Belfast BT7 2GP
Northern Ireland

Tel: 048 9064 8467

Composes and arranges classical, jazz, celtic, soundtrack, jingles, choral, traditional, theatre music and music for children, tv/film. Qualified with BMus from The Queen's University Belfast. Has worked with UTV, BBC, Ulster Orchestra and others.

Roger Doyle

Rynville Mews
Killarney Road
Bray
Co. Wicklow

Tel: +353 1 2828098
Email: rogerd@eircom.net
Website: www.cmc.ie/articles/just-discovering.html

Composes electro-acoustic and solo piano music. Has worked with Operating Theatre, Steven Berkoff and The Netherlands Wind Ensemble. Is a member of Aosdána.

John Drummond

Corrageen
Eslinbridge
Carrick on Shannon
Co. Leitrim

Tel/Fax: +353 78 31513/+353 78 31674
Email: jdt@gofree.indigo.ie

Benjamin Dwyer

90 The Steeples
Chapelizod
Dublin 20

Tel/Fax: +353 1 6234397
Email: mmbdwyer@indigo.ie

Composes contemporary classical music. Qualified with BMus, MMus, LTCL, LRSM and Graduate Diploma from DIT.

Trevor Enright

Arywee
Fedamore
Co. Limerick

Tel: +353 61 390198
Mobile: +353 87 2484941
Email: tenright@indigo.ie
Website: www.mediamusiccomposition.com

Composes and arranges contemporary classical, background, theatre music and music for film/tv and children. Has worked with Screen Training Ireland and Ceol Productions @ Keystone Studios.

Eibhlis Farrell

9 Pine Valley
Rostrevor
Co. Down
Northern Ireland

Tel/Fax: 048 4173 8021 or +353 1 4023568/
048 4173 8466 or +353 1 4023549
Email: eibhlis.farrell@sit.ie

Composes and arranges contemporary classical, opera, choral, church, theatre music and music for children. Qualified with BMus from The Queen's University Belfast, MMus from Bristol University, PhD from Rutgers, USA. Has worked with the Contemporary Music Centre and Dublin Institute of Technology Conservatory of Music and Drama. Is a member of Aosdána.

Stephen Gardner

10 Royal Terrace West
Dun Laoghaire
Co. Dublin

Tel: +353 1 2842136

Composes contemporary classical music. Has worked with RTÉ Concert Orchestra, Concorde, Crash Ensemble and others.

John Gibson

41 Cloverhill Estate
Blackrock
Cork

Tel/Fax: +353 21 4357676/+353 21 4276595

Composes and arranges contemporary classical, opera, folk, celtic, church, classical, choral, traditional music and music for film/tv and children. Qualified with

ARCM, LRAM and Music Diploma in Education. Has worked with the National Symphony of Ireland, RTÉ Concert Orchestra, RTÉ Vanbrugh String Quartet and others.

Conall Gleeson

120 Palmerstown Drive
Palmerstown
Dublin 20

Tel/Fax: +353 1 6266484
Mobile: +353 88 2524966
Email: ceoilpro@indigo.ie

Composes and arranges celtic, traditional, theatre music and music for film/tv. Qualified with LTCL and Postgraduate in viola performance from the Royal Northern College of Music, and Film Scoring Programme in UCLA. Has worked with the National Symphony of Ireland and Screen Training Ireland.

Derek Gleeson

C/o 120 Palmerstown Drive
Palmerstown
Dublin 20

Tel/Fax: +353 1 6235744
Email: dgleeson@prodigy.net
Website: www.derekgleeson.com

Composes contemporary classical, jazz, classical, soundtrack music and music for film/tv. Qualified ARCM. Has worked with The Chamber Orchestra of Europe, The London Philharmonic Orchestra, RTÉ Concert Orchestra and others.

Barry Grace & Paul Murphy

Ear 2 Ear
16 Herbert Street
Dublin 2

Tel/Fax: +353 1 6789173/+353 1 6610969
Email: ear2ear@iol.ie
Website: under construction

Composes and arranges music for advertising agencies and others.

Deirdre Gribbin

11 March Terrace
Dinnington
Newcastle Upon Tyne
NE13 7AF
England

Tel: +44 20 7419 7221
Email: deirdregribbin@yahoo.co.uk
Website: www.cmc.ie

Composes contemporary classical music. Qualified with PhD from the Royal Holloway College London, Fulbright Scholar New York 1999-2000, Arts Foundation 1999, Fellow in Opera Composition and Northern Arts Composing Fellow. Has worked with Ulster Orchestra, Sequenza, Joanna MacGregor and others.

Ronan Guilfoyle
10 O'Rourke Park
Sallynoggin
Co. Dublin

Tel/Fax: +353 1 2853497
Email: 251@eircom.ie

Composes contemporary classical, jazz, theatre music and music for film/tv. Has worked with RTÉ Concert Orchestra, Hibernia String Trio, Improvised Music Ensemble and others.

Douglas Gunn
Ballaghmore Castle
Borris-in-Ossory
Co. Laois

Tel: +353 505 23093
Email: dgunn@iol.ie

Composes and arranges contemporary classical, folk, celtic, church, choral and traditional music. Has worked with The Douglas Gunn Ensemble, The Vendon Duo and others.

Barry Guy
Griffinstown
Skeoughvosteen
Near Borris
Co. Kilkenny

Tel/Fax: +353 503 73860/+353 503 73862
Email: maya@eircom.net
Website: www.shef.ac.uk/misc/rec/ps/efi

Composes contemporary classical, electra acoustic, jazz, soundtrack, choral music and music for film/tv. Qualified with AGSM. Has worked with City of London Sinfonia, Medici String Quartet, Hilliard Ensemble and others.

Paul Hayes
Hiroo Heights No 208
5-1-14 Hiroo
Shibuya-Ku
Tokyo 150
Japan

Tel/Fax: +81 3 3407 4318
Email: pyfhayes@gol.com

Composes and arranges contemporary classical, contemporary electronic dance, opera, folk, celtic, soundtrack, church, classical, choral, world, traditional, background, theatre music and music for film/tv and children. Qualified with BA in Music and English and H Dip Ed. Has worked with the Irish Youth Dance Company, New Balance Dance Company, Association of Irish Composers and others.

Piers Hellawell
c/o School of Music
The Queen's University of Belfast
Belfast BT7 1NN
Northern Ireland

Tel/Fax: 048 9033 5404/048 9023 8484
Email: p.hellawell@freenet.co.uk

Composes contemporary classical music. Qualified with MA from Oxford University. Has worked with Michala Petri, London Symphony Orchestra, Hilliard Ensemble and others.

Michael Holohan
Listoke Lodge
Ballymakenny Road
Drogheda
Co. Louth

Tel: +353 41 9834853

Composes and arranges contemporary classical, classical, celtic, church, choral, world, traditional music and music for children. Qualified with BA, HDipEd, Postgraduate student of Dublin Institute of Technology Conservatory of Music and Drama. Has worked with Droichead Arts Centre, IMRO, Association of Irish Composers and others.

Rachel Holstead
c/o Stephanie Holstead
Ardamore House
Graigue
Lispole
Co. Kerry

Tel: +353 66 9157513
Email: holster@tcd.ie

Composes and arranges contemporary classical, choral, classical, soundtrack, church music and music for film/tv and children. Has worked with County Kildare Orchestras, Darragh Morgan, Anthony Byrne and others.

Ciaran Hope
1512 Federal Avenue No 5
Los Angeles
CA 90025
USA

Tel: +1 310 9154018 or +1 310 4455602
Email: cjhope@geocitites.com
Website: http://www.geocities.com/Vienna/Choir/4746

Composes and arranges contemporary classical, opera, jazz, celtic, soundtrack, choral, background music and music for film/tv. Qualified with MSC Audio Acoustics from Trinity College Dublin, MSC Electro-acoustic composition from Dublin Institute of Technology Conservatory of Music and Drama and Advanced Certificate in Film Scoring from University of Los Angeles. Has worked with Concorde, Disney Pictures, London Philharmonic Orchestra and others.

Michael Howard
53 Balkill Park
Howth
Co. Dublin

Tel: +353 1 8323475
Email: howmac@indigo.ie

Composes and arranges contemporary classical, choral, folk, celtic, soundtrack, world, traditional, background, theatre music and music for film/tv. Has worked with RTÉ, John Feeley, The Dubliners and others.

Willie Hughes
The Composer Company
Mount Evans
Rathangan
Co. Kildare

Tel: +353 87 2447847

Composes and arranges contemporary classical, folk, celtic, soundtrack, jingles, church, classical, choral, world, traditional, background, theatre music and music for film/tv and children. Has worked with Windmill Lane Studios, National Symphony of Ireland, Abbey Theatre and others.

Oliver Hynes
Post-primary Inspector of Music
Department of Education and Science
Hawkins House
Dublin 2

Tel/Fax: +353 1 8734700/+353 1 6715270
Email: hyneso@educ.irlgov.ie
Website: www.irlgov.ie/educ

Composes contemporary classical music. Has worked with the Association of Irish Composers and IMRO.

Marian Ingoldsby
c/o 37 St. Nicholas Park
Carrick-on-Suir
Co. Tipperary

Tel: +353 51 641222

Composes contemporary classical, opera, church, choral, background, theatre music and music for children. Qualified with MA in Composition from University College Cork, LTCL and currently completing a DPhil in Composition at the University of York. Has worked with Opera Theatre Company, the National Symphony of Ireland, Cork International Choral Festival and others.

Brian Irvine
North Down Centre
Castle Park Road
Bangor
Northern Ireland

Tel/Fax: 048 9127 0879/048 9188 8669
Email: brian.irvine@btinternet.com
Website: www.coyote_records.com

Areas of special interest include composition, improvisation and creative music making for all ages. Has worked with The Queen's University Belfast, Moving on Music, the Arts Council of Northern Ireland, Mater Hospital, Ards Borough Council, Drake Music Project and the Crescent Arts Centre. Examples of activities offered within projects includes creative music making through improvisation and composition, with the use of technology. Works with all age groups. Qualifications include a BMus.

Fergus Johnston
16 Trader's Wharf
40-43 Usher's Quay
Dublin 8

Tel: +353 1 6728864

Composes contemporary classical, choral, electronic, interactive dance, theatre music and music for children. Qualified with BA (Mod Music), MPhil in Music and Media Technology. Has worked with Opera Theatre Company, Irish Chamber Orchestra, National Concert Hall Education and Outreach Programme and others. Is a member of Aosdána.

Noel Kelehan
40 Anne Devlin Road
Dublin 14

Tel: +353 1 4945396

Composes and arranges jazz, choral, traditional, soundtrack, jingles, background, theatre music and music for film/tv. Chief arranger for over 25 years with RTÉ. Has worked with Art Farmer, Bobby Shaw, Ronnie Scott and others.

Denise Kelly
66 Darmouth Square South
Ranelagh
Dublin 6

Tel: +353 1 6689366
Mobile: +353 87 2457037

Composes and arranges contemporary classical and traditional music. Has worked with RTÉ Concert Orchestra, Ulster Orchestra, Orchestra of St. Cecilia and others.

Vincent Kennedy
18 Carriglea Drive
Firhouse
Dublin 24

Tel: +353 1 4525580

Composes and arranges contemporary classical, jazz, jingles, church, theatre music and music for children. Has worked with the National Symphony of Ireland, Concorde, RTÉ and others.

John Kinsella
7 Marley Rise
Grange Road
Rathfarnham
Dublin 16

Tel: +353 1 4936492

Composes contemporary classical and classical music. Has worked with RTÉ, Irish Chamber Orchestra, Eric Sweeney and others. Is a member of Aosdána.

Robert (Bobby) Lamb
15 Arkwright Road
Sanderstead
Surrey CR2 OLN
England

Tel: +44 181 657 6760

Composes contemporary classical, jazz, soundtrack, jingles, classical, choral, world, background, theatre music and music for film/tv and children. HFTCL. Has worked with Paramount, BBC, RTÉ and others.

Michael McGlynn
5 Lakelands Lawn
Stillorgan
Co. Dublin

Tel/Fax: +353 1 2835533
Email: info@anuna.ie
Website: www.anuna.ie

Composes and arranges contemporary classical, folk, celtic, soundtrack, church, classical, choral, world, traditional music and music for film/tv. Qualified with BA and BMus. Has worked with Anúna, Ulster Orchestra, Gate Theatre and others.

Deirdre McKay
21 Hall Road
Ballynahinch
Co. Down BT24 8XY
Northern Ireland

Tel/Fax: 048 9756 2640
Email: d.t.mckay@qub.ac.uk

Composes contemporary classical music. Qualified with BMus and MusM. Has worked with Music Network, Ulster Orchestra, Irish Chamber Orchestra and others.

Mary S. McAuliffe
124 Applewood Heights
Greystones
Co. Wicklow

Tel: +353 1 2876800
Email: mcaul@indigo.ie

Composes and arranges contemporary classical music. Qualified with BMus from University College Cork. Has worked with the Culwick Choral Society, Binneas Chamber Choir, Orla Colgan and others.

Stephen McKeon

Ash Lodge
Blessington
Co. Wicklow

Tel/Fax: +353 45 865861/+353 1 865903
Email: smckeon@indigo.ie

Composes and arranges music for film and tv. Has worked with Temple Films, RTÉ, BBC and others.

John McLachlan

11 Belgrave Road
Rathmines
Dublin 6

Tel/Fax: +353 1 4961484
Email: johnmclachlan@eircom.net

Composes contemporary classical music. Qualified with BA, LTCL and ARIAM. Has worked with Hibernia String Trio and has had works performed in Ireland, Paris, London and elsewhere.

Paul Marshall

32 Rugby Avenue
Bangor
Co. Down BT20 3 PZ

Tel/Fax: 048 9145 5737
Email: paul@drumtec.com
Website: www.drumtec.com

Composes soundtracks, world, film/tv, background, theatre, music for children, ambient, hip-hop, jungle and experimental. Qualified with MBA and DMS. Has worked with Belfast Community Drama circle and Old Museum Arts Centre among others.

Neil Martin

Flying Fox
42 Landsdowne Road
Belfast BT15 4AA
Northern Ireland

Tel/Fax: 048 9024 4811/048 9023 4699
Email: flyingfox.cbn@artservicesireland.com

Composes and arranges folk, celtic, soundtrack, traditional, background, theatre music and music for film/tv. Qualified with BA in Music and Celtic Studies from The Queen's University Belfast. Has worked with the Dubliners, TG4, RTÉ and others.

Philip Martin

Chapel House
Theobalds Green
Calstone
Calne
Wiltshire SN11 8QE
England

Tel: +44 1249 812 508
Email: pmandppj@globalnet.co.uk
Website: robertd.cummingsontcumming@csrlink.net

Composes contemporary classical, opera, church, choral, classical, theatre music and music for film/tv and children. Qualified with LRAM, ARAM and FRAM. Has worked with BBC, RTÉ, various symphony orchestras and others. Is a member of Aosdána.

Colin Mawby

Gerrardstown
Garlow Cross
Navan
Co. Meath

Tel/Fax: +353 46 29394

Composes contemporary classical, opera, choral, church music and music for children. Has worked with the National Chamber Choir, RTÉ Philharmonic Choir, the National Symphony of Ireland and others.

Jules Maxwell

6 Abbey Drive
Bangor
Co. Down BT20 4DA
Northern Ireland

Tel/Fax: 048 4063 1497
Email: jules_music@yahoo.com

Composes and arranges jazz, soundtrack, jingles, background, theatre music and music for film/tv and children. Has worked with Lyric Theatre Belfast, Daghdha Dance Company, UTV and others.

Alan Mills
87 Palmerston Road
Wood Green
London N22 4QS
England

Tel: +44 20 8888 8214

Composes contemporary classical, choral and church music. Qualified with MA in music from Cambridge University and Certificate of Advanced Study from Guildhall School of Music. Has worked with the Arts Council of Northern Ireland, Joanna MacGregor, Finchley Children's Music Group and others.

Dr. David Morris
Music Division
University of Ulster Jordanstown
Co. Antrim BT37 0QB
Northern Ireland

Tel/Fax: 048 9036 6690/048 9036 6870
Email: dmorris@ulst.uk

Composes contemporary classical music. Qualified with BMus, MMus and PhD. Has worked with Ulster Orchestra, London Sinfonietta, Warsaw Symphony Orchestra and others.

Gráinne Mulvey
Church Street
Leighlinbridge
Co. Carlow

Tel: +353 503 21403
Email: geem@eircom.net

Composes contemporary classical music. Qualified with DPhil Composition. Has worked with York University Orchestra, the National Symphony of Ireland, Northern Sinfonia and others.

Gerry Murphy
15 Cullenswood Gardens
Ranelagh
Dublin 6

Tel/Fax: +353 1 4973929/+353 1 4967769
Email: office@gonzaga.ie

Composes and arranges contemporary classical, opera, celtic, church, theatre, classical music and music for children.

Kevin O'Connell
163 Clifden Court
Ellis Quay
Dublin 7

Tel/Fax: +353 1 6710351
Email: kevire@hotmail.com
Website: www.cmc.ie/composers/oconnell.htm

Composes contemporary classical and opera. Qualified with BA and MPhil from Trinity College Dublin. Is a member of Aosdána.

Adele O'Dwyer
Silver River Studios
Acontha
Durrow
Tullamore
Co. Offaly

Tel/Fax: +353 506 24044
Email: silverrivermusic@eircom.net

Composes and arranges contemporary classical, folk, celtic, soundtrack, jingles, classical, world, traditional, theatre music and music for film/tv and children. Qualified with BMus from Northwestern University USA, Film Scoring University of California Los Angeles and FÁS Joint Certification to be awarded. Has worked with the National Symphony of Ireland, DeDannan, BBC and others.

Jane O'Leary
1 Avondale Road
Highfield Park
Galway

Tel/Fax: +353 91 522847/+353 91 582153

Composes contemporary classical music. Qualified with BA, PhD, MFA from Princeton University. Has worked with RTÉ Vanbrugh Quartet, Irish Chamber Orchestra, John Feeley and others. Is a member of Aosdána.

Mícheál Ó Súilleabháin
Irish World Music Centre
University of Limerick
Limerick

Tel/Fax: +353 61 202590/+353 61 202589
Website: www.ul.ie/~lwmc

Composes and arranges contemporary classical, jazz, folk, celtic, church, classical, choral, world, traditional, theatre music and music for film/tv. Qualified with BMus, MA, PhD and LTCL. Has worked with Irish Chamber Orchestra and Irish World Music Centre.

Charles Stephen Parker
19 Raglan House
Ballsbridge Court
Ballsbridge
Dublin 4

Tel: +353 1 6603557

Composes contemporary classical music and music for film. Qualified with a performance degree in piano from the Royal College of Music London and a Licentiate performers diploma from Leister School of Music. Has worked with the Moravian Philharmonic Orchestra and others.

Bernard Reilly
26 Sandyford Downs
Sandyford
Dublin 18

Tel/Fax: +353 1 2958742
Email: breilly@eircom.net

Composes and arranges contemporary classical, jazz, celtic, soundtrack, theatre music and music for film/tv and children. Has worked with RTÉ, the Irish Film Board, TG4 and others.

Kenneth Rice
29 Marine Village
Ballina
Killaloe
Co. Tipperary

Mobile: +353 87 2474360
Fax: +353 61 375271
Email: kenrice@eircom.net

Composes and arranges contemporary classical, jingles music and music for film/tv. Qualified with BMus, MA and LTCL. Has worked with RTÉ, Eleanor Shanley, contemporary groups and others.

Richard C. Shanahan
Dromore House
Farranfore
Killarney

Tel/Fax: +353 66 9764278/+353 66 97664621
Email: rshanahan@eircom.net

Composes church, classical and choral music. Recipient of Fleischmann choral training and conducting. Has worked with Tralee Musical Society, Tralee Orchestral Society, Kerry Chamber Choir and others.

Eric Sweeney
Beaumaris
Summerville Avenue
Waterford

Tel: +353 51 876455
Email: esweeney@wit.ie

Composes contemporary classical music. Qualified with BMus, MA, DPhil, LRAM and LRSM. Has worked with RTÉ, Ronan Guilfoyle, Waterford New Music Ensemble and others. Is a member of Aosdána.

Andrew Synott
98 Wilfield Road
Sandymount
Dublin 4

Tel: +353 1 2696023
Mobile: +353 87 2984245
Email: asynott@eircom.net

Composes and arranges contemporary classical, opera, choral, soundtrack, jingles, church, classical, choral, background, theatre music and music for film/tv and children. Qualified with BMus from Trinity College Dublin. Has worked with Opera Theatre Company, Irish Modern Dance Theatre, Christchurch Cathedral Choir and others.

Joe Thoma
An Droichead
Gortamullin
Kenmare
Co. Kerry

Tel: +353 64 41212

Composes and arranges folk, celtic, jingles, contemporary dance, traditional, theatre music and music for film/tv. Has worked with Kenmare Childrens Orchestra, Dublin Contemporary Dance and others.

Fiachra Trench
Easton House
Delgany
Co. Wicklow

Tel/Fax: +353 1 2875972/+353 1 2873852

Composes and arranges music for film/tv and arranges music for rock and pop music. Qualified with MMus. Has worked with RTÉ and others.

Joan Trimble
The Battery House
Forthill
Enniskillen
Northern Ireland

Tel/Fax: 048 6632 2107/048 6632 5047

Composes and arranges classical music. Qualified with BMus, MA, LRAM and is FRIAM and HRCM. Has worked with RTÉ, BBC, UTV and others.

Ken Tuohy
31 Bayside Square East
Sutton
Dublin 13

Tel/Fax: +353 1 8395151/+353 1 8395526
Email: balfor@iol.ie

Composes contemporary classical, opera, jazz, folk, celtic, soundtrack, jingles, church, choral, classical, world, traditional, background, theatre music and music for film/tv and children.

Kevin Volans
The Stableyard
Knockmaroon
Castleknock
Dublin 15

Tel/Fax: +353 1 8207579
Email: kvolans@iol.ie

Composes contemporary classical and opera music. Qualified with BMus and DMus. Has worked with the Netherlands Wind Ensemble, Siobhan Davies, Jonathan Burrows Dance Companies and others.

John Walsh
20 Herbert Place
Dublin 2
Tel: +353 1 6625775

Composes and arranges soundtrack, jingles music and music for film/ tv. Has worked with ESB, RTÉ, Bank of Ireland and others.

Bill Whelan
30-32 Sir John Rogerson's Quay
Dublin 2

Tel/Fax: +353 1 6777330/+353 6777276
Email: mcgw@numb.ie
Website: www.billwhelan.com

Composes and arranges celtic, soundtracks, choral, world, traditional, theatre music and music for film/tv. Has worked with Planxty, Abbey Theatre, U2 and others.

John Christie Willot
c/o The House of Music Ltd
3 Easons Avenue
Cork

Tel/Fax: +353 21 4509612
Email: homusic@eircom.net
Website: www.homusic.com

Composes and arranges contemporary classical, opera, jazz, soundtrack, jingles, church, choral, theatre music and music for film/tv. Has worked with State Opera Maine, South West German Radio, English Chamber Orchestra and others.

Ian Wilson
c/o Contemporary Music Centre
19 Fishamble Street
Temple Bar
Dublin 8

Tel/Fax: +353 1 6731922/+353 1 6489100
Email: wilsonkul@esatclear.ie
Website: www.cmc.ie

Composes contemporary classical music. Qualified with BA (Hons) Music and DPhil from the University of Ulster. Has worked with the London Mozart Players, BBC National Orchestra of Wales and the Vanbrugh Quartet among others. Is a member of Aosdána.

James Wilson
10a Wyvern
Killiney
Co. Dublin

Tel: +353 1 2850786
Email: jwilson@iol.ie

Composes contemporary classical, opera, choral, theatre music and music for children. Is a member of Aosdána.

John Wolf Brennan
Hofmattstr 5
CH-6353 Weggis
Lucerne
Switzerland

Tel/Fax: +41 41 390 2777/+41 41 390 2761
Email: brennan@swissonline.ch
Website: www.brennan.ch

Composes contemporary classical, opera, jazz, church, choral, theatre music and music for children. Studied piano and composition in Lucerne. Has worked with Association of Irish Composers, Pago Libre, Groupe Lacroix and others.

Norman Yourell-Keating
2 Butterfield Orchard
Rathfarnham
Dublin 14

Tel: +353 1 4930805

Composes and arranges theatre music and music for film/tv. Has worked with ensemble groups and soloists.

Patrick Zuk
16 Myrtle Hill Terrace
Lower Glanmire Road
Cork

Composes contemporary classical, choral, church and classical music. Has worked with the National Symphony of Ireland, RTÉ Vanbrugh String Quartet, American Waterways Wind Orchestra and others.

Media

NATIONAL PRINT MEDIA - REPUBLIC OF IRELAND

Classical Ireland
Ellen O'Hea
Editor
11 Clare Street
Dublin 2

Tel: +353 1 6624887/+353 1 6624886
Email: mrs@iol.ie

The Evening Herald
Maurice Haugh
Arts Editor
90 Middle Abbey Street
Dublin 1

Tel: +353 1 7055333 or +353 1 7055667/
+353 1 8720304
Email: m.haugh@unison.ie
Contact: Dave Kenny (Features Editor -
dkenny@unison.ie), Michael Dungan (Classical -
mdbs@indigo.ie), Sarah McQuaid (Folk -
smquaid@indigo.ie), Matt Nugent (Jazz -
herald.news@unison.ie)

The Irish Examiner
Declan Hassett
Arts Editor
PO Box 21
Academy Street
Cork

Tel/Fax: +353 21 4272722/+353 21 4275112
Email: features@examiner.ie
Website: www.examiner.ie
Contact: Declan Townsend (Classical),
Declan Hassett (Classical), Pat Ahern (Traditional),
Paul Dromey (Jazz)

Hot Press Magazine
Niall Stokes
Editor
13 Trinity Street
Dublin 2

Tel/Fax: +353 1 6795077/+353 1 6795097
Email: hotpress@iol.ie
Website: www.hot-press.com

Ireland on Sunday
Fionnuala McCarthy
Features Editor
50 City Quay
Dublin 2

Tel/Fax: +353 1 6718255/+353 1 6718882
Email: info@irelandonsunday.iol.ie
Contact: Eugene Masterson (Music)

Irish Independent
Independent Newspapers Ltd
90 Middle Abbey Street
Dubin 1

Tel/Fax: +353 1 8731333/+353 1 8720304
Email: indo.features@unison.ie
Website: www.unison.ie
Contact: Pat O'Kelly (Classical Reviews),
John Boland (Classical)

Irish Music Magazine
Sean Laffey
Editor
11 Clare Street
Dublin 2

Tel/Fax: +353 1 6624887/+353 1 6624886
Email: mrs@iol.ie
Website: www.mayo-ireland.ie/irishmusic.htm

The Irish Times
Victoria White
Arts Editor
10-16 D'Olier Street
Dublin 2

Tel/Fax: +353 1 6792022/+353 1 6779181
Email: vwhite@irish-times.ie or
ydrysdale@irish-times.ie
Website: www.ireland.com
Contact: Michael Dervan (Music Critic -
mdervan@irish-times.ie), Tony Clayton-Lea
(Traditional - tclaytonlea@irish-times.ie),
Ray Comiskey (Jazz - rcomiskey@irish-times.ie),
Sheila Wayman (Features Editor - swayman@irish-times.ie),
Patsy Murphy (Weekend Editor - pmurphy@irish-times.ie), Willie Clingan (News Editor - wclingan@
irish-times.ie)

Additional Information: 'Michael Dervan's Classical
Music' on the Irish Times portal website at
www.ireland.com/dublin/, provides a weekly classical

news column and countrywide concert guide. Selected features and reviews from the newspaper and a selective guide to other music and entertainment events can be accessed.

RTÉ Guide
RTÉ
Donnybrook
Dublin 4

Tel/Fax: +353 1 2082920/+353 2083085
Email: corra@rte.ie
Contact: Alan Corr (Music Journalist)

The Star
Danny Smyth
Features Editor
Star House
62a Terenure Road North
Dublin 6W

Tel/Fax: +353 1 4901228/+353 1 4902193
Email: danny.smyth@the-star.ie

The Sunday Business Post
Joanne Hayden
Arts Editor
80 Harcourt Street
Dublin 2

Tel/Fax: +353 1 6026000/+353 1 6796496
Email: sbpost@iol.ie
Website: www.sbpost.ie
Contact: Jennifer O'Connell (Agenda Section - jennifer@rbport.ie)

The Sunday Times
Michael Ross
Huguenot House
35 St. Stephen's Green
Dublin 2

Tel/Fax: +353 1 6028859/+353 1 6028847
Email: culture.ireland@sunday-times.co.uk
Website: www.sunday-times.co.uk
Contact: Dermot Murphy (Classical and Jazz), Mick Heaney (traditional)

The Sunday Tribune
Lise Hand
Arts Editor

15 Lower Baggot Street
Dublin 2

Tel/Fax: +353 1 6314300 or +353 1 6314366/ +353 1 6766420
Email: features@tribune.ie
Contact: Ian Fox (Classical), Fintan Vallely (Traditional), Colm O'Sullivan (Jazz)

The Sunday World
John Sheils
Features Editor
18 Rathfarnham Road
Dublin 6

Tel/Fax: +353 1 4063500/+353 1 4908592
Contact: Eddie Rowley (Music - eddierowley@sundayworld.com)

NATIONAL PRINT MEDIA - NORTHERN IRELAND

Belfast Telegraph
Neil Johnston
Arts Editor
124-144 Royal Avenue
Belfast BT1 1EB
Northern Ireland

Tel/Fax: 048 9026 4409/048 9055 4517
Contact: Rathcol (classical), Neil Johnston (Traditional and Jazz)

Irish News
Anna Marie McFaul
Features Editor
113-117 Donegall Street
Belfast BT1 2GE
Northern Ireland

Tel/Fax: 048 9032 2226/048 9033 7505
Website: www.irishnews.com

News Letter
Ian Hill
Arts Editor
46-56 Boucher Crescent
Belfast BT12 6QY
Northern Ireland

Tel/Fax: 048 9068 2860
Contact: Ian Hill (Classical), Geoff Harden (Traditional and Jazz - geoff.harden@dnet.co.uk)

Sunday Life
124-144 Royal Avenue
Belfast BT1 1EB
Northern Ireland

Tel/Fax: 048 9026 4300/048 9055 4507
Contact: John McGurk (Music)

LOCAL PRINT MEDIA - CONNACHT

ArtsWest
Ian Wieczorek
Editor
Annagh
Castlebar
Co. Mayo

Tel/Fax: +353 94 25011
Email: artswest@eircom.net

The Connacht Sentinel
Brendan Carroll
The Editor
15 Market Street
Galway

Tel/Fax: +353 91 567251/+353 91 567970
Email: ctribune@iol.ie
Website: www.iol.ie/ctribune

Connacht Telegraph
Tom Gillespie
The Editor
Ellison Street
Castlebar
Co. Mayo

Tel/Fax: +353 94 21711/+353 94 24002
Email: conntel@eircom.net
Website: www.con-telegraph.ie

Connacht Tribune
John Cunningham
The Editor
15 Market Street
Galway

Tel/Fax: +353 91 567251 or +353 91 567259/
+353 91 567970

Galway Advertiser (free)
Jeff O'Connell
Entertainments Editor
2-3 Church Lane
Galway

Tel/Fax: +353 91 567077/+353 91 565627
Email: kbarrett@galwayadvertiser.ie
Website: www.galwayadvertiser.ie

Leitrim Observer
Claire Casserly
The Editor
St. George's Terrace
Carrick-on-Shannon
Co. Leitrim

Tel/Fax: +353 78 20025/+353 76 20112
Email: leitrimobserver@eircom.net

Magpie
Declan Varley
The Editor
Odeon House
Eyre Square
Galway

Tel/Fax: +353 91 567600/+353 91 567635
Email: info@magpie.ie
Website: www.magpie.ie

Mayo News
Declan McGuire
General Manager
The Fairgreen
Westport
Co. Mayo

Tel/Fax: +353 98 25311/+353 98 26108
Email: mayonews@anu.ie
Website: www.mayonews.ie

Roscommon Champion
Paul Healy
The Editor
Abbey Street
Roscommon

Tel/Fax: +353 903 25051 or +353 903 25053/
+353 903 25053
Email: roscommonchampion@eircom.net

Website: homepage.eircom.net/~
roscommonchampion

Roscommon Herald
Christina McHugh
The Editor
Patrick Street
Boyle
Co. Roscommon

Tel/Fax: +353 79 62004/+353 79 62926
Website: www.roscommonherald.ie

Sligo Champion
Jim Gray
Arts Editor
Wine Street
Sligo

Tel/Fax: +353 71 69222 or +353 71 69133/
+353 71 69040

Sligo Weekender
Robert Cullen
Entertainments Editor
Waterfront House
Bridge Street
Sligo

Tel/Fax: +353 71 42140/+353 71 42255
Email: weekender@iol.ie

Tuam Herald
David Burke
The Editor
Dublin Road
Tuam
Co. Galway

Tel/Fax: +353 93 24183/+353 93 24478
Email: tuamherald@iol.ie
Website: www.tuamherald.ie

Western People
David Dwane
Entertainments Editor
Francis Street
Ballina
Co. Mayo

Tel/Fax: +353 96 21188/+353 96 70208
Email: wpeople@iol.ie
Website: www.westernpeople.ie

LOCAL PRINT MEDIA - DUBLIN CITY AND COUNTY

Citywide News (free)
Edel Williams
The Editor
26a Phibsboro Place
Phibsboro
Dublin 7

Tel/Fax: +353 1 8306667/+353 1 8306833
Email: lifetimes@dna.ie
Website: www.irelandplus.com/cwn

Dublin Extra (free)
Edel Williams
The Editor
26a Phibsboro Place
Phibsboro
Dublin 7

Tel/Fax: +353 1 8306667/+353 1 8306833
Email: lifetimes@dna.ie
Website: www.irelandplus.com/cwn

Dublin Mail (free)
William Murray
The Editor
2 Whitehall Road West
Perrystown
Dublin 12

Tel/Fax: +353 1 4552832/+353 1 4552845

The Dublin People
Tony McCullagh
The Editor
85-86 Omni Park Shopping Centre
Santry
Dublin 9

Tel/Fax: +353 1 8621611/+353 1 8621625
Email: news@northsidepeople.ie
Website: www.northsidepeople.ie

The Echo

David Kennedy
The Editor
48 Old Bawn Road
Tallaght
Dublin 24

Tel/Fax: +353 1 4598513/+353 1 4598514
Email: studio@the-echo.ie
Website: www.the-echo.ie

Event Guide (free)

Kieran Owen
The Editor
7 Eustace Street
Dublin 2

Tel/Fax: +353 1 6713377/+353 1 6710502
Email: info@eventguide.ie
Website: www.eventguide.ie

Fingal Independent

Hubert Murphy
The Editor
4 Main Street
Swords
Co. Dublin

Tel/Fax: +353 1 8407107/+353 1 8407022
Email: hmurphy@fingal-independent.ie
Website: www.unison.ie

The Fitzwilliam Post (free)

Michael Dunne
The Editor
Hogan House
15-17 Hogan Place
Grand Canal Street
Dublin 2

Tel/Fax: +353 1 6613022/+353 1 6613130

In Dublin

Jack Brouder
Arts Editor
3-7 Camden Place
Dublin 2

Tel/Fax: +353 1 4784322/+353 1 4781055
Email: info@hoson.com
Website: www.hoson.com

Life Times (free)

Edel Williams
The Editor
26a Phibsboro Place
Phibsboro
Dublin 7

Tel/Fax: +353 1 8306667/+353 1 8306833
Email: lifetimes@dna.ie
Website: www.irelandplus.com/cwn

Liffey Champion

Vincent Sutton
The Editor
3 Captains Hill
Leixlip
Co. Kildare

Tel/Fax: +353 1 6245533/+353 1 6243013
Email: champnews@eircom.net

North County Leader

Fergal O'Connor
The Editor
Unit 4
20 North Street
Swords
Co. Dublin

Tel/Fax: +353 1 8400200/+353 1 8400550
Email: northcol@indigo.ie

Northside People (free)

Tony McCullagh
The Editor
85-86 Omni Park Shopping Centre
Santry
Dublin 9

Tel/Fax: +353 1 8621611/+353 1 8621625
Email: news@northsidepeople.ie
Website: www.northsidepeople.ie

Southside People (free)

Ken Finlay
The Editor
85-86 Omni Park Shoppping Centre
Santry
Dublin 9

Tel/Fax: +353 1 8621611/+353 1 8621625
Email: news@northsidepeople.ie
Website: www.northsidepeople.ie

Southwest Express
John Russell
The Editor
PO Box 3430
Kennedy Centre
Tallaght
Dublin 24

Tel/Fax: +353 1 4519000/+353 1 4519805

South Dublin Life and Leisure
Alice Sheridan
The Editor
6a Church Place
Sallynoggin
Co. Dublin

Tel/Fax: +353 1 2808880/+353 1 2809020
Email: jaguarpublishing@indigo.ie

LOCAL PRINT MEDIA - LEINSTER

The Argus
Kevin Mulligan
The Editor
Park Street
Dundalk
Co. Louth

Tel/Fax: +353 42 9334632/+353 42 9331643
Email: editorial@argus.ie
Website: www.argus.ie

Athlone Observer
Jason Gill
The Editor
Jesmond Lodge
Station Road
Athlone
Co. Westmeath

Tel/Fax: +353 902 74975/+353 902 78668

Athlone Topic
Louis Glennon
News Editor
Mardyke Street
Athlone
Co. Westmeath

Tel/Fax: +353 902 76060/+353 902 74260

Bray People
Eoin Quinn
The Editor
25 Main Street
Bray
Co. Wicklow

Tel/Fax: +353 1 2867393/+353 1 2860879
Email: editor@braypeople.ie
Website: www.braypeople.ie

Carlow Advertiser (free)
Barry Duggan
The Editor
Strawhall Industrial Estate
Athy Road
Carlow

Tel/Fax: +353 503 31512/+353 503 40016
Email: carlowadvertiser@eircom.net

Carlow People
Michael Ryan
The Editor
Lismard House
Tullow Street
Carlow

Tel/Fax: +353 503 42496/+353 503 34185
Email: carlownews@eircom.net
Website: www.peoplenews.ie

Drogheda Independent
Brian Murphy
Editorial Department
Independent House
9 Shop Street
Drogheda
Co. Louth

Tel/Fax: +353 41 9838658/+353 41 9842753
Email: bmurphy@drogheda-independent.ie
Website: www.unison.ie

Drogheda Leader
Desmond Grant
The Editor
Dominic Street
Drogheda
Co. Louth

Tel/Fax: +353 41 9836100/+353 41 9841517
Email: droghedaleader@eircom.net

Dundalk Democrat

Joe Carroll
The Editor
3 Earl Street
Dundalk
Co. Louth

Tel/Fax: +353 42 9334058/+353 42 9331399
Email: dundalkdemo@eircom.net

The Echo Newspaper Group

Tom Mooney
The Editor
Mill Park Road
Enniscorthy
Co. Wexford

Tel/Fax: +353 54 33231/+353 54 33506

The Guardian

Michael Ryan
The Editor
Castle Hill
Enniscorthy
Co. Wexford

Tel/Fax: +353 54 33642/+353 54 35910
Email: dasheria@hotmail.com
Website: www.peoplenews.ie

Kildare Nationalist

Eddie Coffey
The Editor
Liffey House
Edward Street
Newbridge
Co. Kildare

Tel/Fax: +353 45 432147/+353 45 433720
Email: jjreport@indigo.ie

The Kildare Times (free)

Terry O'Mahony
The Editor
Unit 1
Supervalue Shopping Centre
Fairgreen
Naas
Co. Kildare

Tel/Fax: +353 45 895111/+353 45 895099
Email: kildaretimes@eircom.net

Kilkenny People

Sean Hurley
Sub Editor
34 High Street
Kilkenny

Tel/Fax: +353 56 21015/+353 56 21414
Email: info@kilkennypeople.ie
Website: www.kilkennypeople.ie

Leinster Express

John Whelan
The Editor
Dublin Road
Portlaoise
Co. Laois

Tel/Fax: +353 502 21666/+353 502 20491
Email: l.express@indigo.ie
Website: www.unison.ie

Leinster Leader

Michael Shearin
The Editor
19 South Main Street
Naas
Co. Kildare

Tel/Fax: +353 45 897302/+353 45 871168
Email: editor@leinster.leader.ie
Website: www.rmbi.ie

Longford Leader

Eugene McGee
The Editor
Market Square
Longford

Tel/Fax: +353 43 45241/+353 43 41489
Email: ads@longford-leader.iol.ie

Longford News

David Power
Deputy Editor
Earl Street
Longford

Tel/Fax: +353 43 41488/+353 43 41489
Email: info@longford-news.iol.ie
Website: www.unison.ie

Meath Chronicle
Ken Davis
The Editor
Market Square
Navan
Co. Meath

Tel/Fax: +353 46 79600/+353 46 23565
Email: info@meath-chronicle.ie

Midland Tribune
John O'Callaghan
The Editor
Syngefield
Birr
Co. Offaly

Tel/Fax: +353 509 20003/+353 509 20588
Email: midtrib@iol.ie
Website: www.unison.ie

Nationalist and Leinster Times
Eddie Coffey
The Editor
42 Tullow Street
Carlow

Tel/Fax: +353 503 31731/+353 503 31442
Email: news@leinster-times.ie

New Ross Standard
Ian McLure
The Editor
2 Mary Street
New Ross
Co. Wexford

Tel/Fax: +353 51 421184/+353 51 422462
Website: www.peoplenews.ie

Offaly Express
John Whelan
The Editor
Bridge Street
Tullamore
Co. Offaly

Tel/Fax: +353 509 21744/+353 506 51930
Email: lexpress@indigo.ie
Website: www.rmbi.ie

Topic Newspapers Ltd
Richard Hogan
The Editor
6 Dominic Street
Mullingar
Co. Westmeath

Tel/Fax: +353 44 48868/+353 44 43777
Email: topic@indigo.ie

Tullamore Tribune
Gerard Scully
The Editor
Chruch Street
Tullamore
Co. Offaly

Tel/Fax: +353 506 21152/+353 506 21929
Email: midtrib@iol.ie
Website: www.unison.ie

Wexford People
Michael RyanThe Editor
1a North Main Street
Wexford

Tel/Fax: +353 53 22155/+353 53 23228
Email: editor@peoplenews.ie
Website: www.people.ie

Wicklow People
Eoin Quinn
The Editor
Main Street
Wicklow

Tel/Fax: +353 404 67198/+353 404 69937
Email: wicklowpeople@eircom.net
Website: www.peoplenews.ie

The Weekender Newspaper
Fergus Barry
The Editor
6 Charter Buildings
Kennedy Road
Navan
Co. Meath

Tel/Fax: +353 46 22333/+353 46 29864
Email: tebitto@indigo.ie

Westmeath Examiner
Nicholas Nally
The Editor
19 Dominic Street
Mullingar
Co. Westmeath

Tel/Fax: +353 44 48426/+353 44 46040

Westmeath/Offaly Independent
Eilish Ryan
Deputy Editor
11 Sean Costello Street
Athlone
Co. Westmeath

Tel/Fax: +353 902 72003/+353 902 74474
Email: westoff@iol.ie

Wicklow Times (free)
Shane Harrison
Arts Correspondent
1 Eglinton Road
Bray
Co. Wicklow

Tel/Fax: +353 1 2869111/+353 1 2869074
Email: wicklowtime@eircom.net

LOCAL PRINT MEDIA - MUNSTER

The Avondhu
Liam Howard
The Editor
18 Lower Cork Street
Mitchelstown
Co. Cork

Tel/Fax: +353 25 24451/+353 25 84463
Email: info@avondhupress.ie

(see also)

The Ballincollig Newsletter
Derry Costello
The Editor
Parknamore Lodge
West Village

Ballincollig
Co Cork

Tel/Fax: +353 21 871404

The Carrigdhoun Newspaper
Vincent O'Donovan
The Editor
Wylie House
Main Street
Carrigaline
Co. Cork

Tel/Fax: +353 21 4373557/+353 21 4373559
Email: carrigdhoun@eircom.net

Clare Champion
Gerry Collison
The Editor
Barrack Street
Ennis
Co. Clare

Tel/Fax: +353 65 6828105/+353 65 6820374
Email: editor@clarechampion.ie
Website: www.clarechampion.ie

Clare County Express (free)
Seamus O'Reilly
The Editor
25 Abbey Street
Ennis
Co. Clare

Tel: +353 65 6824726

Dungarvan Leader
Colm Nagle
The Editor
78 O'Connell Street
Dungarvan
Co. Waterford

Tel/Fax: +353 58 41203/+353 56 45301
Email: dungarvanleader@cablesurf.ie

Dungarvan Observer
James Lynch
The Editor
Shandon

Dungarvan
Co. Waterford

Tel/Fax: +353 58 41205/+353 58 41559
Email: observer@indigo.ie

Evening Echo
Declan Hassett
Arts Editor
PO Box no 21
Academy Street
Cork

Tel/Fax: +353 21 4272722/+353 21 4275112
Website: www.examiner.ie

Imokilly People
Edmund Fitzgerald
Arts Editor
57 Main Street
Midleton
Co. Cork

Tel/Fax: +353 21 4613333/+353 21 4632500
Email: imokillypeople@eircom.net
Website: www.imokillypeople.ie

Kerry's Eye
Padraig Kennelly
The Editor
22 Ashe Street
Tralee
Co. Kerry

Tel/Fax: +353 66 7123199/+353 66 7123163
Email: news@kerryesye.com
Website: www.kerryseye.com

The Kerryman/Corkman
Declan Malone
Acting Editor
Clash Industrial Estate
Tralee
Co. Kerry

Tel/Fax: +353 66 7145500/+353 66 7145572
Email: kerryman@indigo.ie
Website: www.kerryweb.ie/kerryman

Killarney Advertiser
Daniel Casey
The Editor
'Mounteagle'
Woodlawn
Co. Kerry

Tel/Fax: +353 64 32215/+353 64 32722
Email: kiladv@iol.ie
Website: www.killarneyadvertiser.ie

The Kingdom
John O'Mahony
The Editor
65 New Street
Killarney
Co. Kerry

Tel/Fax: +353 64 31392/+353 64 34609
Email: kkingdom@iol.ie
Website: www.inkerry.com/kingdom.htm

Limerick Chronicle
Brendan Halligan
The Editor
54 O'Connell Street
Limerick

Tel/Fax: +353 61 315233/+353 61 401424
Email: admin@limerick-leader.ie
Website: www.limerick-leader

Limerick Leader
Brendan Halligan
The Editor
54 O'Connell Street
Limerick

Tel/Fax: +353 61 315233/+353 61 401424
Email: admin@limerick-leader.ie
Website: www.limerick-leader

Limerick Post
Claire Connolly-Doyle
Arts Editor
Town Hall Centre
Rutland Street
Limerick

Tel/Fax: +353 61 413322/+353 61 417684

Email: news@limerickpost.ie
Website: www.limerickpost.ie

Munster Express
Liam Murphy
Arts and Theatre Correspondent
37 The Quay
Waterford

Tel/Fax: +353 51 872141/+353 51 873452
Email: news@munster-express.ie
Website: www.munster-express.ie

Muskerry Leader
Eoin English
The Editor
Time Square
Ballincollig
Co. Cork

Tel/Fax: +353 21 4874491/+353 21 4874493
Email: leadergr@indigo.ie

Nationalist and Munster Advertiser
Tom Corr
The Editor
Queen Street
Clonmel
Co. Tipperary

Tel/Fax: +353 52 22211/+353 52 25248
Email: ewynne@nationalist.ie
Website: www.nationalist.ie

Nenagh Guardian
Gerry Slevin
The Editor
13 Summerhill
Nenagh
Co. Tipperary

Tel/Fax: +353 67 31214/+353 67 33401
Email: nenaghg@eircom.net
Website: www.nenagh-guardian.ie

Southern Star
Con Dowling
Assistant Editor
Glen Street
Skibbereen
Co. Cork

Tel/Fax: +353 28 21200/+353 28 21071
Email: cond@southernstar.ie
Website: www.unison.ie

Tipperary Star
Michael Dundon
The Editor
Friar Street
Thurles
Co. Tipperary

Tel/Fax: +353 504 21639/+353 504 21110
Email: info@tipperarystar.ie

Vale Star/Mallow Star
Sharon O'Brien
The Editor
19 Bridge Street
Mallow
Co. Cork

Tel/Fax: +353 22 22910/+353 22 22959
Email: vstar@vso.iol.ie

Waterford News and Star
John O'Shea
Entertainments Correspondent
25 Michael Street
Waterford

Tel/Fax: +353 51 874951/+353 51 855281
Email: editor@waterford-news.ie
Website: www.waterford-news.ie

Waterford Today (free)
Paddy Gallagher
The Editor
36 Mayor's Walk
Waterford

Tel/Fax: +353 51 854135/+353 51 854140
Email: editor@waterford-today.ie
Website: www.waterford-today.ie

Weekly Observer
Sharon O'Brien
The Editor
19 Bridge Street
Mallow
Co. Cork

Tel/Fax: +353 22 22910/+353 22 22959
Email: vstar@vso.iol.ie

LOCAL PRINT MEDIA - ULSTER

Anglo Celt
Johnny O'Hanlon
The Editor
Station House
Cavan

Tel/Fax: +353 49 4331100/+353 49 4332280
Email: anglocelt@iol.ie

Derry Journal
Patrick McArt
The Editor
Buncrana Road
Derry
Northern Ireland

Tel/Fax: 048 7127 2200/048 7127 2260
Email: derryj@iol.co.uk

Derry People and Donegal News
Columba Gill
The Editor
Crossview House
Letterkenny
Co. Donegal

Tel/Fax: +353 74 21014/+353 74 22881
Email: editor@donegalnews.com
Website: www.donegalnews.com

Donegal Democrat
John Bromley
The Editor
Donegal Road
Ballyshannon
Co. Donegal

Tel/Fax: +353 72 51201/+353 72 51945
Editor: donegaldemocrat@eircom.net

Donegal People's Press
Patrick McArt
The Editor
Buncrana Road
Derry
Northern Ireland

Tel/Fax: 048 7127 2200/048 7127 2260
Email: derryj@sol.co.uk

The Inish Times
Liam Porter
The Editor
42 Upper Main Street
Buncrana
Inishowen
Co. Donegal

Tel/Fax: +353 77 41055/+353 77 41059
Email: inishted@eircom.net
Website: www.inishtimes.ie

Northern Standard
Martin Smyth
The Editor
The Diamond
Monaghan

Tel/Fax: +353 47 82188/+353 47 84070
Email: garysmyth@eircom.net
Website: www.unison.ie

Tirconaill Tribune
John McAteer
The Editor
Main Street
Milford
Co. Donegal

Tel/Fax: +353 74 53600/+353 74 53607
Email: tirconailltribune@eircom.net
Website: tirconaill-tribune.com

LOCAL PRINT MEDIA - NORTHERN IRELAND

Andersonstown News
Robin Livingstone
The Editor
Work West Enterprise Centre
301 Glen Road
Belfast BT11 8ER
Northern Ireland

Tel/Fax: 048 9061 9000/048 9062 0602
Email: info@belfast-news.ie
Website: www.beflast-news.ie

Antrim Times
Dessie Blackadder
The Editor
22-24 Ballymoney Street
Ballymena
Co. Antrim BT43 6AL
Northern Ireland

Tel/Fax: 048 2565 3300/048 2564 1517
Email: edbt@mortonnewspapers.com
Website: www.mortonnewspaper.com

Armagh-Down Obeserver
Desmond Mallon
The Editor
Observer Newspaper NI Ltd
Ann Street
Dungarvan
Co. Tyrone BT70 1ET
Northern Ireland

Tel/Fax: 048 8772 2557/048 8772 7334

Ballyclare Gazette
Richard Petrie
The Editor
36 The Square
Ballyclare
Co. Antrim BT39 9BB
Northern Ireland

Tel/Fax: 048 9335 2967/048 9335 2449

Ballymena Chronicle and Antrim Observer
Desmond Mallon
The Editor
Observer Newspapers NI Ltd
Ann Street
Dungannon
Co. Tyrone BT70 1ET
Northern Ireland

Tel/Fax: 048 8772 2557/048 8772 7334

Ballymena Guardian
Maurice O'Neill
The Editor
83 Wellington Street

Ballymena
Co. Antrim BT43 6AD
Northern Ireland

Tel/Fax: 048 2564 1221/048 2565 3920

Ballymena Times
Des Blackadder
The Editor
22-24 Ballymoney Street
Ballymena
Co. Antrim BT43 6AL
Northern Ireland

Tel/Fax: 048 2565 3300/048 2564 1517
Email: edbt@mortonnewspapers.com
Website: www.mortonnewspapers.com

Ballymoney Times
Lyle McMullan
The Editor
6 Church Street
Ballymoney
Co. Antrim BT53 6DL
Northern Ireland

Tel/Fax: 048 2666 6216/048 2766 7066

Banbridge Chronicle
Brian Hooks
The Editor
14 Bridge Street
Banbridge
Co. Down BT32 3JS
Northern Ireland

Tel/Fax: 048 4066 2322/048 4062 4397

The Banbridge Leader
Damien Wilson
The Editor
25 Bridge Street
Banbridge
Co. Down BT32 3JL
Northern Ireland

Tel/Fax: 048 4066 2745/048 4062 6378
Email: eddl@mortonnewspapers.com

Belfast News (free)
Julie McClay
The Editor
46-56 Boucher Crescent
Belfast BT12 6QY
Northern Ireland

Tel/Fax: 048 9068 0000/048 9066 9910
Email: julie.mcclay@mgn.co.uk

Carrickfergus Advertiser
Stephen Kernohan
The Editor
31a High Street
Carrickfergus
Co. Antrim BT38 7AN
Northern Ireland

Tel/Fax: 048 9336 3651/048 9336 3092
Website: www.ulsternet-ni.co.uk

Coleraine Chronicle
Anthony Toner
Deputy Editor
20 Railway Road
Coleraine
Co. Derry BT52 1PD
Northern Ireland

Tel/Fax: 048 7034 3344/048 7032 9672

Coleraine Times
David Rankin
The Editor
71 New Row
Coleraine
Co. Derry BT52 1AF
Northern Ireland

Tel/Fax: 048 7035 5260/048 7035 6186
Email: edcr@mortonnewspapers.com
Website: www.production@mortonnewspapers.com

Community Telegraph
Nigel Tilson
The Editor
124-144 Royal Avenue
Belfast BT1 1EB
Northern Ireland

Tel/Fax: 048 9026 4396/048 9055 4585

County Down Spectator
Paul Flowers
The Editor
109 Main Street
Bangor
Co. Down BT20 4AF
Northern Ireland

Tel/Fax: 048 9127 0270/048 9127 1544
Email: spectator@dial.pipex.com

Craigavon Echo (free)
David Armstrong
The Editor
14 Church Street
Portadown
Co. Down BT62 3LQ
Northern Ireland

Tel/Fax: 048 3835 0041/048 3835 0203
Email: edcr@mortonnewspapers.com
Website: www.mortonnewspapers.com

The Cross Examiner
Gerry Murray
The Editor
Rathkeeland House
1 Blaney Road
Crossmaglen
Co. Armagh BT35 9JJ
Northern Ireland

Tel/Fax: 048 3086 8500/048 3086 8580
Email: gerry.murray@btinternet.com

The Democrat
Desmond Mallon
The Editor
Observer Newspapers Northern Ireland Ltd
Ann Street
Dungannon
Co. Tyrone BT70 12T
Northern Ireland

Tel/Fax: 048 8772 2557/048 8772 7334

Derry Journal
Patrick McArt
The Editor
Buncrana Road
Derry BT48 8AA
Northern Ireland

Tel/Fax: 048 7127 2200/048 7127 2218

Down Recorder

Marcus Crichton
Deputy Editor
2-4 Church Street
Downpatrick
Co. Down BT30 6EJ
Northern Ireland

Tel/Fax: 048 4461 3711/048 4461 4624
Email: downr@sol.co.uk

Dromore Leader

Damien Wilson
The Editor
12 Market Square
Dromore
Co. Down BT25 1AW
Northern Ireland

Tel/Fax: 048 9269 2217/048 9269 9260
Email: eddl@mortonnewspapers.com

Dungannon News and Tyrone Courier

Richard Montgomery
The Editor
58 Scotch Street
Dungarvan
Co. Tyrone BT70 1BD
Northern Ireland

Tel/Fax: 048 8772 2271/048 8772 6271

Dungannon Observer

Desmond Mallon
The Editor
Observer Newspapers Northern Ireland Ltd
Ann Street
Dungannon
Co. Tyrone BT70 1ET
Northern Ireland

Tel/Fax: 048 8772 2557/048 8772 7334

East Antrim Advertiser

Hugh Vance
The Editor
Dunluce Street
Larne
Co. Antrim BT40 1JG
Northern Ireland

Tel/Fax: 048 2827 2303/048 2826 0255

Fermanagh Herald

Pauline Leary
The Editor
30 Bemore Street
Enniskillen
Co. Fermanagh BT74 6AA
Northern Ireland

Tel/Fax: 048 6632 2066/048 6632 5521
Email: editor@fermanaghherald.com
Website: www.fermanaghherald.com

Fermanagh News

Desmond Mallon
The Editor
Observer Newspaper Northern Ireland Ltd
Ann Street
Dungannon
Co. Tyrone BT70 1ET
Northern Ireland

Tel/Fax: 048 8772 2557/048 8772 7334

Impartial Reporter and Lakeland Extra

Lily Dane
Features Correspondent
8-10 East Bridge Street
Enniskillen
Co. Fermanagh BT74 7BY
Northern Ireland

Tel/Fax: 048 6632 4422/048 6632 5047
Email: lilydane@impartialreporter.com
Website: www.impartialreporter.com

Larne Gazette

Stephen Kernohan
The Editor
20 Main Street
Larne
Co. Antrim BT40 1SS
Northern Ireland

Tel/Fax: 048 2827 7450/048 2826 0733

Larne Times

Stephen Kernohan
The Editor
8 Dunluce Street
Larne
Co. Antrim BT40 1JG
Northern Ireland

Tel/Fax: 048 2827 2303/048 2826 0255

The Leader

Anthony Toner
Deputy Editor
20 Railway Road
Coleraine
Co. Derry BT52 1PD
Northern Ireland

Tel/Fax: 048 7034 3344/048 7032 9672

Lisburn Echo (free)

David Fletcher
The Editor
12a Bow Street
Lisburn
Co. Antrim
Northern Ireland

Tel/Fax: 048 9267 9111/048 9260 2904

Londonderry Sentinel

Chris McNab
The Editor
Suite 3 Spencer House
Spencer Road
Derry BT47 6AA
Northern Ireland

Tel/Fax: 048 7134 8889/048 7134 1175
Email: edls@mortonnewspapers.com
Website: www.mortonnewspapers.com

Lurgan Mail

Richard Elliott
The Editor
4 High Street
Lurgan
Co. Armagh BT66 8AW
Northern Ireland

Tel/Fax: 048 3832 7777/048 3832 5271

Email: edlm@nortonnewspapers.com
Website: www.mortonnewspapers.com

Lurgan and Portadown Examiner

Desmond Mallon
The Editor
Observer Newspaper Northern Ireland Ltd
Ann Street
Dungannon
Co. Tyrone BT70 1ET
Northern Ireland

Tel/Fax: 048 8772 2557/048 8772 7334

Mid-Ulster Echo

John Fillis
The Editor
52 Oldtown Street
Cookstown
Co. Tyrone BT80 8BB
Northern Ireland

Tel/Fax: 048 8676 2288/048 8676 4295
Website: www.mortonnewspapers.com

Mid-Ulster Mail

John Fillis
The Editor
52 Oldtown Street
Cookstown
Co. Tyrone BT80 8BB
Northern Ireland

Tel/Fax: 048 8676 2288/048 8676 4295
Website: www.mortonnewspapers.com

Mid Ulster Observer

Desmond Mallon
The Editor
Observer Newspapers Northern Ireland Ltd
Ann Street
Dungannon
Co. Antrim BT70 1ET
Northern Ireland

Tel/Fax: 048 8772 2557/048 8772 7334

Mourne Observer

Terence Bowman
The Editor
Castlewellan Road
Newcastle
Co. Down BT33 OJX
Northern Ireland

Tel/Fax: 048 4372 2666/048 4372 4566

Newry Reporter

Donal O'Donnell
The Editor
4 Margaret Street
Newry
Co. Down BT66 1ET
Northern Ireland

Tel/Fax: 048 3026 7633/048 3026 3157
Email: clint.aiken@btinternet.com

Newtownards Chronicle

John Savage
The Editor
25 Frances Street
Newtownards
Co. Down BT23 3DT
Northern Ireland

Tel/Fax: 048 9181 3333/048 9182 0087

Newtownards Spectator

Paul Flowers
The Editor
109 Main Street
Bangor
Co. Down BT20 4AF
Northern Ireland

Tel/Fax: 048 9127 0270/048 9127 1544
Email: spectator@dial.pipex.com

Northwest Echo (free)

Chris McNab
The Editor
Suite 3 Spencer House
Spencer Road
Derry BT47 6AA
Northern Ireland

Tel/Fax: 048 7134 8889/048 7134 1175
Email: edls@mortonnewspapers.com
Website: www.mortonnewspapers.com

Northern Constitution

Anthony Toner
Deputy Editor
20 Railway Road
Coleraine
Co. Derry BT52 1PD
Northern Ireland

Tel/Fax: 048 7034 3344/048 7032 9672

The Outlook

Stephen Patton
The Editor
Castle Street
Rathfriland
Newry
Co. Down BT34 5QR
Northern Ireland

Tel/Fax: 048 4063 0781/048 4063 1022

Portadown Times

David Armstrong
The Editor
14 Church Street
Portadown
Co. Armagh BT62 3LQ
Northern Ireland

Tel/Fax: 048 3833 6111/048 3835 0203
Website: www.mortonnewspapers.com

Roe Valley Sentinel

Chris McNab
The Editor
32a Market Street
Limavady
Co. Derry BT49 OAA
Northern Ireland

Tel/Fax: 048 7776 4090/048 7772 2234

Strabane Chronicle

Michelle Canning
The Editor
10 John Street

Omagh
Co. Tyrone BT78 1DT
Northern Ireland

Tel/Fax: +353 48 8224 3444/048 8224 2206
Email: editor@ulsterherald.com
Website: www.ulsterherald.com

Tyrone Constitution
Wesley Acheson
The Editor
25-27 High Street
Omagh
Co. Tyrone BT78 1BD
Northern Ireland

Tel/Fax: 048 2824 2721/048 2824 3549
Email: editor@tyroneconstitution.com

Tyrone Times
Paul McCreevy
The Editor
48 Market Square
Dungannon
Co. Tyrone BT70 1JH
Northern Ireland

Tel/Fax: 048 8775 2801/048 8775 2819
Website: www.mortonnewspapers.com

Ulster Gazette and Armagh Standard
Richard Burgen
News Editor
56 Scotch Stret
Armagh BT61 7DF
Northern Ireland

Tel/Fax: 048 3752 2639/048 3752 7029
Email: ulstergazette@ulsternet-ni.co.uk

Ulster Herald
Dominic McClements
The Editor
10 John Street
Omagh
Co. Tyrone BT78 1DT
Northern Ireland

Tel/Fax: 048 8224 3444/048 8224 2206
Email: editor@ulsterherald.com

Ulster Star
David Fletcher
The Editor
12a Bow Street
Lisburn
Co. Armagh BT28 1BN
Northern Ireland

Tel/Fax: 048 9267 9111/048 9260 2904
Email: edus@mortonnewspapers.com
Website: www.mortonnewspapers.com

NATIONAL RADIO - REPUBLIC OF IRELAND

Lyric FM
Seamus Crimmins
Head Lyric FM
Cornmarket Square
Cornmarket
Co. Limerick

Tel/Fax: +353 61 207300/+353 61 207390
Email: lyric@rte.ie
Website: www.lyricfm.ie

Raidío Na Gaeltachta
Máirín Mhic Dhonnchadha
Poiblíocht
Casla
Conamara
Co. na Gallimhe

Tel/Fax: +353 91 506677/+353 91 506666
Email: rnag@rte.ie
Website: www.rnag.ie

RTÉ Radio 1 and 2FM
Press and Information Office
Office Building
RTÉ
Donnybrook
Dublin 4

Tel/Fax: +353 1 2083111/+353 1 2082093
Email: press@rte.ie
Website: www.rte.ie

Today FM
124 Upper Abbey Street
Dublin 1

Tel/Fax: +353 1 8049033/+353 1 8049099
Email: jkelly@todayfm.com
Website: www.todayfm.com

**NATIONAL RADIO -
NORTHERN IRELAND**

BBC Radio Ulster
Broadcasting House
Ormeau Avenue
Belfast BT2 8HQ
Northern Ireland

Tel/Fax: 048 9033 8292/048 9033 8807
Email: stephanie.mckee@bbc.co.uk or
joanne.murphy@bbc.co.uk or
walter.love@bbc.co.uk
Website: www.bbc.co.uk/northernireland
Contact: David Byers (Chief Producer, Music &
Arts, BBC Northern Ireland), Stephanie McKee
(Classical), Joanne Murphy (Traditional), Walter
Love (Jazz)

LOCAL RADIO - CONNACHT

Community Radio Castlebar
Market Square
Castlebar
Co. Mayo

Tel/Fax: +353 94 25555/+353 94 25989
Email: crcfm@eircom.net
Contact: Peter Killeen (Station Manager),
Tomas Lally (Assistant Manager)

Connemara Community Radio
Connemara West Centre
Letterfrack
Co. Galway

Tel/Fax: +353 95 41616/+353 95 41628
Email: ccradio@connemara.net
Website: www.ainu.ie/ccradio
Contact: Brendan O'Scannaill (Classical), Michael
O'Neill (Traditional), Helen King (Traditional),
Mary Ruddy (Jazz)

Flirt FM
c/o Arás na Macléinn
National University of Ireland Galway
Galway

Tel/Fax: +353 91 750445/+353 91 525700
Email: nuigalway.ie
Website: www.flirtfm.nuigalway.ie
Contact: Yvonne Igoe (Station Manager)

Galway Bay FM
Sandy Road
Galway

Tel/Fax: +353 91 770000/+353 91 752689
Email: gbfm@galway.net
Website: www.gbfm.galway.net
Contact: Gary McMahon (Arts), Kevin Rohan
(Traditional)

Mid-West Radio
Abbey Street
Ballyhaunis
Co. Mayo

Tel/Fax: +353 907 30169/+353 907 30285
Email: chris@mwr.ie
Website: under construction
Contact: Chris Carroll (Station Mangaer and
Jazz), Joe Beirne (Traditional), Sean Duffy
(Traditional), John Duggan (Traditional)

Northwest Radio
Market Yard
Sligo

Tel/Fax: +353 71 60108/+353 71 60889
Contact: Mary Daly (Listings), Kerry Donaghue
(Traditional), Joe Beirne (Traditional), John
Duggan (Traditional)

**LOCAL RADIO -
DUBLIN CITY & COUNTY**

Anna Livia FM
Trevor Austin
Head of Arts
Griffith College
South Circular Road
Dublin 8

Tel/Fax: +353 1 4734444/+353 1 4734445

Dublin 98FM

South Block
The Malthouse
Grand Canal Quay
Dublin 2

Tel/Fax: +353 1 6708981/+353 1 6708986
Email: online@98fm.ie
Contact: John Taylor (Programming), Kieran
Murphy (Programming)

Dublin South Community Radio

Old School
Loreto Avenue
Rathfarnham
Dublin 14

Tel/Fax: +353 1 4930377/+353 1 4930520
Email: dscradmin@oceanfree.net
Contact: Brendan Hickey (Head of Programming)

FM 104

Hume House
Ballsbridge
Dublin 4

Tel/Fax: +353 1 6689689/+353 1 6689401
Contact: Leona Gray (Listings)

Near FM

Coolock Development Centre
Bunratty Drive
Dublin 17

Tel/Fax: +353 1 8485211/+353 1 8486111
Email: nearfm@iol.ie
Contact: Ciaran Murray (Station Manager)

Raidio na Life

7 Cearnóg Mhuirfean
Baile Atha Cliath 2

Tel/Fax: +353 1 6616333/+353 1 6763966
Email: rnl102@iol.ie
Contact: Fionnuala MacAodha (Station Manager)

Tallaght Community Radio

Level 3
The Square
Tallaght
Dublin 24

Tel/Fax: +353 1 4623333/+353 1 4623444
Email: tcr@eircom.net
Contact: Declan McLoughlin (Station Manager)

West Dublin Community Radio

Mary McManus
Arts and Entertainment
Ballyfermot Road
Dublin 10

Tel/Fax: +353 1 6261160/+353 1 6261167
Email: wdcr@indigo.ie

LOCAL RADIO - LEINSTER

East Coast Radio

9 Prince of Wales Terrace
Quinsboro Road
Bray
Co. Wicklow

Tel/Fax: +353 1 2866414/+353 1 2861219
Email: online@eastcoastradio.fm
Website: www.eastcoastradio.fm
Contact: Joe Harrington (Head of Programmes
and Listings), Bob Gallico (Classical)

Leinster CKR FM

Lismard House
Tullow Street
Carlow

Tel/Fax: +353 503 41044/+353 503 41047
Email: info@ckrfm.com
Website: www.ckrfm.com
Contact: Terry Martin (Station Manager and
Listings), John Brady (Classical), Brendan
Bambrick (Traditional), Ronan Sirr (Traditional)

LMFM

Boyne Shopping Centre
Drogheda
Co. Louth

Tel/Fax: +353 41 9832000/+353 41 9832957
Email: requestslmfm@eircom.net
Contact: Ray Stone (Classical), Dick Duffin (Jazz),
Eddie Caffrey (Traditional)

Midlands Radio 3
The Mall
William Street
Tullamore
Co. Offaly

Tel/Fax: +353 506 51333/+353 506 52546
Email: midlandsradio@eircom.net
Contact: Mike Reade (Programming Director)

Radio Kilkenny
56 Hebron Road
Kilkenny

Tel/Fax: +353 56 61577/+353 56 63586
Email: onair@radiokilkenny.eircom.net
Contact: Pat Maher

Shannonside Northern Sound
Minard House
Sligo Road
Longford

Tel/Fax: +353 43 46669/+353 43 48171
Email: info@shannonside.eircom.net
Contact: Joe Finnegan (Head of Programmes)

South East Radio
Custom House Quay
Wexford

Tel/Fax: +353 53 45200/+353 53 45295
Email: wexford@iol.ie
Website: www.southeastradio.ie

LOCAL RADIO - MUNSTER

Clare FM
The Abbeyfield Centre
Francis Street
Ennis
Co. Clare

Tel/Fax: +353 65 6828888/+353 65 6829392
Email: info@clarefm.ie
Contact: Liam O'Shea (Music Programmer),
Austen Durack (Classical), Tim Dennehy
(Traditional)

Community Radio Youghal
League of the Cross Hall
Catherine Street
Youghal
Co. Cork

Tel/Fax: +353 24 91199
Email: ycradio@iol.ie
Website: www.iol.ie/~ycradio
Contact: Jim Coleman (Classical), Tim Smith
(Traditional), John Cunningham (Traditional),
Michael McCarthy (Traditional)

Cork Campus Radio
Level 3
Arás na MacLeinn
University College Cork
Cork

Tel/Fax: +353 21 4902008/+353 21 4903108
Email: radio@ucc.ie
Contact: Sinead O'Donnell (Station Manager),
Kieran Hurley (Engineer and Programme Maker)

Cork 96FM/County Sound FM 103
Broadcasting House
Patrick's Place
Cork

Tel/Fax: +353 21 4551596/+353 21 4551500
Email: info@96fm.ie
Website: www.96fm.ie
Contact: Steve Hynes (Music Controller and
Listings), Derry O'Callaghan (Traditional)

95FM Limerick
PO Box 295
88 O'Connell Street
Limerick

Tel/Fax: +353 61 400195/+353 61 419595
Email: 95fm@iol.ie
Contact: Tom O'Sullivan (Classical), Len Dineen
(Classical), Ruth Brophy (Traditional)

Radio Kerry
Main Street
Tralee
Co. Kerry

Tel/Fax: +353 66 7123666/+353 66 7122282
Email: melanie@radiokerry.eircom.net
Contact: Martin Howard (Head of Music),
Ted Carroll (Classical), Colette Numan Kenny
(Classical), Reggie McCrohan (Traditional),
Maura Begley (Traditional)

Tipp FM
Davis Road
Clonmel
Co. Tipperary

Tel/Fax: +353 52 25299/+353 52 25447
Email: tippfm@tippfm.com
Website: www.tippfm.com
Contact: Colette Grufferty (Traditional),
Pat Geary (Classical)

Tipperary Mid-West Radio
St. Michael's Street
Tipperary

Tel/Fax: +353 62 52555/+353 62 52671
Email: 1tipperarymidwest@eircom.net
Contact: Eric Rochford (Classical), Kevin
Muldoon (Classical), Noel Fahy (Traditional),
Donnchadh O'Cinneide (Traditional Ceomhaltas
Programme), Fran Curry (Morning Magazine)

Wired FM Limerick
Mary Immaculate College
South Circular Road
Limerick

Tel/Fax: +353 61 315103/+353 61 315776
Email: wiredfm@mic.ul.ie
Contact: Darren Connolly (Station Manager)

WLR FM
The Radio Centre
George's Street
Waterford

Tel/Fax: +353 51 877479/+353 51 877420
Email: info@wlrfm.com
Website: www.wlrfm.com
Contact: Paul Byrne (Head of Music), Anne
Muldoon (Traditional), Liam Walsh (Classical)

LOCAL RADIO - ULSTER

Highland Radio
Pinehill
Letterkenny
Co. Donegal

Tel/Fax: +353 74 25000/+353 74 25344
Email: enquiries@highlandradio.com
Website: www.highlandradio.com
Contact: Linda McGroarty (Head of Music),
Billy Patterson (Classical and Jazz),
Seamas Gibson (Traditional)

LOCAL RADIO - NORTHERN IRELAND

BBC Foyle
8 Northland Road
Derry BT48 7JD
Northern Ireland

Tel/Fax: 048 7137 8600/048 7137 8666
Email: gerry.anderson@bbc.co.uk
Website: www.bbc.co.uk

Downtown Radio
Newtownards
Co. Down BT23 4ES
Northern Ireland

Tel/Fax: 048 9181 5555/048 9181 5252
Email: programmes@downtown.co.uk
Website: www.downtown.co.uk
Contact: John Rosborough (Head of
Programming), Romilly Burrowes (Classical),
Tommy Sands (Traditional), Jackie Flavelle (Jazz)

Q97
24 Cloyfin Road
Coleraine
Co. Derry BT52 2NU
Northern Ireland

Tel/Fax: 048 7035 9100/048 7032 6666
Email: sales@q97-fm.com
Website: www.q97-fm.com
Contact: John Wright (Station Manager)

TELEVISION

RTÉ 1 and Network 2
Press and Information Office
Office Building
Donnybrook
Dublin 4

Tel/Fax: +353 1 2083111/+353 1 2082093
Email: press@rte.ie
Website: www.rte.ie

BBC Northern Ireland
Broadcasting House
Ormeau Avenue
Belfst BT2 8HQ
Northern Ireland

Tel/Fax: 048 9033 8292/048 9033 8807
Email: david.byers@bbc.co.uk
Website: www.bbc.co.uk/northernireland/
tvr-music-arts.shtml
Contact: David Byers (Chief Producer, Music &
Arts, BBC Northern Ireland), Marie-Claire Doris
(Producer), Declan McGovern (Producer)

TG4
Baile na hAbhann
Co. Gallimhe

Tel/Fax: +353 91 593636/+353 91 505021
Email: eolas@tg4.ie
Website: www.tg4.ie
Contact: Cilian Fennell (Programming
Consultant)

TV3
Westgate Business Park
Ballymount
Dublin 24

Tel/Fax: +353 1 4193333/+353 1 4193322
Email: lorraine.keane@tv3.ie
Contact: Lorraine Keane (Music Correspondent)

UTV
Havelock House
Ormeau Road
Belfast BT7 1EB
Northern Ireland

Tel/Fax: 048 9032 8122/048 9024 6695
Email: emailinfo@utvlive.com
Contact: Orla McKibbin (Press & Public Relations
Officer)

Appendices

Appendix One

(Questionnaires distributed in each category)

Category	No. of Entries	No. of questionnaires distributed
Organisations	251	322
Education	243	300
Music Educationalists/ Community Musicians	49	70
Libraries	57	59
Health	28	52
Promoters	174	199
Venues	255	349
Festivals	231	388
Instrument Makers & Repairers/Sales & Hire	183	193
Piano Tuners	31	31
Recording & Practice facilities	46	52
Music Copyists	9	14
Programme Note Writers	17	18
Performance Agencies	6	6
Arts Consultants	6	14
Event Management	44	16
Competitions, Scholarships & Bursaries	74	89
Composers and Arrangers	102	133
Media	201	201
Total	**2,007**	**2,506**

Appendix Two

If you wish to be added to our database and included in further editions of this handbook, please fill in the following details and send them to us. (This form may be photocopied).

Company name:

Main contact name:

Job title:

Address:

Tel.:

Fax:

Email:

Website:

Nature of Business:

- [ ] Organisations
- [ ] Music Schools
- [ ] Higher Education
- [ ] Summer School/Winter School/Short Courses
- [ ] Examining Institutions
- [ ] Music Educationalists/Community Musicians
- [ ] Health
- [ ] Music Therapists
- [ ] Public Libraries
- [ ] Specialist Libraries
- [ ] Youth Orchestras
- [ ] Youth Choirs
- [ ] Promoters
- [ ] Venues

- [ ] Festivals
- [ ] Instrument Makers and Repairers
- [ ] Instrument Sales
- [ ] Piano Tuners
- [ ] Recording and Practice Facilities
- [ ] Music Copyists and Typesetters
- [ ] Programme Note Writers
- [ ] Performance Agencies
- [ ] Event Management Companies
- [ ] Arts Consultants
- [ ] Competitions, Scholarships and Bursaries
- [ ] Composers
- [ ] Media

Send to: **The Information Department, Music Network, The Coach House, Dublin Castle, Dublin 2.**
Tel/Fax: **+353 1 6719429/+353 1 6719430**
Email: **info@musicnetwork.ie** • Website: **www.musicnetwork.ie**

Index

INDEX OF ADVERTISERS